Sweet & Ma

Property Law Statutes
2003/04

AUSTRALIA
Law Book Co.
Sydney

CANADA and USA
Carswell
Toronto

HONG KONG
Sweet & Maxwell Asia

NEW ZEALAND
Brookers
Wellington

SINGAPORE and MALAYSIA
Sweet & Maxwell Asia
Singapore and Kuala Lumpur

Sweet & Maxwell's

Property Law Statutes 2003/04

9th Edition

PROFESSOR NIGEL P. GRAVELLS, M.A.
of the Middle Temple, Barrister
Professor of English Law,
University of Nottingham

LONDON
SWEET & MAXWELL
2003

Published in 2003 by Sweet & Maxwell Ltd
of 100 Avenue Road, London NW3 3PF
Typeset by MFK Mendip, Frome, Somerset
Printed in Great Britain by Ashford Colour Printers, Hants

No natural forests were destroyed to make this product; only farmed timber was used and replanted

ISBN 0 421 847 204

PREFACE

Sweet & Maxwell's Property Law Statutes is intended primarily as a reference book for students of property law: it seeks to provide a collection of statutory materials that covers as comprehensively as possible the central property law subjects—land law, conveyancing, trusts and succession.

Legislation enacted during the last five years has shifted the chronological balance of the collection so that the statutes of the 1925 property legislation no longer constitute the core. Of those statutes only the Settled Land Act, the Law of Property Act and the Administration of Estates Act remain fully intact (albeit amended). Part I of the Trustee Act 1925 has been repealed and replaced; and the Land Registration Act 1925 (and subsequent amending statutes) will be repealed and replaced on October 13, 2003. With some minor exceptions, the Trustee Investments Act 1961 has also been repealed.

The new generation of property law statutes includes the Trustee Delegation Act 1999, the Trustee Act 2000 and the Land Registration Act 2002. The first two statutes are in force; and the "substantive" registered land provisions of the Land Registration Act 2002 come into force on October 13, 2003 (although the "procedural" electronic conveyancing provisions are not expected to come into force for some years). Part I of the Commonhold and Leasehold Reform Act 2002 is also included: although commonhold is not a new type of estate in land in the strict sense, it does constitute a new method of land ownership.

The statutes are printed in chronological order as amended by subsequent legislation: textual amendments are incorporated in the original statutes and the amending provisions of subsequent legislation are not printed separately. The sources of all amendments, both textual and non-textual, are indicated in the footnotes. In addition, the footnotes seek to provide both internal cross-referencing and selective references to legislation not included in the book.

The Brambles
Wymeswold
July 2003

Nigel P. Gravells

CONTENTS

CHRONOLOGIAL CONTENTS

ALPHABETICAL CONTENTS

Prescription Act 1832[1]

(2 & 3 WILL. 4, C. 71)

Claims to right of common and other profits à prendre, not to be defeated after thirty years' enjoyment by merely showing the commencement; after sixty years' enjoyment the right to be absolute, unless had by consent or agreement

1.[2] No claim which may be lawfully made at the common law, by custom, prescription, or grant, to any right of common or other profit or benefit to be taken and enjoyed from or upon any land of our sovereign Lord the King, [. . .][3] or any land being parcel of the Duchy of Lancaster or of the Duchy of Cornwall, or of any ecclesiastical or lay person, or body corporate, except such matters and things as are herein specially provided for, and except tithes, rent, and services, shall, where such right, profit, or benefit shall have been actually taken and enjoyed by any person claiming right thereto without interruption for the full period of thirty years, be defeated or destroyed by showing only that such right, profit, or benefit was first taken or enjoyed at any time prior to such period of thirty years, but nevertheless such claim may be defeated in any other way by which the same is now liable to be defeated; and when such right, profit, or benefit shall have been so taken and enjoyed as aforesaid for the full period of sixty years, the right thereto shall be deemed absolute and indefeasible, unless it shall appear that the same was taken and enjoyed by some consent or agreement expressly made or given for that purpose by deed or writing. **1–001**

In claims of right of way or other easement the periods to be twenty years and forty years

2.[4] No claim which may be lawfully made at the common law, by custom, prescription, or grant, to any way or other easement, or to any watercourse, or the use of any water, to be enjoyed or derived upon, over, or from any land or water of our said Lord the King, [. . .][5] or being parcel of the Duchy of Lancaster or of the Duchy of Cornwall, or being the property of any ecclesiastical or lay person, or body corporate, when such way or other matter as herein last before mentioned shall have been actually enjoyed by any person claiming right thereto without interruption for the full period of twenty years, shall be defeated or destroyed by showing only that such way or other matter was first enjoyed at any time prior to such period of twenty years, but nevertheless such claim may be defeated in any other way by which the same is now liable to be defeated; and where such way or other matter as herein last before mentioned shall have been so enjoyed as aforesaid for the full period of forty years, the right thereto shall be deemed absolute and indefeasible, unless it shall appear that the same was enjoyed by some consent or agreement expressly given or made for that purpose by deed or writing. **1–002**

---

[1] Saved by the Law of Property Act 1925, s.12, *post*, para. 9–011.
[2] Certain interruptions in prescriptive claims to rights of common are disregarded: Commons Registration Act 1965, s.16(1), *post*, para. 23–016.
[3] Words repealed by the Statute Law Revision Act 1890.
[4] As to the acquisition of *public* rights of way (which cannot be acquired under this Act), see the Highways Act 1980, ss.31–33.
[5] Words repealed by the Statute Law Revision Act 1890.

Claim to the use of light enjoyed for twenty years

1–003 **3.**[6] When the access and use of light to and for any dwelling house, workshop, or other building shall have been actually enjoyed therewith for the full period of twenty years[7] without interruption, the right thereto shall be deemed absolute and indefeasible, any local usage or custom to the contrary notwithstanding, unless it shall appear that the same was enjoyed by some consent or agreement expressly made or given for that purpose by deed or writing.

Before-mentioned periods to be deemed those next before suits

1–004 **4.**[8] Each of the respective periods of years hereinbefore mentioned shall be deemed and taken to be the period next before some suit or action wherein the claim or matter to which such period may relate shall have been or shall be brought into question, and no act or other matter shall be deemed to be an interruption, within the meaning of this statute, unless the same shall have been or shall be submitted to or acquiesced in for one year after the party interrupted shall have had or shall have notice thereof, and of the person making or authorising the same to be made.

In actions on the case, the claimant may allege his right generally, as at present. In pleas to trespass and certain other pleadings the period mentioned in this Act may be alleged. Exceptions, etc. to be replied specially

1–005 **5.** In all actions upon the case and other pleadings, wherein the party claiming may now by law allege his right generally, without averring the existence of such right from time immemorial, such general allegation shall still be deemed sufficient, and if the same shall be denied, all any every the matters in this Act mentioned and provided, which shall be applicable to the case, shall be admissible in evidence to sustain or rebut such allegation; and in all pleadings to actions of trespass, and in all other pleadings wherein before the passing of this Act it would have been necessary to allege the right to have existed from time immemorial, it shall be sufficient to allege the enjoyment thereof as of right by the occupiers of the tenement in respect whereof the same is claimed for and during such of the periods mentioned in this Act as may be applicable to the case, and without claiming in the name or right of the owner of the fee, as is now usually done; and if the other party shall intend to rely on any proviso, exception, incapacity, disability, contract, agreement, or other matter hereinbefore mentioned, or on any cause or matter of fact or of law not inconsistent with the simple fact of enjoyment, the same shall be specially alleged and set forth in answer to the allegation of the party claiming, and shall not be received in evidence on any general traverse or denial of such allegation.

Presumption to be allowed in claims herein provided for

1–006 **6.** In the several cases mentioned in and provided for by this Act, no presumption shall be allowed or made in favour or support of any claim, upon

[6] See the Rights of Light Act 1959, *post*, para. 19–001.
[7] The Rights of Light Act 1959, s.1, which temporarily extended the period to 27 years, was repealed by the Statute Law (Repeals) Act 1974, s.1, Sched., Pt. IV.
[8] See the Rights of Light Act 1959, s.3(6), *post*, para. 19–002, and the Commons Registration Act 1965, s.16(2), *post*, para. 23–016.

proof of the exercise or enjoyment of the right or matter claimed for any less period of time or number of years than for such period or number mentioned in this Act as may be applicable to the case and to the nature of the claim.

Proviso for infants, etc.

7.[9] Provided also, that the time during which any person otherwise capable of resisting any claim to any of the matters before mentioned shall have been or shall be an infant, idiot, non compos mentis, feme covert, or tenant for life, or during which any action or suit shall have been pending, and which shall have been diligently prosecuted, until abated by the death of any party or parties thereto, shall be excluded in the computation of the periods hereinbefore mentioned, except only in cases where the right or claim is hereby declared to be absolute and indefeasible. **1–007**

What time to be excluded in computing the term of forty years appointed by this Act

8. Provided always, that when any land or water upon, over, or from which any such way or other convenient watercourse or use of water shall have been or shall be enjoyed or derived hath been or shall be held under or by virtue of any term of life, or any term of years exceeding three years from the granting thereof, the time of the enjoyment of any such way or other matter as herein last before mentioned, during the continuance of such terms, shall be excluded in the computation of the said period of forty years, in case the claim shall within three years next after the end or sooner determination of such term be resisted by any person entitled to any reversion expectant on the determination thereof. **1–008**

. . . . . .

Wills Act 1837[1]

(7 Will. 4 & 1 Vict. c. 26)

Meaning of certain words in this Act

1. The words and expressions herein-after mentioned, which in their ordinary signification have a more confined or a different meaning, shall in this Act, except where the nature of the provision or the context of the Act shall exclude such construction, be interpreted as follows; (that is to say,) the word "will" shall extend to a testament, and to a codicil, and to an appointment by will or by writing in the nature of a will in exercise of a power, [and also to an appointment by will of a guardian of a child][2] [. . .][3] and to any other testamentary disposition; **2–001**

---

[9] This section does not apply to a woman married since the passing of the Married Women's Property Act 1882; see also the Law Reform (Married Women and Tortfeasors) Act 1935.
[1] For the effect of the Law of Property Act 1922, see the Law of Property (Amendment) Act 1924, s.9, Sched. 9, para. 3.
[2] Words substituted by the Children Act 1989, s.108(5), Sched. 13, para. 1.
[3] Words repealed by the Statute Law (Repeals) Act 1969, s.1, Sched., Pt. III.

and the words "real estate" shall extend to manors, advowsons, messuages, lands tithes, rents, and hereditaments, [. . .][4] whether corporeal, incorporeal, or personal, [. . .][5] and to any estate, right, or interest (other than a chattel interest) therein; and the words "personal estate" shall extend to leasehold estates and other chattels real, and also to monies, shares of government and other funds, securities for money (not being real estates), debts, choses in action, rights, credits, goods, and all other property whatsoever which by law devolves upon the executor or administrator, and to any share or interest therein; and every word importing the singular number only shall extend and be applied to several persons or things as well as one person or thing; and every word importing the masculine gender only shall extend and be applied to a female as well as a male.

2. [*Repealed by the Statute Law Revision Act* 1874.]

All property may be disposed of by will

2–002 **3.**[6] It shall be lawful for every person to devise, bequeath, or dispose of, by his will executed in manner herein-after required, all real estate and all personal estate which he shall be entitled to, either at law or in equity, at the time of his death, and which if not so devised, bequeathed, or disposed of would devolve [. . .][7] upon his executor or administrator; and the power hereby given shall extend [. . .][8] to all contingent, executory, or other future interests in any real or personal estate, whether the testator may or may not be ascertained as the person or one of the persons in whom the same respectively may become vested, and whether he may be entitled thereto under the instrument by which the same respectively were created or under any disposition thereof by deed or will; and also to all rights of entry for conditions broken, and other rights of entry; and also to such of the same estates, interests, and rights respectively, and other real and personal estate, as the testator may be entitled to at the time of his death, notwithstanding that he may become entitled to the same subsequently to the execution of his will.

4–6. [*Repealed by the Statute Law (Repeals) Act* 1969, *s*.1, *Sched*., *Pt.* III.]

No will of a person under age valid

2–003 **7.** No will made by any person under the age of [eighteen years][9] shall be valid.

8. [*Repealed by the Statute Law (Repeals) Act* 1969, *s*.1, *Sched*., *Pt.* III.]

[Signing and attestation of wills

2–004 **9.** No will shall be valid unless—
(a) it is in writing, and signed by the testator, or by some other person in his presence and by his direction; and

---

[4] Words repealed by the Statute Law (Repeals) Act 1969, s.1, Sched., Pt. III.
[5] Words repealed by the Trusts of Land and Appointment of Trustees Act 1996, s.25(2), Sched. 4.
[6] For restrictions on the freedom of testamentary disposition, see the Inheritance (Provision for Family and Dependants) Act 1975, *post*, para. 34–001.
[7] Words repealed by the Statute Law (Repeals) Act 1969, s.1, Sched., Pt. III.
[8] Words repealed by the Statute Law (Repeals) Act 1969, s.1, Sched., Pt. III.
[9] Words substituted (in relation to wills made after 1969) by the Family Law Reform Act 1969, s.3(1)(a).

(b) it appears that the testator intended by his signature to give effect to the will; and
(c) the signature is made or acknowledged by the testator in the presence of two or more witnesses present at the same time; and
(d) each witness either—
(i) attests and signs the will; or
(ii) acknowledges his signature,
in the presence of the testator (but not necessarily in the presence of any other witness),
but no form of attestation shall be necessary.][10]

Appointments by will to be executed like other wills, and to be valid, although other required solemnities are not observed

10. No appointment made by will, in exercise of any power, shall be valid, unless the same be executed in manner herein-before required; and every will executed in manner herein-before required shall, so far as respects the execution and attestation thereof, be a valid execution of a power of appointment by will, notwithstanding it shall have been expressly required that a will made in exercise of such power should be executed with some additional or other form of execution or solemnity. **2–005**

Soldiers and mariners wills excepted

11.[11] Provided always, that any soldier being in actual military service, or any mariner or seaman being at sea, may dispose of his personal estate as he might have done before the making of this Act. **2–006**

12. [*Repealed by the Admiralty, etc., Acts Repeal Act* 1865, *s*.1.]

Publication not to be requisite

13. Every will executed in manner herein-before required shall be valid without any other publication thereof. **2–007**

Will not to be void on account of incompetency of attesting witness

14. If any person who shall attest the execution of a will shall at the time of the execution thereof or at any time afterwards be incompetent to be admitted a witness to prove the execution thereof, such will shall not on that account be invalid. **2–008**

Gifts to an attesting witness to be void

15.[12] If any person shall attest the execution of any will to whom or to whose wife or husband any beneficial devise, legacy, estate, interest, gift, or **2–009**

---

[10] s.9 substituted (in relation to wills taking effect after 1982) by the Administration of Justice Act 1982, ss.17, 73(6).
[11] Explained and extended by the Wills (Soldiers and Sailors) Act 1918, *post*, para. 5–001. See also the Family Law Reform Act 1969, s.3(3), *post*, para. 26–002.
[12] See the Wills Act 1968, s.1, *post*, para. 25–001.

appointment, of or affecting any real or personal estate (other than and except charges and directions for the payment of any debt or debts), shall be thereby given or made, such devise, legacy, estate, interest, gift, or appointment shall, so far only as concerns such person attesting the execution of such will, or the wife or husband of such person, or any person claiming under such person or wife or husband, be utterly null and void, and such person so attesting shall be admitted as a witness to prove the execution of such will, or to prove the validity or invalidity thereof, notwithstanding such devise, legacy, estate, interest, gift, or appointment mentioned in such will.

Creditor attesting to be admitted a witness

2–010 **16.** In case by any will any real or personal estate shall be charged with any debts or debts, and any creditor, or the wife or husband of any creditor, whose debt is so charged, shall attest the execution of such will, such creditor notwithstanding such charge shall be admitted a witness to prove the execution of such will, or to prove the validity or invalidity thereof.

Executor shall be admitted a witness

2–011 **17.** No person shall, on account of his being an executor of a will, be incompetent to be admitted a witness to prove the execution of such will, or a witness to prove the validity or invalidity thereof.

[Wills to be revoked by marriage, except in certain cases

2–012 **18.**—(1) Subject to subsections (2) to (4) below, a will shall be revoked by the testator's marriage.

(2) A disposition in a will in exercise of a power of appointment shall take effect notwithstanding the testator's subsequent marriage unless the property so appointed would in default of appointment pass to his personal representatives.

(3) Where it appears from a will that at the time it was made the testator was expecting to be married to a particular person and that he intended that the will should not be revoked by the marriage, the will shall not be revoked by his marriage to that person.

(4) Where it appears from a will that at the time it was made the testator was expecting to be married to a particular person and that he intended that a disposition in the will should not be revoked by his marriage to that person,—

(a) that disposition shall take effect notwithstanding the marriage; and
(b) any other disposition in the will shall take effect also, unless it appears from the will that the testator intended the disposition to be revoked by the marriage.][13]

[Effect of dissolution or annulment of marriage on wills

2–013 **18A.**—(1) Where, after a testator has made a will, [an order or decree][14] of a court [of civil jurisdiction in England and Wales][15] dissolves or annuls his

[13] s.18 substituted (in relation to wills made after 1982) by the Administration of Justice Act 1982, ss.18(1), 73(7).
[14] Words substituted by the Family Law Act 1996, s.66(1), Sched. 8, Pt. I, para. 1 from a day to be appointed.
[15] Words inserted by the Family Law Act 1986, s.53(a).

marriage [or his marriage is dissolved or annulled and the divorce or annulment is entitled to recognition in England and Wales by virtue of Part II of the Family Law Act 1986][16],—

[(a) provisions of the will appointing executors or trustees or conferring a power of appointment, if they appoint or confer the power on the former spouse, shall take effect as if the former spouse had died on the date on which the marriage is dissolved or annulled, and

(b) any property which, or an interest in which, is devised or bequeathed to the former spouse shall pass as if the former spouse had died on that date,][17]

except in so far as a contrary intention appears by the will.

(2) Subsection (1)(b) above is without prejudice to any right of the former spouse to apply for financial provision under the Inheritance (Provision for Family and Dependants) Act 1975.

(3) [*Repealed by the Law Reform (Succession) Act* 1995, *s*.5, *Sched.*]][18]

No will to be revoked by presumption

19. No will shall be revoked by any presumption of an intention on the ground of an alteration in circumstances. **2–014**

No will to be revoked but by another will or codicil, or by a writing executed like a will, or by destruction

20. No will or codicil, or any part thereof, shall be revoked otherwise than as aforesaid, or by another will or codicil, executed in manner herein-before required, or by some writing declaring an intention to revoke the same, and executed in the manner in which a will is herein-before required to be executed, or by the burning, tearing, or otherwise destroying the same by the testator, or by some person in his presence and by his direction, with the intention of revoking the same. **2–015**

No alteration in a will shall have any effect unless executed as a will

21. No obliteration, interlineation, or other alteration made in any will after the execution thereof shall be valid or have any effect, except so far as the words or effect of the will before such alteration shall not be apparent, unless such alteration shall be executed in like manner as herein-before is required for the execution of the will; but the will, with such alteration as part thereof, shall be deemed to be duly executed if the signature of the testator and the subscription of the witnesses be made in the margin or on some other part of the will opposite or near to such alteration, or at the foot or end of or opposite to a memorandum referring to such alteration, and written at the end or some other part of the will. **2–016**

[16] Words substituted by the Family Law Act 1986, s.53(b).

[17] Paras (a) and (b) substituted (in relation to wills taking effect after 1995) by the Law Reform (Succession) Act 1995, s.3.

[18] s.18A inserted (in relation to wills taking effect after 1982) by the Administration of Justice Act 1982, ss.18(2), 73(6).

No will revoked to be revived otherwise than by re-execution or a codicil to revive it

2–017 **22.** No will or codicil, or any part thereof, which shall be in any manner revoked, shall be revived otherwise than by the re-execution thereof, or by a codicil executed in manner herein-before required and showing an intention to revive the same; and when any will or codicil which shall be partly revoked, and afterwards wholly revoked, shall be revived, such revival shall not extend to so much thereof as shall have been revoked before the revocation of the whole thereof, unless an intention to the contrary shall be shown.

A devise not to be rendered inoperative by any subsequent conveyance or act

2–018 **23.** No conveyance or other act made or done subsequently to the execution of a will of or relating to any real or personal estate therein comprised, except an act by which such will shall be revoked as aforesaid, shall prevent the operation of the will with respect to such estate or interest in such real or personal estate as the testator shall have power to dispose of by will at the time of his death.

A will shall be construed to speak from the death of the testator

2–019 **24.** Every will shall be construed, with reference to the real estate and personal estate comprised in it, to speak and take effect as if it had been executed immediately before the death of the testator, unless a contrary intention shall appear by the will.

Residuary devise shall include estates comprised in lapsed and void devises

2–020 **25.** Unless a contrary intention shall appear by the will, such real estate or interest therein as shall be comprised or intended to be comprised in any devise in such will contained, which shall fail or be void by reason of the death of the devisee in the lifetime of the testator, or by reason of such devise being contrary to law, or otherwise incapable of taking effect, shall be included in the residuary devise (if any) contained in such will.

A general devise of the testator's lands shall include copyhold and leasehold as well as freehold estates

2–021 **26.** A devise of the land of the testator, or of the land of the testator in any place or in the occupation of any person mentioned in his will, or otherwise described in a general manner, and any other general devise which would describe a […][19] leasehold estate if the testator had no freehold estate which could be described by it, shall be construed to include the […][20] leasehold estates of the testator, or his […][21] leasehold estates, or any of them, to which such description shall extend, as the case may be, as well as freehold estates, unless a contrary intention shall appear by the will.

---

[19] Words repealed by the Statute Law (Repeals) Act 1969, s.1, Sched., Pt. III.
[20] Words repealed by the Statute Law (Repeals) Act 1969, s.1, Sched., Pt. III.
[21] Words repealed by the Statute Law (Repeals) Act 1969, s.1, Sched., Pt. III.

A general gift shall include estates over which the testator has a general power of appointment

27. A general devise of the real estate of the testator, or of the real estate of the testator in any place or in the occupation of any person mentioned in his will, or otherwise described in a general manner, shall be construed to include any real estate, or any real estate to which such description shall extend (as the case may be), which he may have power to appoint in any manner he may think proper, and shall operate as an execution of such power, unless a contrary intention shall appear by the will; and in like manner a bequest of the personal estate of the testator, or any bequest of personal property described in a general manner, shall be construed to include any personal estate, or any personal estate to which such description shall extend (as the case may be), which he may have power to appoint in any manner he may think proper, and shall operate as an execution of such power, unless a contrary intention shall appear by the will. **2–022**

A devise without any words of limitation shall be construed to pass the fee

28. Where any real estate shall be devised to any person without any words of limitation, such devise shall be construed to pass the fee simple, or other the whole estate or interest which the testator had power to dispose of by will in such real estate, unless a contrary intention shall appear by the will. **2–023**

The words "die without issue," or "die without leaving issue," shall be construed to mean die without issue living at the death

29. In any devise or bequest of real or personal estate the words "die without issue," or "die without leaving issue," or "have no issue," or any other words which may import either a want or failure of issue of any person in his lifetime or at the time of his death, or an indefinite failure of his issue, shall be construed to mean a want or failure of issue in the lifetime or at the time of the death of such person, and not an indefinite failure of his issue, unless a contrary intention shall appear by the will, by reason of such person having a prior estate tail, or of a preceding gift, being, without any implication arising from such words, a limitation of an estate tail to such person or issue, or otherwise: provided that this Act shall not extend to cases where such words as aforesaid import if no issue described in a preceding gift shall be born, or if there shall be no issue who shall live to attain the age or otherwise answer the description required for obtaining a vested estate by a preceding gift to such issue. **2–024**

No devise to trustees or executors, except for a term or a presentation to a church, shall pass a chattel interest

30. Where any real estate (other than or not being a presentation to a church) shall be devised to any trustee or executor, such devise shall be construed to pass the fee simple or other the whole estate or interest which the testator had power to dispose of by will in such real estate, unless a definite term of years, absolute or determinable, or an estate of freehold, shall thereby be given to him expressly or by implication. **2–025**

Trustees under an unlimited devise, where the trust may endure beyond the life of a person beneficially entitled for life, to take the fee

2–026 **31.** Where any real estate shall be devised to a trustee, without any express limitation of the estate to be taken by such trustee, and the beneficial interest in such real estate, or in the surplus rents and profits thereof, shall not be given to any person for life, or such beneficial interest shall be given to any person for life, but the purposes of the trust may continue beyond the life of such person, such devise shall be construed to vest in such trustee the fee simple, or other the whole legal estate which the testator had power to dispose of by will in such real estate, and not an estate determinable when the purposes of the trust shall be satisfied.

32. [*Repealed by the Trusts of Land and Appointment of Trustees Act* 1996, *s*.25(2), *Sched.* 4.]

[Gifts to children or other issue who leave issue living at the testator's death shall not lapse

2–027 **33.**—(1) Where—

(a) a will contains a devise or bequest to a child or remoter descendant of the testator; and
(b) the intended beneficiary dies before the testator, leaving issue; and
(c) issue of the intended beneficiary are living at the testator's death,

then, unless a contrary intention appears by the will, the devise or bequest shall take effect as a devise or bequest to the issue living at the testator's death.

(2) Where—

(a) a will contains a devise or bequest to a class of persons consisting of children or remoter descendants of the testator; and
(b) a member of the class dies before the testator, leaving issue; and
(c) issue of that member are living at the testator's death,

then, unless a contrary intention appears by the will, the devise or bequest shall take effect as if the class included the issue of its deceased member living at the testator's death.

(3) Issue shall take under this section through all degrees, according to their stock, in equal shares if more than one, any gift or share which their parent would have taken and so that no issue shall take whose parent is living at the testator's death and so capable of taking.

(4) For the purposes of this section—

(a) the illegitimacy of any person is to be disregarded; and
(b) a person conceived before the testator's death and born living thereafter is to be taken to have been living at the testator's death.][22]

. . . . . .

[22] s.33 substituted (in relation to wills taking effect after 1982) by the Administration of Justice Act 1982, ss.19, 73(6).

Schools Sites Act 1841

(4 & 5 VICT. C. 38)

Landlords empowered to convey land to be used as sites for schools, etc.

2.[1] Any person, being seised in fee simple, fee tail, or for life, of and in any manor or lands of freehold, copyhold, or customary tenure, and having the beneficial interest therein, [. . .][2] may grant, convey, or enfranchise by way of gift, sale, or exchange, in fee simple or for a term of years, any quantity not exceeding one acre of such land, as a site for a school for the education of poor persons, or for the residence of the schoolmaster or schoolmistress, or otherwise for the purposes of the education of such poor persons in religious and useful knowledge; provided that no such grant made by any person seised only for life of and in any such manor or lands shall be valid, unless the person next entitled to the same in remainder, in fee simple or fee tail, (if legally competent,) shall be a party to and join in such grant: Provided also, that where any portion of waste or commonable land shall be gratuitously conveyed by any lord or lady of a manor for any such purposes as aforesaid, the rights and interest of all persons in the said land shall be barred and divested by such conveyance; Provided also, that upon the said land so granted as aforesaid, or any part thereof, ceasing to be used for the purposes in this Act mentioned, the same shall thereupon immediately revert to and become a portion of the said estate held in fee simple or otherwise, or of any manor or land as aforesaid, as fully to all intents and purposes as if this Act had not been passed, any thing herein contained to the contrary notwithstanding. **3–001**

Trustees empowered to sell or exchange lands or buildings

14. When any land or building shall have been or shall be given or acquired under the provisions of the said first-recited Act[3] or this Act, or shall be held in trust for the purposes aforesaid, and it shall be deemed advisable to sell or exchange the same for any other more convenient or eligible site, it shall be lawful for the trustees in whom the legal estate in the said land or building shall be vested, by the direction or with the consent of the managers and directors of the said school, if any such there be, to sell or exchange the said land or building, or part thereof, for other land or building suitable to the purposes of their trust, and to receive on any exchange any sum of money by way of effecting an equality of exchange, and to apply the money arising from such sale or given on such exchange in the purchase of another site, or in the improvement of other premises used or to be used for the purposes of such trust; provided that where the land shall have been given by any ecclesiastical corporation sole, the consent of the bishop of the diocese shall be required to be given to such sale or exchange before the same shall take place: Provided also, that where a portion of any **3–002**

[1] See the Reverter of Sites Act 1987, *post*, para. 49–001.
[2] Words repealed by the Statute Law Revision (No. 2) Act 1888.
[3] This is a reference to the Schools Sites Act 1836, which was repealed by the Schools Sites Act 1841, s.1 (itself repealed by the Statute Law Revision (No. 2) Act 1874).

parliamentary grant shall have been or shall be applied towards the erection of any school, no sale or exchange thereof shall take place [unless the Secretary of State[4] consents].[5]

Common Law Procedure Act 1852

(15 & 16 VICT. C. 76)

Ejectment[1]

Proceedings in ejectment by landlord for non-payment of rent

4–001 **210.** In all cases between landlord and tenant, as often as it shall happen that one half year's rent shall be in arrear, and the landlord or lessor, to whom the same is due, hath right by law to re-enter for the non-payment thereof, such landlord or lessor shall and may, without any formal demand or re-entry, serve a writ in ejectment for the recovery of the demised premises, [. . .][2] which service [. . .][3] shall stand in the place and stead of a demand and re-entry; and in case of judgment against the defendant for nonappearance, if it shall be made appear to the court where the said action is depending, by affidavit, or be proved upon the trial in case the defendant appears, that half a year's rent was due before the said writ was served, and that no sufficient distress was to be found on the demised premises, countervailing the arrears then due, and that the lessor had power to re-enter, then and in every such case the lessor shall recover judgment and execution, in the same manner as if the rent in arrear had been legally demanded, and a re-entry made; and in case the lessee or his assignee, or other person claiming or deriving under the said lease, shall permit and suffer judgment to be had and recovered on such trial in ejectment, and execution to be executed thereon, without paying the rent and arrears, together with full costs, and without proceeding for relief in equity within six months after such execution executed, then and in such case the said lessee, his assignee, and all other persons claiming and deriving under the said lease, shall be barred and foreclosed from all relief or remedy in law or equity, other than by bringing error for reversal of such judgment, in case the same shall be erroneous, and the said landlord or lessor shall from thenceforth hold the said demised premises discharged from such lease; [. . .][4] provided that nothing herein contained shall

[4] The functions of the Secretary of State under this Act, in so far as they are exercisable in relation to Wales, are transferred to the National Assembly for Wales: National Assembly for Wales (Transfer of Functions) Order 1999 (S.I. 1999 No. 672), art. 2(a), Sched. 1.

[5] Words substituted by the Statute Law (Repeals) Act 1978, s.1(2), Sched. 2, para. 1.

[1] In relation to a long lease (generally, any lease originally granted for a term certain exceeding 21 years) of a dwelling, the landlord may not exercise the right of re-entry or forfeiture in relation to a failure to pay rent unless the unpaid amount exceeds a prescribed sum (not exceeding £500) or the unpaid sum includes an amount that has been payable for more than a prescribed period: Commonhold and Leasehold Reform Act 2002, s.167. For restrictions on the recovery of possession of dwellings generally, see the Protection from Eviction Act 1977, *post*, para. 37–001. For jurisdiction to grant relief against forfeiture, see also the Supreme Court Act 1981, s.38, *post*, para. 40–003, the County Courts Act 1984, ss.138–140, *post*, paras 42–007–42–009 *et seq.* and the Law of Property Act 1925, s.146(4), *post*, para. 9–122.

[2] Words repealed by the Statute Law Revision Act 1892.

[3] Words repealed by the Statute Law Revision Act 1892.

[4] Words repealed by the Statute Law Revision Act 1892.

extend to bar the right of any mortgagee of such lease, or any part thereof, who shall not be in possession, so as such mortgagee shall and do, within six months after such judgment obtained and execution executed pay all rent in arrear, and all costs and damages sustained by such lessor or person entitled to the remainder or reversion as aforesaid, and perform all the covenants and agreements which, on the part and behalf of the first lessee, are and ought to be performed.

Lessee proceeding in equity not to have injunction or relief without payment of rent and costs

211. In case the said lessee, his assignee, or other person claiming any right, title, or interest, in law or equity, of, in, or to the said lease, shall, within the time aforesaid, proceed for relief in any court of equity, such person shall not have or continue any injunction against the proceedings at law on such ejectment, unless he does or shall, within forty days next after a full and perfect answer shall be made by the claimant in such ejectment, bring into court, and lodge with the proper officer such sum and sums of money as the lessor or landlord shall in his answer swear to be due and in arrear over and above all just allowances, and also the costs taxed in the said suit, there to remain till the hearing of the cause, or to be paid out to the lessor or landlord on good security, subject to the decree of the court; and in case such proceedings for relief in equity shall be taken within the time aforesaid, and after execution is executed, the lessor or landlord shall be accountable only for so much and no more as he shall really and bona fide, without fraud, deceit, or wilful neglect, make of the demised premises from the time of his entering into the actual possession thereof; and if what shall be so made by the lessor or landlord happen to be less than the rent reserved on the said lease, then the said lessee or his assignee, before he shall be restored to his possession, shall pay such lessor or landlord what the money so by him made fell short of the reserved rent for the time such lessor or landlord held the said lands. **4–002**

Tenant paying all rent with costs, proceedings to cease

212. If the tenant or his assignee do or shall, at any time before the trial in such ejectment, pay or tender to the lessor or landlord, his executors or administrators, or his or their attorney in that cause, or pay into the court where the same cause is depending, all the rent and arrears, together with the costs, then and in such case all further proceedings on the said ejectment shall cease and be discontinued; and if such lessee, his executors, administrators, or assigns, shall, upon such proceedings as aforesaid, be relieved in equity, he and they shall have, hold, and enjoy the demised lands, according to the lease thereof made, without any new lease. **4–003**

Wills (Soldiers and Sailors) Act 1918[1]

(7 & 8 Geo. 5, c. 58)

Explanation of s.11 of Wills Act 1837

5–001 **1.** In order to remove doubts as to the construction of the Wills Act 1837, it is hereby declared and enacted that section eleven of that Act authorises and always has authorised any soldier being in actual military service, or any mariner or seaman being at sea, to dispose of his personal estate as he might have done before the passing of that Act, though under the age of [eighteen years][2].

Extension of s.11 of Wills Act 1837

5–002 **2.** Section eleven of the Wills Act 1837 shall extend to any member of His Majesty's naval or marine forces not only when he is at sea but also when he is so circumstanced that if he were a soldier he would be in actual military service within the meaning of that section.

Validity of testamentary dispositions of real property made by soldiers and sailors

5–003 **3.**—(1) A testamentary disposition of any real estate in England or Ireland made by a person to whom section eleven of the Wills Act 1837 applies, and who dies after the passing of this Act, shall, notwithstanding that the person making the disposition was at the time of making it under [eighteen years][3] of age or that the disposition has not been made in such manner or form as was at the passing of this Act required by law, be valid in any case where the person making the disposition was of such age and the disposition has been made in such manner and form that if the disposition had been a disposition of personal estate made by such a person domiciled in England or Ireland it would have been valid.

(2) A testamentary disposition of any heritable property in Scotland made after the passing of this Act by a person to whom section eleven of the Wills Act 1837 applies or to whom it would apply if he were domiciled in England, shall not be invalid by reason only of the fact that such person is under twenty-one years of age, provided always that he is of such age that he could, if domiciled in Scotland, have made a valid testamentary disposition of moveable property.

Power to appoint testamentary guardians

5–004 **4.** Where any person dies after the passing of this Act having made a will which is, or which, if it had been a disposition of property, would have been rendered valid by section eleven of the Wills Act 1837, any appointment contained in the will of any person as guardian of the infant children of the testator shall be of full force and effect.

[1] See the Family Law Reform Act 1969, s.3(3), *post*, para. 26–002.
[2] Words substituted (in relation to wills made after 1969) by the Family Law Reform Act 1969, s.3(1)(b).
[3] Words substituted (in relation to wills made after 1969) by the Family Law Reform Act 1969, s.3(1)(b).

Short title and interpretation

5.—(1) This Act may be cited as the Wills (Soldiers and Sailors) Act 1918. **5–005**

(2) For the purposes of section eleven of the Wills Act 1837 and this Act the expression "soldier" includes a member of the Air Force, and references in this Act to the said section eleven include a reference to that section as explained and extended by this Act.

Law of Property Act 1922

(12 & 13 Geo. 5, c. 16)

Part VII

Provisions Respecting Leaseholds

Conversion of Perpetually Renewable Leaseholds into Long Terms

Conversion of perpetually renewable leaseholds

145.[1] For the purpose of converting perpetually renewable leases and underleases (not being an interest in perpetually renewable copyhold land enfranchised by Part V of this Act, but including a perpetually renewable underlease derived out of an interest in perpetually renewable copyhold land) into long terms, for preventing the creation of perpetually renewable leasehold interests and for providing for the interests of the persons affected, the provisions contained in the Fifteenth Schedule to this Act shall have effect. **6–001**

Section 145 FIFTEENTH SCHEDULE

PROVISIONS RELATING TO PERPETUALLY RENEWABLE LEASES AND UNDERLEASES

Conversion of Perpetually Renewable Leases into Long Terms

1.—(1) Land comprised in a perpetually renewable lease which was subsisting at the commencement of this Act shall, by virtue of this Act, vest in the person who at such commencement was entitled to such lease, for a term of two thousand years, to be calculated from the date at which the existing term or interest commenced, at the rent and subject to the lessees' covenants and conditions (if any) which under the lease would have been payable or enforceable during the subsistence of such term or interest.

(2) The rent, covenants and conditions (if any) shall (subject to the express provisions of this Act to the contrary) be payable and enforceable during the subsistence of the term created by this Act; and that term shall take effect in substitution for the term or interest created by the lease, and be subject to the like power of re-entry (if any) and other provisions which affected the term or interest created by the lease, but without any right of renewal.

Conversion of Perpetually Renewable Underleases into Long Terms

2.—(1) Land comprised in any underlease, which at the commencement of this Act was perpetually renewable and was derived out of a head term affected by this Act, shall, by virtue of this Act, vest in the person who at such commencement was entitled to the subterm or interest for a term

[1] See the Law of Property Act 1925, s.202, *post*, para. 9–167.

of two thousand years less one day, to be calculated from the date at which the head term created by this Act commenced, at the rent and subject to the underlessee's covenants and conditions (if any) which under the underlease would have been payable or enforceable during the subsistence of such subterm or interest.

(2) The rent, covenants and conditions (if any) shall (subject to the express provisions of this Act to the contrary) be payable and enforceable during the subsistence of the subterm created by this Act; and that subterm shall take effect in substitution for the subterm or interest created by the underlease, and be subject to the like power of re-entry (if any) and other provisions which affected the subterm or interest created by the underlease, but without any right of renewal.

(3) The foregoing provisions of this section shall also apply to any perpetually renewable subterm or interest which, at the commencement of this Act, was derived out of any other subterm or interest, but so that in every case the subterm created by this Act shall be one day less in duration than the derivative term created by this Act, out of which it takes effect.

DISPOSITIONS PURPORTING TO CREATE PERPETUALLY RENEWABLE LEASEHOLDS

5.—(1) A grant, after the commencement of this Act, of a term, subterm, or other leasehold interest with a covenant or obligation for perpetual renewal, which would have been valid if this Part of this Act had not been passed, shall (subject to the express provisions of this Act) take effect as a demise for a term of two thousand years or in the case of a subdemise for a term less in duration by one day than the term out of which it is derived, to commence from the date fixed for the commencement of the term, subterm, or other interest, and in every case free from any obligation for renewal or for payment of any fines, fees, costs, or other money in respect of renewal.

[(2)Sub-paragraph (3) applies where a grant—

(a) relates to commonhold land, and

(b) would take effect by virtue of sub-paragraph (1) as a demise for a term of two thousand years or a subdemise for a fixed term.

(3) The grant shall be treated as if it purported to be a grant of the term referred to in sub-paragraph (2)(b) (and sections 17 and 18 of the Commonhold and Leasehold Reform Act 2002 (residential and non-residential leases) shall apply accordingly).][2]

Settled Land Act 1925[1]

(15 GEO. 5, C. 18)

ARRANGEMENT OF SECTIONS

PART I

GENERAL PRELIMINARY PROVISIONS

Settlements and Settled Land

---

[2] Sub-paras (2) and (3) added by the Commonhold and Leasehold Reform Act 2002, s.68, Sched. 5, para. 1.

[1] See the Trusts of Land and Appointment of Trustees Act 1996, *post*, para. 62–001.

PART I

GENERAL PRELIMINARY PROVISIONS

Settlements and Settled Land[2]

What constitutes a settlement

1.—(1) Any deed, will, agreement for a settlement or other agreement, Act of **7–001**
Parliament, or other instrument, or any number of instruments, whether made

[2] See the Trusts of Land and Appointment of Trustees Act 1996, s.2, *post*, para. 62–002.

or passed before or after, or partly before and partly after, the commencement of this Act, under or by virtue of which instrument or instruments any land, after the commencement of this Act, stands for the time being—

(i) limited in trust for any persons by way of succession; or

(ii) limited in trust for any person in possession—

(a) for an entailed interest whether or not capable of being barred or defeated;

(b) for an estate in fee simple or for a term of years absolute subject to an executory limitation, gift, or disposition over on failure of his issue or in any other event;

(c) for a base or determinable fee [(other than a fee which is a fee simple absolute by virtue of section 7 of the Law of Property Act 1925)][3] or any corresponding interest in leasehold land;

(d) being an infant, for an estate in fee simple or for a term of years absolute; or

(iii) limited in trust for any person for an estate in fee simple or for a term of years absolute contingently on the happening of any event; or

[. . .][4]

(v) charged, whether voluntarily or in consideration of marriage or by way of family arrangement, and whether immediately or after an interval, with the payment of any rentcharge for the life of any person, or any less period, or of any capital, annual or periodical sums for the portions, advancement, maintenance, or otherwise for the benefit of any persons, with or without any term of years for securing or raising the same;

creates or is for the purposes of this Act a settlement and is in this Act referred to as a settlement, or as the settlement, as the case requires:

Provided that, where land is the subject of a compound settlement, references in this Act to the settlement shall be construed as meaning such compound settlement, unless the context otherwise requires.

(2) Where an infant is beneficially entitled to land for an estate in fee simple or for a term of years absolute and by reason of an intestacy or otherwise there is no instrument under which the interest of the infant arises or is acquired, a settlement shall be deemed to have been made by the intestate, or by the person whose interest the infant has acquired.

(3)[5] An infant shall be deemed to be entitled in possession notwithstanding any subsisting right of dower (not assigned by metes and bounds) affecting the land, and such a right of dower shall be deemed to be an interest comprised in the subject of the settlement and coming to the dowress under or by virtue of the settlement.

Where dower has been assigned by metes and bounds, the letters of administration or probate granted in respect of the estate of the husband of the dowress shall be deemed a settlement made by the husband.

(4) An estate or interest not disposed of by a settlement and remaining in or reverting to the settlor, or any person deriving title under him, is for the purposes of this Act an estate or interest comprised in the subject of the settlement and coming to the settlor or such person under or by virtue of the settlement.

(5) Where—

[3] Words inserted by the Trusts of Land and Appointment of Trustees Act 1996, s.25(1), Sched. 3, para. 2(1), (2).

[4] Para. (iv) repealed by the Married Women (Restraint upon Anticipation) Act 1949, s.1(4), Sched. 2.

[5] Dower was abolished by the Administration of Estates Act 1925, s.45(1)(c), *post*, para. 10–036.

(a) a settlement creates an entailed interest which is incapable of being barred or defeated, or a base or determinable fee, whether or not the reversion or right of reverter is in the Crown, or any corresponding interest in leasehold land; or

(b) the subject of a settlement is an entailed interest, or a base or determinable fee, whether or not the reversion or right of reverter is in the Crown, or any corresponding interest in leasehold land;

the reversion or right of reverter upon the cesser of the interest so created or settled shall be deemed to be an interest comprised in the subject of the settlement, and limited by the settlement.

(6) Subsections (4) and (5) of this section bind the Crown.

[(7) This section does not apply to land held upon trust for sale.][6]

What is settled land

2. Land which is or is deemed to be the subject of a settlement is for the purposes of this Act settled land, and is in relation to the settlement referred to in this Act as the settled land. **7–002**

Duration of settlements

3. Land [which has been subject to a settlement which is a settlement for the purposes of this Act][7] shall be deemed for the purposes of this Act to remain and be settled land, and the settlement shall be deemed to be a subsisting settlement for the purposes of this Act so long as— **7–003**

(a) any limitation, charge, or power of charging under the settlement subsists, or is capable of being exercised; or

(b) the person who, if of full age, would be entitled as beneficial owner to have that land vested in him for a legal estate is an infant.

Authorised method of settling land inter vivos

4.—(1) Every settlement of a legal estate in land inter vivos shall, save as in this Act otherwise provided, be effected by two deeds, namely, a vesting deed and a trust instrument and if effected in any other way shall not operate to transfer or create a legal estate. **7–004**

(2) By the vesting deed the land shall be conveyed to the tenant for life or statutory owner (and if more than one as joint tenants) for the legal estate the subject of the intended settlement:

Provided that, where such legal estate is already vested in the tenant for life or statutory owner, it shall be sufficient, without any other conveyance, if the vesting deed declares that the land is vested in him for that estate.

(3) The trust instrument shall—

(a) declare the trusts affecting the settled land;

(b) appoint or constitute trustees of the settlement;

(c) contain the power, if any, to appoint new trustees of the settlement;

(d) set out, either expressly or by reference, any powers intended to be conferred by the settlement in extension of those conferred by this Act;

---

[6] subs. (7) added by the Law of Property (Amendment) Act 1926, s.7, Sched.

[7] Words substituted by the Trusts of Land and Appointment of Trustees Act 1996, s.25(1), Sched. 3, para. 2(1), (3).

(e) bear any ad valorem stamp duty which may be payable (whether by virtue of the vesting deed or otherwise) in respect of the settlement.

Contents of vesting deeds

7–005 **5.**—(1) Every vesting deed for giving effect to a settlement or for conveying settled land to a tenant for life or statutory owner during the subsistence of the settlement (in this Act referred to as a "principal vesting deed") shall contain the following statements and particulars, namely:—

(a) A description, either specific or general, of the settled land;
(b) A statement that the settled land is vested in the person or persons to whom it is conveyed or in whom it is declared to be vested upon the trusts from time to time affecting the settled land;
(c) The names of the persons who are the trustees of the settlement;
(d) Any additional or larger powers conferred by the trust instrument relating to the settled land which by virtue of this Act operate and are exercisable as if conferred by this Act on a tenant for life;
(e) The name of any person for the time being entitled under the trust instrument to appoint new trustees of the settlement.

(2) The statements or particulars required by this section may be incorporated by reference to an existing vesting instrument, and, where there is a settlement subsisting at the commencement of this Act, by reference to that settlement and to any instrument whereby land has been conveyed to the uses or upon the trusts of that settlement, but not (save as last aforesaid) by reference to a trust instrument nor by reference to a disentailing deed.

(3) A principal vesting deed shall not be invalidated by reason only of any error in any of the statements or particulars by this Act required to be contained therein.

Procedure in the case of settlements by will

7–006 **6.** Where a settlement is created by the will of an estate owner who dies after the commencement of this Act—

(a) the will is for the purposes of this Act a trust instrument; and
(b) the personal representatives of the testator shall hold the settled land on trust, if and when required so to do, to convey it to the person who, under the will, or by virtue of this Act, is the tenant for life or statutory owner, and, if more than one, as joint tenants.

Procedure on change of ownership

7–007 **7.**—(1) If, on the death of a tenant for life or statutory owner, or of the survivor of two or more tenants for life or statutory owners, in whom the settled land was vested, the land remains settled land, his personal representatives shall hold the settled land on trust, if and when required so to do, to convey it to the person who under the trust instrument or by virtue of this Act becomes the tenant for life or statutory owner and, if more than one, as joint tenants.

(2) If a person by reason of attaining full age becomes a tenant for life for the purposes of this Act of settled land, he shall be entitled to require the trustees of the settlement, personal representatives, or other persons in whom the settled land is vested, to convey the land to him.

(3) If a person who, when of full age, will together with another person or

other persons constitute the tenant for life for the purposes of this Act of settled land attains that age, he shall be entitled to require the tenant for life, trustees of the settlement, personal representatives or other persons in whom the settled land is vested to convey the land to him and the other person or persons who together with him constitute the tenant for life as joint tenants.

(4) If by reason of forfeiture, surrender, or otherwise the estate owner of any settled land ceases to have the statutory powers of a tenant for life and the land remains settled land, he shall be bound forthwith to convey the settled land to the person who under the trust instrument, or by virtue of this Act, becomes the tenant for life or statutory owner and, if more than one, as joint tenants.

(5) If any person of full age becomes absolutely entitled to the settled land (whether beneficially, or as personal representative, or as [trustee of land][8], or otherwise) free from all limitations, powers, and charges taking effect under the settlement, he shall be entitled to require the trustees of the settlement, personal representatives, or other persons in whom the settled land is vested, to convey the land to him, and if more persons than one being of full age become so entitled to the settled land they shall be entitled to require such persons as aforesaid to convey the land to them as joint tenants.

Mode and costs of conveyance, and saving of rights of personal representatives and equitable chargees

8.—(1) A conveyance by personal representatives under either of the last two preceding sections may be made by an assent in writing signed by them which shall operate as a conveyance. **7–008**

(2) Every conveyance under either of the last two preceding sections shall be made at the cost of the trust estate.

(3) The obligations to convey settled land imposed by the last two preceding sections are subject and without prejudice—

(a) where the settlement is created by a will, to the rights and powers of the personal representatives for purposes of administration; and

(b) in any case, to the person on whom the obligation is imposed being satisfied that provision has been or will be made for the payment of any unpaid death duties in respect of the land or any interest therein for which he is accountable, and any interest and costs in respect of such duties, or that he is otherwise effectually indemnified against such duties, interest and costs.

(4) Where the land is or remains settled land a conveyance under either of the last two preceding sections shall—

(a) if by deed, be a principal vesting deed; and

(b) if by an assent, be a vesting assent, which shall contain the like statements and particulars as are required by this Act in the case of a principal vesting deed.

(5) Nothing contained in either of the last two preceding sections affects the right of personal representatives to transfer or create such legal estates to take effect in priority to a conveyance under either of those sections as may be required for giving effect to the obligations imposed on them by statute.

(6) A conveyance under either of the last two preceding sections, if made by deed, may contain a reservation to the person conveying of a term of years

[8] Words substituted by the Trusts of Land and Appointment of Trustees Act 1996, s.25(1), Sched. 3, para. 2(1), (4).

absolute in the land conveyed, upon trusts for indemnifying him against any unpaid death duties in respect of the land conveyed or any interest therein, and any interest and costs in respect of such duties.

(7) Nothing contained in either of the last two preceding sections affects any right which a person entitled to an equitable charge for securing money actually raised, and affecting the whole estate the subject of the settlement, may have to require effect to be given thereto by a legal mortgage, before the execution of a conveyance under either of those sections.

Procedure in the case of settlements and of instruments deemed to be trust instruments

7–009 **9.**—(1) Each of the following settlements or instruments shall for the purposes of this Act be deemed to be a trust instrument, and any reference to a trust instrument contained in this Act shall apply thereto, namely:—

(i) An instrument executed, or, in case of a will, coming into operation, after the commencement of this Act which by virtue of this Act is deemed to be a settlement;

(ii) A settlement which by virtue of this Act is deemed to have been made by any person after the commencement of this Act;

(iii) An instrument inter vivos intended to create a settlement of a legal estate in land which is executed after the commencement of this Act, and does not comply with the requirements of this Act with respect to the method of effecting such a settlement; and

(iv) A settlement made after the commencement of this Act (including a settlement by the will of a person who dies after such commencement) of any of the following interests—

(a) an equitable interest in land which is capable, when in possession, of subsisting at law; or

(b) an entailed interest; or

(c) a base or determinable fee or any corresponding interest in leasehold land,

but only if and when the interest settled takes effect free from all equitable interests and powers under every prior settlement (if any).

(2) As soon as practicable after a settlement, or an instrument which for the purposes of this Act is deemed to be a trust instrument, takes effect as such, the trustees of the settlement may, and on the request of the tenant for life or statutory owner shall, execute a principal vesting deed, containing the proper statements and particulars, declaring that the legal estate in the settled land shall vest or is vested in the person or persons therein named, being the tenant for life or statutory owner, and including themselves if they are the statutory owners, and such deed shall, unless the legal estate is already so vested, operate to convey or vest the legal estate in the settled land to or in the person or persons aforesaid and, if more than one, as joint tenants.

(3) If there are no trustees of the settlement, then (in default of a person able and willing to appoint such trustees) an application under this Act shall be made to the court for the appointment of such trustees.

(4) The provisions of the last preceding section with reference to a conveyance shall apply, so far as they are applicable, to a principal vesting deed under this section.

Procedure on acquisition of land to be made subject to a settlement

10.—(1) Where after the commencement of this Act land is acquired with capital money arising under this Act or in exchange for settled land, or a rentcharge is reserved on a grant of settled land, the land shall be conveyed to, and the rentcharge shall by virtue of this Act become vested in, the tenant for life or statutory owner, and such conveyance or grant is in this Act referred to as a subsidiary vesting deed: **7–010**

Provided that, where an instrument is subsisting at the commencement of this Act, or is made or comes into operation after such commencement, by virtue of which any money or securities are liable under this Act, or the Acts which it replaces, or under a trust or direction contained in the instrument, to be invested in the purchase of land to be conveyed so as to become settled land, but at the commencement of this Act, or when such instrument is made or comes into operation after such commencement, as the case may be, there is no land in respect of which a principal vesting deed is capable of being executed, the first deed after the commencement of this Act by which any land is acquired as aforesaid shall be a principal vesting deed and shall be framed accordingly.

(2) A subsidiary vesting deed executed on the acquisition of land to be made subject to a settlement shall contain the following statements and particulars, namely—

(a) particulars of the last or only principal vesting instrument affecting land subject to the settlement;

(b) a statement that the land conveyed is to be held upon and subject to the same trusts and powers as the land comprised in such last or only principal vesting instrument;

(c) the names of the persons who are the trustees of the settlement;

(d) the name of any person for the time being entitled to appoint new trustees of the settlement.

(3) A subsidiary vesting deed reserving a rentcharge on a grant of settled land shall contain the following statements and particulars—

(a) a statement that the rentcharge is vested in the grantor and is subject to the settlement which, immediately before the grant, was subsisting with respect to the land out of which it was reserved;

(b) particulars of the last or only principal vesting instrument affecting such land.

(4) A subsidiary vesting deed shall not be invalidated by reason only of any error in any of the statements or particulars by this Act required to be contained therein.

(5) The acquisition of the land shall not operate to increase or multiply charges or powers of charging.

As to contracts for the settlement of land

11.—(1) A contract made or other liability created or arising after the commencement of this Act for the settlement of land— **7–011**

(i) by or on the part of an estate owner; or

(ii) by a person entitled to—

(a) an equitable interest which is capable when in possession of subsisting at law; or

(b) an entailed interest; or

(c) a base or determinable fee or any corresponding interest in leasehold land;

shall, but in cases under paragraph (ii) only if and when the interest of the person entitled takes effect free from all equitable interests and powers under every prior settlement, if any, be deemed an estate contract within the meaning of the Land Charges Act 1925[9], and may be registered as a land charge accordingly, and effect shall be given thereto by a vesting deed and a trust instrument in accordance with this Act.

(2) A contract made or other liability created or arising before the commencement of this Act to make a settlement of land shall be deemed to be sufficiently complied with if effect is given thereto by a vesting deed and a trust instrument in accordance with this Act.

Power to make vesting orders as to settled land

7–012 **12.**—(1) If—

(a) any person who is bound under this Part of this Act to execute a conveyance, vesting deed or vesting assent or in whom settled land is wrongly vested refuses or neglects to execute the requisite conveyance, vesting deed or vesting assent within one month after demand in writing; or

(b) any such person is outside the United Kingdom, or cannot be found, or it is not known whether he is alive or dead; or

(c) for any reason the court is satisfied that the conveyance, vesting deed or vesting assent cannot be executed, or cannot be executed without undue delay or expense;

the court may, on the application of any person interested, make an order vesting the settled land in the tenant for life or statutory owner or person, if any, of full age absolutely entitled (whether beneficially or as personal representative or [trustee of land][10] or otherwise), and, if the land remains settled land, the provisions of this Act relating to a principal vesting deed or a subsidiary vesting deed, as the case may be, shall apply to any order so made and every such order shall contain the like statements and particulars.

(2) No stamp duty shall be payable in respect of a vesting order made in place of a vesting or other assent.

Dispositions not to take effect until vesting instrument is made

7–013 **13.** Where a tenant for life or statutory owner has become entitled to have a principal vesting deed or a vesting assent executed in his favour, then until a vesting instrument is executed or made pursuant to this Act in respect of the settled land, any purported disposition thereof inter vivos by any person, other than a personal representative (not being a disposition which he has power to make in right of his equitable interests or powers under a trust instrument), shall not take effect except in favour of a purchaser of a legal estate [without notice of such tenant for life or statutory owner having become so entitled as aforesaid][11], but, save as aforesaid, shall operate only as a contract for valuable consideration to carry out the transaction after the requisite vesting instrument has been executed or made, and a purchaser of a legal estate shall not be concerned with such disposition unless the contract is registered as a land charge.

[9] Now the Land Charges Act 1972, s.2(4), *post*, para. 31–002.

[10] Words substituted by the Trusts of Land and Appointment of Trustees Act 1996, s.25(1), Sched. 3, para. 2(1), (5).

[11] Words substituted by the Law of Property (Amendment) Act 1926, s.7, Sched.

[Nothing in this section affects the creation or transfer of a legal estate by virtue of an order of the court or the Minister or other competent authority.][12]

Forfeiture and stamps

14.—(1) Any vesting effected under the powers conferred by this Act in relation to settled land shall not operate as a breach of a covenant or condition against alienation or give rise to a forfeiture. **7–014**

(2) Nothing in this Act shall operate to impose any stamp duty on a vesting or other assent.

Examples of instruments

15. Examples of instruments framed in accordance with the provisions of this Act are contained in the First Schedule to this Act. **7–015**

Enforcement of Equitable Interests and Powers against Estate Owner and discharge on termination of Settlement

Enforcement of equitable interests and powers against estate owner

16.[13]—(1) All equitable interests and powers in or over settled land (whether created before or after the date of any vesting instrument affecting the legal estate) shall be enforceable against the estate owner in whom the settled land is vested (but in the case of personal representatives without prejudice to their rights and powers for purposes of administration) in manner following (that is to say):— **7–016**

(i) The estate owner shall stand possessed of the settled land and the income thereof upon such trusts and subject to such powers and provisions as may be requisite for giving effect to the equitable interests and powers affecting the settled land or the income thereof of which he has notice according to their respective priorities;

(ii) Where any person of full age becomes entitled to require a legal estate in the settled land to be vested in him in priority to the settlement, by reason of a right of reverter, statutory or otherwise, or an equitable right of entry taking effect, or on the ground that his interest ought no longer to be capable of being over-reached under the powers of this Act, the estate owner shall be bound, if so requested in writing, to transfer or create such legal estate as may be required for giving legal effect to the rights of the person so entitled;

(iii) Where—

(a) any principal sum is required to be raised on the security of the settled land, by virtue of any trust, or by reason of the exercise of an equitable power affecting the settled land, or by any person or persons who under the settlement is or are entitled or together entitled to or has or have a general power of appointment over the settled land, whether subject to any equitable charges or powers of charging subsisting under the settlement or not; or

[12] Words added by the Law of Property (Amendment) Act 1926, s.6.
[13] See the Law of Property (Amendment) Act 1926, s.1(2), *post*, para. 11–001.

(b) the settled land is subject to any equitable charge for securing money actually raised and affecting the whole estate the subject of the settlement;

the estate owner shall be bound, if so requested in writing, to create such legal estate or charge by way of legal mortgage as may be required for raising the money or giving legal effect to the equitable charge:

Provided that, so long as the settlement remains subsisting, any legal estate or charge by way of legal mortgage so created shall take effect and shall be expressed to take effect subject to any equitable charges or powers of charging subsisting under the settlement which have priority to the interests or powers of the person or persons by or on behalf of whom the money is required to be raised or legal effect is required to be given to the equitable charge, unless the persons entitled to the prior charges or entitled to exercise the powers consent in writing to the same being postponed, but it shall not be necessary for such consent to be expressed in the instrument creating such legal estate or charge by way of legal mortgage.

(2) Where a mortgage or charge is expressed to be made by an estate owner pursuant to this section, then, in favour of the mortgagee or chargee and persons deriving title under him, the same shall take effect in priority to all the trusts of the settlement and all equitable interests and powers subsisting or to arise under the settlement except those to which it is expressly made subject, and shall so take effect, whether the mortgagee or chargee has notice of any such trusts, interests, or powers, or not, and the mortgagee or chargee shall not be concerned to see that a case had arisen to authorise the mortgage or charge, or that no more money than was wanted was raised.

(3) Nothing contained in paragraph (iii) of subsection (1) of this section affects the power conferred by this Act on a tenant for life of raising money by mortgage or of directing capital money to be applied in discharge of incumbrances.

(4) Effect may be given by means of a legal mortgage to an agreement for a mortgage, or a charge or lien, whether or not arising by operation of law, if the agreement charge or lien ought to have priority over the settlement.

(5) Save as hereinbefore expressly provided, no legal estate shall, so long as the settlement is subsisting, be transferred or created by the estate owner for giving effect to any equitable interest or power under the settlement.

(6) If a question arises or a doubt is entertained whether any and what legal estate ought to be transferred or created pursuant to this section, an application may be made to the court for directions as hereinafter provided.

(7) If an estate owner refuses or neglects for one month after demand in writing to transfer or create any such legal estate, or if by reason of his being outside the United Kingdom, or being unable to be found, or by reason of the dissolution of a corporation, or for any other reason, the court is satisfied that the transaction cannot otherwise be effected, or cannot be effected without undue delay or expense, the court may, on the application of any person interested, make a vesting order transferring or creating the requisite legal estate.

(8) This section does not affect a purchaser of a legal estate taking free from any equitable interest or power.

Deed of discharge on termination of settlement

7–017 **17.**—(1) Where the estate owner of any settled land holds the land free from all equitable interests and powers under a trust instrument, the persons who in the last or only principal vesting instrument or the last or only endorsement on or annex thereto are declared to be the trustees of the settlement or the survivors of them shall, save as hereinafter mentioned, be bound to execute, at the cost of the trust estate, a deed declaring that they are discharged from the trust so far as regards that land:

Provided that, if the trustees have notice of any derivative settlement, [trust of land][14] or equitable charge affecting such land, they shall not execute a deed of discharge until—

(a) in the case of a derivative settlement, or [trust of land][15], a vesting instrument or a conveyance has been executed or made for giving effect thereto; and

(b) in the case of an equitable charge, they are satisfied that the charge is or will be secured by a legal mortgage, or is protected by registration as a land charge, or by deposit of the documents of title, or that the owner thereof consents to the execution of the deed of discharge.

Where the land is affected by a derivative settlement or [trust of land][16], the deed of discharge shall contain a statement that the land is settled land by virtue of such vesting instrument as aforesaid and the trust instrument therein referred to, or is [subject to a trust of land][17] by virtue of such conveyance as aforesaid, as the case may require.

(2) If, in the circumstances mentioned in subsection (1) of this section and when the conditions therein mentioned have been complied with, the trustees of a settlement on being requested to execute a deed of discharge—

(a) by the estate owner; or

(b) by a person interested under, or by the trustees of, a derivative settlement; or

(c) by the trustees of [land][18];

refuse to do so, or if for any reason the discharge cannot be effected without undue delay or expense, the estate owner, person interested, or trustees may apply to the court for an order discharging the first mentioned trustees as respects the whole or any part of the settled land, and the court may make such order as it may think fit.

(3) Where a deed or order of discharge contains no statement to the contrary, a purchaser of a legal estate in the land to which the deed or order relates shall be entitled to assume that the land has ceased to be settled land, and is not subject to [a trust of land][19].

[14] Words substituted by the Trusts of Land and Appointment of Trustees Act 1996, s.25(1), Sched. 3, para. 2(1), (6).
[15] Words substituted by the Trusts of Land and Appointment of Trustees Act 1996, s.25(1), Sched. 3, para. 2(1), (6).
[16] Words substituted by the Trusts of Land and Appointment of Trustees Act 1996, s.25(1), Sched. 3, para. 2(1), (6).
[17] Words substituted by the Trusts of Land and Appointment of Trustees Act 1996, s.25(1), Sched. 3, para. 2(1), (6).
[18] Words substituted by the Trusts of Land and Appointment of Trustees Act 1996, s.25(1), Sched. 3, para. 2(1), (6).
[19] Words substituted by the Trusts of Land and Appointment of Trustees Act 1996, s.25(1), Sched. 3, para. 2(1), (6).

Restrictions on dispositions of Settled Land where Trustees have not been Discharged

Restrictions on dispositions of settled land where trustees have not been discharged

7–018 **18.**—(1) Where land is the subject of a vesting instrument and the trustees of the settlement have not been discharged under this Act, then—

(a) any disposition by the tenant for life or statutory owner of the land, other than a disposition authorised by this Act or any other statute, or made in pursuance of any additional or larger powers mentioned in the vesting instrument, shall be void, except for the purpose of conveying or creating such equitable interests as he has power, in right of his equitable interests and powers under the trust instrument, to convey or create; and

(b) if any capital money is payable in respect of a transaction, a conveyance to a purchaser of the land shall only take effect under this Act if the capital money is paid to or by the direction of the trustees of the settlement or into court; and

(c) notwithstanding anything to the contrary in the vesting instrument, or the trust instrument, capital money shall not, except where the trustee is a trust corporation, be paid to or by the direction of fewer persons than two as trustees of the settlement.

(2) The restrictions imposed by this section do not affect—

(a) the right of a personal representative in whom the settled land may be vested to convey or deal with the land for the purposes of administration;

(b) the right of a person of full age who has become absolutely entitled (whether beneficially or as [trustee of land][20] or personal representative or otherwise) to the settled land, free from all limitations, powers, and charges taking effect under the trust instrument, to require the land to be conveyed to him;

(c) the power of the tenant for life, statutory owner, or personal representative in whom the settled land is vested to transfer or create such legal estates, to take effect in priority to the settlement as may be required for giving effect to any obligations imposed on him by statute, but where any capital money is raised or received in respect of the transaction the money shall be paid to or by the direction of the trustees of the settlement or in accordance with an order of the court.

Tenants for Life and Persons with Powers of Tenant for Life

Who is tenant for life

7–019 **19.**—(1) The person of full age who is for the time being beneficially entitled under a settlement to possession of settled land for his life is for the purposes of this Act the tenant for life of that land and the tenant for life under that settlement.

(2) If in any case there are two or more persons of full age so entitled as joint tenants, they together constitute the tenant for life for the purposes of this Act.

(3) If in any case there are two or more persons so entitled as joint tenants and

[20] Words substituted by the Trusts of Land and Appointment of Trustees Act 1996, s.25(1), Sched. 3, para. 2(1), (7).

they are not all of full age, such one or more of them as is or are for the time being of full age is or (if more than one) together constitute the tenant for life for the purposes of this Act, but this subsection does not affect the beneficial interests of such of them as are not for the time being of full age.

(4) A person being tenant for life within the foregoing definitions shall be deemed to be such notwithstanding that, under the settlement or otherwise, the settled land, or his estate or interest therein, is incumbered or charged in any manner or to any extent, and notwithstanding any assignment by operation of law or otherwise of his estate or interest under the settlement, whether before or after it came into possession, other than an assurance which extinguishes that estate or interest.

Other limited owners having powers of tenant for life

20.—(1) Each of the following persons being of full age shall, when his estate or interest is in possession, have the powers of a tenant for life under this Act, (namely):— **7–020**

(i) A tenant in tail, including a tenant in tail after possibility of issue extinct, and a tenant in tail who is by Act of Parliament restrained from barring or defeating his estate tail, and although the reversion is in the Crown, but not including such a tenant in tail where the land in respect whereof he is so restrained was purchased with money provided by Parliament in consideration of public services;

(ii) A person entitled to land for an estate in fee simple or for a term of years absolute with or subject to, in any of such cases, an executory limitation, gift, or disposition over on failure of his issue or in any other event;

(iii) A person entitled to a base or determinable fee, although thereversion or right of reverter is in the Crown, or to any corresponding interest in leasehold land;

(iv) A tenant for years determinable on life, not holding merely under a lease at a rent;

(v) A tenant for the life of another, not holding merely under a lease at a rent;

(vi) A tenant for his own or any other life, or for years determinable on life, whose estate is liable to cease in any event during that life, whether by expiration of the estate, or by conditional limitation, or otherwise, or to be defeated by an executory limitation, gift, or disposition over, or is subject to a trust for accumulation of income for any purpose;

(vii)[21] A tenant by the curtesy;

(viii) A person entitled to the income of land under a trust or direction for payment thereof to him during his own or any other life, whether or not subject to expenses of management or to a trust for accumulation of income for any purpose, or until sale of the land, or until forfeiture, cesser or determination by any means of his interest therein, unless the land is subject to [a trust of land][22];

(ix)[23] A person beneficially entitled to land for an estate in fee simple or for a term of years absolute subject to any estates, interests, charges, or

---

[21] Courtesy was abolished by the Administration of Estates Act 1925, s.45(1)(b), *post*, para. 10–036.
[22] Words substituted by the Trusts of Land and Appointment of Trustees Act 1996, s.25(1), Sched. 3, para. 2(1), (8).
[23] See the Law of Property (Amendment) Act 1926, s.1, *post*, para. 11–001.

powers of charging, subsisting or capable of being exercised under a settlement;

[. . .][24]

(2) In every such case as is mentioned in subsection (1) of this section, the provisions of this Act referring to a tenant for life, either as conferring powers on him or otherwise, shall extend to each of the persons aforesaid, and any reference in this Act to death as regards a tenant for life shall, where necessary, be deemed to refer to the determination by death or otherwise of the estate or interest of the person on whom the powers of a tenant for life are conferred by this section.

(3) For the purposes of this Act the estate or interest of a tenant by the curtesy shall be deemed to be an estate or interest arising under a settlement made by his wife.

(4) Where the reversion or right of reverter or other reversionary right is in the Crown, the exercise by a person on whom the powers of a tenant for life are conferred by this section of his powers under this Act, binds the Crown.

Absolute owners subject to certain interests to have the powers of tenant for life

7–021 **21.**—(1) Where a person of full age is beneficially entitled in possession to a legal estate subject to any equitable interests or powers, then, for the purpose of overreaching such interests or powers, he may, notwithstanding any stipulation to the contrary, by deed (which shall have effect as a principal vesting deed within the meaning of this Act) declare that the legal estate is vested in him on trust to give effect to all equitable interests and powers affecting the legal estate, and that deed shall be executed by two or more individuals approved or appointed by the court or a trust corporation, who shall be stated to be the trustees of the settlement for the purposes of this Act.

Thereupon so long as any of the equitable interests and powers are subsisting the following provisions shall have effect:—

(a) The person so entitled as aforesaid and each of his successors in title being an estate owner shall have the powers of a tenant for life and the land shall be deemed to be settled land;

(b) The instrument (if any) under which his estate arises or is acquired, and the instrument (if any) under which the equitable interests or powers are subsisting or capable of taking effect shall be deemed to be the trust instrument:

Provided that where there is no such instrument as last aforesaid then a deed (which shall take effect as a trust instrument) shall be executed contemporaneously with the vesting deed and shall declare the trusts affecting the land;

(c) The persons stated in the principal vesting deed to be the trustees of the settlement for the purposes of this Act shall also be the trustees of the trust instrument for those purposes; and

(d) Capital money arising on any disposition of the land shall be paid to or by the direction of the trustees of the settlement or into court, and shall be applicable towards discharging or providing for payment in due order of any principal money payable in respect of such interests or charges as are overreached by such disposition, and until so applied shall be invested or applied as capital money under the trust instrument, and the [resultant

[24] Para. (x) repealed by the Married Women (Restraint upon Anticipation) Act 1949, s.1(4), Sched. 2.

profits][25] shall be applied as the income of such capital money, and be liable for keeping down in due order any annual or periodical sum which may be overreached by the disposition.

(2) The following equitable interests and powers are excepted from the operation of subsection (1) of this section, namely—

(i) an equitable interest protected by a deposit of documents relating to the legal estate affected;

(ii) the benefit of a covenant or agreement restrictive of the user of land;

(iii) an easement, liberty or privilege over or affecting land and being merely an equitable interest;

(iv) the benefit of a contract to convey or create a legal estate, including a contract conferring either expressly or by statutory implication a valid option of purchase, a right of pre-emption, or any other like right;

(v) any equitable interest protected by registration under the Land Charges Act 1925[26] other than—

(a) an annuity within the meaning of Part II of that Act;

(b) a limited owner's charge or a general equitable charge within the meaning of that Act.

(3) Subject to the powers conferred by this Act on a tenant for life, nothing contained in this section shall deprive an equitable chargee of any of his rights or of his remedies for enforcing those rights.

Provisions applicable where interest in settled land is restored

22.—(1) Where by a disentailing assurance settled land is expressed to be limited (whether subject or not to any estates, interests, charges or powers expressly created or conferred thereby) upon the trusts subsisting with respect thereto immediately before the execution of such disentailing assurance, or any of such trusts, then, for the purposes of this Act and otherwise, a person entitled to any estate or interest in the settled land under any such previously subsisting trust is entitled thereto after the execution of such disentailing assurance as of his former estate or interest. **7–022**

(2) Where by a resettlement of settled land any estate or interest therein is expressed to be limited to any person (whether subject or not to any estate, interest, charge or power expressly created or conferred by the resettlement) in restoration or confirmation of his estate or interest under a prior settlement, then, for the purposes of this Act and otherwise, that person is entitled to the estate or interest so restored or confirmed as of his former estate or interest, and in addition to the powers exercisable by him in respect of his former estate or interest, he is capable of exercising all such further powers as he could have exercised by virtue of the resettlement, if his estate or interest under the prior settlement had not been so restored or confirmed, but he had been entitled under the resettlement only.

Powers of trustees, etc. when there is no tenant for life

23.—(1) Where under a settlement there is no tenant for life nor, independently of this section, a person having by virtue of this Act the powers of a tenant for life then— **7–023**

[25] Words substituted by the Trustee Act 2000, s.40(1), Sched. 2, Pt. II, para. 7.
[26] Now the Land Charges Act 1972, s.2, *post*, para. 31–002.

(a) any person of full age on whom such powers are by the settlement expressed to be conferred; and

(b) in any other case the trustees of the settlement;

shall have the powers of a tenant for life under this Act.

(2) This section applies to trustees of settlements of land purchased with money provided by Parliament in consideration of public services where the tenant in tail is restrained from barring or defeating his estate tail, except that, if the tenant in tail is of full age and capacity, the powers shall not be exercised without his consent, but a purchaser shall not be concerned to see or inquire whether such consent has been given.

As to a tenant for life who has parted with his interest

7–024 **24.**—(1) If it is shown to the satisfaction of the court that a tenant for life, who has by reason of bankruptcy, assignment, incumbrance, or otherwise ceased in the opinion of the court to have a substantial interest in his estate or interest in the settled land or any part thereof, has unreasonably refused to exercise any of the powers conferred on him by this Act, or consents to an order under this section, the court may, on the application of any person interested in the settled land or the part thereof affected, make an order authorising the trustees of the settlement, to exercise, in the name and on behalf of the tenant for life, any of the powers of a tenant for life under this Act, in relation to the settled land or the part thereof affected, either generally and in such manner and for such period as the court may think fit, or in a particular instance, and the court may by the order direct that any documents of title in the possession of the tenant for life relating to the settled land be delivered to the trustees of the settlement.

(2) While any such order is in force, the tenant for life shall not, in relation to the settled land or the part thereof affected, exercise any of the powers thereby authorised to be exercised in his name and on his behalf, but no person dealing with the tenant for life shall be affected by any such order, unless the order is for the time being registered as an order affecting land.

(3) An order may be made under this section at any time after the estate or interest of the tenant for life under the settlement has taken effect in possession, and notwithstanding that he disposed thereof when it was an estate or interest in remainder or reversion.

Married woman, how to be affected

7–025 **25.**—(1) The foregoing provisions of this Act apply to a married woman of full age, whether or not she is entitled to her estate or interest for her separate use or as her separate property, and she, without her husband, may exercise the powers of a tenant for life under this Act.

(2) [*Repealed by the Married Women (Restraint upon Anticipation) Act* 1949, *s.*1(4), *Sched.* 2.]

Infants, how to be affected

7–026 **26.**—(1) Where an infant is beneficially entitled in possession to land for an estate in fee simple or for a term of years absolute or would if of full age be a tenant for life of or have the powers of a tenant for life over settled land, then, during the minority of the infant—

(a) if the settled land is vested in a personal representative, the personal representative, until a principal vesting instrument has been executed pursuant to the provisions of this Act; and

(b) in every other case, the trustees of the settlement;

shall have, in reference to the settled land and capital money, all the powers conferred by this Act and the settlement on a tenant for life, and on the trustees of the settlement.

(2) If the settled land is vested in a personal representative, then, if and when during the minority the infant, if of full age, would have been entitled to have the legal estate in the settled land conveyed to or otherwise vested in him pursuant to the provisions of this Act, a principal vesting instrument shall, if the trustees of the settlement so require, be executed, at the cost of the trust estate, for vesting the legal estate in themselves, and in the meantime the personal representatives shall, during the minority, give effect to the directions of the trustees of the settlement, and shall not be concerned with the propriety of any conveyance directed to be made by those trustees if the conveyance appears to be a proper conveyance under the powers conferred by this Act or by the settlement, and the capital money, if any, arising under the conveyance is paid to or by the direction of the trustees of the settlement or into court, but a purchaser dealing with the personal representative and paying the capital money, if any, to him shall not be concerned to see that the money is paid to trustees of the settlement or into court, or to inquire whether the personal representative is liable to give effect to any such directions, or whether any such directions have been given.

(3) Subsection (2) of this section applies whether the infant becomes entitled before or after the commencement of this Act, and has effect during successive minorities until a person of full age becomes entitled to require the settled land to be vested in him.

(4) This section does not apply where an infant is beneficially entitled in possession to land for an estate in fee simple or for a term of years absolute jointly with a person of full age (for which case provision is made in the Law of Property Act 1925), but it applies to two or more infants entitled as aforesaid jointly, until one of them attains full age.

(5) This section does not apply where an infant would, if of full age, constitute the tenant for life or have the powers of a tenant for life together with another person of full age, but it applies to two or more infants who would, if all of them were of full age, together constitute the tenant for life or have the powers of a tenant for life, until one of them attains full age.

(6) Nothing in this section affects prejudicially any beneficial interest of an infant.

27. [*Repealed by the Trusts of Land and Appointment of Trustees Act 1996, s.25(2), Sched. 4.*]

28. [*Repealed by the Mental Health Act 1959, s.149(2), Sched. 8, Pt. I.*]

29. [*Repealed by the Trusts of Land and Appointment of Trustees Act 1996, s.25(2), Sched. 4.*]

Trustees of Settlement

Who are trustees for purposes of Act

7–027 **30.**—(1) Subject to the provisions of this Act, the following persons are trustees of a settlement for the purposes of this Act, and are in this Act referred to as the "trustees of the settlement" or "trustees of a settlement," namely—

(i) the persons, if any, who are for the time being under the settlement, trustees with power of sale of the settled land (subject or not to the consent of any person), or with power of consent to or approval of the exercise of such a power of sale, or if there are no such persons; then

(ii) the persons, if any, for the time being, who are by the settlement declared to be trustees thereof for the purposes of the Settled Land Acts 1882 to 1890, or any of them, or this Act, or if there are no such persons; then

(iii) the persons, if any, who are for the time being under the settlement trustees with [a power or duty to sell][27] any other land comprised in the settlement and subject to the same limitations as the land to be sold or otherwise dealt with, or with power of consent to or approval of the exercise of such a power of sale, or, if there are no such persons; then

(iv) the persons, if any, who are for the time being under the settlement trustees with [a future power or duty to sell][28] the settled land, or with power of consent to or approval of the exercise of such a future power of sale, and whether the power [or duty][29] takes effect in all events or not, or, if there are no such persons; then

(v) the persons, if any, appointed by deed to be trustees of the settlement by all the persons who at the date of the deed were together able, by virtue of their beneficial interests or by the exercise of an equitable power, to dispose of the settled land in equity for the whole estate the subject of the settlement.

(2) Paragraphs (i) (iii) and (iv) of the last preceding subsection take effect in like manner as if the powers therein referred to had not by this Act been made exercisable by the tenant for life or statutory owner.

(3) Where a settlement is created by will or a settlement has arisen by the effect of an intestacy, and apart from this subsection there would be no trustees for the purposes of this Act of such settlement, then the personal representatives of the deceased shall, until other trustees are appointed, be by virtue of this Act the trustees of the settlement, but where there is a sole personal representative, not being a trust corporation, it shall be obligatory on him to appoint an additional trustee to act with him for the purposes of this Act, and the provisions of the Trustee Act 1925 relating to the appointment of new trustees and the vesting of trust property shall apply accordingly.

As to trustees of compound settlements

7–028 **31.**—(1) Persons who are for the time being trustees for the purposes of this Act of an instrument which is a settlement, or is deemed to be a subsisting settlement for the purposes of this Act, shall be the trustees for the purposes of

[27] Words substituted by the Trusts of Land and Appointment of Trustees Act 1996, s.25(1), Sched. 3, para. 2(1), (9).

[28] Words substituted by the Trusts of Land and Appointment of Trustees Act 1996, s.25(1), Sched. 3, para. 2(1), (9).

[29] Words substituted by the Trusts of Land and Appointment of Trustees Act 1996, s.25(1), Sched. 3, para. 2(1), (9).

this Act of any settlement constituted by that instrument and any instruments subsequent in date or operation.

[Where there are trustees for the purposes of this Act of the instrument under which there is a tenant for life or statutory owner but there are no trustees for those purposes of a prior instrument, being one of the instruments by which a compound settlement is constituted, those trustees shall, unless and until trustees are appointed of the prior instrument or of the compound settlement, be the trustees for the purposes of this Act of the compound settlement.][30]

(2) This section applies to instruments coming into operation before as well as after the commencement of this Act, but shall have effect without prejudice to any appointment made by the court before such commencement of trustees of a settlement constituted by more than one instrument, and to the power of the court in any case after such commencement to make any such appointment, and where any such appointment has been made before such commencement or is made thereafter this section shall not apply or shall cease to apply to the settlement consisting of the instruments to which the appointment relates.

As to trustees of referential settlements

32.—(1) Where a settlement takes or has taken effect by reference to another **7–029**
settlement, the trustees for the time being of the settlement to which reference is made shall be the trustees of the settlement by reference, but this section does not apply if the settlement by reference contains an appointment of trustees thereof for the purposes of the Settled Land Acts 1882 to 1890, or any of them, or this Act.

(2) This section applies to instruments coming into operation before as well as after the commencement of this Act, but shall have effect without prejudice to any appointment made by the court before such commencement of trustees of a settlement by reference, or of the compound settlement consisting of a settlement and any other settlement or settlements made by reference thereto, and to the power of the court in any case after such commencement to make any such appointment, and where any such appointment has been made before such commencement or is made thereafter this section shall not apply or shall cease to apply.

(3) In this section "a settlement by reference to another settlement" means a settlement of property upon the limitations and subject to the powers and provisions of an existing settlement, with or without variation.

Continuance of trustees in office, and as to certain compound settlements

33.—(1) Where any persons have been appointed or constituted trustees of a **7–030**
settlement, whether by an order of the court or otherwise, or have by reason of [a power or duty to sell][31], or by reason of a power of consent to, or approval of, the exercise of a power of sale, or by virtue of this Act, or otherwise at any time become trustees of a settlement for the purposes of the Settled Land Acts 1882 to 1890 or this Act, then those persons or their successors in office shall remain and be trustees of the settlement as long as that settlement is subsisting or deemed to be subsisting for the purposes of this Act.

[30] Words added by the Law of Property (Amendment) Act 1926, s.7, Sched.
[31] Words substituted by the Trusts of Land and Appointment of Trustees Act 1996, s.25(1), Sched. 3, para. 2(1), (10).

In this subsection "successors in office" means the persons who, by appointment or otherwise, have become trustees for the purposes aforesaid.

(2) Where settled land is or has been expressed to be disposed of under a compound settlement of which trustees were appointed by the court, and the capital money (if any) arising on the disposition is or was paid to the persons who by virtue of the order or any subsequent appointment appear to be or to have been the trustees of that settlement, and where the person by or on whose behalf the disposition is or was made is or was the tenant for life or statutory owner of the land disposed of under an instrument mentioned in the order as constituting part of such compound settlement (in this subsection called "the principal instrument") then the title of the person to whom the disposition is made shall not be impeachable on the ground—

(a) that the instruments mentioned in the order did not constitute a compound settlement; or

(b) that those instruments were not all the instruments at the date of the order or of the disposition constituting the compound settlement of the land disposed of; or

(c) that any of the instruments mentioned in the order did not form part of the settlement of the land disposed of, or had ceased to form part of the settlement at the date of the disposition;

but nothing in this subsection shall prejudice the rights of any person in respect of any estate, interest or charge under any instrument existing at the date of the order and not mentioned therein which would not have been overreached if the disposition had been made by or on behalf of the tenant for life or statutory owner under the principal instrument as such, and there had been trustees of that instrument for the purposes of the Settled Land Acts 1882 to 1890 or this Act, and the capital money, if any, arising on the disposition had been paid to the trustees.

(3) The foregoing provisions of this section operate to confirm all dispositions made before the commencement of this Act, but not so as to render invalid or prejudice any order of the court, or any title or right acquired before the commencement of this Act, and operates without prejudice to any appointment already made by the court of trustees of a settlement, and to the power of the court in any case hereafter to make any such appointment.

Appointment of trustees by court

7–031 **34.**—(1) If at any time there are no trustees of a settlement, or where in any other case it is expedient, for the purposes of this Act, that new trustees of a settlement be appointed, the court may, if it thinks fit, on the application of the tenant for life, statutory owner, or of any other person having, under the settlement, an estate or interest in the settled land, in possession, remainder or otherwise, or, in the case of an infant, of his testamentary or other guardian or next friend, appoint fit persons to be trustees of the settlement.

(2) The persons so appointed, and the survivors and survivor of them, while continuing to be trustees or trustee, and, until the appointment of new trustees, the personal representatives or representative for the time being of the last surviving or continuing trustee, shall become and be the trustees or trustee of the settlement.

Procedure on appointment of new trustees

35.—(1) Whenever a new trustee for the purposes of this Act is appointed of a trust instrument or a trustee thereof for the purposes aforesaid is discharged from the trust without a new trustee being appointed, a deed shall be executed supplemental to the last or only principal vesting instrument containing a declaration that the persons therein named, being the persons who after such appointment or discharge, as the case may be, are the trustees of the trust instrument for the purposes aforesaid, are the trustees of the settlement for those purposes; and a memorandum shall be endorsed on or annexed to the last or only principal vesting instrument in accordance with the Trustee Act 1925. **7–032**

(2) Every such deed as aforesaid shall, if the trustee was appointed or discharged by the court, be executed by such person as the court may direct, and, in any other case, shall be executed by—

(i) the person, if any, named in the principal vesting instrument as the person for the time being entitled to appoint new trustees of the settlement, or if no person is so named, or the person is dead or unable or unwilling to act, the persons who if the principal vesting instrument had been the only instrument constituting the settlement would have had power to appoint new trustees thereof;

(ii) the persons named in the deed of declaration as the trustees of the settlement; and

(iii) any trustee who is discharged as aforesaid or retires.

(3) A statement contained in any such deed of declaration as is mentioned in this section to the effect that the person named in the principal vesting instrument as the person for the time being entitled to appoint new trustees of the settlement is unable or unwilling to act, or that a trustee has remained outside the United Kingdom for more than twelve months, or refuses or is unfit to act, or is incapable of acting, shall in favour of a purchaser of a legal estate be conclusive evidence of the matter stated.

Provisions as to Undivided Shares

Undivided shares to take effect behind a [trust of land][32]

36.—(1) If and when, after the commencement of this Act, settled land is held in trust for persons entitled in possession under a trust instrument in undivided shares, the trustees of the settlement (if the settled land is not already vested in them) may require the estate owner in whom the settled land is vested (but in the case of a personal representative subject to his rights and powers for purposes of administration), at the cost of the trust estate, to convey the land to them, or assent to the land vesting in them as joint tenants, and in the meantime the land shall be held on the same trusts as would have been applicable thereto if it had been so conveyed to or vested in the trustees. **7–033**

(2) If and when the settled land so held in trust in undivided shares is or becomes vested in the trustees of the settlement, the land shall be held by them (subject to any incumbrances affecting the settled land which are secured by a legal mortgage, but freed from any incumbrances affecting the undivided shares or not secured as aforesaid, and from any interests, powers and charges subsisting under the trust instrument which have priority to the trust for the

[32] Words substituted by the Trusts of Land and Appointment of Trustees Act 1996, s.25(1), Sched. 3, para. 2(1), (11).

persons entitled to the undivided shares) [in trust for the persons interested in the land][33].

(3) If the estate owner refuses or neglects for one month after demand in writing to convey the settled land so held in trust in undivided shares in manner aforesaid, or if by reason of his being outside the United Kingdom or being unable to be found, or by reason of the dissolution of a corporation, or for any other reason, the court is satisfied that the conveyance cannot otherwise be made, or cannot be made without undue delay or expense, the court may, on the application of the trustees of the settlement, make an order vesting the settled land in them [in trust for the persons interested in the land][34].

(4) An undivided share in land shall not be capable of being created except under a trust instrument or under the Law of Property Act 1925, and shall then only take effect behind a [trust of land][35].

(5) Nothing in this section affects the priority inter se of any incumbrances whether affecting the entirety of the land or an undivided share.

[(6) In subsections (2) and (3) of this section references to the persons interested in the land include persons interested as trustees or personal representatives (as well as persons beneficially interested).][36]

(7) The provisions of this section bind the Crown.

Transitional Provisions

Transitional provisions with respect to existing settlements, etc.

7–034 **37.** The transitional provisions set out in the Second Schedule to this Act shall have effect as regards settlements existing at the commencement of this Act.

PART II

POWERS OF A TENANT FOR LIFE

Sale and Exchange

Powers of sale and exchange

7–035 **38.** A tenant for life—

(i) May sell the settled land, or any part thereof, or any easement, right or privilege of any kind over or in relation to the land; and

[...][37]

(iii) May make an exchange of the settled land, or any part thereof, or of any easement, right, or privilege of any kind, whether or not newly created, over or in relation to the settled land, or any part thereof, for other land, or for any easement, right or privilege of any kind, whether or not newly created, over or in relation to other land, including an exchange in consideration of money paid for equality of exchange.

---

[33] Words substituted by the Trusts of Land and Appointment of Trustees Act 1996, s.25(1), Sched. 3, para. 2(1), (11).

[34] Words substituted by the Trusts of Land and Appointment of Trustees Act 1996, s.25(1), Sched. 3, para. 2(1), (11).

[35] Words substituted by the Trusts of Land and Appointment of Trustees Act 1996, s.25(1), Sched. 3, para. 2(1), (11).

[36] Subs. (6) substituted by the Trusts of Land and Appointment of Trustees Act 1996, s.25(1), Sched. 3, para. 2(1), (11).

[37] Para. (ii) repealed by the Statute Law (Repeals) Act 1969, s.1, Sched., Pt. III.

Regulations respecting sales

39.—(1) Save as hereinafter provided every sale shall be made for the best consideration in money that can reasonably be obtained. **7–036**

(2) A sale may be made in consideration wholly or partially of a perpetual rent, or a terminable rent consisting of principal and interest combined, payable yearly or half yearly to be secured upon the land sold, or the land to which the easement, right or privilege sold is to be annexed in enjoyment or an adequate part thereof.

In the case of a terminable rent, the conveyance shall distinguish the part attributable to principal and that attributable to interest, and the part attributable to principal shall be capital money arising under this Act:

Provided that, unless the part of the terminable rent attributable to interest varies according to the amount of the principal repaid, the trustees of the settlement shall, during the subsistence of the rent, [accumulate the profits from the capital money by investing them and any resulting profits under the general power of investment in section 3 of the Trustee Act 2000 and shall add the accumulations to the capital.][38]

(3) The rent to be reserved on any such sale shall be the best rent that can reasonably be obtained, regard being had to any money paid as part of the consideration, or laid out, or to be laid out, for the benefit of the settled land, and generally to the circumstances of the case, but a peppercorn rent, or a nominal or other rent less than the rent ultimately payable, may be made payable during any period not exceeding five years from the date of the conveyance.

(4) Where a sale is made in consideration of a rent, the following provisions shall have effect:—

- (i) The conveyance shall contain a covenant by the purchaser for payment of the rent, and [the statutory powers and remedies for the recovery of the rent shall apply][39];
- (ii) A duplicate of the conveyance shall be executed by the purchaser and delivered to the tenant for life or statutory owner, of which execution and delivery the execution of the conveyance by the tenant for life or statutory owner shall be sufficient evidence;
- (iii) A statement, contained in the conveyance or in an indorsement thereon, signed by the tenant for life or statutory owner, respecting any matter of fact or of calculation under this Act in relation to the sale, shall, in favour of the purchaser and of those claiming under him, be sufficient evidence of the matter stated.

(5) The consideration on a sale to any company incorporated by special Act of Parliament or by provisional order confirmed by Parliament or by any other order, scheme or certificate having the force of an Act of Parliament, may, with the consent of the tenant for life, consist, wholly or in part, of fully-paid securities of any description of the company, and such securities shall be vested in the trustees of the settlement and shall be subject to the provisions of this Act relating to securities representing capital money arising under this Act, and may be retained and held by the trustees in like manner as if they had been authorised by this Act for the investment of capital money.

(6) A sale may be made in one lot or in several lots, and either by auction or by private contract, and may be made subject to any stipulations respecting title, or evidence of title, or other things.

[38] Words substituted by the Trustee Act 2000, s.40(1), Sched. 2, Pt. II, para. 8.
[39] Words substituted by the Law of Property (Amendment) Act 1926, s.7, Sched.

(7) On a sale the tenant for life may fix reserve biddings and may buy in at an auction.

Regulations respecting exchanges

7–037 **40.**—(1) Save as in this Part of this Act provided, every exchange shall be made for the best consideration in land or in land and money that can reasonably be obtained.

(2) An exchange may be made subject to any stipulations respecting title, or evidence of title, or other things.

(3) Settled land in England or Wales shall not be given in exchange for land out of England and Wales.

Leasing Powers

Power to lease for ordinary or building or mining or forestry purposes

7–038 **41.** A tenant for life may lease the settled land, or any part thereof, or any easement, right, or privilege of any kind over or in relation to the land, for any purpose whatever, whether involving waste or not, for any term not exceeding—

(i) In case of a building lease, nine hundred and ninety-nine years;
(ii) In case of a mining lease, one hundred years;
(iii) In case of a forestry lease, nine hundred and ninety-nine years;
(iv) In case of any other lease, fifty years.

Regulations respecting leases generally

7–039 **42.**—(1) Save as hereinafter provided, every lease—

(i) shall be by deed, and be made to take effect in possession not later than twelve months after its date, or in reversion after an existing lease having not more than seven years to run at the date of the new lease;
(ii) shall reserve the best rent that can reasonably be obtained, regard being had to any fine taken, and to any money laid out or to be laid out for the benefit of the settled land, and generally to the circumstances of the case;
(iii) shall contain a covenant by the lessee for payment of the rent, and a condition of re-entry on the rent not being paid within a time therein specified not exceeding thirty days.

(2) A counterpart of every lease shall be executed by the lessee and delivered to the tenant for life or statutory owner, of which execution and delivery the execution of the lease by the tenant for life or statutory owner shall be sufficient evidence.

(3) A statement, contained in a lease or in an indorsement thereon, signed by the tenant for life or statutory owner, respecting any matter of fact or of calculation under this Act in relation to the lease, shall, in favour of the lessee and of those claiming under him, be sufficient evidence of the matter stated.

(4) A fine received on the grant of a lease under any power conferred by this Act shall be deemed to be capital money arising under this Act.

(5) A lease at the best rent that can be reasonably obtained without fine, and whereby the lessee is not exempted from punishment for waste, may be made—

(i) Where the term does not exceed twenty-one years—
  (a) Without any notice of an intention to make the lease having been given under this Act; and

(b) notwithstanding that there are no trustees of the settlement; and

(ii) Where the term does not extend beyond three years from the date of the writing, by any writing under hand only containing an agreement instead of a covenant by the lessee for payment of rent.

Leasing powers for special objects

43. The leasing power of a tenant for life extends to the making of— **7–040**

(i) a lease for giving effect (in such manner and so far as the law permits) to a covenant of renewal, performance whereof could be enforced against the owner for the time being of the settled land; and

(ii) a lease for confirming, as far as may be, a previous lease being void or voidable, but so that every lease, as and when confirmed, shall be such a lease as might at the date of the original lease have been lawfully granted under this Act or otherwise, as the case may require.

Provisions as to building, mining and forestry leases

Regulations respecting building leases

44.—(1) Every building lease shall be made partly in consideration of the lessee, or some person by whose direction the lease is granted, or some other person, having erected or agreeing to erect buildings, new or additional, or having improved or repaired or agreeing to improve or repair buildings, or having executed or agreeing to execute on the land leased, an improvement authorised by this Act for or in connexion with building purposes. **7–041**

(2) A peppercorn rent or a nominal or other rent less than the rent ultimately payable, may be made payable for the first five years or any less part of the term.

(3) Where the land is contracted to be leased in lots, the entire amount of rent to be ultimately payable may be apportioned among the lots in any manner:

Provided that—

(i) the annual rent reserved by any lease shall not be less than ten shillings[40]; and

(ii) the total amount of the rents reserved on all leases for the time being granted shall not be less than the total amount of the rents which, in order that the leases may be in conformity with this Act, ought to be reserved in respect of the whole land for the time being leased; and

(iii) the rent reserved by any lease shall not exceed one-fifth part of the full annual value of the land comprised in that lease with the buildings thereon when completed.

Regulations respecting mining leases

45.—(1) In a mining lease— **7–042**

(i) the rent may be made to be ascertainable by or to vary according to the acreage worked, or by or according to the quantities of any mineral or substance gotten, made merchantable, converted, carried away, or disposed of, in or from the settled land, or any other land, or by or according to any facilities given in that behalf; and

---

[40] Amount to be read as fifty pence: Decimal Currency Act 1969, s.10(1).

(ii) the rent may also be made to vary according to the price of the minerals or substances gotten, or any of them, and such price may be the saleable value, or the price or value appearing in any trade or market or other price list or return from time to time, or may be the marketable value as ascertained in any manner prescribed by the lease (including a reference to arbitration), or may be an average of any such prices or values taken during a specified period; and

(iii) a fixed or minimum rent may be made payable, with or without power for the lessee, in case the rent, according to acreage or quantity or otherwise, in any specified period does not produce an amount equal to the fixed or minimum rent, to make up the deficiency in any subsequent specified period, free of rent other than the fixed or minimum rent.

(2) A lease may be made partly in consideration of the lessee having executed, or agreeing to execute, on the land leased an improvement authorised by this Act, for or in connexion with mining purposes.

Variation of building or mining lease according to circumstances of district

7–043 **46.**—(1) Where it is shown to the court with respect to the district in which any settled land is situate, either—

(i) that it is the custom for land therein to be leased for building or mining purposes for a longer term or on other conditions than the term or conditions specified in that behalf in this Act; or

(ii) that it is difficult to make leases for building or mining purposes of land therein, except for a longer term or on other conditions than the term and conditions specified in that behalf in this Act;

the court may, if it thinks fit, authorise generally the tenant for life or statutory owner to make from time to time leases of or affecting the settled land in that district, or parts thereof for any term or on any conditions as in the order of the court expressed, or may, if it thinks fit, authorise the tenant for life or statutory owner to make any such lease in any particular case.

(2) Thereupon the tenant for life or statutory owner, and, subject to any direction in the order of the court to the contrary, each of his successors in title being a tenant for life or statutory owner, may make in any case, or in the particular case, a lease of the settled land, or part thereof, in conformity with the order.

Capitalisation of part of mining rent

7–044 **47.** Under a mining lease, whether the mines or minerals leased are already opened or in work or not, unless a contrary intention is expressed in the settlement, there shall be from time to time set aside, as capital money arising under this Act, part of the rent as follows, namely—where the tenant for life or statutory owner is impeachable for waste in respect of minerals, three fourth parts of the rent, and otherwise one fourth part thereof, and in every such case the residue of the rent shall go as rents and profits.

Regulations respecting forestry leases

7–045 **48.**—(1) In the case of a forestry lease—

(i) a peppercorn rent or a nominal or other rent less than the rent ultimately payable, may be made payable for the first ten years or any less part of the term;

(ii) the rent may be made to be ascertainable by, or to vary according to the value of the timber on the land comprised in the lease, or the produce thereof, which may during any year be cut, converted, carried away, or otherwise disposed of;

(iii) a fixed or minimum rent may be made payable, with or without power for the lessee, in case the rent according to value in any specified period does not produce an amount equal to the fixed or minimum rent, to make up the deficiency in any subsequent specified period, free of rent other than the fixed or minimum rent; and

(iv) any other provisions may be made for the sharing of the proceeds or profits of the user of the land between the reversioner and the Forestry Commissioners[41].

(2) In this section the expression "timber" includes all forest products.

Miscellaneous Powers

Power on dispositions to impose restrictions and make reservations and stipulations

49.—(1) On a sale or other disposition or dealing under the powers of this Act— **7–046**

(a) any easement, right, or privilege of any kind may be reserved or granted over or in relation to the settled land or any part thereof or other land, including the land disposed of, and, in the case of an exchange, the land taken in exchange; and

(b) any restriction with respect to building on or other user of land, or with respect to mines and minerals, or with respect to or for the purpose of the more beneficial working thereof, or with respect to any other thing, may be imposed and made binding, as far as the law permits, by covenant, condition or otherwise, on the tenant for life or statutory owner and the settled land or any part thereof, or on the other party and any land disposed of to him; and

(c) the whole or any part of any capital or annual sum (and in the case of an annual sum whether temporary or perpetual) charged on or payable out of the land disposed of, or any part thereof, and other land subject to the settlement, may as between the tenant for life or statutory owner and his successors in title, and the other party and persons deriving title under or in succession to him (but without prejudice to the rights of the person entitled to such capital or annual sum) be charged exclusively on the land disposed of, or any part thereof, or such other land as aforesaid, or any part thereof, in exoneration of the rest of the land on or out of which such capital or annual sum is charged or payable.

(2) A sale of land may be made subject to a stipulation that all or any of the timber and other trees, pollards, tellers, underwood, saplings and plantations on the land sold (in this section referred to as "timber") or any articles attached to the land (in this section referred to as "fixtures") shall be taken by the purchaser at a valuation, and the amount of the valuation shall form part of the price of the land, and shall be capital money accordingly.

[41] The reference to the Forestry Commissioners is to be construed as a reference to the appropriate Minister: Forestry Act 1967, s.50(1), Sched. 6, para. 5.

(3) Where on a sale the consideration attributable to any timber or fixtures is by mistake paid to a tenant for life or other person not entitled to receive it, then, if such person or the purchaser or the persons deriving title under either of them subsequently pay the aforesaid consideration, with such interest, if any, thereon as the court may direct, to the trustees of the settlement or other persons entitled thereto or into court, the court may, on the application of the purchaser or the persons deriving title under him, declare that the disposition is to take effect as if the whole of the consideration had at the date thereof been duly paid to the trustees of the settlement or other persons entitled to receive the same.

The person not entitled to receive the same, to whom the consideration is paid, and his estate and effects shall remain liable to make good any loss attributable to the mistake.

Separate dealing with surface and minerals, with or without wayleaves, etc.

7–047 **50.** A sale, exchange, lease or other authorised disposition, may be made either of land, with or without an exception or reservation of all or any of the mines and minerals therein, or of any mines and minerals, and in any such case with or without a grant or reservation of powers of working, wayleaves or rights of way, rights of water and drainage, and other powers, easements, rights, and privileges for or incident to or connected with mining purposes, in relation to the settled land, or any part thereof, or any other land.

Power to grant options

7–048 **51.**—(1) A tenant for life may at any time, either with or without consideration, grant by writing an option to purchase or take a lease of the settled land, or any part thereof, or any easement, right, or privilege over or in relation to the same at a price or rent fixed at the time of the granting of the option.

(2) Every such option shall be made exercisable within an agreed number of years not exceeding ten.

(3) The price or rent shall be the best which, having regard to all the circumstances, can reasonably be obtained and either—

(a) may be a specified sum of money or rent, or at a specified rate according to the superficial area of the land with respect to which the option is exercised, or the frontage thereof or otherwise; or

(b) in the case of an option to purchase contained in a lease or agreement for a lease, may be a stated number of years' purchase of the highest rent reserved by the lease or agreement; or

(c) if the option is exercisable as regards part of the land comprised in the lease or agreement, may be a proportionate part of such highest rent;

and any aggregate price or rent may be made to be apportionable in any manner, or according to any system, or by reference to arbitration.

(4) An option to take a mining lease may be coupled with the grant of a licence to search for and prove any mines or minerals under the settled land, or any part thereof, pending the exercise of the option.

(5) The consideration for the grant of the option shall be capital money arising under this Act.

Surrenders and re-grants

52.—(1) A tenant for life may accept, with or without consideration, a surrender of any lease of settled land, whether made under this Act or not, or a regrant of any land granted in fee simple, whether under this Act or not, in respect of the whole land leased or granted, or any part thereof, with or without an exception of all or any of the mines and minerals therein, or in respect of mines and minerals, or any of them, and with or without an exception of any easement, right or privilege of any kind over or in relation to the land surrendered or regranted. **7–049**

(2) On a surrender of a lease, or a regrant of land granted in fee simple, in respect of part only of the land or mines and minerals leased or granted, the rent or rentcharge may be apportioned.

(3) On a surrender or regrant, the tenant for life may in relation to the land or mines and minerals surrendered or regranted, or of any part thereof, make a new or other lease, or grant in fee simple, or new or other leases, or grants in fee simple, in lots.

(4) A new or other lease, or grant in fee simple, may comprise additional land or mines and minerals, and may reserve any apportioned or other rent or rentcharge.

(5) On a surrender or regrant, and the making of a new or other lease, whether for the same or for any extended or other term, or of a new or other grant in fee simple, and whether or not subject to the same or to any other covenants, provisions, or conditions, the value of the lessee's or grantee's interest in the lease surrendered, or the land regranted, may be taken into account in the determination of the amount of the rent or rentcharge to be reserved, and of any fine or consideration in money to be taken, and of the nature of the covenants, provisions, and conditions to be inserted in the new or other lease, or grant in fee simple.

(6) Every new or other lease, or grant in fee simple, shall be in conformity with this Act.

(7) All money, not being rent or a rentcharge, received on the exercise by the tenant for life of the powers conferred by this section, shall, unless the court, on an application made within six months after the receipt thereof or within such further time as the court may in special circumstances allow, otherwise directs, be capital money arising under this Act.

(8) A regrant shall be made to the tenant for life or statutory owner, and shall be deemed a subsidiary vesting deed, and the statements and particulars required in the case of subsidiary vesting deeds shall be inserted therein.

(9) In this section "land granted in fee simple" means land so granted with or subject to a reservation thereout of a perpetual or terminable rentcharge which is or forms part of the settled land, and "grant in fee simple" has a corresponding meaning.

Acceptance of leases

53.—(1) A tenant for life may accept a lease of any land, or of any mines and minerals or of any easement, right, or privilege, convenient to be held or worked with or annexed in enjoyment to the settled land, or any part thereof, for such period, and upon such terms and conditions, as the tenant for life thinks fit: **7–050**

Provided that no fine shall be paid out of capital money in respect of such lease.

(2) The lease shall be granted to the tenant for life or statutory owner, and shall be deemed a subsidiary vesting deed, and the statements and particulars required in the case of subsidiary vesting deeds shall either be inserted therein or endorsed thereon.

(3) The lease may contain an option to purchase the reversion expectant on the term thereby granted.

Power to grant water rights to statutory bodies

7–051 **54.**—(1) For the development, improvement, or general benefit of the settled land, or any part thereof, a tenant for life may make a grant in fee simple or absolutely, or a lease for any term of years absolute, for a nominal price or rent, or for less than the best price or rent that can reasonably be obtained, or gratuitously, to any statutory authority, of any water or streams or springs of water in, upon, or under the settled land, and of any rights of taking, using, enjoying and conveying water, and of laying, constructing, maintaining, and repairing mains, pipes, reservoirs, dams, weirs and other works of any kind proper for the supply and distribution of water, and of any part of the settled land required as a site for any of the aforesaid works, and of any easement, right or privilege over or in relation to the settled land or any part thereof in connexion with any of the aforesaid works.

(2) This section does not authorise the creation of any greater rights than could have been created by a person absolutely entitled for his own benefit to the settled land affected.

(3) In this section "statutory authority" means an authority or company for the time being empowered by any Act of Parliament, public general, or local or private, or by any order or certificate having the force of an Act of Parliament, to provide with a supply of water any town, parish or place in which the settled land or any part thereof is situated.

(4) All money, not being rent, received on the exercise of any power conferred by this section shall be capital money arising under this Act.

Power to grant land for public and charitable purposes

7–052 **55.**—(1) For the development, improvement, or general benefit of the settled land, or any part thereof, a tenant for life may make a grant in fee simple, or absolutely, or a lease for any term of years absolute, for a nominal price or rent, or for less than the best price or rent that can reasonably be obtained, or gratuitously, of any part of the settled land, with or without any easement, right or privilege over or in relation to the settled land or any part thereof, for all or any one or more of the following purposes, namely:—

(i) For the site, or the extension of any existing site, of a place of religious worship, residence for a minister of religion, school house, town hall, market house, public library, public baths, museum, hospital, infirmary, or other public building, literary or scientific institution, drill hall, working-men's club, parish room, reading room or village institute, with or without in any case any yard, garden, or other ground to be held with any such building; or

(ii) For the construction, enlargement, or improvement of any railway, canal, road (public or private), dock, sea-wall, embankment, drain, watercourse, or reservoir; or

(iii) For any other public or charitable purpose in connexion with the settled land, or any part thereof, or tending to the benefit of the persons residing, or for whom dwellings may be erected, on the settled land, or any part thereof.

Not more than one acre shall in any particular case be conveyed for any purpose mentioned in paragraphs (i) and (iii) of this subsection, nor more than five acres for any purpose mentioned in paragraph (ii) of this subsection, unless the full consideration be paid or reserved in respect of the excess.

(2) All money, not being rent, received on the exercise of any power conferred by this section shall be capital money arising under this Act.

Dedication for streets, open spaces, etc.

56.—(1) On or after or in connexion with a sale or grant for building purposes, or a building lease, or the development as a building estate of the settled land, or any part thereof, or at any other reasonable time, the tenant for life, for the general benefit of the residents on the settled land, or on any part thereof— **7–053**

(i) may cause or require any parts of the settled land to be appropriated and laid out for streets, roads, paths, squares, gardens, or other open spaces, for the use, gratuitously or on payment, of the public or of individuals, with sewers, drains, watercourses, fencing, paving, or other works necessary or proper in connexion therewith; and

(ii) may provide that the parts so appropriated shall be conveyed to or vested in the trustees of the settlement, or other trustees, or any company or public body, on trusts or subject to provisions for securing the continued appropriation thereof to the purposes aforesaid, and the continued repair or maintenance of streets and other places and works aforesaid, with or without provision for appointment of new trustees when required; and

(iii) may execute any general or other deed necessary or proper for giving effect to the provisions of this section (which deed may be enrolled in the Central Office of the Supreme Court), and thereby declare the mode, terms, and conditions of the appropriation, and the manner in which and the persons by whom the benefit thereof is to be enjoyed, and the nature and extent of the privileges and conveniences granted.

(2) In regard to the dedication of land for the public purposes aforesaid, a tenant for life shall be in the same position as if he were an absolute owner.

(3) A tenant for life shall have power—

(a) to enter into any agreement for the recompense to be made for any part of the settled land which is required for the widening of a highway under [the Highways Act 1980][42] or otherwise;

(b) to consent to the diversion of any highway over the settled land under [the Highways Act 1980][43] or otherwise;

[. . .][44]

and any agreement or consent so made or given shall be as valid and effectual, for all purposes, as if made or given by an absolute owner of the settled land.

(4) All money, not being rent, received on the exercise of any power conferred by this section shall be capital money arising under this Act.

[42] Words substituted by the Highways Act 1980, s.343(2), Sched. 24, para. 2.
[43] Words substituted by the Highways Act 1980, s.343(2), Sched. 24, para. 2.
[44] Para. (c) repealed by the Highways Act 1959, s.312(2), Sched. 25.

Provision of land for small dwellings, small holdings and dwellings for working classes

7–054 **57.**—(1) Where land is sold, or given in exchange or leased—

(a) for the purpose of the erection on such land of small dwellings; or

(b) to the council of a county or county borough for the purposes of small holdings;

the sale, exchange, or lease may, notwithstanding anything contained in this Act, be made for such consideration in money, or land, or in land and money, or may reserve such rent, as having regard to the said purposes and to all the circumstances of the case, is the best that can reasonably be obtained, notwithstanding that a better consideration or rent might have been obtained if the land were sold, exchanged, or leased, for another purpose.

(2) Notwithstanding anything contained in, and in addition to the other powers conferred by this Act, a tenant for life may at any time—

(a) for the purpose of the erection of dwellings for the working classes, or the provision of gardens to be held therewith; or

(b) for the purpose of the Small Holdings and Allotments Acts 1908 to 1919[45];

make a grant in fee simple or absolutely, or a lease for any term of years absolute of any part of the settled land, with or without any easement, right or privilege of any kind over or in relation to the settled land or any part thereof, for a nominal price or rent, or for less than the best price or rent that can reasonably be obtained or gratuitously:

Provided that, except under an order of the court, not more than two acres in the case of land situate in an urban district, or ten acres in the case of land situate in a rural district, in any one parish shall be granted or leased under the powers conferred by this subsection, unless the full consideration be paid or reserved in respect of the excess.

(3) All money, not being rent, received on the exercise of any power conferred by this section shall be capital money arising under this Act.

Power to compromise claims and release restrictions, etc.

7–055 **58.**—(1) A tenant for life may, with the consent in writing of the trustees of the settlement, either with or without giving or taking any consideration in money or otherwise, compromise, compound, abandon, submit to arbitration or otherwise settle any claim, dispute, or question whatsoever relating to the settled land, or any part thereof, including in particular claims, disputes or questions as to boundaries, the ownership of mines and minerals, rights and powers of working mines and minerals, local laws and customs relative to the working of mines and minerals, and other matters, [...][46] easements, and restrictive covenants, and for any of those purposes may enter into, give, execute, and do such agreements, assurances, releases, and other things as the tenant for life may, with such consent as aforesaid, think proper.

(2) A tenant for life may, with the consent in writing of the trustees of the settlement, at any time, by deed or writing, either with or without consideration in money or otherwise, release, waive, or modify, or agree to release, waive, or modify, any covenant, agreement, or restriction imposed on any other land for

[45] Now the Small Holdings and Allotments Acts 1908–31.
[46] Words repealed by the Statute Law (Repeals) Act 1969, s.1, Sched., Pt. III.

the benefit of the settled land, or any part thereof, or release, or agree to release, any other land from any easement, right or privilege, including a right of pre-emption, affecting the same for the benefit of the settled land, or any part thereof.

(3) A tenant for life may contract that a transaction effected before or after the commencement of this Act, which (whether subject or not to any variation authorised by this subsection) is affected by section seventy-eight of the Railway Clauses Consolidation Act 1845 or by section twenty-two of the Waterworks Clauses Act 1847 (relating to support by minerals) shall take effect as if some other distance than forty yards or the prescribed distance had been mentioned in such sections or had been otherwise prescribed.

In any case where section seventy-eight aforesaid has effect as amended and re-enacted by Part II of the Mines (Working Facilities and Support) Act 1923 a tenant for life may make any agreement authorised by section eighty-five A of the Railway Clauses Consolidation Act 1845 as enacted in the said Part II.

Power to vary leases and grants and to give licences and consents

59.—(1) A tenant for life may, at any time, by deed, either with or without consideration in money or otherwise, vary, release, waive or modify, either absolutely or otherwise, the terms of any lease whenever made of the settled land or any part thereof, or any covenants or conditions contained in any grant in fee simple whenever made of land with or subject to a reservation thereout of a rent which is or forms part of the settled land, and in either case in respect of the whole or any part of the land comprised in any such lease or grant, but so that every such lease or grant shall, after such variation, release, waiver or modification as aforesaid, be such a lease or grant as might then have been lawfully made under this Act if the lease had been surrendered, or the land comprised in the grant had never been so comprised, or had been regranted. **7–056**

(2) Where land is or has been disposed of subject to any covenant requiring the licence, consent, or approval of the covenantee or his successors in title as to—

(a) the user of the land in any manner; or
(b) the erection construction or alteration of or addition to buildings or works of any description on the land; or
(c) the plans or elevations of any proposed buildings or other works on the land; or
(d) any other act, matter, or thing relating to the land, or any buildings or works thereon; or
(e) any assignment, under-letting or parting with the possession of all or any part of the property comprised in any lease affecting the settled land;

and the covenant enures for the benefit of settled land (including, where the disposition is a lease, the reversion expectant on the determination thereof), the licence, consent or approval may be given by the tenant for life of the settled land affected.

Power to apportion rents

60.—(1) A tenant for life may, at any time, by deed either with or without consideration in money or otherwise, agree for the apportionment of any rent **7–057**

reserved or created by any such lease or grant as mentioned in the last preceding section, or any rent being or forming part of the settled land, so that the apportioned parts of such rent shall thenceforth be payable exclusively out of or in respect of such respective portions of the land subject thereto as may be thought proper, and also agree that any covenants, agreements, powers, or remedies for securing such rent and any other covenants or agreements by the lessee or grantee and any conditions shall also be apportioned and made applicable exclusively to the respective portions of the land out of or in respect of which the apportioned parts of such rent shall thenceforth be payable.

(2) Where the settled land, or any part thereof, is held or derived under a lease, or under a grant reserving rent, or subject to covenants, agreements or conditions, whether such lease or grant comprises other land or not, the tenant for life may at any time by deed, with or without giving or taking any consideration in money or otherwise, procure the variation, release, waiver, or modification, either absolutely or otherwise, of the terms, covenants, agreements, or conditions contained in such lease or grant, in respect of the whole or any part of the settled land comprised therein, including the apportionment of any rent, covenants, agreements, conditions, and provisions reserved, or created by, or contained in, such lease or grant.

(3) This section applies to leases or grants made either before or after the commencement of this Act.

Provisions as to consideration

7–058 **61.**—(1) All money, not being rent, payable by the tenant for life in respect of any transaction to which any of the three last preceding sections relates shall be paid out of capital money arising under this Act, and all money, not being rent, received on the exercise by the tenant for life of the powers conferred by any of those sections, shall, unless the court, on an application made within six months after the receipt thereof or within such further time as the court may in special circumstances allow, otherwise directs, be capital money arising under this Act.

(2) For the purpose of the three last preceding sections "consideration in money or otherwise" means—

(a) a capital sum of money or a rent;
(b) land being freehold or leasehold for any term of years whereof not less than sixty years shall be unexpired;
(c) any easement, right or privilege over or in relation to the settled land, or any part thereof, or any other land;
(d) the benefit of any restrictive covenant or condition; and
(e) the release of the settled land, or any part thereof, or any other land, from any easement, right or privilege, including a right of pre-emption, or from the burden of any restrictive covenant or condition affecting the same.

Special provisions as to manorial incidents, etc.

7–059 **62.**—(1)–(3) [*Repealed by the Statute Law (Repeals) Act 1969, s.1, Sched., Pt. III.*]

(4) In reference to the conversion of a perpetually renewable lease or underlease into a long term, a tenant for life may enter into such agreements and

do such acts and things as the lessor or lessee or underlessee, as the case may require, is, by any enactment authorised to enter into or do.

Power to complete predecessor's contracts

63.—A tenant for life may make any disposition which is necessary or proper for giving effect to a contract entered into by a predecessor in title, and which if made by that predecessor would have been valid as against his successors in title. **7–060**

General power for the tenant for life to effect any transaction under an order of the court

64.—(1) Any transaction affecting or concerning the settled land, or any part thereof, or any other land (not being a transaction otherwise authorised by this Act, or by the settlement) which in the opinion of the court would be for the benefit of the settled land, or any part thereof, or the persons interested under the settlement, may, under an order of the court, be effected by a tenant for life, if it is one which could have been validly effected by an absolute owner. **7–061**

(2) In this section "transaction" includes any sale, [. . .][47] exchange, assurance, grant, lease, surrender, reconveyance, release, reservation, or other disposition, and any purchase or other acquisition, and any covenant, contract, or option, and any application of capital money [...][48], and any compromise or other dealing, or arrangement; [. . .][49] and "effected" has the meaning appropriate to the particular transaction; and the references to land include references to restrictions and burdens affecting land.

Provisions as to special classes of property

Power to dispose of mansion

65.—(1) The powers of disposing of settled land conferred by this Act on a tenant for life may be exercised as respects the principal mansion house, if any, on any settled land, and the pleasure grounds and park and lands, if any, usually occupied therewith: **7–062**

Provided that those powers shall not be exercised without the consent of the trustees of the settlement or an order of the court—

(a) if the settlement is a settlement made or coming into operation before the commencement of this Act and the settlement does not expressly provide to the contrary; or

(b) if the settlement is a settlement made or coming into operation after the commencement of this Act and the settlement expressly provides that these powers or any of them shall not be exercised without such consent or order.

(2) Where a house is usually occupied as a farmhouse, or where the site of any house and the pleasure grounds and park and lands, if any, usually occupied therewith do not together exceed twenty-five acres in extent, the house is not to be deemed a principal mansion house within the meaning of this section, and

[47] Words repealed by the Statute Law (Repeals) Act 1969, s.1, Sched., Pt. III.
[48] Words repealed by the Settled Land and Trustee Acts (Court's General Powers) Act 1943, s.2.
[49] Words substituted by the Mental Health Act 1959, s.149(1), Sched. 7, Pt. I.

may accordingly be disposed of in like manner as any other part of the settled land.

Cutting and sale of timber, and capitalisation of part of proceeds

7–063 **66.**—(1) Where a tenant for life is impeachable for waste in respect of timber, and there is on the settled land timber ripe and fit for cutting, the tenant for life, on obtaining the consent of the trustees of the settlement or an order of the court, may cut and sell that timber, or any part thereof.

(2) Three fourth parts of the net proceeds of the sale shall be set aside as and be capital money arising under this Act, and the other fourth part shall go as rents and profits.

Sale and purchase of heirlooms under order of court

7–064 **67.**—(1) Where personal chattels are settled so as to devolve with settled land, or to devolve therewith as nearly as may be in accordance with the law or practice in force at the date of the settlement, or are settled together with land, or upon trusts declared by reference to the trusts affecting land, a tenant for life of the land may sell the chattels or any of them.

(2) The money arising by the sale shall be capital money arising under this Act, and shall be paid, invested, or applied and otherwise dealt with in like manner in all respects as by this Act directed with respect to other capital money arising under this Act, or may be invested in the purchase of other chattels of the same or any other nature, which, when purchased, shall be settled and held on the same trusts, and shall devolve in the same manner as the chattels sold.

(3) A sale or purchase of chattels under this section shall not be made without an order of the court.

(4) Any reference in any enactment to personal chattels settled as heirlooms shall extend to any chattels to which this section applies.

Dealings as between tenants for life and the estate

Provision enabling dealings with tenant for life

7–065 **68.**—(1) In the manner mentioned and subject to the provisions contained in this section—

(a) a sale, grant, lease, mortgage, charge or other disposition of settled land, or of any easement, right, or privilege over the same may be made to the tenant for life; or

(b) capital money may be advanced on mortgage to him; or

(c) a purchase may be made from him of land to be made subject to the limitations of the settlement; or

(d) an exchange may be made with him of settled land for other land; and

(e) any such disposition, advance, purchase, or exchange as aforesaid may be made to, from, or with any persons of whom the tenant for life is one.

(2) In every such case the trustees of the settlement shall, in addition to their powers as trustees, have all the powers of a tenant for life in reference to negotiating and completing the transaction, and shall have power to enforce any covenants by the tenant for life, or, where the tenant for life is himself one of the trustees, then the other or others of them shall have such power, and the said

powers of a tenant for life may be exercised by the trustees of the settlement in the name and on behalf of the tenant for life.

(3) This section applies, notwithstanding that the tenant for life is one of the trustees of the settlement, or that an order has been made authorising the trustees to act on his behalf, or that he is [suffering from mental disorder][50] but does not apply to dealings with any body of persons which includes a trustee of the settlement, not being the tenant for life, unless the transaction is either previously or subsequently approved by the court.

Incumbrances

Shifting of incumbrances

69. Where there is an incumbrance affecting any part of the settled land (whether capable of being overreached on the exercise by the tenant for life of his powers under this Act or not), the tenant for life, with the consent of the incumbrancer, may charge that incumbrance on any other part of the settled land, or on all or any part of the capital money or securities representing capital money subject or to become subject to the settlement, whether already charged therewith or not, in exoneration of the first mentioned part, and, by a legal mortgage, or otherwise, make provision accordingly. **7–066**

Power to vary provisions of an incumbrance and to charge by way of additional security

70.—(1) Where an incumbrance affects any part of the settled land, the tenant for life may, with the consent of the incumbrancer, vary the rate of interest charged and any of the other provisions of the instrument, if any, creating the incumbrance, and with the like consent charge that incumbrance on any part of the settled land, whether already charged therewith or not, or on all or any part of the capital money or securities representing capital money subject or to become subject to the settlement, by way of additional security, or of consolidation of securities, and by a legal mortgage or otherwise, make provision accordingly. **7–067**

(2) "Incumbrance" in this section includes any annual sum payable during a life or lives or during a term of years absolute or determinable, but in any such case an additional security shall be effected so as only to create a charge or security similar to the original charge or security.

Raising of Money

Power to raise money by mortgage

71.—(1) Where money is required for any of the following purposes namely:— **7–068**

(i) Discharging an incumbrance on the settled land or part thereof;

(ii) Paying for any improvement authorised by this Act or by the settlement;

(iii) Equality of exchange;

[. . .][51]

---

[50] Words substituted by the Mental Health Act 1959, s.149(1), Sched. 7, Pt. I.

[51] Paras (iv) and (v) repealed by the Statute Law (Repeals) Act 1969, s.1, Sched., Pt. III.

(vi) Redeeming a compensation rentcharge in respect of the extinguishment of manorial incidents and affecting the settled land;

(vii) Commuting any additional rent made payable on the conversion of a perpetually renewable leasehold interest into a long term;

(viii) Satisfying any claims for compensation on the conversion of a perpetually renewable leasehold interest into a long term by any officer, solicitor, or other agent of the lessor in respect of fees or remuneration which would have been payable by the lessee or under-lessee on any renewal;

(ix) Payment of the costs of any transaction authorised by this section or either of the two last preceding sections;

the tenant for life may raise the money so required, on the security of the settled land, or of any part thereof, by a legal mortgage, and the money so raised shall be capital money for that purpose, and may be paid or applied accordingly.

(2) "Incumbrance" in this section does not include any annual sum payable only during a life or lives or during a term of years absolute or determinable.

(3) The restrictions imposed by this Part of this Act on the leasing powers of a tenant for life do not apply in relation to a mortgage term created under this Act.

Conveyance

Completion of transactions by conveyance

7–069 **72.**—(1) On a sale, exchange, lease, mortgage, charge, or other disposition, the tenant for life may, as regards land sold, given in exchange, leased, mortgaged, charged, or otherwise disposed of, or intended so to be, or as regards easements or other rights or privileges sold, given in exchange, leased, mortgaged, or otherwise disposed of, or intended so to be, effect the transaction by deed to the extent of the estate or interest vested or declared to be vested in him by the last or only vesting instrument affecting the settled land or any less estate or interest, in the manner requisite for giving effect to the sale, exchange, lease, mortgage, charge, or other disposition, but so that a mortgage shall be effected by the creation of a term of years absolute in the settled land or by charge by way of legal mortgage, and not otherwise.

(2) Such a deed, to the extent and in the manner to and in which it is expressed or intended to operate and can operate under this Act, is effectual to pass the land conveyed, or the easements, rights, privileges or other interests created, discharged from all the limitations, powers, and provisions of the settlement, and from all estates, interests, and charges subsisting or to arise thereunder, but subject to and with the exception of—

(i) all legal estates and charges by way of legal mortgage having priority to the settlement; and

(ii) all legal estates and charges by way of legal mortgage which have been conveyed or created for securing money actually raised at the date of the deed; and

(iii) all leases and grants at fee-farm rents or otherwise, and all grants of easements, rights of common, or other rights or privileges which—

(a) were before the date of the deed granted or made for value in money or money's worth, or agreed so to be, by the tenant for life or statutory owner, or by any of his predecessors in title, or any trustees for them, under the settlement, or under any statutory power, or are at that date otherwise binding on the successors in title of the tenant for life or statutory owner; and

(b) are at the date of the deed protected by registration under the Land Charges Act 1925[52] if capable of registration thereunder.

(3) Notwithstanding registration under the Land Charges Act 1925[53] of—

(a) an annuity within the meaning of Part II of that Act;

(b) a limited owner's charge or a general equitable charge within the meaning of that Act;

a disposition under this Act operates to overreach such annuity or charge which shall, according to its priority, take effect as if limited by the settlement.

(4) Where a lease is by this Act authorised to be made by writing under hand only, such writing shall have the same operation under this section as if it had been a deed.

Part III

Investment or Other Application of Capital Money

Modes of investment or application

73.—(1) Capital money arising under this Act, subject to payment of claims properly payable thereout and to the application thereof for any special authorised object for which the capital money was raised, shall, when received, be invested or otherwise applied wholly in one, or partly in one and partly in another or others, of the following modes (namely):— **7–070**

[(i) In investment in securities either under the general power of investment in section 3 of the Trustee Act 2000 or under a power to invest conferred on the trustees of the settlement by the settlement;][54]

(ii) In discharge, purchase, or redemption of incumbrances affecting the whole estate the subject of the settlement, or of [. . .][55] rentcharge in lieu of tithe[56], Crown rent, chief rent, or quit rent, charged on or payable out of the settled land, or of any charge in respect of an improvement created on a holding under the [Agricultural Holdings Act 1986][57] or any similar previous enactment;

(iii) In payment for any improvement authorised by this Act;

(iv) In payment as for an improvement authorised by this Act of any money expended and costs incurred by a landlord under or in pursuance of the [Agricultural Holdings Act 1986][58] or any similar previous enactment, or under custom or agreement or otherwise, in or about the execution of any improvement comprised in [Schedule 7][59] to the said Agricultural Holdings Act;

(v) In payment for equality of exchange of settled land;

[. . .][60]

(viii) In redemption of any compensation rentcharge created in respect of the extinguishment of manorial incidents, and affecting the settled land;

---

[52] Now the Land Charges Act 1972, s.2, *post*, para. 31–002.
[53] Now the Land Charges Act 1972, s.2, *post*, para. 31–002.
[54] Para. (i) substituted by the Trustee Act 2000, s.40(1), Sched. 2, Pt. II, para. 9.
[55] Words repealed by the Finance Act 1963, s.73(8)(b), Sched. 14, Pt. VI.
[56] Tithe rentcharge was extinguished by the Tithe Act 1936, ss.1, 30.
[57] Words substituted by the Agricultural Holdings Act 1986, s.100, Sched. 14, para. 11.
[58] Words substituted by the Agricultural Holdings Act 1986, s.100, Sched. 14, para. 11.
[59] Words substituted by the Agricultural Holdings Act 1986, s.100, Sched. 14, para. 11.
[60] Paras (vi) and (vii) repealed by the Statute Law (Repeals) Act 1969, s.1, Sched., Pt. III.

(ix) In commuting any additional rent made payable on the conversion of a perpetually renewable leasehold interest into a long term, and in satisfying any claim for compensation on such conversion by any officer, solicitor, or other agent of the lessor in respect of fees or remuneration which would have been payable by the lessee or under-lessee on any renewal;

(x) In purchase of the freehold reversion in fee of any part of the settled land, being leasehold land held for years;

(xi) In purchase of land in fee simple, or of leasehold land held for sixty years or more unexpired at the time of purchase, subject or not to any exception or reservation of or in respect of mines or minerals therein, or of or in respect of rights or powers relative to the working of mines or minerals therein, or in other land;

(xii) In purchase either in fee simple, or for a term of sixty years or more, of mines and minerals convenient to be held or worked with the settled land, or of any easement, right, or privilege convenient to be held with the settled land for mining or other purposes;

(xiii) In redemption of an improvement rentcharge, that is to say, a rentcharge (temporary or permanent) created, whether before or after the commencement of this Act, in pursuance of any Act of Parliament, with the object of paying off any money advanced for defraying the expenses of an improvement of any kind authorised by Part I of the Third Schedule to this Act;

(xiv) In the purchase, with the leave of the court, of any leasehold interest where the immediate reversion is settled land, so as to merge the leasehold interest (unless the court otherwise directs) in the reversion, and notwithstanding that the leasehold interest may have less than sixty years to run;

(xv) In payment of the costs and expenses of all plans, surveys, and schemes, including schemes under the Town Planning Act 1925 or any similar previous enactment, made with a view to, or in connexion with the improvement or development of the settled land, or any part thereof, or the exercise of any statutory powers, and of all negotiations entered into by the tenant for life with a view to the exercise of any of the said powers, notwithstanding that such negotiations may prove abortive, and in payment of the costs and expenses of opposing any such proposed scheme as aforesaid affecting the settled land, whether or not the scheme is made;

[…][61]

(xvii) In payment to a local or other authority of such sum as may be agreed in consideration of such authority taking over and becoming liable to repair a private road on the settled land or a road for the maintenance whereof a tenant for life is liable ratione tenurae;

(xviii) In financing any person who may have agreed to take a lease or grant for building purposes of the settled land, or any part thereof, by making advances to him in the usual manner on the security of an equitable mortgage of his building agreement;

(xix) In payment to any person becoming absolutely entitled or empowered to give an absolute discharge;

[61] Para. (xvi) repealed by the Statute Law (Repeals) Act 1998, s.1, Sched., Pt. II.

(xx) In payment of costs, charges, and expenses of or incidental to the exercise of any of the powers, or the execution of any of the provisions of this Act including the costs and expenses incidental to any of the matters referred to in this section;

(xxi) In any other mode authorised by the settlement with respect to money produced by the sale of the settled land.

(2) Notwithstanding anything in this section capital money arising under this Act from settled land in England or Wales shall not be applied in the purchase of land out of England and Wales, unless the settlement expressly authorises the same.

Power to acquire land subject to certain incumbrances

74.—(1) Land may be acquired on a purchase or exchange to be made subject **7–071** to a settlement, notwithstanding that the land is subject to any Crown rent, quit rent, chief rent, or other incident of tenure, or to any easement, right or privilege, or to any restrictive covenant, or to any liability to maintain or repair walls, fences, sea-walls, river banks, dykes, roads, streets, sewers, or drains, or to any improvement rentcharge which is capable under this Act of being redeemed out of capital money.

(2) The acquisition on a purchase or exchange before the commencement of this Act of any land subject to any such burden as aforesaid is hereby confirmed.

Regulations respecting investment, devolution, and income of securities, etc.

75.—(1) Capital money arising under this Act shall, in order to its being **7–072** invested or applied as aforesaid, be paid either to the trustees of the settlement or into court at the option of the tenant for life, and shall be invested or applied by the trustees, or under the direction of the court, as the case may be, accordingly.

[(2) Subject to Part IV of the Trustee Act 2000, to section 75A of this Act to the following provisions of this section—

(a) the investment or other application by the trustees shall be made according to the discretion of the trustees, but subject to any consent required or direction given by the settlement with respect to the investment or other application by the trustees of trust money of the settlement, and

(b) any investment shall be made in the names or under the control of the trustees.][62]

(3) The investment or other application under the direction of the court shall be made on the application of the tenant for life, or of the trustees.

[(4) The trustees, in exercising their power to invest or apply capital money, shall—

(a) so far as practicable, consult the tenant for life; and

(b) so far as consistent with the general interest of the settlement, give effect to his wishes.

(4A) Any investment or other application of capital money under the direction of the court shall not during the subsistence of the beneficial interest of the tenant for life be altered without his consent.

(4B) The trustees may not under section 11 of the Trustee Act 2000 authorise

[62] subs. (2) substituted by the Trustee Act 2000, s.40(1), Sched. 2, Pt. II, para. 10(1).

a person to exercise their functions with respect to the investment or application of capital money on terms that prevent them from complying with subsection (4) of this section.

(4C) A person who is authorised under section 11 of the Trustee Act 2000 to exercise any of their functions with respect to the investment or application of capital money is not subject to subsection (4) of this section.][63]

(5) Capital money arising under this Act while remaining uninvested or unapplied, and securities on which an investment of any such capital money is made shall for all purposes of disposition, transmission and devolution be treated as land, and shall be held for and go to the same persons successively, in the same manner and for and on the same estates, interests, and trusts, as the land wherefrom the money arises would, if not disposed of, have been held and have gone under the settlement.

(6) The income of those securities shall be paid or applied as the income of that land, if not disposed of, would have been payable or applicable under the settlement.

(7) Those securities may be converted into money, which shall be capital money arising under this Act.

(8) All or any part of any capital money paid into court may, if the court thinks fit, be at any time paid out to the trustees of the settlement.

[Power to accept charge as security for part payment for land sold

7–073 **75A.**—(1) Where—

(a) land subject to the settlement is sold by the tenant for life or statutory owner, for an estate in fee simple or a team having at least five hundred years to run, and

(b) the proceeds of sale are liable to be invested, the tenant for life or statutory owner may, with the consent of the trustees of the settlement, contract that the payment of any part, not exceeding two-thirds, of the purchase money shall be secured by a charge by way of legal mortgage of the land sold, with or without the security of any other property.

(2) If any buildings are comprised in the property secured by the charge, the charge must contain a covenant by the mortgagor to keep them insured for their full value against the loss or damage due to any event.

(3) A person exercising the power under subsection (1) of this section, or giving consent for the purpose of that subsection—

(a) is not required to comply with section 5 of the Trustee Act 2000 before giving his consent, and

(b) is not liable for any loss incurred merely because the security is insufficient at the date of the charge.

(4) The power under subsection (1) of this section is exercisable subject to the consent of any person whose consent to a change of investment is required by the instrument, if any, creating the trust.

(5) Where the sale referred to in a subsection (1) of this section is made under the order of the court, the power under that subsection applies only if and as far as the court may by order direct.][64]

[63] substs. (4)–(4C) substituted (for subs. (4)) by the Trustee Act 2000, s.40(1), Sched. 2, Pt. II, para. 10(2).

[64] s.75A inserted by the Trustee Act 2000, s.40(1), Sched. 2, Pt. II, para. 11.

Application of money in court under Lands Clauses and other Acts

76. Where, under an Act, or an order or scheme confirmed by or having the force of an Act of Parliament, incorporating or applying, wholly or in part, the Lands Clauses Acts, or under any Act, public general or local or private, money is at the commencement of this Act in court, or is afterwards paid into court, and is liable to be laid out in the purchase of land to be made subject to a settlement, then, in addition to any mode of dealing therewith authorised by the Act under which the money is in court, that money may be invested or applied as capital money arising under this Act, on the like terms, if any, respecting costs and other things, as nearly as circumstances admit, and notwithstanding anything in this Act according to the same procedure, as if the modes of investment or application authorised by this Act were authorised by the Act under which the money is in court. **7–074**

Application of money in hands of trustees under powers of settlement

77. Where— **7–075**

(a) under any instrument coming into operation either before or after the commencement of this Act money is in the hands of trustees, and is liable to be laid out in the purchase of land to be made subject to the trusts declared by that instrument; or

(b) under any instrument coming into operation after the commencement of this Act money or securities or the proceeds of sale of any property is or are held by trustees on trusts creating entailed interests therein;

then, in addition to such powers of dealing therewith as the trustees have independently of this Act, they may, at the option of the tenant for life, invest or apply the money securities or proceeds as if they were capital money arising under this Act.

Provision as to personal estate settled by reference to capital money, or on trusts corresponding with the limitations of land

78.—(1) Where money or securities or the proceeds of sale of any property is or are by any instrument coming into operation either before or after the commencement of this Act directed to be held on trusts declared by reference to capital money arising under this Act from land settled by that instrument or any other instrument, the money securities or proceeds shall be held on the like trusts as if the same had been or represented money which had actually arisen under this Act from the settled land. **7–076**

[This subsection operates without prejudice to the rights of any person claiming under a disposition for valuable consideration of any such money securities or proceeds, made before the commencement of this Act.][65]

(2) Where money or securities or the proceeds of sale of any property is or are by any instrument coming into operation after the commencement of this Act directed to be held on the same trusts as, or on trusts corresponding as nearly as may be with the limitations of land settled by that instrument or any other instrument, the money, securities or proceeds shall be held on the like trusts as if the same had been or represented capital money arising under this Act from the settled land.

[65] Words added by the Law of Property (Amendment) Act 1926, s.7, Sched.

(3) Such money, securities, or proceeds of sale shall be paid or transferred to or retained by the trustees of the settlement of the settled land, or paid or transferred into court and invested or applied accordingly.

(4) Where the settled land includes freehold land, the money, securities, or proceeds of sale aforesaid shall be held on the like trusts as if the same had been or represented capital money arising from the freehold land.

(5) This section has effect notwithstanding any direction in the instrument creating the trust that the trust property is not to vest absolutely in any tenant in tail or in tail male or in tail female under the limitations of the settled land who dies under a specified age, or before the happening of a specified event, but, save as aforesaid, has effect with any variations and subject to any contrary intention expressed in the instrument creating the trust.

Application of money paid for lease or reversion

7–077 **79.** Where capital money arising under this Act is purchase-money paid in respect of—

(a) a lease for years; or

(b) any other estate or interest in land less than the fee simple; or

(c) a reversion dependent on any such lease, estate, or interest;

the trustees of the settlement or the court, as the case may be, and in the case of the court on the application of any party interested in that money, may, notwithstanding anything in this Act, require and cause the same to be laid out, invested, accumulated, and paid in such manner as, in the judgment of the trustees of the court, as the case may be, will give to the parties interested in that money the like benefit therefrom as they might lawfully have had from the lease, estate, interest, or reversion in respect whereof the money was paid, or as near thereto as may be.

As to money received by way of damages for breach of covenant

7–078 **80.**—(1) Money, not being rent, received by way of damages or compensation for breach of any covenant by a lessee or grantee contained in any lease or grant of settled land shall, unless in any case the court on the application of the tenant for life or the trustees of the settlement otherwise directs, be deemed to be capital money arising under this Act, and shall be paid to or retained by the trustees of the settlement, or paid into court, and invested or applied, accordingly.

(2) In addition to the other modes in which capital money may be applied under this Act or the settlement, money so received as aforesaid or any part thereof may, if the circumstances permit, be applied at any time within twelve months after such receipt, or such extended period as the court may allow, in or towards payment of the costs of making good in whole or in part the breach of covenant in respect of which it was so received, or the consequences thereof, and the trustees of the settlement, if they think fit, may require any money so received or any part thereof to be so applied.

(3) In the application of any such money in or towards payment of the cost of making good any such breach or the consequences of any such breach as aforesaid, the work required to be done for the purpose shall be deemed to be an improvement authorised by Part I of the Third Schedule to this Act.

(4) This section does not apply to money received by way of damages or compensation for the breach of a covenant to repay to the lessor or grantor

money laid out or expended by him, or to any case in which if the money received were applied in making good the breach of covenant or the consequences thereof such application would not enure for the benefit of the settled land, or any buildings thereon.

(5) This section does not apply to money received by way of damages or compensation before the commencement of this Act, but it applies whether the lease or grant was made before or after the commencement of this Act, and whether under the powers conferred by the Settled Land Acts 1882 to 1890 or this Act or not.

(6) The provisions of this section apply only if and as far as a contrary intention is not expressed in the settlement, and have effect subject to the terms of the settlement, and to any provisions therein contained, but a contrary intention shall not be deemed to be expressed merely by words negativing impeachment for waste.

As to capital arising otherwise than under the Act

81. Any money which after the commencement of this Act arises from settled **7–079**
land otherwise than under this Act, as well as any money or securities in the names or under the control of the tenant for life or the trustees of the settlement, being or representing money which had arisen before the commencement of this Act from the settled land otherwise than under the Settled Land Acts 1882 to 1890, and which ought, as between the persons interested in the settled land, to be or to have been treated as capital, shall (without prejudice to any other statutory provisions affecting the same) be deemed to be or to represent capital money arising under this Act, and shall be paid or transferred to or retained by the trustees of the settlement, or paid or transferred into court, and invested or applied, accordingly.

Land acquired may be made a substituted security for released charges

82.—(1) Land acquired by purchase or in exchange or otherwise under the **7–080**
powers of this Act, may be made a substituted security for any charge from which the settled land or any part thereof has theretofore been released on the occasion and in order to the completion of a sale, exchange or other disposition:

Provided that, where a charge does not affect the whole of the settled land, the land acquired shall not be subjected thereto, unless the land is acquired either by purchase with money arising from sale of land which was before the sale subject to the charge, or by an exchange of land which was before the exchange subject to the charge.

(2) On land being so acquired, any person who, by the direction of the tenant for life, so conveys the land as to subject it to any legal estate or charge by way of legal mortgage, is not concerned to inquire whether or not it is proper that the land should be subjected to such legal estate or charge.

Part IV

Improvements

Improvements with Capital Money

Description of improvements authorised by Act

7–081 **83.** Improvements authorised by this Act are the making or execution on, or in connexion with, and for the benefit of settled land, of any of the works mentioned in the Third Schedule to this Act, or of any works for any of the purposes mentioned in that Schedule, and any operation incident to or necessary or proper in the execution of any of those works, or necessary or proper for carrying into effect any of those purposes, or for securing the full benefit of any of those works or purposes.

Mode of application of capital money

7–082 **84.**—(1) Capital money arising under this Act may be applied in or towards payment for any improvement authorised by this Act or by the settlement, without any scheme for the execution of the improvement being first submitted for approval to, or approved by, the trustees of the settlement or the court.

(2) Where the capital money to be expended is in the hands of the trustees of the settlement, they may apply that money in or towards payment for the whole or any part of any work or operation comprised in the improvement, on—

(i) a certificate to be furnished by a competent engineer or able practical surveyor employed independently of the tenant for life, certifying that the work or operation comprised in the improvement or some specific part thereof, has been properly executed, and what amount is properly payable in respect thereof, which certificate shall be conclusive in favour of the trustees as an authority and discharge for any payment made by them in pursuance thereof; or

(ii) an order of the court directing or authorising the trustees so to apply a specified portion of the capital money:

Provided that—

(a) In the case of improvements not authorised by Part I of the Third Schedule to this Act or by the settlement, the trustees may, if they think fit, and shall if so directed by the court, before they make any such application of capital money require that that money, or any part thereof, shall be repaid to them out of the income of the settled land by not more than fifty half-yearly instalments, the first of such instalments to be paid or to be deemed to have become payable at the expiration of six months from the date when the work or operation, in payment for which the money is to be applied, was completed;

(b) No capital money shall be applied by the trustees in payment for improvements not authorised by Parts I and II of the Third Schedule to this Act, or by the settlement, except subject to provision for the repayment thereof being made in manner mentioned in the preceding paragraph of this proviso.

(3) Where the capital money to be expended is in court, the court may, if it thinks fit, on a report or certificate of the [Secretary of State],[66] or of a competent engineer or able practical surveyor approved by the court, or on such other evidence as the court may think sufficient, make such order and give such directions as it thinks fit for the application of the money, or any part thereof, in or towards payment for the whole or any part of any work or operation comprised in the improvement.

(4) Where the court authorises capital money to be applied in payment for any improvement or intended improvement not authorised by Part I of the Third Schedule to this Act or by the settlement, the court, as a condition of making the order, may in any case require that the capital money or any part thereof, and shall as respects an improvement mentioned in Part III of that Schedule (unless the improvement is authorised by the settlement), require that the whole of the capital money shall be repaid to the trustees of the settlement out of the income of the settled land by a fixed number of periodical instalments to be paid at the times appointed by the court, and may require that any incumbrancer of the estate or interest of the tenant for life shall be served with notice of the proceedings.

(5) All money received by the trustees of the settlement in respect of any instalments under this section shall be held by them as capital money arising from freehold land under the settlement, unless the court otherwise directs.

Creation of rentcharges to discharge instalments

85.—(1) When the tenant for life is required by the trustees to repay by instalments the capital money expended, or any part thereof, the tenant for life is by this section authorised to create out of the settled land, or any part thereof, a yearly rentcharge in favour of the trustees of the settlement sufficient in amount to discharge the said half-yearly instalments. **7–083**

(2) Where an order is made requiring repayment by instalments, the settled land shall stand charged with the payment to the trustees of the settlement of a yearly rentcharge sufficient in amount to discharge the periodical instalments, and the rentcharge shall accrue from day to day, and be payable at the times appointed for payment of the periodical instalments, and shall have effect as if limited by the settlement prior to the estate of the tenant for life, and the trustees of the settlement shall have all statutory and other powers for recovery thereof.

(3) A rentcharge created by or under this section shall not be redeemed out of capital money, but may be overreached in like manner as if the same were limited by the settlement, and shall cease if and when the land affected by the improvement ceases to be settled or is sold or exchanged, but if part of the land so affected remains subject to the settlement the rentcharge shall remain in force in regard to the settled land.

Sundry Provisions as to Improvements

Concurrence in improvements

86. The tenant for life may join or concur with any other person interested in executing any improvement authorised by this Act, or in contributing to the cost thereof. **7–084**

[66] Words substituted by the Ministry of Agriculture, Fisheries and Food (Dissolution) Order 2002 (S.I. 2002 No. 794), art. 5(1), Sched. 1, para. 2.

Court may order payment for improvements executed

7–085 **87.** The court may, in any case where it appears proper, make an order directing or authorising capital money to be applied in or towards payment for any improvement authorised by the Settled Land Acts 1882 to 1890 or this Act, notwithstanding that a scheme was not, before the execution of the improvement, submitted for approval, as required by the Settled Land Act 1882 to the trustees of the settlement or to the court, and notwithstanding that no capital money is immediately available for the purpose.

Obligation on tenant for life and successors to maintain, insure, etc.

7–086 **88.**—(1) The tenant for life, and each of his successors in title having under the trust instrument a limited estate or interest only in the settled land, shall, during such period, if any, as the [Secretary of State][67] by certificate in any case prescribes, maintain and repair, at his own expense, every improvement executed under the foregoing provisions of this Act or the enactments replaced thereby, and where a building or work in its nature insurable against damage by fire is comprised in the improvement, shall at his own expense insure and keep insured the improvement in such amount, if any, as the [Secretary of State][68] by certificate in any case prescribes.

(2) The tenant for life, or any of his successors as aforesaid, shall not cut down or knowingly permit to be cut down, except in proper thinning, any trees planted as an improvement under the foregoing provisions of this Act, or under the enactments replaced by those provisions.

(3) The tenant for life, and each of his successors as aforesaid, shall from time to time, if required by the [Secretary of State][69] on or without the application of any person having under the trust instrument any estate or interest in the settled land in possession, remainder, or otherwise, report to the [Secretary of State][70] the state of every improvement executed under this Act, and the fact and particulars of fire insurance, if any.

(4) The [Secretary of State][71] may vary any certificate made by him under this section in such manner or to such extent as circumstances appear to him to require, but not so as to increase the liabilities of the tenant for life, or any of his successors as aforesaid.

(5) If the tenant for life, or any of his successors as aforesaid, fails in any respect to comply with the requisitions of this section, or does any act in contravention thereof, any person having, under the trust instrument, any estate or interest in the settled land in possession, remainder, or reversion, shall have a right of action, in respect of that default or act, against the tenant for life; and the estate of the tenant for life, after his death, shall be liable to make good to the persons entitled under the trust instrument any damages occasioned by that default or act.

(6) Where in connexion with any improvement an improvement rentcharge,

[67] Words substituted by the Ministry of Agriculture, Fisheries and Food (Dissolution) Order 2002 (S.I. 2002 No. 794), art. 5(1), Sched. 1, para. 3.
[68] Words substituted by the Ministry of Agriculture, Fisheries and Food (Dissolution) Order 2002 (S.I. 2002 No. 794), art. 5(1), Sched. 1, para. 3.
[69] Words substituted by the Ministry of Agriculture, Fisheries and Food (Dissolution) Order 2002 (S.I. 2002 No. 794), art. 5(1), Sched. 1, para. 3.
[70] Words substituted by the Ministry of Agriculture, Fisheries and Food (Dissolution) Order 2002 (S.I. 2002 No. 794), art. 5(1), Sched. 1, para. 3.
[71] Words substituted by the Ministry of Agriculture, Fisheries and Food (Dissolution) Order 2002 (S.I. 2002 No. 794), art. 5(1), Sched. 1, para. 3.

as hereinbefore defined, has been created, and that rentcharge has been redeemed out of capital money, this section shall apply to the improvement as if it had been an improvement executed under this Act.

Protection as regards waste in execution and repair of improvements

89. The tenant for life, and each of his successors in title having, under the trust instrument, a limited estate or interest only in the settled land, and all persons employed by or under contract with the tenant for life or any such successor, may from time to time enter on the settled land, and, without impeachment of waste by any remainderman or reversioner, thereon execute any improvement authorised by this Act, or inspect, maintain, and repair the same, and for the purposes thereof do, make, and use on the settled land, all acts, works, and conveniences proper for the execution, maintenance, repair, and use thereof, and get and work freestone, limestone, clay, sand, and other substances, and make tramways and other ways, and burn and make bricks, tiles, and other things, and cut down and use timber and other trees not planted or left standing for shelter or ornament. **7–087**

PART V

MISCELLANEOUS PROVISIONS

Power for tenant for life to enter into contracts

90.—(1) A tenant for life— **7–088**

(i) may contract to make any sale, exchange, mortgage, charge or other disposition authorised by this Act; and

(ii) may vary or rescind, with or without consideration, the contract in the like cases and manner in which, if he were absolute owner of the settled land, he might lawfully vary or rescind the same, but so that the contract as varied be in conformity with this Act; and

(iii) may contract to make any lease, and in making the lease may vary the terms, with or without consideration, but so that the lease be in conformity with this Act; and

(iv) may accept a surrender of a contract for a lease or a grant in fee simple at a rent, in like manner and on the like terms in and on which he might accept a surrender of a lease or a regrant, and thereupon may make a new or other contract for or relative to a lease or leases, or a grant or grants in fee simple at a rent, in like manner and on the like terms in and on which he might make a new or other lease or grant, or new or other leases or grants, where a lease or a grant in fee simple at a rent had been executed; and

(v) may enter into a contract for or relating to the execution of any improvement authorised by this Act, and may vary or rescind any such contract; and

(vi) may, in any other case, enter into a contract to do any act for carrying into effect any of the purposes of this Act, and may vary or rescind any such contract.

(2) Every contract, including a contract arising by reason of the exercise of an option, shall be binding on and shall enure for the benefit of the settled land, and shall be enforceable against and by every successor in title for the time being of the tenant for life, or statutory owner, and may be carried into effect by any such

successor, but so that it may be varied or rescinded by any such successor, in the like case and manner, if any, as if it had been made by himself.

(3) The court may, on the application of the tenant for life, or statutory owner, or of any such successor as aforesaid, or of any person interested in any contract, give directions respecting the enforcing, carrying into effect, varying, or rescinding thereof.

(4) A preliminary contract under this Act for or relating to a lease, and a contract conferring an option, shall not form part of the title or evidence of the title of any person to the lease, or to the benefit thereof, or to the land the subject of the option.

(5) All money, not being rent, received on the exercise by the tenant for life or statutory owner of the powers conferred by subsection (1) of this section, shall, unless the court on an application made within six months after the receipt of the money, or within such further time as the court may in special circumstances allow, otherwise directs, be capital money arising under this Act.

Provisions as to different estates settled upon the same limitations

7–089 **91.**—(1) Where estates are settled by different settlements upon the same limitations, whether by reference or otherwise, the following provisions shall have effect:—

(i) The estates or any two or more of them, as the case may require, may be treated as one aggregate estate, in which case the aggregate estate shall be the settled land for all the purposes of this Act;

(ii) Where the trustees for the purposes of this Act of the two or several settlements are the same persons they shall be the trustees of the settlement of the aggregate estate for all the purposes of this Act, and all or any part of the capital money arising from one of the estates may be applied by the direction of the tenant for life or statutory owner as if the same had arisen from any other of the estates;

(iii) Where the trustees for the purposes of this Act of the settlements or of any two or more of them are not the same persons—

(a) any notice required to be given by this Act to the trustees of the settlement and to the solicitor of such trustees shall be given to the trustees of every settlement which comprises any part of the land to which such notice relates and to the solicitor of such trustees;

(b) any capital money arising on any sale, exchange, lease, mortgage, charge, or other disposition of land comprised in more than one settlement, shall be apportioned between the trustees of the different settlements in such manner as the tenant for life or statutory owner may think fit;

(c) all or any part of the capital money arising from the land comprised in one of the settlements may be paid by the trustees of that settlement, by such direction as aforesaid, to the trustees of any of the other settlements, to be applied by such last-mentioned trustees as if the same had arisen from land comprised in that other settlement:

(iv) For the purposes of this subsection, money liable to be laid out in the purchase of land to be settled upon the same limitations as other land may be applied and dealt with in like manner in all respects as if land had been purchased and settled, and the money were capital money arising therefrom.

(2) Estates shall be deemed to be settled upon the same limitations, notwithstanding that any of them may be subject to incumbrances, charges, or powers of charging to which the other or others of them may not be subject:

Provided that, in any such case as last aforesaid, the powers of this section relating to the payment or application of capital money shall not, unless the settlement under which the capital money is held otherwise provides, be exercisable without an order of the court.

(3) This section has effect without prejudice to any appointment made by the court before the commencement of this Act of trustees of the settlement of an aggregate estate, and to the power of the court in any case after such commencement to make any such appointment, and where any such appointment has been made before such commencement, or is made thereafter, this section has effect as if the trustees so appointed and their successors in office were the trustees for the purposes of this Act of each of the settlements constituting the settlement of the aggregate estate, and there were no other trustees thereof for the purposes of this Act.

(4) In this section "estate" means the land, capital money, and securities representing capital money for the time being subject to a particular settlement.

Proceedings for protection or recovery of land settled or claimed as settled

92. The court may, if it thinks fit, approve of any action, defence, petition to Parliament, parliamentary opposition, or other proceeding taken or proposed to be taken for the protection of settled land, or of any action or proceeding taken or proposed to be taken for the recovery of land being or alleged to be subject to a settlement, and may direct that any costs, charges, or expenses incurred or to be incurred in relation thereto, or any part thereof, be paid out of property subject to the settlement. **7–090**

Reference of questions to court

93. If a question arises or a doubt is entertained— **7–091**

(a) respecting the exercise or intended exercise of any of the powers conferred by this Act, or any enactment replaced by this Act, or the settlement, or any matter relating thereto; or

(b) as to the person in whose favour a vesting deed or assent ought to be executed, or as to the contents thereof; or

(c) otherwise in relation to property subject to a settlement;

the tenant for life or statutory owner, or the trustees of the settlement, or any other person interested under the settlement, may apply to the court for its decision or directions thereon, or for the sanction of the court to any conditional contract, and the court may make such order or give such directions respecting the matter as the court thinks fit.

Part VI

General Provisions as to Trustees

Number of trustees to act

94.—(1) Notwithstanding anything in this Act, capital money arising under this Act shall not be paid to fewer than two persons as trustees of a settlement, unless the trustee is a trust corporation. **7–092**

(2) Subject as aforesaid the provisions of this Act referring to the trustees of a settlement apply to the surviving or continuing trustees or trustee of the settlement for the time being.

Trustees' receipts

7–093 **95.** The receipt or direction in writing of or by the trustees of the settlement, or where a sole trustee is a trust corporation, of or by that trustee, or of or by the personal representatives of the last surviving or continuing trustee, for or relating to any money or securities, paid or transferred to or by the direction of the trustees, trustee, or representatives, as the case may be, effectually discharges the payer or transferor therefrom, and from being bound to see to the application or being answerable for any loss or misapplication thereof, and, in case of a mortgagee or other person advancing money, from being concerned to see that any money advanced by him is wanted for any purpose of this Act, or that no more than is wanted is raised.

96. [*Repealed by the Trustee Act 2000, s.40(1), (3), Sched. 2, Pt. II, para. 12, Sched. 4, Pt. II.*]

Protection of trustees generally

7–094 **97.** The trustees of a settlement, or any of them—

(a) are not liable for giving any consent, or for not making, bringing, taking, or doing any such application, action, proceeding, or thing, as they might make, bring, take, or do; and

(b) in case of a purchase of land with capital money arising under this Act, or of an exchange, lease, or other disposition, are not liable for adopting any contract made by the tenant for life or statutory owner, or bound to inquire as to the propriety of the purchase, exchange, lease, or other disposition, or answerable as regards any price, consideration, or fine; and

(c) are not liable to see to or answerable for the investigation of the title, or answerable for a conveyance of land, if the conveyance purports to convey the land in the proper mode; and

(d) are not liable in respect of purchase-money paid by them by the direction of the tenant for life or statutory owner to any person joining in the conveyance as a conveying party, or as giving a receipt for the purchase-money, or in any other character, or in respect of any other money paid by them by the direction of the tenant for life or statutory owner on the purchase, exchange, lease, or other disposition.

Protection of trustees in particular cases

7–095 **98.**—(1), (2) [*Repealed by the Trustee Act 2000, s.40(1), (3), Sched. 2, Pt. II, para. 13, Sched. 4, Pt. II.*]

(3) The trustees of the settlement shall not be liable in any way on account of any vesting instrument or other documents of title relating to the settled land, other than securities for capital money, being placed in the possession of the tenant for life or statutory owner:

Provided that where, if the settlement were not disclosed, it would appear that the tenant for life had a general power of appointment over, or was absolutely and beneficially entitled to the settled land, the trustees of the settlement shall, before they deliver the documents to him, require that notice of the last or only principal vesting instrument be written on one of the documents under which the tenant for life acquired his title, and may, if the documents are not in their possession, require such notice to be written as aforesaid, but, in the latter case, they shall not be liable in any way for not requiring the notice to be written.

(4) This section applies to dealings and matters effected before as well as after the commencement of this Act.

Indemnities to personal representatives and others

99. Personal representatives, trustees, or other persons who have in good faith, pursuant to this Act, executed a vesting deed, assent, or other conveyance of the settled land, or a deed of discharge of trustees, shall be absolutely discharged from all liability in respect of the equitable interests and powers taking effect under the settlement, and shall be entitled to be kept indemnified at the cost of the trust estate from all liabilities affecting the settled land, but the person to whom the settled land is conveyed (not being a purchaser taking free therefrom) shall hold the settled land upon the trusts, if any, affecting the same. **7–096**

100. [*Repealed by the Trustee Act 2000, s.40(1), (3), Sched. 2, Pt. II, para. 12, Sched. 4, Pt. II.*]

Notice to trustees

101.—(1) Save as otherwise expressly provided by this Act, a tenant for life or statutory owner, when intending to make a sale, exchange, lease, mortgage, or charge or to grant an option— **7–097**

(a) shall give notice of his intention in that behalf to each of the trustees of the settlement, by posting registered letters, containing the notice, addressed to the trustees severally, each at his usual or last known place of abode in the United Kingdom; and

(b) shall give a like notice to the solicitor for the trustees, if any such solicitor is known to the tenant for life or statutory owner, by posting a registered letter, containing the notice, addressed to the solicitor at his place of business in the United Kingdom;

every letter under this section being posted not less than one month before the making or granting by the tenant for life or statutory owner of the sale, exchange, lease, mortgage, charge, or option, or of a contract for the same:

Provided that a notice under this section shall not be valid unless at the date thereof the trustee is a trust corporation, or the number of trustees is not less than two.

(2) The notice required by this section of intention to make a sale, exchange, or lease, or to grant an option, may be notice of a general intention in that behalf.

(3) The tenant for life or statutory owner is, upon request by a trustee of the settlement, to furnish to him such particulars and information as may reasonably be required by him from time to time with reference to sales, exchanges, or leases effected, or in progress, or immediately intended.

(4) Any trustee, by writing under his hand, may waive notice either in any particular case, or generally, and may accept less than one month's notice.

(5) A person dealing in good faith with the tenant for life is not concerned to inquire respecting the giving of any such notice as is required by this section.

Management of land during minority or pending contingency

7–098 **102.**—(1) If and as long as any person who is entitled to a beneficial interest in possession affecting land is an infant, the trustees appointed for this purpose by the settlement, or if there are none so appointed, then the trustees of the settlement, unless the settlement or the order of the court whereby they or their predecessors in office were appointed to be such trustees expressly provides to the contrary, or if there are none, then any persons appointed as trustees for this purpose by the court on the application of a guardian or next friend of the infant, may enter into and continue in possession of the land on behalf of the infant, and in every such case the subsequent provisions of this section shall apply.

(2) The trustees shall manage or superintend the management of the land, with full power—

(a) to fell timber or cut underwood from time to time in the usual course for sale, or for repairs or otherwise; and
(b) to erect, pull down, rebuild, and repair houses, and other buildings and erections; and
(c) to continue the working of mines, minerals, and quarries which have usually been worked; and
(d) to drain or otherwise improve the land or any part thereof; and
[(e) to insure against risks of loss or damage due to any event under section 19 of the Trustee Act 1925;][72] and
(f) to make allowances to and arrangements with tenants and others; and
(g) to determine tenancies, and to accept surrenders of leases and tenancies; and
(h) generally to deal with the land in a proper and due course of management;

but so that, where the infant is impeachable for waste, the trustees shall not commit waste, and shall cut timber on the same terms only, and subject to the same restrictions, on and subject to which the infant could, if of full age, cut the same.

(3) The trustees may from time to time, out of the income of the land, including the produce of the sale of timber and underwood, pay the expenses incurred in the management, or in the exercise of any power conferred by this section, or otherwise in relation to the land, and all outgoings not payable by any tenant or other person, and shall keep down any annual sum, and the interest of any principal sum, charged on the land.

(4) This section has effect subject to an express appointment by the settlement, or the court, of trustees for the purposes of this section or of any enactment replaced by this section.

(5) Where any person is contingently entitled to land, this section shall, subject to any prior interests or charges affecting that land, apply until his interest vests, or, if his interest vests during his minority, until he attains the age of [eighteen years][73].

This subsection applies only where a person becomes contingently entitled under an instrument coming into operation after the commencement of this Act.

[72] Para. (e) substituted by the Trustee Act 2000, s.40(1), Sched. 2, Pt. II, para. 15.
[73] Words substituted by the Family Law Reform Act 1969, s.1(3), Sched. 1, Pt. I.

(6) This section applies only if and as far as a contrary intention is not expressed in the instrument, if any, under which the interest of the infant or person contingently entitled as aforesaid arises, and has effect subject to the terms of that instrument and to the provisions therein contained.

PART VII

RESTRICTIONS, SAVINGS, AND PROTECTION OF PURCHASERS

Legal estate in settled land not to vest in trustee in bankruptcy of estate owner

103. [For the purposes of determining, where the estate owner of any settled land is bankrupt, whether the legal estate in the settled land is comprised in, or is capable of being claimed for, the bankrupt's estate, the legal estate in the settled land shall be deemed not to vest in the][74] estate owner unless and until the estate owner becomes absolutely and beneficially entitled to the settled land free from all limitations, powers, and charges taking effect under the settlement. **7–099**

Powers not assignable, and contract not to exercise powers void

104.—(1) The powers under this Act of a tenant for life are not capable of assignment or release, and do not pass to a person as being, by operation of law or otherwise, an assignee of a tenant for life, and remain exercisable by the tenant for life after and notwithstanding any assignment, by operation of law or otherwise, of his estate or interest under the settlement. **7–100**

This subsection applies notwithstanding that the estate or interest of the tenant for life under the settlement was not in possession when the assignment was made or took effect by operation of law.

(2) A contract by a tenant for life not to exercise his powers under this Act or any of them shall be void.

(3) Where an assignment for value of the estate or interest of the tenant for life was made before the commencement of this Act, this section shall operate without prejudice to the rights of the assignee, and in that case the assignee's rights shall not be affected without his consent, except that—

(a) unless the assignee is actually in possession of the settled land or the part thereof affected, his consent shall not be requisite for the making of leases thereof by the tenant for life or statutory owner, provided the leases are made at the best rent that can reasonably be obtained, without fine, and in other respects are in conformity with this Act; and

(b) the consent of the assignee shall not be required to an investment of capital money for the time being affected by the assignment in securities [. . .][75].

(4) Where such an assignment for value is made or comes into operation after the commencement of this Act, the consent of the assignee shall not be requisite for the exercise by the tenant for life of any of the powers conferred by this Act:

Provided that—

(a) the assignee shall be entitled to the same or the like estate or interest in or charge on the land, money, or securities for the time being representing the land, money, or securities comprised in the assignment,

[74] Words substituted by the Insolvency Act 1985, s.235(1), Sched. 8, para. 3.
[75] Words repealed by the Trustee Act 2000, s.40(1), (3), Sched. 2, Pt. II, para. 16, Sched. 4, Pt. II.

as he had by virtue of the assignment in the last-mentioned land, money, or securities; and

(b) if the assignment so provides, or if it takes effect by operation of the law of bankruptcy, and after notice thereof to the trustees of the settlement, [the consent of the assignee shall be required to an investment of capital money for the time being affected by the assignment in investments other than securities, and to any application of such capital money;][76] and

(c) notice of the intended transaction shall, unless the assignment otherwise provides, be given to the assignee, but a purchaser shall not be concerned to see or inquire whether such notice has been given.

(5) Where such an assignment for value was made before the commencement of this Act, then on the exercise by the tenant for life after such commencement of any of the powers conferred by this Act—

(a) a purchaser shall not be concerned to see or inquire whether the consent of the assignee has been obtained; and

(b) the provisions of paragraph (a) of the last subsection shall apply for the benefit of the assignee.

(6) A trustee or personal representative who is an assignee for value shall have power to consent to the exercise by the tenant for life of his powers under this Act, or to any such investment or application of capital money as aforesaid, and to bind by such consent all persons interested in the trust estate, or the estate of the testator or intestate.

(7) If by the original assignment, or by any subsequent disposition, the estate or interest assigned or created by the original assignment, or any part thereof, or any derivative interest is settled on persons in succession, whether subject to any prior charge or not, and there is no trustee or personal representative in whom the entirety of the estate or interest so settled is vested, then the person for the time being entitled in possession under the limitations of that settlement, whether as trustee or beneficiary, or who would, if of full age, be so entitled, and notwithstanding any charge or incumbrance subsisting or to arise under such settlement, shall have power to consent to the exercise by the tenant for life of his powers under this Act, or to any such investment or application of capital money as aforesaid, and to bind by such consent all persons interested or to become interested under such settlement.

(8) Where an assignee for value, or any person who has power to consent as aforesaid under this section, is an infant, the consent may be given on his behalf by his parents or parent or testamentary or other guardian in the order named.

(9) The court shall have power to authorise any person interested under any assignment to consent to the exercise by the tenant for life of his powers under this Act, or to any such investment or application of capital money as aforesaid, on behalf of himself and all other persons interested, or who may become interested under such assignment.

(10) An assignment by operation of the law of bankruptcy, where the assignment comes into operation after the commencement of this Act, shall be deemed to be an assignment for value for the purposes of this section.

(11) An instrument whereby a tenant for life, in consideration of marriage or as part or by way of any family arrangement, not being a security for payment of money advanced, makes an assignment of or creates a charge upon his estate or interest under the settlement is to be deemed one of the instruments creating the settlement, and not an assignment for value for the purposes of this section:

Provided that this subsection shall not have effect with respect to any

[76] Words substituted by the Trustee Act 2000, s.40(1), Sched. 2, Pt. II, para. 16.

disposition made before the eighteenth day of August, eighteen hundred and ninety, if inconsistent with the nature or terms of the disposition.

(12) This section extends to assignments made or coming into operation before or after the commencement of this Act, and in this section "assignment" includes assignment by way of mortgage, and any partial or qualified assignment, and any charge or incumbrance, "assignee" has a corresponding meaning, and "assignee for value" includes persons deriving title under the original assignee.

Effect of surrender of life estate to the next remainderman

105.—(1) Where the estate or interest of a tenant for life under the settlement has been or is absolutely assured with intent to extinguish the same, either before or after the commencement of this Act, to the person next entitled in remainder or reversion under the settlement, then, [. . .][77] the statutory powers of the tenant for life under this Act shall, in reference to the property affected by the assurance, and notwithstanding the provisions of the last preceding section, cease to be exercisable by him, and the statutory powers shall thenceforth become exercisable as if he were dead, but without prejudice to any incumbrance affecting the estate or interest assured, and to the rights to which any incumbrancer would have been entitled if those powers had remained exercisable by the tenant for life. **7–101**

This subsection applies whether or not any term of years or charge intervenes, or the estate of the remainderman or reversioner is liable to be defeated, and whether or not the estate or interest of the tenant for life under the settlement was in possession at the date of the assurance.

This subsection does not prejudice anything done by the tenant for life before the commencement of this Act, in exercise of any power operating under the Settled Land Acts 1882 to 1890, or, unless the assurance provides to the contrary, operate to accelerate any such intervening term of years or charge as aforesaid.

(2) In this section "assurance" means any surrender, conveyance, assignment or appointment under a power (whether vested in any person solely, or jointly in two or more persons) which operates in equity to extinguish the estate or interest of the tenant for life, and "assured" has a corresponding meaning.

Prohibition or limitation against exercise of powers void, and provision against forfeiture

106.—(1) If in a settlement, will, assurance, or other instrument executed or made before or after, or partly before and partly after, the commencement of this Act a provision is inserted— **7–102**

(a) purporting or attempting, by way of direction, declaration, or otherwise, to forbid a tenant for life or statutory owner to exercise any power under this Act, or his right to require the settled land to be vested in him; or

(b) attempting, or tending, or intended, by a limitation, gift, or disposition over of settled land, or by a limitation, gift, or disposition of other real or any personal property, or by the imposition of any condition, or by forfeiture, or in any other manner whatever, to prohibit or prevent him

[77] Words repealed by the Law of Property (Amendment) Act 1926, s.7, Sched.

Provided that, as regards the first vesting instrument executed for the purpose of giving effect to—

(a) a settlement subsisting at the commencement of this Act; or
(b) an instrument which by virtue of this Act is deemed to be a settlement; or
(c) a settlement which by virtue of this Act is deemed to have been made by any person after the commencement of this Act; or
(d) an instrument inter vivos intended to create a settlement of a legal estate in land which is executed after the commencement of this Act and does not comply with the requirements of this Act with respect to the method of effecting such a settlement;

a purchaser shall be concerned to see—

(i) that the land disposed of to him is comprised in such settlement or instrument;
(ii) that the person in whom the settled land is by such vesting instrument vested, or declared to be vested, is the person in whom it ought to be vested as tenant for life or statutory owner;
(iii) that the persons thereby stated to be the trustees of the settlement are the properly constituted trustees of the settlement.

(3) A purchaser of a legal estate in settled land from a personal representative shall be entitled to act on the following assumptions:—

(i) If the capital money, if any, payable in respect of the transaction is paid to the personal representative, that such representative is acting under his statutory or other powers and requires the money for purposes of administration;
(ii) If such capital money is, by the direction of the personal representative, paid to persons who are stated to be the trustees of a settlement, that such persons are the duly constituted trustees of the settlement for the purposes of this Act, and that the personal representative is acting under his statutory powers during a minority;
(iii) In any other case, that the personal representative is acting under his statutory or other powers.

(4) Where no capital money arises under a transaction, a disposition by a tenant for life or statutory owner shall, in favour of a purchaser of a legal estate, have effect under this Act notwithstanding that at the date of the transaction there are no trustees of the settlement.

(5) If a conveyance of or an assent relating to land formerly subject to a vesting instrument does not state who are the trustees of the settlement for the purposes of this Act, a purchaser of a legal estate shall be bound and entitled to act on the assumption that the person in whom the land was thereby vested was entitled to the land free from all limitations, powers, and charges taking effect under that settlement, absolutely and beneficially, or, if so expressed in the conveyance or assent, as personal representative, or [trustee of land][79] or otherwise, and that every statement of fact in such conveyance or assent is correct.

[79] Words substituted by the Trusts of Land and Appointment of Trustees Act 1996, s.25(1), Sched. 3, para. 2(1), (12).

Purchaser of beneficial interest of tenant for life to have remedies of a legal owner

111. Where— **7–107**

(a) at the commencement of this Act the legal beneficial interest of a tenant for life under a settlement is vested in a purchaser; or

(b) after the commencement of this Act a tenant for life conveys or deals with his beneficial interest in possession in favour of a purchaser, and the interest so conveyed or created would, but for the restrictions imposed by statute on the creation of legal estates, have been a legal interest;

the purchaser shall (without prejudice to the powers conferred by this Act on the tenant for life) have and may exercise all the same rights and remedies as he would have had or have been entitled to exercise if the interest had remained or been a legal interest and the reversion, if any, on any leases or tenancies derived out of the settled land had been vested in him:

Provided that, where the conveyance or dealing is effected after the commencement of this Act, the purchaser shall not be entitled to the possession of the documents of title relating to the settled land, but shall have the same rights with respect thereto as if the tenant for life had given to him a statutory acknowledgment of his right to production and delivery of copies thereof, and a statutory undertaking for the safe custody thereof.

The tenant for life shall not deliver any such documents to a purchaser of his beneficial interest, who is not also a purchaser of the whole of the settled land to which such documents relate.

Exercise of powers; limitation of provisions, etc.

112.—(1) Where a power of sale, exchange, leasing, mortgaging, charging, or other power is exercised by a tenant for life, or statutory owner or by the trustees of a settlement, he and they may respectively execute, make, and do all deeds, instruments, and things necessary or proper in that behalf. **7–108**

(2) Where any provision in this Act refers to sale, purchase, exchange, mortgaging, charging, leasing, or other disposition or dealing, or to any power, consent, payment, receipt, deed, assurance, contract, expenses, act, or transaction, it shall (unless the contrary appears) be construed as extending only to sales, purchases, exchanges, mortgages, charges, leases, dispositions, dealings, powers, consents, payments, receipts, deeds, assurances, contracts, expenses, acts, and transactions under this Act.

. . . . . .

PART IX

SUPPLEMENTARY PROVISIONS

Definitions

117.—(1) In this Act, unless the context otherwise requires, the following expressions have the meanings hereby assigned to them respectively, that is to say:— **7–109**

(i) "Building purposes" include the erecting and the improving of, and the adding to, and the repairing of buildings; and a "building lease" is a lease for any building purposes or purposes connected therewith;

(ii) "Capital money arising under this Act" means capital money arising under the powers and provisions of this Act or the Acts replaced by this Act, and receivable for the trusts and purposes of the settlement and includes securities representing capital money;

(iii) "Death duty" means estate duty, [...][80] and every other duty leviable or payable on death;

(iv) "Determinable fee" means a fee determinable whether by limitation or condition;

(v) "Disposition" and "conveyance" include a mortgage, charge by way of legal mortgage, lease, assent, vesting declaration, vesting instrument, disclaimer, release and every other assurance of property or of an interest therein by any instrument, except a will, and "dispose of" and "convey" have corresponding meanings;

(vi) "Dower" includes "freebench";

(vii) "Hereditaments" mean real property which on an intestacy might before the commencement of this Act have devolved on an heir;

(viii) "Instrument" does not include a statute unless the statute creates a settlement;

(ix) "Land" includes land of any tenure, and mines and minerals whether or not held apart from the surface, buildings or parts of buildings (whether the division is horizontal, vertical or made in any other way) and other corporeal hereditaments; also a manor, an advowson, and a rent and other incorporeal hereditaments, and an easement, right, privilege, or benefit in, over, or derived from land, and any estate or interest in land [, but does not (except in the phrase "trust of land") include][81] an undivided share in land;

(x) "Lease" includes an agreement for a lease, and "forestry lease" means a lease to the Forestry Commissioners[82] for any purpose for which they are authorised to acquire land by the Forestry Act 1919;

(xi) "Legal mortgage" means a mortgage by demise or subdemise or a charge by way of legal mortgage, and "legal mortgagee" has a corresponding meaning; "legal estate" means an estate interest or charge in or over land (subsisting or created at law) which is by statute authorised to subsist or to be created at law; and "equitable interests" mean all other interests and charges in or over land or in the proceeds of sale thereof; an equitable interest "capable of subsisting at law" means such an equitable interest as could validly subsist at law, if clothed with the legal estate; and "estate owner" means the owner of a legal estate;

(xii) "Limitation" includes a trust, and "trust" includes an implied or constructive trust;

[...][83]

(xiv) "Manor" includes lordship, and reputed manor or lordship; and "manorial incident" has the same meaning as in the Law of Property Act 1922;

[80] Words repealed by the Finance Act 1949, s.52, Sched. 11, Pt. IV, and the Finance Act 1975, s.59(5), Sched. 13.

[81] Words substituted by the Trusts of Land and Appointment of Trustees Act 1996, s.25(1), Sched. 3, para. 2(1), (13)(a).

[82] The reference to the Forestry Commissioners is to be construed as a reference to the appropriate Minister: Forestry Act 1967, s.50(1), Sched. 6, para. 5.

[83] Definition of "lunatic" repealed by the Mental Health Act 1959, s.149(2), Sched. 8, Pt. I.

(xv) "Mines and minerals" mean mines and minerals whether already opened or in work or not, and include all minerals and substances in, on, or under the land, obtainable by underground or by surface working; and "mining purposes" include the sinking and searching for, winning, working, getting, making merchantable, smelting or otherwise converting or working for the purposes of any manufacture, carrying away, and disposing of mines and minerals, in or under the settled land, or any other land, and the erection of buildings, and the execution of engineering and other works suitable for those purposes; and a "mining lease" is a lease for any mining purposes or purposes connected therewith, and includes a grant or licence for any mining purposes;

[. . .][84]

(xvii) "Notice" includes constructive notice;

(xviii) "Personal representative" means the executor, original or by representation, or administrator, for the time being of a deceased person, and where there are special personal representatives for the purposes of settled land means those personal representatives;

(xix) "Possession" includes receipt of rents and profits, or the right to receive the same, if any; and "income" includes rents and profits;

(xx) "Property" includes any thing in action, and any interest in real or personal property;

(xxi) "Purchaser" means a purchaser in good faith for value, and includes a lessee, mortgagee or other person who in good faith acquires an interest in settled land for value; and in reference to a legal estate includes a chargee by way of legal mortgage;

(xxii) "Rent" includes yearly or other rent, and toll, duty, royalty, or other reservation, by the acre, or the ton, or otherwise; and, in relation to rent, "payment" includes delivery; and "fine" includes premium or fore-gift, and any payment, consideration, or benefit in the nature of a fine, premium, or fore-gift;

(xxiii) "Securities" include stocks, funds, and shares;

(xxiv) "Settled land" includes land which is deemed to be settled land; "settlement" includes an instrument or instruments which under this Act or the Acts which it replaces is or are deemed to be or which together constitute a settlement, and a settlement which is deemed to have been made by any person or to be subsisting for the purposes of this Act; "a settlement subsisting at the commencement of his Act" includes a settlement created by virtue of this Act immediately on the commencement thereof; and "trustees of the settlement" mean the trustees thereof for the purposes of this Act howsoever appointed or constituted;

(xxv) "Small dwellings" mean dwelling-houses of a rateable value not exceeding one hundred pounds per annum;

(xxvi) "Statutory owner" means the trustees of the settlement or other persons who, during a minority, or at any other time when there is no tenant for life, have the powers of a tenant for life under this Act, but does not include the trustees of the settlement, where by virtue of an order of the court or otherwise the trustees have power to convey the settled land in the name of the tenant for life;

[84] Definition of "Minister" repealed by the Ministry of Agriculture, Fisheries and Food (Dissolution) Order 2002 (S.I. 2002 No. 794), art. 5(2), Sched. 2.

(xxvii) "Steward" includes deputy steward, or other proper officer, of a manor;

(xxviii) "Tenant for life" includes a person (not being a statutory owner) who has the powers of a tenant for life under this Act, and also (where the context requires) one of two or more persons who together constitute the tenant for life, or have the powers of a tenant for life; and "tenant in tail" includes a person entitled to an entailed interest in any property; and "entailed interest" has the same meaning as in the Law of Property Act 1925;

(xxix) A "term of years absolute" means a term of years, taking effect either in possession or in reversion, with or without impeachment for waste, whether at a rent or not and whether subject or not to another legal estate, and whether certain or liable to determination by notice, re-entry, operation of law, or by a provision for cesser on redemption, or in any other event (other than the dropping of a life, or the determination of a determinable life interest), but does not include any term of years determinable with life or lives or with the cesser of a determinable life interest, nor, if created after the commencement of this Act, a term of years which is not expressed to take effect in possession within twenty-one years after the creation thereof where required by statute to take effect within that period; and in this definition the expression "term of years" includes a term for less than a year, or for a year or years and a fraction of a year or from year to year;

(xxx) "Trust corporation"[85] means the Public Trustee or a corporation either appointed by the court in any particular case to be a trustee or entitled by rules made under subsection (3) of section four of the Public Trustee Act 1906 to act as custodian trustee, and "trust for sale" [has the same meaning][86] as in the Law of Property Act 1925;

(xxxi) In relation to settled land "vesting deed" or "vesting order" means the instrument whereby settled land is conveyed to or vested or declared to be vested in a tenant for life or statutory owner; "vesting assent" means the instrument whereby a personal representative, after the death of a tenant for life or statutory owner, or the survivor of two or more tenants for life or statutory owners, vests settled land in a person entitled as tenant for life or statutory owner; "vesting instrument" means a vesting deed, a vesting assent or, where the land affected remains settled land, a vesting order; "principal vesting instrument" includes any vesting instrument other than a subsidiary vesting deed; and "trust instrument" means the instrument whereby the trusts of the settled land are declared, and includes any two or more such instruments and a settlement or instrument which is deemed to be a trust instrument;

(xxxii) "United Kingdom" means Great Britain and Northern Ireland;

(xxxiii) "Will" includes codicil.

[(1A) Any references in this Act to money, securities or proceeds of sale being paid or transferred into court shall be construed as referring to the money,

---

85 Definition of "trust corporation" extended by the Law of Property (Amendment) Act 1926, s.3, *post*, para. 11–002, and the Charities Act 1993, s.35, *post*, para. 56–034.

86 Words substituted by the Trusts of Land and Appointment of Trustees Act 1996, s.25(1), Sched. 3, para. 2(1), (13)(b).

securities or proceeds being paid or transferred into the Supreme Court or any other court that has jurisdiction, and any reference in this Act to the court, in a context referring to the investment or application of money, securities or proceeds of sale paid or transferred into court, shall be construed, in the case of money, securities or proceeds paid or transferred into the Supreme Court, as referring to the High Court, and, in the case of money, securities or proceeds paid or transferred into another court, as referring to that other court.][87]

(2) Where an equitable interest in or power over property arises by statute or operation of law, references to the "creation" of an interest or power include any interest or power so arising.

(3) References to registration under the Land Charges Act 1925[88] apply to any registration made under any statute which is by the Land Charges Act 1925[89] to have effect as if the registration had been made under that Act.

. . . . . .

Trustee Act 1925[1]

(15 Geo. 5, c. 19)

Arrangement of Sections

Part II

General Powers of Trustees and Personal Representatives

General Powers

Indemnities

Maintenance, Advancement and Protective Trusts

---

[87] subs. (1A) inserted by the Administration of Justice Act 1965, s.17(1), Sched. 1.
[88] Now the Land Charges Act 1972, *post*, para. 31–001.
[89] Now the Land Charges Act 1972, *post*, para. 31–001.
[1] Applied to vesting orders under the Settled Land Act 1925, s.113(9), the Law of Property Act 1925, s.9(3), *post*, para. 9–009, the Administration of Estates Act 1925, s.43(2), *post*, para. 10–034.

PART III

APPOINTMENT AND DISCHARGE OF TRUSTEES

PART IV

POWERS OF THE COURT

Appointment of New Trustees

Vesting Orders

Jurisdiction to make other Orders

Payment into Court

PART V

GENERAL PROVISIONS

PART I

INVESTMENTS[2]

1. [*Repealed by the Trustee Investments Act* 1961, *s.16(2), Sched. 5.*]

2–11. [*Repealed by the Trustee Act 2000, s.40(1), (3), Sched. 2, Pt. II, para. 18, Sched. 4, Pt. II.*]

PART II

GENERAL POWERS OF TRUSTEES AND PERSONAL REPRESENTATIVES

General Powers

Power of trustees for sale to sell by auction, etc.

12.—(1) Where [a trustee has a duty or power to sell property][3], he may sell or concur with any other person in selling all or any part of the property, either subject to prior charges or not, and either together or in lots, by public auction or by private contract, subject to any such conditions respecting title or evidence of title or other matter as the trustee thinks fit, with proper to vary any contract for sale, and to buy in at any auction, or to rescind any contract for sale and to re-sell, without being answerable for any loss. **8–001**

(2) A [duty][4] or power to sell or dispose of land includes a [duty][5] or power to sell or dispose of part thereof, whether the division is horizontal, vertical, or made in any other way.

(3) This section does not enable an express power to sell settled land to be exercised where the power is not vested in the tenant for life or statutory owner.

Power to sell subject to depreciatory conditions

13.—(1) No sale made by a trustee shall be impeached by any beneficiary upon the ground that any of the conditions subject to which the sale was made may have been unnecessarily depreciatory, unless it also appears that the consideration for the sale was thereby rendered inadequate. **8–002**

(2) No sale made by a trustee shall, after the execution of the conveyance, be impeached as against the purchaser upon the ground that any of the conditions subject to which the sale was made may have been unnecessarily depreciatory, unless it appears that the purchaser was acting in collusion with the trustee at the time when the contract for sale was made.

(3) No purchaser, upon any sale made by a trustee, shall be at liberty to make any objection against the title upon any of the grounds aforesaid.

---

[2] See the Trustee Act 2000, Pt. II, *post*, paras 64–003 *et seq.*

[3] Words substituted by the Trusts of Land and Appointment of Trustees Act 1996, s.25(1), Sched. 3, para. 3(1), (2).

[4] Words substituted by the Trusts of Land and Appointment of Trustees Act 1996, s.25(1), Sched. 3, para. 3(1), (2).

[5] Words substituted by the Trusts of Land and Appointment of Trustees Act 1996, s.25(1), Sched. 3, para. 3(1), (2).

(4) This section applies to sales made before or after the commencement of this Act.

Power of trustees to give receipts

8–003 **14.**—(1) The receipt in writing of a trustee for any money, securities, [investments][6] or other personal property or effects payable, transferable, or deliverable to him under any trust or power shall be a sufficient discharge to the person paying, transferring, or delivering the same and shall effectively exonerate him from seeing to the application or being answerable for any loss or misapplication thereof.

(2) This section does not, except where the trustee is a trust corporation, enable a sole trustee to give a valid receipt for—

[(a) proceeds of sale or other capital money arising under a trust of land;][7]

(b) capital money arising under the Settled Land Act 1925.

(3) This section applies notwithstanding anything to the contrary in the instrument, if any, creating the trust.

Power to compound liabilities

8–004 **15.** A personal representative, or two or more trustees acting together, or, subject to the restrictions imposed in regard to receipts by a sole trustee not being a trust corporation, a sole acting trustee where by the instrument, if any, creating the trust, or by statute, a sole trustee is authorised to execute the trusts and powers reposed in him, may, if and as he or they think fit—

(a) accept any property, real or personal, before the time at which it is made transferable or payable; or

(b) sever and apportion any blended trust funds or property; or

(c) pay or allow any debt or claim on any evidence that he or they think sufficient; or

(d) accept any composition or any security, real or personal, for any debt or for any property, real or personal, claimed; or

(e) allow any time of payment of any debt; or

(f) compromise, compound, abandon, submit to arbitration, or otherwise settle any debt, account, claim, or thing whatever relating to the testator's or intestate's estate or to the trust;

and for any of those purposes may enter into, give, execute, and do such agreements, instruments of composition or arrangement, releases, and other things as to him or them seem expedient, without being responsible for any loss occasioned by any act or thing so done by him or them [if he has or they have discharged the duty of care set out in section 1(1) of the Trustee Act 2000][8].

Power to raise money by sale, mortgage, etc.

8–005 **16.**—(1) Where trustees are authorised by the instrument, if any, creating the trust or by law to pay or apply capital money subject to the trust for any purpose or in any manner, they shall have and shall be deemed always to have had power

[6] Word inserted by the Trustee Act 2000, s.40(1), Sched. 2, Pt. II, para. 19.

[7] Para. (a) substituted by the Trusts of Land and Appointment of Trustees Act 1996, s.25(1), Sched. 3, para. 3(1), (3).

[8] Words substituted by the Trustee Act 2000, s.40(1), Sched. 2, Pt. II, para. 20.

to raise the money required by sale, conversion, calling in, or mortgage of all or any part of the trust property for the time being in possession.

(2) This section applies notwithstanding anything to the contrary contained in the instrument, if any, creating the trust, but does not apply to trustees of property held for charitable purposes, or to trustees of a settlement for the purposes of the Settled Land Act 1925, not being also the statutory owners.

Protection to purchasers and mortgagees dealing with trustees

17. No purchaser or mortgagee, paying or advancing money on a sale or mortgage purporting to be made under any trust or power vested in trustees, shall be concerned to see that such money is wanted, or that no more than is wanted is raised, or otherwise as to the application thereof. **8–006**

Devolution of powers or trusts

18.—(1) Where a power or trust is given to or imposed on two or more trustees jointly, the same may be exercised or performed by the survivors or survivor of them from the time being. **8–007**

(2) Until the appointment of new trustees, the personal representatives or representative for the time being of a sole trustee, or, where there were two or more trustees of the last surviving or continuing trustee, shall be capable of exercising or performing any power or trust which was given to, or capable of being exercised by, the sole or last surviving or continuing trustee, or other the trustees or trustee for the time being of the trust.

(3) This section takes effect subject to the restrictions imposed in regard to receipts by a sole trustee, not being a trust corporation.

(4) In this section "personal representative" does not include an executor who has renounced or has not proved.

[**Power to insure**

19.—(1) A trustee may— **8–008**

(a) insure any property which is subject to the trust against risks of loss or damage due to any event, and

(b) pay the premiums out of the trust funds.

(2) In the case of property held on a bare trust, the power to insure is subject to any direction given by the beneficiary or each of the beneficiaries—

(a) that any property specified in the direction is not to be insured;

(b) that any property specified in the direction is not to be insured except on such conditions as may be so specified.

(3) Property is held on a bare trust if it is held on trust for—

(a) a beneficiary who is full age and capacity and absolutely entitles to the property subject to the trust, or

(b) beneficiaries each of whom is of full age and capacity and who (taken together) are absolutely entitled to the property subject to the trust.

(4) If a direction under subsection (2) of this section is given, the power to insure, so far as it is subject to the direction, ceases to be a delegable function for the purposes of section 11 of the Trustee Act 2000 (power to employ agents).

(5) In this section "trust funds" means any income or capital funds of a trust.][9]

[9] s.19 substituted by the Trustee Act 2000, s.34(1).

Application of insurance money where policy kept up under any trust, power or obligation

8–009 **20.**—(1) Money receivable by trustees or any beneficiary under a policy of insurance against the loss or damage of any property subject to a trust or to a settlement within the meaning of the Settled Land Act 1925 [...][10] shall, where the policy has been kept up under any trust in that behalf or under any power statutory or otherwise, or in performance of any covenant or of any obligation statutory or otherwise, or by a tenant for life impeachable for waste, be capital money for the purposes of the trust or settlement, as the case may be.

(2) If any such money is receivable by any person, other than the trustees of the trust or settlement, that person shall use his best endeavours to recover and receive the money, and shall pay the net residue thereof, after discharging any costs of recovering and receiving it, to the trustees of the trust or settlement, or, if there are no trustees capable of giving a discharge therefor, into court.

(3) Any such money—

(a) if it was receivable in respect of settled land within the meaning of the Settled Land Act 1925, or any building or works thereon, shall be deemed to be capital money arising under that Act from the settled land, and shall be invested or applied by the trustees, or, if in court, under the direction of the court, accordingly;

(b) if it was receivable in respect of personal chattels settled as heirlooms within the meaning of the Settled Land Act 1925, shall be deemed to be capital money arising under that Act, and shall be applicable by the trustees, or, if in court, under the direction of the court, in like manner as provided by that Act with respect to money arising by a sale of chattels settled as heirlooms as aforesaid;

(c) if it was receivable in respect of [land subject to a trust of land or personal property held on trust for sale][11], shall be held upon the trusts and subject to the powers and provisions applicable to money arising by a sale under such trust;

(d) in any other case, shall be held upon trusts corresponding as nearly as may be with the trusts affecting the property in respect of which it was payable.

(4) Such money, or any part thereof, may also be applied by the trustees, or, if in court, under the direction of the court, in rebuilding, reinstating, replacing, or repairing the property lost or damaged, but any such application by the trustees shall be subject to the consent of any person whose consent is required by the instrument, if any, creating the trust to the investment of money subject to the trust, and, in the case of money which is deemed to be capital money arising under the Settled Land Act 1925, be subject to the provisions of that Act with respect to the application of capital money by the trustees of the settlement.

(5) Nothing contained in this section prejudices or affects the right of any person to require any such money or any part thereof to be applied in rebuilding, reinstating, or repairing the property lost or damaged, or the rights of any mortgagee, lessor, or lessee, whether under any statute or otherwise.

(6) This section applies to policies affected either before or after the commencement of this Act, but only the money received after such commencement.

[10] Words repealed by the Trustee Act 2000, s.34(2), 40(3), Sched. 4, Pt II.
[11] Words substituted by the Trusts of Land and Appointment of Trustees Act 1996, s.25(1), Sched. 3, para. 3(1), (5).

Deposit of documents for safe custody

21. [*Repealed by the Trustee Act 2000, s.40(1), (3), Sched. 2, Pt. II, para. 21, Sched. 4, Pt. II.*]

Reversionary interests, valuations, and audit

22.—(1) Where trust property includes any share or interest in property not vested in the trustees, or the proceeds of the sale of any such property, or any other thing in action, the trustees on the same falling into possession, or becoming payable or transferable may— **8–010**

(a) agree or ascertain the amount or value thereof or any part thereof in such manner as they may think fit;

(b) accept in or towards satisfaction thereof, at the market or current value, or upon any valuation or estimate of value which they may think fit, any authorised investments;

(c) allow any deductions for duties, costs, charges and expenses which they may think proper or reasonable;

(d) execute any release in respect of the premises so as effectually to discharge all accountable parties from all liability in respect of any matters coming within the scope of such release;

without being responsible in any such case for any loss occasioned by any act or thing so done by them [if they have discharged the duty of care set out in section 1(1) of the Trustee Act 2000][12].

(2) The trustees shall not be under any obligation and shall not be chargeable with any breach of trust by reason of any omission—

(a) to place any distringas notice or apply for any stop or other like order upon any securities or other property out of or on which such share or interest or other thing in action as aforesaid is derived, payable or charged; or

(b) to take any proceedings on account of any act, default, or neglect on the part of the persons in whom such securities or other property or any of them or any part thereof are for the time being, or had at any time been, vested;

unless and until required in writing so to do by some person, or the guardian of some person, beneficially interested under the trust, and unless also due provision is made to their satisfaction for payment of the costs of any proceedings required to be taken:

Provided that nothing in this subsection shall relieve the trustees of the obligation to get in and obtain payment or transfer of such share or interest or other thing in action on the same falling into possession.

(3) Trustees may, for the purpose of giving effect to the trust, or any of the provisions of the instrument, if any, creating the trust or of any statute, from time to time (by duly qualified agents) ascertain and fix the value of any trust property in such manner as they think proper, and any valuation so made [. . .][13] shall be binding upon all persons interested under the trust [if the trustees have discharged the duty of care set out in section 1(1) of the Trustee Act 2000].[14]

(4) Trustees may, in their absolute discretion, from time to time, but not more

[12] Words substituted by the Trustee Act 2000, s.40(1), Sched. 2, Pt. II, para. 22(a).
[13] Words repealed by the Trustee Act 2000, s.40(1), Sched. 2, Pt. II, para. 22(b).
[14] Words added by the Trustee Act 2000, s.40(1), Sched. 2, Pt. II, para. 22(b).

than once in every three years unless the nature of the trust or any special dealings with the trust property make a more frequent exercise of the right reasonable, cause the accounts of the trust property to be examined or audited by an independent accountant, and shall, for that purpose, produce such vouchers and give such information to him as he may require; and the costs of such examination or audit, including the fee of the auditor, shall be paid out of the capital or income of the trust property, or partly in one way and partly in the other, as the trustees, in their absolute discretion, think fit, but in default of any direction by the trustees to the contrary in any special case, costs attributable to capital shall be borne by capital and those attributable to income by income.

23. [*Repealed by the Trustee Act 2000, s.40(1), (3), Sched. 2, Pt. II, para. 23, Sched. 4, Pt. II.*]

Power to concur with others

8–011 **24.** Where an undivided share in [any][15] property, is subject to a trust, or forms part of the estate of a testator or intestate, the trustees or personal representatives may (without prejudice to the [trust][16] affecting the entirety of the land and the powers of the [trustees][17] in reference thereto) execute or exercise any [duty or][18] power vested in them in relation to such share in conjunction with the persons entitled to or having power in that behalf over the other share or shares, and notwithstanding that any one or more of the trustees or personal representatives may be entitled to or interested in any such other share, either in his or their own right or in a fiduciary capacity.

[Delegation of trustee's functions by power of attorney

8–012 **25.**—(1) Notwithstanding any rule of law or equity to the contrary, a trustee may, by power of attorney, delegate the execution or exercise of all or any of the trusts, powers and discretions vested in him as trustee either alone or jointly with any other person or persons.

(2) A delegation under this section—

(a) commences as provided by the instrument creating the power or, if the instrument makes no provision as to the commencement of the delegation with the date of the execution of the instrument by the donor; and

(b) continues for a period of twelve months or any shorter period provided by the instrument creating the power.

(3) The persons who may be donees of a power of attorney under this section include a trusts corporation.

(4) Before or within seven days after giving power of attorney under this section the donor shall give written notice of it (specifying the date on which the power comes into operation and its duration, the donee of the power, the reason

[15] Words substituted by the Trusts of Land and Appointment of Trustees Act 1996, s.25(1), Sched. 3, para. 3(1), (6).
[16] Words substituted by the Trusts of Land and Appointment of Trustees Act 1996, s.25(1), Sched. 3, para. 3(1), (6).
[17] Words substituted by the Trusts of Land and Appointment of Trustees Act 1996, s.25(1), Sched. 3, para. 3(1), (6).
[18] Words substituted by the Trusts of Land and Appointment of Trustees Act 1996, s.25(1), Sched. 3, para. 3(1), (6).

why the power is given and, where some only are delegated, the trusts, powers and discretions delegated) to—

(a) each person (other than himself), if any, who under any instrument creating the trusts has power (whether alone or jointly) to appoint a new trustee; and

(b) each of the other trustees, if any;

but failure to comply with this subsection shall not, in favour of a person dealing with the donee of the power, invalidate any act done or instrument executed by the donee.

(5) A power of attorney given under this section by a single donor—

(a) in the form set out in subsection (6) of this section; or

(b) in a form to the like effect but expressed to be made under this subsection,

shall operate to delegate to the person identified in the form as the single donee of the power the execution and exercise of all the trusts, powers and discretions vested in the donor as trustee (either alone or jointly with any other person or persons) under the single trust so identified.

(6) The form referred to in subsection (5) of this section is as follows—

"THIS GENERAL TRUSTEE POWER OF ATTORNEY is made on [*date*] by [*name of donor*] of [*address of donor*] as trustee of [*name or details of one trust*].

I appoint [*name of one donee*] of [*address of donee*] to be my attorney [*if desired, the date on which the delegation commences or the period for which it continues(or both)*] in accordance with section 25(5) of the Trustee Act 1925.

[*To be executed as a deed*]".

(7) The donor of a power of attorney given under this section shall be liable for the acts or defaults of the donee in the same manner as if they were the acts or defaults of the donor.

(8) For the purpose of executing or exercising the trusts or powers delegated to him, the donee may exercise any of the powers conferred on the donor as trustee by statute or by the instrument creating the trust, including power, for the purpose of the transfer of any inscribed stock, himself to delegate to an attorney power to transfer, but not including the power of delegation conferred by this section.

(9) The fact that it appears from any power of attorney given under this section, or from any evidence required for the purposes of any such power of attorney or otherwise, that in dealing with any stock the donee of the power is acting in the execution of a trust shall not be deemed for any purpose to affect any person in whose books the stock is inscribed or registered with any notice of the trust.

(10) This section applies to a personal representative, tenant for life and statutory owner as it applies to a trustee except that subsection (4) shall apply as if it required the notice there mentioned to be given—

(a) in the case of a personal representative, to each of the other personal representatives, if any, except any executor who has renounced probate;

(b) in the case of a tenant for life, to the trustees of the settlement and to each person, if any, who together with the person giving the notice constitutes the tenant for life; and

(c) in the case of a statutory owner, to each of the persons, if any, who together with the person giving the notice constitute the statutory owner and, in the case of a statutory owner by virtue of section 23(1)(a) of the Settled Land Act 1925, to the trustees of the settlement.][19–20]

Indemnities

Protection against liability in respect of rents and covenants

8–013 **26.**—(1) Where a personal representative or trustee liable as such for—

(a) any rent, covenant, or agreement reserved by or contained in any lease; or

(b) any rent, covenant or agreement payable under or contained in any grant made in consideration of a rentcharge; or

(c) any indemnity given in respect of any rent, covenant or agreement referred to in either of the foregoing paragraphs;

satisfies all liabilities under the lease or grant [which may have accrued and been claimed][21] up to the date of the conveyance hereinafter mentioned, and, where necessary, sets apart a sufficient fund to answer any future claim that may be made in respect of any fixed and ascertained sum which the lessee or grantee agreed to lay out on the property demised or granted, although the period for laying out the same may not have arrived, then and in any such case the personal representative or trustee may convey the property demised or granted to a purchaser, legatee, devisee, or other person entitled to call for a conveyance thereof and thereafter—

(i) he may distribute the residuary real and personal estate of the deceased testator or intestate, or, as the case may be, the trust estate (other than the fund, if any, set apart as aforesaid) to or amongst the persons entitled thereto, without appropriating any part, or any further part, as the case may be, of the estate of the deceased or of the trust estate to meet any future liability under the said lease or grant;

(ii) notwithstanding such distribution, he shall not be personally liable in respect of any subsequent claim under the said lease or grant.

[(1A) Where a personal representative or trustee has as such entered into, or may as such be required to enter into, an authorised guarantee agreement with respect to any lease comprised in the estate of a deceased testator or intestate or a trust estate (and, in a case where he has entered into such an agreement, he has satisfied all liabilities under it which may have accrued and been claimed up to the date of distribution)—

(a) he may distribute the residuary real and personal estate of the deceased testator or intestate, or the trust estate, to or amongst the persons entitled thereto—

(i) without appropriating any part of the estate of the deceased, or the trust estate, to meet any future liability (or, as the case may be, any liability) under any such agreement, and

(ii) notwithstanding any potential liability of his to enter into any such agreement; and

(b) notwithstanding such distribution, he shall not be personally liable in

---

19–20 s.25 substituted by the Trustee Delegation Act 1999, s.5(1). For collective delegation by trustees, see the Trustee Act 2000, Pt. IV, *post*, paras 64–011 *et seq.*

21 Words substituted by the Law of Property (Amendment) Act 1926, s.7, Sched.

respect of any subsequent claim (or, as the case may be, any claim) under any such agreement.

In this subsection "authorised guarantee agreement" has the same meaning as in the Landlord and Tenant (Covenants) Act 1995.][22]

(2) This section operates without prejudice to the right of the lessor or grantor, or the persons deriving title under the lessor or grantor, to follow the assets of the deceased or the trust property into the hands of the persons amongst whom the same may have been respectively distributed, and applies notwithstanding anything to the contrary in the will or other instrument, if any, creating the trust.

(3) In this section "lease" includes an underlease and an agreement for a lease or underlease and any instrument giving any such indemnity as aforesaid or varying the liabilities under the lease; "grant" applies to a grant whether the rent is created by limitation, grant, reservation, or otherwise, and includes an agreement for a grant and any instrument giving any such indemnity as aforesaid or varying the liabilities under the grant; "lessee" and "grantee" include persons respectively deriving title under them.

Protection by means of advertisements

27.—(1) With a view to the conveyance to or distribution among the persons entitled to any real or personal property, the trustees of a settlement [, trustees of land, trustees for sale of personal property][23] or personal representatives, may give notice by advertisement in the Gazette, and [in a newspaper circulating in the district in which the land is situated][24], and such other like notices, including notices elsewhere than in England and Wales, as would, in any special case, have been directed by a court of competent jurisdiction in an action for administration, of their intention to make such conveyance or distribution as aforesaid, and requiring any person interested to send to the trustees or personal representatives within the time, not being less than two months, fixed in the notice or, where more than one notice is given, in the last of the notices, particulars of his claim in respect of the property or any part thereof to which the notice relates. **8–014**

(2) At the expiration of the time fixed by the notice the trustees or personal representatives may convey or distribute the property or any part thereof to which the notice relates, to or among the persons entitled thereto, have regard only to the claims, whether formal or not, of which the trustees or personal representatives then had notice and shall not, as respects the property so conveyed or distributed, be liable to any person of whose claim the trustees or personal representatives have not had notice at the time of conveyance or distribution; but nothing in this section—

(a) prejudices the right of any person to follow the property, or any property representing the same, into the hands of any person, other than a purchaser, who may have received it; or

(b) frees the trustees or personal representatives from any obligation to make searches or obtain official certificates of search similar to those which an intending purchaser would be advised to make or obtain.

---

[22] subs. (1A) inserted by the Landlord and Tenant (Covenants) Act 1995, s.30(1), Sched. 1, para. 1.

[23] Words substituted by the Trusts of Land and Appointment of Trustees Act 1996, s.25(1), Sched. 3, para. 3(1), (7).

[24] Words substituted by the Law of Property (Amendment) Act 1926, s.7, Sched.

(3) This section applies notwithstanding anything to the contrary in the will or other instrument, if any, creating the trust.

Protection in regard to notice

8–015 **28.** A trustee or personal representative acting for the purposes of more than one trust or estate shall not, in the absence of fraud, be affected by notice of any instrument, matter, fact or thing in relation to any particular trust or estate if he has obtained notice thereof merely by reason of his acting or having acted for the purposes of another trust or estate.

29. [*Repealed by the Powers of Attorney Act 1971, s.11(2), (4), Sched. 2.*][25]

30. [*Repealed by the Trustee Act 2000, s.40(1), (3), Sched. 2, Pt. II, para. 24, Sched. 4, Pt. II.*]

Maintenance, Advancement and Protective Trusts

Power to apply income for maintenance and to accumulate surplus income during a minority

8–016 **31.**—(1) Where any property is held by trustees in trust for any person for any interest whatsoever, whether vested or contingent, then, subject to any prior interests or charges affecting that property—

(i) during the infancy of any such person, if his interest so long continues, the trustees may, at their sole discretion, pay to his parent or guardian, if any, or otherwise apply for or towards his maintenance, education, or benefit, the whole or such part, if any, of the income of that property as may, in all the circumstances, be reasonable, whether or not there is—
   (a) any other fund applicable to the same purpose; or
   (b) any person bound by law to provide for his maintenance or education; and

(ii) if such person on attaining the age of [eighteen years][26] has not a vested interest in such income, the trustees shall thenceforth pay the income of that property and of any accretion thereto under subsection (2) of this section to him, until he either attains a vested interest therein or dies, or until failure of his interest:

Provided that, in deciding whether the whole or any part of the income of the property is during a minority to be paid or applied for the purposes aforesaid, the trustees shall have regard to the age of the infant and his requirements and generally to the circumstances of the case, and in particular to what other income, if any, is applicable for the same purposes; and where trustees have notice that the income of more than one fund is applicable for those purposes, then, so far as practicable, unless the entire income of the funds is paid or applied as aforesaid or the court otherwise directs, a proportionate part only of the income of each fund shall be so paid or applied.

(2) During the infancy of any such person, if his interest so long continues, the trustees shall accumulate all the residue of that income [by investing it, and any

[25] See now the Powers of Attorney Act 1971, s.5, *post*, para. 30–004.
[26] Words substituted by the Family Law Reform Act 1969, s.1(3), (4), Sched. 1, Pt. I, Sched. 3, paras 5(1)(a), 9.

profits from so investing it][27] from time to time in authorised investments, and shall hold those accumulations as follows:—

(i) If any such person—

(a) attains the age of [eighteen years][28], or marries under that age, and his interest in such income during his infancy or until his marriage is a vested interest; or

(b) on attaining the age of [eighteen years][29] or on marriage under that age becomes entitled to the property from which such income arose in fee simple, absolute or determinable, or absolutely, or for an entailed interest;

the trustees shall hold the accumulations in trust for such person absolutely, but without prejudice to any provision with respect thereto contained in any settlement by him made under any statutory powers during his infancy, and so that the receipt of such person after marriage, and though still an infant, shall be a good discharge; and

(ii) In any other case the trustees shall, notwithstanding that such person had a vested interest in such income, hold the accumulations as an accretion to the capital of the property from which such accumulations arose, and as one fund with such capital for all purposes, and so that, if such property is settled land, such accumulations shall be held upon the same trusts as if the same were capital money arising therefrom;

but the trustees may, at any time during the infancy of such person if his interest so long continues, apply those accumulations, or any part thereof, as if they were income arising in the then current year.

(3) This section applies in the case of a contingent interest only if the limitation or trust carries the intermediate income of the property, but it applies to a future or contingent legacy by the parent of, or a person standing in loco parentis to, the legatee, if and for such period as, under the general law, the legacy carries interest for the maintenance of the legatee, and in any such case as last aforesaid the rate of interest shall (if the income available is sufficient, and subject to any rules of court to the contrary) be five pounds per centum per annum.

(4) This section applies to a vested annuity in like manner as if the annuity were the income of property held by trustees in trust to pay the income thereof to the annuitant for the same period for which the annuity is payable, save that in any case accumulations made during the infancy of the annuitant shall be held in trust for the annuitant or his personal representatives absolutely.

(5) This section does not apply where the instrument, if any, under which the interest arises came into operation before the commencement of this Act.

Power of advancement

32.—(1) Trustees may at any time or times pay or apply any capital money subject to a trust, for the advancement or benefit, in such manner as they may, in their absolute discretion, think fit, of any person entitled to the capital of the trust property or of any share thereof, whether absolutely or contingently on his attaining any specified age or on the occurrence of any other event, or subject to **8–017**

[27] Words substituted by the Trustee Act 2000, s.40(1), Sched. 2, Pt. II, para. 25.

[28] Words substituted by the Family Law Reform Act 1969, s.1(3), (4), Sched. 1, Pt. I, Sched. 3, paras 5(1)(a), 9.

[29] Words substituted by the Family Law Reform Act 1969, s.1(3), (4), Sched. 1, Pt. I, Sched. 3, paras 5(1)(a), 9.

a gift over on his death under any specified age or on the occurrence of any other event, and whether in possession or in remainder or reversion, and such payment or application may be made notwithstanding that the interest of such person is liable to be defeated by the exercise of a power of appointment or revocation, or to be diminished by the increase of the class to which he belongs:

Provided that—

(a) the money so paid or applied for the advancement or benefit of any person shall not exceed altogether in amount one-half of the presumptive or vested share or interest of that person in the trust property; and

(b) if that person is or becomes absolutely and indefeasibly entitled to a share in the trust property the money so paid or applied shall be brought into account as part of such share; and

(c) no such payment or application shall be made so as to prejudice any person entitled to any prior life or other interest, whether vested or contingent, in the money paid or applied unless such person is in existence and of full age and consents in writing to such payment or application.

[(2) This section does not apply to capital money arising under the Settled Land Act 1925.][30]

(3) This section does not apply to trusts constituted or created before the commencement of this Act.

Protective trusts

8–018 **33.**—(1) Where any income, including an annuity or other periodical income payment, is directed to be held on protective trusts for the benefit of any person (in this section called "the principal beneficiary") for the period of his life or for any less period, then, during that period (in this section called the "trust period") the said income shall, without prejudice to any prior interest, be held on the following trusts, namely:—

(i) Upon trust for the principal beneficiary during the trust period or until he, whether before or after the termination of any prior interest, does or attempts to do or suffers any act or thing, or until any event happens, other than an advance under any statutory or express power, whereby, if the said income were payable during the trust period to the principal beneficiary absolutely during that period, he would be deprived of the right to receive the same or any part thereof, in any of which cases, as well as on the termination of the trust period, whichever first happens, this trust of the said income shall fail or determine;

(ii) If the trust aforesaid fails or determines during the subsistence of the trust period, then, during the residue of that period, the said income shall be held upon trust for the application thereof for the maintenance or support, or otherwise for the benefit, of all or any one or more exclusively of the other or others of the following persons (that is to say)—

(a) the principal beneficiary and his wife or husband, if any, and his or her children or more remote issue, if any; or

(b) if there is no wife or husband or issue of the principal beneficiary in existence, the principal beneficiary and the persons who would, if he

---

[30] subs. (2) substituted by the Trusts of Land and Appointment of Trustees Act 1996, s.25(1), Sched. 3, para. 3(1), (8).

were actually dead, be entitled to the trust property or the income thereof or the annuity fund, if any, or arrears of the annuity, as the case may be;

as the trustees in their absolute discretion, without being liable to account for the exercise of such discretion, think fit.

(2) This section does not apply to trusts coming into operation before the commencement of this Act, and has effect subject to any variation of the implied trusts aforesaid contained in the instrument creating the trust.

(3) Nothing in this section operates to validate any trust which would, if contained in the instrument creating the trust, be liable to be set aside.

[(4) In relation to the dispositions mentioned in section 19(1) of the Family Law Reform Act 1987, this section shall have effect as if any reference (however expressed) to any relationship between two persons were construed in accordance with section 1 of that Act[31].][32]

PART III

APPOINTMENT AND DISCHARGE OF TRUSTEES[33]

Limitation of the number of trustees

34.—(1) Where, at the commencement of this Act, there are more than four trustees of a settlement of land, or more than four trustees holding land on trust for sale, no new trustees shall (except where as a result of the appointment the number is reduced to four or less) be capable of being appointed until the number is reduced to less than four, and thereafter the number shall not be increased beyond four. **8–019**

(2) In the case of settlements and dispositions [creating trusts of land][34] made or coming into operation after the commencement of this Act—

(a) the number of trustees thereof shall not in any case exceed four, and where more than four persons are named as such trustees, the four first named (who are able and willing to act) shall alone be the trustees, and the other persons named shall not be trustees unless appointed on the occurrence of a vacancy;

(b) the number of the trustees shall not be increased beyond four.

(3) This section only applies to settlements and dispositions of land, and the restrictions imposed on the number of trustees do not apply—

(a) in the case of land vested in trustees for charitable, ecclesiastical, or public purposes; or

(b) where the net proceeds of the sale of the land are held for like purposes; or

(c) to the trustees of a term of years absolute limited by a settlement on trusts for raising money, or of a like term created under the statutory remedies relating to annual sums charged on land.

---

[31] See the Family Law Reform Act 1987, *post*, para. 50–001. The repeal of s.15 of the Family Law Reform Act 1969 (Family Law Reform Act 1987, s.33(4), Sched. 4) and its replacement by section 19 of the Family Law Reform Act 1987 do not affect the operation of this section in relation to: (a) any disposition *inter vivos* made before April 4, 1988 (the date on which the repeal came into force); or (b) any disposition by will or codicil executed before that date: Family Law Reform Act 1987, s.33(2), Sched. 3, para. 9.

[32] subs. (4) added by the Family Law Reform Act 1987, s.33(1), Sched. 2, para. 2.

[33] See also the Trusts of Land and Appointment of Trustees Act 1996, Pt. II, *post*, paras 60–020 *et seq.*

[34] Words substituted by the Trusts of Land and Appointment of Trustees Act 1996, s.25(1), Sched. 3, para. 3(1), (9).

Appointments of trustees of settlements and [trustees of land][35]

8–020 **35.**—[(1) Appointments of new trustees of land and of new trustees of any trust of the proceeds of sale of the land shall, subject to any order of the court, be effected by separate instruments, but in such manner as to secure that the same persons become trustees of land and trustees of the trust of the proceeds of sale.][36]

(2) Where new trustees of a settlement are appointed, a memorandum of the names and addresses of the persons who are for the time being the trustees thereof for the purposes of the Settled Land Act 1925 shall be endorsed on or annexed to the last or only principal vesting instrument by or on behalf of the trustees of the settlement, and such vesting instrument shall, for that purpose, be produced by the person having the possession thereof to the trustees of the settlement when so required.

[(3) Where new trustees of land are appointed, a memorandum of the persons who are for the time being the trustees of the land shall be endorsed on or annexed to the conveyance by which the land was vested in trustees of land; and that conveyance shall be produced to the persons who are for the time being the trustees of the land by the person in possession of it in order for that to be done when the trustees require its production.][37]

(4) This section applies only to settlements and dispositions of land.

Power of appointing new or additional trustees

8–021 **36.**—(1) Where a trustee, either original or substituted, and whether appointed by a court or otherwise, is dead, or remains out of the United Kingdom for more than twelve months, or desires to be discharged from all or any of the trusts or powers reposed in or conferred on him, or refuses or is unfit to act therein, or is incapable of acting therein, or is an infant, then, subject to the restrictions imposed by this Act on the number of trustees,—

(a) the person or persons nominated for the purpose of appointing new trustees by the instrument, if any, creating the trust; or
(b) if there is no such person, or no such person able and willing to act, then the surviving or continuing trustees or trustee for the time being, or the personal representatives of the last surviving or continuing trustee;

may, by writing, appoint one or more other person (whether or not being the persons exercising the power) to be a trustee or trustees in the place of the trustee so deceased remaining out of the United Kingdom, desiring to be discharged, refusing, or being unfit or being incapable, or being an infant, as aforesaid.

(2) Where a trustee has been removed under a power contained in the instrument creating the trust, a new trustee or new trustees may be appointed in the place of the trustee who is removed, as if he were dead, or, in the case of a corporation, as if the corporation desired to be discharged from the trust, and the provisions of this section shall apply accordingly, but subject to the restrictions imposed by this Act on the number of trustees.

(3) Where a corporation being a trustee is or has been dissolved, either before

[35] Words substituted by the Trusts of Land and Appointment of Trustees Act 1996, s.25(1), Sched. 3, para. 3(1), (10)(c).
[36] subs. (1) substituted by the Trusts of Land and Appointment of Trustees Act 1996, s.25(1), Sched. 3, para. 3(1), (10)(a).
[37] subs. (3) substituted by the Trusts of Land and Appointment of Trustees Act 1996, s.25(1), Sched. 3, para. 3(1), (10)(b).

or after the commencement of this Act, then, for the purposes of this section and of any enactment replaced thereby, the corporation shall be deemed to be and to have been from the date of the dissolution incapable of acting in the trusts or powers reposed in or conferred on the corporation.

(4) The power of appointment given by subsection (1) of this section or any similar previous enactment to the personal representatives of a last surviving or continuing trustee shall be and shall be deemed always to have been exercisable by the executors for the time being (whether original or by representation) of such surviving or continuing trustee who have proved the will of their testator or by the administrators for the time being of such trustee without the concurrence of any executor who has renounced or has not proved.

(5) But a sole or last surviving executor intending to renounce, or all the executors where they all intend to renounce, shall have and shall be deemed always to have had power, at any time before renouncing probate, to exercise the power of appointment given by this section, or by any similar previous enactment, if willing to act for that purpose and without thereby accepting the office of executor.

[(6) Where, in the case of any trust, there are not more than three trustees—][38]

(a) the person or persons nominated for the purpose of appointing new trustees by the instrument, if any, creating the trust; or

(b) if there is no such person, or no such person able and willing to act, then the trustee or trustees for the time being;

may, by writing, appoint another person or other persons to be an additional trustee or additional trustees, but it shall not be obligatory to appoint any additional trustee, unless the instrument, if any, creating the trust, or any statutory enactment provides to the contrary, nor shall the number of trustees be increased beyond four by virtue of any such appointment.

[(6A) A person who is either—

(a) both a trustee and attorney for the other trustee (if one other), or for both of the other trustees (if two others), under a registered power; or

(b) attorney under a registered power for the trustee (if one) or for both or each of the trustees (if two or three),

may, if subsection (6B) of this section is satisfied in relations to him, make an appointment under subsection (6)(b) of this section on behalf of the trustee or trustees.

(6B) This subsection is satisfied in relation to an attorney under a registered power for one or more trustees if (as attorney under the power)—

(a) he intends to exercise any function of the trustee or trustees by virtue of section 1(1) of the Trustee Delegation Act 1999, or

(b) he intends to exercise any function of the trustee or trustees in relation to any land, capital proceeds of a conveyance of land or income from land by virtue of its delegation to him under section 25 of this Act or the instrument (if any) creating the trust.

(6C) In subsections (6A) and (6B) of this section "registered power" means a power of attorney created by an instrument which is for the time being registered under section 6 of the Enduring Powers of Attorney Act 1985.

(6D) Subsection (6A) of this section—

(a) applied only if and so far as a contrary intention is not expressed in the instrument creating the power of attorney (or, where more than one, any of them) or the instrument (if any) creating the trust; and

[38] Words substituted by the Trusts of Land and Appointment of Trustees Act 1996, s.25(1), Sched. 3, para. 3(1), (11).

(b) has effect subject to the terms of those instruments.][39]

(7) Every new trustee appointed under this section as well before as after all the trust property becomes by law, or by assurance, or otherwise, vested in him, shall have the same powers, authorities, and discretions, and may in all respects act as if he had been originally appointed a trustee by the instrument, if any, creating the trust.

(8) The provisions of this section relating to a trustee who is dead include the case of a person nominated trustee in a will but dying before the testator, and those relative to a continuing trustee include a refusing or retiring trustee, if willing to act in the execution of the provisions of this section.

[(9) Where a trustee is incapable, by reason of mental disorder within the meaning of [the Mental Health Act 1983][40], of exercising his functions as trustee and is also entitled in possession to some beneficial interest in the trust property, no appointment of a new trustee in his place shall be made by virtue of paragraph (b) of subsection (1) of this section unless leave to make the appointment has been given by the authority having jurisdiction under [Part VII of the Mental Health Act 1983][41].][42]

Supplemental provisions as to appointment of trustees

8–022 **37.**—(1) On the appointment of a trustee for the whole or any part of trust property—

(a) the number of trustees may, subject to the restrictions imposed by this Act on the number of trustees, be increased; and

(b) a separate set of trustees, not exceeding four, may be appointed for any part of the trust property held on trusts distinct from those relating to any other part or parts of the trust property, notwithstanding that no new trustees or trustee are or is to be appointed for other parts of the trust property, and any existing trustee may be appointed or remain one of such separate set of trustees, or, if only one trustee was originally appointed, then, save as hereinafter provided, one separate trustee may be so appointed; and

(c) it shall not be obligatory, save as hereinafter provided, to appoint more than one new trustee where only one trustee was originally appointed, or to fill up the original number of trustees where more than two trustees were originally appointed, but, except where only one trustee was originally appointed, and a sole trustee when appointed will be able to give valid receipts for all capital money, a trustee shall not be discharged from his trust unless there will be either a trust corporation or at least two [persons][43] to act as trustees to perform the trust; and

(d) any assurance or thing requisite for vesting the trust property, or any part thereof, in a sole trustee, or jointly in the persons who are the trustees, shall be executed or done.

(2) Nothing in this Act shall authorise the appointment of a sole trustee, not being a trust corporation, where the trust, when appointed, would not be able to give valid receipts for all capital money arising under the trust.

---

[39] subss. (6A)–(6D) inserted by the Trustee Delegation Act 1999, s.8(1).
[40] Words substituted by the Mental Health Act 1983, s.148, Sched. 4, para. 4(a).
[41] Words substituted by the Mental Health Act 1983, s.148, Sched. 4, para. 4(a).
[42] subs. (9) substituted by the Mental Health Act 1959, s.149(1), Sched. 7, Pt. I.
[43] Word substituted by the Trusts of Land and Appointment of Trustees Act 1996, s.25(1), Sched. 3, para. 3(1), (12).

Evidence as to a vacancy in a trust

38.—(1) A statement, contained in any instrument coming into operation after the commencement of this Act by which a new trustee is appointed for any purpose connected with land, to the effect that a trustee has remained out of the United Kingdom for more than twelve months or refuses or is unfit to act, or is incapable of acting, or that he is not entitled to a beneficial interest in the trust property in possession, shall, in favour of a purchaser of a legal estate, be conclusive evidence of the matter stated. **8–023**

(2) In favour of such purchaser any appointment of a new trustee depending on that statement, and any vesting declaration, express or implied, consequent on the appointment, shall be valid.

Retirement of trustee without a new appointment

39.—(1) Where a trustee is desirous of being discharged from the trust, and after his discharge there will be either a trust corporation or at least two [persons][44] to act as trustees to perform the trust, then, if such trustee as aforesaid by deed declares that he is desirous of being discharged from the trust, and if his co-trustees and such other person, if any, as is empowered to appoint trustees, by deed consent to the discharge of the trustee, and to the vesting in the co-trustees alone of the trust property, the trustee desirous of being discharged shall be deemed to have retired from the trust, and shall, by the deed, be discharged therefrom under this Act, without any new trustee being appointed in his place. **8–024**

(2) Any assurance or thing requisite for vesting the trust property in the continuing trustees alone shall be executed or done.

Vesting of trust property in new or continuing trustees

40.—(1) Where by a deed a new trustee is appointed to perform any trust, then— **8–025**

(a) if the deed contains a declaration by the appointor to the effect that any estate or interest in any land subject to the trust, or in any chattel so subject, or the right to recover or receive any debt or other thing in action so subject, shall vest in the persons who by virtue of the deed become or are the trustees for performing the trust, the deed shall operate, without any conveyance or assignment, to vest in those persons as joint tenants and for the purposes of the trust the estate interest or right to which the declaration relates; and

(b) if the deed is made after the commencement of this Act and does not contain such a declaration, the deed shall, subject to any express provision to the contrary therein contained, operate as if it had contained such a declaration by the appointor extending to all the estates interests and rights with respect to which a declaration could have been made.

(2) Where by a deed a retiring trustee is discharged under [section 39 of this

[44] Word substituted by the Trusts of Land and Appointment of Trustees Act 1996, s.25(1), Sched. 3, para. 3(1), (13).

Act or section 19 of the Trusts of Land and Appointment of Trustees Act 1996][45] without a new trustee being appointed, then—

(a) if the deed contains such a declaration as aforesaid by the retiring and continuing trustees, and by the other person, if any, empowered to appoint trustees, the deed shall, without any conveyance or assignment, operate to vest in the continuing trustees alone, as joint tenants, and for the purposes of the trust, the estate, interest, or right to which the declaration relates; and

(b) if the deed is made after the commencement of this Act and does not contain such a declaration, the deed shall, subject to any express provision to the contrary therein contained, operate as if it had contained such a declaration by such persons as aforesaid extending to all the estates, interests and rights with respect to which a declaration could have been made.

(3) An express vesting declaration, whether made before or after the commencement of this Act, shall, notwithstanding that the estate, interest or right to be vested is not expressly referred to, and provided that the other statutory requirements were or are complied with, operate and be deemed always to have operated (but without prejudice to any express provision to the contrary contained in the deed of appointment or discharge) to vest in the persons respectively referred to in subsections (1) and (2) of this section, as the case may require, such estates, interests and rights as are capable of being and ought to be vested in those persons.

(4) This section does not extend—

(a) to land conveyed by way of mortgage for securing money subject to the trust, except land conveyed on trust for securing debentures or debenture stock;

(b) to land held under a lease which contains any covenant, condition or agreement against assignment or disposing of the land without licence or consent, unless, prior to the execution of the deed containing expressly or impliedly the vesting declaration, the requisite licence or consent has been obtained, or unless, by virtue of any statute or rule of law, the vesting declaration, express or implied, would not operate as a breach of covenant or give rise to a forfeiture;

(c) to any share, stock, annuity or property which is only transferable in books kept by a company or other body, or in manner directed by or under an Act of Parliament.

In this subsection "lease" includes an underlease and an agreement for a lease or underlease.

(5) For purposes of registration of the deed in any registry, the person or persons making the declaration expressly or impliedly, shall be deemed the conveying party or parties, and the conveyance shall be deemed to be made by him or them under a power conferred by this Act.

(6) This section applies to deeds of appointment or discharge executed on or after the first day of January, eighteen hundred and eighty-two.

[45] Words substituted by the Trusts of Land and Appointment of Trustees Act 1996, s.25(1), Sched. 3, para. 3(1), (14).

Part IV

Powers of the Court[46]

Appointment of new Trustees

Power of court to appoint new trustees

41.—(1) The court may, whenever it is expedient to appoint a new trustee or new trustees, and it is found inexpedient difficult or impracticable so to do without the assistance of the court, make an order appointing a new trustee or new trustees either in substitution for or in addition to any existing trustee or trustees, or although there is no existing trustee. **8–026**

In particular and without prejudice to the generality of the foregoing provision, the court may make an order appointing a new trustee in substitution for a trustee who [. . .][47] is [incapable, by reason of mental disorder within the meaning of [the Mental Health Act 1983][48], of exercising his functions as trustee][49] or is a bankrupt, or is a corporation which is in liquidation or has been dissolved.

(2) The power conferred by this section may, in the case of a deed of arrangement within the meaning of the Deeds of Arrangement Act 1914 be exercised either by the High Court or by the court having jurisdiction in bankruptcy in the district in which the debtor resided or carried on business at the date of the execution of the deed.

(3) An order under this section, and any consequential vesting order or conveyance, shall not operate further or otherwise as a discharge to any former or continuing trustee than an appointment of new trustees under any power for that purpose contained in any instrument would have operated.

(4) Nothing in this section gives power to appoint an executor or administrator.

Power to authorise remuneration

42. Where the court appoints a corporation, other than the Public Trustee, to be a trustee either solely or jointly with another person, the court may authorise the corporation to charge such remuneration for its services as trustee as the court may think fit. **8–027**

Powers of new trustee appointed by the court

43. Every trustee appointed by a court of competent jurisdiction shall, as well before as after the trust property becomes by law, or by assurance, or otherwise, vested in him, have the same powers, authorities, and discretions, and may in all respects act as if he had been originally appointed a trustee by the instrument, if any, creating the trust. **8–028**

[46] For the jurisdiction of the county court under Pt. IV, see s.63A, *post*, para. 8–049.
[47] Words repealed by the Criminal Law Act 1967, s.10, Sched. 3, Pt. III.
[48] Words substituted by the Mental Health Act 1983, s.148, Sched. 4, para. 4(b).
[49] Words substituted by the Mental Health Act 1959, s.149(1), Sched. 7, Pt. I.

Vesting Orders

Vesting orders of land

8–029 **44.** In any of the following cases, namely:—

(i) Where the court appoints or has appointed a trustee, or where a trustee has been appointed out of court under any statutory or express power;

(ii) Where a trustee entitled to or possessed of any land or interest therein, whether by way of mortgage or otherwise, or entitled to a contingent right therein, either solely or jointly with any other person—

(a) is under disability; or

(b) is out of the jurisdiction of the High Court; or

(c) cannot be found, or, being a corporation, has been dissolved;

(iii) Where it is uncertain who was the survivor of two or more trustees jointly entitled to or possessed of any interest in land;

(iv) Where it is uncertain whether the last trustee known to have been entitled to or possessed of any interest in land is living or dead;

(v) Where there is no personal representative of a deceased trustee who was entitled to or possessed of any interest in land, or where it is uncertain who is the personal representative of a deceased trustee who was entitled to or possessed of any interest in land;

(vi) Where a trustee jointly or solely entitled to or possessed of any interest in land, or entitled to a contingent right therein, has been required, by or on behalf of a person entitled to require a conveyance of the land or interest or a release of the right, to convey the land or interest or to release the right, and has wilfully refused or neglected to convey the land or interest or release the right for twenty-eight days after the date of the requirement;

(vii) Where land or any interest therein is vested in a trustee whether by way of mortgage or otherwise, and it appears to the court to be expedient;

the court may make an order (in this Act called a vesting order) vesting the land or interest therein in any such person in any such manner and for any such estate or interest as the court may direct, or releasing or disposing of the contingent right to such person as the court may direct:

Provided that—

(a) Where the order is consequential on the appointment of a trustee the land or interest therein shall be vested for such estate as the court may direct in the persons who on the appointment are the trustees; and

(b) Where the order relates to a trustee entitled or formerly entitled jointly with another person, and such trustee is under disability or out of the jurisdiction of the High Court or cannot be found, or being a corporation has been dissolved, the land interest or right shall be vested in such other person who remains entitled, either alone or with any other person the court may appoint.

Orders as to contingent rights of unborn persons

8–030 **45.** Where any interest in land is subject to a contingent right in an unborn person or class or unborn persons who, on coming into existence would, in respect thereof, become entitled to or possessed of that interest on any trust, the court may make an order releasing the land or interest therein from the contingent right, or may make an order vesting in any person the estate or interest to or of which the unborn person or class of unborn persons would, on coming into existence, be entitled or possessed in the land.

Vesting order in place of conveyance by infant mortgagee

46. Where any person entitled to or possessed of any interest in land, or entitled to a contingent right in land, by way of security for money, is an infant, the court may make an order vesting or releasing or disposing of the interest in the land or the right in like manner as in the case of a trustee under disability. **8–031**

Vesting order consequential on order for sale or mortgage of land

47. Where any court gives a judgment or makes an order directing the sale or mortgage of any land, every person who is entitled to or possessed of any interest in the land, or entitled to a contingent right therein, and is a party to the action or proceeding in which the judgment or order is given or made or is otherwise bound by the judgment or order, shall be deemed to be so entitled or possessed, as the case may be, as a trustee for the purposes of this Act, and the court may, if it thinks expedient, make an order vesting the land or any part thereof for such estate or interest as that court thinks fit in the purchaser or mortgagee or in any other person: **8–032**

Provided that, in the case of a legal mortgage, the estate to be vested in the mortgagee shall be a term of years absolute.

Vesting order consequential on judgment for specific performance, etc.

48. Where a judgment is given for the specific performance of a contract concerning any interest in land, or for sale or exchange of any interest in land, or generally where any judgment is given for the conveyance of any interest in land either in cases arising out of the doctrine of election or otherwise, the court may declare— **8–033**

(a) that any of the parties to the action are trustees of any interest in the land or any part thereof within the meaning of this Act; or
(b) that the interests of unborn persons who might claim under any party to the action, or under the will or voluntary settlement of any deceased person who was during his lifetime a party to the contract or transaction concerning which the judgment is given, are the interests of persons who, on coming into existence, would be trustees within the meaning of this Act;

and thereupon the court may make a vesting order relating to the rights of those persons, born and unborn, as if they had been trustees.

Effect of vesting order

49. A vesting order under any of the foregoing provisions shall in the case of a vesting order consequential on the appointment of a trustee, have the same effect— **8–034**

(a) as if the persons who before the appointment were the trustees, if any, had duly executed all proper conveyances of the land for such estate or interest as the court directs; or
(b) if there is no such person, or no such person of full capacity, as if such person had existed and been of full capacity and had duly executed all

proper conveyances of the land for such estate or interest as the court directs;

and shall in every other case have the same effect as if the trustee or other person or description or class of persons to whose rights or supposed rights the said provisions respectively relate had been an ascertained and existing person of full capacity, and had executed a conveyance or release to the effect intended by the order.

Power to appoint person to convey

8–035 **50.** In all cases where a vesting order can be made under any of the foregoing provisions, the court may, if it is more convenient, appoint a person to convey the land or any interest therein or release the contingent right, and a conveyance or release by that person in conformity with the order shall have the same effect as an order under the appropriate provision.

Vesting orders as to stock and things in action

8–036 **51.**—(1) In any of the following cases, namely:—

(i) Where the court appoints or has appointed a trustee, or where a trustee has been appointed out of court under any statutory or express power;

(ii) Where a trustee entitled, whether by way of mortgage or otherwise, alone or jointly with another person to stock or to a thing in action—

(a) is under disability; or

(b) is out of the jurisdiction of the High Court; or

(c) cannot be found, or, being a corporation, has been dissolved; or

(d) neglects or refuses to transfer stock or receive the dividends or income thereof, or to sue for or recover a thing in action, according to the direction of the person absolutely entitled thereto for twenty-eight days next after a request in writing has been made to him by the person so entitled; or

(e) neglects or refuses to transfer stock or receive the dividends or income thereof, or to sue for or recover a thing in action for twenty-eight days next after an order of the court for that purpose has been served on him;

(iii) Where it is uncertain whether a trustee entitled alone or jointly with another person to stock or to a thing in action is alive or dead;

(iv) Where stock is standing in the name of a deceased person whose personal representative is under disability;

(v) Where stock or a thing in action is vested in a trustee whether by way of mortgage or otherwise and it appears to the court to be expedient;

the court may make an order vesting the right to transfer or call for a transfer of stock, or to receive the dividends or income thereof, or to sue for or recover the thing in action, in any such person as the court may appoint:

Provided that—

(a) Where the order is consequential on the appointment of a trustee, the right shall be vested in the persons who, on the appointment, are the trustees; and

(b) where the person whose right is dealt with by the order was entitled jointly with another person, the right shall be vested in that last-mentioned person either alone or jointly with any other person whom the court may appoint.

(2) In all cases where a vesting order can be made under this section, the court may, if it is more convenient, appoint some proper person to make or join in making the transfer:

Provided that the person appointed to make or join in making a transfer of stock shall be some proper officer of the bank, or the company or society whose stock is to be transferred.

(3) The person in whom the right to transfer or call for the transfer of any stock is vested by an order of the court under this Act, may transfer the stock to himself or any other person, according to the order, and the Bank of England and all other companies shall obey every order under this section according to its tenor.

(4) After notice in writing of an order under this section it shall not be lawful for the Bank of England or any other company to transfer any stock to which the order relates or to pay any dividends thereon except in accordance with the order.

(5) The court may make declarations and give directions concerning the manner in which the right to transfer any stock or thing in action vested under the provisions of this Act is to be exercised.

(6) The provisions of this Act as to vesting orders shall apply to shares in ships registered under the [Merchant Shipping Act 1995][50] as if they were stock.

Vesting orders of charity property

52. The powers conferred by this Act as to vesting orders may be exercised for vesting any interest in land, stock, or thing in action in any trustee of a charity or society over which the court would have jurisdiction upon action duly instituted, whether the appointment of the trustee was made by instrument under a power or by the court under its general or statutory jurisdiction. **8–037**

Vesting orders in relation to infant's beneficial interests

53. Where an infant is beneficially entitled to any property the court may, with a view to the application of the capital or income thereof for the maintenance, education, or benefit of the infant, make an order— **8–038**

(a) appointing a person to convey such property; or
(b) in the case of stock, or a thing in action, vesting in any person the right to transfer or call for a transfer of such stock, or to receive the dividends or incomes thereof, or to sue for and recover such thing in action, upon such terms as the court may think fit.

[Jurisdiction in regard to mental patients

54.—(1) Subject to the provisions of this section, the authority having jurisdiction under [Part VII of the Mental Health Act 1983][51] shall not have power to make any order, or give any direction or authority, in relation to a patient who is a trustee if the High Court has power under this Act to make an order to the like effect. **8–039**

(2) Where a patient is a trustee and a receiver appointed by the said authority is acting for him or an application for the appointment of a receiver has been

[50] Words substituted by the Merchant Shipping Act 1995, s.314(2), Sched. 13, para. 13.
[51] Words substituted by the Mental Health Act 1983, s.148, Sched. 4, para. 4(c).

made but not determined, then, except as respects a trust which is subject to an order for administration made by the High Court, the said authority shall have concurrent jurisdiction with the High Court in relation to—

(a) mortgaged property of which the patient has become a trustee merely by reason of the mortgage having been paid off;

(b) matters consequent on the making of provision by the said authority for the exercise of a power of appointing trustees or retiring from a trust;

(c) matters consequent on the making of provision by the said authority for the carrying out of any contract entered into by the patient;

(d) property to some interest in which the patient is beneficially entitled but which, or some interest in which, is held by the patient under an express, implied or constructive trust.

The Lord Chancellor may make rules with respect to the exercise of the jurisdiction referred to in this subsection.

(3) In this section "patient" means a patient as defined by [section 94 of the Mental Health Act 1983][52] or a person as to whom powers are [exercisable under section 98 of that Act and have been exercised under that section or section 104 of the Mental Health Act 1959][53].][54]

Orders made upon certain allegations to be conclusive evidence

8–040 **55.** Where a vesting order is made as to any land under this Act or under [Part VII of the Mental Health Act 1983][55], as amended by any subsequent enactment, or under any Act relating to lunacy in Northern Ireland, founded on an allegation of any of the following matters namely—

(a) the personal incapacity of a trustee or mortgagee; or

(b) that a trustee or mortgagee or the personal representative of or other person deriving title under a trustee or mortgagee is out of the jurisdiction of the High Court or cannot be found, or being a corporation has been dissolved; or

(c) that it is uncertain which of two or more trustees, or which of two or more persons interested in a mortgage, was the survivor; or

(d) that it is uncertain whether the last trustee or the personal representative of or other person deriving title under a trustee or mortgagee, or the last surviving person interested in a mortgage is living or dead; or

(e) that any trustee or mortgagee has died intestate without leaving a person beneficially interested under the intestacy or has died and it is not known who is his personal representative or the person interested;

the fact that the order has been so made shall be conclusive evidence of the matter so alleged in any court upon any question as to the validity of the order; but this section does not prevent the court from directing a reconveyance or surrender or the payment of costs occasioned by any such order if improperly obtained.

Application of vesting order to property out of England

8–041 **56.** The powers of the court to make vesting orders under this Act shall extend to all property in any part of His Majesty's dominions except Scotland.

[52] Words substituted by the Mental Health Act 1983, s.148, Sched. 4, para. 4(c).
[53] Words substituted by the Mental Health Act 1983, s.148, Sched. 4, para. 4(c).
[54] s.54 substituted by the Mental Health Act 1959, s.149(1), Sched. 7, Pt. I.
[55] Words substituted by the Mental Health Act 1983, s.148, Sched. 4, para. 4(d).

Jurisdiction to make other Orders

Power of court to authorise dealings with trust property

57.[56]—(1) Where in the management or administration of any property vested in trustees, any sale, lease, mortgage, surrender, release, or other disposition, or any purchase, investment, acquisition, expenditure, or other transaction, is in the opinion of the court expedient, but the same cannot be effected by reason of the absence of any power for that purpose vested in the trustees by the trust instrument, if any, or by law, the court may by order confer upon the trustees, either generally or in any particular instance, the necessary power for the purpose, on such terms, and subject to such provisions and conditions, if any, as the court may think fit and may direct in what manner any money authorised to be expended, and the costs of any transaction, are to be paid or borne as between capital and income. **8–042**

(2) The court may, from time to time, rescind or vary any order made under this section, or may make any new or further order.

(3) An application to the court under this section may be made by the trustees, or by any of them, or by any person beneficially interested under the trust.

(4) This section does not apply to trustees of a settlement for the purposes of the Settled Land Act 1925.

Persons entitled to apply for orders

58.—(1) An order under this Act for the appointment of a new trustee or concerning any interest in land, stock, or thing in action subject to a trust, may be made on the application of any person beneficially interested in the land, stock, or thing in action, whether under disability or not, or on the application of any person duly appointed trustee thereof. **8–043**

(2) An order under this Act concerning any interest in land, stock, or thing in action subject to a mortgage may be made on the application of any person beneficially interested in the equity of redemption, whether under disability or not, or of any person interested in the money secured by the mortgage.

Power to give judgment in absence of a trustee

59. Where in any action the court is satisfied that diligent search has been made for any person who, in the character of trustee, is made a defendant in any action, to serve him with a process of the court, and that he cannot be found, the court may hear and determine the action and give judgment therein against that person in his character of a trustee as if he had been duly served, or had entered an appearance in the action, and had also appeared by his counsel and solicitor at the hearing, but without prejudice to any interest he may have in the matters in question in the action in any other character. **8–044**

Power to charge costs on trust estate

60. The court may order the costs and expenses of and incident to any application for an order appointing a new trustee, or for a vesting order, or of **8–045**

[56] The powers of the court are extended by the Settled Land and Trustee Acts (Court's General Powers) Act 1943, s.1.

and incident to any such order, or any conveyance or transfer in pursuance thereof, to be raised and paid out of the property in respect whereof the same is made, or out of the income thereof, or to be borne and paid in such manner and by such persons as to the court may seem just.

Power to relieve trustee from personal liability

8–046 **61.** If it appears to the court that a trustee, whether appointed by the court or otherwise, is or may be personally liable for any breach of trust, whether the transaction alleged to be a breach of trust occurred before or after the commencement of this Act, but has acted honestly and reasonably, and ought fairly to be excused for the breach of trust and for omitting to obtain the directions of the court in the matter in which he committed such breach, then the court may relieve him either wholly or partly from personal liability for the same.

Power to make beneficiary indemnify for breach of trust

8–047 **62.**—(1) Where a trustee commits a breach of trust at the instigation or request or with the consent in writing of a beneficiary, the court may, if it thinks fit, [. . .][57] make such order as to the court seems just, for impounding all or any part of the interest of the beneficiary in the trust estate by way of indemnity to the trustee or persons claiming through him.

(2) This section applies to breaches of trust committed as well before as after the commencement of this Act.

Payment into Court

Payment into court by trustees

8–048 **63.**—(1) Trustees, or the majority of trustees, having in their hands or under their control money or securities belonging to a trust, may pay the same into court; [. . .][58]

(2) The receipt or certificate of the proper officer shall be a sufficient discharge to trustees for the money or securities so paid into court.

(3) Where money or securities are vested in any persons as trustees, and the majority are desirous of paying the same into court, but the concurrence of the other or others cannot be obtained, the court may order the payment into court to be made by the majority without the concurrence of the other or others.

(4) Where any such money or securities are deposited with any banker, broker, or other depositary, the court may order payment or delivery of the money or securities to the majority of the trustees for the purpose of payment into court.

(5) Every transfer payment and delivery made in pursuance of any such order shall be valid and take effect as if the same had been made on the authority or by the act of all the persons entitled to the money and securities so transferred, paid, or delivered.

[57] Words repealed by the Married Women (Restraint upon Anticipation) Act 1949, s.1(4), Sched. 2.
[58] Words repealed by the Administration of Justice Act 1965, s.36(4), Sched. 3.

[Jurisdiction of County Court

63A.—(1) The county court has jurisdiction under the following provisions where the amount or value of the trust estate or fund to be dealt with in the court does not exceed the county court limit— **8–049**

section 41;
section 42;
section 51;
section 57;
section 60;
section 61;
section 62.

(2) The county court has jurisdiction under the following provisions where the land or the interest or contingent right in land which is to be dealt with in the court forms part of a trust estate which does not exceed in amount or value the county court limit—

section 44;
section 45;
section 46.

(3) The county court has jurisdiction—

(a) under section 47 and 48 of this Act, where the judgment is given or order is made by the court;
(b) under sections 50 and 56, where a vesting order can be made by the court;
(c) under section 53, where the amount or value of the property to be dealt with in the court does not exceed the county court limit; and
(d) under section 63 (including power to receive payment of money or securities into court) where the money or securities to be paid into court do not exceed in amount or value the county court limit.

(4) Any reference to the court in section 59 of this Act includes a reference to the county court.

(5) In this section, in its application to any enactment, "the county court limit" means the amount for the time being specified by an Order in Council under section 145 of the County Courts Act 1984 as the county court limit for the purposes of that enactment (or, where no such Order in Council has been made, the corresponding limit specified by Order in Council under section 192 of the County Courts Act 1959).][59]

Part V

General Provisions

Application of Act to Settled Land Act Trustees

64.—(1) All the powers and provisions contained in this Act with reference to the appointment of new trustees, and the discharge and retirement of trustees, apply to and include trustees for the purposes of the Settled Land Act 1925 and trustees for the purpose of the management of land during a minority, whether such trustees are appointed by the court or by the settlement, or under provisions contained in any instrument. **8–050**

---

[59] s.63A inserted by the County Courts Act 1984, s.148(1), Sched. 2, Pt. I, para. 1. For the jurisdiction of the county court by agreement, see the County Courts Act 1984, s.24, *post*, para. 42–003.

(2) Where, either before or after the commencement of this Act, trustees of a settlement have been appointed by the court for the purposes of the Settled Land Acts 1882 to 1890 or of the Settled Land Act 1925, then, after the commencement of this Act—

(a) the person or persons nominated for the purpose of appointing new trustees by the instrument, if any, creating the settlement, though no trustees for the purposes of the said Acts were thereby appointed; or

(b) if there is no such person, or no such person able and willing to act, the surviving or continuing trustees or trustee for the time being for the purposes of the said Acts or the personal representatives of the last surviving or continuing trustee for those purposes,

shall have the powers conferred by this Act to appoint new or additional trustees of the settlement for the purposes of the said Acts.

(3) Appointments of new trustees for the purposes of the said Acts made or expressed to be made before the commencement of this Act by the trustees or trustee or personal representatives referred to in paragraph (b) of the last preceding subsection or by the persons referred to in paragraph (a) of that subsection are, without prejudice to any order of the court made before such commencement, hereby confirmed.

65. [*Repealed by the Criminal Law Act* 1967, *s.10*, *Sched. 3*, *Pt. I.*]

Indemnity to banks, etc.

8–051 **66.** This Act, and every order purporting to be made under this Act, shall be a complete indemnity to the Bank of England, and to all persons for any acts done pursuant thereto, and it shall not be necessary for the Bank or for any person to inquire concerning the propriety of the order, or whether the court by which the order was made had jurisdiction to make it.

Jurisdiction of the "court"

8–052 **67.**—(1) In this Act "the court" means the High Court […][60] or the county court, where those courts respectively have jurisdiction.

(2) The procedure under this Act in […][61] county courts shall be in accordance with the Acts and rules regulating the procedure of those courts.

Definitions

8–053 **68.**—(1) In this Act, unless the context otherwise requires, the following expressions having the meanings hereby assigned to them respectively, that is to say:—

(1) "Authorised investments" means investments authorised by the instrument, if any, creating the trust for the investment of money subject to the trust, or by law;

(2) "Contingent right" as applied to land includes a contingent or executory interest, a possibility coupled with an interest, whether the object of the

[60] Words repealed by the Courts Act 1971, s.56(4), Sched. 11, Pt. II.
[61] Words repealed by the Courts Act 1971, s.56(4), Sched. 11, Pt. II.

gift or limitation of the interest, or possibility is or is not ascertained, also a right of entry, whether immediate or future, and whether vested or contingent;

(3) "Convey" and "conveyance" as applied to any person include the execution by that person of every necessary or suitable assurance (including an assent) for conveying, assigning, appointing, surrendering, or otherwise transferring or disposing of land whereof he is seised or possessed, or wherein he is entitled to a contingent right, either for his whole estate or for any less estate, together with the performance of all formalities required by law for the validity of the conveyance; "sale" includes an exchange;

(4) "Gazette" means the London Gazette;

(5) "Instrument" includes Act of Parliament;

(6) "Land" includes land of any tenure, and mines and minerals whether or not severed from the surface, buildings or parts of buildings, whether the division is horizontal, vertical or made in any other way, and other corporeal hereditaments; also a manor, an advowson, and a rent and other incorporeal hereditaments, and an easement, right, privilege, or benefit in, over, or derived from land [...][62]; and in this definition "mines and minerals" include any strata or seam of minerals or substances in or under any land, and powers of working and getting the same, [...][63]; and "hereditaments" mean real property which under an intestacy occurring before the commencement of this Act might have devolved on an heir;

(7) "Mortgage" and "mortgagee" include a charge or chargee by way of legal mortgage, and relate to every estate and interest regarded in equity as merely a security for money, and every person deriving title under the original mortgagee;

[...][64]

(9) "Personal representative" means the executor, original or by representation, or administrator for the time being of a deceased person;

(10) "Possession" includes receipt of rent and profits or the right to receive the same, if any; "income" includes rents and profits; and "possessed" applies to receipt of income of and to any vested estate less than a life interest in possession or in expectancy in any land;

(11) "Property" includes real and personal property, and any estate share and interest in any property, real or personal, and any debt, and any thing in action, and any other right or interest, whether in possession or not;

(12) "Rights" include estates and interests;

(13) "Securities" include stocks, funds, and shares; [...][65] and "securities payable to bearer" include securities transferable by delivery or by delivery and endorsement;

(14) "Stock" includes fully paid up shares, and so far as relates to vesting orders made by the court under this Act, includes any fund, annuity, or security transferable in books kept by any company or society, or by instrument of transfer either alone or accompanied by other formalities, and any share or interest therein;

(15) "Tenant for life," "statutory owner," "settled land," "settlement," "trust

[62] Words repealed by the Trusts of Land and Appointment of Trustees Act 1996, s.25(2), Sched. 4.
[63] Words repealed by the Trusts of Land and Appointment of Trustees Act 1996, s.25(2), Sched. 4.
[64] Definition of "payment into court" repealed by the Administration of Justice Act 1965, s.17(1), Sched. 1.
[65] Words repealed by the Administration of Justice Act 1965, s.17(1), Sched. 1.

instrument," "trustees of the settlement" [...][66] "term of years absolute" and "vesting instrument" have the same meanings as in the Settled Land Act 1925, and "entailed interest" has the same meaning as in the Law of Property Act 1925;

(16) "Transfer" in relation to stock or securities, includes the performance and execution of every deed, power of attorney, act, and thing on the part of the transferor to effect and complete the title in the transferee;

(17) "Trust" does not include the duties incident to an estate conveyed by way of mortgage, but with this exception the expressions "trust" and "trustee" extend to implied and constructive trusts, and to cases where the trustee has a beneficial interest in the trust property, and to the duties incident to the office of a personal representative, and "trustee" where the context admits, includes a personal representative, and "new trustee" includes an additional trustee;

(18) "Trust corporation"[67] means the Public Trustee or a corporation either appointed by the court in any particular case to be a trustee, or entitled by rules made under subsection (3) of section four of the Public Trustee Act 1906 to act as custodian trustee;

(19) "Trust for sale" in relation to land means an immediate [...][68] trust for sale, whether or not exercisable at the request or with the consent of any person [...][69]; [...][70];

(20) "United Kingdom" means Great Britain and Northern Ireland.

[(2) Any reference in this Act to paying money or securities into court shall be construed as referring to paying the money or transferring or depositing the securities into or in the Supreme Court or into or in any other court that has jurisdiction, and any reference in this Act to payment of money or securities into court shall be construed—

(a) with reference to an order of the High Court, as referring to payment of the money or transfer or deposit of the securities into or in the Supreme Court; and

(b) with reference to an order of any other court, as referring to payment of the money or transfer or deposit of the securities into or in that court.][71]

Application of Act

8–054 **69.**—(1) This Act, except where otherwise expressly provided, applies to trusts including, so far as this Act applies thereto, executorships and administratorships constituted or created either before or after the commencement of this Act.

(2) The powers conferred by this Act on trustees are in addition to the powers conferred by the instrument, if any, creating the trust, but those powers, unless otherwise stated, apply if and so far only as a contrary intention is not expressed in the instrument, if any, creating the trust, and have effect subject to the terms of that instrument.

---

[66] Words repealed by the Mental Health Act 1959, s.149(2), Sched. 8, Pt. I.

[67] Definition of "trust corporation" extended by the Law of Property (Amendment) Act 1926, s.3, *post*, para. 11–002, and the Charities Act 1993, s.35, *post*, para. 56–034.

[68] Words repealed by the Trusts of Land and Appointment of Trustees Act 1996, s.25(2), Sched. 4.

[69] Words repealed by the Trusts of Land and Appointment of Trustees Act 1996, s.25(2), Sched. 4.

[70] Definition of "trustees for sale" repealed by the Trusts of Land and Appointment of Trustees Act 1996, s.25(2), Sched. 4.

[71] subs. (2) added (and subs. (1) numbered) by the Administration of Justice Act 1965, s.17(1), Sched. 1.

(3) [*Repealed by the Statute Law (Repeals) Act 1978, s.1, Sched. 1, Pt. XVII.*]

Enactments repealed

70. [. . .][72] without prejudice to the provisions of section thirty-eight of the Interpretation Act 1889[73]: **8–055**

(a) Nothing in this repeal shall affect any vesting order or appointment made or other thing done under any enactment so repealed, and any order or appointment so made may be revoked or varied in like manner as if it had been made under this Act;

(b) References in any document to any enactment repealed by this Act shall be construed as references to this Act or to the corresponding enactment in this Act.

Law of Property Act 1925

(15 Geo. 5, c. 20)

Arrangement of Sections

Part I

General Principles as to Legal Estates, Equitable Interests and Powers

sect.

---

[72] Words repealed by the Statute Law Revision Act 1950.
[73] Now the Interpretation Act 1978, ss.16(1), 17(2)(a).

Part III

Mortgages, Rentcharges and Powers of Attorney

Mortgages

Rentcharges

Powers of Attorney

Part IV

Equitable Interests and things in Action

PART V

LEASES AND TENANCIES

PART VI

POWERS

PART VII

PERPETUITIES AND ACCUMULATIONS

Perpetuities

Accumulations

PART IX

VOIDABLE DISPOSITIONS

PART X

WILLS

PART I

GENERAL PRINCIPLES AS TO LEGAL ESTATES, EQUITABLE INTERESTS AND POWERS

Legal estates and equitable interests

1.—(1) The only estates in land which are capable of subsisting or of being **9–001**
conveyed or created at law are—

(a) An estate in fee simple absolute in possession;

(b) A term of years absolute.

(2) The only interests or charges in or over land which are capable of subsisting or of being conveyed or created at law are—

(a) An easement, right, or privilege in or over land for an interest equivalent to an estate in fee simple absolute in possession or a term of years absolute;

(b) A rentcharge[1] in possession issuing out of or charged on land being either perpetual or for a term of years absolute;

(c) A charge by way of legal mortgage;

(d) [. . .][2] and any other similar charge on land which is not created by an instrument;

(e) Rights of entry exercisable over or in respect of a legal term of years absolute, or annexed, for any purpose, to a legal rentcharge.

(3) All other estates, interests, and charges in or over land take effect as equitable interests.

(4) The estates, interests, and charges which under this section are authorised to subsist or to be conveyed or created at law are (when subsisting or conveyed or created at law) in this Act referred to as "legal estates," and have the same incidents as legal estates subsisting at the commencement of this Act; and the owner of a legal estate is referred to as "an estate owner" and his legal estate is referred to as his estate.

(5) A legal estate may subsist concurrently with or subject to any other legal estate in the same land in like manner as it could have done before the commencement of this Act.

(6) A legal estate is not capable of subsisting or of being created in an undivided share in land or of being held by an infant.

(7) Every power of appointment over, or power to convey or charge land or any interest therein, whether created by a statute or other instrument or implied by law, and whether created before or after the commencement of this Act (not being a power vested in a legal mortgagee or an estate owner in right of his estate and exercisable by him or by another person in his name and on his behalf), operates only in equity.

(8) Estates, interests, and charges in or over land which are not legal estates are in this Act referred to as "equitable interests," and powers which by this Act are to operate in equity only are in this Act referred to as "equitable powers."

(9) The provisions in any statute or other instrument requiring land to be conveyed to uses shall take effect as directions that the land shall (subject to creating or reserving thereout any legal estate authorised by this Act which may be required) be conveyed to a person of full age upon the requisite trusts.

(10) The repeal of the Statute of Uses (as amended) does not affect the operation thereof in regard to dealings taking effect before the commencement of this Act.

---

[1] For the definition of "rentcharge," see the Law of Property (Entailed Interests) Act 1932, s.2, *post*, para. 13–001.

[2] Words repealed by the Tithe Act 1936, s.48(3), Sched. 9, and the Finance Act 1963, s.73(8)(b), Sched. 14, Pt. VI.

Conveyances overreaching certain equitable interests and powers

2.—(1) A conveyance to a purchaser of a legal estate in land shall overreach any equitable interest or power affecting that estate, whether or not he has notice thereof, if— **9–002**

(i) the conveyance is made under the powers conferred by the Settled Land Act 1925, or any additional powers conferred by a settlement, and the equitable interest or power is capable of being overreached thereby, and the statutory requirements respecting the payment of capital money arising under the settlement are complied with;

(ii) the conveyance is made by [trustees of land][3] and the equitable interest or power is at the date of the conveyance capable of being overreached by such trustees under the provisions of subsection (2) of this section or independently of that subsection, and [the requirements of section 27 of this Act respecting the payment of capital money arising on such a conveyance][4] are complied with;

(iii) the conveyance is made by a mortgagee or personal representative in the exercise of his paramount powers, and the equitable interest or power is capable of being overreached by such conveyance, and any capital money arising from the transaction is paid to the mortgagee or personal representative;

(iv) the conveyance is made under an order of the court and the equitable interest or power is bound by such order, and any capital money arising from the transaction is paid into, or in accordance with the order of, the court.

[(1A) An equitable interest in land subject to a trust of land which remains in, or is to revert to, the settlor shall (subject to any contrary intention) be overreached by the conveyance if it would be so overreached were it an interest under the trust.][5]

(2) [Where the legal estate affected is subject to [a trust of land][6], then if at the date of a conveyance made after the commencement of this Act [by the trustees][7], the trustees (whether original or substituted) are either—][8]

(a) two or more individuals approved or appointed by the court or the successors in office of the individuals so approved or appointed; or

(b) a trust corporation,

[any equitable interest or power having priority [to the trust][9]][10] shall, notwithstanding any stipulation to the contrary, be overreached by the conveyance, and shall, according to its priority, take effect as if created or arising by means of a primary trust affecting the proceeds of sale and the income of the land until sale.

(3) The following equitable interests and powers are excepted from the operation of subsection (2) of this section, namely—

[3] Words substituted by the Trusts of Land and Appointment of Trustees Act 1996, s.25(1), Sched. 3, para. 4(1), (2)(a).
[4] Words substituted by the Trusts of Land and Appointment of Trustees Act 1996, s.25(1), Sched. 3, para. 4(1), (2)(a).
[5] subs. (1A) inserted by the Trusts of Land and Appointment of Trustees Act 1996, s.25(1), Sched. 3, para. 4(1), (2)(b).
[6] Words substituted by the Trusts of Land and Appointment of Trustees Act 1996, s.25(1), Sched. 3, para. 4(1), (2)(c).
[7] Words substituted by the Trusts of Land and Appointment of Trustees Act 1996, s.25(1), Sched. 3, para. 4(1), (2)(c).
[8] Words substituted by the Law of Property (Amendment) Act 1926, s.7, Sched.
[9] Words substituted by the Trusts of Land and Appointment of Trustees Act 1996, s.25(1), Sched. 3, para. 4(1), (2)(c).
[10] Words substituted by the Law of Property (Amendment) Act 1926, s.7, Sched.

(i) Any equitable interest protected by a deposit of documents relating to the legal estate affected;
(ii) The benefit of any covenant or agreement restrictive of the user of land;
(iii) Any easement, liberty, or privilege over or affecting land and being merely an equitable interest (in this Act referred to as an "equitable easement");
(iv) The benefit of any contract (in this Act referred to as an "estate contract") to convey or create a legal estate, including a contract conferring either expressly or by statutory implication a valid option to purchase, a right of pre-emption, or any other like right;
(v) Any equitable interest protected by registration under the Land Charges Act 1925[11] other than—
(a) an annuity within the meaning of Part II of that Act;
(b) a limited owner's charge or a general equitable charge within the meaning of that Act.

(4) Subject to the protection afforded by this section to the purchaser of a legal estate, nothing contained in this section shall deprive a person entitled to an equitable charge of any of his rights or remedies for enforcing the same.

(5) So far as regards the following interests, created before the commencement of this Act (which accordingly are not within the provisions of the Land Charges Act 1925[12]), namely—
(a) the benefit of any covenant or agreement restrictive of the user of the land;
(b) any equitable easement;
(c) the interest under a puisne mortgage within the meaning of the Land Charges Act 1925[13], unless and until acquired under a transfer made after the commencement of this Act;
(d) the benefit of an estate contract, unless and until the same is acquired under a conveyance made after the commencement of this Act;

a purchaser of a legal estate shall only take subject thereto if he has notice thereof, and the same are not overreached under the provisions contained or in the manner referred to in this section.

Manner of giving effect to equitable interests and powers

9–003 **3.**—(1) All equitable interests and powers in or over land shall be enforceable against the estate owner of the legal estate affected in manner following (that is to say):—
(a) Where the legal estate affected is settled land, the tenant for life or statutory owner shall be bound to give effect to the equitable interests and powers in manner provided by the Settled Land Act 1925;
[...][14]
(c) [In any other case][15], the estate owner shall be bound to give effect to the equitable interests and powers affecting his estate of which he has notice according to their respective priorities. This provision does not affect the priority or powers of a legal mortgagee, or the powers of personal representatives for purposes of administration.

[11] Now the Land Charges Act 1972, *post*, para. 31–001.
[12] Now the Land Charges Act 1972, *post*, para. 31–001.
[13] Now the Land Charges Act 1972, *post*, para. 31–001.
[14] Para. (b) repealed by the Trusts of Land and Appointment of Trustees Act 1996, s.25(2), Sched. 4.
[15] Words substituted by the Trusts of Land and Appointment of Trustees Act 1996, s.25(1), Sched. 3, para. 4(1), (3).

(2) [*Repealed by the Trusts of Land and Appointment of Trustees Act 1996, s.25(2), Sched. 4.*]

(3) Where, by reason [. . .][16] of an equitable right of entry taking effect, or for any other reason, a person becomes entitled to require a legal estate to be vested in him, then and in any such case the estate owner whose estate is affected shall be bound to convey or create such legal estate as the case may require.

(4) If any question arises whether any and what legal estate ought to be transferred or created as aforesaid, any person interested may apply to the court for directions in the manner provided by this Act.

(5) If the [. . .][17] estate owners refuse or neglect for one month after demand to transfer or create any such legal estate, or if by reason of their being out of the United Kingdom or being unable to be found, or by reason of the dissolution of a corporation, or for any other reason, the court is satisfied that the transaction cannot otherwise be effected, or cannot be effected without undue delay or expense, the court may, on the application of any person interested, make a vesting order transferring or creating a legal estate in the manner provided by this Act.

(6) This section does not affect a purchaser of a legal estate taking free from an equitable interest or power.

[(7) The county court has jurisdiction under this section where the land which is to be dealt with in the court does not exceed [£30,000][18] in capital value [. . .][19].][20]

Creation and disposition of equitable interests

4.—(1) Interests in land validly created or arising after the commencement of this Act, which are not capable of subsisting as legal estates, shall take effect as equitable interests, and, save as otherwise expressly provided by statute, interests in land which under the Statute of Uses or otherwise could before the commencement of this Act have been created as legal interests, shall be capable of being created as equitable interests: **9–004**

Provided that, after the commencement of this Act (and save as hereinafter expressly enacted), an equitable interest in land shall only be capable of being validly created in any case in which an equivalent equitable interest in property real or personal could have been validly created before such commencement.

(2) All rights and interests in land may be disposed of, including—

(a) a contingent, executory or future equitable interest in any land, or a possibility coupled with an interest in any land, whether or not the object of the gift or limitation of such interest or possibility be ascertained;

(b) a right of entry, into or upon land whether immediate or future, and whether vested or contingent.

(3) All rights of entry affecting a legal estate which are exercisable on condition broken or for any other reason may after the commencement of this Act, be made exercisable by any person and the persons deriving title under him, but, in regard to an estate in fee simple (not being a rentcharge held for a

[16] Words repealed by the Reverter of Sites Act 1987, s.8(2), (3), Sched.

[17] Words repealed by the Trusts of Land and Appointment of Trustees Act 1996, s.25(2), Sched. 4.

[18] Figure substituted by the High Court and County Courts Jurisdiction Order 1991 (S.I. 1991 No. 724), art. 2(8), Sched.

[19] Words repealed by the High Court and County Courts Jurisdiction Order 1991 (S.I. 1991 No. 724), art. 2(8), Sched.

[20] subs. (7) added by the County Courts Act 1984, s.148(1), Sched. 2, Pt. II, para. 2(1), (3). For the jurisdiction of the county court by agreement, see the County Courts Act 1984, s.24, *post*, para. 42–003.

legal estate) only within the period authorised by the rule relating to perpetuities.

Satisfied terms, whether created out of freehold or leasehold land to cease

9–005 **5.**—(1) Where the purposes of a term of years created or limited at any time out of freehold land, become satisfied either before or after the commencement of this Act (whether or not that term either by express declaration or by construction of law becomes attendant upon the freehold reversion) it shall merge in the reversion expectant thereon and shall cease accordingly.

(2) Where the purposes of a term of years created or limited, at any time, out of leasehold land, become satisfied after the commencement of this Act, that term shall merge in the reversion expectant thereon and shall cease accordingly.

(3) Where the purposes are satisfied only as respects part of the land comprised in a term, this section shall have effect as if a separate term had been created in regard to that part of the land.

Saving of lessors' and lessees' covenants

9–006 **6.**—(1) Nothing in this Part of this Act affects prejudicially the right to enforce any lessor's or lessee's covenants, agreements or conditions (including a valid option to purchase or right of pre-emption over the reversion), contained in any such instrument as is in this section mentioned, the benefit or burden of which runs with the reversion or the term.

(2) This section applies where the covenant, agreement or condition is contained in any instrument—

(a) creating a term of years absolute, or
(b) varying the rights of the lessor or lessee under the instrument creating the term.

Saving of certain legal estates and statutory powers

9–007 **7.**—(1) A fee simple which, by virtue of the Lands Clauses Acts, [. . .][21] or any similar statute, is liable to be divested, is for the purposes of this Act a fee simple absolute, and remains liable to be divested as if this Act had not been passed [and a fee simple subject to a legal or equitable right of entry or re-entry is for the purposes of this Act a fee simple absolute][22].

(2) A fee simple vested in a corporation which is liable to determine by reason of the dissolution of the corporation is, for the purposes of this Act, a fee simple absolute.

(3) The provisions of—

[. . .][23]

(b) the Friendly Societies Act 1896[24] in regard to land to which that Act applies;
(c) any other statutes conferring special facilities or prescribing special modes (whether by way of registered memorial or otherwise) for disposing of or acquiring land, or providing for the vesting (by conveyance or otherwise) of the land in trustees or any person, or the

[21] Words repealed by the Reverter of Sites Act 1987, s.8(2), (3), Sched.
[22] Words added by the Law of Property (Amendment) Act 1926, s.7, Sched.
[23] Para. (a) repealed by the Criminal Justice Act 1948, s.83, Sched. 10.
[24] Now the Friendly Societies Act 1974.

holder for the time being of an office or any corporation sole or aggregate (including the Crown);

shall remain in full force.

[...][25]

(4) Where any such power for disposing of or creating a legal estate is exercisable by a person who is not the estate owner, the power shall, when practicable, be exercised in the name and on behalf of the estate owner.

Saving of certain legal powers to lease

8.—(1) All leases or tenancies at a rent for a term of years absolute authorised to be granted by a mortgagor or mortgagee or by the Settled Land Act 1925 or any other statute (whether or not extended by any instrument) may be granted in the name and on behalf of the estate owner by the person empowered to grant the same, whether being an estate owner or not, with the same effect and priority as if this Part of this Act had not been passed; but this section does not (except as respects the usual qualified covenant for quiet enjoyment) authorise any person granting a lease in the name of an estate owner to impose any personal liability on him. **9–008**

(2) Where a rentcharge is held for a legal estate, the owner thereof may under the statutory power or under any corresponding power, create a legal term of years absolute for securing or compelling payment of the same; but in other cases terms created under any such power shall, unless and until the estate owner of the land charged gives legal effect to the transaction, take effect only as equitable interests.

Vesting orders and dispositions of legal estates operating as conveyances by an estate owner

9.—(1) Every such order, declaration, or conveyance as is hereinafter mentioned, namely— **9–009**

(a) every vesting order made by any court or other competent authority;

(b) every vesting declaration (express or implied) under any statutory power;

(c) every vesting instrument made by the trustees of a settlement or other persons under the provisions of the Settled Land Act 1925;

(d) every conveyance by a person appointed for the purpose under an order of the court or authorised under any statutory power to convey in the name or on behalf of an estate owner;

(e) every conveyance made under any power reserved or conferred by this Act,

which is made or executed for the purpose of vesting, conveying, or creating a legal estate, shall operate to convey or create the legal estate disposed of in like manner as if the same had been a conveyance executed by the estate owner of the legal estate to which the order, declaration, vesting instrument, or conveyance relates.

(2) Where the order, declaration, or conveyance is made in favour of a purchaser, the provisions of this Act relating to a conveyance of a legal estate to a purchaser shall apply thereto.

[25] Words repealed by the Trusts of Land and Appointment of Trustees Act 1996, s.25(2), Sched. 4.

(3) The provisions of the Trustee Act 1925 relating to vesting orders and orders appointing a person to convey shall apply to all vesting orders authorised to be made by this Part of this Act.

Title to be shown to legal estates

9–010 **10.**—(1) Where title is shown to a legal estate in land, it shall be deemed not necessary or proper to include in the abstract of title an instrument relating only to interests or powers which will be over-reached by the conveyance of the estate to which title is being shown; but nothing in this Part of this Act affects the liability of any person to disclose an equitable interest or power which will not be so over-reached, or to furnish an abstract of any instrument creating or affecting the same.

(2)[26] A solicitor delivering an abstract framed in accordance with this Part of this Act shall not incur any liability on account of an omission to include therein an instrument which, under this section, is to be deemed not necessary or proper to be included, nor shall any liability be implied by reason of the inclusion of any such instrument.

11. [*Repealed by the Law of Property Act 1969, s.16(2), Sched. 2, Pt. I.*]

Limitation and Prescription Acts

9–011 **12.** Nothing in this Part of this Act affects the operation of any statute, or of the general law for the limitation of actions or proceedings relating to land or with reference to the acquisition of easements or rights over or in respect of land.

Effect of possession of documents

9–012 **13.** This Act shall not prejudicially affect the right or interest of any person arising out of or consequent on the possession by him of any documents relating to a legal estate in land, nor affect any question arising out of or consequent upon any omission to obtain or any other absence of possession by any person of any documents relating to a legal estate in land.

Interests of persons in possession

9–013 **14.** This Part of this Act shall not prejudicially affect the interest of any person in possession or in actual occupation of land to which he may be entitled in right of such possession or occupation.

Presumption that parties are of full age

9–014 **15.** The persons expressed to be parties to any conveyance shall, until the contrary is proved, be presumed to be of full age at the date thereof.

[26] In s.10(2) (and in ss.48 and 182) any reference to a solicitor is to be construed as including a reference to a licensed conveyancer or to a body recognised by the Council for Licensed Conveyancers as suitable to provide conveyancing services (Administration of Justice Act 1985, ss.32, 34(2)), or to an institution or practitioner recognised by the Lord Chancellor as suitable to provide such services (Building Societies Act 1982, s.124, Sched. 21).

16–18. [*Repealed by the Finance Act 1975, ss.52(2), 59(5), Sched. 13, Pt. I.*]

Infants and Lunatics

19. [*Repealed by the Trusts of Land and Appointment of Trustees Act 1996, s.25(2), Sched. 4.*]

Infants not to be appointed trustees

20. The appointment of an infant to be a trustee in relation to any settlement or trust shall be void, but without prejudice to the power to appoint a new trustee to fill the vacancy. **9–015**

Receipts by married infants

21. A married infant shall have power to give valid receipts for all income (including statutory accumulations of income made during the minority) to which the infant may be entitled in like manner as if the infant were of full age. **9–016**

[Conveyances on behalf of persons suffering from mental disorder and as to land held by them [in trust][27]

22.—(1) Where a legal estate in land (whether settled or not) is vested in a person suffering from mental disorder, either solely or jointly with any other person or persons, his receiver or (if no receiver is acting for him) any person authorised in that behalf shall, under an order of the authority having jurisdiction under [Part VII of the Mental Health Act 1983][28] or of the court, or under any statutory power, make or concur in making all requisite dispositions for conveying or creating a legal estate in his name and on his behalf. **9–017**

(2) If land [subject to a trust of land][29] is vested, either solely or jointly with any other person or persons, in a person who is incapable, by reason of mental disorder, of exercising his functions as trustee, a new trustee shall be appointed in the place of that person, or he shall be otherwise discharged from the trust, before the legal estate is dealt with [by the trustees][30].

[(3) Subsection (2) of this section does not prevent a legal estate being dealt with without the appointment of a new trustee, or the discharge of the incapable trustee, at a time when the donee of an enduring power (within the meaning of the Enduring Powers of Attorney Act 1985) is entitled to act for the incapable trustee in the dealing.][31]][32]

23. [*Repealed by the Trusts of Land and Appointment of Trustees Act 1996, s.25(2), Sched. 4.*]

[27] Words substituted by the Trusts of Land and Appointment of Trustees Act 1996, s.25(1), Sched. 3, para. 4(1), (6).
[28] Words substituted by the Mental Health Act 1983, s.148(1), Sched. 4, para. 5(a).
[29] Words substituted by the Trusts of Land and Appointment of Trustees Act 1996, s.25(1), Sched. 3, para. 4(1), (6)(a)
[30] Words substituted by the Trusts of Land and Appointment of Trustees Act 1996, s.25(1), Sched. 3, para. 4(1), (6)(a)
[31] subs. (3) added by the Trustee Delegation Act 1999, s.9.
[32] s.22 substituted by the Mental Health Act 1959, s.149(1), Sched. 7, Pt. I.

[Trusts of land

Appointment of trustees of land

9–018 **24.**—(1) The persons having power to appoint new trustees of land shall be bound to appoint the same persons (if any) who are for the time being trustees of any trust of the proceeds of sale of the land.

(2) A purchaser shall not be concerned to see that subsection (1) of this section has been complied with.

(3) This section applies whether the trust of land and the trust of proceeds of sale are created, or arise, before or after the commencement of this Act.][33]

25–26. [*Repealed by the Trusts of Land and Appointment of Trustees Act 1996, s.25(2), Sched. 4.*]

Purchaser not to be concerned with the trusts of the proceeds of sale which are to be paid to two or more trustees or to a trust corporation

9–019 **27.**—[(1) A purchaser of a legal estate from trustees of land shall not be concerned with the trusts affecting the land, the net income of the land or the proceeds of sale of the land whether or not those trusts are declared by the same instrument as that by which the trust of land is created.][34]

[(2) Notwithstanding anything to the contrary in the instrument (if any) creating a [trust][35] of land or in [any trust affecting the net proceeds of sale of the land if it is sold][36], the proceeds of sale or other capital money shall not be paid to or applied by the direction of fewer than two persons as [trustees][37], except where the trustee is a trust corporation, but this subsection does not affect the right of a sole personal representative as such to give valid receipts for, or direct the application of, proceeds of sale or other capital money, nor, except where capital money arises of the transaction, render it necessary to have more than one trustee.][38]

28–30. [*Repealed by the Trusts of Land and Appointment of Trustees Act 1996, s.25(2), Sched. 4.*]

[Trust][39] of mortgaged property where right of redemption is barred

9–020 **31.**—(1) Where any property, vested in trustees by way of security, becomes, by virtue of the statutes of limitation, or of an order for foreclosure or otherwise, discharged from the right of redemption, it shall be held by them [in trust—

33 s.24 substituted by the Trusts of Land and Appointment of Trustees Act 1996, s.25(1), Sched. 3, para. 4(1), (7).
34 subs. (1) substituted by the Trusts of Land and Appointment of Trustees Act 1996, s.25(1), Sched. 3, para. 4(1), (8)(a).
35 Word substituted by the Trusts of Land and Appointment of Trustees Act 1996, s.25(1), Sched. 3, para. 4(1), (8)(b).
36 Words substituted by the Trusts of Land and Appointment of Trustees Act 1996, s.25(1), Sched. 3, para. 4(1), (8)(b).
37 Word substituted by the Trusts of Land and Appointment of Trustees Act 1996, s.25(1), Sched. 3, para. 4(1), (8)(b).
38 subs. (2) substituted by the Law of Property (Amendment) Act 1926, s.7, Sched.
39 Word substituted by the Trusts of Land and Appointment of Trustees Act 1996, s.5(1), Sched. 2, para. 1(1), (6).

(a) to apply the income from the property in the same manner as interest paid on the mortgage debt would have been applicable; and
(b) if the property is sold, to apply the net proceeds of sale, after payment of costs and expenses, in the same manner as repayment of the mortgage debt would have been applicable.][40]

[(2) Subsection (1) of this section][41] operates without prejudice to any rule of law relating to the apportionment of capital and income between tenant for life and remainderman.

(3) [*Repealed by the Trusts of Land and Appointment of Trustees Act 1996, ss.5(1), 25(2), Sched. 2, para. 1(1), (4), Sched. 4.*]

[(4) Where—
(a) the mortgage money is capital money for the purposes of the Settled Land Act 1925;
(b) land other than any forming the whole or part of the property mentioned in subsection (1) of this section is, or is deemed to be, subject to the settlement; and
(c) the tenant for life or statutory owner requires the trustees to execute with respect to land forming the whole or part of that property a vesting deed such as would have been required in relation to the land if it had been acquired on a purchase with capital money,

the trustees shall execute such a vesting deed.][42]

(5) This section applies whether the right of redemption was discharged before or after the first day of January, nineteen hundred and twelve, but has effect without prejudice to any dealings or arrangements made before that date.

32. [*Repealed by the Trusts of Land and Appointment of Trustees Act 1996, ss.5(1), 25(2), Sched. 2, para. 2(1), Sched. 4.*]

Application of Part I to personal representatives

33. The provisions of this Part of this Act relating to [trustees of land][43] apply **9–021**
to personal representatives holding [land in trust][44], but without prejudice to their rights and powers for purposes of administration.

Undivided Shares and Joint Ownership

Effect of future dispositions to tenants in common

34.—(1) An undivided share in land shall not be capable of being created **9–022**
except as provided by the Settled Land Act 1925 or as hereinafter mentioned.

(2) Where, after the commencement of this Act, land is expressed to be conveyed to any persons in undivided shares and those persons are of full age, the conveyance shall (notwithstanding anything to the contrary in this Act) operate as if the land had been expressed to be conveyed to the grantees, or, if

---

[40] Words substituted by the Trusts of Land and Appointment of Trustees Act 1996, s.5(1), Sched. 2, para. 1(1), (2).
[41] Words substituted by the Trusts of Land and Appointment of Trustees Act 1996, s.5(1), Sched. 2, para. 1(1), (3).
[42] subs. (4) substituted by the Trusts of Land and Appointment of Trustees Act 1996, s.5(1), Sched. 2, para. 1(1), (5).
[43] Words substituted by the Trusts of Land and Appointment of Trustees Act 1996, s.25(1), Sched. 3, para. 4(1), (9).
[44] Words substituted by the Trusts of Land and Appointment of Trustees Act 1996, s.25(1), Sched. 3, para. 4(1), (9).

there are more than four grantees, to the four first named in the conveyance, as joint tenants [in trust for the persons interested in the land][45]:

Provided that, where the conveyance is made by way of mortgage the land shall vest in the grantees or such four of them as aforesaid for a term of years absolute (as provided by this Act) as joint tenants subject to cesser on redemption in like manner as if the mortgage money had belonged to them on a joint account, but without prejudice to the beneficial interests in the mortgage money and interest.

(3) A devise bequest or testamentary appointment, coming into operation after the commencement of this Act, of land to two or more persons in undivided shares shall operate as a devise bequest or appointment of the land to […][46] the personal representatives of the testator, and […][47] (but without prejudice to the rights and powers of the personal representatives for purposes of administration) [in trust for the persons interested in the land][48].

[(3A) In subsections (2) and (3) of this section references to the persons interested in the land include persons interested as trustees or personal representatives (as well as persons beneficially interested).][49]

(4) [*Repealed by the Trusts of Land and Appointment of Trustees Act 1996, ss.5(1), 25(2), Sched. 2, para. 3(1), (5), Sched. 4.*]

35. [*Repealed by the Trusts of Land and Appointment of Trustees Act 1996, s.25(2), Sched. 4.*]

Joint tenancies

9–023 **36.**—(1) Where a legal estate (not being settled land) is beneficially limited to or held in trust for any persons as joint tenants, the same shall be held [in trust][50], in like manner as if the persons beneficially entitled were tenants in common, but not so as to sever their joint tenancy in equity.

(2)[51] No severance of a joint tenancy of a legal estate, so as to create a tenancy in common in land, shall be permissible, whether by operation of law or otherwise, but this subsection does not affect the right of a joint tenant to release his interest to the other joint tenants, or the right to sever a joint tenancy in an equitable interest whether or not the legal estate is vested in the joint tenants:

Provided that, where a legal estate (not being settled land) is vested in joint tenants beneficially, and any tenant desires to sever the joint tenancy in equity, he shall give to the other joint tenants a notice in writing of such desire or do such other acts or things as would, in the case of personal estate, have been effectual to sever the tenancy in equity, and thereupon [the land shall be held in

[45] Words substituted by the Trusts of Land and Appointment of Trustees Act 1996, s.5(1), Sched. 2, para. 3(1), (2).
[46] Words repealed by the Trusts of Land and Appointment of Trustees Act 1996, ss.5(1), 25(2), Sched. 2, para. 3(1), (3)(a), Sched. 4.
[47] Words repealed by the Trusts of Land and Appointment of Trustees Act 1996, ss.5(1), 25(2), Sched. 2, para. 3(1), (3)(a), Sched. 4.
[48] Words substituted by the Trusts of Land and Appointment of Trustees Act 1996, s.5(1), Sched. 2, para. 3(1), (3)(b).
[49] subs. (3A) inserted by the Trusts of Land and Appointment of Trustees Act 1996, s.5(1), Sched. 2, para. 3(1), (4).
[50] Words substituted by the Trusts of Land and Appointment of Trustees Act 1996, s.5(1), Sched. 2, para. 4(1), (2).
[51] Extended retrospectively with regard to assumptions on the sale of land by the survivor of joint tenants: see the Law of Property (Joint Tenants) Act 1964, ss.1, 2, *post*, para. 22–002.

trust on terms][52] which would have been requisite for giving effect to the beneficial interests if there had been an actual severance.

[Nothing in this Act affects the right of a survivor of joint tenants, who is solely and beneficially interested, to deal with his legal estate as if it were not held [in trust][53].][54]

(3) Without prejudice to the right of a joint tenant to release his interest to the other joint tenants no severance of a mortgage term or trust estate so as to create a tenancy in common, shall be permissible.

Rights of husband and wife

37. A husband and wife shall, for all purposes of acquisition of any interest in property, under a disposition made or coming into operation after the commencement of this Act, be treated as two persons. **9–024**

Party structures

38.—(1) Where under a disposition or other arrangement which, if a holding in undivided shares had been permissible, would have created a tenancy in common, a wall or other structure is or is expressed to be made a party wall or structure, that structure shall be and remain severed vertically as between the respective owners, and the owner of each part shall have such rights to support and user over the rest of the structure as may be requisite for conferring rights corresponding to those which would have subsisted if a valid tenancy in common had been created. **9–025**

(2) Any person interested may, in case of dispute, apply to the court for an order declaring the rights and interests under this section of the persons interested in any such party structure, and the court may make such order as it thinks fit.

Transitional Provisions

Transitional provisions in First Schedule

39. For the purpose of effecting the transition from the law existing prior to the commencement of the Law of Property Act 1922 to the law enacted by that Act (as amended), the provisions set out in the First Schedule to this Act shall have effect— **9–026**

(1) for converting existing legal estates, interests and charges not capable under the said Act of taking effect as legal interests into equitable interests;
(2) for discharging, getting in or vesting outstanding legal estates;
(3) for making provision with respect to legal estates vested in infants;
(4) for subjecting land held in undivided shares to [trusts][55];
(5) for dealing with party structures and open spaces held in common;
(6) for converting tenancies by entireties into joint tenancies;

[52] Words substituted by the Trusts of Land and Appointment of Trustees Act 1996, s.5(1), Sched. 2, para. 4(1), (3).
[53] Words substituted by the Trusts of Land and Appointment of Trustees Act 1996, s.5(1), Sched. 2, para. 4(1), (3).
[54] Words added by the Law of Property (Amendment) Act 1926, s.7, Sched.
[55] Word substituted by the Trusts of Land and Appointment of Trustees Act 1996, s.25(1), Sched. 3, para. 4(1), (10).

(7) for converting existing freehold mortgages into mortgages by demise;
(8) for converting existing leasehold mortgages into mortgages by sub-demise.

PART II

CONTRACTS, CONVEYANCES AND OTHER INSTRUMENTS

Contracts

40. [*Repealed by the Law of Property (Miscellaneous Provisions) Act 1989, ss.2(8), 4, Sched. 2.*][56]

Stipulations not of the essence of a contract

9–027 **41.** Stipulations in a contract, as to time or otherwise, which according to rules of equity are not deemed to be or to have become of the essence of the contract, are also construed and have effect at law in accordance with the same rules.

Provisions as to contracts

9–028 **42.**—(1) A stipulation that a purchaser of a legal estate in land shall accept a title made with the concurrence of any person entitled to an equitable interest shall be void, if a title can be made discharged from the equitable interest without such concurrence—
(a) under a [trust of land][57]; or
(b) under this Act, or the Settled Land Act 1925, or any other statute.

(2) A stipulation that a purchaser of a legal estate in land shall pay or contribute towards the costs of or incidental to—
(a) obtaining a vesting order, or the appointment of trustees of a settlement, or the appointment of trustees of [land][58]; or
(b) the preparation stamping or execution of a conveyance [in trust][59], or of a vesting instrument for bringing into force the provisions of the Settled Land Act 1925;

shall be void.

(3) A stipulation contained in any contract for sale or exchange of land made after the commencement of this Act, to the effect that an outstanding legal estate is to be traced or got in by or at the expense of a purchaser or that no objection is to be taken on account of an outstanding legal estate, shall be void.

(4) If the subject matter of any contract for the sale or exchange of land—
(i) is a mortgage term and the vendor has power to convey the fee simple in the land, or, in the case of a mortgage of a term of years absolute, the leasehold reversion affected by the mortgage, the contract shall be deemed to extend to the fee simple in the land or such leasehold reversion;

[56] See now the Law of Property (Miscellaneous Provisions) Act 1989, s.2, *post*, para. 53–002.
[57] Word(s) substituted by the Trusts of Land and Appointment of Trustees Act 1996, s.25(1), Sched. 3, para. 4(1), (11).
[58] Word substituted by the Trusts of Land and Appointment of Trustees Act 1996, s.25(1), Sched. 3, para. 4(1), (11).
[59] Words substituted by the Trusts of Land and Appointment of Trustees Act 1996, s.25(1), Sched. 3, para. 4(1), (11).

(ii) is an equitable interest capable of subsisting as a legal estate, and the vendor has power to vest such legal estate in himself or in the purchaser or to require the same to be so vested, the contract shall be deemed to extend to such legal estate;

(iii) is an entailed interest in possession and the vendor has power to vest in himself or in the purchaser the fee simple in the land, (or, if the entailed interest is an interest in a term of years absolute, such term,) or to require the same to be so vested, the contract shall be deemed to extend to the fee simple in the land or the term of years absolute.

(5) This section does not affect the right of a mortgagee of leasehold land to sell his mortgage term only if he is unable to convey or vest the leasehold reversion expectant thereon.

(6) [*Repealed by the Trusts of Land and Appointment of Trustees Act 1996, s.25(2), Sched. 4.*]

(7) Where a purchaser has power to acquire land compulsorily, and a contract, whether by virtue of a notice to treat or otherwise, is subsisting under which title can be made without payment of the compensation money into court, title shall be made in that way unless the purchaser, to avoid expense or delay or for any special reason, considers it expedient that the money should be paid into court.

(8) A vendor shall not have any power to rescind a contract by reason only of the enforcement of any right under this section.

(9) This section only applies in favour of a purchaser for money or money's worth.

Rights protected by registration

43.—(1) Where a purchaser of a legal estate is entitled to acquire the same discharged from an equitable interest which is protected by registration as a pending action, annuity, writ, order, deed of arrangement or land charge, and which will not be over-reached by the conveyance to him, he may notwithstanding any stipulation to the contrary, require— **9–029**

(a) that the registration shall be cancelled; or

(b) that the person entitled to the equitable interest shall concur in the conveyance;

and in either case free of expense to the purchaser.

(2) Where that registration cannot be cancelled or the person entitled to the equitable interest refuses to concur in the conveyance, this section does not affect the right of any person to rescind the contract.

Statutory commencement of title

44.—(1) After the commencement of this Act thirty years[60] shall be substituted for forty years as the period of commencement of title which a purchaser of land may require; nevertheless earlier title than thirty years may be required in cases similar to those in which earlier title than forty years might immediately before the commencement of this Act be required. **9–030**

(2) Under a contract to grant or assign a term of years, whether derived or to

[60] s.44 has effect, in its application to contracts made after 1969, as if it specified 15 years instead of 30 years as the period of commencement of title which may be required: Law of Property Act 1969, s.23, *post*, para. 27–001.

be derived out of freehold or leasehold land, the intended lessee or assign shall not be entitled to call for the title to the freehold.

(3) Under a contract to sell and assign a term of years derived out of a leasehold interest in land, the intended assign shall not have the right to call for the title to the leasehold reversion.

(4) On a contract to grant a lease for a term of years to be derived out of a leasehold interest, with a leasehold reversion, the intended lessee shall not have the right to call for the title to that reversion.

[(4A) Subsections (2) and (4) of this section do not apply to a contract to grant a term of years if the grant will be an event within section 4(1) of the Land Registration Act 2002 (events which trigger compulsory first registration of title).][61]

(5) Where by reason of any of [subsections (2) to (4) of this section][62] an intending lessee or assign is not entitled to call for the title to the freehold or to a leasehold reversion, as the case may be, he shall not, where the contract is made after the commencement of this Act, be deemed to be affected with notice of any matter or thing of which, if he had contracted that such title should be furnished, he might have had notice.

(6) Where land of copyhold or customary tenure has been converted into freehold by enfranchisement, then, under a contract to sell and convey the freehold, the purchaser shall not have the right to call for the title to make the enfranchisement.

(7) Where the manorial incidents formerly affecting any land have been extinguished, then, under a contract to sell and convey the freehold, the purchaser shall not have the right to call for the title of the person entering into any compensation agreement or giving a receipt for the compensation money to enter into such agreement or to give such receipt, and shall not be deemed to be affected with notice of any matter or thing of which, if he had contracted that such title should be furnished, he might have had notice.

(8) A purchaser shall not be deemed to be or ever to have been affected with notice of any matter or thing of which, if he had investigated the title or made enquiries in regard to matters prior to the period of commencement of title fixed by this Act, or by any other statute, or by any rule of law, he might have had notice, unless he actually makes such investigation or enquiries.

(9) Where a lease whether made before or after the commencement of this Act, is made under a power contained in a settlement, will, Act of Parliament, or other instrument, any preliminary contract for or relating to the lease shall not, for the purpose of the deduction of title to an intended assign, form part of the title, or evidence of the title, to the lease.

(10) This section, save where otherwise expressly provided, applies to contracts for sale whether made before or after the commencement of this Act, and applies to contracts for exchange in like manner as to contracts for sale, save that it applies only to contracts for exchange made after such commencement.

(11) This section applies only if and so far as a contrary intention is not expressed in the contract.

[(12) Nothing in this section applies in relation to registered land or to a term of years to be derived out of registered land.][63]

[61] subs. (4A) inserted by the Land Registration Act 2002, s.133, Sched. 11, para. 2(1), (2).
[62] Words substituted by the Land Registration Act 2002, s.133, Sched. 11, para. 2(1), (3).
[63] subs. (12) added by the Land Registration Act 2002, s.133, Sched. 11, para. 2(1), (4).

Other statutory conditions of sale

45.—(1) A purchaser of any property shall not— **9–031**

(a) require the production, or any abstract or copy, of any deed, will, or other document, dated or made before the time prescribed by law, or stipulated, for the commencement of the title, even though the same creates a power subsequently exercised by an instrument abstracted in the abstract furnished to the purchaser; or

(b) require any information, or make any requisition, objection or inquiry, with respect to any such deed, will, or document, or the title prior to that time, notwithstanding that any such deed, will, or other document, or that prior title, is recited, agreed to be produced, or noticed;

and he shall assume, unless the contrary appears, that the recitals, contained in the abstracted instruments, of any deed, will, or other document, forming part of that prior title, are correct, and give all the material contents of the deed, will, or other document so recited, and that every document so recited was duly executed by all necessary parties, and perfected, if and as required, by fine, recovery, acknowledgment, enrolment, or otherwise:

Provided that this subsection shall not deprive a purchaser of the right to require the production, or an abstract or copy of—

(i) any power of attorney under which any abstracted document is executed; or

(ii) any document creating or disposing of an interest, power or obligation which is not shown to have ceased or expired, and subject to which any part of the property is disposed of by an abstracted document; or

(iii) any document creating any limitation or trust by reference to which any part of the property is disposed of by an abstracted document.

(2) Where land sold is held by lease (other than an under-lease), the purchaser shall assume, unless the contrary appears, that the lease was duly granted; and, on production of the receipt for the last payment due for rent under the lease before the date of actual completion of the purchase, he shall assume, unless the contrary appears, that all the covenants and provisions of the lease have been duly performed and observed up to the date of actual completion of the purchase.

(3) Where land sold is held by under-lease, the purchaser shall assume, unless the contrary appears, that the under-lease and every superior lease were duly granted; and, on production of the receipt for the last payment due for rent under the under-lease before the date of actual completion of the purchase, he shall assume, unless the contrary appears, that all the covenants and provisions of the under-lease have been duly performed and observed up to the date of actual completion of the purchase, and further that all rent due under every superior lease, and all the covenants and provisions of every superior lease, have been paid and duly performed and observed up to that date.

(4) On a sale of any property, the following expenses shall be borne by the purchaser where he requires them to be incurred for the purpose of verifying the abstract or any other purpose, that is to say—

(a) the expenses of the production and inspection of all Acts of Parliament, inclosure awards, records, proceedings of courts, court rolls, deeds, wills, probates, letters of administration, and other documents, not in the possession of the vendor or his mortgagee or trustee, and the expenses of all journeys incidental to such production or inspection; and

(b) the expenses of searching for, procuring, making, verifying, and producing all certificates, declarations, evidences, and information not in the possession of the vendor or his mortgagee or trustee, and all attested, stamped, office, or other copies or abstracts of, or extracts from, any Acts of Parliament or other documents aforesaid, not in the possession of the vendor or his mortgagee or trustee;

and where the vendor or his mortgagee or trustee retains possession of any document, the expenses of making any copy thereof, attested or unattested, which a purchaser requires to be delivered to him, shall be borne by that purchaser.

(5) On a sale of any property in lots, a purchaser of two or more lots, held wholly or partly under the same title, shall not have a right to more than one abstract of the common title, except at his own expense.

(6) Recitals, statements, and descriptions of facts, matters, and parties contained in deeds, instruments, Acts of Parliament, or statutory declarations, twenty years old at the date of the contract, shall, unless and except so far as they may be proved to be inaccurate, be taken to be sufficient evidence of the truth of such facts, matters, and descriptions.

(7) The inability of a vendor to furnish a purchaser with an acknowledgment of his right to production and delivery of copies of documents of title or with a legal covenant to produce and furnish copies of documents of title shall not be an objection to title in case the purchaser will, on the completion of the contract, have an equitable right to the production of such documents.

(8) Such acknowledgments of the right of production or covenants for production and such undertakings or covenants for safe custody of documents as the purchaser can and does require shall be furnished or made at his expense, and the vendor shall bear the expense of perusal and execution on behalf of and by himself, and on behalf of and by necessary parties other than the purchaser.

(9) A vendor shall be entitled to retain documents of title where—

(a) he retains any part of the land to which the documents relate; or

(b) the document consists of a trust instrument or other instrument creating a trust which is still subsisting, or an instrument relating to the appointment or discharge of a trustee of a subsisting trust.

(10) This section applies to contracts for sale made before or after the commencement of this Act, and applies to contracts for exchange in like manner as to contracts for sale, except that it applies only to contracts for exchange made after such commencement:

Provided that this section shall apply subject to any stipulation or contrary intention expressed in the contract.

(11) Nothing in this section shall be construed as binding a purchaser to complete his purchase in any case where, on a contract made independently of this section, and containing stipulations similar to the provisions of this section, or any of them, specific performance of the contract would not be enforced against him by the court.

Forms of contracts and conditions of sale

9–032 **46.** The Lord Chancellor may from time to time prescribe and publish forms of contracts and conditions of sale of land, and the forms so prescribed shall, subject to any modification, or any stipulation or intention to the contrary, expressed in the correspondence, apply to contracts by correspondence, and may, but only by express reference thereto, be made to apply to any other cases for which the forms are made available.

Application of insurance money on completion of a sale or exchange

47.—(1) Where after the date of any contract for sale or exchange of property, money becomes payable under any policy of insurance maintained by the vendor in respect of any damage to or destruction of property included in the contract, the money shall, on completion of the contract, be held or receivable by the vendor on behalf of the purchaser and paid by the vendor to the purchaser on completion of the sale or exchange, or so soon thereafter as the same shall be received by the vendor. **9–033**

(2) This section applies only to contracts made after the commencement of this Act, and has effect subject to—

(a) any stipulation to the contrary contained in the contract,
(b) any requisite consents of the insurers,
(c) the payment by the purchaser of the proportionate part of the premium from the date of the contract.

(3) This section applies to a sale or exchange by an order of the court, as if—

(a) for references to the "vendor" there were substituted references to the "person bound by the order";
(b) for the reference to the completion of the contract there were substituted a reference to the payment of the purchase or equality money (if any) into court;
(c) for the reference to the date of the contract there were substituted a reference to the time when the contract becomes binding.

Stipulations preventing a purchaser, lessee or underlessee from employing his own solicitor to be void

48.[64]—(1) Any stipulation made on the sale of any interest in land after the commencement of this Act to the effect that the conveyance to, or the registration of the title of, the purchaser shall be prepared or carried out at the expense of the purchaser by a solicitor appointed by or acting for the vendor, and any stipulation which might restrict a purchaser in the selection of the solicitor to act on his behalf in relation to any interest in land agreed to be purchased, shall be void; and, if a sale is effected by demise or subdemise, then, for the purposes of this subsection, the instrument required for giving effect to the transaction shall be deemed to be a conveyance: **9–034**

Providing that nothing in this subsection shall affect any right reserved to a vendor to furnish a form of conveyance to a purchaser from which the draft can be prepared, or to charge a reasonable fee therefor, or, where a perpetual rentcharge is to be reserved as the only consideration in money or money's worth, the right of a vendor to stipulate that the draft conveyance is to be prepared by his solicitor at the expense of the purchaser.

(2) Any covenant or stipulation contained in, or entered into with reference to any lease or underlease made before or after the commencement of this Act—

(a) whereby the right of preparing, at the expense of a purchaser, any conveyance of the estate or interest of the lessee or underlessee in the

[64] See *ante*, para. 9–010, n. 93.

demised premises or in any part thereof, or of otherwise carrying out, at the expense of the purchaser, any dealing with such estate or interest, is expressed to be reserved to or vested in the lessor or underlessor or his solicitor; or

(b) which in any way restricts the right of the purchaser to have such conveyance carried out on his behalf by a solicitor appointed by him;

shall be void:

Provided that, where any covenant or stipulation is rendered void by this subsection, there shall be implied in lieu thereof a covenant or stipulation that the lessee or underlessee shall register with the lessor or his solicitor within six months from the date thereof, or as soon after the expiration of that period as may be practicable, all conveyances and devolutions (including probates or letters of administration) affecting the lease or underlease and pay a fee of one guinea in respect of each registration, and the power of entry (if any) on breach of any covenant contained in the lease or underlease shall apply and extend to the breach of any covenant so to be implied.

(3) Save where a sale is effected by demise or subdemise, this section does not affect the law relating to the preparation of a lease or underlease or the draft thereof.

(4) In this section "lease" and "underlease" include any agreement therefor or other tenancy, and "lessee" and "underlessee" and "lessor" and "underlessor" have corresponding meanings.

Applications to the court by vendor and purchaser

9–035 **49.**—(1) A vendor or purchaser of any interest in land, or their representatives respectively, may apply in a summary way to the court, in respect of any requisitions or objections, or any claim for compensation, or any other question arising out of or connected with the contract (not being a question affecting the existence or validity of the contract), and the court may make such order upon the application as to the court may appear just, and may order how and by whom all or any of the costs of and incident to the application are to be borne and paid.

(2) Where the court refuses to grant specific performance of a contract, or in any action for the return of a deposit, the court may, if it thinks fit, order the repayment of any deposit.

(3) This section applies to a contract for the sale or exchange of any interest in land.

[(4) The county court has jurisdiction under this section where the land which is to be dealt with in the court does not exceed [£30,000][65] in capital value [. . .][66].][67]

Discharge of incumbrances by the court on sales or exchanges

9–036 **50.**—(1) Where land subject to any incumbrance, whether immediately realizable or payable or not, is sold or exchanged by the court, or out of court,

[65] Figure substituted by the High Court and County Courts Jurisdiction Order 1991 (S.I. 1991 No. 724), art. 2(8), Sched.

[66] Words repealed by the High Court and County Courts Jurisdiction Order 1991 (S.I. 1991 No. 724), art. 2(8), Sched.

[67] subs. (4) added by the County Courts Act 1984, s.148(1), Sched. 2, Pt. II, para. 2(1), (3). For the jurisdiction of the county court by agreement, see the County Courts Act 1984, s.24, *post*, para. 42–003.

the court may, if it thinks fit, on the application of any party to the sale or exchange, direct or allow payment into court of such sum as is hereinafter mentioned, that is to say—

(a) in the case of an annual sum charged on the land, or of a capital sum charged on a determinable interest in the land, the sum to be paid into court shall be of such amount as, when invested in Government securities, the court considers will be sufficient, by means of the dividends thereof, to keep down or otherwise provide for that charge; and

(b) in any other case of capital money charged on the land, the sum to be paid into court shall be of an amount sufficient to meet the incumbrance and any interest due thereon;

but in either case there shall also be paid into court such additional amount as the court considers will be sufficient to meet the contingency of further costs, expenses and interest, and any other contingency, except depreciation of investments, not exceeding one-tenth part of the original amount to be paid in, unless the court for special reason thinks fit to require a larger additional amount.

(2) Thereupon, the court may, if it thinks fit, and either after or without any notice to the incumbrancer, as the court thinks fit, declare the land to be freed from the incumbrance, and make any order for conveyance, or vesting order, proper for giving effect to the sale or exchange, and give directions for the retention and investment of the money in court and for the payment or application of the income thereof.

(3) The court may declare all other land, if any, affected by the incumbrance (besides the land sold or exchanged) to be freed from the incumbrance, and this power may be exercised either after or without notice to the incumbrancer, and notwithstanding that on a previous occasion an order, relating to the same incumbrance, has been made by the court which was confined to the land then sold or exchanged.

(4) On any application under this section the court may, if it thinks fit, as respects any vendor or purchaser, dispense with the service of any notice which would otherwise be required to be served on the vendor or purchaser.

(5) After notice served on the persons interested in or entitled to the money or fund in court, the court may direct payment or transfer thereof to the persons entitled to receive or give a discharge for the same, and generally may give directions respecting the application or distribution of the capital or income thereof.

(6) This section applies to sales or exchanges whether made before or after the commencement of this Act, and to incumbrances whether created by statute or otherwise.

Conveyances and other Instruments

Lands lie in grant only

51.—(1) All lands and all interests therein lie in grant and are incapable of being conveyed by livery or livery and seisin, or by feoffment, or by bargain and sale; and a conveyance of an interest in land may operate to pass the possession or right to possession thereof, without actual entry, but subject to all prior rights thereto. **9–037**

(2) The use of the word grant is not necessary to convey land or to create any interest therein.

Conveyances to be by deed

9–038 **52.**—(1) All conveyances of land or of any interest therein are void for the purpose of conveying or creating a legal estate unless made by deed.

(2) This section does not apply to—

(a) assents by a personal representative;
(b) disclaimers made in accordance with [sections 178 to 180 or sections 315 to 319 of the Insolvency Act 1986][68], or not required to be evidenced in writing;
(c) surrenders by operation of law, including surrenders which may, by law, be effected without writing;
(d) leases or tenancies or other assurances not required by law to be made in writing;
(e) receipts [other than those falling within section 115 below][69];
(f) vesting orders of the court or other competent authority;
(g) conveyances taking effect by operation of law.

Instruments required to be in writing

9–039 **53.**—(1) Subject to the provisions hereinafter contained with respect to the creation of interests in land by parol—

(a) no interest in land can be created or disposed of except by writing signed by the person creating or conveying the same, or by his agent thereunto lawfully authorised in writing, or by will, or by operation of law;
(b) a declaration of trust respecting any land or any interest therein must be manifested and proved by some writing signed by some person who is able to declare such trust or by his will;
(c) a disposition of an equitable interest or trust subsisting at the time of the disposition, must be in writing signed by the person disposing of the same, or by his agent thereunto lawfully authorised in writing or by will.

(2) This section does not affect the creation or operation of resulting, implied or constructive trusts.

Creation of interests in land by parol

9–040 **54.**—(1) All interests in land created by parol and not put in writing and signed by the persons so creating the same, or by their agents thereunto lawfully authorised in writing, have, notwithstanding any consideration having been given for the same, the force and effect of interests at will only.

(2) Nothing in the foregoing provisions of this Part of this Act shall affect the creation by parol of leases taking effect in possession for a term not exceeding three years (whether or not the lessee is given power to extend the term) at the best rent which can be reasonably obtained without taking a fine.

Savings in regard to last two sections

9–041 **55.** Nothing in the last two foregoing sections shall—

(a) invalidate dispositions by will; or

[68] Words substituted by the Insolvency Act 1986, s.439(2), Sched. 14.
[69] Words substituted by the Law of Property (Miscellaneous Provisions) Act 1989, s.1(8) Sched. 1, para. 2.

(b) affect any interest validly created before the commencement of this Act; or
(c) affect the right to acquire an interest in land by virtue of taking possession; or
(d) affect the operation of the law relating to part performance.

Persons taking who are not parties and as to indentures

56.—(1) A person may take an immediate or other interest in land or other property, or the benefit of any condition, right of entry, covenant or agreement over or respecting land or other property, although he may not be named as a party to the conveyance or other instrument. **9–042**

(2) A deed between parties, to effect its objects, has the effect of an indenture though not indented or expressed to be an indenture.

Description of deeds

57. Any deed, whether or not being an indenture, may be described (at the commencement thereof or otherwise) as a deed simply, or as a conveyance, deed of exchange, vesting deed, trust instrument, settlement, mortgage, charge, transfer of mortgage, appointment, lease or otherwise according to the nature of the transaction intended to be effected. **9–043**

Provisions as to supplemental instruments

58. Any instrument (whether executed before or after the commencement of this Act) expressed to be supplemental to a previous instrument, shall, as far as may be, be read and have effect as if the supplemental instrument contained a full recital of the previous instrument, but this section does not operate to give any right to an abstract or production of any such previous instrument, and a purchaser may accept the same evidence that the previous instrument does not affect the title as if it had merely been mentioned in the supplemental instrument. **9–044**

Conditions and certain covenants not implied

59.—(1) An exchange or other conveyance of land made by deed after the first day of October, eighteen hundred and forty-five, does not imply any condition in law. **9–045**

(2) The word "give" or "grant" does not, in a deed made after the date last aforesaid, imply any covenant in law, save where otherwise provided by statute.

Abolition of technicalities in regard to conveyances and deeds

60.—(1) A conveyance of freehold land to any person without words of limitation, or any equivalent expression, shall pass to the grantee the fee simple or other the whole interest which the grantor had power to convey in such land, unless a contrary intention appears in the conveyance. **9–046**

(2) A conveyance of freehold land to a corporation sole by his corporate

designation without the word "successors" shall pass to the corporation the fee simple or other the whole interest which the grantor had power to convey in such land, unless a contrary intention appears in the conveyance.

(3) In a voluntary conveyance a resulting trust for the grantor shall not be implied merely by reason that the property is not expressed to be conveyed for the use or benefit of the grantee.

(4) The foregoing provisions of this section apply only to conveyances and deeds executed after the commencement of this Act:

Provided that in a deed executed after the thirty-first day of December, eighteen hundred and eighty-one, it is sufficient—

(a) In the limitation of an estate in fee simple, to use the words "in fee simple," without the word "heirs";

[...][70]

Construction of expressions used in deeds and other instruments

9–047 **61.** In all deeds, contracts, wills, orders and other instruments executed, made or coming into operation after the commencement of this Act, unless the context otherwise requires—

(a) "Month" means calendar month;
(b) "Person" includes a corporation;
(c) The singular includes the plural and vice versa;
(d) The masculine includes the feminine and vice versa.

General words implied in conveyances

9–048 **62.**[71]—(1) A conveyance of land shall be deemed to include and shall by virtue of this Act operate to convey, with the land, all buildings, erections, fixtures, commons, hedges, ditches, fences, ways, waters, watercourses, liberties, privileges, easements, rights, and advantages whatsoever, appertaining or reputed to appertain to the land, or any part thereof, or, at the time of conveyance, demised, occupied, or enjoyed with, or reputed or known as part or parcel of or appurtenant to the land or any part thereof.

(2) A conveyance of land, having houses or other buildings thereon, shall be deemed to include and shall by virtue of this Act operate to convey, with the land, houses, or other buildings, all outhouses, erections, fixtures, cellars, areas, courts, courtyards, cisterns, sewers, gutters, drains, ways, passages, lights, watercourses, liberties, privileges, easements, rights, and advantages whatsoever, appertaining or reputed to appertain to the land, houses, or other buildings conveyed, or any of them, or any part thereof, or, at the time of conveyance, demised, occupied, or enjoyed with, or reputed or known as part or parcel of or appurtenant to, the land, houses, or other buildings conveyed, or any of them, or any part thereof.

(3) A conveyance of a manor shall be deemed to include and shall by virtue of

[70] Paras (b) and (c) repealed by the Trusts of Land and Appointment of Trustees Act 1996, s.25(2), Sched. 4.

[71] s.62 is saved in relation to conveyances pursuant to the right of enfranchisement under the Leasehold Reform Act 1967 (s.10(1)) and the right to buy under Pt. V of the Housing Act 1985 (ss.139(1), 151(1), Sched. 6, Pt. I, paras 1, 7), conveyances executed for the purposes of the Leasehold Reform, Housing and Urban Development Act 1993, Pt. I, Chap. I, and leases granted back to the freeholder in accordance with s.36 of the 1993 Act (ss.34(9), 36(4), Sched. 7, para. 2(1), Sched. 9, Pt. IV, para. 9).

this Act operate to convey, with the manor, all pastures, feedings, wastes, warrens, commons, mines, minerals, quarries, furzes, trees, woods, underwoods, coppices, and the ground and soil thereof, fishings, fisheries, fowlings, courts leet, courts baron, and other courts, view of frankpledge and all that to view of frankpledge doth belong, mills, mulctures, customs, tolls, duties, reliefs, heriots, fines, sums of money, amerciaments, waifs, estrays, chief-rents, quitrents, rentscharge, rents seck, rents of assize, fee farm rents, services, royalties jurisdictions, franchises, liberties, privileges, easements, profits, advantages, rights, emoluments, and hereditaments whatsoever, to the manor appertaining or reputed to appertain, or, at the time of conveyance, demised, occupied, or enjoyed with the same, or reputed or known as part, parcel, or member thereof.

For the purposes of this subsection the right to compensation for manorial incidents on the extinguishment thereof shall be deemed to be a right appertaining to the manor.

(4) This section applies only if and as far as a contrary intention is not expressed in the conveyance, and has effect subject to the terms of the conveyance and to the provisions therein contained.

(5) This section shall not be construed as giving to any person a better title to any property, right, or thing in this section mentioned than the title which the conveyance gives to him to the land or manor expressed to be conveyed, or as conveying to him any property, right, or thing in this section mentioned, further or otherwise than as the same could have been conveyed to him by the conveying parties.

(6) This section applies to conveyances made after the thirty-first day of December, eighteen hundred and eighty-one.

All estate clause implied

63.[72]—(1) Every conveyance is effectual to pass all the estate, right, title, interest, claim, and demand which the conveying parties respectively have, in, to, or on the property conveyed, or expressed or intended so to be, or which they respectively have power to convey in, to, or on the same. **9–049**

(2) This section applies only if and as far as a contrary intention is not expressed in the conveyance, and has effect subject to the terms of the conveyance and to the provisions therein contained.

(3) This section applies to conveyances made after the thirty-first day of December, eighteen hundred and eighty-one.

Production and safe custody of documents

64.—(1) Where a person retains possession of documents, and gives to another an acknowledgment in writing of the rights of that other to production of those documents, and to delivery of copies thereof (in this section called an acknowledgment), that acknowledgment shall have effect as in this section provided. **9–050**

(2) An acknowledgment shall bind the documents to which it relates in the possession or under the control of the person who retains them, and in the

[72] s.63 is saved in relation to conveyances pursuant to the right of enfranchisement under the Leasehold Reform Act 1967 (s.10(1)) and the right to buy under Pt. V of the Housing Act 1985 (s.139(1), Sched. 6, Pt. II, para. 8) and conveyances executed for the purposes of the Leasehold Reform, Housing and Urban Development Act 1993, Pt. I, Chap. I (s.34(9), Sched. 7, para. 2(1)).

possession or under the control of every other person having possession or control thereof from time to time, but shall bind each individual possessor or person as long only as he has possession or control thereof; and every person so having possession or control from time to time shall be bound specifically to perform the obligations imposed under this section by an acknowledgment, unless prevented from so doing by fire or other inevitable accident.

(3) The obligations imposed under this section by an acknowledgment are to be performed from time to time at the request in writing of the person to whom an acknowledgment is given, or of any person, not being a lessee at a rent, having or claiming any estate, interest, or right through or under that person, or otherwise becoming through or under that person interested in or affected by the terms of any document to which the acknowledgment relates.

(4) The obligations imposed under this section by an acknowledgment are—

(i) An obligation to produce the documents or any of them at all reasonable times for the purpose of inspection, and of comparison with abstracts or copies thereof, by the person entitled to request production or by any person by him authorised in writing; and

(ii) An obligation to produce the documents or any of them at any trial, hearing, or examination in any court, or in the execution of any commission, or elsewhere in the United Kingdom, on any occasion on which production may properly be required, for proving or supporting the title or claim of the person entitled to request production, or for any other purpose relative to that title or claim; and

(iii) An obligation to deliver to the person entitled to request the same true copies or extracts, attested or unattested, of or from the documents or any of them.

(5) All costs and expenses of or incidental to the specific performance of any obligation imposed under this section by an acknowledgment shall be paid by the person requesting performance.

(6) An acknowledgment shall not confer any right to damages for loss or destruction of, or injury to, the documents to which it relates, from whatever cause arising.

(7) Any person claiming to be entitled to the benefit of an acknowledgment may apply to the court for an order directing the production of the documents to which it relates, or any of them, or the delivery of copies of or extracts from those documents or any of them to him, or some person on his behalf; and the court may, if it thinks fit, order production, or production and delivery, accordingly, and may give directions respecting the time, place, terms, and mode of production or delivery, and may make such order as it thinks fit respecting the costs of the application, or any other matter connected with the application.

(8) An acknowledgment shall by virtue of this Act satisfy any liability to give a covenant for production and delivery of copies of or extracts from documents.

(9) Where a person retains possession of documents and gives to another an undertaking in writing for safe custody thereof, that undertaking shall impose on the person giving it, and on every person having possession or control of the documents from time to time, but on each individual possessor or person as long only as he has possession or control thereof, an obligation to keep the documents safe, whole, uncancelled, and undefaced, unless prevented from so doing by fire or other inevitable accident.

(10) Any person claiming to be entitled to the benefit of such an undertaking may apply to the court to assess damages for any loss or destruction of, or injury

to, the documents or any of them, and the court may, if it thinks fit, direct an inquiry respecting the amount of damages, and order payment thereof by the person liable, and make such order as it thinks fit respecting the costs of the application, or any other matter connected with the application.

(11) An undertaking for safe custody of documents shall by virtue of this Act satisfy any liability to give a covenant for safe custody of documents.

(12) The rights conferred by an acknowledgment or an undertaking under this section shall be in addition to all such other rights relative to the production, or inspection, or the obtaining of copies of documents, as are not, by virtue of this Act, satisfied by the giving of the acknowledgment or undertaking, and shall have effect subject to the terms of the acknowledgment or undertaking, and to any provisions therein contained.

(13) This section applies only if and as far as a contrary intention is not expressed in the acknowledgment or undertaking.

(14) This section applies to an acknowledgment or undertaking given, or a liability respecting documents incurred, after the thirty-first day of December, eighteen hundred and eighty-one.

Reservation of legal estates

65.—(1) A reservation of a legal estate shall operate at law without any **9–051**
execution of the conveyance by the grantee of the legal estate out of which the reservation is made, or any regrant by him, so as to create the legal estate reserved, and so as to vest the same in possession in the person (whether being the grantor or not) for whose benefit the reservation is made.

(2) A conveyance of a legal estate expressed to be made subject to another legal estate not in existence immediately before the date of the conveyance, shall operate as a reservation, unless a contrary intention appears.

(3) This section applies only to reservations made after the commencement of this Act.

Confirmation of past transactions

66.—(1) A deed containing a declaration by the estate owner that his estate **9–052**
shall go and devolve in such a manner as may be requisite for confirming any interests intended to affect his estate and capable under this Act of subsisting as legal estates which, at some prior date, were expressed to have been transferred or created, and any dealings therewith which would have been legal if those interests had been legally and validly transferred or created, shall, to the extent of the estate of the estate owner, but without prejudice to the restrictions imposed by this Act in the case of mortgages, operate to give legal effect to the interests so expressed to have been transferred or created and to the subsequent dealings aforesaid.

(2) The powers conferred by this section may be exercised by a tenant for life or statutory owner, [trustee of land][73] or a personal representative (being in each case an estate owner) as well as by an absolute owner, but if exercised by any person, other than an absolute owner, only with the leave of the court.

(3) This section applies only to deeds containing such a declaration as aforesaid if executed after the commencement of this Act.

[(4) The county court has jurisdiction under this section where the land which

[73] Words substituted by the Trusts of Land and Appointment of Trustees Act 1996, s.25(1) Sched. 3, para. 4(1), (12).

is to be dealt with in the court does not exceed [£30,000][74] in capital value [. . .][75].][76]

Receipt in deed sufficient

9–053 **67.**—(1) A receipt for consideration money or securities in the body of a deed shall be a sufficient discharge for the same to the person paying or delivering the same, without any further receipt for the same being indorsed on the deed.

(2) This section applies to deeds executed after the thirty-first day of December, eighteen hundred and eighty-one.

Receipt in deed or indorsed evidence

9–054 **68.**—(1) A receipt for consideration money or other consideration in the body of a deed or indorsed thereon shall, in favour of a subsequent purchaser, not having notice that the money or other consideration thereby acknowledged to be received was not in fact paid or given, wholly or in part, be sufficient evidence of the payment or giving of the whole amount thereof.

(2) This section applies to deeds executed after the thirty-first day of December, eighteen hundred and eighty-one.

Receipt in deed or indorsed authority for payment to solicitor

9–055 **69.**[77]—(1) Where a solicitor produces a deed, having in the body thereof or indorsed thereon a receipt for consideration money or other consideration, the deed being executed, or the indorsed receipt being signed, by the person entitled to give a receipt for that consideration, the deed shall be a sufficient authority to the person liable to pay or give the same for his paying or giving the same to the solicitor, without the solicitor producing any separate or other direction or authority in that behalf from the person who executed or signed the deed or receipt.

(2) This section applies whether the consideration was paid or given before or after the commencement of this Act.

Partial release of security from rentcharge

9–056 **70.**—(1) A release from a rentcharge of part of the land charged therewith does not extinguish the whole rentcharge, but operates only to bar the right to recover any part of the rentcharge out of the land released, without prejudice to the rights of any persons interested in the land remaining unreleased, and not concurring in or confirming the release.

(2) This section applies to releases made after the twelfth day of August, eighteen hundred and fifty-nine.

---

[74] Figure substituted by the High Court and County Courts Jurisdiction Order 1991 (S.I. 1991 No. 724), art. 2(8), Sched.

[75] Words repealed by the High Court and County Courts Jurisdiction Order 1991 (S.I. 1991 No. 724), art. 2(8), Sched.

[76] subs. (4) added by the County Courts Act 1984, s.148(1), Sched. 2, Pt. II, para. 2(1), (3). For the jurisdiction of the county court by agreement, see the County Courts Act 1984, s.24, *post*, para. 42–003.

[77] In s.69 (and in s.75(1)) any reference to a solicitor is to be construed as including a reference to a licensed conveyancer: Administration of Justice Act 1985, s.34(1).

Release of part of land affected from a judgment

71.—(1) A release from a judgment (including any writ or order imposing a charge) of part of any land charged therewith does not effect the validity of the judgment as respects any land not specifically released. **9–057**

(2) This section operates without prejudice to the rights of any persons interested in the property remaining unreleased and not concurring in or confirming the release.

(3) This section applies to releases made after the twelfth day of August, eighteen hundred and fifty-nine.

Conveyances by a person to himself, etc.

72.—(1) In conveyances made after the twelfth day of August, eighteen hundred and fifty-nine, personal property, including chattels real, may be conveyed by a person to himself jointly with another person by the like means by which it might be conveyed by him to another person. **9–058**

(2) In conveyances made after the thirty-first day of December, eighteen hundred and eighty-one, freehold land, or a thing in action, may be conveyed by a person to himself jointly with another person, by the like means by which it might be conveyed by him to another person; and may, in like manner, be conveyed by a husband to his wife, and by a wife to her husband, alone or jointly with another person.

(3) After the commencement of this Act a person may convey land to or vest land in himself.

(4) Two or more persons (whether or not being trustees or personal representatives) may convey, and shall be deemed always to have been capable of conveying, any property vested in them to any one or more of themselves in like manner as they could have conveyed such property to a third party; provided that if the persons in whose favour the conveyance is made are, by reason of any fiduciary relationship or otherwise, precluded from validly carrying out the transaction, the conveyance shall be liable to be set aside.

73. [*Repealed by the Law of Property (Miscellaneous Provisions) Act 1989, s.4, Sched. 2.*]

Execution of instruments by or on behalf of corporations

74.—(1) In favour of a purchaser a deed shall be deemed to have been duly executed by a corporation aggregate if its seal be affixed thereto in the presence of and attested by its clerk, secretary or other permanent officer or his deputy, and a member of the board of directors, council or other governing body of the corporation, and where a seal purporting to be the seal of a corporation has been affixed to a deed, attested by persons purporting to be persons holding such offices as aforesaid, the deed shall be deemed to have been executed in accordance with the requirements of this section, and to have taken effect accordingly. **9–059**

(2) The board of directors, council or other governing body of a corporation aggregate may, by resolution or otherwise, appoint an agent either generally or in any particular case, to execute on behalf of the corporation any agreement or

other instrument [which is not a deed][78] in relation to any matter within the powers of the corporation.

(3)[79] Where a person is authorised under a power of attorney or under any statutory or other power to convey any interest in property in the name or on behalf of a corporation sole or aggregate, he may as attorney execute the conveyance by signing the name of the corporation in the presence of at least one witness, [...][80] and such execution shall take effect and be valid in like manner as if the corporation had executed the conveyance.

(4)[81] Where a corporation aggregate is authorised under a power of attorney or under any statutory or other power to convey any interest in property in the name or on behalf of any other person (including another corporation), an officer appointed for that purpose by the board of directors, council or other governing body of the corporation by resolution or otherwise, may execute the deed or other instrument in the name of such other person; and where an instrument appears to be executed by an officer so appointed, then in favour of a purchaser the instrument shall be deemed to have been executed by an officer duly authorised.

(5) The foregoing provisions of this section apply to transactions wherever effected, but only to deeds and instruments executed after the commencement of this Act, except that, in the case of powers or appointments of an agent or officer, they apply whether the power was conferred or the appointment was made before or after the commencement of this Act or by this Act.

(6) Notwithstanding anything contained in this section, any mode of execution or attestation authorised by law or by practice or by the statute, charter, memorandum or articles, deed of settlement or other instrument constituting the corporation or regulating the affairs thereof, shall (in addition to the modes authorised by this section) be as effectual as if this section had not been passed.

Rights of purchaser as to execution

9–060 **75.**—(1) On a sale, the purchaser shall not be entitled to require that the conveyance to him be executed in his presence, or in that of his solicitor, as such; but shall be entitled to have, at his own cost, the execution of the conveyance attested by some person appointed by him, who may, if he thinks fit, be his solicitor.

(2) This section applies to sales made after the thirty-first day of December, eighteen hundred and eighty-one.

Covenants

76. [*Repealed by the Law of Property (Miscellaneous Provisions) Act 1994, ss. 10(1), 21(2), (3), Sched. 2.*][82]

[78] Words substituted by the Law of Property (Miscellaneous Provisions) Act 1989, s.1(8), Sched. 1, para. 3.

[79] An instrument to which subss. (3) and (4) apply may be executed either as provided thereby or as provided by the Powers of Attorney Act 1971, s.7, whenever the power of attorney was created, but without prejudice to any statutory direction requiring an instrument to be executed in the name of an estate owner within the meaning of this Act: Powers of Attorney Act 1971, s.7(2)–(4), *post*, para. 30–006.

[80] Words repealed by the Law of Property (Miscellaneous Provisions) Act 1989, s.4, Sched. 2.

[81] See n. 79, *supra*.

[82] See now the Law of Property (Miscellaneous Provisions) Act 1994, Pt. I, *post*, paras 57–001 *et seq*.

Implied covenants in conveyances subject to rents

77.—(1) In addition to the covenants implied under [Part I of the Law of Property (Miscellaneous Provisions) Act 1994][83], there shall in the several cases in this section mentioned, be deemed to be included and implied, a covenant to the effect in this section stated, by and with such persons as are hereinafter mentioned, that is to say:— **9–061**

(A) In a conveyance for valuable consideration, other than a mortgage, of the entirety of the land affected by a rentcharge, a covenant by the grantee or joint and several covenants by the grantees, if more than one, with the conveying parties and with each of them, if more than one, in the terms set out in Part VII of the Second Schedule to this Act. Where a rentcharge has been apportioned in respect of any land, with the consent of the owner of the rentcharge, the covenants in this paragraph shall be implied in the conveyance of that land in like manner as if the apportioned rentcharge were the rentcharge referred to, and the document creating the rentcharge related solely to that land:

(B) In a conveyance for valuable consideration, other than a mortgage, of part of land affected by a rentcharge, subject to a part of that rentcharge which has been or is by that conveyance apportioned (but in either case without the consent of the owner of the rentcharge) in respect of the land conveyed:—

(i) A covenant by the grantee of the land or joint and several covenants by the grantees, if more than one, with the conveying parties and with each of them, if more than one, in the terms set out in paragraph (i) of Part VIII of the Second Schedule to this Act;

(ii) A covenant by a person who conveys or is expressed to convey as beneficial owner, or joint and several covenants by the persons who so convey or are expressed to so convey, if at the date of the conveyance any part of the land affected by such rentcharge is retained, with the grantees of the land and with each of them (if more than one) in the terms set out in paragraph (ii) of Part VIII of the Second Schedule to this Act:

[. . .][84]

[(2) Where in a conveyance for valuable consideration, other than a mortgage, part of land affected by a rentcharge is, without the consent of the owner of the rentcharge, expressed to be conveyed subject to or charged with the entire rent, paragraph (B)(i) of subsection (1) to this section shall apply as if, in paragraph (i) of Part VIII of the Second Schedule to this Act—

(a) any reference to the apportioned rent were to the entire rent; and

(b) the words "(other than the covenant to pay the entire rent)" were omitted.

(2A) Where in a conveyance for valuable consideration, other than a mortgage, part of land affected by a rentcharge is, without the consent of the owner of the rentcharge, expressed to be conveyed discharged or exonerated from the entire rent, paragraph (B)(ii) of subsection (1) of this section shall apply as if, in paragraph (ii) of Part VIII of the Second Schedule to this Act—

(a) any reference to the balance of the rent were to the entire rent; and

83 Words substituted by the Law of Property (Miscellaneous Provisions) Act 1994, s.21(1), Sched. 1, para. 1.

84 Paras (C) and (D) repealed in relation to "new tenancies" (as defined by the Landlord and Tenant (Covenants) Act 1995, s.1, *post*, para. 58–001): Landlord and Tenant (Covenants) Act 1995, ss.14(a), 30(2), (3), Sched. 2.

(b) the words ", other than the covenant to pay the entire rent," were omitted.][85]

(3) In this section "conveyance" does not include a demise by way of lease at a rent.

(4) Any covenant which would be implied under this section by reason of a person conveying or being expressed to convey as beneficial owner may, by express reference to this section, be implied, with or without variation, in a conveyance, whether or not for valuable consideration, by a person who conveys or is expressed to convey as settlor, or as trustee, or as mortgagee, or as personal representative of a deceased person, [...][86] or under an order of the court.

(5) The benefit of a covenant implied as aforesaid shall be annexed and incident to, and shall go with, the estate or interest of the implied covenantee, and shall be capable of being enforced by every person in whom that estate or interest is, for the whole or any part thereof, from time to time vested.

(6) A covenant implied as aforesaid may be varied or extended by deed, and, as so varied or extended, shall, as far as may be, operate in the like manner, and with all the like incidents, effects and consequences, as if such variations or extensions were directed in this section to be implied.

(7) In particular any covenant implied under this section may be extended by providing that—

(a) the land conveyed; or

(b) the part of the land affected by the rentcharge which remains vested in the covenantor;

[...][87]

shall, as the case may require, stand charged with the payment of all money which may become payable under the implied covenant.

(8) This section applies only to conveyances made after the commencement of this Act.

Benefit of covenants relating to land

9–062 **78.**[88]—(1) A covenant relating to any land of the covenantee shall be deemed to be made with the covenantee and his successors in title and the persons deriving title under him or them, and shall have effect as if such successors and other persons were expressed.

For the purposes of this subsection in connection with covenants restrictive of the user of land "successors in title" shall be deemed to include the owners and occupiers for the time being of the land of the covenantee intended to be benefited.

(2) This section applies to covenants made after the commencement of this Act, but the repeal of section fifty-eight of the Conveyancing Act 1881 does not affect the operation of covenants to which that section applied.

---

85 subss. (2) and (2A) substituted (for subs. (2)) in relation to "new tenancies" (as defined by the Landlord and Tenant (Covenants) Act 1995, s.1, *post*, para. 58–001): Landlord and Tenant (Covenants) Act 1995, s.30(1), (3), Sched. 1, para. 2.

86 Words repealed by the Mental Health Act 1959, s.149(2), Sched. 8, Pt. I.

87 Para. (c) repealed in relation to "new tenancies" (as defined by the Landlord and Tenant (Covenants) Act 1995, s.1, *post*, para. 58–001): Landlord and Tenant (Covenants) Act 1995, s.30(2), (3), Sched. 2.

88 ss.78 and 79 do not apply to "new tenancies" (as defined in the Landlord and Tenant (Covenants) Act 1995, s.1, *post*, para. 58–001): Landlord and Tenant (Covenants) Act 1995, s.30(4)(a).

Burden of covenants relating to land

79.[89]—(1) A covenant relating to any land of a covenantor or capable of being bound by him, shall, unless a contrary intention is expressed, be deemed to be made by the covenantor on behalf of himself his successors in title and the persons deriving title under him or them, and, subject as aforesaid, shall have effect as if such successors and other persons were expressed. **9–063**

This subsection extends to a covenant to do some act relating to the land, notwithstanding that the subject-matter may not be in existence when the covenant is made.

(2) For the purpose of this section in connection with covenants restrictive of the user of land "successors in title" shall be deemed to include the owners and occupiers for the time being of such land.

(3) This section applies only to covenants made after the commencement of this Act.

Covenants binding land

80.—(1) A covenant and a bond and an obligation or contract [made under seal after 31 December, 1881 but before the coming into force of section 1 of the Law of Property (Miscellaneous Provisions) Act 1989 or executed as a deed in accordance with that section after its coming into force][90] binds the real estate as well as the personal estate of the person making the same if and so far as a contrary intention is not expressed in the covenant, bond, obligation, or contract. **9–064**

This subsection extends to a covenant implied by virtue of this Act.

(2) Every covenant running with the land, whether entered into before or after the commencement of this Act, shall take effect in accordance with any statutory enactment affecting the devolution of the land, and accordingly the benefit or burden of every such covenant shall vest in or bind the persons who by virtue of any such enactment or otherwise succeed to the title of the covenantee or the covenantor, as the case may be.

(3) The benefit of a covenant relating to land entered into after the commencement of this Act may be made to run with the land without the use of any technical expression if the covenant is of such a nature that the benefit could have been made to run with the land before the commencement of this Act.

(4) For the purposes of this section, a covenant runs with the land when the benefit or burden of it, whether at law or in equity, passes to the successors in title of the covenantee or the covenantor, as the case may be.

Effect of covenant with two or more jointly

81.[91]—(1) A covenant, and a contract under seal, and a bond or obligation under seal, made with two or more jointly, to pay money or to make a conveyance, or to do any other act, to them or for their benefit, shall be deemed to include, and shall, by virtue of this Act, imply, an obligation to do the act to, or **9–065**

---

[89] ss.78 and 79 do not apply to "new tenancies" (as defined in the Landlord and Tenant (Covenants) Act 1995, s.1, *post*, para. 58–001): Landlord and Tenant (Covenants) Act 1995, s.30(4)(a).

[90] Words substituted by the Law of Property (Miscellaneous Provisions) Act 1989, s.1(8), Sched 1, para. 4.

[91] ss.81 and 83 apply to covenants implied by virtue of the Law of Property (Miscellaneous Provisions) Act 1994: Law of Property (Miscellaneous Provisions) Act 1994, s.8(2).

accepted by the applicant; and the Lands Tribunal may accordingly refuse to modify a restriction without some such addition.][4]

(2) The court shall have power on the application of any person interested—

(a) To declare whether or not in any particular case any freehold land is [or would in any given event be][5] affected by a restriction imposed by any instrument; or

(b) To declare what, upon the true construction of any instrument purporting to impose a restriction, is the nature and extent of the restriction thereby imposed and whether the same is [or would in any given event be][6] enforceable and if so by whom.

[Neither subsections (7) and (11) of this section nor, unless the contrary is expressed, any later enactment providing for this section not to apply to any restrictions shall affect the operation of this subsection or the operation for the purposes of this subsection of any other provisions of this section.][7]

(3) The [Lands Tribunal][8] shall, before making any order under this section, direct such enquiries, if any, to be made of any [Government department or][9] local authority, and such notices, if any, whether by way of advertisement or otherwise, to be given to such of the persons who appear to be entitled to the benefit of the restriction intended to be discharged, modified, or dealt with as, having regard to any enquiries notices or other proceedings previously made, given or taken, the [Lands Tribunal][10] may think fit.

[(3A) On an application to the Lands Tribunal under this section the Lands Tribunal shall give any necessary directions as to the persons who are or are not to be admitted (as appearing to be entitled to the benefit of the restriction) to oppose the application, and no appeal shall lie against any such direction; but rules under the Lands Tribunal Act 1949 shall make provision whereby, in cases in which there arises on such application (whether or not in connection with the admission of persons to oppose) any such question as is referred to in subsection (2)(a) or (b) of this section, the proceedings on the application can and, if the rules so provide, shall be suspended to enable the decision of the court to be obtained on that question by an application under that subsection, or by means of a case stated by the Lands Tribunal, or otherwise, as may be provided by those rules or by rules of court.][11]

(4) [*Repealed by the Lands Tribunal Act 1949, s.10, Sched. 2.*]

(5) Any order made under this section shall be binding on all persons, whether ascertained or of full age or capacity or not, then entitled or thereafter capable of becoming entitled to the benefit of any restriction, which is thereby discharged, modified, or dealt with, and whether such persons are parties to the proceedings or have been served with notice or not [. . .][12]

(6) An order may be made under this section notwithstanding that any instrument which is alleged to impose the restriction intended to be discharged, modified, or dealt with, may not have been produced to the court or the [Lands

[4] subss.(1A)-(1C) inserted by the Law of Property Act 1969, s.28(2).
[5] Words inserted by the Law of Property Act 1969, s.28(4).
[6] Words inserted by the Law of Property Act 1969, s.28(4).
[7] Words added by the Law of Property Act 1969, s.28(4).
[8] Words substituted by the Law of Property Act 1969, s.28(1)(a).
[9] Words inserted by the Law of Property Act 1969, s.28(5).
[10] Words substituted by the Law of Property Act 1969, s.28(1)(a).
[11] subs. (3A) inserted by the Law of Property Act 1969, s.28(6).
[12] Words repealed by the Lands Tribunal Act 1949, s.10, Sched. 2.

Tribunal][13], and the court or the [Lands Tribunal][14] may act on such evidence of that instrument as it may think sufficient.

(7) This section applies to restrictions whether subsisting at the commencement of this Act or imposed thereafter, but this section does not apply where the restriction was imposed on the occasion of a disposition made gratuitously or for a nominal consideration for public purposes.

(8) This section applies whether the land affected by the restrictions is registered or not [...][15]

(9) Where any proceedings by action or otherwise are taken to enforce a restrictive covenant, any person against whom the proceedings are taken, may in such proceedings apply to the court for an order giving leave to apply to the [Lands Tribunal][16] under this section, and staying the proceedings in the meantime.

(10) [*Repealed by the Lands Tribunal Act 1949, s.10, Sched. 2.*]

(11) This section does not apply to restrictions imposed by the Commissioners of Works[17] under any statutory power for the protection of any Royal Park or Garden or to restrictions of a like character imposed upon the occasion of any enfranchisement effected before the commencement of this Act in any manor vested in His Majesty in right of the Crown or the Duchy of Lancaster, nor [subject to subsection (11A) below][18] to restrictions created or imposed—

(a) for Naval, Military or Air Force purposes,

[(b) for civil aviation purposes under the powers of the Air Navigation Act 1920, of section 19 or 23 of the Civil Aviation Act 1949 or of section 30 or 41 of the Civil Aviation Act 1982][19].

[(11A) Subsection (11) of this section—

(a) shall exclude the application of this section to a restriction falling within subsection (11)(a), and not created or imposed in connection with the use of any land as an aerodrome, only so long as the restriction is enforceable by or on behalf of the Crown; and

(b) shall exclude the application of this section to a restriction falling within subsection (11)(b), or created or imposed in connection with the use of any land as an aerodrome, only so long as the restriction is enforceable by or on behalf of the Crown or any public or international authority.][20]

(12) Where a term of more than [forty][21] years is created in land (whether before or after the commencement of this Act) this section shall after the expiration of [twenty-five][22] years of the term, apply to restrictions affecting such leasehold land in like manner as it would have applied had the land been freehold:

Provided that this subsection shall not apply to mining leases.

[13] Words substituted by the Law of Property Act 1969, s.28(1)(a).
[14] Words substituted by the Law of Property Act 1969, s.28(1)(a).
[15] Words repealed by the Land Registration Act 2002, ss.133, Sched. 11, para. 2(1), (5), Sched. 13.
[16] Words substituted by the Law of Property Act 1969, s.28(1)(a).
[17] Now the Secretary of State for the Environment: Secretary of State for the Environment Order 1970 (S.I. 1970 No. 1681).
[18] Words inserted by the Law of Property Act 1969, s.28(9).
[19] Para. (b) substituted by the Civil Aviation Act 1982, s.109(2), Sched. 15, para. 1.
[20] subs. (11A) inserted by the Law of Property Act 1969, s.28(9).
[21] Word substituted by the Landlord and Tenant Act 1954, s.52(1).
[22] Word substituted by the Landlord and Tenant Act 1954, s.52(1).

Part III

Mortgages, Rentcharges, and Powers of Attorney

Mortgages

Mode of mortgaging freeholds

9–069 **85.**—(1) A mortgage of an estate in fee simple shall only be capable of being effected at law either by a demise for a term of years absolute, subject to a provision for cesser on redemption, or by a charge by deed expressed to be by way of legal mortgage:

Provided that a first mortgagee shall have the same right to the possession of documents as if his security included the fee simple.

(2) Any purported conveyance of an estate in fee simple by way of mortgage made after the commencement of this Act shall (to the extent of the estate of the mortgagor) operate as a demise of the land to the mortgagee for a term of years absolute, without impeachment for waste, but subject to cesser on redemption, in manner following, namely:—

(a) A first or only mortgagee shall take a term of three thousand years from the date of the mortgage:

(b) A second or subsequent mortgagee shall take a term (commencing from the date of the mortgage) one day longer than the term vested in the first or other mortgagee whose security ranks immediately before that of such second or subsequent mortgagee:

and, in this subsection, any such purported conveyance as aforesaid includes an absolute conveyance with a deed of defeasance and any other assurance which, but for this subsection, would operate in effect to vest the fee simple in a mortgagee subject to redemption.

(3) [Subsection (2) does not apply to registered land, but, subject to that, this section applies whether or not the land is registered land and whether or not][23] the mortgage is expressed to be made by way of trust for sale or otherwise.

(4) Without prejudice to the provisions of this Act respecting legal and equitable powers, every power to mortgage or to lend money on mortgage of an estate in fee simple shall be construed as a power to mortgage the estate for a term of years absolute, without impeachment for waste, or by a charge by way of legal mortgage or to lend on such security.

Mode of mortgaging leaseholds

9–070 **86.**—(1) A mortgage of a term of years absolute shall only be capable of being effected at law either by a subdemise for a term of years absolute, less by one day at least than the term vested in the mortgagor, and subject to a provision for cesser on redemption, or by a charge by deed expressed to be by way of legal mortgage; and where a licence to subdemise by way of mortgage is required, such licence shall not be unreasonably refused:

Provided that a first mortgagee shall have the same right to the possession of documents as if his security had been effected by assignment.

(2) Any purported assignment of a term of years absolute by way of mortgage made after the commencement of this Act shall (to the extent of the estate of the

[23] Words substituted by the Land Registration Act 2002, s.133, Sched. 11, para. 2(1), (6).

mortgagor) operate as a subdemise of the leasehold land to the mortgagee for a term of years absolute but subject to cesser on redemption, in manner following, namely:—

(a) The term to be taken by a first or only mortgagee shall be 10 days less than the term expressed to be assigned:

(b) The term to be taken by a second or subsequent mortgagee shall be one day longer than the term vested in the first or other mortgagee whose security ranks immediately before that of the second or subsequent mortgagee, if the length of the last mentioned term permits, and in any case for a term less by one day at least than the term expressed to be assigned:

and, in this subsection, any such purported assignment as aforesaid includes an absolute assignment with a deed of defeasance and any other assurance which, but for this subsection, would operate in effect to vest the term of the mortgagor in a mortgagee subject to redemption.

(3) [Subsection (2) does not apply to registered land, but, subject to that, this section applies whether or not the land is registered land and whether or not][24] the mortgage is made by way of sub-mortgage of a term of years absolute, or is expressed to be by way of trust for sale or otherwise.

(4) Without prejudice to the provisions of this Act respecting legal and equitable powers, every power to mortgage for or to lend money on mortgage of a term of years absolute by way of assignment shall be construed as a power to mortgage the term by subdemise for a term of years absolute or by a charge by way of legal mortgage, or to lend on such security.

Charges by way of legal mortgage

87.—(1) Where a legal mortgage of land is created by a charge by deed **9–071**
expressed to be by way of legal mortgage, the mortgagee shall have the same protection, powers and remedies (including the right to take proceedings to obtain possession from the occupiers and the persons in receipt of rents and profits, or any of them) as if—

(a) where the mortgage is a mortgage of an estate in fee simple, a mortgage term for three thousand years without impeachment of waste had been thereby created in favour of the mortgagee; and

(b) where the mortgage is a mortgage of a term of years absolute, a sub-term less by one day than the term vested in the mortgagor had been thereby created in favour of the mortgagee.

(2) Where an estate vested in a mortgagee immediately before the commencement of this Act has by virtue of this Act been converted into a term of years absolute or sub-term, the mortgagee may, by a declaration in writing to that effect signed by him, convert the mortgage into a charge by way of legal mortgage, and in that case the mortgage term shall be extinguished in the inheritance or in the head term as the case may be, and the mortgagee shall have the same protection, powers and remedies (including the right to take proceedings to obtain possession from the occupiers and the persons in receipt of rents and profits or any of them) as if the mortgage term or sub-term had remained subsisting.

The power conferred by this subsection may be exercised by a mortgagee notwithstanding that he is a trustee or personal representative.

[24] Words substituted by the Land Registration Act 2002, s.133, Sched. 11, para. 2(1), (7).

(3) Such declaration shall not affect the priority of the mortgagee or his right to retain possession of documents, nor affect his title to or right over any fixtures or chattels personal comprised in the mortgage.

[(4) Subsection (1) of this section shall not be taken to be affected by section 23(1)(a) of the Land Registration Act 2002 (under which owner's powers in relation to a registered estate do not include power to mortgage by demise or sub-demise).][25]

Realisation of freehold mortgages

9–072 **88.**—(1) Where an estate in fee simple has been mortgaged by the creation of a term of years absolute limited thereout or by a charge by way of legal mortgage and the mortgagee sells under his statutory or express power of sale—

(a) the conveyance by him shall operate to vest in the purchaser the fee simple in the land conveyed subject to any legal mortgage having priority to the mortgage in right of which the sale is made and to any money thereby secured and thereupon;

(b) the mortgage term or the charge by way of legal mortgage and any subsequent mortgage term or charges shall merge or be extinguished as respects the land conveyed;

and such conveyance may, as respects the fee simple, be made in the name of the estate owner in whom it is vested.

(2) Where any such mortgagee obtains an order for foreclosure absolute, the order shall operate to vest the fee simple in him (subject to any legal mortgage having priority to the mortgage in right of which the foreclosure is obtained and to any money thereby secured), and thereupon the mortgage term, if any, shall thereby be merged in the fee simple, and any subsequent mortgage term or charge by way of legal mortgage bound by the order shall thereupon be extinguished.

(3) Where any such mortgagee acquires a title under the Limitation Acts, he, or the persons deriving title under him, may enlarge the mortgage term into a fee simple under the statutory power for that purpose discharged from any legal mortgage affected by the title so acquired, or in the case of a chargee by way of legal mortgage may by deed declare that the fee simple is vested in him discharged as aforesaid, and the same shall vest accordingly.

(4) Where the mortgage includes fixtures or chattels personal any statutory power of sale and any right to foreclosure or take possession shall extend to the absolute or other interest therein affected by the charge.

(5) In the case of a sub-mortgage by subdemise of a long term (less a nominal period) itself limited out of an estate in fee simple, the foregoing provisions of this section shall operate as if the derivative term, if any, created by the sub-mortgage had been limited out of the fee simple, and so as to enlarge the principal term and extinguish the derivative term created by the sub-mortgage as aforesaid, and to enable the sub-mortgagee to convey the fee simple or acquire it by foreclosure, enlargement, or otherwise as aforesaid.

(6) This section applies to a mortgage whether created before or after the commencement of this Act, and to a mortgage term created by this Act, but does not operate to confer a better title to the fee simple than would have been acquired if the same had been conveyed by the mortgage (being a valid mortgage) and the restrictions imposed by this Act in regard to the effect and

[25] subs. (4) added by the Land Registration Act 2002, s.133, Sched. 11, para. 2(1), (8).

creation of mortgages were not in force, and all prior mortgages (if any) not being merely equitable charges had been created by demise or by charge by way of legal mortgage.

Realisation of leasehold mortgages

89.—(1) Where a term of years absolute has been mortgaged by the creation of another term of years absolute limited thereout or by a charge by way of legal mortgage, and the mortgagee sells under his statutory or express power of sale,— **9–073**

(a) the conveyance by him shall operate to convey to the purchaser not only the mortgage term, if any, but also (unless expressly excepted with the leave of the court) the leasehold reversion affected by the mortgage, subject to any legal mortgage having priority to the mortgage in right of which the sale is made and to any money thereby secured, and thereupon

(b) the mortgage term, or the charge by way of legal mortgage and any subsequent mortgage term or charge, shall merge in such leasehold reversion or be extinguished unless excepted as aforesaid;

and such conveyance may, as respects the leasehold reversion, be made in the name of the estate owner in whom it is vested.

Where a licence to assign is required on a sale by a mortgagee, such licence shall not be unreasonably refused.

(2) Where any such mortgagee obtains an order for foreclosure absolute, the order shall, unless it otherwise provides, operate (without giving rise to a forfeiture for want of a licence to assign) to vest the leasehold reversion affected by the mortgage and any subsequent mortgage term in him, subject to any legal mortgage having priority to the mortgage in right of which the foreclosure is obtained and to any money thereby secured, and thereupon the mortgage term and any subsequent mortgage term or charge by way of legal mortgage bound by the order shall, subject to any express provision to the contrary contained in the order, merge in such leasehold reversion or be extinguished.

(3) Where any such mortgagee acquires a title under the Limitation Acts, he, or the persons deriving title under him, may by deed declare that the leasehold reversion affected shall vest in him, free from any right of redemption which is barred, and the same shall (without giving rise to a forfeiture for want of a licence to assign) vest accordingly, and thereupon the mortgage term, if any, and any other mortgage term or charge by way of legal mortgage affected by the title so acquired shall, subject to any express provision to the contrary contained in the deed, merge in such leasehold reversion or be extinguished.

(4) Where the mortgage includes fixtures or chattels personal, any statutory power of sale and any right to foreclose or take possession shall extend to the absolute or other interest therein affected by the charge.

(5) In the case of a sub-mortgage by subdemise of a term (less a nominal period) itself limited out of a leasehold reversion, the foregoing provisions of this section shall operate as if the derivative term created by the sub-mortgage had been limited out of the leasehold reversion, and so as (subject as aforesaid) to merge the principal mortgage term therein as well as the derivative term created by the sub-mortgage and to enable the sub-mortgagee to convey the leasehold reversion or acquire it by foreclosure, vesting, or otherwise as aforesaid.

(6) This section takes effect without prejudice to any incumbrance or trust affecting the leasehold reversion which has priority over the mortgage in right of

which the sale, foreclosure, or title is made or acquired, and applies to a mortgage whether executed before or after the commencement of this Act, and to a mortgage term created by this Act, but does not apply where the mortgage term does not comprise the whole of the land included in the leasehold reversion unless the rent (if any) payable in respect of that reversion has been apportioned as respects the land affected, or the rent is of no money value or no rent is reserved, and unless the lessee's covenants and conditions (if any) have been apportioned, either expressly or by implication, as respects the land affected.

[In this subsection references to an apportionment include an equitable apportionment made without the consent of the lessor.][26]

[(7) The county court has jurisdiction under this section where the amount owing in respect of the mortgage or charge at the commencement of the proceedings does not exceed [£30,000][27].][28]

Realisation of equitable charges by the court

9–074 **90.**—(1) Where an order for sale is made by the court in reference to an equitable mortgage on land (not secured by a legal term of years absolute or by a charge by way of legal mortgage) the court may, in favour of a purchaser, make a vesting order conveying the land or may appoint a person to convey the land or create and vest in the mortgagee a legal term of years absolute to enable him to carry out the sale, as the case may require, in like manner as if the mortgage had been created by deed by way of legal mortgage pursuant to this Act, but without prejudice to any incumbrance having priority to the equitable mortgage unless the incumbrancer consents to the sale.

(2) This section applies to equitable mortgages made or arising before or after the commencement of this Act, but not to a mortgage which has been over-reached under the powers conferred by this Act or otherwise.

[(3) The county court has jurisdiction under this section where the amount owing in respect of the mortgage or charge at the commencement of the proceedings does not exceed [£30,000][29].][30]

Sale of mortgaged property in action for redemption or foreclosure

9–075 **91.**—(1) Any person entitled to redeem mortgaged property may have a judgment or order for sale instead of for redemption in an action brought by him either for redemption alone, or for sale alone, or for sale or redemption in the alternative.

(2) In any action, whether for foreclosure, or for redemption, or for sale, or for the raising and payment in any manner of mortgage money, the court, on the request of the mortgagee, or of any person interested either in the mortgage money or in the right of redemption, and, notwithstanding that—

(a) any other person dissents; or

[26] Words added by the Law of Property (Amendment) Act 1926, s.7, Sched.

[27] Figure substituted by the High Court and County Courts Jurisdiction Order 1991 (S.I. 1991 No. 724), art. 2(8), Sched.

[28] subs. (7) added by the County Courts Act 1984, s.148(1), Sched. 2, Pt. II, para. 3(1), (3). For the jurisdiction of the county court by agreement, see the County Courts Act 1984, s. 24, *post*, para. 42–003.

[29] Figure substituted by the High Court and County Courts Jurisdiction Order 1991 (S.I. 1991 No. 724), art. 2(8), Sched.

[30] subs. (3) added by the County Courts Act 1984, s.148(1), Sched. 2, Pt. II, para. 3(1), (3). For the jurisdiction of the county court by agreement, see the County Courts Act 1984, s.24, *post*, para. 42–003.

(b) the mortgagee or any person so interested does not appear in the action; and without allowing any time for redemption or for payment of any mortgage money, may direct a sale of the mortgaged property, on such terms as it thinks fit, including the deposit in court of a reasonable sum fixed by the court to meet the expenses of sale and to secure performance of the terms.

(3) But, in an action brought by a person interested in the right of redemption and seeking a sale, the court may, on the application of any defendant, direct the plaintiff to give such security for costs as the court thinks fit, and may give the conduct of the sale to any defendant, and may give such directions as it thinks fit respecting the costs of the defendants or any of them.

(4) In any case within this section the court may, if it thinks fit, direct a sale without previously determining the priorities of incumbrancers.

(5) This section applies to actions brought either before or after the commencement of this Act.

(6) In this section "mortgaged property" includes the estate or interest which a mortgagee would have had power to convey if the statutory power of sale were applicable.

(7) For the purposes of this section the court may, in favour of a purchaser, make a vesting order conveying the mortgaged property, or appoint a person to do so, subject or not to any incumbrance, as the court may think fit; or, in the case of an equitable mortgage, may create and vest a mortgage term in the mortgagee to enable him to carry out the sale as if the mortgage had been made by deed by way of legal mortgage.

[(8) The county court has jurisdiction under this section where the amount owing in respect of the mortgage or charge at the commencement of the proceedings does not exceed [£30,000][31].][32]

Power to authorise land and minerals to be dealt with separately

92.—(1) Where a mortgagee's power of sale in regard to land has become exercisable but does not extend to the purposes mentioned in this section, the court may, on his application, authorise him and the persons deriving title under him to dispose— **9–076**

(a) of the land, with an exception or reservation of all or any mines and minerals, and with or without rights and powers of or incidental to the working, getting or carrying away of minerals; or

(b) of all or any mines and minerals, with or without the said rights or powers separately from the land;

and thenceforth the powers so conferred shall have effect as if the same were contained in the mortgage.

[(2) The county court has jurisdiction under this section where the amount owing in respect of the mortgage or charge at the commencement of the proceedings does not exceed [£30,000][33].][34]

[31] Figure substituted by the High Court and County Courts Jurisdiction Order 1991 (S.I. 1991 No. 724), art. 2(8), Sched.

[32] subs. (8) added by the County Courts Act 1984, s.148(1), Sched. 2, Pt. II, para. 3(1), (3). For the jurisdiction of the county court by agreement, see the County Courts Act 1984, s.24, *post*, para. 42–003.

[33] Figure substituted by the High Court and County Courts Jurisdiction Order 1991 (S.I. 1991 No. 724), art. 2(8), Sched.

[34] subs. (2) added (and subs.(1) numbered) by the County Courts Act 1984, s.148(1), Sched. 2, Pt. II, para. 3(1), (2), (3). For the jurisdiction of the county court by agreement, see the County Courts Act 1984, s.24, *post*, para. 42–003.

Restriction on consolidation of mortgages

9–077 **93.**—(1) A mortgagor seeking to redeem any one mortgage is entitled to do so without paying money due under any separate mortgage made by him, or by any person through whom he claims, solely on property other than that comprised in the mortgage which he seeks to redeem.

This subsection applies only if and as far as a contrary intention is not expressed in the mortgage deeds or one of them.

(2) This section does not apply where all the mortgages were made before the first day of January, eighteen hundred and eighty-two.

(3) Save as aforesaid, nothing in this Act, in reference to mortgages, affects any right of consolidation or renders inoperative a stipulation in relation to any mortgage made before or after the commencement of this Act reserving a right to consolidate.

Tacking and further advances

9–078 **94.**—(1) After the commencement of this Act, a prior mortgagee shall have a right to make further advances to rank in priority to subsequent mortgages (whether legal or equitable)—

(a) if an arrangement has been made to that effect with the subsequent mortgagees; or

(b) if he had no notice of such subsequent mortgages at the time when the further advance was made by him; or

(c) whether or not he had such notice as aforesaid, where the mortgage imposes an obligation on him to make such further advances.

This subsection applies whether or not the prior mortgage was made expressly for securing further advances.

(2) In relation to the making of further advances after the commencement of this Act a mortgagee shall not be deemed to have notice of a mortgage merely by reason that it was registered as a land charge [. . .][35] if it was not so registered at the [time when the original mortgage was created][36] or when the last search (if any) by or on behalf of the mortgagee was made, whichever last happened.

This subsection only applies where the prior mortgage was made expressly for securing a current account or other further advances.

(3) Save in regard to the making of further advances as aforesaid, the right to tack is hereby abolished:

Provided that nothing in this Act shall affect any priority acquired before the commencement of this Act by tacking, or in respect of further advances made without notice of a subsequent incumbrance or by arrangement with the subsequent incumbrancer.

(4) This section applies to mortgages of land made before or after the commencement of this Act, but not to charges [on registered land][37].

Obligation to transfer instead of reconveying, and as to right to take possession

9–079 **95.**—(1) Where a mortgagor is entitled to redeem, then subject to compliance with the terms on compliance with which he would be entitled to require a

[35] Words repealed by the Law of Property Act 1969, s.16(2), Sched. 2, Pt. I.
[36] Words substituted by the Law of Property (Amendment) Act 1926, s.7, Sched.
[37] Words substituted by the Land Registration Act 2002, s.133, Sched. 11, para. 2(1), (9).

reconveyance or surrender, he shall be entitled to require the mortgagee, instead of re-conveying or surrendering, to assign the mortgage debt and convey the mortgaged property to any third person, as the mortgagor directs; and the mortgagee shall be bound to assign and convey accordingly.

(2) The rights conferred by this section belong to and are capable of being enforced by each incumbrancer, or by the mortgagor, notwithstanding any intermediate incumbrance; but a requisition of an incumbrancer prevails over a requisition of the mortgagor, and, as between incumbrancers, a requisition of a prior incumbrancer prevails over a requisition of a subsequent incumbrancer.

(3) The foregoing provisions of this section do not apply in the case of a mortgagee being or having been in possession.

(4) Nothing in this Act affects prejudicially the right of a mortgagee of land whether or not his charge is secured by a legal term of years absolute to take possession of the land, but the taking of possession by the mortgagee does not convert any legal estate of the mortgagor into an equitable interest.

(5) This section applies to mortgages made either before or after the commencement of this Act, and takes effect notwithstanding any stipulation to the contrary.

Regulations respecting inspection, production and delivery of documents, and priorities

96.—(1) A mortgagor, as long as his right to redeem subsists, shall be entitled from time to time, at reasonable times, on his request, and at his own cost, and on payment of the mortgagee's costs and expenses in this behalf, to inspect and make copies or abstracts of or extracts from the documents of title relating to the mortgaged property in the custody or power of the mortgagee. **9–080**

This subsection applies to mortgages made after the thirty-first day of December, eighteen hundred and eighty-one, and takes effect notwithstanding any stipulation to the contrary.

(2) A mortgagee, whose mortgage is surrendered or otherwise extinguished, shall not be liable on account of delivering documents of title in his possession to the person not having the best right thereto, unless he has notice of the right or claim of a person having a better right, whether by virtue of a right to require a surrender or re-conveyance or otherwise.

[In this subsection notice does not include notice implied by reason of registration under the Land Charges Act 1925[38] [. . .][39].][40]

Priorities as between puisne mortgages

97. Every mortgage affecting a legal estate in land made after the commencement of this Act, whether legal or equitable (not being a mortgage protected by the deposit of documents relating to the legal estate affected) shall rank according to its date of registration as a land charge pursuant to the Land Charges Act 1925.[41] **9–081**

This section does not apply [to mortgages or charges to which the Land Charges Act 1972 does not apply by virtue of section 14(3) of that Act (which excludes certain land charges created by instruments necessitating registration

[38] Now the Land Charges Act 1972, *post*, para. 31–001.
[39] Words repealed by the Law of Property Act 1969, s.16(2), Sched. 2, Pt. I.
[40] Words added by the Law of Property (Amendment) Act 1926, s.7, Sched.
[41] Now the Land Charges Act 1972, *post*, para. 31–001.

under the [Land Registration Act 2002][42]), or][43] to mortgages or charges of registered land […][44]

Actions for possession by mortgagors

9–082 **98.**—(1) A mortgagor for the time being entitled to the possession or receipt of the rents and profits of any land, as to which the mortgagee has not given notice of his intention to take possession or to enter into the receipt of the rents and profits thereof, may sue for such possession, or for the recovery of such rents or profits, or to prevent or recover damages in respect of any trespass or other wrong relative thereto, in his own name only, unless the cause of action arises upon a lease or other contract made by him jointly with any other person.

(2) This section does not prejudice the power of a mortgagor independently of this section to take proceedings in his own name only, either in right of any legal estate vested in him or otherwise.

(3) This section applies whether the mortgage was made before or after the commencement of this Act.

Leasing powers of mortgagor and mortgagee in possession

9–083 **99.**—(1) A mortgagor of land while in possession shall, as against every incumbrancer, have power to make from time to time any such lease of the mortgaged land, or any part thereof, as is by this section authorised.

(2) A mortgagee of land while in possession shall, as against all prior incumbrancers, if any, and as against the mortgagor, have power to make from time to time any such lease as aforesaid.

(3) The leases which this section authorises are—

(i) agricultural or occupation leases for any term not exceeding twenty-one years, or, in the case of a mortgage made after the commencement of this Act, fifty years; and

(ii) building leases for any term not exceeding ninety-nine years, or, in the case of a mortgage made after the commencement of this Act, nine hundred and ninety-nine years.

(4) Every person making a lease under this section may execute and do all assurances and things necessary or proper in that behalf.

(5) Every such lease shall be made to take effect in possession not later than twelve months after its date.

(6) Every such lease shall reserve the best rent that can reasonably be obtained, regard being had to the circumstances of the case, but without any fine being taken.

(7) Every such lease shall contain a covenant by the lessee for payment of the rent, and a condition of re-entry on the rent not being paid within a time therein specified not exceeding thirty days.

(8) A counterpart of every such lease shall be executed by the lessee and delivered to the lessor, of which execution and delivery the execution of the lease by the lessor shall, in favour of the lessee and all persons deriving title under him, be sufficient evidence.

(9) Every such building lease shall be made in consideration of the lessee, or some person by whose direction the lease is granted, having erected, or agreeing

[42] Words substituted by the Land Registration Act 2002, s.133, Sched. 11, para. 2(1), (10).
[43] Words substituted by the Land Charges Act 1972, s.18(1), Sched. 3, para. 1.
[44] Words repealed by the Law of Property Act 1969, s.16(2), Sched. 2, Pt. I.

to erect within not more than five years from the date of the lease, buildings, new or additional, or having improved or repaired buildings, or agreeing to improve or repair buildings within that time, or having executed, or agreeing to execute within that time, on the land leased, an improvement for or in connection with building purposes.

(10) In any such building lease a peppercorn rent, or a nominal or other rent less than the rent ultimately payable, may be made payable for the first five years, or any less part of the term.

(11) In case of a lease by the mortgagor, he shall, within one month after making the lease, deliver to the mortgagee, or, where there are more than one, to the mortgagee first in priority, a counterpart of the lease duly executed by the lessee, but the lessee shall not be concerned to see that this provision is complied with.

(12) A contract to make or accept a lease under this section may be enforced by or against every person on whom the lease if granted would be binding.

(13) [Subject to subsection (13A) below,][45] this section applies only if and as far as a contrary intention is not expressed by the mortgagor and mortgagee in the mortgage deed, or otherwise in writing, and has effect subject to the terms of the mortgage deed or of any such writing and to the provisions therein contained.

[(13A) Subsection (13) of this section—

(a) shall not enable the application of any provision of this section to be excluded or restricted in relation to any mortgage of agricultural land made after 1st March 1948 but before 1st September 1995, and

(b) shall not enable the power to grant a lease of an agricultural holding to which, by virtue of section 4 of the Agricultural Tenancies Act 1995, the Agricultural Holdings Act 1986 will apply, to be excluded or restricted in relation to any mortgage of agricultural land made on or after 1st September 1995.

(13B) In subsection (13A) of this section—

"agricultural holding" has the same meaning as in the Agricultural Holdings Act 1986; and

"agricultural land" has the same meaning as in the Agriculture Act 1947.][46]

(14) The mortgagor and mortgagee may, by agreement in writing, whether or not contained in the mortgage deed, reserve to or confer on the mortgagor or the mortgagee, or both, any further or other powers of leasing or having reference to leasing; and any further or other powers so reserved or conferred shall be exercisable, as far as may be, as if they were conferred by this Act, and with all the like incidents, effects, and consequences:

Provided that the powers so reserved or conferred shall not prejudicially affect the rights of any mortgagee interested under any other mortgage subsisting at the date of the agreement, unless that mortgagee joins in or adopts the agreement.

(15) Nothing in this Act shall be construed to enable a mortgagor or mortgagee to make a lease for any longer term or on any other conditions than such as could have been granted or imposed by the mortgagor, with the concurrence of all the incumbrancers, if this Act and the enactments replaced by this section had not been passed:

Provided that, in the case of a mortgage of leasehold land, a lease granted under this section shall reserve a reversion of not less than one day.

[45] Words inserted by the Agricultural Tenancies Act 1995, s.31(1), (2).
[46] subss.(13A) and (13B) inserted by the Agricultural Tenancies Act 1995, s.31(1), (3).

(16) Subject as aforesaid, this section applies to any mortgage made after the thirty-first day of December, eighteen hundred and eighty-one, but the provisions thereof, or any of them, may, by agreement in writing made after that date between mortgagor and mortgagee, be applied to a mortgage made before that date, so nevertheless that any such agreement shall not prejudicially affect any right or interest of any mortgagee not joining in or adopting the agreement.

(17) The provisions of this section referring to a lease shall be construed to extend and apply, as far as circumstances admit, to any letting, and to an agreement, whether in writing or not, for leasing or letting.

(18) For the purposes of this section "mortgagor" does not include an incumbrancer deriving title under the original mortgagor.

(19) The powers of leasing conferred by this section shall, after a receiver of the income of the mortgaged property or any part thereof has been appointed by a mortgagee under his statutory power, and so long as the receiver acts, be exercisable by such mortgagee instead of by the mortgagor, as respects any land affected by the receivership, in like manner as if such mortgagee were in possession of the land, and the mortgagee may, by writing, delegate any of such powers to the receiver.

Powers of mortgagor and mortgagee in possession to accept surrenders of leases

9–084 **100.**—(1) For the purpose only of enabling a lease authorised under the last preceding section, or under any agreement made pursuant to that section, or by the mortgage deed (in this section referred to as an authorised lease) to be granted, a mortgagor of land while in possession shall, as against every incumbrancer, have, by virtue of this Act, power to accept from time to time a surrender of any lease of the mortgaged land or any part thereof comprised in the lease, with or without an exception of or in respect of all or any of the mines and minerals therein, and, on a surrender of the lease so far as it comprises part only of the land or mines and minerals leased, the rent may be apportioned.

(2) For the same purpose, a mortgagee of land while in possession shall, as against all prior or other incumbrancers, if any, and as against the mortgagor, have, by virtue of this Act, power to accept from time to time any such surrender as aforesaid.

(3) On a surrender of part only of the land or mines and minerals leased, the original lease may be varied, provided that the lease when varied would have been valid as an authorised lease if granted by the person accepting the surrender; and, on a surrender and the making of a new or other lease, whether for the same or for any extended or other term, and whether subject or not to the same or to any other covenants, provisions, or conditions, the value of the lessee's interest in the lease surrendered may, subject to the provisions of this section, be taken into account in the determination of the amount of the rent to be reserved, and of the nature of the covenants, provisions, and conditions to be inserted in the new or other lease.

(4) Where any consideration for the surrender, other than an agreement to accept an authorised lease, is given by or on behalf of the lessee to or on behalf of the person accepting the surrender, nothing in this section authorises a surrender to a mortgagor without the consent of the incumbrancers, or authorises a surrender to a second or subsequent incumbrancer without the consent of every prior incumbrancer.

(5) No surrender shall, by virtue of this section, be rendered valid unless:—

(a) An authorised lease is granted of the whole of the land or mines and minerals comprised in the surrender to take effect in possession immediately or within one month after the date of the surrender; and

(b) The term certain or other interest granted by the new lease is not less in duration than the unexpired term or interest which would have been subsisting under the original lease if that lease had not been surrendered; and

(c) Where the whole of the land mines and minerals originally leased has been surrendered, the rent reserved by the new lease is not less than the rent which would have been payable under the original lease if it had not been surrendered; or where part only of the land or mines and minerals has been surrendered, the aggregate rents respectively remaining payable or reserved under the original lease and new lease are not less than the rent which would have been payable under the original lease if no partial surrender had been accepted.

(6) A contract to make or accept a surrender under this section may be enforced by or against every person on whom the surrender, if completed, would be binding.

(7) This section applies only if and as far as a contrary intention is not expressed by the mortgagor and mortgagee in the mortgage deed, or otherwise in writing, and shall have effect subject to the terms of the mortgage deed or of any such writing and to the provisions therein contained.

(8) This section applies to a mortgage made after the thirty-first day of December, nineteen hundred and eleven, but the provisions of this section, or any of them, may, by agreement in writing made after that date, between mortgagor and mortgagee, be applied to a mortgage made before that date, so nevertheless that any such agreement shall not prejudicially affect any right or interest of any mortgagee not joining in or adopting the agreement.

(9) The provisions of this section referring to a lease shall be construed to extend and apply, as far as circumstances admit, to any letting, and to any agreement, whether in writing or not, for leasing or letting.

(10) The mortgagor and mortgagee may, by agreement in writing, whether or not contained in the mortgage deed, reserve or confer on the mortgagor or mortgagee, or both, any further or other powers relating to the surrender of leases; and any further or other powers so conferred or reserved shall be exercisable, as far as may be, as if they were conferred by this Act, and with all the like incidents, effects and consequences:

Provided that the powers so reserved or conferred shall not prejudicially affect the rights of any mortgagee interested under any other mortgage subsisting at the date of the agreement, unless that mortgagee joins in or adopts the agreement.

(11) Nothing in this section operates to enable a mortgagor or mortgagee to accept a surrender which could not have been accepted by the mortgagor with the concurrence of all the incumbrancers if this Act and the enactments replaced by this section had not been passed.

(12) For the purposes of this section "mortgagor" does not include an incumbrancer deriving title under the original mortgagor.

(13) The powers of accepting surrenders conferred by this section shall, after a receiver of the income of the mortgaged property or any part thereof has been appointed by the mortgagee, under the statutory power, and so long as the receiver acts, be exercisable by such mortgagee instead of by the mortgagor, as respects any land affected by the receivership, in like manner as if such

mortgagee were in possession of the land; and the mortgagee may, by writing, delegate any of such powers to the receiver.

Powers incident to estate or interest of mortgagee

9–085 **101.**—(1) A mortgagee, where the mortgage is made by deed, shall, by virtue of this Act, have the following powers, to the like extent as if they had been in terms conferred by the mortgage deed, but not further (namely):

(i) A power, when the mortgage money has become due, to sell, or to concur with any other person in selling, the mortgaged property, or any part thereof, either subject to prior charges or not, and either together or in lots, by public auction or by private contract, subject to such conditions respecting title, or evidence of title, or other matter, as the mortgagee thinks fit, with power to vary any contract for sale, and to buy in at an auction, or to rescind any contract for sale, and to re-sell, without being answerable for any loss occasioned thereby; and

(ii) A power, at any time after the date of the mortgage deed, to insure and keep insured against loss or damage by fire any building, or any effects or property of an insurable nature, whether affixed to the freehold or not, being or forming part of the property which or an estate or interest wherein is mortgaged, and the premiums paid for any such insurance shall be a charge on the mortgaged property or estate or interest, in addition to the mortgage money, and with the same priority, and with interest at the same rate, as the mortgage money; and

(iii) A power, when the mortgage money has become due, to appoint a receiver of the income of the mortgaged property, or any part thereof; or, if the mortgaged property consists of an interest in income, or of a rentcharge or an annual or other periodical sum, a receiver of that property or any part thereof; and

(iv) A power, while the mortgagee is in possession, to cut and sell timber and other trees ripe for cutting, and not planted or left standing for shelter or ornament, or to contract for any such cutting and sale, to be completed within any time not exceeding twelve months from the making of the contract.

[(1A) Subsection (1)(i) is subject to section 21 of the Commonhold and Leasehold Reform Act 2002 (no disposition of part-units).][47]

(2) Where the mortgage deed is executed after the thirty-first day of December, nineteen hundred and eleven, the power of sale aforesaid includes the following powers as incident thereto (namely):—

(i) A power to impose or reserve or make binding, as far as the law permits, by covenant, condition, or otherwise, on the unsold part of the mortgaged property or any part thereof, or on the purchaser and any property sold, any restriction or reservation with respect to building on or other user of land, or with respect to mines and minerals, or for the purpose of the more beneficial working thereof, or with respect to any other thing:

(ii) A power to sell the mortgaged property or any part thereof, or all or any mines and minerals apart from the surface:—

(a) With or without a grant or reservation of rights of way, rights of water, easements, rights, and privileges, for or con- nected with building

[47] subs. (1A) inserted by the Commonhold and Leasehold Reform Act 2002, s.68, Sched. 5, para. 2.

or other purposes in relation to the property remaining in mortgage or any part thereof, or to any property sold: and

(b) With or without an exception or reservation of all or any of the mines and minerals in or under the mortgaged property, and with or without a grant or reservation of powers of working, wayleaves, or rights of way, rights of water and drainage and other powers, easements, rights, and privileges for or connected with mining purposes in relation to the property remaining unsold or any part thereof, or to any property sold: and

(c) With or without covenants by the purchaser to expend money on the land sold.

(3) The provisions of this Act relating to the foregoing powers, comprised either in this section, or in any other section regulating the exercise of those powers, may be varied or extended by the mortgage deed, and, as so varied or extended, shall, as far as may be, operate in the like manner and with all the like incidents, effects, and consequences, as if such variations or extensions were contained in this Act.

(4) This section applies only if and as far as a contrary intention is not expressed in the mortgage deed, and has effect subject to the terms of the mortgage deed and to the provisions therein contained.

(5) Save as otherwise provided, this section applies where the mortgage deed is executed after the thirty-first day of December, eighteen hundred and eighty-one.

(6) The power of sale conferred by this section includes such power of selling the estate in fee simple or any leasehold reversion as is conferred by the provisions of this Act relating to the realisation of mortgages.

Provision as to mortgages of undivided shares in land

102.—(1) A person who was before the commencement of this Act a mortgagee of an undivided share in land shall have the same power to sell his [interest under the trust to which the land is subject][48], as, independently of this Act, he would have had in regard to the share in the land; and shall also have a right to require the [trustees][49] in whom the land is vested to account to him for the income attributable to that share or to appoint a receiver to receive the same from such trustees corresponding to the right which, independently of this Act, he would have had to take possession or to appoint a receiver of the rents and profits attributable to the same share. **9–086**

(2) The powers conferred by this section are exercisable by the persons deriving title under such mortgagee.

Regulation of exercise of power of sale

103. A mortgagee shall not exercise the power of sale conferred by this Act unless and until— **9–087**

(i) Notice requiring payment of the mortgage money has been served on the mortgagor or one of two or more mortgagors, and default has been made

[48] Words substituted by the Trusts of Land and Appointment of Trustees Act 1996, s.25(1), Sched. 3, para. 4(1), (13).

[49] Word substituted by the Trusts of Land and Appointment of Trustees Act 1996, s.25(1), Sched. 3, para. 4(1), (13).

in payment of the mortgage money, or of part thereof for three months after such service; or

(ii) Some interest under the mortgage is in arrear and unpaid for two months after becoming due; or

(iii) There has been a breach of some provision contained in the mortgage deed or in this Act, or in an enactment replaced by this Act, and on the part of the mortgagor, or of some person concurring in making the mortgage, to be observed or performed, other than and besides a covenant for payment of the mortgage money or interest thereon.

Conveyance on sale

9–088 **104.**—(1) A mortgagee exercising the power of sale conferred by this Act shall have power, by deed, to convey the property sold, for such estate and interest therein as he is by this Act authorised to sell or convey or may be the subject of the mortgage, freed from all estates, interests, and rights to which the mortgage has priority, but subject to all estates, interests, and rights which have priority to the mortgage.

(2) Where a conveyance is made in exercise of the power of sale conferred by this Act, or any enactment replaced by this Act, the title of the purchaser shall not be impeachable on the ground—

(a) that no case had arisen to authorise the sale; or
(b) that due notice was not given; or
(c) where the mortgage is made after the commencement of this Act, that leave of the court, when so required, was not obtained; or
(d) whether the mortgage was made before or after such commence-ment, that the power was otherwise improperly or irregularly exercised;

and a purchaser is not, either before or on conveyance, concerned to see or inquire whether a case has arisen to authorise the sale, or due notice has been given, or the power is otherwise properly and regularly exercised; but any person damnified by an unauthorised, or improper, or irregular exercise of the power shall have his remedy in damages against the person exercising the power.

(3) A conveyance on sale by a mortgagee, made after the commencement of this Act, shall be deemed to have been made in exercise of the power of sale conferred by this Act unless a contrary intention appears.

Application of proceeds of sale

9–089 **105.** The money which is received by the mortgagee, arising from the sale, after discharge of prior incumbrances to which the sale is not made subject, if any, or after payment into court under this Act of a sum to meet any prior incumbrance, shall be held by him in trust to be applied by him, first, in payment of all costs, charges, and expenses properly incurred by him as incident to the sale or any attempted sale, or otherwise; and secondly, in discharge of the mortgage money, interest, and costs, and other money, if any, due under the mortgage; and the residue of the money so received shall be paid to the person entitled to the mortgaged property, or authorised to give receipts for the proceeds of the sale thereof.

Provisions as to exercise of power of sale

106.—(1) The power of sale conferred by this Act may be exercised by any person for the time being entitled to receive and give a discharge for the mortgage money. **9–090**

(2) The power of sale conferred by this Act does not affect the right of foreclosure.

(3) The mortgagee shall not be answerable for any involuntary loss happening in or about the exercise or execution of the power of sale conferred by this Act, or of any trust connected therewith, or, where the mortgage is executed after the thirty-first day of December, nineteen hundred and eleven, of any power or provision contained in the mortgage deed.

(4) At any time after the power of sale conferred by this Act has become exercisable, the person entitled to exercise the power may demand and recover from any person, other than a person having in the mortgaged property an estate, interest, or right in priority to the mortgage, all the deeds and documents relating to the property, or to the title thereto, which a purchaser under the power of sale would be entitled to demand and recover from him.

Mortgagee's receipts, discharges, etc.

107.—(1) The receipt in writing of a mortgagee shall be a sufficient discharge for any money arising under the power of sale conferred by this Act, or for any money or securities comprised in his mortgage, or arising thereunder; and a person paying or transferring the same to the mortgagee shall not be concerned to inquire whether any money remains due under the mortgage. **9–091**

(2) Money received by a mortgagee under his mortgage or from the proceeds of securities comprised in his mortgage shall be applied in like manner as in this Act directed respecting money received by him arising from a sale under the power of sale conferred by this Act, but with this variation, that the costs, charges, and expenses payable shall include the costs, charges, and expenses properly incurred of recovering and receiving the money or securities, and of conversion of securities into money, instead of those incident to sale.

Amount and application of insurance money

108.—(1) The amount of an insurance effected by a mortgagee against loss or damage by fire under the power in that behalf conferred by this Act shall not exceed the amount specified in the mortgage deed, or, if no amount is therein specified, two third parts of the amount that would be required, in case of total destruction, to restore the property insured. **9–092**

(2) An insurance shall not, under the power conferred by this Act, be effected by a mortgagee in any of the following cases (namely):

(i) Where there is a declaration in the mortgage deed that no insurance is required:

(ii) Where an insurance is kept up by or on behalf of the mortgagor in accordance with the mortgage deed:

(iii) Where the mortgage deed contains no stipulation respecting insurance, and an insurance is kept up by or on behalf of the mortgagor with the consent of the mortgagee to the amount to which the mortgagee is by this Act authorised to insure.

(3) All money received on an insurance of mortgaged property against loss or

damage by fire or otherwise effected under this Act, or any enactment replaced by this Act, or on an insurance for the maintenance of which the mortgagor is liable under the mortgage deed, shall, if the mortgagee so requires, be applied by the mortgagor in making good the loss or damage in respect of which the money is received.

(4) Without prejudice to any obligation to the contrary imposed by law, or by special contract, a mortgagee may require that all money received on an insurance of mortgaged property against loss or damage by fire or otherwise effected under this Act, or any enactment replaced by this Act, or on an insurance for the maintenance of which the mortgagor is liable under the mortgage deed, be applied in or towards the discharge of the mortgage money.

Appointment, powers, remuneration and duties of receiver

9–093 **109.**—(1) A mortgagee entitled to appoint a receiver under the power in that behalf conferred by this Act shall not appoint a receiver until he has become entitled to exercise the power of sale conferred by this Act, but may then, by writing under his hand, appoint such person as he thinks fit to be receiver.

(2) A receiver appointed under the powers conferred by this Act or any enactment replaced by this Act, shall be deemed to be the agent of the mortgagor; and the mortgagor shall be solely responsible for the receiver's acts or defaults unless the mortgage deed otherwise provides.

(3) The receiver shall have power to demand and recover all the income of which he is appointed receiver, by action, distress, or otherwise, in the name either of the mortgagor or of the mortgagee, to the full extent of the estate or interest which the mortgagor could dispose of, and to give effectual receipts accordingly for the same, and to exercise any powers which may have been delegated to him by the mortgagee pursuant to this Act.

(4) A person paying money to the receiver shall not be concerned to inquire whether any case has happened to authorise the receiver to act.

(5) The receiver may be removed, and a new receiver may be appointed, from time to time by the mortgagee by writing under his hand.

(6) The receiver shall be entitled to retain out of any money received by him, for his remuneration, and in satisfaction of all costs, charges, and expenses incurred by him as receiver, a commission at such rate, not exceeding five per centum on the gross amount of all money received, as is specified in his appointment, and if no rate is so specified, then at the rate of five per centum on that gross amount, or at such other rate as the court thinks fit to allow, on application made by him for that purpose.

(7) The receiver shall, if so directed in writing by the mortgagee, insure to the extent, if any, to which the mortgagee might have insured and keep insured against loss or damage by fire, out of the money received by him, any building, effects, or property comprised in the mortgage, whether affixed to the freehold or not, being of an insurable nature.

(8) Subject to the provisions of this Act as to the application of insurance money, the receiver shall apply all money received by him as follows, namely:

(i) In discharge of all rents, taxes, rates, and outgoings whatever affecting the mortgaged property; and

(ii) In keeping down all annual sums or other payments, and the interest on all principal sums, having priority to the mortgage in right whereof he is receiver; and

(iii) In payment of his commission, and of the premiums on fire, life, or other insurances, if any, properly payable under the mortgage deed or under this Act, and the cost of executing necessary or proper repairs directed in writing by the mortgagee; and

(iv) In payment of the interest accruing due in respect of any principal money due under the mortgage; and

(v) In or towards discharge of the principal money if so directed in writing by the mortgagee;

and shall pay the residue, if any, of the money received by him to the person who, but for the possession of the receiver, would have been entitled to receive the income of which he is appointed receiver, or who is otherwise entitled to the mortgaged property.

Effect of bankruptcy of the mortgagor on the power to sell or appoint a receiver

110.—(1) Where the statutory or express power for a mortgagee either to sell or to appoint a receiver is made exercisable by reason of the mortgagor [...][50] being adjudged a bankrupt, such power shall not be exercised only on account of the [...][51] adjudication, without the leave of the court. **9–094**

(2) This section applies only where the mortgage deed is executed after the commencement of this Act; [...][52]

Effect of advance on joint account

111.—(1) Where— **9–095**

(a) in a mortgage, or an obligation for payment of money, or a transfer of a mortgage or of such an obligation, the sum, or any part of the sum, advanced or owing is expressed to be advanced by or owing to more persons than one out of money, or as money, belonging to them on a joint account; or

(b) a mortgage, or such an obligation, or such a transfer is made to more persons than one, jointly;

the mortgage money, or other money or money's worth, for the time being due to those persons on the mortgage or obligation, shall, as between them and the mortgagor or obligor, be deemed to be and remain money or money's worth belonging to those persons on a joint account; and the receipt in writing of the survivors or last survivor of them, or of the personal representative of the last survivor, shall be a complete discharge for all money or money's worth for the time being due, notwithstanding any notice to the payer of a severance of the joint account.

(2) This section applies if and so far as a contrary intention is not expressed in the mortgage, obligation, or transfer, and has effect subject to the terms of the mortgage, obligation, or transfer, and to the provisions therein contained.

(3) This section applies to any mortgage obligation or transfer made after the thirty-first day of December eighteen hundred and eighty-one.

. . . . . .

Notice of trusts affecting mortgage debts

113.—(1) A person dealing in good faith with a mortgagee, or with the mortgagor if the mortgage has been discharged released or postponed as to the **9–096**

[50] Words repealed by the Insolvency Act 1985, s.235(3), Sched. 10, Pt. III.
[51] Words repealed by the Insolvency Act 1985, s.235(3), Sched. 10, Pt. III.
[52] Words repealed by the Insolvency Act 1985, s.235(3), Sched. 10, Pt. III.

whole or any part of the mortgaged property, shall not be concerned with any trust at any time affecting the mortgage money or the income thereof, whether or not he has notice of the trust, and may assume unless the contrary is expressly stated in the instruments relating to the mortgage—

(a) that the mortgagees (if more than one) are or were entitled to the mortgage money on a joint account; and

(b) that the mortgagee has or had power to give valid receipts for the purchase money or mortgage money and the income thereof (including any arrears of interest) and to release or postpone the priority of the mortgage debt or any part thereof or to deal with the same or the mortgaged property or any part thereof;

without investigating the equitable title to the mortgage debt or the appointment or discharge of trustees in reference thereto.

(2) This section applies to mortgages made before or after the commencement of this Act, but only as respects dealings effected after such commencement.

(3) This section does not affect the liability of any person in whom the mortgage debt is vested for the purposes of any trust to give effect to that trust.

Transfers of mortgages

9–097 **114.**—(1) A deed executed by a mortgagee purporting to transfer his mortgage or the benefit thereof shall, unless a contrary intention is therein expressed, and subject to any provisions therein contained, operate to transfer to the transferee—

(a) the right to demand, sue for, recover, and give receipts for, the mortgage money or the unpaid part thereof, and the interest then due, if any, and thenceforth to become due thereon; and

(b) the benefit of all securities for the same, and the benefit of and the right to sue on all covenants with the mortgagee, and the right to exercise all powers of the mortgagee; and

(c) all the estate and interest in the mortgaged property then vested in the mortgagee subject to redemption or cesser, but as to such estate and interest subject to the right of redemption then subsisting.

(2) In this section "transferee" includes his personal representatives and assigns.

(3) A transfer of mortgage may be made in the form contained in the Third Schedule to this Act with such variations and additions, if any, as the circumstances may require.

(4) This section applies, whether the mortgage transferred was made before or after the commencement of this Act, but applies only to transfers made after the commencement of this Act.

(5) This section does not extend to a transfer of a bill of sale of chattels by way of security.

Reconveyances of mortgages by endorsed receipts

9–098 **115.**—(1) A receipt endorsed on, written at the foot of, or annexed to, a mortgage for all money thereby secured, which states the name of the person who pays the money and is executed by the chargee by way of legal mortgage or the person in whom the mortgaged property is vested and who is legally entitled to give a receipt for the mortgage money shall operate, without any reconveyance, surrender, or release—

(a) Where a mortgage takes effect by demise or subdemise, as a surrender of the term, so as to determine the term or merge the same in the reversion immediately expectant thereon;

(b) Where the mortgage does not take effect by demise or subdemise, as a reconveyance thereof to the extent of the interest which is the subject matter of the mortgage, to the person who immediately before the execution of the receipt was entitled to the equity of redemption;

and in either case, as a discharge of the mortgaged property from all principal money and interest secured by, and from all claims under the mortgage, but without prejudice to any term or other interest which is paramount to the estate or interest of the mortgagee or other person in whom the mortgaged property was vested.

(2) Provided that, where by the receipt the money appears to have been paid by a person who is not entitled to the immediate equity of redemption, the receipt shall operate as if the benefit of the mortgage had by deed been transferred to him; unless—

(a) it is otherwise expressly provided; or

(b) the mortgage is paid off out of capital money, or other money in the hands of a personal representative or trustee properly applicable for the discharge of the mortgage, and it is not expressly provided that the receipt is to operate as a transfer.

(3) Nothing in this section confers on a mortgagor a right to keep alive a mortgage paid off by him, so as to affect prejudicially any subsequent incumbrancer; and where there is no right to keep the mortgage alive, the receipt does not operate as a transfer.

(4) This section does not affect the right of any person to require a reassignment, surrender, release, or transfer to be executed in lieu of a receipt.

(5) A receipt may be given in the form contained in the Third Schedule to this Act, with such variations and additions, if any, as may be deemed expedient; [. . .][53]

(6) In a receipt given under this section the same covenants shall be implied as if the person who executes the receipt had by deed been expressed to convey the property as mortgagee, subject to any interest which is paramount to the mortgage.

(7) Where the mortgage consists of a mortgage and a further charge or of more than one deed, it shall be sufficient for the purposes of this section, if the receipt refers either to all the deeds whereby the mortgage money is secured or to the aggregate amount of the mortgage money thereby secured and for the time being owing, and is endorsed on, written at the foot of, or annexed to, one of the mortgage deeds.

(8) This section applies to the discharge of a charge by way of legal mortgage, and to the discharge of a mortgage, whether made by way of statutory mortgage or not, executed before or after the commencement of this Act, but only as respects discharges effected after such commencement.

[53] Words repealed by the Finance Act 1971, s.69(7), Sched. 14, Pt. VI.

(9) The provisions of this section relating to the operation of a receipt shall (in substitution for the like statutory provisions relating to receipts given by or on behalf of a building [...][54] [...][55] society) apply to the discharge of a mortgage made to any such society, provided that the receipt is executed in the manner required by the statute relating to the society [...][56]

(10) This section does not apply to the discharge of a [registered charge (within the meaning of the Land Registration Act 2002)].[57]

(11) In this section "mortgaged property" means the property remaining subject to the mortgage at the date of the receipt.

Cesser of mortgage terms

9–099 **116.** Without prejudice to the right of a tenant for life or other person having only a limited interest in the equity of redemption to require a mortgage to be kept alive by transfer or otherwise, a mortgage term shall, when the money secured by the mortgage has been discharged, become a satisfied term and shall cease.

Forms of statutory legal charges

9–100 **117.**—(1) As a special form of charge by way of legal mortgage, a mortgage of freehold or leasehold land may be made by a deed expressed to be made by way of statutory mortgage, being in one of the forms (Nos. 1 or 4) set out in the Fourth Schedule to this Act, with such variations and additions, if any, as circumstances may require, and if so made the provisions of this section shall apply thereto.

(2) There shall be deemed to be included, and there shall by virtue of this Act be implied, in such a mortgage deed—

First, a covenant with the mortgagee by the person therein expressed to charge as mortgagor to the effect following, namely:

> That the mortgagor will, on the stated day, pay to the mortgagee the stated mortgage money, with interest thereon in the meantime at the stated rate, and will thereafter, if and as long as the mortgage money or any part thereof remains unpaid, pay to the mortgagee (as well after as before any judgment is obtained under the mortgage) interest thereon, or on the unpaid part thereof, at the stated rate, by equal half-yearly payments the first thereof to be made at the end of six months from the day stated for payment of the mortgage money:

Secondly, a provision to the following effect (namely):

> That if the mortgagor on the stated day pays to the mortgagee the stated mortgage money, with interest thereon in the meantime at the stated rate, the mortgagee at any time thereafter, at the request and cost of the mortgagor, shall discharge the mortgaged property or transfer the benefit of the mortgage as the mortgagor may direct.

This subsection applies to a mortgage deed made under section twenty-six of the Conveyancing Act 1881 with a substitution of a reference to "the person therein expressed to convey as mortgagor" for the reference in this subsection to "the person therein expressed to charge as mortgagor."

[54] Words repealed by the Friendly Societies Act 1971, s.14(2), Sched. 3.
[55] Words repealed by the Industrial and Provident Societies Act 1965, s.77(1), Sched. 5.
[56] Words repealed by the Finance Act 1971, s.69(7), Sched. 14, Pt. VI.
[57] Words substituted by the Land Registration Act 2002, s.133, Sched. 11, para. 2(1), (11).

Forms of statutory transfers of legal charges

118.—(1) A transfer of a statutory mortgage may be made by a deed expressed to be made by way of statutory transfer of mortgage, being in such one of the three forms (Nos. 2, 3 or 4) set out in the Fourth Schedule to this Act as may be appropriate to the case with such variations and additions, if any, as circumstances may require, and if so made the provisions of this section shall apply thereto. **9–101**

(2) In whichever of those three forms the deed of transfer is made, it shall have effect as follows (namely):—

(i) There shall become vested in the person to whom the benefit of the mortgage is expressed to be transferred (who, with his personal representatives and assigns, is in this section designated the transferee), the right to demand, sue for, recover, and give receipts for the mortgage money, or the unpaid part thereof, and the interest then due, if any, and thenceforth to become due thereon, and the benefit of all securities for the same, and the benefit of and the right to sue on all covenants with the mortgagee, and the right to exercise all powers of the mortgagee:

(ii) All the term and interest, if any, subject to redemption, of the mortgagee in the mortgaged land shall vest in the transferee, subject to redemption.

(3) If a covenantor joins in the deed of transfer, there shall also be deemed to be included, and there shall by virtue of this Act be implied therein, a covenant with the transferee by the person expressed to join therein as covenantor to the effect following (namely):

That the covenantor will, on the next of the days by the mortgage deed fixed for payment of interest pay to the transferee the stated mortgage money, or so much thereof as then remains unpaid, with interest thereon, or on the unpaid part thereof, in the meantime, at the rate stated in the mortgage deed; and will thereafter, as long as the mortgage money or any part thereof remains unpaid, pay to the transferee interest on that sum, or the unpaid part thereof, at the same rate, on the successive days by the mortgage deed fixed for payment of interest.

(4) If the deed of transfer is made in the Form No. 4, it shall, by virtue of this Act, operate not only as a statutory transfer of mortgage, but also as a statutory mortgage, and the provisions of this section shall have effect in relation thereto accordingly; but it shall not be liable to any increased stamp duty by reason only of it being designated a mortgage.

(5) This section applies to the transfer of a statutory mortgage created under any enactment replaced by this Act.

Implied covenants, joint and several

119. In a deed of statutory mortgage, or of statutory transfer of mortgage, where more persons than one are expressed to convey or charge as mortgagors, or to join as covenantors, the implied covenant on their part shall be deemed to be a joint and several covenant by them; and where there are more mortgagees or more transferees than one, the implied covenant with them shall be deemed to be a covenant with them jointly, unless the amount secured is expressed to be secured to them in shares or distinct sums, in which latter case the implied covenant with them shall be deemed to be a covenant with each severally in respect of the share or distinct sum secured to him. **9–102**

Form of discharge of statutory mortgage or charge

9–103 **120.** A statutory mortgage may be surrendered or discharged by a receipt in the form (No. 5) set out in the Fourth Schedule to this Act with such variations and additions, if any, as circumstances may require.

Rentcharges[58]

Remedies for the recovery of annual sums charged on land

9–104 **121.**—(1) Where a person is entitled to receive out of any land, or out of the income of any land, any annual sum, payable half-yearly or otherwise, whether charged on the land or on the income of the land, and whether by way of rentcharge or otherwise, not being rent incident to a reversion, then, subject and without prejudice to all estates, interests, and rights having priority to the annual sum, the person entitled to receive the annual sum shall have such remedies for recovering and compelling payment thereof as are described in this section, as far as those remedies might have been conferred by the instrument under which the annual sum arises, but not further.

(2) If at any time the annual sum or any part thereof is unpaid for twenty-one days next after the time appointed for any payment in respect thereof, the person entitled to receive the annual sum may enter into and distrain on the land charged or any part thereof, and dispose according to law of any distress found, to the intent that thereby or otherwise the annual sum and all arrears thereof, and all costs and expenses occasioned by non-payment thereof, may be fully paid.

(3) If at any time the annual sum or any part thereof is unpaid for forty days next after the time appointed for any payment in respect thereof, then, although no legal demand has been made for payment thereof, the person entitled to receive the annual sum may enter into possession of and hold the land charged or any part thereof, and take the income thereof, until thereby or otherwise the annual sum and all arrears thereof due at the time of his entry, or afterwards becoming due during his continuance in possession, and all costs and expenses occasioned by non-payment of the annual sum, are fully paid; and such possession when taken shall be without impeachment of waste.

(4) In the like case the person entitled to the annual sum, whether taking possession or not, may also by deed demise the land charged or any part thereof, to a trustee for a term of years, with or without impeachment of waste, on trust, by all or any of the means hereinafter mentioned, or by any other reasonable means, to raise and pay the annual sum and all arrears thereof due or to become due, and all costs and expenses occasioned by non-payment of the annual sum, or incurred in compelling or obtaining payment thereof, or otherwise relating thereto, including the costs of the preparation and execution of the deed of demise, and the costs of the execution of the trusts of that deed:

Provided that this subsection shall not authorise the creation of a legal term of years absolute after the commencement of this Act, save where the annual sum is a rentcharge held for a legal estate.

The surplus, if any, of the money raised, or of the income received, under the trusts of the deed shall be paid to the person for the time being entitled to the land therein comprised in reversion immediately expectant on the term thereby created.

[58] See the Perpetuities and Accumulations Act 1964, s.11(1), *post*, para. 21–011.

The means by which such annual sum, arrears, costs, and expenses may be raised includes—

(a) the creation of a legal mortgage or a sale (effected by assignment or subdemise) of the term created in the land charged or any part thereof,

(b) the receipt of the income of the land comprised in the term.

(5) This section applies only if and as far as a contrary intention is not expressed in the instrument under which the annual sum arises, and has effect subject to the terms of that instrument and to the provisions therein contained.

(6) The rule of law relating to perpetuities does not apply to any powers or remedies conferred by this section [...][59]

(7) The powers and remedies conferred by this section apply where the instrument creating the annual sum comes into operation after the thirty-first day of December, eighteen hundred and eighty-one, and whether the instrument conferring the power under which the annual sum was authorised to be created came into operation before or after that date, unless the instrument creating the power or under which the annual sum is created otherwise directs.

Creation of rentcharges charged on another rentcharge and remedies for recovery thereof

122.—(1) A rentcharge or other annual sum (not being rent incident to a reversion) payable half yearly or otherwise may be granted, reserved, charged or created out of or on another rentcharge or annual sum (not being rent incident to a reversion) charged on or payable out of land or on or out of the income of land, in like manner as the same could have been made to issue out of land. **9–105**

(2) If at any time the annual sum so created or any part thereof is unpaid for twenty-one days next after the time appointed for any payment in respect thereof, the person entitled to receive the annual sum shall (without prejudice to any prior interest or charge) have power to appoint a receiver of the annual sum charged or any part thereof, and the provisions of this Act relating to the appointment, powers, remuneration and duties of a receiver, shall apply in like manner as if such person were a mortgagee entitled to exercise the power of sale conferred by this Act, and the annual sum charged were the mortgaged property and the person entitled thereto were the mortgagor.

(3) The power to appoint a receiver conferred by this section shall (where the annual sum is charged on a rentcharge) take effect in substitution for the remedies conferred, in the case of annual sums charged on land, by the last preceding section, but subsection (6) of that section shall apply and have effect as if herein re-enacted and in terms made applicable to the powers conferred by this section.

(4) This section applies to annual sums expressed to be created before as well as after the commencement of this Act, and, but without prejudice to any order of the court made before the commencement of this Act, operates to confirm any annual sum which would have been validly created if this section had been in force.

Powers of Attorney[60]

123, 124. [*Repealed by the Powers of Attorney Act 1971, s.11(2), Sched. 2.*]

[59] Words repealed by the Perpetuities and Accumulations Act 1964, s.11(2).
[60] See now the Powers of Attorney Act 1971, ss.4–7, *post*, paras 30–003 *et seq.*

Powers of attorney relating to land to be filed

9–106 **125.**—(1) [*Repealed by the Powers of Attorney Act 1971, s.11(2), Sched. 2.*]

(2) Notwithstanding any stipulation to the contrary, a purchaser of any interest in or charge upon land [(not registered land)][61] shall be entitled to have any instrument creating a power of attorney which affects his title, or [a copy][62] thereof or of the material portions thereof delivered to him free of expense.

(3) This section only applies to instruments executed after the commencement of this Act, and no right to rescind a contract shall arise by reason of the enforcement of the provisions of this section.

126–128. [*Repealed by the Powers of Attorney Act 1971, s.11(2), Sched. 2.*]

129. [*Repealed by the Powers of Attorney Act 1971, ss.8, 11(2), Sched. 2.*]

PART IV

EQUITABLE INTERESTS AND THINGS IN ACTION

[. . .][63] **Entailed interests in real and personal property**

9–107 **130.**—(1)–(3) [*Repealed by the Trusts of Land and Appointment of Trustees Act 1996, s.25(2), Sched. 4.*]

(4) In default of and subject to the execution of a disentailing assurance or the exercise of the testamentary power conferred by this Act, an entailed interest (to the extent of the property affected) shall devolve as an equitable interest, from time to time, upon the persons who would have been successively entitled thereto as the heirs of the body (either generally or of a particular class) of the tenant in tail or other person, or as tenant by the curtesy, if the entailed interest had, before the commencement of this Act, been limited in respect of freehold land governed by the general law in force immediately before such commencement, and such law had remained unaffected.

(5) Where personal chattels are settled without reference to settled land on trusts creating entailed interests therein, the trustees, with the consent of the usufructuary for the time being if of full age, may sell the chattels or any of them, and the net proceeds of any such sale shall be held in trust for and shall go to the same persons successively, in the same manner and for the same interests, as the chattels sold would have been held and gone if they had not been sold, and the income of investments representing such proceeds of sale shall be applied accordingly.

(6) [*Repealed by the Trusts of Land and Appointment of Trustees Act 1996, s.25(2), Sched. 4.*]

(7) In this Act where the context so admits "entailed interest" includes an estate tail (now made to take effect as an equitable interest) created before the commencement of this Act.

[61] Words substituted by the Land Registration Act 2002, s.133, Sched. 11, para. 2(1), (12).
[62] Words substituted by the Law of Property (Amendment) Act 1926, s.7, Sched.
[63] Words repealed by the Trusts of Land and Appointment of Trustees Act 1996, s.25(2), Sched. 4.

Abolition of the rule in Shelley's case

131. Where by any instrument coming into operation after the commencement of this Act an interest in any property is expressed to be given to the heir or heirs or issue or any particular heir or any class of the heirs or issue of any person in words which, but for this section [(and paragraph 5 of Schedule 1 to the Trusts of Land and Appointment of Trustees Act 1996)][64] would, under the rule of law known as the Rule in Shelley's case, have operated to give that person an interest in fee simple or an entailed interest, such words shall operate in equity as words of purchase and not of limitation, and shall be construed and have effect accordingly, and in the case of an interest in any property expressed to be given to an heir or heirs or any particular heir or class of heirs, the same person or persons shall take as would in the case of freehold land have answered that description under the general law in force before the commencement of this Act. **9–108**

As to heirs taking by purchase

132.—(1) A limitation of real or personal property in favour of the heir, either general or special, of a deceased person which, if limited in respect of freehold land before the commencement of this Act, would have conferred on the heir an estate in the land by purchase, shall operate to confer a corresponding equitable interest in the property on the person who would, if the general law in force immediately before such commencement had remained unaffected, have answered the description of the heir, either general or special, of the deceased in respect of his freehold land, either at the death of the deceased or at the time named in the limitation, as the case may require. **9–109**

(2) This section applies whether the deceased person dies before or after the commencement of this Act, but only applies to limitations or trusts created by an instrument coming into operation after such commencement.

133. [*Repealed by the Statute Law (Repeals) Act 1969, s.1, Sched., Pt. III.*]

Restriction on executory limitations

134.—(1) Where there is a person entitled to— **9–110**

(a) an equitable interest in land for an estate in fee simple or for any less interest not being an entailed interest, or

(b) any interest in other property, not being an entailed interest,

with an executory limitation over on default or failure of all or any of his issue, whether within or at any specified period or time or not, that executory limitation shall be or become void and incapable of taking effect, if and as soon as there is living any issue who has attained the age of [eighteen years][65] of the class on default or failure whereof the limitation over was to take effect.

(2) This section applies where the executory limitation is contained in an instrument coming into operation after the thirty-first day of December, eighteen hundred and eighty-two, save that, as regards instruments coming into

[64] Words inserted by the Trusts of Land and Appointment of Trustees Act 1996, s.25(1), Sched. 3, para. 4(1), (14).

[65] Words substituted by the Family Law Reform Act 1969, s.1(3), Sched. 1, Pt. I.

operation before the commencement of this Act, it only applies to limitations of land for an estate in fee, or for a term of years absolute or determinable on life or for a term of life.

Equitable waste

9–111 **135.** An equitable interest for life without impeachment of waste does not confer upon the tenant for life any right to commit waste of the description known as equitable waste, unless an intention to confer such right expressly appears by the instrument creating such equitable interest.

Legal assignments of things in action

9–112 **136.**—(1) Any absolute assignment by writing under the hand of the assignor (not purporting to be by way of charge only) of any debt or other legal thing in action, of which express notice in writing has been given to the debtor, trustee or other person from whom the assignor would have been entitled to claim such debt or thing in action, is effectual in law (subject to equities having priority over the right of the assignee) to pass and transfer from the date of such notice—

(a) the legal right to such debt or thing in action;

(b) all legal and other remedies for the same; and

(c) the power to give a good discharge for the same without the concurrence of the assignor:

Provided that, if the debtor, trustee or other person liable in respect of such debt or thing in action has notice—

(a) that the assignment is disputed by the assignor or any person claiming under him; or

(b) of any other opposing or conflicting claims to such debt or thing in action;

he may, if he thinks fit, either call upon the persons making claim thereto to interplead concerning the same, or pay the debt or other thing in action into court under the provisions of the Trustee Act 1925.

(2) This section does not affect the provisions of the Policies of Assurance Act 1867.

[(3) The county court has jurisdiction (including power to receive payment of money or securities into court) under the proviso to subsection (1) of this section where the amount or value of the debt or thing in action does not exceed [£30,000][66].][67]

Dealings with life interests, reversions and other equitable interests

9–113 **137.**—(1)[68] The law applicable to dealings with equitable things in action which regulates the priority of competing interests therein, shall, as respects

[66] Figure substituted by the High Court and County Courts Jurisdiction Order 1991 (S.I. 1991 No. 724), art. 2(8), Sched.

[67] subs. (3) added by the County Courts Act 1984, s.148(1), Sched. 2, Pt. II, para. 4. For the jurisdiction of the county court by agreement, see the County Courts Act 1984, s.24, *post*, para. 42–003.

[68] Consequent upon the repeal of section 102(2) of the Land Registration Act 1925 (the discontinuance of the Minor Interests Index), the rule of law referred to in this subsection (commonly known as the rule in *Dearle v. Hall*) now determines questions of priority which previously fell to be determined in accordance with the order of lodging of priority cautions and inhibitions in the Minor Interests Index: Land Registration Act 1986, s.5(1), *post*, para. 46–001. As to existing entries in the Minor Interests Index, see the Land Registration Act 1986, s.5(2), *post*, para. 46–001.

dealings with equitable interests in land, capital money, and securities representing capital money effected after the commencement of this Act, apply to and regulate the priority of competing interests therein.

This subsection applies whether or not the money or securities are in court.

(2) (i) In the case of a dealing with an equitable interest in settled land, capital money or securities representing capital money, the persons to be served with notice of the dealing shall be the trustees of the settlement; and where the equitable interest is created by a derivative or subsidiary settlement, the persons to be served with notice shall be the trustees of that settlement.

(ii) In the case of a dealing with an equitable interest in [land subject to a trust of land, or the proceeds of the sale of such land, the persons to be served with notice shall be the trustees][69].

(iii) In any other case the person to be served with notice of a dealing with an equitable interest in land shall be the estate owner of the land affected.

The persons on whom notice is served pursuant to this subsection shall be affected thereby in the same manner as if they had been trustees of personal property out of which the equitable interest was created or arose.

This subsection does not apply where the money or securities are in court.

(3) A notice, otherwise than in writing, given to, or received by, a trustee after the commencement of this Act as respects any dealing with an equitable interest in real or personal property, shall not affect the priority of competing claims of purchasers in that equitable interest.

(4) Where, as respects any dealing with an equitable interest in real or personal property—

(a) the trustees are not persons to whom a valid notice of the dealing can be given; or

(b) there are no trustees to whom a notice can be given; or

(c) for any other reason a valid notice cannot be served, or cannot be served without unreasonable cost or delay;

a purchaser may at his own cost require that—

(i) a memorandum of the dealing be endorsed, written on or permanently annexed to the instrument creating the trust;

(ii) the instrument be produced to him by the person having the possession or custody thereof to prove that a sufficient memorandum has been placed thereon or annexed thereto.

Such memorandum shall, as respects priorities, operate in like manner as if notice in writing of the dealing had been given to trustees duly qualified to receive the notice at the time when the memorandum is placed on or annexed to the instrument creating the trust.

(5) Where the property affected is settled land, the memorandum shall be placed on or annexed to the trust instrument and not the vesting instrument.

Where the property affected is land [subject to a trust of land][70], the memorandum shall be placed on or annexed to the instrument whereby the equitable interest is created.

(6) Where the trust is created by statute or by operation of law, or in any other case where there is no instrument whereby the trusts are declared, the instrument under which the equitable interest is acquired or which is evidence of

[69] Words substituted by the Trusts of Land and Appointment of Trustees Act 1996, s.25(1), Sched. 3, para. 4(1), (15).

[70] Words substituted by the Trusts of Land and Appointment of Trustees Act 1996, s.25(1), Sched. 3, para. 4(1), (15).

the devolution thereof shall, for the purposes of this section, be deemed the instrument creating the trust.

In particular, where the trust arises by reason of an intestacy, the letters of administration or probate in force when the dealing was effected shall be deemed such instrument.

(7) Nothing in this section affects any priority acquired before the commencement of this Act.

(8) Where a notice in writing of a dealing with an equitable interest in real or personal property has been served on a trustee under this section, the trustees from time to time of the property affected shall be entitled to the custody of the notice, and the notice shall be delivered to them by any person who for the time being may have the custody thereof; and subject to the payment of costs, any person interested in the equitable interest may require production of the notice.

(9) The liability of the estate owner of the legal estate affected to produce documents and furnish information to persons entitled to equitable interests therein shall correspond to the liability of a trustee for sale to produce documents and furnish information to persons entitled to equitable interests in the proceeds of sale of the land.

(10) This section does not apply until a trust has been created, and in this section "dealing" includes a disposition by operation of law.

Power to nominate a trust corporation to receive notices

9–114 **138.**—(1) By any settlement or other instrument creating a trust, a trust corporation may be nominated to whom notices of dealings affecting real or personal property may be given, whether or not under the foregoing section, and in default of such nomination the trustees (if any) of the instrument, or the court on the application of any person interested, may make the nomination.

(2) The person having the possession or custody of any instrument on which notices under that section may be endorsed shall cause the name of the trust corporation to whom notices may be given to be endorsed upon that instrument.

(3) Notice given to any trust corporation whose name is so endorsed shall operate in the same way as a notice or endorsement under the foregoing section.

(4)[71] Where a trust corporation is acting for the purposes of this section a notice given to a trustee of the trust instrument of a dealing relating to the trust property shall forthwith be delivered or sent by post by the trustee to the trust corporation, and until received by the corporation shall not affect any priority.

(5) A trust corporation shall not be nominated for the purposes of this section—

(a) unless that corporation consents to act; or
(b) where that corporation has any beneficial interest in or charge upon the trust property; or
(c) where a trust corporation is acting as the trustee or one of the trustees of the instrument creating the trust.

(6) Where a trust corporation acting for the purposes of this section becomes entitled to any beneficial interest in or charge upon the trust property, another trust corporation shall be nominated in its place and all documents relating to notices affecting the trust shall be delivered to the corporation so nominated.

(7) A trust corporation acting for the purposes of this section shall be bound

[71] See the Land Registration Act 1986, s.5(2), *post*, para. 46–001.

to keep a separate register of notices of dealings in respect of each equitable interest and shall enter therein—

(a) the date of the notice;
(b) the name of the person giving the notice;
(c) short particulars of the equitable interest intended to be affected; and
(d) short particulars of the effect of the dealing if mentioned in the notice.

(8) The trust corporation may, before making any entry in the register, require the applicant to pay a fee not exceeding the prescribed fee.

(9) Subject to the payment of a fee not exceeding the prescribed fee, the trust corporation shall permit any person who would, if the corporation had been the trustee of the trust instrument, have been entitled to inspect notices served on the trustee, to inspect and take copies of the register and any notices held by the corporation.

(10) Subject to the payment by the applicant of a fee not exceeding the prescribed fee, the trust corporation shall reply to all inquiries respecting notices received by the corporation in like manner and in the same circumstances as if the corporation had been the trustee of the trust instrument.

(11) In this section "prescribed fee" means the fee prescribed [by the Lord Chancellor][72], in cases where the Public Trustee acts as a trust corporation for the purposes of this section.

PART V

LEASES AND TENANCIES

Effect of extinguishment of reversion

139.—(1)[73] Where a reversion expectant on a lease of land is surrendered or merged, the estate or interest which as against the lessee for the time being confers the next vested right to the land, shall be deemed the reversion for the purpose of preserving the same incidents and obligations as would have affected the original reversion had there been no surrender or merger thereof. **9–115**

(2) This section applies to surrenders or mergers effected after the first day of October, eighteen hundred and forty-five.

Apportionment of conditions on severance

140.[74]—(1) Notwithstanding the severance by conveyance, surrender, or otherwise of the reversionary estate in any land comprised in a lease, and notwithstanding the avoidance or cesser in any other manner of the term granted by a lease as to part only of the land comprised therein, every condition or right of re-entry, and every other condition contained in the lease, shall be apportioned, and shall remain annexed to the severed parts of the reversionary estate as severed, and shall be in force with respect to the term whereon each **9–116**

[72] Words substituted by the Public Trustee (Liability and Fees) Act 2002, s. 2(2).
[73] subs. (1) applies where the exercise of the right to buy under Part V of the Housing Act 1985 terminates a secure tenancy: Housing Act 1985, ss.139(2), 151(2).
[74] For special provisions relating to agricultural holdings, see the Agricultural Holdings Act 1986, ss.31–33 (notices to quit part of an agricultural holding), s.74(3), (4) (compensation for termination of tenancy of part of an agricultural holding); for special provision relating to new tenancies beginning after August 30, 1995 and to farm business tenancies, see Agricultural Tenancies Act 1995, ss.4–7, 24(1).

severed part is reversionary, or the term in the part of the land as to which the term has not been surrendered, or has not been avoided or has not otherwise ceased, in like manner as if the land comprised in each severed part, or the land as to which the term remains subsisting, as the case may be, had alone originally been comprised in the lease.

(2) In this section "right of re-entry" includes a right to determine the lease by notice to quit or otherwise; but where the notice is served by a person entitled to a severed part of the reversion so that it extends to part only of the land demised, the lessee may within one month determine the lease in regard to the rest of the land by giving to the owner of the reversionary estate therein a counter notice expiring at the same time as the original notice.

(3) This section applies to leases made before or after the commencement of this Act and whether the severance of the reversionary estate or the partial avoidance or cesser of the term was effected before or after such commencement:

Provided that, where the lease was made before the first day of January eighteen hundred and eighty-two nothing in this section shall affect the operation of a severance of the reversionary estate or partial avoidance or cesser of the term which was effected before the commencement of this Act.

Rent and benefit of lessee's covenants to run with the reversion

9–117 **141.**[75]—(1) Rent reserved by a lease, and the benefit of every covenant or provision therein contained, having reference to the subject-matter thereof, and on the lessee's part to be observed or performed, and every condition of re-entry and other condition therein contained, shall be annexed and incident to and shall go with the reversionary estate in the land, or in any part thereof, immediately expectant on the term granted by the lease, notwithstanding severance of that reversionary estate, and without prejudice to any liability affecting a covenantor or his estate.

(2) Any such rent, covenant or provision shall be capable of being recovered, received, enforced, and taken advantage of, by the person from time to time entitled, subject to the term, to the income of the whole or any part, as the case may require, of the land leased.

(3) Where that person becomes entitled by conveyance or otherwise, such rent, covenant or provision may be recovered, received, enforced or taken advantage of by him notwithstanding that he becomes so entitled after the condition of re-entry or forfeiture has become enforceable, but this subsection does not render enforceable any condition of re-entry or other condition waived or released before such person becomes entitled as aforesaid.

(4) This section applies to leases made before or after the commencement of this Act, but does not affect the operation of—

(a) any severance of the reversionary estate; or

(b) any acquisition by conveyance or otherwise of the right to receive or enforce any rent covenant or provision;

effected before the commencement of this Act.

[75] ss.141 and 142 do not apply to "new tenancies" (as defined in the Landlord and Tenant (Covenants) Act 1995, s.1, *post*, para. 58–001): Landlord and Tenant (Covenants) Act 1995, s.30(4)(b). Section 141 is excluded in relation to transfers of land from a local housing authority to a housing action trust (Housing Act 1988, s.74(4)), transfers by a housing action trust (Housing Act 1988, s.84A(4)), and changes of landlord under Part IV of the Housing Act 1988 (Housing Act 1988, s.104(4)).

Obligation of lessor's covenants to run with reversion

142.[76]—(1) The obligation under a condition or of a covenant entered into by a lessor with reference to the subject-matter of the lease shall, if and as far as the lessor has power to bind the reversionary estate immediately expectant on the term granted by the lease, be annexed and incident to and shall go with that reversionary estate, or the several parts thereof, notwithstanding severance of that reversionary estate, and may be taken advantage of and enforced by the person in whom the term is from time to time vested by conveyance, devolution in law, or otherwise; and, if and as far as the lessor has power to bind the person from time to time entitled to that reversionary estate, the obligation aforesaid may be taken advantage of and enforced against any person so entitled. **9–118**

(2) This section applies to leases made before or after the commencement of this Act, whether the severance of the reversionary estate was effected before or after such commencement:

Provided that, where the lease was made before the first day of January eighteen hundred and eighty-two, nothing in this section shall affect the operation of any severance of the reversionary estate effected before such commencement.

This section takes effect without prejudice to any liability affecting a covenantor or his estate.

Effect of licences granted to lessees

143.—(1) Where a licence is granted to a lessee to do any act, the licence, unless otherwise expressed, extends only— **9–119**

(a) to the permission actually given; or

(b) to the specific breach of any provision or covenant referred to; or

(c) to any other matter thereby specifically authorised to be done;

and the licence does not prevent any proceeding for any subsequent breach unless otherwise specified in the licence.

(2) Notwithstanding any such licence—

(a) All rights under covenants and powers of re-entry contained in the lease remain in full force, and are available as against any subsequent breach of covenant, condition or other matter not specifically authorised or waived, in the same manner as if no licence had been granted; and

(b) The condition or right of entry remains in force in all respects as if the licence had not been granted, save in respect of the particular matter authorised to be done.

(3) Where in any lease there is a power or condition of re-entry on the lessee assigning, subletting or doing any other specified act without a licence, and a licence is granted—

(a) to any one of two or more lessees to do any act, or to deal with his equitable share or interest; or

(b) to any lessee, or to any one of two or more lessees to assign or underlet part only of the property, or to do any act in respect of part only of the property;

[76] ss.141 and 142 do not apply to "new tenancies" (as defined in the Landlord and Tenant (Covenants) Act 1995, s.1, *post*, para. 58–001): Landlord and Tenant (Covenants) Act 1995, s.30(4)(b). Section 141 is excluded in relation to transfers of land from a local housing authority to a housing action trust (Housing Act 1988, s.74(4)), transfers by a housing action trust (Housing Act 1988, s.84A(4)), and changes of landlord under Part IV of the Housing Act 1988 (Housing Act 1988, s.104(4)).

the licence does not operate to extinguish the right of entry in case of any breach of covenant or condition by the co-lessees of the other shares or interests in the property, or by the lessee or lessees of the rest of the property (as the case may be) in respect of such shares or interests or remaining property, but the right of entry remains in force in respect of the shares, interests or property not the subject of the licence.

This subsection does not authorise the grant after the commencement of this Act of a licence to create an undivided share in a legal estate.

(4) This section applies to licences granted after the thirteenth day of August, eighteen hundred and fifty-nine.

No fine to be exacted for licence to assign

9–120 **144.** In all leases containing a covenant, condition, or agreement against assigning, underletting, or parting with the possession, or disposing of the land or property leased without licence or consent, such covenant, condition, or agreement shall, unless the lease contains an express provision to the contrary, be deemed to be subject to a proviso to the effect that no fine or sum of money in the nature of a fine shall be payable for or in respect of such licence or consent; but this proviso does not preclude the right to require the payment of a reasonable sum in respect of any legal or other expense incurred in relation to such licence or consent.

Lessee to give notice of ejectment to lessor

9–121 **145.** Every lessee to whom there is delivered any writ for the recovery of premises demised to or held by him, or to whose knowledge any such writ comes, shall forthwith give notice thereof to his lessor or his bailiff or receiver, and, if he fails so to do, he shall be liable to forfeit to the person of whom he holds the premises an amount equal to the value of three years' improved or rack rent of the premises, to be recovered by action in any court having jurisdiction in respect of claims for such an amount.

Restrictions on and relief against forfeiture of leases and underleases

9–122 **146.**[77]—(1) A right of re-entry or forfeiture under any proviso or stipulation in a lease for a breach of any covenant or condition in the lease shall not be enforceable, by action or otherwise, unless and until the lessor serves on the lessee a notice—

(a) specifying the particular breach complained of; and

(b) if the breach is capable of remedy, requiring the lessee to remedy the breach; and

(c) in any case, requiring the lessee to make compensation in money for the breach;

and the lessee fails, within a reasonable time thereafter, to remedy the breach, if

[77] In relation to a long lease (generally, any lease originally granted for a term certain exceeding 21 years) of a dwelling, the landlord may not serve a notice under subs.(1) in respect of a breach of covenant or condition unless the tenant has admitted the breach or a court or tribunal has determined that the breach has occurred: Commonhold and Leasehold Reform Act 2002, ss.168–169. For restrictions on the enforcement of repairing covenants in long leases of small houses, see the Leasehold Property (Repairs) Act 1938, *post*, paras 14–001 *et seq*. For provisions relating to notices, see s.196 of this Act, *post*, para. 9–162, and the Landlord and Tenant Act 1927, s.18(2), *post*, para. 12–001.

it is capable of remedy, and to make reasonable compensation in money, to the satisfaction of the lessor, for the breach.

(2) Where a lessor is proceeding, by action or otherwise, to enforce such a right of re-entry or forfeiture, the lessee may, in the lessor's action, if any, or in any action brought by himself, apply to the court for relief; and the court may grant or refuse relief, as the court, having regard to the proceedings and conduct of the parties under the foregoing provisions of this section, and to all the other circumstances, thinks fit; and in case of relief may grant it on such terms, if any, as to costs, expenses, damages, compensation, penalty, or otherwise, including the granting of an injunction to restrain any like breach in the future, as the court, in the circumstances of each case, thinks fit.

(3) A lessor shall be entitled to recover as a debt due to him from a lessee, and in addition to damages (if any), all reasonable costs and expenses properly incurred by the lessor in the employment of a solicitor and surveyor or valuer, or otherwise, in reference to any breach giving rise to a right of re-entry or forfeiture which, at the request of the lessee, is waived by the lessor, or from which the lessee is relieved, under the provisions of this Act.

(4)[78] Where a lessor is proceeding by action or otherwise to enforce a right of re-entry or forfeiture under any covenant, proviso, or stipulation in a lease, or for non-payment of rent, the court may, on application by any person claiming as under-lessee any estate or interest in the property comprised in the lease or any part thereof, either in the lessor's action (if any) or in any action brought by such person for that purpose, make an order vesting, for the whole term of the lease or any less term, the property comprised in the lease or any part thereof in any person entitled as under-lessee to any estate or interest in such property upon such conditions as to execution of any deed or other document, payment of rent, costs, expenses, damages, compensation, giving security, or otherwise, as the court in the circumstances of each case may think fit, but in no case shall any such under-lessee be entitled to require a lease to be granted to him for any longer term than he had under his original sub-lease.

(5)[79] For the purposes of this section—

(a) "Lease" includes an original or derivative under-lease; also an agreement for a lease where the lessee has become entitled to have his lease granted; also a grant at a fee farm rent, or securing a rent by condition;

(b) "Lessee" includes an original or derivative under-lessee, and the persons deriving title under a lessee; also a grantee under any such grant as aforesaid and the persons deriving title under him;

(c) "Lessor" includes an original or derivative under-lessor, and the persons deriving title under a lessor; also a person making such grant as aforesaid and the persons deriving title under him;

(d) "Under-lease" includes an agreement for an under-lease where the under-lessee has become entitled to have his under-lease granted;

(e) "Under-lessee" includes any person deriving title under an under-lessee.

(6) This section applies although the proviso or stipulation under which the right of re-entry or forfeiture accrues is inserted in the lease in pursuance of the directions of any Act of Parliament.

---

[78] Nothing in subss. (8)–(10) of this section shall affect the provisions of subs. (4): Law of Property (Amendment) Act 1929, s.1. See also the Common Law Procedure Act 1852, ss.210–212, *ante*, paras 4–001 *et seq*. the Supreme Court Act 1981, s.38, *post*, para. 40–003 and the County Courts Act 1984, s.138(10), *post*, para. 42–007.

[79] The definitions in subs.(5) are applied in restricted form by the Leasehold Property (Repairs) Act 1938, s.7, *post*, para. 14–006.

(7) For the purposes of this section a lease limited to continue as long only as the lessee abstains from committing a breach of covenant shall be and take effect as a lease to continue for any longer term for which it could subsist, but determinable by a proviso for re-entry on such a breach.

(8)[80] This section does not extend—

(i) To a covenant or condition against assigning, underletting, parting with the possession, or disposing of the land leased where the breach occurred before the commencement of this Act; or

(ii) In the case of a mining lease, to a covenant or condition for allowing the lessor to have access to or inspect books, accounts, records, weighing machines or other things, or to enter or inspect the mine or the workings thereof.

(9)[81] This section does not apply to a condition for forfeiture on the bankruptcy of the lessee or on taking in execution of the lessee's interest if contained in a lease of—

(a) Agricultural or pastoral land;

(b) Mines or minerals;

(c) A house used or intended to be used as a public-house or beershop;

(d) A house let as a dwelling-house, with the use of any furniture, books, works of art, or other chattels not being in the nature of fixtures;

(e) Any property with respect to which the personal qualifications of the tenant are of importance for the preservation of the value or character of the property, or on the ground of neighbourhood to the lessor, or to any person holding under him.

(10)[82] Where a condition of forfeiture on the bankruptcy of the lessee or on taking in execution of the lessee's interest is contained in any lease, other than a lease of any of the classes mentioned in the last subsection, then—

(a) if the lessee's interest is sold within one year from the bankruptcy or taking in execution, this section applies to the forfeiture condition aforesaid;

(b) if the lessee's interest is not sold before the expiration of that year, this section only applies to the forfeiture condition aforesaid during the first year from the date of the bankruptcy or taking in execution.

(11) This section does not, save as otherwise mentioned, affect the law relating to re-entry or forfeiture or relief in case of non-payment of rent.

(12) This section has effect notwithstanding any stipulation to the contrary.

[(13) The county court has jurisdiction under this section [. . .][83].][84]

Relief against notice to effect decorative repairs

9–123 **147.**—(1) After a notice is served on a lessee relating to the internal decorative repairs to a house or other building, he may apply to the court for relief, and if, having regard to all the circumstances of the case (including in particular the length of the lessee's term or interest remaining unexpired), the

---

80 See *ante*, para. 9–122, n. 78.

81 See *ante*, para. 9–122, n. 78.

82 See *ante*, para. 9–122, n. 78.

83 Words repealed by the High Court and County Courts Jurisdiction Order 1991 (S.I. 1991 No. 724), art. 2(8), Sched.

84 subs. (13) added by the County Courts Act 1984, s.148(1), Sched. 2, Pt. II, para. 5. For the jurisdiction of the county court by agreement, see the County Courts Act 1984, s.24, *post*, para. 42–003.

court is satisfied that the notice is unreasonable, it may, by order, wholly or partially relieve the lessee from liability for such repairs.

(2) This section does not apply:—

(i) where the liability arises under an express covenant or agreement to put the property in a decorative state of repair and the covenant or agreement has never been performed;

(ii) to any matter necessary or proper—

(a) for putting or keeping the property in a sanitary condition, or

(b) for the maintenance or preservation of the structure;

(iii) to any statutory liability to keep a house in all respects reasonably fit for human habitation;

(iv) to any covenant or stipulation to yield up the house or other building in a specified state of repair at the end of the term.

(3) In this section "lease" includes an underlease and an agreement for a lease, and "lessee" has a corresponding meaning and includes any person liable to effect the repairs.

(4) This section applies whether the notice is served before or after the commencement of this Act, and has effect notwithstanding any stipulation to the contrary.

[(5) The county court has jurisdiction under this section [. . .][85].][86]

Waiver of a covenant in a lease

148.—(1) Where any actual waiver by a lessor or the persons deriving title under him of the benefit of any covenant or condition in any lease is proved to have taken place in any particular instance, such waiver shall not be deemed to extend to any instance, or to any breach of covenant or condition save that to which such waiver specially relates, nor operate as a general waiver of the benefit of any such covenant or condition. **9–124**

(2) This section applies unless a contrary intention appears and extends to waivers effected after the twenty-third day of July, eighteen hundred and sixty.

Abolition of interesse termini, and as to reversionary leases and leases for lives

149.—(1) The doctrine of interesse termini is hereby abolished. **9–125**

(2) As from the commencement of this Act all terms of years absolute shall, whether the interest is created before or after such commencement, be capable of taking effect at law or in equity, according to the estate interest or powers of the grantor, from the date fixed for commencement of the term, without actual entry.

(3) A term, at a rent or granted in consideration of a fine, limited after the commencement of this Act to take effect more than twenty-one years from the date of the instrument purporting to create it, shall be void, and any contract made after such commencement to create such a term shall likewise be void; but this subsection does not apply to any term taking effect in equity under a settlement, or created out of an equitable interest under a settlement, or under an equitable power for mortgage, indemnity or other like purposes.

[85] Words repealed by the High Court and County Courts Jurisdiction Order 1991 (S.I. 1991 No. 724), art. 2(8), Sched.

[86] subs. (5) added by the County Courts Act 1984, s.148(1), Sched. 2, Pt. II, para. 6. For the jurisdiction of the county court by agreement, see the County Courts Act 1984, s.24, *post*, para. 42–003.

(4) Nothing in subsections (1) and (2) of this section prejudicially affects the right of any person to recover any rent or to enforce or take advantage of any covenants or conditions, or, as respects terms or interests created before the commencement of this Act, operates to vary any statutory or other obligations imposed in respect of such terms or interests.

(5) Nothing in this Act affects the rule of law that a legal term, whether or not being a mortgage term, may be created to take effect in reversion expectant on a longer term, which rule is hereby confirmed.

(6) Any lease or underlease, at a rent, or in consideration of a fine, for life or lives or for any term of years determinable with life or lives, or on the marriage of the lessee, or any contract therefor, made before or after the commencement of this Act, or created by virtue of Part V of the Law of Property Act 1922, shall take effect as a lease, underlease or contract therefor, for a term of ninety years determinable after the death or marriage (as the case may be) of the original lessee, or of the survivor of the original lessees, by at least one month's notice in writing given to determine the same on one of the quarter days applicable to the tenancy, either by the lessor or the persons deriving title under him, to the person entitled to the leasehold interest, or if no such person is in existence by affixing the same to the premises, or by the lessee or other persons in whom the leasehold interest is vested to the lessor or the persons deriving title under him:

Provided that—

(a) this subsection shall not apply to any term taking effect in equity under a settlement or created out of an equitable interest under a settlement for mortgage, indemnity, or other like purposes;

(b) the person in whom the leasehold interest is vested by virtue of Part V of the Law of Property Act 1922 shall, for the purposes of this subsection, be deemed an original lessee;

(c) if the lease, underlease, or contract therefor is made determinable on the dropping of the lives of persons other than or besides the lessees, then the notice shall be capable of being served after the death of any person or of the survivor of any persons (whether or not including the lessees) on the cesser of whose life or lives the lease, underlease, or contract is made determinable, instead of after the death of the original lessee or of the survivor of the original lessees;

(d) if there are no quarter days specially applicable to the tenancy, notice may be given to determine the tenancy on one of the usual quarter days.

[(7) Subsection (8) applies where a lease, underlease or contract—

(a) relates to commonhold land, and

(b) would take effect by virtue of subsection (6) as a lease, underlease or contract of the kind mentioned in that subsection.

(8) The lease, underlease or contract shall be treated as if it purported to be a lease, underlease or contract of the kind referred to in subsection (7)(b) (and sections 17 and 18 of the Commonhold and Leasehold Reform Act 2002 (residential and non-residential leases) shall apply accordingly).][87]

Surrender of a lease, without prejudice to underleases with a view to the grant of a new lease

9–126 **150.**—(1) A lease may be surrendered with a view to the acceptance of a new lease in place thereof, without a surrender of any under-lease derived thereout.

[87] subss. (7) and (8) added by the Commonhold and Leasehold Reform Act 2002, s.68, Sched. 5, para. 3.

(2) A new lease may be granted and accepted, in place of any lease so surrendered, without any such surrender of an under-lease as aforesaid, and the new lease operates as if all under-leases derived out of the surrendered lease had been surrendered before the surrender of that lease was effected.

(3) The lessee under the new lease and any person deriving title under him is entitled to the same rights and remedies in respect of the rent reserved by and the covenants, agreements and conditions contained in any under-lease as if the original lease had not been surrendered but was or remained vested in him.

(4) Each under-lessee and any person deriving title under him is entitled to hold and enjoy the land comprised in his under-lease (subject to the payment of any rent reserved by and to the observance of the covenants agreements and conditions contained in the under-lease) as if the lease out of which the under-lease was derived had not been surrendered.

(5) The lessor granting the new lease and any person deriving title under him is entitled to the same remedies, by distress or entry in and upon the land comprised in any such under-lease for rent reserved by or for breach of any covenant, agreement or condition contained in the new lease (so far only as the rents reserved by or the covenants, agreements or conditions contained in the new lease do not exceed or impose greater burdens than those reserved by or contained in the original lease out of which the under-lease is derived) as he would have had—

(a) If the original lease had remained on foot; or

(b) If a new under-lease derived out of the new lease had been granted to the under-lessee or a person deriving title under him;

as the case may require.

(6) This section does not affect the powers of the court to give relief against forfeiture.

Provision as to attornments by tenants

151.—(1) Where land is subject to a lease— **9–127**

(a) the conveyance of a reversion in the land expectant on the determination of the lease; or

(b) the creation or conveyance of a rentcharge to issue or issuing out of the land;

shall be valid without any attornment of the lessee:

Nothing in this subsection—

(i) affects the validity of any payment of rent by the lessee to the person making the conveyance or grant before notice of the conveyance or grant is given to him by the person entitled thereunder; or

(ii) renders the lessee liable for any breach of covenant to pay rent, on account of his failure to pay rent to the person entitled under the conveyance or grant before such notice is given to the lessee.

(2) An attornment by the lessee in respect of any land to a person claiming to be entitled to the interest in the land of the lessor, if made without the consent of the lessor, shall be void.

This subsection does not apply to an attornment—

(a) made pursuant to a judgment of a court of competent jurisdiction; or

(b) to a mortgagee, by a lessee holding under a lease from the mortgagor where the right of redemption is barred; or

(c) to any other person rightfully deriving title under the lessor.

Leases invalidated by reason of non-compliance with terms of powers under which they are granted

9–128 **152.**—(1) Where in the intended exercise of any power of leasing, whether conferred by an Act of Parliament or any other instrument, a lease (in this section referred to as an invalid lease) is granted, which by reason of any failure to comply with the terms of the power is invalid, then—

(a) as against the person entitled after the determination of the interest of the grantor to the reversion; or

(b) as against any other person who, subject to any lease properly granted under the power, would have been entitled to the land comprised in the lease;

the lease, if it was made in good faith, and the lessee has entered thereunder, shall take effect in equity as a contract for the grant, at the request of the lessee, of a valid lease under the power, of like effect as the invalid lease, subject to such variations as may be necessary in order to comply with the terms of the power:

Provided that a lessee under an invalid lease shall not, by virtue of any such implied contract, be entitled to obtain a variation of the lease if the other persons who would have been bound by the contract are willing and able to confirm the lease without variation.

(2) Where a lease granted in the intended exercise of such a power is invalid by reason of the grantor not having power to grant the lease at the date thereof, but the grantor's interest in the land comprised therein continues after the time when he might, in the exercise of the power, have properly granted a lease in the like terms, the lease shall take effect as a valid lease in like manner as if it had been granted at that time.

(3) Where during the continuance of the possession taken under an invalid lease the person for the time being entitled, subject to such possession, to the land comprised therein or to the rents and profits thereof, is able to confirm the lease without variation, the lessee, or other person who would have been bound by the lease had it been valid, shall, at the request of the person so able to confirm the lease, be bound to accept a confirmation thereof, and thereupon the lease shall have effect and be deemed to have had effect as a valid lease from the grant thereof.

Confirmation under this subsection may be by a memorandum in writing signed by or on behalf of the persons respectively confirming and accepting the confirmation of the lease.

(4) Where a receipt or a memorandum in writing confirming an invalid lease is, upon or before the acceptance of rent thereunder, signed by or on behalf of the person accepting the rent, that acceptance shall, as against that person, be deemed to be a confirmation of the lease.

(5) The foregoing provisions of this section do not affect prejudicially—

(a) any right of action or other right or remedy to which, but for those provisions or any enactment replaced by those provisions, the lessee named in an invalid lease would or might have been entitled under any covenant on the part of the grantor for title or quiet enjoyment contained therein or implied thereby; or

(b) any right of re-entry or other right or remedy to which, but for those provisions or any enactment replaced thereby, the grantor or other person for the time being entitled to the reversion expectant on the termination of the lease, would or might have been entitled by reason of any breach of the covenants, conditions or provisions contained in the lease and binding on the lessee.

(6) Where a valid power of leasing is vested in or may be exercised by a person who grants a lease which, by reason of the determination of the interest of the grantor or otherwise, cannot have effect and continuance according to the terms thereof independently of the power, the lease shall for the purposes of this section be deemed to have been granted in the intended exercise of the power although the power is not referred to in the lease.

(7) This section does not apply to a lease of land held on charitable, ecclesiastical or public trusts.

(8) This section takes effect without prejudice to the provision in this Act for the grant of leases in the name and on behalf of the estate owner of the land affected.

Enlargement of residue of long terms into fee simple estates

153.—(1) Where a residue unexpired of not less than two hundred years of a term, which, as originally created, was for not less than three hundred years, is subsisting in land, whether being the whole land originally comprised in the term, or part only thereof,— **9–129**

(a) without any trust or right of redemption affecting the term in favour of the freeholder, or other person entitled in reversion expectant on the term; and

(b) without any rent, or with merely a peppercorn rent or other rent having no money value, incident to the reversion, or having had a rent, not being merely a peppercorn rent or other rent having no money value, originally so incident, which subsequently has been released or has become barred by lapse of time, or has in any other way ceased to be payable;

the term may be enlarged into a fee simple in the manner, and subject to the restrictions in this section provided.

(2) This section applies to and includes every such term as aforesaid whenever created, whether or not having the freehold as the immediate reversion thereon; but does not apply to—

(i) Any term liable to be determined by re-entry for condition broken; or

(ii) Any term created by subdemise out of a superior term, itself incapable of being enlarged into fee simple.

(3) This section extends to mortgage terms, where the right of redemption is barred.

(4) A rent not exceeding the yearly sum of one pound which has not been collected or paid for a continuous period of twenty years or upwards shall, for the purposes of this section, be deemed to have ceased to be payable:

Provided that, of the said period, at least five years must have elapsed after the commencement of this Act.

(5) Where a rent incident to a reversion expectant on a term to which this section applies is deemed to have ceased to be payable for the purposes aforesaid, no claim for such rent or for any arrears thereof shall be capable of being enforced.

(6) Each of the following persons, namely—

(i) Any person beneficially entitled in right of the term, whether subject to any incumbrance or not, to possession of any land comprised in the term, and, in the case of a married woman without the concurrence of her husband, whether or not she is entitled for her separate use or as her separate property [...][88]

(ii) Any person being in receipt of income as trustee, in right of the term, or having the term vested in him [as a trustee of land][89], whether subject to any incumbrance or not;

(iii) Any person in whom, as personal representative of any deceased person, the term is vested, whether subject to any incumbrance or not;

shall, so far as regards the land to which he is entitled, or in which he is interested in right of the term, in any such character as aforesaid, have power by deed to declare to the effect that, from and after the execution of the deed, the term shall be enlarged into a fee simple.

(7) Thereupon, by virtue of the deed and of this Act, the term shall become and be enlarged accordingly, and the person in whom the term was previously vested shall acquire and have in the land a fee simple instead of the term.

(8) The estate in fee simple so acquired by enlargement shall be subject to all the same trusts, powers, executory limitations over, rights, and equities, and to all the same covenants and provisions relating to user and enjoyment, and to all the same obligations of every kind, as the term would have been subject to if it had not been so enlarged.

(9) But where—

(a) any land so held for the residue of a term has been settled in trust by reference to other land, being freehold land, so as to go along with that other land, or, in the case of settlements coming into operation before the commencement of this Act, so as to go along with that other land as far as the law permits; and

(b) at the time of enlargement, the ultimate beneficial interest in the term, whether subject to any subsisting particular estate or not, has not become absolutely and indefeasibly vested in any person, free from charges or powers of charging created by a settlement;

the estate in fee simple acquired as aforesaid shall, without prejudice to any conveyance for value previously made by a person having a contingent or defeasible interest in the term, be liable to be, and shall be, conveyed by means of a subsidiary vesting instrument and settled in like manner as the other land, being freehold land, aforesaid, and until so conveyed and settled shall devolve beneficially as if it had been so conveyed and settled.

(10) The estate in fee simple so acquired shall, whether the term was originally created without impeachment of waste or not, include the fee simple in all mines and minerals which at the time of enlargement have not been severed in right or in fact, or have not been severed or reserved by an inclosure Act or award.

Application of Part V to existing leases

9–130 **154.**[90] This Part of this Act, except where otherwise expressly provided, applies to leases created before or after the commencement of this Act, and "lease" includes an under-lease or other tenancy.

[88] Words repealed by the Married Women (Restraint upon Anticipation) Act 1949, s.1, Sched. 2.
[89] Words substituted by the Trusts of Land and Appointment of Trustees Act 1996, s.25(1), Sched. 3, para. 4(1), (16).
[90] Applied in restricted form by the Leasehold Property (Repairs) Act 1938, s.7(1), *post*, para. 14–006.

Part VI

Powers

Release of powers simply collateral

155. A person to whom any power, whether coupled with an interest or not, is given may by deed release, or contract not to exercise, the power. **9–131**

Disclaimer of power

156.—(1) A person to whom any power, whether coupled with an interest or not, is given may by deed disclaim the power, and, after disclaimer, shall not be capable of exercising or joining in the exercise of the power. **9–132**

(2) On such disclaimer, the power may be exercised by the other person or persons or the survivor or survivors of the other persons, to whom the power is given, unless the contrary is expressed in the instrument creating the power.

Protection of purchasers claiming under certain void appointments

157.—(1) An instrument purporting to exercise a power of appointment over property, which, in default of and subject to any appointment, is held in trust for a class or number of persons of whom the appointee is one, shall not (save as hereinafter provided) be void on the ground of fraud on the power as against a purchaser in good faith: **9–133**

Provided that, if the interest appointed exceeds, in amount or value, the interest in such property to which immediately before the execution of the instrument the appointee was presumptively entitled under the trust in default of appointment, having regard to any advances made in his favour and to any hotchpot provision, the protection afforded by this section to a purchaser shall not extend to such excess.

(2) In this section "a purchaser in good faith" means a person dealing with an appointee of the age of not less than twenty-five years for valuable consideration in money or money's worth, and without notice of the fraud, or of any circumstances from which, if reasonable inquiries had been made, the fraud might have been discovered.

(3) Persons deriving title under any purchaser entitled to the benefit of this section shall be entitled to the like benefit.

(4) This section applies only to dealings effected after the commencement of this Act.

Validation of appointments where objects are excluded or take illusory shares

158.—(1) No appointment made in exercise of any power to appoint any property among two or more objects shall be invalid on the ground that— **9–134**

(a) an unsubstantial, illusory, or nominal share only is appointed to or left unappointed to devolve upon any one or more of the objects of the power; or

(b) any object of the power is thereby altogether excluded;

but every such appointment shall be valid notwithstanding that any one or more of the objects is not thereby, or in default of appointment, to take any share in the property.

(2) This section does not affect any provision in the instrument creating the power which declares the amount of any share from which any object of the power is not to be excluded.

(3) This section applies to appointments made before or after the commencement of this Act.

Execution of powers not testamentary

9–135 **159.**—(1) A deed executed in the presence of and attested by two or more witnesses (in the manner in which deeds are ordinarily executed and attested) is so far as respects the execution and attestation thereof, a valid execution of a power of appointment by deed or by any instrument in writing, not testamentary, notwithstanding that it is expressly required that a deed or instrument in writing, made in exercise of the power, is to be executed or attested with some additional or other form of execution or attestation or solemnity.

(2) This section does not operate to defeat any direction in the instrument creating the power that—

- (a) the consent of any particular person is to be necessary to a valid execution;
- (b) in order to give validity to any appointment, any act is to be performed having no relation to the mode of executing and attesting the instrument.

(3) This section does not prevent the donee of a power from executing it in accordance with the power by writing, or otherwise than by an instrument executed and attested as a deed; and where a power is so executed this section does not apply.

(4) This section applies to appointments by deed made after the thirteenth day of August, eighteen hundred and fifty-nine.

Application of Part VI to existing powers

9–136 **160.** This Part of this Act applies to powers created or arising either before or after the commencement of this Act.

PART VII

PERPETUITIES AND ACCUMULATIONS[91]

Perpetuities

Abolition of the double possibility rule

9–137 **161.**—(1) The rule of law prohibiting the limitation, after a life interest to an unborn person, of an interest in land to the unborn child or other issue of an unborn person is hereby abolished, but without prejudice to any other rule relating to perpetuities.

(2) This section only applies to limitations or trusts created by an instrument coming into operation after the commencement of this Act.

[91] See the Perpetuities and Accumulations Act 1964, *post*, paras 21–001 *et seq.*

Restrictions on the perpetuity rule

162.—(1) For removing doubts, it is hereby declared that the rule of law relating to perpetuities does not apply and shall be deemed never to have applied— **9–138**

(a) To any power to distrain on or to take possession of land or the income thereof given by way of indemnity against a rent, whether charged upon or payable in respect of any part of that land or not; or

(b) To any rentcharge created only as an indemnity against another rentcharge, although the indemnity rentcharge may only arise or become payable on breach of a condition or stipulation; or

(c) To any power, whether exercisable on breach of a condition or stipulation or not, to retain or withhold payment of any instalment of a rentcharge as an indemnity against another rentcharge; or

(d) To any grant, exception, or reservation of any right of entry on, or user of, the surface of land or of any easements, rights, or privileges over or under land for the purpose of—

(i) winning, working, inspecting, measuring, converting, manufacturing, carrying away, and disposing of mines and minerals;

(ii) inspecting, grubbing up, felling and carrying away timber and other trees, and the tops and lops thereof;

(iii) executing repairs, alterations, or additions to any adjoining land, or the buildings and erections thereon;

(iv) constructing, laying down, altering, repairing, renewing, cleansing, and maintaining sewers, watercourses, cesspools, gutters, drains, water-pipes, gas-pipes, electric wires or cables or other like works.

(2) This section applies to instruments coming into operation before or after the commencement of this Act.

163. [*Repealed by the Perpetuities and Accumulations Act 1964, s.4(6).*]

Accumulations

General restrictions on accumulation of income

164.[92]—(1) No person may by any instrument or otherwise settle or dispose of any property in such manner that the income thereof shall, save as hereinafter mentioned, be wholly or partially accumulated for any longer period than one of the following, namely:— **9–139**

(a) the life of the grantor or settlor; or

(b) a term of twenty-one years from the death of the grantor, settlor or testator; or

(c) the duration of the minority or respective minorities of any person or persons living or en ventre sa mere at the death of the grantor, settlor or testator; or

(d) the duration of the minority or respective minorities only of any person or persons who under the limitations of the instrument directing the accumulations would, for the time being, if of full age, be entitled to the income directed to be accumulated.

[92] For extensions and restrictions relating to the power to accumulate income, see the Perpetuities and Accumulations Act 1964, s.13, *post*, para. 21–013.

In every case where any accumulation is directed otherwise than as aforesaid, the direction shall (save as hereinafter mentioned) be void; and the income of the property directed to be accumulated shall, so long as the same is directed to be accumulated contrary to this section, go to and be received by the person or persons who would have been entitled thereto if such accumulation had not been directed.

(2) This section does not extend to any provision—

(i) for payment of the debts of any grantor, settlor, testator or other person;

(ii) for raising portions for—

(a) any child, children or remoter issue of any grantor, settlor or testator; or

(b) any child, children or remoter issue of a person taking any interest under any settlement or other disposition directing the accumulations or to whom any interest is thereby limited;

(iii) respecting the accumulation of the produce of timber or wood;

and accordingly such provisions may be made as if no statutory restrictions on accumulation of income had been imposed.

(3) The restrictions imposed by this section apply to instruments made on or after the twenty-eighth day of July, eighteen hundred, but in the case of wills only where the testator was living and of testamentary capacity after the end of one year from that date.

Qualification of restrictions on accumulation

9–140 **165.** Where accumulations of surplus income are made during a minority under any statutory power or under the general law, the period for which such accumulations are made is not (whether the trust was created or the accumulations were made before or after the commencement of this Act) to be taken into account in determining the periods for which accumulations are permitted to be made by the last preceding section, and accordingly an express trust for accumulation for any other permitted period shall not be deemed to have been invalidated or become invalid, by reason of accumulations also having been made as aforesaid during such minority.

Restriction on accumulation for the purchase of land

9–141 **166.**—(1) No person may settle or dispose of any property in such manner that the income thereof shall be wholly or partially accumulated for the purchase of land only, for any longer period than the duration of the minority or respective minorities of any person or persons who, under the limitations of the instrument directing the accumulation, would be for the time being, if of full age, be entitled to the income so directed to be accumulated.

(2) This section does not, nor do the enactments which it replaces, apply to accumulations to be held as capital money for the purposes of the Settled Land Act 1925 or the enactments replaced by that Act, whether or not the accumulations are primarily liable to be laid out in the purchase of land.

(3) This section applies to settlements and dispositions made after the twenty-seventh day of June eighteen hundred and ninety-two.

PART VIII

167–170. [*Repealed by the Statute Law (Repeals) Act 1969, s.1, Sched., Pt. III.*]

171. [*Repealed by the Mental Health Act 1959, s.149(2), Sched. 8, Pt. I.*]

Part IX

Voidable Dispositions

172. [*Repealed by the Insolvency Act 1985, s.235(3), Sched. 10, Pt. IV.*][93]

Voluntary disposition of land how far voidable as against purchasers

173.—(1) Every voluntary disposition of land made with intent to defraud a subsequent purchaser is voidable at the instance of that purchaser. **9–142**

(2) For the purposes of this section, no voluntary disposition, whenever made, shall be deemed to have been made with intent to defraud by reason only that a subsequent conveyance for valuable consideration was made, if such subsequent conveyance was made after the twenty-eight day of June, eighteen hundred and ninety-three.

Acquisitions of reversions at an under value

174.—(1) No acquisition made in good faith, without fraud or unfair dealing, of any reversionary interest in real or personal property, for money or money's worth, shall be liable to be opened or set aside merely on the ground of under value. **9–143**

In this subsection "reversionary interest" includes an expectancy or possibility.

(2) This section does not affect the jurisdiction of the court to set aside or modify unconscionable bargains.

Part X

Wills

Contingent and future testamentary gifts to carry the intermediate income

175.—(1) A contingent or future specific devise or bequest of property, whether real or personal, and a contingent residuary devise of freehold land, and a specific or residuary devise of freehold land to trustees upon trust for persons whose interests are contingent or executory shall, subject to the statutory provisions relating to accumulations, carry the intermediate income of that property from the death of the testator, except so far as such income, or any part thereof, may be otherwise expressly disposed of. **9–144**

(2) This section applies only to wills coming into operation after the commencement of this Act.

Power for tenant in tail in possession to dispose of property by specific devise or bequest

176.—(1) A tenant in tail of full age shall have power to dispose by will, by means of a devise or bequest referring specifically either to the property or to the instrument under which it was acquired or to entailed property generally— **9–145**

---

[93] See the Insolvency Act 1986, ss.423–425, *post*, paras 47–012 *et seq*.

(a) of all property of which he is tenant in tail in possession at his death; and
(b) of money (including the proceeds of property directed to be sold) subject to be invested in the purchase of property, of which if it had been so invested he would have been tenant in tail in possession at his death;

in like manner as if, after barring the entail, he had been tenant in fee-simple or absolute owner thereof for an equitable interest at his death, but, subject to and in default of any such disposition by will, such property shall devolve in the same manner as if this section had not been passed.

(2) This section applies to entailed interests authorised to be created by this Act as well as to estates tail created before the commencement of this Act, but does not extend to a tenant in tail who is by statute restrained from barring or defeating his estate tail, whether the land or property in respect whereof he is so restrained was purchased with money provided by Parliament in consideration of public services or not, or to a tenant in tail after possibility of issue extinct, and does not render any interest which is not disposed of by the will of the tenant in tail liable for his debts or other liabilities.

(3) In this section "tenant in tail" includes an owner of a base fee in possession who has power to enlarge the base fee into a fee-simple without the concurrence of any other person.

(4) This section only applies to wills executed after the commencement of this Act, or confirmed or republished by codicil executed after such commencement.

177. [*Repealed by the Administration of Justice Act 1982, s.75(1), Sched. 9, Pt. I.*][94]

178. [*Repealed by the Statute Law (Repeals) Act 1969, s.1, Sched., Pt. III.*]

Prescribed forms for reference in wills

9–146 **179.** The Lord Chancellor may from time to time prescribe and publish forms to which a testator may refer in his will, and give directions as to the manner in which they may be referred to, but, unless so referred to, such forms shall not be deemed to be incorporated in a will.

PART XI

MISCELLANEOUS

Miscellaneous

Provisions as to corporations

9–147 **180.**—(1) Whether either after or before the commencement of this Act any property or any interest therein is or has been vested in a corporation sole (including the Crown), the same shall, unless and until otherwise disposed of by the corporation, pass and devolve to and vest in and be deemed always to have passed and devolved to or vested in the successors from time to time of such corporation.

[94] See the Wills Act 1837, s.18, *ante*, para. 2–012.

(2) Where either after or before the commencement of this Act there is or has been a vacancy in the office of a corporation sole or in the office of the head of a corporation aggregate (in any case in which the vacancy affects the status or powers of the corporation) at the time when, if there had been no vacancy, any interest in or charge on property would have been acquired by the corporation, such interest shall notwithstanding such vacancy vest and be deemed to have vested in the successor to such office on his appointment as a corporation sole, or in the corporation aggregate (as the case may be), but without prejudice to the right of such successor, or of the corporation aggregate after the appointment of its head officer, to disclaim that interest or charge.

(3) Any contract or other transaction expressed or purported to be made with a corporation sole, or any appointment of a corporation sole as a custodian or other trustee or as a personal representative, at a time (either after or before the commencement of this Act) when there was a vacancy in the office, shall on the vacancy being filled take effect and be deemed to have taken effect as if the vacancy had been filled before the contract, transaction or appointment was expressed to be made or was capable of taking effect, and on the appointment of a successor shall be capable of being enforced, accepted, disclaimed or renounced by him.

Dissolution of a corporation

181.—(1) Where, by reason of the dissolution of a corporation either before or after the commencement of this Act, a legal estate in any property has determined, the court may by order create a corresponding estate and vest the same in the person who would have been entitled to the estate which determined had it remained a subsisting estate. **9–148**

[(2) The county court has jurisdiction under this section where the amount or value of the property or of the interest in the property which is to be dealt with in the court does not exceed [£30,000][95].][96]

Protection of solicitor and trustees adopting Act

182.[97]—(1) The powers given by this Act to any person, and the covenants, provisions, stipulations, and words which under this Act are to be deemed to be included or implied in any instrument, or are by this Act made applicable to any contract for sale or other transaction, are and shall be deemed in law proper powers, covenants, provisions, stipulations, and words, to be given by or to be contained in any such instrument, or to be adopted in connection with, or applied to, any such contract or transaction, and a solicitor shall not be deemed guilty of neglect or breach of duty, or become in any way liable, by reason of his omitting, in good faith, in any such instrument, or in connection with any such contract or transaction, to negative the giving, inclusion, implication, or application of any of those powers, covenants, provisions, stipulations, or words, or to insert or apply any others in place thereof, in any case where the provisions of this Act would allow of his doing so. **9–149**

[95] Figure substituted by the High Court and County Courts Jurisdiction Order 1991 (S.I. 1991 No. 724), art. 2(8), Sched.

[96] subs. (2) added (and subs. (1) numbered) by the County Courts Act 1984, s.148(1), Sched. 2, Pt. II, para. 7(1), (2). For the jurisdiction of the county court by agreement, see the County Courts Act 1984, s.24, *post*, para. 42–003.

[97] See *ante*, para. 9–010, n. 26.

(2) But, save as expressly provided by this Act, nothing in this Act shall be taken to imply that the insertion in any such instrument, or the adoption in connection with, or the application to, any contract or transaction, of any further or other powers, covenants, provisions, stipulations, or words is improper.

(3) Where the solicitor is acting for trustees, executors, or other persons in a fiduciary position, those persons shall also be protected in like manner.

(4) Where such persons are acting without a solicitor, they shall also be protected in like manner.

Fraudulent concealment of documents and falsification of pedigrees

9–150 **183.**—(1) Any person disposing of property or any interest therein for money or money's worth to a purchaser, or the solicitor or other agent of such person, who—

(a) conceals from the purchaser any instrument or incumbrance material to the title; or

(b) falsifies any pedigree upon which the title may depend in order to induce the purchaser to accept the title offered or produced;

with intent in any of such cases to defraud, is guilty of a misdemeanour punishable by fine, or by imprisonment for a term not exceeding two years, or by both.

(2) Any such person or his solicitor or agent is also liable to an action for damages by the purchaser or the persons deriving title under him for any loss sustained by reason of—

(a) the concealment of the instrument or incumbrance; or

(b) any claim made by a person under such pedigree whose right was concealed by such falsification as aforesaid.

(3) In estimating damages, where the property or any interest therein is recovered from the purchaser or the persons deriving title under him, regard shall be had to any expenditure by him or them in improvements of any land.

(4) No prosecution for any offence under this section shall be commenced without the leave of the Attorney-General.

(5) Before leave to prosecute is granted there shall be given to the person intended to be prosecuted such notice of the application for leave to prosecute as the Attorney-General may direct.

Presumption of survivorship in regard to claims to property

9–151 **184.**[98] In all cases where, after the commencement of this Act, two or more persons have died in circumstances rendering it uncertain which of them survived the other or others, such deaths shall (subject to any order of the court), for all purposes affecting the title to property, be presumed to have occurred in order of seniority, and accordingly the younger shall be deemed to have survived the elder.

Merger

9–152 **185.** There is no merger by operation of law only of any estate the beneficial interest in which would not be deemed to be merged or extinguished in equity.

[98] Excluded in the case of husband and wife, one or both of whom die intestate, by the Administration of Estates Act 1925, s.46(3), *post*, para. 10–037.

Rights of pre-emption capable of release

186. All statutory and other rights of pre-emption affecting a legal estate shall be and be deemed always to have been capable of release, and unless released shall remain in force as equitable interests only. **9–153**

Legal easements

187.—(1) Where an easement, right or privilege for a legal estate is created, it shall enure for the benefit of the land to which it is intended to be annexed. **9–154**

(2) Nothing in this Act affects the right of a person to acquire, hold or exercise an easement, right or privilege over or in relation to land for a legal estate in common with any other person, or the power of creating or conveying such an easement right or privilege.

Power to direct division of chattels

188.—(1) Where any chattels belong to persons in undivided shares, the persons interested in a moiety or upwards may apply to the court for an order for division of the chattels or any of them, according to a valuation or otherwise, and the court may make such order and give any consequential directions as it thinks fit. **9–155**

[(2) The county court has jurisdiction under this section where the amount or value of the property or of the interest in the property which is to be dealt with in the court does not exceed [£30,000][99].][1]

Indemnities against rents

189.—(1) A power of distress given by way of indemnity against a rent or any part thereof payable in respect of any land, or against the breach of any covenant or condition in relation to land, is not and shall not be deemed ever to have been a bill of sale within the meaning of the Bills of Sale Acts 1878 and 1882 as amended by any subsequent enactment. **9–156**

(2) The benefit of all covenants and powers given by way of indemnity against a rent or any part thereof payable in respect of land, or against the breach of any covenant or condition in relation to land, is and shall be deemed always to have been annexed to the land to which the indemnity is intended to relate, and may be enforced by the estate owner for the time being of the whole or any part of that land, notwithstanding that the benefit may not have been expressly apportioned or assigned to him or to any of his predecessors in title.

[99] Figure substituted by the High Court and County Courts Jurisdiction Order 1991 (S.I. 1991 No. 724), art. 2(8), Sched.

[1] subs. (2) added (and subs. (1) numbered) by the County Courts Act 1984, s.148(1), Sched. 2, Pt. II, para. 8(1), (2). For the jurisdiction of the county court by agreement, see the County Courts Act 1984, s.24, *post*, para. 42–003.

Redemption and Apportionment of Rents, etc.

Equitable apportionment of rents and remedies for non-payment or breach of covenant

9–157 **190.**—(1) Where in a conveyance for valuable consideration, other than a mortgage, of part of land which is affected by a rentcharge, such rentcharge or a part thereof is, without the consent of the owner thereof, expressed to be—

(a) charged exclusively on the land conveyed or any part thereof in exoneration of the land retained or other land; or

(b) charged exclusively on the land retained or any part thereof in exoneration of the land conveyed or other land; or

(c) apportioned between the land conveyed or any part thereof, and the land retained by the grantor or any part thereof;

then, without prejudice to the rights of the owner of the rentcharge, such charge or apportionment shall be binding as between the grantor and the grantee under the conveyance and their respective successors in title.

(2) Where—

(a) any default is made in payment of the whole or part of a rentcharge by the person who, by reason of such charge or apportionment as aforesaid, is liable to pay the same; or

(b) any breach occurs of any of the covenants (other than in the case of an apportionment the covenant to pay the entire rentcharge) or conditions contained in the deed or other document creating the rentcharge, so far as the same relate to the land retained or conveyed, as the case may be;

the owner for the time being of any other land affected by the entire rentcharge who—

(i) pays or is required to pay the whole or part of the rentcharge which ought to have been paid by the defaulter aforesaid; or

(ii) incurs any costs, damages or expenses by reason of the breach of covenant or condition aforesaid;

may enter into and distrain on the land in respect of which the default or breach is made or occurs, or any part of that land, and dispose according to law of any distress found, and may also take possession of the income of the same land until, by means of such distress and receipt of income or otherwise the whole or part of the rentcharge (charged or apportioned as aforesaid) so unpaid and all costs, damages and expenses incurred by reason of the non-payment thereof or of the breach of the said covenants and conditions, are fully paid or satisfied.

(3) Where in a conveyance for valuable consideration, other than a mortgage, of part of land comprised in a lease, for the residue of the term or interest created by the lease, the rent reserved by such lease or a part thereof is, without the consent of the lessor, expressed to be—

(a) charged exclusively on the land conveyed or any part thereof in exoneration of the land retained by the assignor or other land; or

(b) charged exclusively on the land retained by the assignor or any part thereof in exoneration of the land conveyed or other land; or

(c) apportioned between the land conveyed or any part thereof and the land retained by the assignor or any part thereof;

then, without prejudice to the rights of the lessor, such charge or apportionment shall be binding as between the assignor and the assignee under the conveyance and their respective successors in title.

(4) Where—

(a) any default is made in payment of the whole or part of a rent by the person who, by reason of such charge or apportionment as aforesaid, is liable to pay the same; or

(b) any breach occurs of any of the lessee's covenants (other than in the case of an apportionment the covenant to pay the entire rent) or conditions contained in the lease, so far as the same relate to the land retained or conveyed, as the case may be;

the lessee for the time being of any other land comprised in the lease, in whom, as respects that land, the residue of the term or interest created by the lease is vested, who—

(i) pays or is required to pay the whole or part of the rent which ought to have been paid by the defaulter aforesaid; or

(ii) incurs any costs, damages or expenses by reason of the breach of covenant or condition aforesaid;

may enter into and distrain on the land comprised in the lease in respect of which the default or breach is made or occurs, or any part of that land, and dispose according to law of any distress found, and may also take possession of the income of the same land until (so long as the term or interest created by the lease is subsisting) by means of such distress and receipt of income or otherwise, the whole or part of the rent (charged or apportioned as aforesaid) so unpaid and all costs, damages and expenses incurred by reason of the non-payment thereof or of the breach of the said covenants and conditions, are fully paid or satisfied.

(5) The remedies conferred by this section take effect so far only as they might have been conferred by the conveyance whereby the rent or any part thereof is expressed to be charged or apportioned as aforesaid, but a trustee, personal representative, mortgagee or other person in a fiduciary position has, and shall be deemed always to have had, power to confer the same or like remedies.

(6) This section applies only if and so far as a contrary intention is not expressed in the conveyance whereby the rent or any part thereof is expressed to be charged or apportioned as aforesaid, and takes effect subject to the terms of that conveyance and to the provisions therein contained.

(7) The remedies conferred by this section apply only where the conveyance whereby the rent or any part thereof is expressed to be charged or apportioned is made after the commencement of this Act, and do not apply where the rent is charged exclusively as aforesaid or legally apportioned with the consent of the owner or lessor.

(8) The rule of law relating to perpetuities does not affect the powers or remedies conferred by this section or any like powers or remedies expressly conferred, before or after the commencement of this Act, by an instrument.

191. [*Repealed by the Rentcharges Act 1977, s.17(2), Sched. 2.*]

Apportionment of charges payable for redemption of tithe rentcharge

192. An order of apportionment of a charge on land by way of annuity for redemption of tithe rentcharge may be made by the Minister[2] under sections ten to fourteen (inclusive) of the Inclosure Act 1854 on the application of any person interested, according to the provisions of the Inclosure Acts 1845 to **9–158**

[2] The functions of the Minister, in so far as they concern annuities charged on land for the redemption of rentcharges or money payments redeemed under the Title Acts 1836 to 1936, are transferred to the Commissioners of Inland Revenue: Tithe Act 1951, s.10(4), and the Tithe Redemption Commission (Transfer of Functions and Dissolution) Order 1959 (S.I. 1959 No. 1971).

1882, in the land charged or any part thereof without the concurrence of any other person:

Provided that the Minister may, in any such case, on the application of any person interested in the annuity, require as a condition of making the order that any apportioned part of the annuity which does not exceed the yearly sum of two pounds shall be redeemed forthwith.

Commons and Waste Lands

Rights of the public over commons and waste lands

9–159 **193.**—(1) Members of the public shall, subject as hereinafter provided, have rights of access for air and exercise to any land which is a metropolitan common within the meaning of the Metropolitan Commons Acts 1866 to 1898, or manorial waste, or a common which is wholly or partly situated within [an area which immediately before 1 April 1974 was][3] a borough or urban district, and to any land which at the commencement of this Act is subject to rights of common and to which this section may from time to time be applied in manner hereinafter provided:

Provided that—

(a) such rights of access shall be subject to any Act, scheme, or provisional order for the regulation of the land, and to any byelaw, regulation or order made thereunder or under any other statutory authority; and

(b) the Minister[4] shall, on the application of any person entitled as lord of the manor or otherwise to the soil of the land, or entitled to any commonable rights affecting the land, impose such limitations on and conditions as to the exercise of the rights of access or as to the extent of the land to be affected as, in the opinion of the Minister, are necessary or desirable for preventing any estate, right or interest of a profitable or beneficial nature in, over, or affecting the land from being injuriously affected, [for conserving flora, fauna or geological or physiographical features of the land,][5] or for protecting any object of historical interest and, where any such limitations or conditions are so imposed, the rights of access shall be subject thereto; and

(c) such rights of access shall not include any right to draw or drive upon the land a carriage, cart, caravan, truck, or other vehicle, or to camp or light any fire thereon; and

(d) the rights of access shall cease to apply—

(i) to any land over which the commonable rights are extinguished under any statutory provision;

(ii) to any land over which the commonable rights are otherwise extinguished if the council of the county [, county borough][6] [. . .][7] [or metropolitan district][8] in which the land is situated by resolution assent

[3] Words inserted by the Local Government Act 1972, s.189(4).
[4] In ss.193 and 194 "the Minister" means the Secretary of State for the Environment or, in so far as the functions of the Minister are exercisable in relation to Wales, the National Assembly for Wales: Ministry of Land and Natural Resources Order 1965 (S.I. 1965 No. 143); Ministry of Land and Natural Resources (Dissolution) Order 1967 (S.I. 1967 No. 156); Secretary of State for the Environment Order 1970 (S.I. 1970 No. 1681); and the National Assembly for Wales (Transfer of Functions) Order 1999 (S.I. 1999 No. 672), art. 2(a), Sched. 1. But see n. 52, *supra*.
[5] Words inserted by the Countryside and Rights of Way Act 2000, s.46(3), Sched. 4, para. 1.
[6] Words inserted by the Local Government (Wales) Act 1994, s.66(6), Sched. 16, para. 7(1).
[7] Words repealed by the Local Government Act 1972, s.272(1), Sched. 30.
[8] Words inserted by the Local Government Act 1985, s.16, Sched. 8, para. 10(5).

to its exclusion from the operation of this section, and the resolution is approved by the Minister.

(2)[9] The lord of the manor or other person entitled to the soil of any land subject to rights of common may by deed, revocable or irrevocable, declare that this section shall apply to the land, and upon such deed being deposited with the Minister the land shall, so long as the deed remains operative, be land to which this section applies.

(3) Where limitations or conditions are imposed by the Minister under this section, they shall be published by such person and in such manner as the Minister may direct.

(4) Any person who, without lawful authority, draws or drives upon any land to which this section applies any carriage, cart, caravan, truck, or other vehicle, or camps or lights any fire thereon, or who fails to observe any limitation or condition imposed by the Minister under this section in respect of any such land, shall be liable on summary conviction to a fine not exceeding [level 1 on the standard scale][10] for each offence.

(5) Nothing in this section shall prejudice or affect the right of any person to get and remove mines or minerals or to let down the surface of the manorial waste or common.

(6) This section does not apply to any common or manorial waste which is for the time being held for Naval, Military or Air Force purposes and in respect of which rights of common have been extinguished or cannot be exercised.

Restrictions on inclosure of commons

194.—(1) The erection of any building or fence, or the construction of any other work, whereby access to land to which this section applies is prevented or impeded, shall not be lawful unless the consent of the Minister[11] thereto is obtained, and in giving or withholding his consent the Minister shall have regard to the same considerations and shall, if necessary, hold the same inquiries as are directed by the Commons Act 1876 to be taken into consideration and held by the Minister before forming an opinion whether an application under the Inclosure Acts 1845 to 1882 shall be acceded to or not. **9–160**

(2) Where any building or fence is erected, or any other work constructed without such consent as is required by this section, the county court within whose jurisdiction the land is situated, shall, on an application being made by the council of any county [or county borough][12] [. . .][13] or district concerned, or by the lord of the manor or any other person interested in the common, have power to make an order for the removal of the work, and the restoration of the land to the condition in which it was before the work was erected or constructed, but any such order shall be subject to the like appeal as an order made under section thirty of the Commons Act 1876.

(3) This section applies to any land which at the commencement of this Act is subject to rights of common:

Provided that this section shall cease to apply—

(a) to any land over which the rights of common are extinguished under any statutory provision;

---

[9] subs. (2) repealed by the Countryside and Rights of Way Act 2000, ss.46(1)(a), 102, Sched. 16, Pt. 1, from a day to be appointed.

[10] Words substituted by virtue of the Criminal Justice Act 1982, ss.38, 46.

[11] See *ante*, para. 9–159, n. 44.

[12] Words inserted by the Local Government (Wales) Act 1994, s.66(6), Sched. 16, para. 7(2)(a).

[13] Words repealed by the Local Government Act 1972, s.272(1), Sched. 30.

(b) to any land over which the rights of common are otherwise extinguished, if the council of the county [, county borough][14] [...][15] [or metropolitan district][16] in which the land is situated by resolution assent to its exclusion from the operation of this section and the resolution is approved by the Minister.

(4) This section does not apply to any building or fence erected or work constructed if specially authorised by Act of Parliament, or in pursuance of an Act of Parliament or Order having the force of an Act, or if lawfully erected or constructed in connection with the taking or working of minerals in or under any land to which the section is otherwise applicable, or to any [telecommunication apparatus installed for the purposes of a telecommunications code system][17].

Judgments, etc. affecting Land

Equitable charges in right of judgment debt, etc.

9–161 **195.**—(1)–(3) [*Repealed by the Administration of Justice Act 1956, ss.34(2), 57(2), Sched. 2.*]

(4) A recognisance, on behalf of the Crown or otherwise, whether entered into before or after the commencement of this Act, and an inquisition finding a debt due to the Crown, and any obligation or specialty made to or in favour of the Crown, whatever may have been its date, shall not operate as a charge on any interest in land, or on the unpaid purchase money for any land, unless or until a writ or order, for the purpose of enforcing it, is registered in the register of writs and orders at the Land Registry.

(5) [*Repealed by the Administration of Justice Act 1956, ss.34(2), 57(2), Sched. 2.*]

Notices

Regulations respecting notices

9–162 **196.**[18]—(1) Any notice required or authorised to be served or given by this Act shall be in writing.

(2) Any notice required or authorised by this Act to be served on a lessee or mortgagor shall be sufficient, although only addressed to the lessee or mortgagor by that designation, without his name, or generally to the persons interested, without any name, and notwithstanding that any person to be affected by the notice is absent, under disability, unborn, or unascertained.

(3)[19] Any notice required or authorised by this Act be served shall be sufficiently served if it is left at the last-known place of abode or business in the United Kingdom of the lessee, lessor, mortgagee, mortgagor, or other person to be served, or, in case of a notice required or authorised to be served on a lessee or mortgagor, is affixed or left for him on the land or any house or building comprised in the lease or mortgage, or, in case of a mining lease, is left for the lessee at the office or counting-house of the mine.

(4)[20] Any notice required or authorised by this Act to be served shall also be

[14] Words inserted by the Local Government (Wales) Act 1994, s.66(6), Sched. 16, para. 7(2)(b).
[15] Words repealed by the Local Government Act 1972, s.272(1), Sched. 30.
[16] Words inserted by the Local Government Act 1985, s.16, Sched. 8, para. 10(5).
[17] Words substituted by the Telecommunications Act 1984, s.109(1), Sched. 4, para. 16.
[18] Applied by the Leasehold Property (Repairs) Act 1938, s.7(2), *post*, para. 14–006.
[19] See the Landlord and Tenant Act 1987, s.49.
[20] See the Landlord and Tenant Act 1987, s.49.

sufficiently served, if it is sent by post in a registered letter[21] addressed to the lessee, lessor, mortgagee, mortgagor, or other person to be served, by name, at the aforesaid place of abode or business, office, or counting-house, and if that letter is not returned [by the postal operator (within the meaning of the Postal Services Act 2000) concerned][22] undelivered; and that service shall be deemed to be made at the time at which the registered letter would in the ordinary course be delivered.

(5) The provisions of this section shall extend to notices required to be served by any instrument affecting property executed or coming into operation after the commencement of this Act unless a contrary intention appears.

(6) This section does not apply to notices served in proceedings in the court.

197. [*Repealed by the Law of Property Act 1969, s.16(2), Sched. 2, Pt. I.*]

Registration under the Land Charges Act 1925[23] to be notice

198.[24]—(1) The registration of any instrument or matter [in any register kept under the Land Charges Act 1972 or any local land charges register][25], shall be deemed to constitute actual notice of such instrument or matter, and of the fact of such registration, to all persons and for all purposes connected with the land affected, as from the date of registration or other prescribed date and so long as the registration continues in force. **9–163**

(2) This section operates without prejudice to the provisions of this Act respecting the making of further advances by a mortgagee, and applies only to instruments and matters required or authorised to be registered [in any such register][26].

Restrictions on constructive notice

199.—(1) A purchaser shall not be prejudicially affected by notice of— **9–164**

(i) any instrument or matter capable of registration under the provisions of the Land Charges Act 1925[27], or any enactment which it replaces, which is void or not enforceable as against him under that Act or enactment, by reason of the non-registration thereof;

(ii) any other instrument or matter or any fact or thing unless—

(a) it is within his own knowledge, or would have come to his knowledge if such inquiries and inspections had been made as ought reasonably to have been made by him; or

(b) in the same transaction with respect to which a question of notice to the purchaser arises, it has come to the knowledge of his counsel, as such, or of his solicitor or other agent, as such, or would have come to the knowledge of his solicitor or other agent, as such, if such inquiries and inspections had been made as ought reasonably to have been made by the solicitor or other agent.

---

[21] Any reference to the registered post is to be construed as including a reference to the recorded delivery service: Recorded Delivery Service Act 1962, s.1, Sched.

[22] Words substituted by the Postal Services Act 2000 (Consequential Modifications No. 1) Order 2001 (S.I. 2001 No. 1149), art. 3(1), Sched., para. 7.

[23] Now the Land Charges Act 1972, *post*, para. 31–001.

[24] Excluded by the Law of Property Act 1969, ss.24(1), 25(2), *post*, paras 27–002, 27–003.

[25] Words substituted by the Local Land Charges Act 1975, s.17(2), Sched. 1.

[26] Words substituted by the Local Land Charges Act 1975, s.17(2), Sched. 1.

[27] Now the Land Charges Act 1972, *post*, para. 31–001.

(2) Paragraph (ii) of the last subsection shall not exempt a purchaser from any liability under, or any obligation to perform or observe, any covenant, condition, provision, or restriction contained in any instrument under which his title is derived, mediately, or immediately; and such liability or obligation may be enforced in the same manner and to the same extent as if that paragraph had not been enacted.

(3) A purchaser shall not by reason of anything in this section be affected by notice in any case where he would not have been so affected if this section had not been enacted.

(4) This section applies to purchases made either before or after the commencement of this Act.

Notice of restrictive covenants and easements

9–165 **200.**—(1) Where land having a common title with other land is disposed of to a purchaser (other than a lessee or a mortgagee) who does not hold or obtain possession of the documents forming the common title, such purchaser, notwithstanding any stipulation to the contrary, may require that a memorandum giving notice of any provision contained in the disposition to him restrictive of user of, or giving rights over, any other land comprised in the common title, shall, where practicable, be written or indorsed on, or, where impracticable, be permanently annexed to some one document selected by the purchaser but retained in the possession or power of the person who makes the disposition, and being or forming part of the common title.

(2) The title of any person omitting to require an indorsement to be made or a memorandum to be annexed shall not, by reason only of this enactment, be prejudiced or affected by the omission.

(3) This section does not apply to dispositions of registered land.

(4) Nothing in this section affects the obligation to register a land charge in respect of—

(a) any restrictive covenant or agreement affecting freehold land; or
(b) any estate contract; or
(c) any equitable easement, liberty or privilege.

PART XII

CONSTRUCTION, JURISDICTION, AND GENERAL PROVISIONS

Provisions of Act to apply to incorporeal hereditaments

9–166 **201.**—(1) The provisions of this Act relating to freehold land apply to manors, reputed manors, lordships, advowsons, [...][28] perpetual rent-charges, and other incorporeal hereditaments, subject only to the qualifications necessarily arising by reason of the inherent nature of the hereditament affected.

(2) This Act does not affect the special restrictions imposed on dealings with advowsons by the Benefices Act 1898 or any other statute or measure, nor affect the limitation of, or authorise any disposition to be made of, a title or dignity of honour which in its nature is inalienable.

(3) [*Repealed by the Trusts of Land and Appointment of Trustees Act 1996, s.25(2), Sched. 4.*]

[28] Words repealed by the Title Act 1936, s.48(3), Sched. 9.

Provisions as to enfranchisement of copyholds, etc.

202. For giving effect to this Act, the enfranchisement of copyhold land, and the conversion into long terms of perpetually renewable leaseholds, and of leases for lives and of leases for years terminable with life or lives or on marriage, effected by the Law of Property Act 1922 as amended by any subsequent enactment, shall be deemed to have been effected immediately before the commencement of this Act. **9–167**

Payment into court, jurisdiction and procedure

203.—(1) Payment of money into court effectually exonerates therefrom the person making the payment. **9–168**

(2) Subject to any rules of court to the contrary—

(a) Every application to the court under this Act shall, save as otherwise expressly provided, be by summons at chambers;

(b) On an application by a purchaser notice shall be served in the first instance on the vendor;

(c) On an application by a vendor notice shall be served in the first instance on the purchaser;

(d) On any application notice shall be served on such persons, if any, as the court thinks fit.

(3) In this Act, unless the contrary intention appears, "the court" means the High Court [...][29] or the county court, where those courts respectively have jurisdiction.

(4) All matters within the jurisdiction of the High Court under this Act shall, save as otherwise expressly provided, and subject to the enactments for the time being in force with respect to the Supreme Court of Judicature, be assigned to the Chancery Division of the court.

(5) The court shall have full power and discretion to make such order as it thinks fit respecting the costs, charges and expenses of all or any of the parties to any application.

Orders of court conclusive

204.—(1) An order of the court under any statutory or other jurisdiction shall not, as against a purchaser, be invalidated on the ground of want of jurisdiction, or of want of any concurrence, consent, notice, or service, whether the purchaser has notice of any such want or not. **9–169**

(2) This section has effect with respect to any lease, sale, or other act under the authority of the court, and purporting to be in pursuance of any statutory power notwithstanding any exception in such statute.

(3) This section applies to all orders made before or after the commencement of this Act.

General definitions

205.—(1) In this Act unless the context otherwise requires, the following expressions have the meanings hereby assigned to them respectively, that is to say:— **9–170**

[29] Words repealed by the Courts Act 1971, s.56(4), Sched. 11, Pt. II.

(i) "Bankruptcy" includes liquidation by arrangement; also in relation to a corporation means the winding up thereof;

(ii) "Conveyance" includes a mortgage, charge, lease, assent, vesting declaration, vesting instrument, disclaimer, release and every other assurance of property or of an interest therein by any instrument, except a will; "convey" has a corresponding meaning; and "disposition" includes a conveyance and also a devise, bequest, or an appointment of property contained in a will; and "dispose of" has a corresponding meaning;

(iii) "Building purposes" include the erecting and improving of, and the adding to, and the repairing of buildings; and a "building lease" is a lease for building purposes or purposes connected therewith;

[. . .][30]

(iv) "Death duty" means estate duty, [. . .][31] and every other duty leviable or payable on a death;

(v) "Estate owner" means the owner of a legal estate, but an infant is not capable of being an estate owner;

(vi) "Gazette" means the London Gazette;

(vii) "Incumbrance" includes a legal or equitable mortgage and a trust for securing money, and a lien, and a charge of a portion, annuity, or other capital or annual sum; and "incumbrancer" has a meaning corresponding with that of incumbrance, and includes every person entitled to the benefit of an incumbrance, or to require payment or discharge thereof;

(viii) "Instrument" does not include a statute, unless the statute creates a settlement;

(ix) "Land" includes land of any tenure, and mines and minerals, whether or not held apart from the surface, buildings or parts of buildings (whether the division is horizontal, vertical or made in any other way) and other corporeal hereditaments; also a manor, an advowson, and a rent and other incorporeal hereditaments, and an easement, right, privilege, or benefit in, over, or derived from land; [. . .][32] and "mines and minerals" include any strata or seam of minerals or substances in or under any land, and powers of working and getting the same [...][33]; and "manor" includes a lordship, and reputed manor or lordship; and "hereditament" means any real property which on an intestacy occurring before the commencement of this Act might have devolved upon an heir;

(x) "Legal estates" mean the estates, interests and charges, in or over land (subsisting or created at law) which are by this Act authorised to subsist or to be created as legal estates; "equitable interests" mean all the other interests and charges in or over land [. . .][34]; and equitable interest "capable of subsisting as a legal estate" means such as could validly subsist or be created as a legal estate under this Act;

(xi) "Legal powers" include the powers vested in a chargee by way of legal mortgage or in an estate owner under which a legal estate can be

[30] Definition of "the county court limit" (inserted by the County Courts Act 1984, s.148(1), Sched. 2, Pt. II, para. 9) repealed by the High Court and County Courts Jurisdiction Order 1991 (S.I. 1991 No. 724), art. 2(8), Sched.

[31] Words repealed by the Finance Act 1949, s.52(10), Sched. 11, Pt. IV, and the Finance Act 1975, s.59(5), Sched. 13.

[32] Words repealed by the Trusts of Land and Appointment of Trustees Act 1996, s.25(2), Sched. 4.

[33] Words repealed by the Trusts of Land and Appointment of Trustees Act 1996, s.25(2), Sched. 4.

[34] Words repealed by the Trusts of Land and Appointment of Trustees Act 1996, s.25(2), Sched. 4.

transferred or created; and "equitable powers" mean all the powers in or over land under which equitable interests or powers only can be transferred or created;

(xii) "Limitation Acts" mean the Real Property Limitation Acts 1833, 1837 and 1874 and "limitation" includes a trust;

[(xiii) "Mental disorder" has the meaning assigned to it by [section 1 of the Mental Health Act 1983][35] and "receiver," in relation to a person suffering from mental disorder, means a receiver appointed for that person under [Part VIII of the Mental Health Act 1959 or Part VII of the said Act of 1983][36]][37];

(xiv)

A "mining lease" means a lease for mining purposes, that is, the searching for, winning, working, getting, making merchantable, carrying away, or disposing of mines and minerals, or purposes connected therewith, and includes a grant or licence for mining purposes;

(xv) "Minister" means the Minister of Agriculture and Fisheries[38];

(xvi) "Mortgage" includes any charge or lien on any property for securing money or money's worth; "legal mortgage" means a mortgage by demise or subdemise or a charge by way of legal mortgage and "legal mortgagee" has a corresponding meaning; "mortgage money" means money or money's worth secured by a mortgage; "mortgagor" includes any person from time to time deriving title under the original mortgagor or entitled to redeem a mortgage according to his estate interest or right in the mortgaged property; "mortgagee" includes a chargee by way of legal mortgage and any person from time to time deriving title under the original mortgagee; and "mortgagee in possession" is, for the purposes of this Act, a mortgagee who, in right of the mortgage, has entered into and is in possession of the mortgaged property; and "right of redemption" includes an option to repurchase only if the option in effect creates a right of redemption;

(xvii) "Notice" includes constructive notice;

(xviii) "Personal representative" means the executor, original or by representation, or administrator for the time being of a deceased person, and as regards any liability for the payment of death duties includes any person who takes possession of or intermeddles with the property of a deceased person without the authority of the personal representatives or the court;

(xix) "Possession" includes receipt of rents and profits or the right to receive the same, if any; and "income" includes rents and profits;

(xx) "Property" includes any thing in action, and any interest in real or personal property;

(xxi) "Purchaser" means a purchaser in good faith for valuable consideration and includes a lessee, mortgagee or other person who for valuable consideration acquires an interest in property except that in Part I of this Act and elsewhere where so expressly provided

[35] Words substituted by the Mental Health Act 1983, s.148(1), Sched. 4, para. 5(b).
[36] Words substituted by the Mental Health Act 1983, s.148(1), Sched. 4, para. 5(b).
[37] Para. (xiii) substituted by the Mental Health Act 1959, s.149(1), Sched. 7, Pt. I.
[38] Now the Minister of Environment, Food and Rural Affairs (Ministry for Environment, Food and Rural Affairs) Order 1955 (S.I. 1995 No. 554). This definition does not apply to ss.192–194, *ante*, paras 9–158 *et seq*.

"purchaser" only means a person who acquires an interest in or charge on property for money or money's worth; and in reference to a legal estate includes a chargee by way of legal mortgage; and where the context so requires "purchaser" includes an intending purchaser; "purchase" has a meaning corresponding with that of "purchaser"; and "valuable consideration" includes marriage but does not include a nominal consideration in money;

(xxii) "Registered land" has the same meaning as in the [Land Registration Act 2002][39] […][40]

(xxiii) "Rent" includes a rent service or a rentcharge, or other rent, toll, duty, royalty, or annual or periodical payment in money or money's worth, reserved or issuing out of or charged upon land, but does not include mortgage interest; "rentcharge" includes a fee farm rent; "fine" includes a premium or foregift and any payment, consideration, or benefit in the nature of a fine, premium or foregift; "lessor" includes an underlessor and a person deriving title under a lessor or underlessor; and "lessee" includes an underlessee and a person deriving title under a lessee or under-lessee, and "lease" includes an underlease or other tenancy;

(xxiv) "Sale" includes an extinguishment of manorial incidents, but in other respects means a sale properly so called;

(xxv) "Securities" include stocks, funds and shares;

(xxvi) "Tenant for life," "statutory owner," "settled land," "settlement," "vesting deed," "subsidiary vesting deed," "vesting order," "vesting instrument," "trust instrument," "capital money," and "trustees of the settlement" have the same meanings as in the Settled Land Act 1925;

(xxvii) "Term of years absolute" means a term of years (taking effect either in possession or in reversion whether or not at a rent) with or without impeachment for waste, subject or not to another legal estate, and either certain or liable to determination by notice, re-entry, operation of law, or by a provision for cesser on redemption, or in any other event (other than the dropping of a life, or the determination of a determinable life interest); but does not include any term of years determinable with life or lives or with the cesser of a determinable life interest, nor, if created after the commencement of this Act, a term of years which is not expressed to take effect in possession within twenty-one years after the creation thereof where required by this Act to take effect within that period; and in this definition the expression "term of years" includes a term for less than a year, or for a year or years and a fraction of a year or from year to year;

(xxviii) "Trust Corporation"[41] means the Public Trustee or a corporation either appointed by the court in any particular case to be a trustee or entitled by rules made under subsection (3) of section four of the Public Trustee Act 1906 to act as custodian trustee;

(xxix) "Trust for sale," in relation to land, means an immediate […][42] trust for sale, whether or not exercisable at the request or with the consent

[39] Words substituted by the Land Registration Act 2002, s.133, Sched. 11, para. 2(1), (13)(a).
[40] Definition of "Land Registrar" repealed by the Land Registration Act 2002, ss.133, 135, Sched. 11, para. 2(1), (13)(b), Sched. 13.
[41] Definition of "trust corporation" extended by the Law of Property (Amendment) Act 1926, s.3, *post*, para. 11–002, and the Charities Act 1993, s.35, *post*, para. 56–034.
[42] Words repealed by the Trusts of Land and Appointment of Trustees Act 1996, s.25(2), Sched. 4.

of any person [. . .][43]; "trustees for sale" mean the persons (including a personal representative) holding land on trust for sale; [. . .][44];

(xxx) "United Kingdom" means Great Britain and Northern Ireland;

(xxxi) "Will" includes codicil.

[(1A) Any reference in this Act to money being paid into court shall be construed as referring to the money being paid into the Supreme Court or any other court that has jurisdiction, and any reference in this Act to the court, in a context referring to the investment or application of money paid into court, shall be construed, in the case of money paid into the Supreme Court, as referring to the High Court, and in the case of money paid into another court, as referring to that other court.][45]

(2) Where an equitable interest in or power over property arises by statute or operation of law, references to the creation of an interest or power include references to any interest or power so arising.

(3) References to registration under the Land Charges Act 1925[46] apply to any registration made under any other statute which is by the Land Charges Act 1925[47] to have effect as if the registration had been made under that Act.

Forms of instruments and examples of abstracts

206.—(1) Instruments in the form of, and using the expressions in the forms given in the Fifth Schedule to this Act, or in the like form or using expressions to the like effect, shall, in regard to form and expression be sufficient. **9–171**

(2) Examples of abstracts of title framed in accordance with the enactments which will take effect at the commencement of this Act are contained in the Sixth Schedule to this Act.

Repeals as respects England and Wales

207. [. . .][48] without prejudice to the provisions of section thirty-eight of the Interpretation Act 1889[49]:— **9–172**

(a) Nothing in this repeal shall affect the validity or legality of any dealing in property or other transaction completed before the commencement of this Act, or any title or right acquired or appointment made before such commencement, but, subject as aforesaid, this Act shall, except where otherwise expressly provided, apply to and in respect of instruments whether made or coming into operation before or after such commencement:

(b) Nothing in this repeal shall affect any rules, orders, or other instruments made under any enactment so repealed, but all such rules, orders and instruments shall continue in force as if made under the corresponding enactment in this Act:

(c) References in any document to any enactment repealed by this Act shall be construed as references to this Act or to the corresponding enactment in this Act.

[43] Words repealed by the Trusts of Land and Appointment of Trustees Act 1996, s.25(2), Sched. 4.
[44] Definition of "power to postpone sale" repealed by the Trusts of Land and Appointment of Trustees Act 1996, s.25(2), Sched. 4.
[45] subs. (1A) inserted by the Administration of Justice Act 1965, s.17(1), Sched. 1.
[46] Now the Land Charges Act 1972, *post*, para. 31–001.
[47] Now the Land Charges Act 1972, *post*, para. 31–001.
[48] Words repealed by the Statute Law Revision Act 1950.
[49] Now the Interpretation Act 1978, ss.16(1), 17(2)(a).

Application to the Crown

9–173 **208.**—(1) Nothing in this Act shall be construed as rendering any property of the Crown subject to distress, or liable to be taken or disposed of by means of any distress.

(2) This Act shall not in any manner (save as otherwise expressly provided and except so far as it relates to undivided shares, joint ownership, leases for lives or leases for years terminable with life or marriage) affect or alter the descent, devolution or tenure or the nature of the estates and interests of or in any land for the time being vested in His Majesty either in right of the Crown or of the Duchy of Lancaster or of or in any land for the time being belonging to the Duchy of Cornwall and held in right or in respect of the said Duchy, but so nevertheless that, after the commencement of this Act, no estates, interests or charges in or over any such lands as aforesaid shall be conveyed or created, except such estates, interests or charges as are capable under this Act of subsisting or of being conveyed or created.

(3) Subject as aforesaid the provisions of this Act bind the Crown.

SCHEDULES

Section 39 FIRST SCHEDULE[50]

TRANSITIONAL PROVISIONS

PART I

CONVERSION OF CERTAIN EXISTING LEGAL ESTATES INTO EQUITABLE INTERESTS

All estates, interests and charges in or over land, including fees determinable whether by limitation or condition, which immediately before the commencement of this Act were estates, interests or charges, subsisting at law, or capable of taking effect as such, but which by virtue of Part I of this Act are not capable of taking effect as legal estates, shall as from the commencement of this Act be converted into equitable interests, and shall not fail by reason of being so converted into equitable interests either in the land or in the proceeds of sale thereof, nor shall the priority of any such estate, charge or interest over other equitable interests be affected.

PART II

VESTING OF LEGAL ESTATES

1. Where the purposes of a term of years, created or limited out of leasehold land, are satisfied at the commencement of this Act, that term shall merge in the reversion expectant thereon and shall cease accordingly; but where the term was vested in the owner of the reversion, the merger and cesser shall take effect without prejudice to any protection which would have been afforded to the owner for the time being of that reversion had the term remained subsisting.

Where the purposes are satisfied only as respects part of the land comprised in a term, this provision has effect as if a separate term had been created in regard to that part of the land.

2. Where immediately after the commencement of this Act any owner of a legal estate is entitled, subject or not to the payment of the costs of tracing the title and of conveyance, to require any other legal estate in the same land to be surrendered, released or conveyed to him so as to merge or be extinguished, the last-mentioned estate shall by virtue of this Part of this Schedule be extinguished, but without prejudice to any protection which would have been afforded to him had that estate remained subsisting.

3. Where immediately after the commencement of this Act any person is entitled, subject or not to

[50] Where, at the commencement of the Trusts of Land and Appointment of Trustees Act 1996, any land is held on trust for sale or on the statutory trusts by virtue of this Schedule, it shall after that commencement be held in trust for the persons entitled in the land; and references in this Schedule to trusts for sale or trustees for sale or to the statutory trusts shall be construed accordingly: Trusts of Land and Appointment of Trustees Act 1996, s.5(1), Sched. 2, para. 7.

the payment of the costs of tracing the title and of conveyance, to require any legal estate (not vested in trustees for sale) to be conveyed to or otherwise vested in him, such legal estate shall, by virtue of this Part of this Schedule, vest in manner hereinafter provided. [The divesting of a legal estate by virtue of this paragraph shall not, where the person from whom the estate is so divested was a trustee, operate to prevent the legal estate being conveyed, or a legal estate being created, by him in favour of a purchaser for money or money's worth, if the purchaser has no notice of the trust and if the documents of title relating to the estate divested are produced by the trustee or by persons deriving title under him.][51]

This paragraph shall (without prejudice to any claim, in respect of fines, fees, and other customary payments) apply to a person who, under a surrender or any disposition having the effect of a surrender, or under a covenant to surrender or otherwise, was, immediately before the commencement of this Act, entitled to require a legal customary estate of inheritance to be vested in him, or who, immediately after such commencement becomes entitled to enfranchised land.

4. Any person who, immediately after the commencement of this Act, is entitled to an equitable interest capable of subsisting as a legal estate which has priority over any legal estate in the same land, shall be deemed to be entitled for the foregoing purposes to require a legal estate to be vested in him for an interest of a like nature not exceeding in extent or duration the equitable interest:

Provided that this paragraph shall not—

(a) apply where the equitable interest is capable of being over-reached by virtue of a subsisting trust for sale or a settlement;
(b) operate to prevent such person from acquiring any other legal estate under this Part of this Schedule to which he may be entitled.

5. For the purposes of this Part of this Schedule, a tenant for life, statutory owner or personal representative, shall be deemed to be entitled to require to be vested in him any legal estate in settled land (whether or not vested in the Crown) which he is, by the Settled Land Act 1925, given power to convey.

6. Under the provisions of this Part of this Schedule, the legal estate affected (namely, any estate which a person is entitled to require to be vested in him as aforesaid) shall vest as follows:—

(a) Where at the commencement of this Act land is subject to a mortgage (not being an equitable charge unsecured by any estate), the legal estate affected shall vest in accordance with the provisions relating to mortgages contained in this Schedule;
(b) Where the land is at the commencement or by virtue of this Act or any Act coming into operation at the same time subject or is by virtue of any statute made subject to a trust for sale, the legal estate affected shall vest in the trustees for sale (including personal representatives holding land on trust for sale) but subject to any mortgage term subsisting or created by this Act;
(c) Where at the commencement of this Act or by virtue of any statute coming into operation at the same time the land is settled land, the legal estate affected shall vest in the tenant for life or statutory owner entitled under the Settled Land Act 1925 to require a vesting deed to be executed in his favour, or in the personal representative, if any, in whom the land may be vested or the Public Trustee, as the case may require but subject to any mortgage term subsisting or created by this Act;
(d) In any case to which the foregoing sub-paragraphs do not apply the legal estate affected shall vest in the person of full age who, immediately after the commencement of this Act, is entitled (subject or not to the payment of costs and any customary payments) to require the legal estate to be vested in him, but subject to any mortgage term subsisting or created by this Act.

7. Nothing in this Part of this Schedule shall operate—

(a) To vest in a mortgagee of a term of years absolute any nominal leasehold reversion which is held in trust for him subject to redemption; or
(b) To vest in a mortgagee any legal estate except a term of years absolute; or
(c) To vest in a person entitled to a leasehold interest, as respects such interest, any legal estate except a term of years absolute; or
(d) To vest in a person entitled to a rentcharge (either perpetual or held for a term of years absolute) as respects such rentcharge, any legal estate except a legal estate in the rentcharge; or
(e) To vest in a person entitled to an easement, right or privilege with reference thereto, any legal estate except a legal estate in the easement, right or privilege; or
(f) To vest any legal estate in a person for an undivided share; or
(g) To vest any legal estate in an infant; or
(h) To affect prejudicially the priority of any mortgage or other incumbrance or interest subsisting at the commencement of this Act; or

[51] Words inserted by the Law of Property (Amendment) Act 1926, s.7, Sched.

(i) To render invalid any limitation or trust which would have been capable of taking effect as an equitable limitation or trust; or

(j) To vest in a purchaser or his personal representatives any legal estate which he has contracted to acquire and in regard to which a contract, including an agreement to create a legal mortgage, is pending at the commencement of this Act, although the consideration may have been paid or satisfied and the title accepted, or to render unnecessary the conveyance of such estate; or

(k) To vest in the managing trustees or committee of management of a charity any legal estate vested in the Official Trustee of Charity Lands; or

(l) To vest in any person any legal estate which failed to pass to him by reason of his omission to be registered as proprietor under the Land Transfer Acts 1875 and 1897 until brought into operation by virtue of the Land Registration Act 1925.

[(m) To vest in any person any legal estate affected by any rent covenants or conditions if, before any proceedings are commenced in respect of the rent covenants or conditions, and before any conveyance of the legal estate or dealing therewith inter vivos is effected, he or his personal representatives disclaim it in writing signed by him or them.][52]

8. Any legal estate acquired by virtue of this Part of this Schedule shall be held upon the trusts and subject to the powers, provisions, rents, covenants, conditions, rights of redemption (as respects terms of years absolute) and other rights, burdens and obligations, if any, upon or subject to which the estate acquired ought to be held.

9. No stamp duty shall become payable by reason only of any vesting surrender or release effected by this Schedule.

PART III

PROVISIONS AS TO LEGAL ESTATE VESTED IN INFANT

1. Where immediately before the commencement of this Act a legal estate in land is vested in one or more infants beneficially, or where immediately after the commencement of this Act a legal estate in land would by virtue of this Act have become vested in one or more infants beneficially if he or they had been of full age, the legal estate shall vest in the manner provided by the Settled Land Act 1925.

2. Where immediately before the commencement of this Act a legal estate in land is vested in an infant jointly with one or more other persons of full age beneficially, the legal estate shall by virtue of this Act vest in that other person or those other persons on the statutory trusts, but not so as to sever any joint tenancy in the net proceeds of sale or in the rents and profits until sale:

Provided that, if, by virtue of this paragraph the legal estate becomes vested in one person as trustee, then, if no other person is able and willing to do so, the parents or parent testamentary or other guardian of the infant, if respectively able and willing to act, (in the order named) may, and at the request of any person interested shall (subject to the costs being provided for) by writing appoint an additional trustee and thereupon by virtue of this Act the legal estate shall vest in the additional trustee and existing trustee as joint tenants.

3. Where, immediately before the commencement of this Act, a legal estate in land is vested solely in an infant as a personal representative, or a trustee of a settlement, or on trust for sale or on any other trust, or by way of mortgage, or where immediately after the commencement of this Act a legal estate in land would by virtue of any provision of this Act or otherwise have been so vested if the infant were of full age, the legal estate and the mortgage debt (if any) and interest thereon shall, by virtue of this Act, vest in the Public Trustee, pending the appointment of trustees as hereinafter provided—

(a) as to the land, upon the trusts, and subject to the equities affecting the same (but in the case of a mortgage estate for a term of years absolute in accordance with this Act); and

(b) as to the mortgage debt and interest, upon such trusts as may be requisite for giving effect to the rights (if any) of the infant or other persons beneficially interested therein:

Provided that—

(i) The Public Trustee shall not be entitled to act in the trust, or charge any fee, or be liable in any manner, unless and until requested in writing to act by or on behalf of the persons interested in the land or the income thereof, or in the mortgage debt or interest thereon (as the case may be), which request may be made on behalf of the infant by his parents or parent, or testamentary or other guardian (in the order named), and those persons may, in the order aforesaid (if no other person is able and willing to do so) appoint new trustees in the place of the Public Trustee, and thereupon by virtue of this Act the land or term and mortgage money shall vest in the trustees so appointed upon the trusts and subject to the equities aforesaid:

[52] para. (m) added by the Law of Property (Amendment) Act 1926, s.7, Sched.

Provided that the Public Trustee may, before he accepts the trust, but subject to the payment of his costs, convey to a person of full age who becomes entitled;

(ii) After the Public Trustee has been so requested to act, and has accepted the trust, no trustee shall (except by an order of the court) be appointed in his place without his consent;

(iii) Any person interested in the land or the income thereof, or in the mortgage debt or in the interest thereon (as the case may be), may, at any time during the minority, apply to the court for the appointment of trustees of the trust, and the court may make such order as it thinks fit, and if thereby new trustees are appointed the legal estate (but in the case of a mortgage estate only for a term of years absolute as aforesaid) and the mortgage debt (if any) and interest shall, by virtue of this Act, vest in the trustees as joint tenants upon the trusts and subject to the equities aforesaid;

(iv) Neither a purchaser of the land nor a transferee for money or money's worth of the mortgage shall be concerned in any way with the trusts affecting the legal estate or the mortgage debt and interest thereon;

(v) The vesting in the Public Trustee of a legal estate or a mortgage debt by virtue of this Part of this Schedule shall not affect any directions previously given as to the payment of income or of interest on any mortgage money, but such instructions may, until he accepts the trust, continue to be acted on as if no such vesting had been effected.

[3A. The county court has jurisdiction under proviso (iii) to paragraph 3 of this Part where the land which is to be dealt with in the court does not exceed [£30,000][53] in capital value [. . .][54].][55]

4. Where, immediately before the commencement of this Act, a legal estate in land is vested in two or more persons jointly as personal representatives, trustees, or mortgagees, and anyone of them is an infant, or where immediately after the commencement of this Act a legal estate in land would, by virtue of this Act, or otherwise have been so vested if the infant were of full age, the legal estate in the land with the mortgage debt (if any) and the interest thereon shall, by virtue of this Act, vest in the other person or persons of full age—

(a) as to the legal estate, upon the trusts and subject to the equities affecting the same (but in the case of a mortgage estate only for a term of years absolute as aforesaid); and

(b) as to the mortgage debts and interest, upon such trusts as may be requisite for giving effect to the rights (if any) of the infant or other persons beneficially interested therein;

but neither a purchaser of the land nor a transferee for money or money's worth of the mortgage shall be concerned in any way with the trusts affecting the legal estate or the mortgage debt and interest thereon:

Provided that, if by virtue of this paragraph, the legal estate and mortgage debt, if any, become vested in a sole trustee, then, if no other person is able and willing to do so, the parents or parent, testamentary or other guardian of the infant (in the order named) may, and at the request of any person interested shall, (subject to the costs being provided for) by writing appoint a new trustee in place of the infant, and thereupon by virtue of this Act the legal estate and mortgage money shall vest in the new and continuing trustees upon the trusts and subject to the equities aforesaid.

5. This Part of this Schedule does not affect the estate or powers of an administrator durante minore aetate, nor, where there is a tenant for life or statutory owner of settled land, operate to vest the legal estate therein in the Public Trustee.

Part IV

Provisions subjecting Land held in Undivided Shares to a Trust for Sale

1. Where, immediately before the commencement of this Act, land is held at law or in equity in undivided shares vested in possession, the following provisions shall have effect:—

(1) If the entirety of the land is vested in trustees or personal representatives (whether subject or not to incumbrances affecting the entirety or an undivided share) in trust for persons entitled in undivided shares, then—

(a) if the land is subject to incumbrances affecting undivided shares or to incumbrances affecting the entirety which under this Act or otherwise are not secured by legal terms of years absolute, the entirety of the land shall vest free from such incumbrances in such trustees or personal representatives and be held by them upon the statutory trusts; and

[53] Figure substituted by the High Court and County Courts Jurisdiction Order 1991 (S.I. 1991 No. 724), art. 2(8), Sched.

[54] Words repealed by the High Court and County Courts Jurisdiction Order 1991 (S.I. 1991 No. 724), art. 2(8), Sched.

[55] Para. 3A inserted by the County Courts Act 1984, s.148(1), Sched. 2, Pt. II, para. 10(a). For the jurisdiction of the county court by agreement, see the County Courts Act 1984, s.24, *post*, para. 42–003.

(b) in any other case, the land shall be held by such trustees or personal representatives upon the statutory trusts;

subject in the case of personal representatives, to their rights and powers for the purposes of administration.

(2) If the entirety of the land (not being settled land) is vested absolutely and beneficially in not more than four persons of full age entitled thereto in undivided shares free from incumbrances affecting undivided shares, but subject or not to incumbrances affecting the entirety, it shall, by virtue of this Act, vest in them as joint tenants upon the statutory trusts.

(3) If the entirety of the land is settled land (whether subject or not to incumbrances affecting the entirety or an undivided share) held under one and the same settlement, it shall, by virtue of this Act, vest, free from incumbrances affecting undivided shares, and from incumbrances affecting the entirety, which under this Act or otherwise are not secured by a legal [mortgage, and free from any interests, powers and charges subsisting under the settlement, which have priority to the interests of the persons entitled to the undivided shares][56], in the trustees (if any) of the settlement as joint tenants upon the statutory trusts.

Provided that if there are no such trustees, then—

(i) pending their appointment, the land shall, by virtue of this Act, vest (free as aforesaid) in the Public Trustee upon the statutory trusts;

(ii) the Public Trustee shall not be entitled to act in the trust, or charge any fee, or be liable in any manner, unless and until requested in writing to act by or on behalf of persons interested in more than an undivided half of the land or the income thereof;

(iii) after the Public Trustee has been so requested to act, and has accepted the trust, no trustee shall (except by an order of the court) be appointed in the place of the Public Trustee without his consent;

(iv) if, before the Public Trustee has accepted the trust, trustees of the settlement are appointed, the land shall, by virtue of this Act, vest (free as aforesaid) in them as joint tenants upon the statutory trusts;

(v) if, before the Public Trustee has accepted the trust, the persons having power to appoint new trustees are unable or unwilling to make an appointment, or if the tenant for life having power to apply to the court for the appointment of trustees of the settlement neglects to make the application for at least three months after being requested by any person interested in writing so to do, or if the tenants for life of the undivided shares are unable to agree, any person interested under the settlement may apply to the court for the appointment of such trustees.

[(3A) The county court has jurisdiction under proviso (v) to sub-paragraph (3) of this paragraph where the land to be dealt with in the court does not exceed [£30,000][57] in capital value [. . .][58].][59]

(4) In any case to which the foregoing provisions of this Part of this Schedule do not apply, the entirety of the land shall vest (free as aforesaid) in the Public Trustee upon the statutory trusts:

Provided that—

(i) The Public Trustee shall not be entitled to act in the trust, or charge any fee, or be liable in any manner, unless and until requested in writing to act by or on behalf of the persons interested in more than an undivided half of the land or the income thereof;

(ii) After the Public Trustee has been so requested to act, and has accepted the trust, no trustee shall (except by an order of the court) be appointed in the place of the Public Trustee without his consent;

(iii) Subject as aforesaid, any person interested in more than an undivided half of the land or the income thereof may appoint new trustees in the place of the Public Trustee with the consent of any incumbrancers of undivided shares (but so that a purchaser shall not be concerned to see whether any such consent has been given) and [thereupon the land shall by virtue of this Act vest][60] in the persons so appointed (free as aforesaid) upon the statutory trusts; or such persons may (without such consent as aforesaid), at any time, whether or not the Public Trustee has accepted the trust, apply to the court for the appointment of trustees of the land, and the court may make such order as it thinks fit, and if thereby trustees of the

---

[56] Words substituted by the Law of Property (Amendment) Act 1926, s.7, Sched.

[57] Figure substituted by the High Court and County Courts Jurisdiction Order 1991 (S.I. 1991 No. 724), art. 2(8), Sched.

[58] Words repealed by the High Court and County Courts Jurisdiction Order 1991 (S.I. 1991 No. 724), art. 2(8), Sched.

[59] Sub-para. (3A) inserted by the County Courts Act 1984, s.148(1), Sched. 2, Pt. II, para. 10(b). For the jurisdiction of the county court by agreement, see the County Courts Act 1984, s.24, *post*, para. 42–003.

[60] Words substituted by the Law of Property (Amendment) Act 1926, s.7, Sched.

land are appointed, the same shall by virtue of this Act, vest (free as aforesaid) in the trustees as joint tenants upon the statutory trusts;

(iv) If the persons interested in more than an undivided half of the land or the income thereof do not either request the Public Trustee to act, or (whether he refuses to act or has not been requested to act) apply to the court for the appointment of trustees in his place, within three months from the time when they have been requested in writing by any person interested so to do, then and in any such case, any person interested may apply to the court for the appointment of trustees in the place of the Public Trustee, and the court may make such order as it thinks fit, and if thereby trustees of the land are appointed the same shall by virtue of this Act, vest (free as aforesaid) in the trustees upon the statutory trusts;

[(4A) The county court has jurisdiction under provisos (iii) and (iv) to sub-paragraph (4) of this paragraph where the land which is to be dealt with in the court does not exceed [£30,000][61] in capital value [. . .][62].][63]

(5) The vesting in the Public Trustee of land by virtue of this Part of this Schedule shall not affect any directions previously given as to the payment of income or of interest on any mortgage money, but such instructions may, until he accepts the trust, continue to be acted on as if no such vesting had been effected.

(6) The court or the Public Trustee may act on evidence given by affidavit or by statutory declaration as respects the undivided shares without investigating the title to the land.

(7) Where all the undivided shares in the land are vested in the same mortgagees for securing the same mortgage money and the rights of redemption affecting the land are the same as might have been subsisting if the entirety had been mortgaged by an owner before the undivided shares were created, the land shall, by virtue of this Act, vest in the mortgagees as joint tenants for a legal term of years absolute (in accordance with this Act) subject to cesser on redemption by the trustees for sale in whom the right of redemption is vested by this Act, and for the purposes of this Part of this Schedule the mortgage shall be deemed an incumbrance affecting the entirety.

(8) This Part of this Schedule does not (except where otherwise expressly provided) prejudice incumbrancers whose incumbrances affect the entirety of the land at the commencement of this Act, but (if the nature of the incumbrance admits) the land shall vest in them for legal terms of years absolute in accordance with this Act but not so as to affect subsisting priorities.

(9) The trust for sale and powers of management vested in persons who hold the entirety of the land on trust for sale shall, save as hereinafter mentioned, not be exercisable without the consent of any incumbrancer, being of full age, affected whose incumbrance is divested by this Part of this Schedule, but a purchaser shall not be concerned to see or inquire whether any such consent has been given, nor, where the incumbrancer is not in possession, shall any such consent be required if, independently of this Part of this Schedule or any enactment replaced thereby the transaction would have been binding on him, had the same been effected by the mortgagor.

(10) This Part of this Schedule does not apply to land in respect of which a subsisting contract for sale (whether made under an order in a partition action or by or on behalf of all the tenants in common or coparceners) is in force at the commencement of this Act if the contract is completed in due course (in which case title may be made in like manner as if this Act, and any enactment thereby replaced, had not been passed), nor to the land in respect of which a partition action is pending at such commencement if an order for a partition or sale is subsequently made in such action [within eighteen months from the commencement of this Act][64].

(11) The repeal of the enactments relating to partition shall operate without prejudice to any proceedings thereunder commenced before the commencement of this Act, and to the jurisdiction of the court to make any orders in reference thereto, and subject to the following provisions, namely:—

(i) In any such proceedings, and at any stage thereof, any person or persons interested

---

[61] Figure substituted by the High Court and County Courts Jurisdiction Order 1991 (S.I. 1991 No. 724), art. 2(8), Sched.

[62] Words repealed by the High Court and County Courts Jurisdiction Order 1991 (S.I. 1991 No. 724), art. 2(8), Sched.

[63] Sub-para. (4A) inserted by the County Courts Act 1984, s.148(1), Sched. 2, Pt. II, para. 10(b). For the jurisdiction of the county court by agreement, see the County Courts Act 1984, s.24, *post*, para. 42–003.

[64] Words added by the Law of Property (Amendment) Act 1926, s.7, Sched.

individually or collectively in [one half or upwards][65] of the land to which the proceedings relate, may apply to the court for an order staying such proceedings;

(ii) The court may upon such application make an order staying the proceedings as regards the whole or any part, not being an undivided share, of the land;

(iii) As from the date of such order the said enactments shall cease to apply to the land affected by the order and the provisions of this Part of this Schedule shall apply thereto;

(iv) The court may by such order appoint trustees of the land and the same shall by virtue of this Act vest (free as aforesaid) in the trustees as joint tenants upon the statutory trusts;

(v) The court may order that the costs of the proceedings and of the application shall be raised by the trustees, by legal mortgage of the land or any part thereof, and paid either wholly or partially into court or to the trustees;

(vi) The court may act on such evidence as appears to be sufficient, without investigating the title to the land.

(12) In this Part of this Schedule "incumbrance" does not include [a legal rentcharge affecting the entirety][66] land tax, tithe rentcharge, or any similar charge on the land not created by an instrument.

2. Where undivided shares in land, created before the commencement of this Act, fall into possession after such commencement, and the land is not settled land when the shares fall into possession, the personal representatives (subject to their rights and powers for purposes of administration) or other estate owners in whom the entirety of the land is vested shall, by an assent or a conveyance, give effect to the foregoing provisions of this Part of this Schedule in like manner as if the shares had fallen into possession immediately before the commencement of this Act, and in the meantime the land shall be held on the statutory trusts.

3. This Part of this Schedule shall not save as hereinafter mentioned apply to party structures and open spaces within the meaning of the next succeeding Part of this Schedule.

[4. Where, immediately before the commencement of this Act there are two or more tenants for life of full age entitled under the same settlement in undivided shares, and, after the cesser of all their interests in the income of the settled land, the entirety of the land is limited so as to devolve together (not in undivided shares), their interests shall, but without prejudice to any beneficial interest, be converted into a joint tenancy; and the joint tenants and the survivor of them shall, until the said cesser occurs, constitute the tenant for life for the purposes of the Settled Land Act 1925 and this Act.][67]

Part V

Provisions as to Party Structures and Open Spaces

1. Where, immediately before the commencement of this Act, a party wall or other party structure is held in undivided shares, the ownership thereof shall be deemed to be severed vertically as between the respective owners, and the owner of each part shall have such rights to support and of user over the rest of the structure as may be requisite for conferring rights corresponding to those subsisting at the commencement of this Act.

2. Where, immediately before the commencement of this Act, an open space of land (with or without any building used in common for the purposes of any adjoining land) is held in undivided shares, in right whereof each owner has rights of access and user over the open space, the ownership thereof shall vest in the Public Trustee on the statutory trusts which shall be executed only with the leave of the court, and, subject to any order of the court to the contrary, each person who would have been a tenant in common shall, until the open space is conveyed to a purchaser, have rights of access and user over the open space corresponding to those which would have subsisted if the tenancy in common had remained subsisting.

3. Any person interested may apply to the court for an order declaring the rights and interests under this Part of this Schedule, of the persons interested in any such party structure or open space, or generally may apply in relation to the provisions of this Part of this Schedule, and the court may make such order as it thinks fit.

[65] Words substituted by the Law of Property (Amendment) Act 1926, s.7, Sched.
[66] Words inserted by the Law of Property (Amendment) Act 1926, s.7, Sched.
[67] Para. 4 added by the Law of Property (Amendment) Act 1926, s.7, Sched.

PART VI

CONVERSION OF TENANCIES BY ENTIRETIES INTO JOINT TENANCIES

Every tenancy by entireties existing immediately before the commencement of this Act shall, but without prejudice to any beneficial interest, as from such commencement be converted into a joint tenancy.

PART VII

CONVERSION OF EXISTING FREEHOLD MORTGAGES INTO MORTGAGES BY DEMISE

1. All land, which immediately before the commencement of this Act, was vested in a first or only mortgagee for an estate in fee simple in possession, whether legal or equitable, shall, from and after the commencement of this Act, vest in the first or only mortgagee for a term of three thousand years from such commencement, without impeachment of waste, but subject to a provision for cesser corresponding to the right of redemption which, at such commencement, was subsisting with respect to the fee simple.

2. All land, which immediately before the commencement of this Act, was vested in a second or subsequent mortgagee for an estate in fee simple in possession, whether legal or equitable, shall, from and after the commencement of this Act, vest in the second or subsequent mortgagee for a term one day longer than the term vested in the first or other mortgagee whose security ranks immediately before that of such second or subsequent mortgagee, without impeachment of waste, but subject to the term or terms vested in such first or other prior mortgagee and subject to a provision for cesser corresponding to the right of redemption which, at such commencement, was subsisting with respect to the fee simple.

3. The estate in fee simple which, immediately before the commencement of this Act, was vested in any such mortgagee shall, from and after such commencement, vest in the mortgagor or tenant for life, statutory owner, trustee for sale, personal representative, or other person of full age who, if all money owing on the security of the mortgage and all other mortgages or charges (if any) had been discharged at the commencement of this Act, would have been entitled to have the fee simple conveyed to him, but subject to any mortgage term created by this Part of this Schedule or otherwise and to the money secured by any such mortgage or charge.

4. If a sub-mortgage by conveyance of the fee simple is subsisting immediately before the commencement of this Act, the principal mortgagee shall take the principal term created by paragraphs 1 or 2 of this Part of this Schedule (as the case may require) and the sub-mortgagee shall take a derivative term less by one day than the term so created, without impeachment of waste, subject to a provision for cesser corresponding to the right of redemption subsisting under the sub-mortgage.

5. This Part of this Schedule applies to land enfranchised by statute as well as to land which was freehold before the commencement of this Act, and (save where expressly excepted) whether or not the land is registered under the Land Registration Act 1925, or the mortgage is made by way of trust for sale or otherwise.

6. A mortgage affecting a legal estate made before the commencement of this Act which is not protected, either by a deposit of documents of title relating to the legal estate or by registration as a land charge, shall not, as against a purchaser in good faith without notice thereof, obtain any benefit by reason of being converted into a legal mortgage by this Schedule, but shall, in favour of such purchaser, be deemed to remain an equitable interest.

This paragraph does not apply to mortgages or charges registered or protected under the Land Registration Act 1925, or to mortgages or charges registered in a local deeds register.

7. Nothing in this Part of this Schedule shall affect priorities or the right of any mortgagee to retain possession of documents, nor affect his title to or rights over any fixtures or chattels personal comprised in the mortgage.

8. This Part of this Schedule does not apply unless a right of redemption is subsisting immediately before the commencement of this Act.

PART VIII

CONVERSION OF EXISTING LEASEHOLD MORTGAGES INTO MORTGAGES BY SUBDEMISE

1. All leasehold land, which immediately before the commencement of this Act, was vested in a first or only mortgagee by way of assignment of a term of years absolute shall, from and after the commencement of this Act, vest in the first or only mortgagee for a term equal to the term assigned by the mortgage, less the last ten days thereof, but subject to a provision for cesser corresponding to

the right of redemption which at such commencement was subsisting with respect to the term assigned.

2. All leasehold land, which immediately before the commencement of this Act, was vested in a second or subsequent mortgagee by way of assignment of a term of years absolute (whether legal or equitable) shall, from and after the commencement of this Act, vest in the second or subsequent mortgagee for a term one day longer than the term vested in the first or other mortgagee whose security ranks immediately before that of such second or subsequent mortgagee if the length of the last-mentioned term permits, and in any case for a term less by one day at least than the term assigned by the mortgage, but subject to the term or terms vested in such first or other prior mortgagee, and subject to a provision for cesser corresponding to the right of redemption which, at the commencement of this Act, was subsisting with respect to the term assigned by the mortgage.

3. The term of years absolute which was assigned by any such mortgage shall, from and after the commencement of this Act, vest in the mortgagor or tenant for life, statutory owner, trustee for sale, personal representative, or other person of full age who, if all the money owing on the security of the mortgage and all other mortgages or charges, if any, had been discharged at the commencement of this Act, would have been entitled to have the term assigned or surrendered to him, but subject to any derivative mortgage term created by this Part of this Schedule or otherwise and to the money secured by any such mortgage or charge.

4. If a sub-mortgage by assignment of a term is subsisting immediately before the commencement of this Act, the principal mortgagee shall take the principal derivative term created by paragraphs 1 or 2 of this Part of this Schedule or the derivative term created by his mortgage (as the case may require), and the sub-mortgagee shall take a derivative term less by one day than the term so vested in the principal mortgagee, subject to a provision for cesser corresponding to the right of redemption subsisting under the sub-mortgage.

5. A mortgage affecting a legal estate made before the commencement of this Act which is not protected, either by a deposit of documents of title relating to the legal estate or by registration as a land charge shall not, as against a purchaser in good faith without notice thereof, obtain any benefit by reason of being converted into a legal mortgage by this Schedule, but shall, in favour of such purchaser, be deemed to remain an equitable interest.

This paragraph does not apply to mortgages or charges registered or protected under the Land Registration Act 1925, or to mortgages or charges registered in a local deeds register.

6. This Part of this Schedule applies to perpetually renewable leaseholds, and to leaseholds for lives, which are by statute converted into long terms, with the following variations, namely:—

(a) The term to be taken by a first or only mortgagee shall be ten days less than the term created by such statute:

(b) The term to be taken by a second or subsequent mortgagee shall be one day longer than the term vested in the first or other mortgagee whose security ranks immediately before that of the second or subsequent mortgagee, if the length of the last-mentioned term permits, and in any case for a term less by one day at least than the term created by such statute:

(c) The term created by such statute shall, from and after the commencement of this Act, vest in the mortgagor or tenant for life, statutory owner, trustee for sale, personal representative, or other person of full age, who if all the money owing on the security of the mortgage and all other mortgages or charges, if any, had been discharged at the commencement of this Act, would have been entitled to have the term assigned or surrendered to him, but subject to any derivative mortgage term created by this Part of this Schedule or otherwise and to the money secured by any such mortgage or charge.

7. This Part of this Schedule applies (save where expressly excepted) whether or not the leasehold land is registered under the Land Registration Act 1925, or the mortgage is made by way of trust for sale or otherwise.

8. Nothing in this Part of this Schedule shall affect priorities or the right of any mortgagee to retain possession of documents, nor affect his title to or rights over any fixtures or chattels personal comprised in the mortgage, but this Part of this Schedule does not apply unless a right of redemption is subsisting at the commencement of this Act.

Administration of Estates Act 1925

(15 & 16 GEO. 5, C. 23)

ARRANGEMENT OF SECTIONS

PART I

DEVOLUTION OF REAL ESTATE

PART IV

DISTRIBUTION OF RESIDUARY ESTATE

PART V

SUPPLEMENTAL

PART I

DEVOLUTION OF REAL ESTATE

Devolution of real estate on personal representative

10–001 **1.**—(1) Real estate to which a deceased person was entitled for an interest not ceasing on his death shall on his death, and notwithstanding any testamentary disposition thereof, devolve from time to time on the personal representative of the deceased, in like manner as before the commencement of this Act chattels real devolved on the personal representative from time to time of a deceased person.

(2) The personal representatives for the time being of a deceased person are deemed in law his heirs and assigns within the meaning of all trusts and powers.

(3) The personal representatives shall be the representative of the deceased in regard to his real estate to which he was entitled for an interest not ceasing on his death as well as in regard to his personal estate.

Application to real estate of law affecting chattels real

10–002 **2.**[1]—(1) Subject to the provisions of this Act, all enactments and rules of law, and all jurisdiction of any court with respect to the appointment of administrators or to probate or letters of administration, or to dealings before

[1] See also s.39, *post*, para. 10–030.

probate in the case of chattels real, and with respect to costs and other matters in the administration of personal estate, in force before the commencement of this Act, and all powers, duties, rights, equities, obligations, and liabilities of a personal representative in force at the commencement of this Act with respect to chattels real, shall apply and attach to the personal representative and shall have effect with respect to real estate vested in him, and in particular all such powers of disposition and dealing as were before the commencement of this Act exercisable as respects chattels real by the survivor or survivors of two or more personal representatives, as well as by a single personal representative, or by all the personal representatives together, shall be exercisable by the personal representatives or representative of the deceased with respect to his real estate.

(2)[2] Where as respects real estate there are two or more personal representatives, a conveyance of real estate devolving under this Part of this Act [or a contract for such a conveyance][3] shall not [...][4] be made without the concurrence therein of all such representatives or an order of the court, but where probate is granted to one or some of two or more persons named as executors, whether or not power is reserved to the other or others to prove, any conveyance of the real estate [or contract for such a conveyance][5] may be made by the proving executor or executors for the time being, without an order of the court, and shall be as effectual as if all the persons named as executors had concurred therein.

(3) Without prejudice to the rights and powers of a personal representative, the appointment of a personal representative in regard to real estate shall not, save as hereinafter provided, affect—

(a) any rule as to marshalling or as to administration of assets;
(b) the beneficial interest in real estate under any testamentary disposition;
(c) any mode of dealing with any beneficial interest in real estate, or the proceeds of sale thereof;
(d) the right of any person claiming to be interested in the real estate to take proceedings for the protection or recovery thereof against any person other than the personal representative.

Interpretation of Part I

3.—(1) In this Part of this Act "real estate" includes— **10–003**

(i) Chattels real, and land in possession, remainder, or reversion, and every interest in or over land to which a deceased person was entitled at the time of his death; and
(ii) Real estate held on trust (including settled land) or by way of mortgage or security, but not [...][6] money secured or charged on land.

(2) A testator shall be deemed to have been entitled at his death to any interest in real estate passing under any gift contained in his will which operates as an appointment under a general power to appoint by will, or operates under the testamentary power conferred by statute to dispose of an entailed interest.

(3) An entailed interest of a deceased person shall (unless disposed of under

---

[2] The amendments to subs. (2) apply to contracts made after June 30, 1995: Law of Property (Miscellaneous Provisions) Act 1994, s. 16(3).
[3] Words inserted by the Law of Property (Miscellaneous Provisions) Act 1994, s.16(1)(a).
[4] Words repealed by the Law of Property (Miscellaneous Provisions) Act 1994, ss.16(1)(b), 21(2), Sched. 2.
[5] Words inserted by the Law of Property (Miscellaneous Provisions) Act 1994, s.16(1)(c).
[6] Words repealed by the Trusts of Land and Appointment of Trustees Act 1996, s.25(2), Sched. 4.

the testamentary power conferred by statute) be deemed an interest ceasing on his death, but any further or other interest of the deceased in the same property in remainder or reversion which is capable of being disposed of by his will shall not be deemed to be an interest so ceasing.

(4) The interest of a deceased person under a joint tenancy where another tenant survives the deceased is an interest ceasing on his death.

(5) On the death of a corporator sole his interest in the corporation's real and personal estate shall be deemed to be an interest ceasing on his death and shall devolve to his successor.

This subsection applies on the demise of the Crown as respects all property, real and personal, vested in the Crown as a corporation sole.

PART II

EXECUTORS AND ADMINISTRATORS

General Provisions

4. [*Repealed by the Supreme Court of Judicature (Consolidation) Act 1925, s.226, Sched. 6.*]

Cesser of right of executor to prove

10–004 **5.** Where a person appointed executor by a will—

(i) survives the testator but dies without having taken out probate of the will; or
(ii) is cited to take out probate of the will and does not appear to the citation; or
(iii) renounces probate of the will;

his rights in respect of the executorship shall wholly cease, and the representation to the testator and the administration of his real and personal estate shall devolve and be committed in like manner as if that person had not been appointed executor.

Withdrawal of renunciation

10–005 **6.**—(1) Where an executor who has renounced probate has been permitted, whether before or after the commencement of this Act, to withdraw the renunciation and prove the will, the probate shall take effect and be deemed always to have taken effect without prejudice to the previous acts and dealings of and notices to any other personal representative who has previously proved the will or taken out letters of administration, and a memorandum of the subsequent probate shall be endorsed on the original probate or letters of administration.

(2) This section applies whether the testator died before or after the commencement of this Act.

Executor of executor represents original testator

10–006 **7.**[7]—(1) An executor of a sole or last surviving executor of a testator is the executor of that testator.

[7] Excluded by the Administration of Estates Act 1971, s.1(2)(a), (3).

This provision shall not apply to an executor who does not prove the will of his testator, and, in the case of an executor who on his death leaves surviving him some other executor of his testator who afterwards proves the will of that testator, it shall cease to apply on such probate being granted.

(2) So long as the chain of such representation is unbroken, the last executor in the chain is the executor of every preceding testator.

(3) The chain of such representation is broken by—

(a) an intestacy; or

(b) the failure of a testator to appoint an executor; or

(c) the failure to obtain probate of a will;

but is not broken by a temporary grant of administration if probate is subsequently granted.

(4) Every person in the chain of representation to a testator—

(a) has the same rights in respect of the real and personal estate of that testator as the original executor would have had if living; and

(b) is, to the extent to which the estate whether real or personal of that testator has come to his hands, answerable as if he were an original executor.

Right of proving executors to exercise powers

8.—(1) Where probate is granted to one or some of two or more persons named as executors, whether or not power is reserved to the others or other to prove, all the powers which are by law conferred on the personal representative may be exercised by the proving executor or executors for the time being and shall be as effectual as if all the persons named as executors had concurred therein. **10–007**

(2) This section applies whether the testator died before or after the commencement of this Act.

[Vesting of estate in Public Trustee where intestacy or lack of executors

9.—(1) Where a person dies intestate, his real and personal estate shall vest in the Public Trustee until the grant of administration. **10–008**

(2) Where a testator dies and—

(a) at the time of his death there is no executor with power to obtain probate of the will, or

(b) at any time before probate of the will is granted there ceases to be any executor with power to obtain probate,

the real and personal estate of which he disposes by the will shall vest in the Public Trustee until the grant of representation.

(3) The vesting of real or personal estate in the Public Trustee by virtue of this section does not confer on him any beneficial interest in, or impose on him any duty, obligation or liability in respect of, the property.][8]

10–14. [*Repealed by the Supreme Court of Judicature (Consolidation) Act 1925, s.226, Sched. 6.*]

[8] s.9 substituted by the Law of Property (Miscellaneous Provisions) Act 1994, s.14(1).

Executor not to act while administration is in force

10–009 **15.** Where administration has been granted in respect of any real or personal estate of a deceased person, no person shall have power to bring any action or otherwise act as executor of the deceased person in respect of the estate comprised in or affected by the grant until the grant has been recalled or revoked.

16. [*Repealed by the Supreme Court of Judicature (Consolidation) Act 1925, s.226, Sched. 6.*]

Continuance of legal proceedings after revocation of temporary administration

10–010 **17.**—(1) If, while any legal proceeding is pending in any court by or against an administrator to whom a temporary administration has been granted, that administration is revoked, that court may order that the proceeding be continued by or against the new personal representative in like manner as if the same had been originally commenced by or against him, but subject to such conditions and variations, if any, as that court directs.

[(2) The county court has jurisdiction under this section where the proceedings are pending in that court.][9]

18–20. [*Repealed by the Supreme Court of Judicature (Consolidation) Act 1925, s.226, Sched. 6.*]

Rights and liabilities of administrator

10–011 **21.** Every person to whom administration of the real and personal estate of a deceased person is granted, shall, subject to the limitations contained in the grant, have the same rights and liabilities and be accountable in like manner as if he were the executor of the deceased.

[Debtor who becomes creditor's executor by representation or administrator to account for debt to estate

10–012 **21A.**—(1) Subject to subsection (2) of this section, where a debtor becomes his deceased creditor's executor by representation or administrator—

(a) his debt shall thereupon be extinguished; but

(b) he shall be accountable for the amount of the debt as part of the creditor's estate in any case where he would be so accountable if he had been appointed as an executor by the creditor's will.

(2) Subsection (1) of this section does not apply where the debtor's authority to act as executor or administrator is limited to part only of the creditor's estate which does not include the debt; and a debtor whose debt is extinguished by virtue of paragraph (a) shall not be accountable for its amount by virtue of paragraph (b) of that subsection in any case where the debt was barred by the Limitation Act 1939[10] before he became the creditor's executor or administrator.

[9] subs. (2) added (and subs. (1) numbered) by the County Courts Act 1984, s.14(1), Sched. 2, Pt. III, para. 11(1), (2). For the jurisdiction of the county court by agreement, see the County Courts Act 1984, s.24, *post*, para. 42–003.

[10] The reference to the Limitation Act 1939 is to be construed as including a reference to the Limitation Act 1980: Limitation Act 1980, s.40(2), Sched. 3, para. 2.

(3) In this section "debt" includes any liability, and "debtor" and "creditor" shall be construed accordingly.][11]

Special Provisions as to Settled Land

Special executors as respects settled land

22.—(1) A testator may appoint, and in default of such express appointment shall be deemed to have appointed, as his special executors in regard to settled land, the persons, if any, who are at his death the trustees of the settlement thereof, and probate may be granted to such trustees specially limited to the settled land. **10–013**

In this subsection "settled land" means land vested in the testator which was settled previously to his death and not by his will.

(2) A testator may appoint other persons either with or without such trustees as aforesaid or any of them to be his general executors in regard to his other property and assets.

Provisions where, as respects settled land, representation is not granted to the trustees of the settlement

23.—(1) Where settled land becomes vested in a personal representative, not being a trustee of the settlement, upon trust to convey the land to or assent to the vesting thereof in the tenant for life or statutory owner in order to give effect to a settlement created before the death of the deceased and not by his will, or would, on the grant of representation to him, have become so vested, such representative may— **10–014**

(a) before representation has been granted, renounce his office in regard only to such settled land without renouncing it in regard to other property;

(b) after representation has been granted, apply to the court for revocation of the grant in regard to the settled land without applying in regard to other property.

(2) Whether such renunciation or revocation is made or not, the trustees of the settlement, or any person beneficially interested thereunder, may apply to the High Court for an order appointing a special or additional personal representative in respect of the settled land, and a special or additional personal representative, if and when appointed under the order, shall be in the same position as if representation had originally been granted to him alone in place of the original personal representative, if any, or to him jointly with the original personal representative, as the case may be, limited to the settled land, but without prejudice to the previous acts and dealings, if any, of the personal representative originally constituted or the effect of notices given to such personal representative.

(3) The court may make such order as aforesaid subject to such security, if any, being given by or on behalf of the special or additional personal representative, as the court may direct, and shall, unless the court considers that special considerations apply, appoint such persons as may be necessary to secure that the persons to act as representatives in respect of the settled land shall, if willing to act, be the same persons as are the trustees of the settlement, and an office copy of the order when made shall be furnished to the [principal

[11] s.21A inserted by the Limitation Amendment Act 1980, s.10.

registry of the Family Division of the High Court][12] for entry, and a memorandum of the order shall be endorsed on the probate or administration.

(4) The person applying for the appointment of a special or additional personal representative shall give notice of the application to the [principal registry of the Family Division of the High Court][13] in the manner prescribed.

(5) Rules of court may be made for prescribing for all matters required for giving effect to the provisions of this section, and in particular—

(a) for notice of any application being given to the proper officer;
(b) for production of orders, probates, and administration to the registry;
(c) for the endorsement on a probate or administration of a memorandum of an order, subject or not to any exceptions;
(d) for the manner in which the costs are to be borne;
(e) for protecting purchasers and trustees and other persons in a fiduciary position, dealing in good faith with or giving notices to a personal representative before notice of any order has been endorsed on the probate or administration or a pending action has been registered in respect of the proceedings.

Power for special personal representatives to dispose of settled land

10–015 **24.**—(1) The special personal representatives may dispose of the settled land without the concurrence of the general personal representatives, who may likewise dispose of the other property and assets of the deceased without the concurrence of the special personal representatives.

(2) In this section the expression "special personal representatives" means the representatives appointed to act for the purposes of settled land and includes any original personal representative who is to act with an additional personal representative for those purposes.

Duties, Rights, and Obligations

[Duty of personal representatives

10–016 **25.** The personal representatives of a deceased person shall be under a duty to—

(a) collect and get in the real and personal estate of the deceased and administer it according to law;
(b) when required to do so by the court, exhibit on oath in the court a full inventory of the estate and when so required render an account of the administration of the estate to the court;
(c) when required to do so by the High Court, deliver up the grant of probate or administration to that court.][14]

Rights of action by and against personal representative

10–017 **26.**—(1), (2) [*Repealed by the Law Reform (Miscellaneous Provisions) Act 1934, s.1(7).*]

(3) A personal representative may distrain for arrears of a rentcharge due or accruing to the deceased in his lifetime on the land affected or charged

[12] Words substituted by the Administration of Justice Act 1970, s.1(6), Sched. 2, para. 3.
[13] Words substituted by the Administration of Justice Act 1970, s.1(6), Sched. 2, para. 3.
[14] s.25 substituted by the Administration of Estates Act 1971, s.9, as restricted by s.1(5).

therewith, so long as the land remains in the possession of the person liable to pay the rentcharge or of the persons deriving title under him, and in like manner as the deceased might have done had he been living.

(4) A personal representative may distrain upon land for arrears of rent due or accruing to the deceased in like manner as the deceased might have done had he been living.

Such arrears may be distrained for after the termination of the lease or tenancy as if the term or interest had not determined, if the distress is made—

(a) within six months after the termination of the lease or tenancy;
(b) during the continuance of the possession of the lessee or tenant from whom the arrears were due.

The statutory enactments relating to distress for rent apply to any distress made pursuant to this subsection.

(5), (6) [*Repealed by the Law Reform (Miscellaneous Provisions) Act 1934, s.1(7).*]

Protection of persons acting on probate or administration

27.[15]—(1) Every person making or permitting to be made any payment or disposition in good faith under a representation shall be indemnified and protected in so doing, notwithstanding any defect or circumstance whatsoever affecting the validity of the representation. **10–018**

(2) Where a representation is revoked, all payments and dispositions made in good faith to a personal representative under the representation before the revocation thereof are a valid discharge to the person making the same; and the personal representative who acted under the revoked representation may retain and reimburse himself in respect of any payments or dispositions made by him which the person to whom representation is afterwards granted might have properly made.

Liability of person fraudulently obtaining or retaining estate of deceased

28. If any person, to the defrauding of creditors or without full valuable consideration, obtains, receives or holds any real or personal estate of a deceased person or effects the release of any debt or liability due to the estate of the deceased, he shall be charged as executor in his own wrong to the extent of the real and personal estate received or coming to his hands, or the debt or liability released, after deducting— **10–019**

(a) any debt for valuable consideration and without fraud due to him from the deceased person at the time of his death; and
(b) any payment made by him which might properly be made by a personal representative.

Liability of estate of personal representative

29. Where a person as personal representative of a deceased person (including an executor in his own wrong) wastes or converts to his own use any part of the real or personal estate of the deceased, and dies, his personal representative shall to the extent of the available assets of the defaulter be liable **10–020**

[15] See also s.37, *post*, para. 10–028, and the Law of Property Act 1925, s.204, *ante*, para. 9–169.

and chargeable in respect of such waste or conversion in the same manner as the defaulter would have been if living.

Provisions applicable where administration granted to nominee of the Crown

10–021 **30.**—(1) Where the administration of the real and personal estate of any deceased person is granted to a nominee of the Crown (whether the Treasury Solicitor, or a person nominated by the Treasury Solicitor, or any other person), any legal proceeding by or against that nominee for the recovery of the real or personal estate, or any part or share thereof, shall be of the same character, and be instituted and carried on in the same manner, and be subject to the same rules of law and equity (including, except as otherwise provided by this Act, the rules of limitation under the statutes of limitation or otherwise), in all respects as if the administration had been granted to such nominee as one of the persons interested under this Act in the estate of the deceased.

(2) An information or other proceeding on the part of His Majesty shall not be filed or instituted, and a petition of right shall not be presented, in respect of the real or personal estate of any deceased person or any part or share thereof, or any claim thereon, except [. . .][16] subject to the same rules of law and equity within and subject to which a proceeding for the like purposes might be instituted by or against a subject.

(3) The Treasury Solicitor shall not be required, when applying for or obtaining administration of the estate of a deceased person for the use or benefit of His Majesty, to deliver, nor shall [. . .][17] the High Court or the Commissioners of Inland Revenue be entitled to receive in connection with any such application or grant of administration, any affidavit, statutory declaration, account, certificate, or other statement verified on oath; but the Treasury Solicitor shall deliver and the said Division and Commissioners respectively shall accept, in lieu thereof, an account or particulars of the estate of the deceased by or on behalf of the Treasury Solicitor.

(4) References in sections two, four [. . .][18] and seven of the Treasury Solicitor Act 1876 and in subsection (3) of section three of the Duchy of Lancaster Act 1920 to "personal estate" shall include real estate.

Power to make rules

10–022 **31.** Provision may be made by rules of court for giving effect to the provisions of this Part of this Act so far as relates to real estate and in particular for adapting the procedure and practice on the grant of letters of administration to the case of real estate.

PART III

ADMINISTRATION OF ASSETS

Real and personal estate of deceased are assets for payment of debts

10–023 **32.**—(1) The real and personal estate, whether legal or equitable, of a deceased person, to the extent of his beneficial interest therein, and the real and

[16] Words repealed by the Limitation Act 1939, s.34(4), Sched.
[17] Words repealed by the Administration of Justice Act 1970, s.54(3), Sched. 11.
[18] Word repealed by the Statute Law (Repeals) Act 1981, s.1(1), Sched. 1, Pt. I.

personal estate of which a deceased person in pursuance of any general power (including the statutory power to dispose of entailed interests) disposes by his will, are assets for payment of his debts (whether by specialty or simple contract) and liabilities, and any disposition by will inconsistent with this enactment is void as against the creditors, and the court shall, if necessary, administer the property for the purpose of the payment of the debts and liabilities.

This subsection takes effect without prejudice to the rights of incumbrancers.

(2) If any person to whom any such beneficial interest devolves or is given, or in whom any such interest vests, disposes thereof in good faith before an action is brought or process is sued out against him, he shall be personally liable for the value of the interest so disposed of by him, but that interest shall not be liable to be taken in execution in the action or under the process.

Trust for sale

33.—[(1) On the death of a person intestate as to any real or personal estate, that estate shall be held in trust by his personal representatives with the power to sell it.][19] **10–024**

[(2) The personal representative shall pay out of—

(a) the ready money of the deceased (so far as not disposed of by his will, if any); and

(b) any net money arising from disposing of any other part of his estate (after payment of costs),

all][20] such funeral, testamentary and administration expenses, debts and other liabilities as are properly payable thereout having regard to the rules of administration contained in this Part of this Act, and out of the residue of the said money the personal representative shall set aside a fund sufficient to provide for any pecuniary legacies bequeathed by the will (if any) of the deceased.

(3) During the minority of any beneficiary or the subsistence of any life interest and pending the distribution of the whole or any part of the estate of the deceased, the person representatives may invest the residue of the said money, or so much thereof as may not have been distributed, [under the Trustee Act 2000.][21]

(4) The residue of the said money and any investments for the time being representing the same, [and any part of the estate of the deceased which remains][22] unsold and is not required for the administration purposes aforesaid, is in this Act referred to as "the residuary estate of the intestate."

(5) The income (including net rents and profits of real estate and chattels real after payment of rates, taxes, rent, costs of insurance, repairs and other outgoings properly attributable to income) of so much of the real and personal estate of the deceased as may not be disposed of by his will, if any, or may not be required for the administration purposes aforesaid, may, however such estate is invested, as from the death of the deceased, be treated and applied as income, and for that purpose any necessary apportionment may be made between tenant for life and remainderman.

[19] subs. (1) substituted by the Trusts of Land and Appointment of Trustees Act 1996, s.5(1), Sched. 2, para. 5(1), (2).

[20] Words substituted by the Trusts of Land and Appointment of Trustees Act 1996, s.5(1), Sched. 2, para. 5(1), (3).

[21] Words substituted by the Trustee Act 2000, s.40(1), Sched. 2, Pt. II, para. 27.

[22] Words substituted by the Trusts of Land and Appointment of Trustees Act 1996, s.5(1), Sched. 2, para. 5(1), (4).

(6) Nothing in this section affects the rights of any creditor of the deceased or the rights of the Crown in respect of death duties.

(7) Where the deceased leaves a will, this section has effect subject to the provisions contained in the will.

Administration of assets

10–025 **34.**—(1) [*Repealed by the Insolvency Act 1985, s.235(3), Sched. 10, Pt. III.*][23]

(2) [*Repealed by the Administration of Estates Act 1971, s.12, Sched. 2, Pt. II.*]

(3) Where the estate of a deceased person is solvent his real and personal estate shall, subject to rules of court and the provisions hereinafter contained as to charges on property of the deceased, and to the provisions, if any, contained in his will, be applicable towards the discharge of the funeral, testamentary and administration expenses, debts and liabilities payable thereout in the order mentioned in Part II of the First Schedule to this Act.

Charges on property of deceased to be paid primarily out of the property charged

10–026 **35.**—(1) Where a person dies possessed of, or entitled to, or, under a general power of appointment (including the statutory power to dispose of entailed interests) by his will disposes of, an interest in property, which at the time of his death is charged with the payment of money, whether by way of legal mortgage, equitable charge or otherwise (including a lien for unpaid purchase money), and the deceased has not by will deed or other document signified a contrary or other intention, the interest so charged shall, as between the different persons claiming through the deceased, be primarily liable for the payment of the charge; and every part of the said interest, according to its value, shall bear a proportionate part of the charge on the whole thereof.

(2) Such contrary or other intention shall not be deemed to be signified—

(a) by a general direction for the payment of debts or of all the debts of the testator out of his personal estate, or his residuary real and personal estate, or his residuary real estate; or

(b) by a charge of debts upon any such estate;

unless such intention is further signified by words expressly or by necessary implication referring to all or some part of the charge.

(3) Nothing in this section affects the right of a person entitled to the charge to obtain payment or satisfaction thereof either out of the other assets of the deceased or otherwise.

Effect of assent or conveyance by personal representative

10–027 **36.**—(1) A personal representative may assent to the vesting, in any person who (whether by devise, bequest, devolution, appropriation or otherwise) may be entitled thereto, either beneficially or as a trustee or personal representative, of any estate or interest in real estate to which the testator or intestate was entitled or over which he exercised a general power of appointment by his will, including the statutory power to dispose of entailed interests, and which devolved upon the personal representative.

[23] See the Insolvency Act 1986, s.421, and the Administration of Insolvent Estates of Deceased Persons Order 1986 (S.I. 1986 No. 1999).

(2) The assent shall operate to vest in that person the estate or interest to which the assent relates, and, unless a contrary intention appears, the assent shall relate back to the death of the deceased.

(3) [*Repealed by the Law of Property (Miscellaneous Provisions) Act 1994, s.21(1), Sched. 2.*]

(4) An assent to the vesting of a legal estate shall be in writing, signed by the personal representative, and shall name the person in whose favour it is given and shall operate to vest in that person the legal estate to which it relates; and an assent not in writing or not in favour of a named person shall not be effectual to pass a legal estate.

(5) Any person in whose favour an assent or conveyance of a legal estate is made by a personal representative may require that notice of the assent or conveyance be written or endorsed on or permanently annexed to the probate or letters of administration, at the cost of the estate of the deceased, and that the probate or letters of administration be produced, at the like cost, to prove that the notice has been placed thereon or annexed thereto.

(6) A statement in writing by a personal representative that he has not given or made an assent or conveyance in respect of a legal estate, shall, in favour of a purchaser, but without prejudice to any previous disposition made in favour of another purchaser deriving title mediately or immediately under the personal representative, be sufficient evidence that an assent or conveyance has not been given or made in respect of the legal estate to which the statement relates, unless notice of a previous assent or conveyance affecting that estate has been placed on or annexed to the probate or administration.

A conveyance by a personal representative of a legal estate to a purchaser accepted on the faith of such a statement shall (without prejudice as aforesaid and unless notice of a previous assent or conveyance affecting that estate has been placed on or annexed to the probate or administration) operate to transfer or create the legal estate expressed to be conveyed in like manner as if no previous assent or conveyance had been made by the personal representative.

A personal representative making a false statement, in regard to any such matter, shall be liable in like manner as if the statement had been contained in a statutory declaration.

(7) An assent or conveyance by a personal representative in respect of a legal estate shall, in favour of a purchaser, unless notice of a previous assent or conveyance affecting that legal estate has been placed on or annexed to the probate or administration, be taken as sufficient evidence that the person in whose favour the assent or conveyance is given or made is the person entitled to have the legal estate conveyed to him, and upon the proper trusts, if any, but shall not otherwise prejudicially affect the claim of any person rightfully entitled to the estate vested or conveyed or any charge thereon.

(8) A conveyance of a legal estate by a personal representative to a purchaser shall not be invalidated by reason only that the purchaser may have notice that all the debts, liabilities, funeral, and testamentary or administration expenses, duties, and legacies of the deceased have been discharged or provided for.

(9) An assent or conveyance given or made by a personal representative shall not, except in favour of a purchaser of a legal estate, prejudice the right of the personal representative or any other person to recover the estate or interest to which the assent or conveyance relates, or to be indemnified out of such estate or interest against any duties, debt, or liability to which such estate or interest would have been subject if there had not been any assent or conveyance.

(10) A personal representative may, as a condition of giving an assent or making a conveyance, require security for the discharge of any such duties, debt,

towards satisfaction of any legacy bequeathed by the deceased, or of any other interest or share in his property, whether settled or not, as to the personal representative may seem just and reasonable, according to the respective rights of the persons interested in the property of the deceased:

Provided that—

(i) an appropriation shall not be made under this section so as to affect prejudicially any specific devise or bequest;

(ii) an appropriation of property, whether or not being an investment authorised by law or by the will, if any, of the deceased for the investment of money subject to the trust, shall not (save as hereinafter mentioned) be made under this section except with the following consents:—

(a) when made for the benefit of a person absolutely and beneficially entitled in possession, the consent of that person;

(b) when made in respect of any settled legacy share or interest, the consent of either the trustee thereof, if any (not being also the personal representative), or the person who may for the time being be entitled to the income:

If the person whose consent is so required as aforesaid is an infant or [is incapable, by reason of mental disorder within the meaning of [the Mental Health Act 1983][33] of managing and administering his property and affairs][34], the consent shall be given on his behalf by his parents or parent, testamentary or other guardian […][35] or receiver, or if, in the case of an infant, there is no such parent or guardian, by the court on the application of his next friend;

(iii) no consent (save of such trustee as aforesaid) shall be required on behalf of a person who may come into existence after the time of appropriation, or who cannot be found or ascertained at that time;

(iv) if no [receiver is acting for a person suffering from mental disorder][36], then, if the appropriation is of an investment authorised by law or by the will, if any, of the deceased for the investment of money subject to the trust, no consent shall be required on behalf of the [said person][37];

(v) if, independently of the personal representative, there is no trustee of a settled legacy share or interest, and no person of full age and capacity entitled to the income thereof, no consent shall be required to an appropriation in respect of such legacy share or interest, provided that the appropriation is of an investment authorised as aforesaid.

[(1A) The county court has jurisdiction under proviso (ii) to subsection (1) of this section where the estate in respect of which the application is made does not exceed in amount or value the county court limit.][38]

(2) Any property duly appropriated under the powers conferred by this section shall thereafter be treated as an authorised investment, and may be retained or dealt with accordingly.

(3) For the purposes of such appropriation, the personal representative may ascertain and fix the value of the respective parts of the real and personal estate and the liabilities of the deceased as he may think fit, and shall for that purpose employ a duly qualified valuer in any case where such employment may be

[33] Words substituted by the Mental Health Act 1983, s.148(1), Sched. 4, para. 7.
[34] Words substituted by the Mental Health Act 1959, s.149(1), Sched. 7, Pt. I.
[35] Words repealed by the Mental Health Act 1959, s.149(1), Sched. 7, Pt. I.
[36] Words substituted by the Mental Health Act 1959, s.149(1), Sched. 7, Pt. I.
[37] Words substituted by the Mental Health Act 1959, s.149(1), Sched. 7, Pt. I.
[38] subs. (1A) inserted by the County Courts Act 1984, s.148(1), Sched. 2, Pt. III, para. 13. For the jurisdiction of the county court by agreement, see the County Courts Act 1984, s.24, *post*, para. 42–003.

necessary; and may make any conveyance (including an assent) which may be requisite for giving effect to the appropriation.

(4) An appropriation made pursuant to this section shall bind all persons interested in the property of the deceased whose consent is not hereby made requisite.

(5)[39] The personal representative shall, in making the appropriation, have regard to the rights of any person who may thereafter come into existence, or who cannot be found or ascertained at the time of appropriation, and of any other person whose consent is not required by this section.

(6) This section does not prejudice any other power of appropriation conferred by law or by the will (if any) of the deceased, and takes effect with any extended powers conferred by the will (if any) of the deceased, and where an appropriation is made under this section, in respect of a settled legacy, share or interest, the property appropriated shall remain subject to all [trusts][40] and powers of leasing, disposition, and management or varying investments which would have been applicable thereto or to the legacy, share or interest in respect of which the appropriation is made, if no such appropriation had been made.

(7) If after any real estate has been appropriated in purported exercise of the powers conferred by this section, the person to whom it was conveyed disposes of it or any interest therein, then, in favour of a purchaser, the appropriation shall be deemed to have been made in accordance with the requirements of this section and after all the requisite consents, if any, had been given.

(8) In this section, a settled legacy, share or interest includes any legacy, share or interest to which a person is not absolutely entitled in possession at the date of the appropriation, also an annuity, and "purchaser" means a purchaser for money or money's worth.

(9) This section applies whether the deceased died intestate or not, and whether before or after the commencement of this Act, and extends to property over which a testator exercises a general power of appointment, including the statutory power to dispose of entailed interests, and authorises the setting apart of a fund to answer an annuity by means of the income of that fund or otherwise.

Power to appoint trustees of infants' property

42.—(1) Where an infant is absolutely entitled under the will or on the **10–033** intestacy of a person dying before or after the commencement of this Act (in this subsection called "the deceased") to a devise or legacy, or to the residue of the estate of the deceased, or any share therein, and such devise, legacy, residue or share is not under the will, if any, of the deceased, devised or bequeathed to trustees for the infant, the personal representatives of the deceased may appoint a trust corporation or two or more individuals not exceeding four (whether or not including the personal representatives or one or more of the personal representatives), to be the trustee or trustees of such devise, legacy, residue or share for the infant, and to be trustees of any land devised or any land being or forming part of such residue or share for the purposes of the Settled Land Act 1925, and of the statutory provisions relating to the management of land during a minority, and may execute or do any assurance or thing requisite for vesting such devise, legacy, residue or share in the trustee or trustees so appointed.

[39] For the rights of the surviving spouse in relation to the matrimonial home, see the Intestates' Estates Act 1952, s.5, Sched. 2, para. 1(3), *post*, para. 15–001.

[40] Word substituted by the Trusts of Land and Appointment of Trustees Act 1996, s.25(1), Sched. 3, para. 6(1), (3).

On such appointment the personal representatives, as such, shall be discharged from all further liability in respect of such devise, legacy, residue, or share, and the same may be retained in its existing condition or state of investment, or may be converted into money, and such money may be invested in any authorised investment.

(2) Where a personal representative has before the commencement of this Act retained or sold any such devise, legacy, residue or share, and invested the same or the proceeds thereof in any investments in which he was authorised to invest money subject to the trust, then, subject to any order of the court made before such commencement, he shall not be deemed to have incurred any liability on that account, or by reason of not having paid or transferred the money or property into court.

Obligations of personal representative as to giving possession of land and powers of the court

10–034 **43.**—(1) A personal representative, before giving an assent or making a conveyance in favour of any person entitled, may permit that person to take possession of the land, and such possession shall not prejudicially affect the right of the personal representative to take or resume possession nor his power to convey the land as if he were in possession thereof, but subject to the interest of any lessee, tenant or occupier in possession or in actual occupation of the land.

(2) Any person who as against the personal representative claims possession of real estate, or the appointment of a receiver thereof, or a conveyance thereof, or an assent to the vesting thereof, or to be registered as proprietor thereof under the [Land Registration Act 2002][41], may apply to the court for directions with reference thereto, and the court may make such vesting or other order as may be deemed proper, and the provisions of the Trustee Act 1925, relating to vesting orders and to the appointment of a person to convey, shall apply.

(3) This section applies whether the testator or intestate died before or after the commencement of this Act.

[(4) The county court has jurisdiction under this section where the estate in respect of which the application is made does not exceed in amount or value the county court limit.][42]

Power to postpone distribution

10–035 **44.** Subject to the foregoing provisions of this Act, a personal representative is not bound to distribute the estate of the deceased before the expiration of one year from the death.

[41] Words substituted by the Land Registration Act 2002, s.133, Sched. 11, para. 3.

[42] subs. (4) added by the County Courts Act 1984, s.148(1), Sched. 2, Pt. III, para. 14. For the jurisdiction of the county court by agreement, see the County Courts Act 1984, s.24, *post*, para. 42–003.

Part IV

Distribution of Residuary Estate[43]

Abolition of descent to heir, curtesy, dower and escheat

45.—(1) With regard to the real estate and personal inheritance of every person dying after the commencement of this Act, there shall be abolished— **10–036**

(a) All existing modes rules and canons of descent, and of devolution by special occupancy or otherwise, of real estate, or of a personal inheritance, whether operating by the general law or by the custom of gavelkind or borough english or by any other custom of any county, locality, or manor, or otherwise howsoever; and

(b) Tenancy by the curtesy and every other estate and interest of a husband in real estate as to which his wife dies intestate, whether arising under the general law or by custom or otherwise; and

(c) Dower and freebench and every other estate and interest of a wife in real estate as to which her husband dies intestate, whether arising under the general law or by custom or otherwise: Provided that where a right (if any) to freebench or other like right has attached before the commencement of this Act which cannot be barred by a testamentary or other disposition made by the husband, such right shall, unless released, remain in force as an equitable interest; and

(d) Escheat to the Crown or the Duchy of Lancaster or the Duke of Cornwall or to a mesne lord for want of heirs.

(2) Nothing in this section affects the descent or devolution of an entailed interest.

Succession to real and personal estate on intestacy

46.[44]—(1) The residuary estate of an intestate shall be distributed in the manner or be held on the trusts mentioned in this section, namely:— **10–037**

[(i) If the intestate leaves a husband or wife, then in accordance with the following Table:

Table

If the intestate— (1) leaves— (a) no issue, and (b) no parent, or brother or sister of the whole blood, or issue of a brother or sister of the whole blood	the residuary estate shall be held in trust for the surviving husband or wife absolutely.

[43] See the Family Law Reform Act 1987, ss.1, 18, *post*, paras 50–001, 50–002.

[44] The amendments to ss.46–49 have effect in relation to persons dying intestate after 1952.

(2) leaves issue (whether or not persons mentioned in sub-paragraph (b) above also survive)

the surviving husband or wife shall take the personal chattels absolutely and, in addition, the residuary estate of the intestate (other than the personal chattels) shall stand charged with the payment of a [fixed net sum][45], free of death duties and costs, to the surviving husband or wife with interest thereon from the date of the death [at such rate as the Lord Chancellor may specify by order][46] until paid or appropriated, and, subject to providing for that sum and the interest thereon, the residuary estate (other than the personal chattels) shall be held—

(a) as to one half upon trust for the surviving husband or wife during his or her life, and, subject to such life interest, on the statutory trusts for the issue of the intestate, and

(b) as to the other half, on the statutory trusts for the issue of the intestate.

(3) leaves one or more of the following, that is to say, a parent, a brother or sister of the whole blood, or issue of a brother or sister of the whole blood, but leaves no issue

the surviving husband or wife shall take the personal chattels absolutely and, in addition, the residuary estate of the intestate (other than the personal chattels) shall stand charged with the payment of a [fixed net sum][47], free of death duties and costs, to the surviving husband or wife with interest thereon from the date of the death [at such rate as the Lord Chancellor may specify by order][48] until paid or appropriated, and, subject to providing for that sum and the interest thereon, the residuary estate (other than the personal chattels) shall be held—

(a) as to one half in trust for the surviving husband or wife absolutely, and

---

[45] Words substituted by the Family Provisions Act 1966, s.1(2)(a). The current sum is £125,000: Family Provision (Intestate Succession) Order 1993 (S.I. 1993 No. 2906).

[46] Words substituted by the Administration of Justice Act 1977, s.28(1)(a). See the Intestate Succession (Interest and Capitalisation) Order 1977 (S.I. 1977 No. 1491), as amended by the Intestate Succession (Interest and Capitalisation) Amendment Order 1983 (S.I. 1983 No. 1374), which provides that the specified rate of interest shall be 6 per cent per annum.

[47] Words substituted by the Family Provision Act 1966, s.1(2)(a). The current sum is £200,000: Family Provision (Intestate Succession) Order 1993 (S.I. 1993 No. 2906).

[48] See *ante*, n. 46.

(b) as to the other half—

(i) where the intestate leaves one parent or both parents (whether or not brothers or sisters of the intestate or their issue also survive) in trust for the parent absolutely or, as the case may be, for the two parents in equal shares absolutely

(ii) where the intestate leaves no parent, on the statutory trusts for the brothers and sisters of the whole blood of the intestate.][49]

[The fixed net sums referred to in paragraphs (2) and (3) of this Table shall be of the amounts provided by or under section 1 of the Family Provision Act 1966.][50]

(ii) If the intestate leaves issue but no husband or wife, the residuary estate of the intestate shall be held on the statutory trusts for the issue of the intestate;

(iii) If the intestate leaves [no husband or wife and][51] no issue but both parents, then [...][52] the residuary estate of the intestate shall be held in trust for the father and mother in equal shares absolutely;

(iv) If the intestate leaves [no husband or wife and][53] no issue but one parent, then [...][54] the residuary estate of the intestate shall be held in trust for the surviving father or mother absolutely;

(v) If the intestate leaves no [husband or wife and no issue and no][55] parent, then [...][56] the residuary estate of the intestate shall be held in trust for the following persons living at the death of the intestate, and in the following order and manner, namely:—

First, on the statutory trusts for the brothers and sisters of the whole blood of the intestate; but if no person takes an absolutely vested interest under such trusts; then

Secondly, on the statutory trusts for the brothers and sisters of the half blood of the intestate; but if no person takes an absolutely vested interest under such trusts; then

Thirdly, for the grandparents of the intestate and, if more than one survive the intestate, in equal shares; but if there is no member of this class; then

Fourthly, on the statutory trusts for the uncles and aunts of the intestate (being brothers or sisters of the whole blood of a parent of the intestate); but if no person takes an absolutely vested interest under such trusts; then

Fifthly, on the statutory trusts for the uncles and aunts of the intestate

[49] s.46(1)(i) substituted by the Intestates' Estates Act 1952, s.1(2).
[50] Words added by the Family Provision Act 1966, s.1(2)(a).
[51] Words inserted by the Intestates' Estates Act 1952, s.1(3)(a).
[52] Words repealed by the Intestates' Estates Act 1952, s.1(3)(a).
[53] Words inserted by the Intestates' Estates Act 1952, s.1(3)(a).
[54] Words repealed by the Intestates' Estates Act 1952, s.1(3)(a).
[55] Words substituted by the Intestates' Estates Act 1952, s.1(3)(b).
[56] Words repealed by the Intestates' Estates Act 1952, s.1(3)(b).

[Right of surviving spouse to have own life interest redeemed[67]

10–039 **47A.**—(1) Where a surviving husband or wife is entitled to a life interest in part of the residuary estate, and so elects, the personal representative shall purchase or redeem the life interest by paying the capital value thereof to the tenant for life, or the persons deriving title under the tenant for life, and the costs of the transaction; and thereupon the residuary estate of the intestate may be dealt with and distributed free from the life interest.

(2) [*Repealed by the Administration of Justice Act 1977, ss.28(2), 32(4), Sched. 5, Pt. VI.*]

(3) An election under this section shall only be exercisable if at the time of the election the whole of the said part of the residuary estate consists of property in possession, but, for the purposes of this section, a life interest in property partly in possession and partly not in possession shall be treated as consisting of two separate life interests in those respective parts of the property.

[(3A) The capital value shall be reckoned in such manner as the Lord Chancellor may by order direct, and an order under this subsection may include transitional provisions.

(3B) The power to make orders under subsection (3A) above shall be exercisable by statutory instrument subject to annulment in pursuance of a resolution of either House of Parliament; and any such order may be varied or revoked by a subsequent order made under the power.][68]

(4) [*Repealed by the Administration of Justice Act 1977, ss.28(2), 32(4), Sched. 5, Pt. VI.*]

(5) An election under this section shall be exercisable only within the period of twelve months from the date on which representation with respect to the estate of the intestate is first taken out:

Provided that if the surviving husband or wife satisfies the court that the limitation to the said period of twelve months will operate unfairly—

(a) in consequence of the representation first taken out being probate of a will subsequently revoked on the ground that the will was invalid, or

(b) in consequence of a question whether a person had an interest in the estate, or as to the nature of an interest in the estate, not having been determined at the time when representation was first taken out, or

(c) in consequence of some other circumstances affecting the administration or distribution of the estate,

the court may extend the said period.

(6) An election under this section shall be exercisable, except where the tenant for life is the sole personal representative, by notifying the personal representative (or, where there are two or more personal representatives of whom one is the tenant for life, all of them except the tenant for life) in writing; and a notification in writing under this subsection shall not be revocable except with the consent of the personal representative.

(7) Where the tenant for life is the sole personal representative an election under this section shall not be effective unless written notice thereof is given to the [[Senior Registrar][69] of the Family Division of the High Court][70] within the

[67] Sidenote as printed in the Intestates' Estates Act 1952, Sched. 1, which sets out the Administration of Estates Act 1925, ss.46 to 49, as amended.

[68] subss. (3A) and (3B) inserted by the Administration of Justice Act 1977, s.28(3); and see the Intestate Succession (Interest and Capitalisation) Order 1977 (S.I. 1977 No. 1491), as amended by the Intestate Succession (Interest and Capitalisation) Amendment Order 1983 (S.I. 1983 No. 1374).

[69] Words substituted by the Supreme Court Act 1981, s.152(1), Sched. 5.

[70] Words substituted by the Administration of Justice Act 1970, s.1(6), Sched. 2, para. 4.

period within which it must be made; and provision may be made by probate rules for keeping a record of such notices and making that record available to the public.

In this subsection the expression "probate rules" means rules [of court made under section 127 of the Supreme Court Act 1981][71].

(8) An election under this section by a tenant for life who is an infant shall be as valid and binding as it would be if the tenant for life were of age; but the personal representative shall, instead of paying the capital value of the life interest to the tenant for life, deal with it in the same manner as with any other part of the residuary estate to which the tenant for life is absolutely entitled.

(9)[72] In considering for the purposes of the foregoing provisions of this section the question when representation was first taken out, a grant limited to settled land or to trust property shall be left out of account and a grant limited to real estate or to personal estate shall be left out of account unless a grant limited to the remainder of the estate has previously been made or is made at the same time.][73]

Powers of personal representative in respect of interests of surviving spouse

48.—(1) [*Repealed by the Intestates' Estates Act 1952, s.2(a).*] **10–040**

(2) The personal representatives may raise—

(a) [the fixed net sum][74] or any part thereof and the interest thereon payable to the surviving husband or wife of the intestate on the security of the whole or any part of the residuary estate of the intestate (other than the personal chattels), so far as that estate may be sufficient for the purpose or the said sum and interest may not have been satisfied by an appropriation under the statutory power available in that behalf; and

(b) in like manner the capital sum, if any, required for the purchase or redemption of the life interest of the surviving husband or wife of the intestate, or any part thereof not satisfied by the application for that purpose of any part of the residuary estate of the intestate;

and in either case the amount, if any, properly required for the payment of the costs of the transaction.

Application to cases of partial intestacy

49.—(1) Where any person dies leaving a will effectively disposing of part of his property, this Part of this Act shall have effect as respects the part of his property not so disposed of subject to the provisions contained in the will and subject to the following modifications:— **10–041**

[. . .][75]

(b) The personal representative shall, subject to his rights and powers for the purposes of administration, be a trustee for the persons entitled under

[71] Words substituted by the Supreme Court Act 1981, s.152(1), Sched. 5.

[72] See the Intestates' Estates Act 1952, s.5, Sched. 2, para. 3(3), *post*, para. 15–001.

[73] s.47A inserted by the Intestates' Estates Act 1952, s.2(b).

[74] Words substituted by the Family Provision Act 1966, s.1(2)(b). The current sum is £125,000 if the intestate leaves issue; or £200,000 if the intestate leaves no issue: Family Provision (Intestate Succession) Order 1993 (S.I. 1993 No. 2906).

[75] Paras (aa) (inserted by the Intestates' Estates Act 1952, s.3(2)) and (a) repealed (in relation to persons dying intestate after 1995) by the Law Reform (Succession) Act 1995, ss.1(2)(b), (3), 5, Sched.

this Part of this Act in respect of the part of the estate not expressly disposed of unless it appears by the will that the personal representative is intended to take such part beneficially.

[(2),(3) [*Repealed by the Law Reform (Succession) Act 1994, ss.1(2)(b), 5, Sched.*]

(4) The references in subsection (3) of section forty-seven A of this Act to property are references to property comprised in the residuary estate and, accordingly, where a will of the deceased creates a life interest in property in possession, and the remaining interest in that property forms part of the residuary estate, the said references are references to that remaining interest (which, until the life interest determines, is property not in possession).][76]

Construction of documents

10–042 **50.**[77]—(1) References to any Statutes of Distribution in an instrument inter vivos made or in a will coming into operation after the commencement of this Act, shall be construed as references to this Part of this Act; and references in such an instrument or will to statutory next of kin shall be construed, unless the context otherwise requires, as referring to the persons who would take beneficially on an intestacy under the foregoing provisions of this Part of this Act.

(2) Trusts declared in an instrument inter vivos made, or in a will coming into operation, before the commencement of this Act by reference to the Statutes of Distribution, shall, unless the contrary thereby appears, be construed as referring to the enactments (other than the Intestates' Estates Act 1890) relating to the distribution of effects of intestates which were in force immediately before the commencement of this Act.

[(3) In subsection (1) of this section the reference to this Part of this Act, or the foregoing provisions of this Part of this Act, shall in relation to an instrument inter vivos made, or a will or codicil coming into operation, after the coming into force of section 18 of the Family Law Reform Act 1987 (but not in relation to instruments inter vivos made or wills or codicils coming into operation earlier) be construed as including references to that section.][78]

Savings

10–043 **51.**—(1) Nothing in this Part of this Act affects the right of any person to take beneficially, by purchase, as heir either general or special.

(2) The foregoing provisions of this Part of this Act do not apply to any beneficial interest in real estate (not including chattels real) to which a [person of unsound mind][79] or defective living and of full age at the commencement of

[76] subss. (2)–(4) added by the Intestates' Estates Act 1952, s.3(3).

[77] References to this Part of this Act shall, in relation to instruments made or wills or codicils coming into operation after the commencement of the Intestates' Estates Act 1952, include references to Part I of that Act: Intestates' Estates Act 1952, s.6(2); after the commencement of the Family Law Reform Act 1969, shall include references to Part IV of that Act: Family Law Reform Act 1969, s.14(6); after the commencement of the Family Law Reform Act 1987, shall include references to s.18 of that Act: Family Law Reform Act 1987, s.18(3), *post*, para. 50–002; and after the commencement of the Law Reform (Succession) Act 1995, shall include references to s.1 of that Act: Law Reform (Succession) Act 1995, s.1(4).

[78] subs. (3) added by the Family Law Reform Act 1987, s.33(1), Sched. 2, para. 3.

[79] Words substituted by the Mental Treatment Act 1930, s.20(5), as saved by the Mental Health Act 1983, s.148, Sched. 5, para. 29.

this Act, and unable, by reason of his incapacity, to make a will, who thereafter dies intestate in respect of such interest without having recovered his testamentary capacity, was entitled at his death, and any such beneficial interest (not being an interest ceasing on his death) shall, without prejudice to any will of the deceased, devolve in accordance with the general law in force before the commencement of this Act applicable to freehold land, and that law shall, notwithstanding any repeal, apply to the case.

For the purposes of this subsection, a [person of unsound mind][80] or defective who dies intestate as respects any beneficial interest in real estate shall not be deemed to have recovered his testamentary capacity unless his [...][81] receiver has been discharged.

(3) Where an infant dies after the commencement of this Act without having been married [and without issue][82], and independently of this subsection he would, at his death, have been equitably entitled under a [trust or][83] settlement (including a will) to a vested estate in fee simple or absolute interest in freehold land, or in any property [...][84] to devolve therewith or as freehold land, such infant shall be deemed to have had [a life interest][85], and the [trust or][86] settlement shall be construed accordingly.

(4) [*Repealed by the Trusts of Land and Appointment of Trustees Act 1996, s.25(2), Sched. 4.*]

Interpretation of Part IV

52. In this Part of this Act "real and personal estate" means every beneficial interest (including rights of entry and reverter) of the intestate in real and personal estate which (otherwise than in right of a power of appointment or of the testamentary power conferred by statute to dispose of entailed interests) he could, if of full age and capacity, have disposed of by his will [and references (however expressed) to any relationship between two persons shall be construed in accordance with section 1 of the Family Law Reform Act 1987][87]. **10–044**

Part V

Supplemental

General savings

53.—(1) Nothing in this Act shall derogate from the powers of the High Court which exist independently of this Act or alter the distribution of business between the several divisions of the High Court, or operate to transfer any jurisdiction from the High Court to any other court. **10–045**

[80] Words substituted by the Mental Treatment Act 1930, s.20(5), as saved by the Mental Health Act 1983, s.148, Sched. 5, para. 29.
[81] Words repealed by the Mental Health Act 1959, s.149(2), Sched. 8, Pt. I.
[82] Words inserted by the Trusts of Land and Appointment of Trustees Act 1996, s.25(1), Sched. 3, para. 6(1), (4)(a).
[83] Words inserted by the Trusts of Land and Appointment of Trustees Act 1996, s.25(1), Sched. 3, para. 6(1), (4)(b).
[84] Word repealed by the Trusts of Land and Appointment of Trustees Act 1996, s.25(1), Sched. 4.
[85] Words substituted by the Trusts of Land and Appointment of Trustees Act 1996, s.25(1), Sched. 3, para. 6(1), (4)(c).
[86] Words inserted by the Trusts of Land and Appointment of Trustees Act 1996, s.25(1), Sched. 3, para. 6(1), (4)(b).
[87] Words added by the Family Law Reform Act 1987, s.33(1), Sched. 2, para. 4.

(2) Nothing in this Act shall affect any unrepealed enactment in a public general Act dispensing with probate or administration as respects personal estate not including chattels real.

(3) [*Repealed by the Finance Act 1975, ss.52(2), 59(5), Sched. 13, Pt. I.*]

Application of Act

10–046 **54.** Save as otherwise expressly provided, this Act does not apply in any case where the death occurred before the commencement of this Act.

Definitions

10–047 **55.**—(1) In this Act, unless the context otherwise requires, the following expressions have the meanings hereby assigned to them respectively, that is to say:—

(i) "Administration" means, with reference to the real and personal estate of a deceased person, letters of administration, whether general or limited, or with the will annexed or otherwise:

(ii) "Administrator" means a person to whom administration is granted:

(iii) "Conveyance" includes a mortgage, charge by way of legal mortgage, lease, assent, vesting declaration, vesting instrument, disclaimer, release and every other assurance of property or of an interest therein by any instrument, except a will, and "convey" has a corresponding meaning, and "disposition" includes a "conveyance" also a devise bequest and an appointment of property contained in a will, and "dispose of" has a corresponding meaning:

[(iiiA) "the County Court limit", in relation to any enactment contained in this Act, means the amount for the time being specified by an Order in Council under section 145 of the County Courts Act 1984 as the county court limit for the purposes of that enactment (or, where no such Order in Council has been made, the corresponding limit specified by Order in Council under section 192 of the County Courts Act 1959;][88]

(iv) "the Court" means the High Court, and also the county court, where that court has jurisdiction […][89]

(v) "Income" includes rents and profits:

(vi) "Intestate" includes a person who leaves a will but dies intestate as to some beneficial interest in his real or personal estate:

[(via) "Land" has the same meaning as in the Law of Property Act 1925;][90]

(vii) "Legal estates" mean the estates charges and interests in or over land (subsisting or created at law) which are by statute authorised to subsist or to be created at law; and "equitable interests" mean all other interests and charges in or over land […][91]:

(viii) "[Person of unsound mind]"[92] includes a [person of unsound mind][93]

---

[88] Definition inserted by the County Courts Act 1984, s.148(1), Sched. 2, Pt. III, para. 15.

[89] Words repealed by the Courts Act 1971, s.56(4), Sched. 11, Pt. II.

[90] Definition inserted by the Trusts of Land and Appointment of Trustees Act 1996, s.25(1), Sched. 3, para. 6(1), (5).

[91] Words repealed by the Trusts of Land and Appointment of Trustees Act 1996, s.25(2), Sched. 4.

[92] Words substituted by the Mental Treatment Act 1930, s.20(5), as saved by the Mental Health Act 1983, s.148, Sched. 5, para. 29.

[93] Words substituted by the Mental Treatment Act 1930, s.20(5), as saved by the Mental Health Act 1983, s.148, Sched. 5, para. 29.

whether so found or not, and in relation to a [person of unsound mind][94] not so found; [...][95] and "defective" includes every person affected by the provisions of section one hundred and sixteen of the Lunacy Act 1890, as extended by section sixty-four of the Mental Deficiency Act 1913, and for whose benefit a receiver has been appointed:

(ix) "Pecuniary legacy" includes an annuity, a general legacy, a demonstrative legacy so far as it is not discharged out of designated property, and any other general direction by a testator for the payment of money, including all death duties free from which any devise, bequest, or payment is made to take effect:

(x) "Personal chattels" mean carriages, horses, stable furniture and effects (not used for business purposes), motor cars and accessories (not used for business purposes), garden effects, domestic animals, plate, plated articles, linen, china, glass, books, pictures, prints, furniture, jewellery, articles of household or personal use or ornament, musical and scientific instruments and apparatus, wines, liquors and consumable stores, but do not include any chattels used at the death of the intestate for business purposes nor money or securities for money:

(xi) "Personal representative" means the executor, original or by representation, or administrator for the time being of a deceased person, and as regards any liability for the payment of death duties includes any person who takes possession of or intermeddles with the property of a deceased person without the authority of the personal representatives or the court, and "executor" includes a person deemed to be appointed executor as respects settled land:

(xii) "Possession" includes the receipt of rents and profits or the right to receive the same, if any:

(xiii) "Prescribed" means prescribed by rules of court [...][96]

(xiv) "Probate" means the probate of a will:

[...][97]

[...][98]

(xvii) "Property" includes a thing in action and any interest in real or personal property:

(xviii) "Purchaser" means a lessee, mortgagee or other person who in good faith acquires an interest in property for valuable consideration, also an intending purchaser and "valuable consideration" includes marriage, but does not include a nominal consideration in money:

(xix) "Real estate" save as provided in Part IV of this Act means real estate, including chattels real, which by virtue of Part I of this Act devolves on the personal representative of a deceased person:

(xx) "Representation" means the probate of a will and administration, and the expression "taking out representation" refers to the obtaining of the probate of a will or of the grant of administration:

(xxi) "Rent" includes a rent service or a rentcharge, or other rent, toll,

---

[94] Words substituted by the Mental Treatment Act 1930, s.20(5), as saved by the Mental Health Act 1983, s.148, Sched. 5, para. 29.

[95] Words repealed by the Mental Health Act 1959, s.149(2), Sched. 8, Pt. I.

[96] Words repealed by the Supreme Court Act 1981, s.152(4), Sched. 7.

[97] Definition of "probate judge" repealed by the Law of Property (Miscellaneous Provisions) Act 1994, s.21(1), Sched. 2.

[98] Definition of "probate rules" repealed by the Supreme Court Act 1981, s.152(4), Sched. 7.

duty, or annual or periodical payment in money or money's worth, issuing out of or charged upon land, but does not include mortgage interest; and "rentcharge" includes a fee farm rent:

[...][99]

(xxiii) "Securities" include stocks, funds, or shares:

(xxiv) "Tenant for life," "statutory owner," [...][1] "settled land," "settlement," "trustees of the settlement," "term of years absolute," "death duties," and "legal mortgage," have the same meanings as in the Settled Land Act 1925 and "entailed interest" and "charge by way of legal mortgage" have the same meanings as in the Law of Property Act 1925:

(xxv) "Treasury solicitor" means the solicitor for the affairs of His Majesty's Treasury, and includes the solicitor for the affairs of the Duchy of Lancaster:

(xxvi) "Trust corporation"[2] means the public trustee or a corporation either appointed by the court in any particular case to be a trustee or entitled by rules made under subsection (3) of section four of the Public Trustee Act 1906 to act as custodian trustee:

[...][3]

(xxviii) "Will" includes codicil.

(2) References to a child or issue living at the death of any person include a child or issue en ventre sa mere at the death.

(3) References to the estate of a deceased person include property over which the deceased exercises a general power of appointment (including the statutory power to dispose of entailed interests) by his will.

. . . .

Application to Crown

10–048 **57.**—(1) The provisions of this Act bind the Crown and the Duchy of Lancaster, and the Duke of Cornwall for the time being, as respects the estates of persons dying after the commencement of this Act, but not so as to affect the time within which proceedings for the recovery of real or personal estate vesting in or devolving on His Majesty in right of His Crown, or His Duchy of Lancaster, or on the Duke of Cornwall, may be instituted.

(2) Nothing in this Act in any manner affects or alters the descent or devolution of any property for the time being vested in His Majesty either in right of the Crown or of the Duchy of Lancaster or of any property for the time being belonging to the Duchy of Cornwall.

[99] Definition of "rules of court" repealed by the Supreme Court Act 1981, s.152(4), Sched. 7.
[1] Word repealed by the Trusts of Land and Appointment of Trustees Act 1996, s.25(2), Sched. 4.
[2] Definition of "trust corporation" extended by the Law of Property (Amendment) Act 1926, s.3(1), *post*, para. 11–002, and by the Charities Act 1993, s.35, *post*, para. 56–034.
[3] Definitions of "trust of sale" and "power to postpone a sale" repealed by the Trusts of Land and Appointment of Trustees Act 1996, s.25(2), Sched. 4.

SCHEDULES

Section 34

FIRST SCHEDULE

PART I

[*Repealed by the Insolvency Act 1985, s.235(3), Sched. 10, Pt. III.*][4]

PART II

ORDER OF APPLICATION OF ASSETS WHERE THE ESTATE IS SOLVENT

1. Property of the deceased undisposed of by will, subject to the retention thereout of a fund sufficient to meet any pecuniary legacies.
2. Property of the deceased not specifically devised or bequeathed but included (either by a specific or general description) in a residuary gift, subject to the retention out of such property of a fund sufficient to meet any pecuniary legacies, so far as not provided for as aforesaid.
3. Property of the deceased specifically appropriated or devised or bequeathed (either by a specific or general description) for the payment of debts.
4. Property of the deceased charged with, or devised or bequeathed (either by a specific or general description) subject to a charge for the payment of debts.
5. The fund, if any, retained to meet pecuniary legacies.
6. Property specifically devised or bequeathed, rateably according to value.
7. Property appointed by will under a general power, including the statutory power to dispose of entailed interests, rateably according to value.
8. The following provisions shall also apply—

(a) The order of application may be varied by the will of the deceased.

[. . .][5]

Law of Property (Amendment) Act 1926

(16 & 17 GEO. 5, C. 11)

Conveyances of legal estates subject to certain interests

1.—(1) Nothing in the Settled Land Act 1925 shall prevent a person on whom the powers of a tenant for life are conferred by paragraph (ix) of subsection (1) of section twenty of that Act from conveying or creating a legal estate subject to a prior interest as if the land had not been settled land. **11–001**

(2) In any of the following cases, namely—

(a) where a legal estate has been conveyed or created under subsection one of this section, or under section sixteen of the Settled Land Act 1925 subject to any prior interest, or

(b) where before the first day of January, nineteen hundred and twenty-six, land has been conveyed to a purchaser for money or money's worth subject to any prior interest whether or not on the purchase the land was expressed to be exonerated from, or the grantor agreed to indemnify the purchaser against, such prior interest,

the estate owner for the time being of the land subject to such prior interest may, notwithstanding any provision contained in the Settled Land Act 1925, but without prejudice to any power whereby such prior interest is capable of being

---

[4] See the Insolvency Act 1986, s.421, and the Administration of Insolvent Estates of Deceased Persons Order 1986 (S.I. 1986 No. 1999).

[5] Sub-para. (b) repealed by the Finance (No. 2) Act 1983, s.16(4), Sched. 2, Pt. II.

overreached, convey or create a legal estate subject to such prior interest as if the instrument creating the prior interest was not an instrument or one of the instruments constituting a settlement of the land.

(3) In this section "interest" means an estate, interest, charge or power of charging subsisting, or capable of arising or of being exercised, under a settlement, and, where a prior interest arises under the exercise of a power, "instrument" includes both the instrument conferring the power and the instrument exercising it.

2. [*Repealed by the Agricultural Holdings Act 1948, ss.98–100, Sched. 8.*]

Meaning of "trust corporation"[1]

11–002 **3.**—(1) For the purposes of the Law of Property Act 1925, the Settled Land Act 1925, the Administration of Estates Act 1925 and the [Supreme Court Act 1981][2], the expression "Trust Corporation" includes the Treasury Solicitor, the Official Solicitor and any person holding any other official position prescribed by the Lord Chancellor, and, in relation to the property of a bankrupt and property subject to a deed of arrangement, includes the trustee in bankruptcy and the trustee under the deed respectively, and, in relation to charitable ecclesiastical and public trusts, also includes any local or public authority so prescribed, and any other corporation constituted under the laws of the United Kingdom or any part thereof which satisfies the Lord Chancellor that it undertakes the administration of any such trusts without remuneration, or that by its constitution it is required to apply the whole of its net income after payment of outgoings for charitable, ecclesiastical or public purposes, and is prohibited from distributing, directly or indirectly, any part thereof by way of profits amongst any of its members, and is authorised by him to act in relation to such trusts as a trust corporation.

(2) For the purposes of this provision, the expression "Treasury Solicitor" means the solicitor for the affairs of His Majesty's Treasury, and includes the solicitor for the affairs of the Duchy of Lancaster.

Landlord and Tenant Act 1927

(17 & 18 Geo. 5, c. 36)

Part II

General Amendments of the Law of Landlord and Tenant

Provisions as to covenants to repair

12–001 **18.**—(1) Damages for a breach of a covenant or agreement to keep or put premises in repair during the currency of a lease, or to leave or put premises in repair at the termination of a lease, whether such covenant or agreement is

---

[1] See also the Charities Act 1993, s.35, *post*, para. 56–034.
[2] Words substituted by the Supreme Court Act 1981, s.152(1), Sched. 5.

expressed or implied, and whether general or specific, shall in no case exceed the amount (if any) by which the value of the reversion (whether immediate or not) in the premises is diminished owing to the breach of such covenant or agreement as aforesaid; and in particular no damage shall be recovered for a breach of any such covenant or agreement to leave or put premises in repair at the termination of a lease, if it is shown that the premises, in whatever state of repair they might be, would at or shortly after the termination of the tenancy have been or be pulled down, or such structural alterations made therein as would render valueless the repairs covered by the covenant or agreement.

(2) A right of re-entry or forfeiture for a breach of any such covenant or agreement as aforesaid shall not be enforceable, by action or otherwise, unless the lessor proves that the fact that such a notice as is required by section one hundred and forty-six of the Law of Property Act 1925 had been served on the lessee was known either—

(a) to the lessee; or
(b) to an under-lessee holding under an under-lease which reserved a nominal reversion only to the lessee; or
(c) to the person who last paid the rent due under the lease either on his own behalf or as agent for the lessee or under-lessee;

and that a time reasonably sufficient to enable the repairs to be executed had elapsed since the time when the fact of the service of the notice came to the knowledge of any such person.

Where a notice has been sent by registered post[1] addressed to a person at his last known place of abode in the United Kingdom, then, for the purposes of this subsection, that person shall be deemed, unless the contrary is proved, to have had knowledge of the fact that the notice had been served as from the time at which the letter would have been delivered in the ordinary course of post.

This subsection shall be construed as one with section one hundred and forty-six of the Law of Property Act 1925.

(3) This section applies whether the lease was created before or after the commencement of this Act.

Provisions as to covenants not to assign, etc. without licence or consent

19.[2]—(1) In all leases whether made before or after the commencement of this Act containing a covenant condition or agreement against assigning, underletting, charging or parting with the possession of demised premises or any part thereof without licence or consent, such covenant condition or agreement shall, notwithstanding any express provision to the contrary, be deemed to be subject— **12–002**

(a) to a proviso to the effect that such licence or consent is not to be unreasonably withheld, but this proviso but does not preclude the right of the landlord to require payment of a reasonable sum in respect of any legal or other expenses incurred in connection with such licence or consent; and
(b) (if the lease is for more than forty years, and is made in consideration wholly or partially of the erection, or the substantial improvement, addition or alteration of buildings, and the lessor is not a Government

[1] Any reference to the registered post is to be construed as including a reference to the recorded delivery service: Recorded Delivery Service Act 1962, s.1, Sched.
[2] Excluded by the Leasehold Reform Act 1967, s.30(5), and the Housing Act 1988, s.15(2). See also the Landlord and Tenant Act 1988, *post*, para. 51–001.

department or local or public authority, or a statutory or public utility company) to a proviso to the effect that in the case of any assignment, under-letting, charging or parting with the possession (whether by the holders of the lease or any under-tenant whether immediate or not) effected more than seven years before the end of the term no consent or licence shall be required, if notice in writing of the transaction is given to the lessor within six months after the transaction is effected.

[(1A) Where the landlord and the tenant under a qualifying lease have entered into an agreement specifying for the purposes of this subsection—

(a) any circumstances in which the landlord may withhold his licence or consent to an assignment of the demised premises or any part of them, or

(b) any conditions subject to which any such licence or consent may be granted,

then the landlord—

(i) shall not be regard as unreasonably withholding his licence or consent to any such assignment if he withholds it on the ground (and it is the case) that any such circumstances exist, and

(ii) if he gives such licence or consent subject to any such conditions, shall not be regarded as giving it subject to unreasonable conditions;

and section 1 of the Landlord and Tenant Act 1988 (qualified duty to consent to assignment etc.) shall have effect subject to the provisions of this subsection.

(1B) Subsection (1A) of this section applies to such an agreement as is mentioned in that subsection—

(a) whether it is contained in the lease or not, and

(b) whether it is made at the time when the lease is granted or at any other time falling before the application for the landlord's licence or consent is made.

(1C) Subsection (1A) shall not, however, apply to any such agreement to the extent that any circumstances or conditions specified in it are framed by reference to any matter falling to be determined by the landlord or by any other person for the purposes of the agreement, unless under the terms of the agreement—

(a) that person's power to determine that matter is required to be exercised reasonably, or

(b) the tenant is given an unrestricted right to have any such determination reviewed by a person independent of both landlord and tenant whose identity is ascertainable by reference to the agreement,

and in the latter case the agreement provides for the determination made by any such independent person on the review to be conclusive as to the matter in question.

(1D) In its application to a qualifying lease, subsection (1)(b) of this section shall not have effect in relation to any assignment of the lease.

(1E) In subsections (1A) and (1D) of this section—

(a) "qualifying lease" means any lease which is a new tenancy for the purposes of section 1 of the Landlord and Tenant (Covenants) Act 1995 other than a residential lease, namely a lease by which a building or part of a building is let wholly or mainly as a single private residence; and

(b) references to assignment include parting with possession on assignment.][3]

(2)[4] In all leases whether made before or after the commencement of this Act

---

[3] subss. (1A)–(1E) inserted by the Landlord and Tenant (Covenants) Act 1995, s.22.
[4] Excluded by the Housing Act 1980, s.81(1) and the Housing Act 1985, s.97(4).

containing a covenant condition or agreement against the making of improvements without licence or consent, such covenant condition or agreement shall be deemed, notwithstanding any express provision to the contrary, to be subject to a proviso that such licence or consent is not to be unreasonably withheld; but this proviso does not preclude the right to require as a condition of such licence or consent the payment of a reasonable sum in respect of any damage to or diminution in the value of the premises or any neighbouring premises belonging to the landlord, and of any legal or other expenses properly incurred in connection with such licence or consent nor, in the case of an improvement which does not add to the letting value of the holding, does it preclude the right to require as a condition of such licence or consent, where such a requirement would be reasonable, an undertaking on the part of the tenant to reinstate the premises in the condition in which they were before the improvement was executed.

(3) In all leases whether made before or after the commencement of this Act containing a covenant condition or agreement against the alteration of the user of the demised premises, without licence or consent, such covenant condition or agreement shall, if the alteration does not involve any structural alteration of the premises, be deemed, notwithstanding any express provision to the contrary, to be subject to a proviso that no fine or sum of money in the nature of a fine, whether by way of increase of rent or otherwise, shall be payable for or in respect of such licence or consent; but this proviso does not preclude the right of the landlord to require payment of a reasonable sum in respect of any damage to or diminution in the value of the premises or any neighbouring premises belonging to him and of any legal or other expenses incurred in connection with such licence or consent.

Where a dispute as to the reasonableness of any such sum has been determined by a court of competent jurisdiction, the landlord shall be bound to grant the licence or consent on payment of the sum so determined to be reasonable.

(4) This section shall not apply to leases of agricultural holdings within the meaning of the [Agricultural Holdings Act 1986][5] [which are leases in relation to which that Act applies, or to farm business tenancies within the meaning of the Agricultural Tenancies Act 1995][6], and paragraph (b) of subsection (1), subsection (2) and subsection (3) of this section shall not apply to mining leases.

Law of Property (Entailed Interests) Act 1932

(22 & 23 Geo. 5, c. 27)

Definition of rent charge

2. For removing doubt it is hereby declared that a rent charge (not being a rent **13–001**
charge limited to take effect in remainder after or expectant on the failure or determination of some other interest) is a rent charge in possession within the

---

[5] Words substituted by the Agricultural Holdings Act 1986, s.100, Sched. 14, para. 15.
[6] Words inserted by the Agricultural Tenancies Act 1995, s.40, Sched., para. 6.

meaning of paragraph (b) of subsection (2) of section one of the Law of Property Act 1925, notwithstanding that the payments in respect thereof are limited to commence or accrue at some time subsequent to its creation.

Leasehold Property (Repairs) Act 1938

(1 & 2 Geo. 6, c. 34)

Restriction on enforcement of repairing covenants in long leases of small houses

14–001 **1.**—(1) Where a lessor serves on a lessee under subsection (1) of section one hundred and forty-six of the Law of Property Act 1925 a notice that relates to a breach of a covenant or agreement to keep or put in repair during the currency of the lease [all or any of the property comprised in the lease][1], and at the date of the service of the notice [three][2] years or more of the term of the lease remain unexpired, the lessee may within twenty-eight days from that date serve on the lessor a counter-notice to the effect that he claims the benefit of this Act.

(2) A right to damages for a breach of such a covenant as aforesaid shall not be enforceable by action commenced at any time at which [three][3] years or more of the term of the lease remain unexpired unless the lessor has served on the lessee not less than one month before the commencement of the action such a notice as is specified in subsection (1) of section one hundred and forty-six of the Law of Property Act 1925, and where a notice is served under this subsection, the lessee may, within twenty-eight days from the date of the service thereof, serve on the lessor a counter-notice to the effect that he claims the benefit of this Act.

(3) Where a counter-notice is served by a lessee under this section, then, notwithstanding anything in any enactment or rule of law, no proceedings, by action or otherwise, shall be taken by the lessor for the enforcement of any right of re-entry or forfeiture under any proviso or stipulation in the lease for breach of the covenant or agreement in question, or for damages for breach thereof, otherwise than with the leave of the court.

(4) A notice served under subsection (1) of section one hundred and forty-six of the Law of Property Act 1925, in the circumstances specified in subsection (1) of this section, and a notice served under subsection (2) of this section shall not be valid unless it contains a statement, in characters not less conspicuous than those used in any other part of the notice, to the effect that the lessee is entitled under this Act to serve on the lessor a counter-notice claiming the benefit of this Act, and a statement in the like characters specifying the time within which, and the manner in which, under this Act a counter-notice may be served and specifying the name and address for service of the lessor.

(5) Leave for the purposes of this section shall not be given unless the lessor proves—

(a) that the immediate remedying of the breach in question is requisite for preventing substantial diminution in the value of his reversion, or that the value thereof has been substantially diminished by the breach;

(b) that the immediate remedying of the breach is required for giving effect

[1] Words substituted by the Landlord and Tenant Act 1954, s.51(2).
[2] Word substituted by the Landlord and Tenant Act 1954, s.51(2).
[3] Word substituted by the Landlord and Tenant Act 1954, s.51(2).

in relation to the [premises][4] to the purposes of any enactment, or of any byelaw or other provision having effect under an enactment, [or for giving effect to any order of a court or requirement of any authority under any enactment or any such byelaw or other provision as aforesaid][5];

(c) in a case in which the lessee is not in occupation of the whole of the [premises as respects which the covenant or agreement is proposed to be enforced][6], that the immediate remedying of the breach is required in the interests of the occupier of [those premises][7] or of part thereof;

(d) that the breach can be immediately remedied at an expense that is relatively small in comparison with the much greater expense that would probably be occasioned by postponement of the necessary work; or

(e) special circumstances which in the opinion of the court, render it just and equitable that leave should be given.

(6) The court may, in granting or in refusing leave for the purposes of this section, impose such terms and conditions on the lessor or on the lessee as it may think fit.

Restriction on right to recover expenses of survey, etc.

2. A lessor on whom a counter-notice is served under the preceding section shall not be entitled to the benefit of subsection (3) of section one hundred and forty-six of the Law of Property Act 1925 (which relates to costs and expenses incurred by a lessor in reference to breaches of covenant), so far as regards any costs or expenses incurred in reference to the breach in question, unless he makes an application for leave for the purposes of the preceding section, and on such an application the court shall have power to direct whether and to what extent the lessor is to be entitled to the benefit thereof. **14–002**

Saving for obligation to repair on taking possession

3. This Act shall not apply to a breach of a covenant or agreement in so far as it imposes on the lessee an obligation to put [premises][8] in repair that is to be performed upon the lessee taking possession of the premises or within a reasonable time thereafter. **14–003**

4. [*Repealed by the Landlord and Tenant Act 1954, s.51(2).*]

Application to past breaches

5. This Act applies to leases created, and to breaches occurring, before or after the commencement of this Act. **14–004**

Court having jurisdiction under this Act

6.—(1) In this Act the expression "the court" means the county court, except in a case in which any proceedings by action for which leave may be given would **14–005**

[4] Word substituted by the Landlord and Tenant Act 1954, s.51(2).
[5] Words substituted by the Landlord and Tenant Act 1954, s.51(2).
[6] Words substituted by the Landlord and Tenant Act 1954, s.51(2).
[7] Words substituted by the Landlord and Tenant Act 1954, s.51(2).
[8] Word substituted by the Landlord and Tenant Act 1954, s.51(2).

have to be taken in a court other than the county court, and means in the said excepted case that other court.

(2) [*Repealed by the County Courts Act 1959, s.204, Sched. 3.*]

Application of certain provisions of Law of Property Act 1925

14–006 **7.**—(1) In this Act the expressions "lessor," "lessee" and "lease" have the meanings assigned to them respectively by sections one hundred and forty-six and one hundred and fifty-four of the Law of Property Act 1925, except that they do not include any reference to such a grant as is mentioned in the said section one hundred and forty-six, or to the person making, or to the grantee under such a grant, or to persons deriving title under such a person; and "lease" means a lease for a term of [seven years or more, not being a lease of an agricultural holding within the meaning of the [Agricultural Holdings Act 1986][9] [which is a lease in relation to which that Act applies and not being a farm business tenancy within the meaning of the Agricultural Tenancies Act 1995][10]][11].

(2) The provisions of section one hundred and ninety-six of the said Act (which relate to the service of notices) shall extend to notices and counter-notices required or authorised by this Act.

Intestates' Estates Act 1952

(15 & 16 Geo. 6 & 1 Eliz. 2, c. 64)

Part I

Amendments of Law of Intestate Succession

1–4. [*Amend the Administration of Estates Act* 1925, *ss.*46–49, *ante, paras* 10–037 *et seq.*]

Rights of surviving spouse as respects the matrimonial home

15–001 **5.** The Second Schedule to this Act shall have effect for enabling the surviving husband or wife of a person dying intestate after the commencement of this Act to acquire the matrimonial home.

SCHEDULES

FIRST SCHEDULE

[*Sets out the Administration of Estates Act* 1925, *ss.*46–49, *ante, paras* 10–037 *et seq., as amended by Part I of this Act.*]

---

[9] Words substituted by the Agricultural Holdings Act 1986, s.100, Sched. 14, para. 17.
[10] Words inserted by the Agricultural Tenancies Act 1995, s.40, Sched., para. 8.
[11] Words substituted by the Landlord and Tenant Act 1954, s.51(2).

Section 5

SECOND SCHEDULE

Rights of Surviving Spouse as respects the Matrimonial Home

1.—(1) Subject to the provisions of this Schedule, where the residuary estate of the intestate comprises an interest in a dwelling-house in which the surviving husband or wife was resident at the time of the intestate's death, the surviving husband or wife may require the personal representative, in exercise of the power conferred by section forty-one of the principal Act (and with due regard to the requirements of that section as to valuation) to appropriate the said interest in the dwelling-house in or towards satisfaction of any absolute interest of the surviving husband or wife in the real and personal estate of the intestate.

(2)[1] The right conferred by this paragraph shall not be exercisable where the interest is—

(a) a tenancy which at the date of the death of the intestate was a tenancy which would determine within the period of two years from that date; or

(b) a tenancy which the landlord by notice given after that date could determine within the remainder of that period.

(3) Nothing in subsection (5) of section forty-one of the principal Act (which requires the personal representative, in making an appropriation to any person under that section, to have regard to the rights of others) shall prevent the personal representative from giving effect to the right conferred by this paragraph.

(4) The reference in this paragraph to an absolute interest in the real and personal estate of the intestate includes a reference to the capital value of a life interest which the surviving husband or wife has under this Act elected to have redeemed.

(5) Where part of a building was, at the date of the death of the intestate, occupied as a separate dwelling, that dwelling shall for the purposes of this Schedule be treated as a dwelling-house.

2. Where—

(a) the dwelling-house forms part of a building and an interest in the whole of the building is comprised in the residuary estate; or

(b) the dwelling-house is held with agricultural land and an interest in the agricultural land is comprised in the residuary estate; or

(c) the whole or part of the dwelling-house was at the time of the intestate's death used as a hotel or lodging house; or

(d) a part of the dwelling-house was at the time of the intestate's death used for purposes other than domestic purposes,

the right conferred by paragraph 1 of this Schedule shall not be exercisable unless the court, on being satisfied that the exercise of that right is not likely to diminish the value of assets in the residuary estate (other than the said interest in the dwelling-house) or make them more difficult to dispose of, so orders.

3.—(1) The right conferred by paragraph 1 of this Schedule—

(a) shall not be exercisable after the expiration of twelve months from the first taking out of representation with respect to the intestate's estate;

(b) shall not be exercisable after the death of the surviving husband or wife;

(c) shall be exercisable, except where the surviving husband or wife is the sole personal representative, by notifying the personal representative (or, where there are two or more personal representatives of whom one is the surviving husband or wife, all of them except the surviving husband or wife) in writing.

(2) A notification in writing under paragraph (c) of the foregoing sub-paragraph shall not be revocable except with the consent of the personal representative; but the surviving husband or wife may require the personal representative to have the said interest in the dwelling-house valued in accordance with section forty-one of the principal Act and to inform him or her of the result of that valuation before he or she decides whether to exercise the right.

(3) Subsection (9) of the section forty-seven A added to the principal Act by section two of this Act shall apply for the purposes of the construction of the reference in this paragraph to the first taking out of representation, and the proviso to subsection (5) of that section shall apply for the purpose of enabling the surviving husband or wife to apply for an extension of the period of twelve months mentioned in this paragraph.

4.—(1) During the period of twelve months mentioned in paragraph 3 of this Schedule the personal representative shall not without the written consent of the surviving husband or wife sell or otherwise dispose of the said interest in the dwelling-house except in the course of administration owing to want of other assets.

(2) An application to the court under paragraph 2 of this Schedule may be made by the personal representative as well as by the surviving husband or wife, and if, on an application under that

[1] Excluded by the Leasehold Reform Act 1967, s.7(8).

paragraph, the court does not order that the right conferred by paragraph 1 of this Schedule shall be exercisable by the surviving husband or wife, the court may authorise the personal representative to dispose of the said interest in the dwelling-house within the said period of twelve months.

(3) Where the court under sub-paragraph (3) of paragraph 3 of this Schedule extends the said period of twelve months, the court may direct that this paragraph shall apply in relation to the extended period as it applied in relation to the original period of twelve months.

(4) This paragraph shall not apply where the surviving husband or wife is the sole personal representative or one of two or more personal representatives.

(5) Nothing in this paragraph shall confer any right on the surviving husband or wife as against a purchaser from the personal representative.

5.—(1) Where the surviving husband or wife is one of two or more personal representatives, the rule that a trustee may not be a purchaser of trust property shall not prevent the surviving husband or wife from purchasing out of the estate of the intestate an interest in a dwelling-house in which the surviving husband or wife was resident at the time of the intestate's death.

(2) The power of appropriation under section forty-one of the principal Act shall include power to appropriate an interest in a dwelling-house in which the surviving husband or wife was resident at the time of the intestate's death partly in satisfaction of an interest of the surviving husband or wife in the real and personal estate of the intestate and partly in return for a payment of money by the surviving husband or wife to the personal representative.

6.—(1) Where the surviving husband or wife is a person of unsound mind or a defective, a requirement or consent under this Schedule may be made or given on his or her behalf by the committee or receiver, if any, or, where there is no committee or receiver, by the court.

(2) A requirement or consent made or given under this Schedule by a surviving husband or wife who is an infant shall be as valid and binding as it would be if he or she were of age; and, as respects an appropriation in pursuance of paragraph 1 of this Schedule, the provisions of section forty-one of the principal Act as to obtaining the consent of the infant's parent or guardian, or of the court on behalf of the infant, shall not apply.

7.—(1) Except where the context otherwise requires, references in this Schedule to a dwelling-house include references to any garden or portion of ground attached to and usually occupied with the dwelling-house or otherwise required for the amenity or convenience of the dwelling-house.

(2) This Schedule shall be construed as one with Part IV of the principal Act.

Charitable Trusts (Validation) Act 1954

(2 & 3 ELIZ. 2, C. 58)

Validation and modification of imperfect trust instruments

16–001 **1.**—(1) In this Act, "imperfect trust provision" means any provision declaring the objects for which property is to be held or applied, and so describing those objects that, consistently with the terms of the provision, the property could be used exclusively for charitable purposes, but could nevertheless be used for purposes which are not charitable.

(2) Subject to the following provisions of this Act, any imperfect trust provision contained in an instrument taking effect before the sixteenth day of December, nineteen hundred and fifty-two, shall have, and be deemed to have had, effect in relation to any disposition or covenant to which this Act applies—

(a) as respects the period before the commencement of this Act, as if the whole of the declared objects were charitable; and

(b) as respects the period after that commencement as if the provision had required the property to be held or applied for the declared objects in so far only as they authorise use for charitable purposes.

(3) A document inviting gifts of property to be held or applied for objects declared by the document shall be treated for the purposes of this section as an instrument taking effect when it is first issued.

(4) In this Act, "covenant" includes any agreement, whether under seal or not, and "covenantor" is to be construed accordingly.

Dispositions and covenants to which the Act applies

2.—(1) Subject to the next following subsection, this Act applies to any disposition of property to be held or applied for objects declared by an imperfect trust provision, and to any covenant to make such a disposition, where apart from this Act the disposition or covenant is invalid under the law of England and Wales, but would be valid if the objects were exclusively charitable. **16–002**

(2) This Act does not apply to a disposition if before the sixteenth day of December, nineteen hundred and fifty-two, property comprised in, or representing that comprised in, the disposition in question or another disposition made for the objects declared by the same imperfect trust provision, or income arising from any such property, has been paid or conveyed to, or applied for the benefit of, the persons entitled by reason of the invalidity of the disposition in question or of such other disposition as aforesaid, as the case may be.

(3) A disposition in settlement or other disposition creating more than one interest in the same property shall be treated for the purposes of this Act as a separate disposition in relation to each of the interests created.

Savings for adverse claims, etc.

3.—(1) Subject to the next following subsection, where a disposition to which this Act applies was made before, and is not confirmed after, the commencement of this Act, the foregoing sections shall not prejudice a person's right, by reason of the invalidity of the disposition, to property comprised in, or representing that comprised in, the disposition as against the persons administering the imperfect trust provision or the persons on whose behalf they do so, unless the right accrued to him or some person through whom he claims more than six years before the sixteenth day of December, nineteen hundred and fifty-two; but the persons administering the imperfect trust provision, and any trustee for them or for the persons on whose behalf they do so, shall be entitled, as against a person whose right to the property is saved by this subsection, to deal with the property as if this subsection had not been passed, unless they have express notice of a claim by him to enforce his right to the property. **16–003**

(2) No proceedings shall be begun by any person to enforce his right to any property by virtue of the foregoing subsection after the expiration of one year beginning with the date of the passing of this Act or the date when the right first accrues to him or to some person through whom he claims, whichever is the later, unless the right (before or after its accrual) either—

(a) has been concealed by the fraud or some person administering the imperfect trust provision or his agent; or

(b) has been acknowledged by some such person or his agent by means of a written acknowledgment given to the person having the right or his agent and signed by the person making it, or by means of a payment or transfer of property in respect of the right;

and if the period prescribed by this subsection for any person to bring proceedings to recover any property expires without his having recovered the property or begun proceedings to do so, his title to the property shall be extinguished.

This subsection shall not be taken as extending the time for bringing any proceedings beyond the period of limitation prescribed by any other enactment.

(3) For the purposes of the foregoing subsections, a right by reason of the invalidity of a disposition to property comprised in, or representing that comprised in, the disposition shall not be deemed to accrue to anyone so long as he is under a disability or has a future interest only, or so long as the disposition is subject to another disposition made by the same person, and the whole of the property or the income arising from it is held or applied for the purposes of that other disposition.

(4) [Subsections (2) to (6) of section thirty-eight of the Limitation Act 1980][1] (which define the circumstances in which, for the purposes of that Act, a person is to be deemed to be under a disability or to claim through another person), shall apply for the purposes of the foregoing subsections as they apply for the purposes of that Act.

(5) Where subsection (1) of this section applies to save a person's right to property comprised in, or representing that comprised in, a disposition, or would have so applied but for some dealing with the property by persons administering the imperfect trust provision, or by any trustee for them or for the persons on whose behalf they do so, the foregoing sections shall not prejudice the first-mentioned person's right by virtue of his interest in the property to damages or other relief in respect of any dealing with the property by any person administering the imperfect trust provision or by any such trustee as aforesaid, if the person dealing with the property had at the time express notice of a claim by him to enforce his right to the property.

(6) A covenant entered into before the commencement of this Act shall not be enforceable by virtue of this Act unless confirmed by the covenantor after that commencement, but a disposition made in accordance with such a covenant shall be treated for the purposes of this Act as confirming the covenant and any previous disposition made in accordance with it.

Provisions as to pending proceedings and past decisions and tax payments

16–004 **4.**—(1) Subject to the next following subsection, effect shall be given to the provisions of this Act in legal proceedings begun before its commencement, as well as in those begun afterwards.

(2) This Act shall not affect any order or judgment made or given before its commencement in legal proceedings begun before the sixteenth day of December, nineteen hundred and fifty-two, or any appeal or other proceedings consequent on any such order or judgment.

(3) Where in legal proceedings begun on or after the said sixteenth day of December, any order or judgment has been made or given before the commencement of this Act which would not have been made or given after that commencement, the court by which the order or judgment was made or given shall, on the application of any person aggrieved thereby, set it aside in whole or in part and make such further order as the court thinks equitable with a view to placing those concerned as nearly as may be in the position they ought to be in having regard to this Act:

[1] Words substituted by the Limitation Act 1980, s.40(2), Sched. 3, para. 4.

Provided that proceedings to have an order or judgment set aside under this subsection shall not be instituted more than six months after the commencement of this Act.

(4) This Act shall not, by its operation on any instrument as respects the period before the commencement of the Act, impose or increase any liability to tax nor entitle any person to reclaim any tax paid or borne before that commencement, nor (save as respects taxation) require the objects declared by the instrument to be treated for the purposes of any enactment as having been charitable so as to invalidate anything done or any determination given before that commencement.

. . . . . .

Recreational Charities Act 1958

(6 & 7 Eliz. 2, c. 17)

General provision as to recreational and similar trusts, etc.

1.—(1) Subject to the provisions of this Act, it shall be and be deemed always to have been charitable to provide, or assist in the provision of, facilities for recreation or other leisure-time occupation, if the facilities are provided in the interests of social welfare: **17–001**

Provided that nothing in this section shall be taken to derogate from the principle that a trust or institution to be charitable must be for the public benefit.

(2) The requirement of the foregoing subsection that the facilities are provided in the interests of social welfare shall not be treated as satisfied unless—

(a) the facilities are provided with the object of improving the conditions of life for the persons for whom the facilities are primarily intended; and

(b) either—

(i) those persons have need of such facilities as aforesaid by reason of their youth, age, infirmity or disablement, poverty or social and economic circumstances; or

(ii) the facilities are to be available to the members or female members of the public at large.

(3) Subject to the said requirement, subsection (1) of this section applies in particular to the provision of facilities at village halls, community centres and women's institutes, and to the provision and maintenance of grounds and buildings to be used for purposes of recreation or leisure-time occupation, and extends to the provision of facilities for those purposes by the organising of any activity.

Miners' welfare trusts

2.—(1) Where trusts declared before the seventeenth day of December, nineteen hundred and fifty-seven, required or purported to require property to be held for the purpose of activities which are social welfare activities within the meaning of the Miners' Welfare Act 1952, and at that date the whole or part of **17–002**

the property held on those trusts or of any property held with that property represented an application of moneys standing to the credit of the miners' welfare fund or moneys provided by the Coal Industry Social Welfare Organisation, those trusts shall be treated as if they were and always had been charitable.

(2) For the purposes of this section property held on the same trusts as other property shall be deemed to be held with it, though vested in different trustees.

Savings and other provisions as to past transactions

17–003 **3.**—(1) Nothing in this Act shall be taken to restrict the purposes which are to be regarded as charitable independently of this Act.

(2) Nothing in this Act—

(a) shall apply to make charitable any trust, or validate any disposition, of property if before the seventeenth day of December, nineteen hundred and fifty-seven, that property or any property representing or forming part of it, or any income arising from any such property, has been paid or conveyed to, or applied for the benefit of, the persons entitled by reason of the invalidity of the trust or disposition; or

(b) shall affect any order or judgment made or given (whether before or after the passing of this Act) in legal proceedings begun before that day; or

(c) shall require anything properly done before that day, or anything done or to be done in pursuance of a contract entered into before that day, to be treated for any purpose as wrongful or ineffectual.

(3) Except as provided by subsections (4) and (5) of this section, nothing in this Act shall require anything to be treated for the purposes of any enactment as having been charitable at a time before the date of the passing of this Act, so as to invalidate anything done or any determination given before that date.

(4) For the purposes of income tax, this Act shall not require anything to be treated as having been charitable at a time before the date of the passing of this Act unless it would have been so treated in accordance with the practice applied by the Commissioners of Inland Revenue immediately before the eighteenth day of December, nineteen hundred and fifty-two; but, subject to that and to paragraphs (a) and (b) of subsection (2) of this section there shall be made all such adjustments, whether by way of repayment of tax, additional assessment or otherwise, as are made necessary in relation to income tax by the retrospective operation of sections one and two of this Act, and nothing in the Income Tax Act 1952 shall preclude the repayment by virtue of this Act of tax for the year 1946–47 or a subsequent year of assessment if a claim is made in that behalf to the Commissioners of Inland Revenue within two years from the date of the passing of this Act.

(5) As respects stamp duty on any instrument executed before the date of the passing of this Act, this Act shall not require anything to be treated as having been charitable for the purposes of subsection (1) of section fifty-four of the Finance Act 1947 (which excepted instruments in favour of charities from certain increases of stamp duty under that Act), unless it would have been so treated in accordance with the practice applied by the Commissioners of Inland Revenue immediately before the eighteenth day of December, nineteen hundred and fifty-two; but subject to that and to paragraphs (a) and (b) of subsection (2) of this section, where more stamp duty has been paid on an instrument executed on or after the said eighteenth day of December and before

the date of the passing of this Act than ought to have been paid having regard to sections one and two of this Act, the provisions of sections ten and eleven of the Stamp Duties Management Act 1891 shall apply as if a stamp of greater value than was necessary had been inadvertently used for the instrument, and relief may be given accordingly, and may be so given notwithstanding that, in accordance with the provisions of section twelve of the Stamp Act 1891, the instrument had been stamped before the passing of this Act with a particular stamp denoting that it was duly stamped.

An application for relief under the said section ten as applied by this subsection may be made at any time within two years from the date of the passing of this Act, notwithstanding that it is made outside the time limited by that section.

. . . . . .

Variation of Trusts Act 1958

(6 & 7 ELIZ. 2, C. 53)

Jurisdiction of courts to vary trusts

1.—(1) Where property, whether real or personal, is held on trusts arising, whether before or after the passing of this Act, under any will, settlement or other disposition, the court may if it thinks fit by order approve on behalf of— **18–001**

(a) any person having, directly or indirectly, an interest, whether vested or contingent, under the trusts who by reason of infancy or other incapacity is incapable of assenting, or

(b) any person (whether ascertained or not) who may become entitled, directly or indirectly, to an interest under the trusts as being at a future date or on the happening of a future event a person of any specified description or a member of any specified class of persons, so however that this paragraph shall not include any person who would be of that description, or a member of that class, as the case may be, if the said date had fallen or the said event had happened at the date of the application to the court, or

(c) any person unborn, or

(d) any person in respect of any discretionary interest of his under protective trusts where the interest of the principal beneficiary has not failed or determined,

any arrangement (by whomsoever proposed, and whether or not there is any other person beneficially interested who is capable of assenting thereto) varying or revoking all or any of the trusts, or enlarging the powers of the trustees of managing or administering any of the property subject to the trusts:

Provided that except by virtue of paragraph (d) of this subsection the court shall not approve an arrangement on behalf of any person unless the carrying out thereof would be for the benefit of that person.

(2) In the foregoing subsection "protective trusts" means the trusts specified in paragraphs (i) and (ii) of subsection (1) of section thirty-three of the Trustee Act 1925 or any like trusts, "the principal beneficiary" has the same meaning as

on the servient land specified in the application, and had been so erected by the person who made the application, and

(b) had remained in that position during the period for which the notice has effect and had been removed at the end of that period.

(2) For the purposes of this section a notice registered under the last preceding section shall be taken to have effect until either—

(a) the registration is cancelled, or

(b) the period of one year beginning with the date of registration of the notice expires, or

(c) in the case of a notice registered in pursuance of an application accompanied by a certificate issued under paragraph (b) of subsection (3) of the last preceding section, the period specified in the certificate expires without such a further certificate as is mentioned in paragraph (c) of subsection (5) of that section having before the end of that period been lodged with the local authority,

and shall cease to have effect on the occurrence of any one of those events.

(3) Subject to the following provisions of this section, any person who, if such a structure as is mentioned in subsection (1) of this section had been erected as therein mentioned, would have had a right of action in any court in respect of that structure, on the grounds that he was entitled to a right to the access of light to the dominant building across the servient land, and that the said right was infringed by that structure, shall have the like right of action in that court in respect of the registration of a notice under the last preceding section:

Provided that an action shall not be begun by virtue of this subsection after the notice in question has ceased to have effect.

(4) Where, at any time during the period for which a notice registered under the last preceding section has effect, the circumstances are such that, if the access of light to the dominant building had been enjoyed continuously from a date one year earlier than the date on which the enjoyment thereof in fact began, a person would have had a right of action in any court by virtue of the last preceding subsection in respect of the registration of the notice, that person shall have the like right of action in that court by virtue of this subsection in respect of the registration of the notice.

(5) The remedies available to the plaintiff in an action brought by virtue of subsection (3) or subsection (4) of this section (apart from any order as to costs) shall be such declaration as the court may consider appropriate in the circumstances, and an order directing the registration of the notice to be cancelled or varied, as the court may determine.

(6) For the purposes of section four of the Prescription Act 1832 (under which a period of enjoyment of any of the rights to which that Act applies is not to be treated as interrupted except by a matter submitted to or acquiesced in for one year after notice thereof)—

(a) as from the date of registration of a notice under the last preceding section, all persons interested in the dominant building or any part thereof shall be deemed to have notice of the registration thereof and of the person on whose application it was registered;

(b) until such time as an action is brought by virtue of subsection (3) or subsection (4) of this section in respect of the registration of a notice under the last preceding section, all persons interested in the dominant building or any part thereof shall be deemed to acquiesce in the obstruction which, in accordance with subsection (1) of this section, is to be treated as resulting from the registration of the notice;

(c) as from the date on which such an action is brought, no person shall be treated as submitting to or acquiescing in that obstruction:

Provided that if, in any such action, the court decides against the claim of the plaintiff, the court may direct that the preceding provisions of this subsection shall apply in relation to the notice as if that action had not been brought.

Application to Crown land

4.—(1) Subject to the next following subsection, this Act shall apply in relation to land in which there is a Crown or Duchy interest as it applies in relation to land in which there is no such interest. **19–003**

(2) Section three of the Prescription Act 1832, as modified by the preceding provisions of this Act, shall not by virtue of this section be construed as applying to any land to which (by reason that there is a Crown or Duchy interest therein) that section would not apply apart from this Act.

(3) In this section "Crown or Duchy interest" means an interest belonging to Her Majesty in right of the Crown or of the Duchy of Lancaster, or belonging to the Duchy of Cornwall, or belonging to a government department, or held in trust for Her Majesty for the purposes of a government department.

Power to make rules

5.—(1) [*Repealed by the Local Land Charges Act 1975, ss.17(2), 19(1), Scheds. 1, 2.*] **19–004**

(2) Any rules made [under section 14 of the Local Land Charges Act 1975 for the purposes of section 2 of this Act][2] shall (without prejudice to the inclusion therein of other provisions as to cancelling or varying the registration of notices or agreements) include provision for giving effect to any order of the court under subsection (5) of section three of this Act.

6. [*Repealed by the Northern Ireland Constitution Act 1973, s.41(1), Sched. 6, Pt. I.*]

Interpretation

7.—(1) In this Act, except in so far as the context otherwise requires, the following expressions have the meanings hereby assigned to them respectively, that is to say:— **19–005**

"action" includes a counterclaim, and any reference to the plaintiff in an action shall be construed accordingly;

["local authority", in relation to land in a district or a London borough, means the council of the district or borough, and, in relation to land in the City of London, means the Common Council of the City;][3]

"owner", in relation to any land, means a person who is the estate owner in respect of the fee simple thereof, or is entitled to a tenancy thereof (within the meaning of the Landlord and Tenant Act 1954) for a term of years certain of which, at the time in question, not less than seven years remain unexpired, or is a mortgagee in possession (within the meaning of the Law of Property Act 1925) where the interest mortgaged is either the fee simple of the land or such a tenancy thereof;

---

[2] Words substituted by the Local Land Charges Act 1975, s.17(2), Sched. 1.
[3] Definition substituted by the Local Land Charges Act 1975, s.17(2), Sched. 1.

(c) a person having a child or grandchild within sub-paragraphs (i) to (iv) of paragraph (b) above, or any of whose children or grandchildren, if subsequently born, would by virtue of his or her descent fall within those sub-paragraphs;
(d) any person on the failure or determination of whose prior interest the disposition is limited to take effect.

Reduction of age and exclusion of class members to avoid remoteness

21–004 **4.**—(1) Where a disposition is limited by reference to the attainment by any person or persons of a specified age exceeding twenty-one years, and it is apparent at the time the disposition is made or becomes apparent at a subsequent time—

(a) that the disposition would, apart from this section, be void for remoteness, but
(b) that it would not be so void if the specified age had been twenty-one years,

the disposition shall be treated for all purposes as if, instead of being limited by reference to the age in fact specified, it had been limited by reference to the age nearest to that age which would, if specified instead, have prevented the disposition from being so void.

(2) Where in the case of any disposition different ages exceeding twenty-one years are specified in relation to different persons—

(a) the reference in paragraph (b) of subsection (1) above to the specified age shall be construed as a reference to all the specified ages, and
(b) that subsection shall operate to reduce each such age so far as is necessary to save the disposition from being void for remoteness.

(3) Where the inclusion of any persons, being potential members of a class or unborn persons who at birth would become members or potential members of the class, prevents the foregoing provisions of this section from operating to save a disposition from being void for remoteness, those persons shall thenceforth be deemed for all the purposes of the disposition to be excluded from the class, and the said provisions shall thereupon have effect accordingly.

(4) Where, in the case of a disposition to which subsection (3) above does not apply, it is apparent at the time the disposition is made or becomes apparent at a subsequent time that, apart from this subsection, the inclusion of any persons, being potential members of a class or unborn persons who at birth would become members or potential members of the class, would cause the disposition to be treated as void for remoteness, those persons shall, unless their exclusion would exhaust the class, thenceforth be deemed for all the purposes of the disposition to be excluded from the class.

(5) Where this section has effect in relation to a disposition to which section 3 above applies, the operation of this section shall not affect the validity of anything previously done in relation to the interest disposed of by way of advancement, application of intermediate income or otherwise.

(6) [*Repeals the Law of Property Act 1925, s.163.*]

[(7) For the avoidance of doubt it is hereby declared that a question arising under section 3 of this Act or subsection (1)(a) above of whether a disposition would be void apart from this section is to be determined as if subsection (6) above had been a separate section of this Act.][1]

[1] subs. (7) added by the Children Act 1975, s.108(1)(a), Sched. 3, para. 43.

Condition relating to death of surviving spouse

5. Where a disposition is limited by reference to the time of death of the survivor of a person in being at the commencement of the perpetuity period and any spouse of that person, and that time has not arrived at the end of the perpetuity period, the disposition shall be treated for all purposes, where to do so would save it from being void for remoteness, as if it had instead been limited by reference to the time immediately before the end of that period. **21–005**

Saving and acceleration of expectant interests

6. A disposition shall not be treated as void for remoteness by reason only that the interest disposed of is ulterior to and dependent upon an interest under a disposition which is so void, and the vesting of an interest shall not be prevented from being accelerated on the failure of a prior interest by reason only that the failure arises because of remoteness. **21–006**

Powers of appointment

7. For the purposes of the rule against perpetuities, a power of appointment shall be treated as a special power unless— **21–007**

(a) in the instrument creating the power it is expressed to be exercisable by one person only, and

(b) it could, at all times during its currency when that person is of full age and capacity, be exercised by him so as immediately to transfer to himself the whole of the interest governed by the power without the consent of any other person or compliance with any other condition, not being a formal condition relating only to the mode of exercise of the power:

Provided that for the purpose of determining whether a disposition made under a power of appointment exercisable by will only is void for remoteness, the power shall be treated as a general power where it would have fallen to be so treated if exercisable by deed.

Administrative powers of trustees

8.—(1) The rule against perpetuities shall not operate to invalidate a power conferred on trustees or other persons to sell, lease, exchange or otherwise dispose of any property for full consideration, or to do any other act in the administration (as opposed to the distribution) of any property, and shall not prevent the payment to trustees or other persons of reasonable remuneration for their services. **21–008**

(2) Subsection (1) above shall apply for the purpose of enabling a power to be exercised at any time after the commencement of this Act notwithstanding that the power is conferred by an instrument which took effect before that commencement.

Options relating to land

9.—(1) The rule against perpetuities shall not apply to a disposition consisting of the conferring of an option to acquire for valuable consideration an interest reversionary (whether directly or indirectly) on the term of a lease if— **21–009**

(a) the option is exercisable only by the lessee or his successors in title, and
(b) it ceases to be exercisable at or before the expiration of one year following the determination of the lease.

This subsection shall apply in relation to an agreement for a lease as it applies in relation to a lease, and "lessee" shall be construed accordingly.

(2) In the case of a disposition consisting of the conferring of an option to acquire for valuable consideration any interest in land, the perpetuity period under the rule against perpetuities shall be twenty-one years, and section 1 of this Act shall not apply:

Provided that this subsection shall not apply to a right of pre-emption conferred on a public or local authority in respect of land used or to be used for religious purposes where the right becomes exercisable only if the land ceases to be used for such purposes.

Avoidance of contractual and other rights in cases of remoteness

21–010 **10.** Where a disposition inter vivos would fall to be treated as void for remoteness if the rights and duties thereunder were capable of transmission to persons other than the original parties and had been so transmitted, it shall be treated as void as between the person by whom it was made and the person to whom or in whose favour it was made or any successor of his, and no remedy shall lie in contract or otherwise for giving effect to it or making restitution for its lack of effect.

Rights for enforcement of rentcharges

21–011 **11.**—(1) The rule against perpetuities shall not apply to any powers or remedies for recovering or compelling the payment of an annual sum to which section 121 or 122 of the Law of Property Act 1925 applies, or otherwise becoming exercisable or enforceable on the breach of any condition or other requirement relating to that sum.

(2) [*Amends the Law of Property Act 1925, s.121(6), ante, para. 9–104.*]

Possibilities of reverter, conditions subsequent, exceptions and reservations

21–012 **12.**—(1) In the case of—

(a) a possibility of reverter on the determination of a determinable fee simple, or
(b) a possibility of a resulting trust on the determination of any other determinable interest in property,

the rule against perpetuities shall apply in relation to the provision causing the interest to be determinable as it would apply if that provision were expressed in the form of a condition subsequent giving rise, on breach thereof, to a right of re-entry or an equivalent right in the case of property other than land, and where the provision falls to be treated as void for remoteness the determinable interest shall become an absolute interest.

(2) Where a disposition is subject to any such provision, or to any such condition subsequent, or to any exception or reservation, the disposition shall be treated for the purposes of this Act as including a separate disposition of any rights arising by virtue of the provision, condition subsequent, exception or reservation.

Accumulations

Amendment of s.164 of Law of Property Act 1925

13.—(1) The periods for which accumulations of income under a settlement or other disposition are permitted by section 164 of the Law of Property Act 1925 shall include— **21–013**

(a) a term of twenty-one years from the date of the making of the disposition, and
(b) the duration of the minority or respective minorities of any person or persons in being at that date.

(2) It is hereby declared that the restrictions imposed by the said section 164 apply in relation to a power to accumulate income whether or not there is a duty to exercise that power, and that they apply whether or not the power to accumulate extends to income produced by the investment of income previously accumulated.

Right to stop accumulations

14. Section 2 above shall apply to any question as to the right of beneficiaries to put an end to accumulations of income under any disposition as it applies to questions arising on the rule against perpetuities. **21–014**

Supplemental

Short title, interpretation and extent

15.—(1) This Act may be cited as the Perpetuities and Accumulations Act 1964. **21–015**

(2) In this Act—

"disposition" includes the conferring of a power of appointment and any other disposition of an interest in or right over property, and references to the interest disposed of shall be construed accordingly;

"in being" means living or en ventre sa mere;

"power of appointment" includes any discretionary power to transfer a beneficial interest in property without the furnishing of valuable consideration;

"will" includes a codicil;

and for the purposes of this Act a disposition contained in a will shall be deemed to be made at the death of the testator.

(3) For the purposes of this Act a person shall be treated as a member of a class if in his case all the conditions identifying a member of the class are satisfied, and shall be treated as a potential member if in his case some only of those conditions are satisfied but there is a possibility that the remainder will in time be satisfied.

(4) Nothing in this Act shall affect the operation of the rule of law rendering void for remoteness certain dispositions under which property is limited to be applied for purposes other than the benefit of any person or class of persons in cases where the property may be so applied after the end of the perpetuity period.

(5) The foregoing sections of this Act shall apply (except as provided in section 8(2) above) only in relation to instruments taking effect after the commencement of this Act, and in the case of an instrument made in the

exercise of a special power of appointment shall apply only where the instrument creating the power takes effect after that commencement:

Provided that section 7 above shall apply in all cases for construing the foregoing reference to a special power of appointment.

(6) This Act shall apply in relation to a disposition made otherwise than by an instrument as if the disposition had been contained in an instrument taking effect when the disposition was made.

(7) This Act binds the Crown.

(8) Except in so far as the contrary intention appears, any enactment of the Parliament of Northern Ireland passed for purposes similar to the purposes of this Act shall bind the Crown.

(9) This Act shall not extend to Scotland or (apart from subsection (8) above) to Northern Ireland.

Law of Property (Joint Tenants) Act 1964

(1964 c. 63)

Assumptions on sale of land by survivor of joint tenants

22–001 **1.**—(1) For the purposes of section 36(2) of the Law of Property Act 1925, as amended by section 7 of and the Schedule to the Law of Property (Amendment) Act 1926, the survivor of two or more joint tenants shall, in favour of a purchaser of the legal estate, be deemed to be solely and beneficially interested if [. . .][1] the conveyance includes a statement that he is so interested.

Provided that the foregoing provisions of this subsection shall not apply if, at any time before the date of the conveyance by the survivor—

(a) a memorandum of severance (that is to say a note or memorandum signed by the joint tenants or one of them and recording that the joint tenancy was severed in equity on a date therein specified) had been endorsed on or annexed to the conveyance by virtue of which the legal estate was vested in the joint tenants; or

(b) [a bankruptcy order][2] made against any of the joint tenants, or a petition for such an order, had been registered under the Land Charges Act 1925[3], being an order or petition of which the purchaser has notice, by virtue of the registration, on the date of the conveyance by the survivor.

(2) The foregoing provisions of this section shall apply with the necessary modifications in relation to a conveyance by the personal representatives of the survivor of joint tenants as they apply in relation to a conveyance by such a survivor.

Retrospective and transitional provisions

22–002 **2.** Section 1 of this Act shall be deemed to have come into force on 1st January 1926, and for the purposes of that section in its application to a conveyance

[1] Words repealed by the Law of Property (Miscellaneous Provisions) Act 1994, s.21(1), (2), Sched. 1, para. 1, Sched. 2.

[2] Words substituted by the Insolvency Act 1985, s.235(1), Sched. 8, para. 13.

[3] Now the Land Charges Act 1972, *post*, para. 31–001.

executed before the passing of this Act a statement signed by the vendor or by his personal representatives that he was solely and beneficially interested shall be treated as if it had been included in the conveyance.

Exclusion of registered land

3. This Act shall not apply to [registered land][4]. **22–003**

Commons Registration Act 1965[1]

(1965 c. 64)

Registration of commons and town or village greens and ownership of and rights over them

1.—(1) There shall be registered, in accordance with the provisions of this Act and subject to the exceptions mentioned therein,— **23–001**

(a) land in England or Wales which is common land or a town or village green;
(b) rights of common over such land; and
(c) persons claiming to be or found to be owners of such land or becoming the owners thereof by virtue of this Act;

and no rights of common over land which is capable of being registered under this Act shall be registered [in the register of title][2].

(2) After the end of such period, not being less than three years from the commencement of this Act, as the Minister may by order determine—

(a) no land capable of being registered under this Act shall be deemed to be common land or a town or village green unless it is so registered; and
(b) no rights of common shall be exercisable over any such land unless they are registered either under this Act or [in the register of title][3].

(3) Where any land is registered under this Act but no person is registered as the owner thereof under this Act or [in the register of title][4], it shall—

(a) if it is a town or village green, be vested in accordance with the following provisions of this Act; and
(b) if it is common land, be vested as Parliament may hereafter determine.

Registration authorities

2.—(1) The registration authority for the purposes of this Act shall be— **23–002**

(a) in relation to any land situated in any county [. . .][5], the council of that county [. . .][6] [or, if the county is a metropolitan county, the council of the metropolitan district in which the land is situated][7]; and

[4] Words substituted by the Land Registration Act 2002, s.133, Sched. 11, para. 5.
[1] See also the Common Land (Rectification of Registers) Act 1989, *post*, para. 52–001.
[2] Words substituted by the Land Registration Act 2002, s.133, Sched. 11, para. 7(1), (2).
[3] Words substituted by the Land Registration Act 2002, s.133, Sched. 11, para. 7(1), (2).
[4] Words substituted by the Land Registration Act 2002, s.133, Sched. 11, para. 7(1), (2).
[5] Words repealed by the Local Government Act 1972, s.272(1), Sched. 30.
[6] Words repealed by the Local Government Act 1972, s.272(1), Sched. 30.
[7] Words inserted by the Local Government Act 1985, s.16, Sched. 8, para. 10(6)(a).

(b) in relation to any land situated in Greater London, the [council of the London borough in which the land is situated][8];

except where an agreement under this section otherwise provides.

(2) Where part of any land is in the area of one registration authority and part in that of another the authorities may by agreement provide for one of them to be the registration authority in relation to the whole of the land.

The registers

23–003 **3.**—(1) For the purpose of registering such land as is mentioned in section 1(1) of this Act and rights of common over and ownership of such land every registration authority shall maintain—

(a) a register of common land; and

(b) a register of town or village greens;

and regulations under this Act may require or authorise a registration authority to note on those registers such other information as may be prescribed.

(2) Any register maintained under this Act shall be open to inspection by the public at all reasonable times.

Provisional registration

23–004 **4.**—(1) Subject to the provisions of this section, a registration authority shall register any land as common land or a town or village green or, as the case may be, any rights of common over or ownership of such land, on application duly made to it and accompanied by such declaration and such other documents (if any) as may be prescribed for the purpose of verification or of proving compliance with any prescribed conditions.

(2) An application for the registration of any land as common land or as a town or village green may be made by any person, and a registration authority—

(a) may so register any land notwithstanding that no application for that registration has been made, and

(b) shall so register any land in any case where it registers any rights over it under this section.

(3) No person shall be registered under this section as the owner of any land which is registered [in the register of title][9] and no person shall be registered under this section as the owner of any other land unless the land itself is registered under this section.

(4) Where, in pursuance of an application under this section, any land would fall to be registered as common land or as a town or village green, but the land is already so registered, the registration authority shall not register it again but shall note the application in the register.

(5) A registration under this section shall be provisional only until it has become final under the following provisions of this Act.

(6) An application for registration under this section shall not be entertained if made after such date, not less than three years from the commencement of this Act, as the Minister may by order specify; and different dates may be so specified for different classes of applications.

(7) Every local authority shall take such steps as may be prescribed for informing the public of the period within which and the manner in which applications for registration under this section may be made.

8 Words substituted by the Local Government Act 1985, s.16, Sched. 8, para. 10(6)(b).
9 Words substituted by the Land Registration Act 2002, s.133, Sched. 11, para. 7(1), (2).

Notification of, and objections to, registration

5.—(1) A registration authority shall give such notices and take such other steps as may be prescribed for informing the public of any registration made by it under section 4 of this Act, of the times and places where copies of the relevant entries in the register may be inspected and of the period during which and the manner in which objections to the registration may be made to the authority. **23–005**

(2) The period during which objections to any registration under section 4 of this Act may be made shall be such period, ending not less than two years after the date of the registration, as may be prescribed.

(3) Where any land or rights over land are registered under section 4 of this Act but no person is so registered as the owner of the land the registration authority may, if it thinks fit, make an objection to the registration notwithstanding that it has no interest in the land.

(4) Where an objection to a registration under section 4 of this Act is made, the registration authority shall note the objection on the register and shall give such notice as may be prescribed to the person (if any) on whose application the registration was made and to any person whose application is noted under section 4(4) of this Act.

(5) Where a person to whom notice has been given under subsection (4) of this section so requests or where the registration was made otherwise than on the application of any person, the registration authority may, if it thinks fit, cancel or modify a registration to which objection is made under this section.

(6) Where such an objection is made, then, unless the objection is withdrawn or the registration cancelled before the end of such period as may be prescribed, the registration authority shall refer the matter to a Commons Commissioner.

(7) An objection to the registration of any land as common land or as a town or village green shall be treated for the purposes of this Act as being also an objection to any registration (whenever made) under section 4 of this Act of any rights over the land.

(8) A registration authority shall take such steps as may be prescribed for informing the public of any objection which they have noted on the register under this section and of the times and places where copies of the relevant entries in the register may be inspected.

(9) Where regulations under this Act require copies of any entries in a register to be sent by the registration authority to another local authority they may require that other authority to make the copies available for inspection in such manner as may be prescribed.

Disposal of disputed claims

6.—(1) The Commons Commissioner to whom any matter has been referred under section 5 of this Act shall inquire into it and shall either confirm the registration, with or without modifications, or refuse to confirm it; and the registration shall, if it is confirmed, become final, and, if the confirmation is refused, become void— **23–006**

(a) if no appeal is brought against the confirmation or refusal, at the end of the period during which such an appeal could have been brought;

(b) if such an appeal is brought, when it is finally disposed of.

(2) On being informed in the prescribed manner that a registration has become final (with or without modifications) or has become void a registration authority shall indicate that fact in the prescribed manner in the register and, if it has become void, cancel the registration.

(3) Where the registration of any land as common land or as a town or village green is cancelled (whether under this section or under section 5(5) of this Act) the registration authority shall also cancel the registration of any person as the owner thereof.

Finality of undisputed registrations

23–007 **7.**—(1) If no objection is made to a registration under section 4 of this Act or if all objections made to such a registration are withdrawn the registration shall become final at the end of the period during which such objections could have been made under section 5 of this Act or, if an objection made during that period is withdrawn after the end thereof, at the date of the withdrawal.

(2) Where by virtue of this section a registration has become final the registration authority shall indicate that fact in the prescribed manner in the register.

Vesting of unclaimed land

23–008 **8.**—(1) Where the registration under section 4 of this Act of any land as common land or as a town or village green has become final but no person is registered under that section as the owner of the land, then, unless the land is registered [in the register of title][10], the registration authority shall refer the question of the ownership of the land to a Commons Commissioner.

(2) After the registration authority has given such notices as may be prescribed, the Commons Commissioner shall inquire into the matter and shall, if satisfied that any person is the owner of the land, direct the registration authority to register that person accordingly; and the registration authority shall comply with the direction.

(3) If the Commons Commissioner is not so satisfied and the land is a town or village green he shall direct the registration authority to register as the owner of the land the local authority specified in subsection (5) of this section; and the registration authority shall comply with the direction.

(4) On the registration under this section of a local authority as the owner of any land the land shall vest in that local authority and, if the land is not regulated by a scheme under the Commons Act 1899, sections 10 and 15 of the Open Spaces Act 1906 (power to manage and make byelaws) shall apply in relation to it as if that local authority had acquired the ownership under the said Act of 1906.

[(5) Subject to subsection (6) of this section, the local authority in which any land is to be vested under this section is—

(a) if the land is in a parish or community where there is a parish or community council, that council, but, if the land is regulated by a scheme under the Commons Act 1899, only if the powers of management under Part I of that Act are, in accordance with arrangements under Part VI of the Local Government Act 1972, being exercised by the parish or community council;

(b) if the land is in a London borough, the council of that borough; and

(c) in any other case, the council of the district in which the land is situated.

(6) Where—

[10] Words substituted by the Land Registration Act 2002, s.133, Sched. 11, para. 7(1), (2).

(a) any land has been vested in a district council in accordance with subsection (5)(c) of this section, and

(b) after the land has been so vested a parish or community council comes into being for the parish or community in which the land is situated (whether by the establishment of a new council or by adding that parish or community to a group of parishes or communities for which a council has already been established),

then, if the circumstances are such that, had the direction under subsection (3) of this section been given at a time after the parish or community council had come into being, the land would in accordance with subsection (5)(a) of this section have been vested in the parish or community council, the district council shall, if requested to do so by the parish or community council, direct the registration authority to register the parish or community council, in place of the district council, as the owner of the land; and the registration authority shall comply with any such direction.

(7) The council of any district, parish or community affected by any registration made in pursuance of subsection (6) above shall pay to the other of those councils so affected such sum, if any, as may be agreed between them to be appropriate to take account of any sums received or to be received, or any expenditure incurred or to be incurred, in respect of the land concerned, and, in default of agreement, the question of what sum, if any, is appropriate for that purpose shall be determined by arbitration.][11]

Protection of unclaimed common land

9. Where the registration under section 4 of this Act of any land as common land has become final but no person is registered under this Act or [in the register of title][12] as the owner of the land, then, until the land is vested under any provision hereafter made by Parliament, any local authority in whose area the land or part of the land is situated may take such steps for the protection of the land against unlawful interference as could be taken by an owner in possession of the land, and may (without prejudice to any power exercisable apart from this section) institute proceedings for any offence committed in respect of the land. **23–009**

Effect of registration

10. The registration under this Act of any land as common land or as a town or village green, or of any rights of common over any such land, shall be conclusive evidence of the matters registered, as at the date of registration, except where the registration is provisional only. **23–010**

Exemption from registration

11.—(1) The foregoing provisions of this Act shall not apply to the New Forest or Epping Forest nor to any land exempted from those provisions by an order of the Minister, and shall not be taken to apply to the Forest of Dean. **23–011**

(2) The Minister shall not make an order under this section except on an application made to him before such date as may be prescribed.

[11] subss. (5)–(7) substituted (for subs. (5)) by the Local Government Act 1972, s.189(2).
[12] Words substituted by the Land Registration Act 2002, s.133, Sched. 11, para. 7(1), (3).

(3) The Minister shall not make an order under this section with respect to any land unless it appears to him—

(a) that the land is regulated by a scheme under the Commons Act 1899 or the Metropolitan Commons Acts 1866 to 1898 or is regulated under a local Act or under an Act confirming a provisional order made under the Commons Act 1876; and

(b) that no rights of common have been exercised over the land for at least thirty years and that the owner of the land is known.

(4) The Minister shall, before dealing with any application under this section, send copies thereof to the registration authority and to such other local authorities as may be prescribed, and shall inform those authorities whether he has granted or refused the application; and those authorities shall take such steps as may be prescribed for informing the public of the application and its grant or refusal.

(5) If any question arises under this Act whether any land is part of the forests mentioned in subsection (1) of this section it shall be referred to and decided by the Minister.

Subsequent registration under Land Registration Acts 1925 and 1936

23–012 **12.** The following provisions shall have effect with respect to the registration [in the register of title][13] of any land after the ownership of the land has been registered under this Act, that is to say—

[...][14]

(b) if the registration authority is notified by the Chief Land Registrar that the land has been registered [in the register of title][15] the authority shall delete the registration of the ownership under this Act and indicate in the register in the prescribed manner that it has been registered under those Acts.

Amendment of registers

23–013 **13.** Regulations under this Act shall provide for the amendment of the registers maintained under this Act where—

(a) any land registered under this Act ceases to be common land or a town or village green; or

(b) any land becomes common land or a town or village green; or

(c) any rights registered under this Act are apportioned, extinguished or released, or are varied or transferred in such circumstances as may be prescribed;

[...][16]

Rectification of registers

23–014 **14.** The High Court may order a register maintained under this Act to be amended if—

[13] Words substituted by the Land Registration Act 2002, s.133, Sched. 11, para. 7(1), (4).
[14] Para. (a) repealed by the Land Registration Act 1997, s.4(2), Sched. 2, Pt. I.
[15] Words substituted by the Land Registration Act 2002, s.133, Sched. 11, para. 7(1), (4).
[16] Words repealed by the Law of Property Act 1969, s.16(2), Sched. 2, Pt. I.

(a) the registration under this Act of any land or rights of common has become final and the court is satisfied that any person was induced by fraud to withdraw an objection to the registration or to refrain from making such an objection; or

(b) the register has been amended in pursuance of section 13 of this Act and it appears to the court that no amendment or a different amendment ought to have been made and that the error cannot be corrected in pursuance of regulations made under this Act;

and, in either case, the court deems it just to rectify the register.

Quantification of certain grazing rights

15.—(1) Where a right of common consists of or includes a right, not limited by number, to graze animals or animals of any class, it shall for the purposes of registration under this Act be treated as exercisable in relation to no more animals, or animals of that class, than a definite number. **23–015**

(2) Any application for the registration of such a right shall state the number of animals to be entered in the register or, as the case may be, the numbers of animals of different classes to be so entered.

(3) When the registration of such a right has become final the right shall accordingly be exercisable in relation to animals not exceeding the number or numbers registered or such other number or numbers as Parliament may hereafter determine.

Disregard of certain interruptions in prescriptive claims to rights of common

16.—(1) Where during any period a right of common claimed over any land was not exercised, but during the whole or part of that period either— **23–016**

(a) the land was requisitioned; or

(b) where the right claimed is a right to graze animals, the right could not be or was not exercised for reasons of animal health;

that period or part shall be left out of account, both—

(i) in determining for the purposes of the Prescription Act 1832 whether there was an interruption within the meaning of that Act of the actual enjoyment of the right; and

(ii) in computing the period of thirty or sixty years mentioned in section 1 of that Act.

(2) For the purposes of the said Act any objection under this Act to the registration of a right of common shall be deemed to be such a suit or action as is referred to in section 4 of that Act.

(3) In this section "requisitioned" means in the possession of a Government department in the exercise or purported exercise of powers conferred by regulations made under the Emergency Powers (Defence) Act 1939 or by Part VI of the Requisitioned Land and War Works Act 1945; and in determining in any proceedings any question arising under this section whether any land was requisitioned during any period a document purporting to be a certificate to that effect issued by a Government department shall be admissible in evidence.

(4) Where it is necessary for the purposes of this section to establish that a right to graze animals on any land could not be or was not exercised for reasons of animal health it shall be sufficient to prove either—

(a) that the movement of the animals to that land was prohibited or restricted by or under the Diseases of Animals Act 1950 or any enactment repealed by that Act; or

(b) that the land was not, but some other land was, approved for grazing under any scheme in force under that Act or any such enactment and the animals were registered, or were undergoing tests with a view to registration, under the scheme.

Commons Commissioners and assessors

23–017 **17.**—(1) The Lord Chancellor shall—

(a) appoint to be Commons Commissioners such number of [persons who have a 7 year general qualification, within the meaning of section 71 of the Courts and Legal Services Act 1990][17] as he may determine; and

(b) draw up and from time to time revise a panel of assessors to assist the Commons Commissioners in dealing with cases calling for special knowledge;

and shall appoint one of the Commons Commissioners to be Chief Commons Commissioner.

[(1A) A Commons Commissioner shall vacate his office on the day on which he attains the age of seventy years; but this subsection is subject to section 26(4) to (6) of the Judicial Pensions and Retirement Act 1993 (power of Lord Chancellor to authorise continuance in office up to the age of seventy-five years).][18]

(2) Any matter referred under this Act to a Commons Commissioner shall be dealt with by such one of the Commissioners as the Chief Commons Commissioner may determine, and that Commissioner may sit with an assessor selected by the Chief Commons Commissioner from the panel appointed under this section.

(3) If at any time the Chief Commons Commissioner is for any reason unable to act, the Lord Chancellor may appoint another Commons Commissioner to act in his stead.

(4) A Commons Commissioner may order any party to any proceedings before him to pay to any other party to the proceedings any costs incurred by that party in respect of the proceedings; and any costs so awarded shall be taxed in the county court according to such of the scales prescribed by county court rules for proceedings in the county court as may be directed by the order, but subject to any modifications specified in the direction, or, if the order gives no direction, by the county court, and shall be recoverable in like manner as costs awarded in the county court.

(5) The Minister shall pay to the Commons Commissioners and assessors appointed under this section such fees and such travelling and other allowances as the Minister may, with the approval of the Treasury, determine, and shall provide the Commons Commissioners with such services and facilities as appear to him required for the discharge of their functions.

Appeals from Commons Commissioners

23–018 **18.**—(1) Any person aggrieved by the decision of a Commons Commissioner as being erroneous in point of law may, within such time as may be limited by rules of court, require the Commissioner to state a case for the decision of the High Court.

[17] Words substituted by the Courts and Legal Services Act 1990, s.71(2), Sched. 10, para. 26.
[18] subs. (1A) inserted by the Judicial Pensions and Retirement Act 1993, s.26(10), Sched. 6, para. 26.

(2) So much of section 63(1) of the Supreme Court of Judicature (Consolidation) Act 1925[19] as requires appeals to the High Court to be heard and determined by a Divisional Court shall not apply to an appeal by way of case stated under this section, but no appeal to the Court of Appeal shall be brought against the decision of the High Court in such a case except with the leave of that Court or the Court of Appeal.

. . . . . .

Orders

20.—(1) Any order made by the Minister under any provision of this Act may be varied or revoked by subsequent order made thereunder. **23–019**

(2) Any such order, other than an order made under section 11 of this Act, shall be made by statutory instrument.

(3) Any statutory instrument made under this section shall be subject to annulment in pursuance of a resolution of either House of Parliament.

Savings

21.—(1) Section 1(2) of this Act shall not affect the application to any land registered under this Act of section 193 or section 194 of the Law of Property Act 1925 (rights of access to, and restriction on inclosure of, land over which rights of common are exercisable). **23–020**

(2) Section 10 of this Act shall not apply for the purpose of deciding whether any land forms part of a highway.

Interpretation

22.—(1) In this Act, unless the context otherwise requires— **23–021**

"common land" means—

(a) land subject to rights of common (as defined in this Act) whether those rights are exercisable at all times or only during limited periods;

(b) waste land of a manor not subject to rights of common;

but does not include a town or village green or any land which forms part of a highway;

"land" includes land covered with water;

"local authority" means [. . .][20] the council of a county, [. . .][21] London borough or county district, the council of a parish [. . .][22];

"the Minister" means the Minister of Land and Natural Resources[23];

"prescribed" means prescribed by regulations under this Act;

["register of title" means the register kept under section 1 of the Land Registration Act 2002;][24]

---

[19] See now the Supreme Court Act 1981, s.66(1).

[20] Words repealed by the Local Government Act 1985, s.102(2), Sched. 17.

[21] Words repealed by the Local Government Act 1972, s.272(1), Sched. 30.

[22] Words repealed by the Local Government Act 1972, s.272(1), Sched. 30.

[23] Now the Secretary of State for the Environment or, in so far as the functions of the Minister are exercisable in relation to Wales, the National Assembly for Wales: Ministry of Land and Natural Resources (Dissolution) Order 1967 (S.I. 1967 No. 156); Secretary of State for the Environment Order 1970 (S.I. 1970 No. 1681); and the National Assembly for Wales (Transfer of Functions) Order 1999 (S.I. 1999 No. 672), art. 2(a), Sched. 1.

[24] Definition inserted by the Land Registration Act 2002, s.133, Sched. 11, para. 7(1), (5).

"registration" includes an entry in the register made in pursuance of section 13 of this Act;

"rights of common" includes cattlegates or beastgates (by whatever name known) and rights of sole or several vesture or herbage or of sole or several pasture, but does not include rights held for a term of years or from year to year;

"town or village green" means land which had been allotted by or under any Act for the exercise or recreation of the inhabitants of any locality or on which the inhabitants of any locality have a customary right to indulge in lawful sports and pastimes [or which falls within subsection (1A) of this section.][25]

[(1A) Land falls within this subsection if it is land on which for not less than twenty years a significant number of the inhabitants of any locality, or of any neighbourhood within a locality, have indulged in a lawful sports and pastimes as of right, and either—

(a) continue to do so, or

(b) have ceased to do so for not more than such period as may be prescribed, or determined in accordance with prescribed provisions.

(1B) If regulations made for the purposes of paragraph (b) of subsection (1A) of this section provide for the period mentioned in that paragraph to come to an end unless prescribed steps are taken, the regulations may also require registration authorities to make available in accordance with the regulations, on payment of any prescribed fee, information relating to the taking of any such steps.][26]

(2) References in this Act to the ownership and the owner of any land are references to the ownership of a legal estate in fee simple in any land and to the person holding that estate, and references to land registered [in the register of title][27] are references to land the fee simple of which is so registered.

Application to Crown

23–022 **23.**—(1) This Act shall apply in relation to land in which there is a Crown or Duchy interest as it applies in relation to land in which there is no such interest.

(2) In this section "Crown or Duchy interest" means an interest belonging to Her Majesty in right of the Crown or of the Duchy of Lancaster, or belonging to the Duchy of Cornwall, or belonging to a Government department, or held in trust for Her Majesty for the purposes of a Government department.

. . . . . .

[25] Words substituted by the Countryside and Rights of Way Act 2000, s.98(1), (2).
[26] subss. (1A) and (1B) inserted by the Countryside and Rights of Way Act 2000, s.98(1), (3).
[27] Words substituted by the Land Registration Act 2002, s.133, Sched. 11, para. 7(1), (6).

Misrepresentation Act 1967

(1967 c. 7)

Removal of certain bars to rescission for innocent misrepresentation

1. Where a person has entered into a contract after a misrepresentation has been made to him, and— **24–001**

(a) the misrepresentation has become a term of the contract; or

(b) the contract has been performed;

or both, then, if otherwise he would be entitled to rescind the contract without alleging fraud, he shall be so entitled, subject to the provisions of this Act, notwithstanding the matters mentioned in paragraphs (a) and (b) of this section.

Damages for misrepresentation

2.—(1) Where a person has entered into a contract after a misrepresentation has been made to him by another party thereto and as a result thereof he has suffered loss, then, if the person making the misrepresentation would be liable to damages in respect thereof had the misrepresentation been made fraudulently, that person shall be so liable notwithstanding that the misrepresentation was not made fraudulently, unless he proves that he had reasonable ground to believe and did believe up to the time the contract was made that the facts represented were true. **24–002**

(2) Where a person has entered into a contract after a misrepresentation has been made to him otherwise than fraudulently, and he would be entitled, by reason of the misrepresentation, to rescind the contract, then, if it is claimed, in any proceedings arising out of the contract, that the contract ought to be or has been rescinded, the court or arbitrator may declare the contract subsisting and award damages in lieu of rescission, if of opinion that it would be equitable to do so, having regard to the nature of the misrepresentation and the loss that would be caused by it if the contract were upheld, as well as to the loss that rescission would cause to the other party.

(3) Damages may be awarded against a person under subsection (2) of this section whether or not he is liable to damages under subsection (1) thereof, but where he is so liable any award under the said subsection (2) shall be taken into account in assessing his liability under the said subsection (1).

[Avoidance of provision excluding liability for misrepresentation

3. If a contract contains a term which would exclude or restrict— **24–003**

(a) any liability to which a party to a contract may be subject by reason of any misrepresentation made by him before the contract was made; or

(b) any remedy available to another party to the contract by reason of such a misrepresentation,

that term shall be of no effect except in so far as it satisfies the requirement of reasonableness as stated in section 11(1) of the Unfair Contract Terms Act

1977[1]; and it is for those claiming that the term satisfies that requirement to show that it does.][2]

Wills Act 1968

(1968 c. 28)

Restriction of operation of Wills Act 1837, s.15

25–001 **1.**—(1) For the purposes of section 15 of the Wills Act 1837 (avoidance of gifts to attesting witnesses and their spouses) the attestation of a will by a person to whom or to whose spouse there is given or made any such disposition as is described in that section shall be disregarded if the will is duly executed without his attestation and without that of any other such person.

(2) This section applies to the will of any person dying after the passing of this Act, whether executed before or after the passing of this Act.

Family Law Reform Act 1969

(1969 c. 46)

PART I

REDUCTION OF AGE OF MAJORITY AND RELATED PROVISIONS

Reduction of age of majority from 21 to 18

26–001 **1.**—(1) As from the date on which this section comes into force a person shall attain full age on attaining the age of eighteen instead of on attaining the age of twenty-one; and a person shall attain full age on that date if he has then already attained the age of eighteen but not the age of twenty-one.

(2) The foregoing subsection applies for the purposes of any rule of law, and, in the absence of a definition or of any indication of a contrary intention, for the construction of "full age", "infant", "infancy", "minor", "minority" and similar expressions in—

(a) any statutory provision, whether passed or made before, on or after the date on which this section comes into force; and

(b) any deed, will or other instrument of whatever nature (not being a statutory provision) made on or after that date.

. . . . .

[1] The requirement of reasonableness is that "the term shall have been a fair and reasonable one to be included having regard to the circumstances which were, or ought reasonably to have been, known to or in the contemplation of the parties when the contract was made."

[2] Section substituted by the Unfair Contract Terms Act 1977, s.8(1).

Provisions relating to wills and intestacy

3.—(1) [*Amends the Wills Act 1837, s.7, ante, para. 2–003, and the Wills (Soldiers and Sailors) Act 1918, ss.1, 3(1), ante, paras 5–001, 5–003.*] **26–002**

(2) [*Amends the Administration of Estates Act 1925, s.47(1)(i), ante, para. 10–038.*]

(3) Any will which—

(a) has been made, whether before or after the coming into force of this section, by a person under the age of eighteen; and

(b) is valid by virtue of the provisions of section 11 of the said Act of 1837 and the said Act of 1918,

may be revoked by that person notwithstanding that he is still under that age whether or not the circumstances are then such that he would be entitled to make a valid will under those provisions.

(4) In this section "will" has the same meaning as in the said Act of 1837 and "intestate" has the same meaning as in the said Act of 1925.

. . . . . .

Time at which a person attains a particular age

9.—(1) The time at which a person attains a particular age expressed in years shall be the commencement of the relevant anniversary of the date of his birth. **26–003**

(2) This section applies only where the relevant anniversary falls on a date after that on which this section comes into force, and, in relation to any enactment, deed, will or other instrument, has effect subject to any provision therein.

. . . . . .

Law of Property Act 1969

(1969 c. 59)

PART III

AMENDMENT OF LAW RELATING TO DISPOSITIONS OF ESTATES AND INTERESTS IN LAND AND TO LAND CHARGES

Reduction of statutory period of title

23. Section 44(1) of the Law of Property Act 1925 (under which the period of commencement of title which may be required under a contract expressing no contrary intention is thirty years except in certain cases) shall have effect, in its application to contracts made after the commencement of this Act, as if it specified fifteen years instead of thirty years as the period of commencement of title which may be so required. **27–001**

Contracts for purchase of land affected by land charge, etc.

27–002 **24.**—(1) Where under a contract for the sale or other disposition of any estate or interest in land the title to which is not registered under the [Land Registration Act 2002][1] or any enactment replaced by it any question arises whether the purchaser had knowledge, at the time of entering into the contract, of a registered land charge, that question shall be determined by reference to his actual knowledge and without regard to the provisions of section 198 of the Law of Property Act 1925 (under which registration under the Land Charges Act 1925[2] or any enactment replaced by it is deemed to constitute actual notice).

(2) Where any estate or interest with which such a contract is concerned is affected by a registered land charge and the purchaser, at the time of entering into the contract, had not received notice and did not otherwise actually know that the estate or interest was affected by the charge, any provision of the contract shall be void so far as it purports to exclude the operation of subsection (1) above or to exclude or restrict any right or remedy that might otherwise be exercisable by the purchaser on the ground that the estate or interest is affected by the charge.

(3) In this section—

"purchaser" includes a lessee, mortgagee or other person acquiring or intending to acquire an estate or interest in land; and

"registered land charge" means any instrument or matter registered, otherwise than in a register of local land charges, under the Land Charges Act 1925[3] or any Act replaced by it.

(4) For the purposes of this section any knowledge acquired in the course of a transaction by a person who is acting therein as counsel, or as solicitor or other agent, for another shall be treated as the knowledge of that other.

(5) This section does not apply to contracts made before the commencement of this Act.

Compensation in certain cases for loss due to undisclosed land charges

27–003 **25.**—(1) Where a purchaser of any estate or interest in land under a disposition to which this section applies has suffered loss by reason that the estate or interest is affected by a registered land charge, then if—

(a) the date of completion was after the commencement of this Act; and
(b) on that date the purchaser had no actual knowledge of the charge; and
(c) the charge was registered against the name of an owner of an estate in the land who was not as owner of any such estate a party to any transaction, or concerned in any event, comprised in the relevant title;

the purchaser shall be entitled to compensation for the loss.

(2) For the purposes of subsection (1)(b) above, the question whether any person had actual knowledge of a charge shall be determined without regard to the provisions of section 198 of the Law of Property Act 1925 (under which registration under the Land Charges Act 1925[4] or any enactment replaced by it is deemed to constitute actual notice).

(3) Where a transaction comprised in the relevant title was affected or evidenced by a document which expressly provided that it should take effect subject to an interest or obligation capable of registration in any of the relevant

[1] Words substituted by the Land Registration Act 2002, s.133, Sched. 11, para. 9.
[2] Now the Land Charges Act 1972, *post*, para. 31–001.
[3] Now the Land Charges Act 1972, *post*, para. 31–001.
[4] Now the Land Charges Act 1972, *post*, para. 31–001.

registers, the transaction which created that interest or obligation shall be treated for the purposes of subsection (1)(c) above as comprised in the relevant title.

(4) Any compensation for loss under this section shall be paid by the Chief Land Registrar, and where the purchaser of the estate or interest in question has incurred expenditure for the purpose—

(a) of securing that the estate or interest is no longer affected by the registered land charge or is so affected to a less extent; or

(b) of obtaining compensation under this section;

the amount of the compensation shall include the amount of the expenditure (so far as it would not otherwise fall to be treated as compensation for loss) reasonably incurred by the purchaser for that purpose.

(5) In the case of an action to recover compensation under this section, the cause of action shall be deemed for the purposes of [the Limitation Act 1980][5] to accrue at the time when the registered land charge affecting the estate or interest in question comes to the notice of the purchaser.

(6) Any proceedings for the recovery of compensation under this section shall be commenced in the High Court; and if in such proceedings the High Court dismisses a claim to compensation it shall not order the purchaser to pay the Chief Land Registrar's costs unless it considers that it was unreasonable for the purchaser to commence the proceedings.

(7) [*Repealed by the Land Charges Act 1972, s.18(3), Sched. 5.*]

(8) Where compensation under this section has been paid in a case where the purchaser would have had knowledge of the registered land charge but for the fraud of any person, the Chief Land Registrar, on behalf of the Crown, may recover the amount paid from that person.

(9) This section applies to the following dispositions, that is to say—

(a) any sale or exchange and, subject to the following provisions of this subsection, any mortgage of an estate or interest in land;

(b) any grant of a lease for a term of years derived out of a leasehold interest;

(c) any compulsory purchase, by whatever procedure, of land; and

(d) any conveyance of a fee simple in land under Part I of the Leasehold Reform Act 1967;

but does not apply to the grant of a term of years derived out of the freehold or the mortgage of such a term by the lessee; and references in this section to a purchaser shall be construed accordingly.

(10) In this section—

"date of completion", in relation to land which vests in the Land Commission or another acquiring authority by virtue of a general vesting declaration under the Land Commission Act 1967 or the Town and Country Planning Act 1968[6], means the date on which it so vests;

"mortgage" includes any charge;

"registered land charge" means any instrument or matter registered, otherwise than in a register of local land charges, under the Land Charges Act 1925[7], or any Act replaced by it, except that—

(a) in relation to an assignment of a lease or underlease or a mortgage by an assignee under such an assignment, it does not include any instrument or matter affecting the title to the freehold or to any relevant leasehold reversion; and

[5] Words substituted by the Limitation Act 1980, s.40(2), Sched. 3, para. 9.
[6] Now the Town and Country Planning Act 1990.
[7] Now the Land Charges Act 1972, *post*, para. 31–001.

(b) in relation to the grant of an underlease or the mortgage by the underlessee of the term of years created by an underlease, it does not include any instrument or matter affecting the title to the freehold or to any leasehold reversion superior to the leasehold interest out of which the term of years is derived;

"relevant registers" means the registers kept under section 1 of the Land Charges Act 1925[8];

"relevant title" means—

(a) in relation to a disposition made under a contract, the title which the purchaser was, apart from any acceptance by him (by agreement or otherwise) of a shorter or an imperfect title, entitled to require; or

(b) in relation to any other disposition, the title which he would have been entitled to require if the disposition had been made under a contract to which section 44(1) of the Law of Property Act 1925 applied and that contract had been made on the date of completion.

(11) For the purposes of this section any knowledge acquired in the course of a transaction by a person who is acting therein as counsel, or as solicitor or other agent, for another shall be treated as the knowledge of that other.

. . . . . .

Administration of Justice Act 1970

(1970 c. 31)

Part IV

Actions by Mortgagees for Possession

Additional powers of court in action by mortgagee for possession of dwelling-house

28–001 **36.**[1]—(1) Where the mortgagee under a mortgage of land which consists of or includes a dwelling-house brings an action in which he claims possession of the mortgaged property, not being an action for foreclosure in which a claim for possession of the mortgaged property is also made, the court may exercise any of the powers conferred on it by subsection (2) below if it appears to the court that in the event of its exercising the power the mortgagor is likely to be able within a reasonable period to pay any sums due under the mortgage or to remedy a default consisting of a breach of any other obligation arising under or by virtue of the mortgage.

(2) The court—

(a) may adjourn the proceedings, or

(b) on giving judgment, or making an order, for delivery of possession of the

---

[8] Now the Land Charges Act 1972, *post*, para. 31–001.

[1] Extended and modified by the Administration of Justice Act 1973, s.8, *post*, para. 32–001.

mortgaged property, or at any time before the execution of such judgment or order, may—

(i) stay or suspend execution of the judgment or order, or

(ii) postpone the date for delivery of possession,

for such period or periods as the court thinks reasonable.

(3) Any such adjournment, stay, suspension or postponement as is referred to in subsection (2) above may be made subject to such conditions with regard to payment by the mortgagor of any sum secured by the mortgage or the remedying of any default as the court thinks fit.

(4) The court may from time to time vary or revoke any condition imposed by virtue of this section.

(5) This section shall have effect in relation to such an action as is referred to in subsection (1) above begun before the date on which this section comes into force unless in that action judgment has been given, or an order made, for delivery of possession of the mortgaged property and that judgment or order was executed before that date.

(6) In the application of this section to Northern Ireland, "the court" means a judge of the High Court in Northern Ireland, and in subsection (1) the words from "not being" to "made" shall be omitted.

37, 38. [*Repealed by the County Courts Act 1984, s.148(3), Sched. 4.*][2]

[**38A.** This Part of this Act shall not apply to a mortgage securing an agreement which is a regulated agreement within the meaning of the Consumer Credit Act 1974.][3]

Interpretation of Part IV

39.—(1) In this Part of this Act— **28–002**

"dwelling-house" includes any building or part thereof which is used as a dwelling;

"mortgage" includes a charge and "mortgagor" and "mortgagee" shall be construed accordingly;

"mortgagor" and "mortgagee" includes any person deriving title under the original mortgagor or mortgagee.

(2) The fact that part of the premises comprised in a dwelling-house is used as a shop or office or for business, trade or professional purposes shall not prevent the dwelling-house from being a dwelling-house for the purposes of this Part of this Act.

[2] For the jurisdiction of the county court, see the County Courts Act 1984, s.21, *post*, para. 42–001.
[3] s.38A inserted by the Consumer Credit Act 1974, s.192(3)(a), Sched. 4, Pt. I, para. 30.

Matrimonial Proceedings and Property Act 1970

(1970 c. 45)

PART II

MISCELLANEOUS PROVISIONS

. . . . . .

Provisions relating to property of married persons

Contributions by spouse in money or money's worth to the improvement of property

29–001 **37.** It is hereby declared that where a husband or wife contributes in money or money's worth to the improvement of real or personal property in which or in the proceeds of sale of which either or both of them has or have a beneficial interest, the husband or wife so contributing shall, if the contribution is of a substantial nature and subject to any agreement between them to the contrary express or implied, be treated as having then acquired by virtue of his or her contribution a share or an enlarged share, as the case may be, in that beneficial interest of such an extent as may have been then agreed or, in default of such agreement, as may seem in all the circumstances just to any court before which the question of the existence or extent of the beneficial interest of the husband or wife arises (whether in proceedings between them or in any other proceedings).

Powers of Attorney Act 1971[1]

(1971 c. 27)

Execution of powers of attorney

30–001 **1.**—(1) An instrument creating a power of attorney shall be [executed as a deed by][2] the donor of the power.

(2) [*Repealed by the Law of Property (Miscellaneous Provisions) Act 1989, ss.1(8), 4, Sched. 1, para. 6(b), Sched. 2.*]

(3) This section is without prejudice to any requirement in, or having effect under, any other Act as to the witnessing of instruments creating powers of attorney and does not affect the rules relating to the execution of instruments by bodies corporate.

2. [*Repealed by the Supreme Court Act 1981, s.152(4), Sched. 7.*]

---

[1] See also the Enduring Powers of Attorney Act 1985, *post*, para. 43–001.

[2] Words substituted by the Law of Property (Miscellaneous Provisions) Act 1989, s.1(8), Sched. 1, para. 6(a).

Proof of instruments creating powers of attorney

3.—(1) The contents of an instrument creating a power of attorney may be proved by means of a copy which— **30–002**

(a) is a reproduction of the original made with a photographic or other device for reproducing documents in facsimile; and

(b) contains the following certificate or certificates signed by the donor of the power or by a solicitor [duly certificated notary public][3] or stockbroker, that is to say—

(i) a certificate at the end to the effect that the copy is a true and complete copy of the original; and

(ii) if the original consists of two or more pages, a certificate at the end of each page of the copy to the effect that it is a true and complete copy of the corresponding page of the original.

(2) Where a copy of an instrument creating a power of attorney has been made which complies with subsection (1) of this section, the contents of the instrument may also be proved by means of a copy of that copy if the further copy itself complies with that subsection, taking references in it to the original as references to the copy from which the further copy is made.

(3) In this section ["duly certificated notary public" has the same meaning as it has in the Solicitors Act 1974 by virtue of section 87(1) of that Act and][4] "stockbroker" means a member of any stock exchange within the meaning of the Stock Transfer Act 1963 or the Stock Transfer Act (Northern Ireland) 1963.

(4) This section is without prejudice to section 4 of the Evidence and Powers of Attorney Act 1940 (proof of deposited instruments by office copy) and to any other method of proof authorised by law.

(5) For the avoidance of doubt, in relation to an instrument made in Scotland the references to a power of attorney in this section and in section 4 of the Evidence and Powers of Attorney Act 1940 include references to a factory and commission.

Powers of attorney given as security

4.—(1) Where a power of attorney is expressed to be irrevocable and is given to secure— **30–003**

(a) a proprietary interest of the donee of the power; or

(b) the performance of an obligation owed to the donee,

then, so long as the donee has that interest or the obligation remains undischarged, the power shall not be revoked—

(i) by the donor without the consent of the donee; or

(ii) by the death, incapacity or bankruptcy of the donor or, if the donor is a body corporate, by its winding up or dissolution.

(2) A power of attorney given to secure a proprietary interest may be given to the person entitled to the interest and persons deriving title under him to that interest, and those persons shall be duly constituted donees of the power for all purposes of the power but without prejudice to any right to appoint substitutes given by the power.

(3) This section applies to powers of attorney whenever created.

[3] Words inserted by the Courts and Legal Services Act 1990, s.125(2), Sched. 17, para. 4.
[4] Words inserted by the Courts and Legal Services Act 1990, s.125(2), Sched. 17, para. 4.

Protection of donee and third persons where power of attorney is revoked

30–004 **5.**—(1) A donee of a power of attorney who acts in pursuance of the power at a time when it has been revoked shall not, by reason of the revocation, incur any liability (either to the donor or to any other person) if at that time he did not know that the power had been revoked.

(2) Where a power of attorney has been revoked and a person, without knowledge of the revocation, deals with the donee of the power, the transaction between them shall, in favour of that person, be as valid as if the power had then been in existence.

(3) Where the power is expressed in the instrument creating it to be irrevocable and to be given by way of security then, unless the person dealing with the donee knows that it was not in fact given by way of security, he shall be entitled to assume that the power is incapable of revocation except by the donor acting with the consent of the donee and shall accordingly be treated for the purposes of subsection (2) of this section as having knowledge of the revocation only if he knows that it has been revoked in that manner.

(4) Where the interest of a purchaser depends on whether a transaction between the donee of a power of attorney and another person was valid by virtue of subsection (2) of this section, it shall be conclusively presumed in favour of the purchaser that that person did not at the material time know of the revocation of the power if—

(a) the transaction between that person and the donee was completed within twelve months of the date on which the power came into operation; or
(b) that person makes a statutory declaration, before or within three months after the completion of the purchase, that he did not at the material time know of the revocation of the power.

(5) Without prejudice to subsection (3) of this section, for the purposes of this section knowledge of the revocation of a power of attorney includes knowledge of the occurrence of any event (such as the death of the donor) which has the effect of revoking the power.

(6) In this section "purchaser" and "purchase" have the meanings specified in section 205(1) of the Law of Property Act 1925.

(7) This section applies whenever the power of attorney was created but only to acts and transactions after the commencement of this Act.

Additional protection for transferees under stock exchange transactions

30–005 **6.**—(1) Without prejudice to section 5 of this Act, where—

(a) the donee of a power of attorney executes, as transferor, an instrument transferring registered securities; and
(b) the instrument is executed for the purposes of a stock exchange transaction,

it shall be conclusively presumed in favour of the transferee that the power had not been revoked at the date of the instrument if a statutory declaration to that effect is made by the donee of the power on or within three months after that date.

(2) In this section "registered securities" and "stock exchange transaction" have the same meanings as in the Stock Transfer Act 1963.

Execution of instruments, etc. by donee of power of attorney

[**7.**—(1) If the donee of a power of attorney is an individual, he may, if he thinks fit— **30–006**

(a) execute any instrument with his own signature, and][5]

(b) do any other thing in his own name,

by the authority of the donor of the power; and any document executed or thing done in that manner shall be as effective as if executed or done by the donee with the signature […][6], or, as the case may be, in the name, of the donor of the power.

(2) For the avoidance of doubt it is hereby declared that an instrument to which subsection (3) […][7] of section 74 of the Law of Property Act 1925 applies may be executed either as provided in [that subsection][8] or as provided in this section.

(3) This section is without prejudice to any statutory direction requiring an instrument to be executed in the name of an estate owner within the meaning of the said Act of 1925.

(4) This section applies whenever the power of attorney was created.

8. [*Repeals the Law of Property Act 1925, s.129.*]

9. [*Repealed by the Trustee Delegation Act 1999, s.12, Sched.*]

Effect of general power of attorney in specified form

10.—(1) Subject to subsection (2) of this section, a general power of attorney in the form set out in Schedule 1 to this Act, or in a form to the like effect but expressed to be made under this Act, shall operate to confer— **30–007**

(a) on the donee of the power; or

(b) if there is more than one donee, on the donees acting jointly or acting jointly or severally, as the case may be,

authority to do on behalf of the donor anything which he can lawfully do by an attorney.

(2) [Subject to section 1 of the Trustee Delegation Act 1999, this section][9] does not apply to functions which the donor has as a trustee or personal representative or as a tenant for life or statutory owner within the meaning of the Settled Land Act 1925.

---

[5] Words substituted by the Law of Property (Miscellaneous Provisions) Act 1989, s.1(8), Sched. 1, para. 7(1).
[6] Words repealed by the Law of Property (Miscellaneous Provisions) Act 1989, s.4, Sched. 2.
[7] Words repealed by the Law of Property (Miscellaneous Provisions) Act 1989, ss.1(8), 4, Sched. 1, para. 7(2)(a), Sched. 2.
[8] Words substituted by the Law of Property (Miscellaneous Provisions) Act 1989, s.1(8), Sched. 1, para. 7(2)(b).
[9] Words substituted by the Trustee Delegation Act 1999, s.3.

Land Charges Act 1972

(1972 c. 61)

ARRANGEMENT OF SECTIONS

Preliminary

The registers and the index

31–001 **1.**—(1) The registrar shall continue to keep at the registry in the prescribed manner the following registers, namely—

(a) a register of land charges;
(b) a register of pending actions;
(c) a register of writs and orders affecting land;
(d) a register of deeds of arrangement affecting land;
(e) a register of annuities,

and shall also continue to keep there an index whereby all entries made in any of those registers can readily be traced.

(2) Every application to register shall be in the prescribed form and shall contain the prescribed particulars.

[(3) Where any charge or other matter is registrable in more than one of the registers kept under this Act, it shall be sufficient if it is registered in one such register, and if it is so registered the person entitled to the benefit of it shall not be prejudicially affected by any provision of this Act as to the effect of non-registration in any other such register.

(3A) Where any charge or other matter is registrable in a register kept under this Act and was also, before the commencement of the Local Land Charges Act 1975, registrable in a local land charges register, then, if before the commencement of the said Act it was registered in the appropriate local land charges register, it shall be treated for the purposes of the provisions of this Act as to the effect of non-registration as if it had been registered in the appropriate register under this Act; and any certificate setting out the result of an official search of the appropriate local land charges register shall, in relation to it, have effect as if it were a certificate setting out the result of an official search under this Act.][1]

(4) Schedule 1 to this Act shall have effect in relation to the register of annuities.

(5) An office copy of an entry in any register kept under this section shall be admissible in evidence in all proceedings and between all parties to the same extent as the original would be admissible.

(6) Subject to the provisions of this Act, registration may be vacated pursuant to an order of the court.

[(6A) The county courts have jurisdiction under subsection (6) above—

(a) in the case of a land charge of Class C(i), C(ii) or D(i), if the amount does not exceed £30,000;

(b) in the case of a land charge of class C(iii), if it is for a specified capital sum of money not exceeding £30,000 or, where it is not for a specified capital sum, if the capital value of the land affected does not exceed £30,000;

(c) in the case of a land charge of Class A, Class B, Class C(iv), Class D(ii), Class D(iii) or Class E if the capital value of the land affected does not exceed £30,000;

(d) in the case of a land charge of Class F, if the land affected by it is thesubject of an order made by the court under section 1 of the Matrimonial Homes Act 1983 [or section 33 of the Family Law Act 1996][2] or an application for an order under [either of those sections][3] relating to that land has been made to the court;

(e) in a case where an application under section 23 of the Deeds of Arrangement Act 1914 could be entertained by the court.][4]

(6B) [*Repealed by the High Court and County Courts Jurisdiction Order* 1991 (*S.I.* 1991 *No.* 724), *art.* 2(8), *Sched.*][5]

(7) In this section "index" includes any device or combination of devices serving the purpose of an index.

Registration in register of land charges

The register of land charges

2.—(1) If a charge on or obligation affecting land falls into one of the classes described in this section, it may be registered in the register of land charges as a land charge of that class. **31–002**

[1] subss. (3) and (3A) substituted (for subs. (3)) by the Local Land Charges Act 1975, s.17(1)(a).
[2] Words inserted by the Family Law Act 1996, s.66(1), Sched. 8, Pt. III, para. 46(a).
[3] Words substituted by the Family Law Act 1996, s.66(1), Sched. 8, Pt. III, para. 46(b).
[4] subs. (6A) substituted by the High Court and County Courts Jurisdiction Order 1991 (S.I. 1991 No. 724), art. 2(8), Sched.
[5] subss. (6A) and (6B) inserted by the County Courts Act 1984, s.148(1), Sched. 2, Pt. IV, para. 16.

(2) A Class A land charge is—

(a) a rent or annuity or principal money payable by instalments or otherwise, with or without interest, which is not a charge created by deed but is a charge upon land (other than a rate) created pursuant to the application of some person under the provisions of any Act of Parliament, for securing to any person either the money spent by him or the costs, charges and expenses incurred by him under such Act, or the money advanced by him for repaying the money spent or the costs, charges and expenses incurred by another person under the authority of an Act of Parliament; or

(b) a rent or annuity or principal money payable as mentioned in paragraph (a) above which is not a charge created by deed but is a charge upon land (other than a rate) created pursuant to the application of some person under any of the enactments mentioned in Schedule 2 to this Act.

(3) A Class B land charge is a charge on land (not being a local land charge [. . .][6]) of any of the kinds described in paragraph (a) of subsection (2) above, created otherwise than pursuant to the application of any person.

(4) A Class C land charge is any of the following [(not being a local land charge)][7], namely—

(i) a puisne mortgage;
(ii) a limited owner's charge;
(iii) a general equitable charge;
(iv) an estate contract;

and for this purpose—

(i) a puisne mortgage is a legal mortgage which is not protected by a deposit of documents relating to the legal estate affected;

(ii) a limited owner's charge is an equitable charge acquired by a tenant for life or statutory owner under [[the Inheritance Tax Act 1984][8] or under][9] any other statute by reason of the discharge by him of any [inheritance tax][10] or other liabilities and to which special priority is given by the statute;

(iii) a general equitable charge is any equitable charge which—

(a) is not secured by a deposit of documents relating to the legal estate affected; and

(b) does not arise or affect an interest arising under a [trust of land][11] or a settlement; and

(c) is not a charge given by way of indemnity against rents equitably apportioned or charged exclusively on land in exoneration of other land and against the breach or non-observance of covenants or conditions; and

(d) is not included in any other class of land charge;

[6] Words repealed by the Local Land Charges Act 1975, s.19(1), Sched. 2.
[7] Words inserted by the Local Land Charges Act 1975, s.17(1)(b).
[8] Words substituted by the Inheritance Tax Act 1984 (formerly the Capital Transfer Tax Act 1984: see the Finance Act 1986, s.100(1)(a)), s.276, Sched. 8, para. 3.
[9] Words substituted by the Finance Act 1975, s.52(1), Sched. 12, para. 18(1), (2).
[10] From July 25, 1986, any reference to capital transfer tax, except where the reference relates to a liability to tax arising before that date, has effect as a reference to inheritance tax: Finance Act 1986, s.100(1)(b), (2).
[11] Words substituted by the Trusts of Land and Appointment of Trustees Act 1996, s.25(1), Sched. 3, para. 12(1), (2).

(iv)[12] an estate contract is a contract by an estate owner or by a person entitled at the date of the contract to have a legal estate conveyed to him to convey or create a legal estate, including a contract conferring either expressly or by statutory implication a valid option to purchase, a right of pre-emption or any other like right.

(5) A Class D land charge is any of the following [(not being a local land charge)][13], namely—

(i) an Inland Revenue charge;
(ii) a restrictive covenant;
(iii) an equitable easement;

and for this purpose—

(i) an Inland Revenue charge is a charge on land, being a charge acquired by the Board under [the Inheritance Tax Act 1984][14];
(ii) a restrictive covenant is a covenant or agreement (other than a covenant or agreement between a lessor and a lessee) restrictive of the user of land and entered into on or after 1st January 1926;
(iii) an equitable easement is an easement, right or privilege over or affecting land created or arising on or after 1st January 1926, and being merely an equitable interest.

(6) A Class E land charge is an annuity created before 1st January 1926 and not registered in the register of annuities.

(7) A Class F land charge is a charge affecting any land by virtue of the [Part IV of the Family Law Act 1996][15].

(8) A charge or obligation created before 1st January 1926 can only be registered as a Class B land charge or a Class C land charge if it is acquired under a conveyance made on or after that date.

(9) [*Repealed by the Finance Act 1977, s.59, Sched. 9, Pt. V.*]

Registration of land charges

3.—(1) A land charge shall be registered in the name of the estate owner whose estate is intended to be affected. **31–003**

[(1A) Where a person has died and a land charge created before his death would apart from his death have been registered in his name, it shall be so registered notwithstanding his death.][16]

(2) A land charge registered before 1st January 1926 under any enactment replaced by the Land Charges Act 1925 in the name of a person other than the estate owner may remain so registered until it is registered in the name of the estate owner in the prescribed manner.

(3) A puisne mortgage created before 1st January 1926 may be registered as a land charge before any transfer of the mortgage is made.

(4) The expenses incurred by the person entitled to the charge in registering a land charge of Class A, Class B or Class C (other than an estate contract) or by the Board in registering an Inland Revenue charge shall be deemed to form part

[12] The following matters may be registered under the Land Charges Act 1972 as if they were estate contracts: notices of desire to have the freehold or an extended lease under the Leasehold Reform Act 1967 (s.5(5)); notices given under ss.13 and 42 of the Leasehold Reform, Housing and Urban Development Act 1993 (s.97(1)); and requests for overriding leases under s.19 of the Landlord and Tenant (Covenants) Act 1995 s.20(6)).
[13] Words inserted by the Local Land Charges Act 1975, s.17(1)(b).
[14] Words substituted by the Inheritance Tax Act 1984 (formerly the Capital Transfer Tax Act 1984: see the Finance Act 1986, s.100(1)(a)), s.276, Sched. 8, para. 3.
[15] Words substituted by the Family Law Act 1996, s.66(1), Sched. 8, Pt. III, para. 47.
[16] subs. (1A) inserted by the Law Reform (Miscellaneous Provisions) Act 1994, s.15(1), (2).

of the land charge, and shall be recoverable accordingly on the day for payment of any part of the land charge next after such expenses are incurred.

(5) Where a land charge is not created by an instrument, short particulars of the effect of the charge shall be furnished with the application to register the charge.

(6) An application to register an Inland Revenue charge shall state the [tax][17] in respect of which the charge is claimed and, so far as possible, shall define the land affected, and such particulars shall be entered or referred to in the register.

(7) In the case of a land charge for securing money created by a company before 1st January 1970 or so created at any time as a floating charge, registration under [Part XII, or Chapter III of Part XXIII, of the Companies Act 1985 (or corresponding earlier enactments)][18] shall be sufficient in place of registration under this Act, and shall have effect as if the land charge had been registered under this Act.

(8) [The corresponding earlier enactments][19] referred to in subsection (7) above are section 93 of the Companies (Consolidation) Act 1908, section 79 of the Companies Act 1929 [. . .][20] section 95 of the Companies Act 1948 [and sections 395 to 398 of the Companies Act 1985][21] [as originally enacted][22].

Effect of land charges and protection of purchasers

31–004 **4.**—(1) A land charge of Class A (other than a land improvement charge registered after 31st December 1969) or of Class B shall, when registered, take effect as if it had been created by a deed of charge by way of legal mortgage, but without prejudice to the priority of the charge.

(2) A land charge of Class A created after 31st December 1888 shall be void as against a purchaser of the land charged with it or of any interest in such land, unless the land charge is registered in the register of land charges before the completion of the purchase.

(3) After the expiration of one year from the first conveyance occurring on or after 1st January 1889 of a land charge of Class A created before that date the person entitled to the land charge shall not be able to recover the land charge or any part of it as against a purchaser of the land charged with it or of any interest in the land, unless the land charge is registered in the register of land charges before the completion of the purchase.

(4) If a land improvement charge was registered as a land charge of Class A before 1st January 1970, and body corporate which, but for the charge, would have power to advance money on the security of the estate or interest affected by it shall have that power notwithstanding the charge.

(5) A land charge of Class B and a land charge of Class C (other than an estate contract) created or arising on or after 1st January 1926 shall be void as against a purchaser of the land charged with it, or of any interest in such land, unless the land charge is registered in the appropriate register before the completion of the purchase.

(6) An estate contract and a land charge of Class D created or entered into on

[17] Word substituted by the Finance Act 1975, s.52(1), Sched. 12, para. 18(1), (4).
[18] Words substituted by the Companies Act 1989, s.107, Sched. 16, para. 1(1), (2).
[19] Words substituted by the Companies Act 1989, s.107, Sched. 16, para. 1(1), (3).
[20] Word repealed by the Companies Consolidation (Consequential Provisions) Act 1985, s.30, Sched. 2.
[21] Words added by the Companies Consolidation (Consequential Provisions) Act 1985, s.30, Sched. 2.
[22] Words added by the Companies Act 1989, s.107, Sched.16, para. 1(1), (3).

or after 1st January 1926 shall be void as against a purchaser for money or money's worth [(or, in the case of an Inland Revenue charge, a purchaser within the meaning of [the Inheritance Tax Act 1984][23])][24] of a legal estate in the land charged with it, unless the land charge is registered in the appropriate register before the completion of the purchase.

(7) After the expiration of one year from the first conveyance occurring on or after 1st January 1926 of a land charge of Class B or Class C created before that date the person entitled to the land charge shall not be able to enforce or recover the land charge or any part of it as against a purchaser of the land charged with it, or of any interest in the land, unless the land charge is registered in the appropriate register before the completion of the purchase.

(8) A land charge of Class F shall be void as against a purchaser of the land charged with it, or of any interest in such land, unless the land charge is registered in the appropriate register before the completion of the purchase.

Registration in registers of pending actions, writs and orders and deeds of arrangement

The register of pending actions

5.[25]—(1) There may be registered in the register of pending actions— **31–005**

(a) a pending land action;

(b) a petition in bankruptcy filed on or after 1st January 1926.

(2) Subject to general rules under section 16 of this Act, every application for registration under this section shall contain particulars of the title of the proceedings and the name, address and description of the estate owner or other person whose estate or interest is intended to be affected.

(3) An application for registration shall also state—

(a) if it relates to a pending land action, the court in which and the day on which the action was commenced; and

(b) if it relates to a petition in bankruptcy, the court in which and the day on which the petition was filed.

(4) The registrar shall forthwith enter the particulars in the register, in the name of the estate owner or other person whose estate or interest is intended to be affected.

[(4A) Where a person has died and a pending land action would apart from his death have been registered in his name, it shall be so registered notwithstanding his death.][26]

(5) An application to register a petition in bankruptcy against a firm shall state the names and addresses of the partners, and the registration shall be effected against each partner as well as against the firm.

(6) No fee shall be charged for the registration of a petition in bankruptcy if the application for registration is made by the registrar of the court in which the petition is filed.

---

[23] Words substituted by the Inheritance Tax Act 1984 (formerly the Capital Transfer Tax Act 1984: see the Finance Act 1986, s.100(1)(a)), s.276, Sched, 8, para. 3.

[24] Words substituted by the Finance Act 1975, s.52(1), Sched. 12, para. 18(1),(5).

[25] s.5 applies to applications for acquisition orders under the Landlord and Tenant Act 1987, s.28 (s.28(5)); for restraint orders under the Criminal Justice Act 1988, s.77 (ss.77(12)(b),79), the Prevention of Terrorism (Temporary Provisions) Act 1989, s.13(8), Sched. 4, Pt. I, para. 3 (para. 6(1)(b)) and the Drug Trafficking Act 1994, s.26 (ss.26(12)(b), 28); for access orders under the Access to Neighbouring Land Act 1992 (s.5(6)); for vesting orders under the Leasehold Reform, Housing and Urban Development Act 1993, ss.26(1), 50(1) (s.97(2)); and for freezing orders under the International Criminal Court Act 2001, s.38, Sched. 6, para. 7(1)(b) (*ibid.*).

[26] subs. (4A) inserted by the Law Reform (Miscellaneous Provisions) Act 1994, s.15(1), (3).

(7) A pending land action shall not bind a purchaser without express notice of it unless it is for the time being registered under this section.

(8) A petition in bankruptcy shall not bind a purchaser of a legal estate in good faith, for money or money's worth, [. . .][27] unless it is for the time being registered under this section.

(9) [*Repealed by the Insolvency Act 1985, s.235(3), Sched. 10, Pt. III.*]

(10) The court, if it thinks fit, may, upon the determination of the proceedings, or during the pendency of the proceedings if satisfied that they are not prosecuted in good faith, make an order vacating a registration under this section, and direct the party on whose behalf it was made to pay all or any of the costs and expenses occasioned by the registration and by its vacation.

[(11) The county court has jurisdiction under subsection (10) of this section where the action was brought or the petition in bankruptcy was filed in that court.][28]

The register of writs and orders affecting land

31–006 **6.**[29]—(1) There may be registered in the register of writs and orders affecting land—

(a) any writ or order affecting land issued or made by any court for the purpose of enforcing a judgment or recognisance;

(b) any order appointing a receiver or sequestrator of land;

[(c) any bankruptcy order, whether or not the bankrupt's estate is known to include land][30];

[(d) any access order under the Access to Neighbouring Land Act 1992.][31]

[(1A) No writ or order affecting an interest under a trust of land may be registered under subsection (1) above.][32]

(2) Every entry made pursuant to this section shall be made in the name of the estate owner or other person whose land, if any, is affected by the writ or order registered.

[(2A) Where a person has died and any such writ or order as is mentioned in subsection (1)(a) or (b) above would apart from his death have been registered in his name, it shall be so registered notwithstanding his death.][33]

(3) No fee shall be charged for the registration of a [bankruptcy order][34] if the application for registration is made by an official receiver.

(4) Except as provided by subsection (5) below and by [section 37(5) of the Supreme Court Act 1981][35] and [section 107(3) of the County Courts Act 1984][36]

[27] Words repealed by the Insolvency Act 1985, s.235(1), (3), Sched. 8, para. 21(2), Sched. 10, Pt. III.

[28] subs. (11) added by the County Courts Act 1984, s.148(1), Sched. 2, Pt. IV, para. 17.

[29] This section applies to charging orders under the Charging Orders Act 1979 (s.3(2), *post*, para. 38–003); orders appointing managers under the Landlord and Tenant Act 1987, s.24 (s.24(8)); acquisition orders under the Landlord and Tenant Act 1987 (s.30(6)); restraint and charging orders under the Criminal Justice Act 1988, ss.77, 78 (ss.77(12)(a), 79); restraint orders under the Prevention of Terrorism (Temporary Provisions) Act 1989, s.13(8), Sched. 4, Pt. I, para. 3 (para. 6(1)(a)) and the Drug Trafficking Act 1994, ss.26, 27 (ss.26(12)(a), 28); charging orders under the Council Tax (Administration and Enforcement) Regulations 1992 (S.I. 1992 No. 613), reg. 50 (reg. 51(1), (6)); vesting orders under the Leasehold Reform, Housing and Urban Development Act 1993, ss.26(1), 50(1) (s.97(2)); and freezing orders under the International Criminal Court Act 2001, s.38, Sched. 6, para. 7(1)(a) (*ibid.*).

[30] Para. (c) substituted by the Insolvency Act 1985, s.235(1), Sched. 8, para. 21(1), (3)(a).

[31] Para. (d) added by the Access to Neighbouring Land Act 1992, s.5(1).

[32] subs. (1A) inserted by the Trusts of Land and Appointment of Trustees Act 1996, s.25(1), Sched. 3, para. 12(1), (3).

[33] subs. (2A) inserted by the Law Reform (Miscellaneous Provisions) Act 1994, s.15(1), (4).

[34] Words substituted by the Insolvency Act 1985, s.235(1), Sched. 8, para. 21(1), (3)(b).

[35] Words substituted by the Supreme Court Act 1981, s.152(1), Sched. 5.

[36] Words substituted by the County Courts Act 1984, s.148(1), Sched. 2, Pt. IV, para. 18.

(which makes special provision as to receiving orders in respect of land of judgment debtors) every such writ and order as is mentioned in subsection (1) above, and every delivery in execution or other proceeding taken pursuant to any such writ or order, or in obedience to any such writ or order, shall be void as against a purchaser of the land unless the writ or order is for the time being registered under this section.

[(5) Subject to subsection (6) below, the title of a trustee in bankruptcy shall be void as against a purchaser of a legal estate in good faith for money or money's worth unless the bankruptcy order is for the time being registered under this section.][37]

(6) Where a petition in bankruptcy has been registered under section 5 above, the title of the trustee in bankruptcy shall be void as against a purchaser of a legal estate in good faith for money or money's worth [...][38] claiming under a conveyance made after the date of registration, unless at the date of the conveyance either the registration of the petition is in force or a receiving order on the petition is registered under this section.

The register of deeds of arrangement affecting land

7.—(1) A deed of arrangement affecting land may be registered in the register **31–007** of deeds of arrangement affecting land, in the name of the debtor, on the application of a trustee of the deed or a creditor assenting to or taking the benefit of the deed.

(2) Every deed of arrangement shall be void as against a purchaser of any land comprised in it or affected by it unless it is for the time being registered under this section.

Expiry and renewal of registrations

8. A registration under section 5, section 6 or section 7 of this Act shall cease **31–008** to have effect at the end of the period of five years from the date on which it is made, but may be renewed from time to time and, if so renewed, shall have effect for five years from the date of renewal.

Searches and official searches

Searches

9.—(1) Any person may search in any register kept under this Act on paying **31–009** the prescribed fee.

(2) Without prejudice to subsection (1) above, the registrar may provide facilities for enabling persons entitled to search in any such register to see photographic or other images or copies of any portion of the register which they may wish to examine.

Official searches

10.—(1) Where any person requires search to be made at the registry for **31–010** entries of any matters or documents, entries of which are required or allowed to

[37] subs. (5) substituted by the Insolvency Act 1985, s.235(1), Sched. 8, para. 21(1), (3)(c).
[38] Words repealed by the Insolvency Act 1985, s.235(1), (3), Sched. 8, para. 21(1), (3)(d), Sched. 10, Pt. III.

be made in the registry by this Act, he may make a requisition in that behalf to the registrar, which may be either—

(a) a written requisition delivered at or sent by post to the registry; or

(b) a requisition communicated by teleprinter, telephone or other means in such manner as may be prescribed in relation to the means in question, in which case it shall be treated as made to the registrar if, but only if, he accepts it;

and the registrar shall not accept a requisition made in accordance with paragraph (b) above unless it is made by a person maintaining a credit account at the registry, and may at his discretion refuse to accept it notwithstanding that it is made by such a person.

(2) The prescribed fee shall be payable in respect of every requisition made under this section; and that fee—

(a) in the case of a requisition made in accordance with subsection (1)(a) above, shall be paid in such manner as may be prescribed for the purposes of this paragraph unless the requisition is made by a person maintaining a credit account at the registry and the fee is debited to that account;

(b) in the case of a requisition made in accordance with subsection (1)(b) above, shall be debited to the credit account of the person by whom the requisition is made.

(3) Where a requisition is made under subsection (1) above and the fee payable in respect of it is paid or debited in accordance with subsection (2) above, the registrar shall thereupon make the search required and—

(a) shall issue a certificate setting out the result of the search; and

(b) without prejudice to paragraph (a) above, may take such other steps as he considers appropriate to communicate that result to the person by whom the requisition was made.

(4) In favour of a purchaser or an intending purchaser, as against persons interested under or in respect of matters or documents entries of which are required or allowed as aforesaid, the certificate, according to its tenor, shall be conclusive, affirmatively or negatively, as the case may be.

(5) If any officer, clerk or person employed in the registry commits, or is party or privy to, any act of fraud or collusion, or is wilfully negligent, in the making of or otherwise in relation to any certificate under this section, he shall be guilty of an offence and shall be liable on conviction on indictment to imprisonment for a term not exceeding two years, or on summary conviction to imprisonment for a term not exceeding three months or to a fine not exceeding [the prescribed sum][39], or to both such imprisonment and fine.

(6) Without prejudice to subsection (5) above, no officer, clerk or person employed in the registry shall, in the absence of fraud on his part, be liable for any loss which may be suffered—

(a) by reason of any discrepancy between—

(i) the particulars which are shown in a certificate under this section as being the particulars in respect of which the search for entries was made, and

(ii) the particulars in respect of which a search for entries was required by the person who made the requisition; or

(b) by reason of any communication of the result of a search under this section made otherwise than by issuing a certificate under this section.

[39] Words substituted by virtue of the Magistrates' Courts Act 1980, s.32(2).

Miscellaneous and supplementary

Date of effective registration and priority notices

11.—(1) Any person intending to make an application for the registration of any contemplated charge, instrument or other matter in pursuance of this Act or any rule made under this Act may give a priority notice in the prescribed form at least the relevant number of days before the registration is to take effect. **31–011**

(2) Where a notice is given under subsection (1) above, it shall be entered in the register to which the intended application when made will relate.

(3) If the application is presented within the relevant number of days thereafter and refers in the prescribed manner to the notice, the registration shall take effect as if the registration had been made at the time when the charge, instrument or matter was created, entered into, made or arose, and the date at which the registration so takes effect shall be deemed to be the date of registration.

(4) Where—

(a) any two charges, instruments or matters are contemporaneous; and

(b) one of them (whether or not protected by a priority notice) is subject to or dependent on the other; and

(c) the latter is protected by a priority notice,

the subsequent or dependent charge, instrument or matter shall be deemed to have been created, entered into or made, or to have arisen, after the registration of the other.

(5) Where a purchaser has obtained a certificate under section 10 above, any entry which is made in the register after the date of the certificate and before the completion of the purchase, and is not made pursuant to a priority notice entered on the register on or before the date of the certificate, shall not affect the purchaser if the purchase is completed before the expiration of the relevant number of days after the date of the certificate.

(6) The relevant number of days is—

(a) for the purposes of subsections (1) and (5) above, fifteen;

(b) for the purposes of subsection (3) above, thirty;

or such other number as may be prescribed; but in reckoning the relevant number of days for any of the purposes of this section any days when the registry is not open to the public shall be excluded.

Protection of solicitors, trustees, etc.

12.[40] A solicitor, or a trustee, personal representative, agent or other person in a fiduciary position, shall not be answerable— **31–012**

(a) in respect of any loss occasioned by reliance on an office copy of an entry in any register kept under this Act;

(b) for any loss that may arise from error in a certificate under section 10 above obtained by him.

---

[40] In s.12 any reference to a solicitor is to be construed as including a reference to a licensed conveyancer or to a body recognised by the Council for Licensed Conveyancers as suitable to provide conveyancing services (Administration of Justice Act 1985, ss.32, 34(2)), or to an institution or practitioner recognised by the Lord Chancellor as suitable to provide such services (Building Societies Act 1986, s.124, Sched. 21).

Saving for overreaching powers

31–013 **13.**—(1) The registration of any charge, annuity or other interest under this Act shall not prevent the charge, annuity or interest being overreached under any other Act, except where otherwise provided by that other Act.

(2) The registration as a land charge of a puisne mortgage or charge shall not operate to prevent that mortgage or charge being overreached in favour of a prior mortgagee or a person deriving title under him where, by reason of a sale or foreclosure, or otherwise, the right of the puisne mortgagee or subsequent chargee to redeem is barred.

Exclusion of matters affecting registered land or created by instruments necessitating registration of land

31–014 **14.**—(1) This Act shall not apply to instruments or matters required to be registered or re-registered on or after 1st January 1926, if and so far as they affect registered land, and can be protected under the [Land Registration Act 2002][41].

(2) Nothing in this Act imposes on the registrar any obligation to ascertain whether or not an instrument or matter affects registered land.

(3) Where an instrument executed on or after 27th July 1971 conveys, grants or assigns an estate in land and creates a land charge affecting that estate, this Act shall not apply to the land charge, so far as it affects that estate, if under [section 7 of the Land Registration Act 2002 (effect of failure to comply with requirement of registration)][42] the instrument will, unless the necessary application for registration under that Act is made within the time allowed by or under [section 6 of that Act][43], become void so far as respects the conveyance, grant or assignment of that estate.

. . . . . .

Interpretation

31–015 **17.**—(1) In this Act, unless the context otherwise requires,—

"annuity" means a rentcharge or an annuity for a life or lives or for any term of years or greater estate determinable on a life or on lives and created after 25th April 1855 and before 1st January 1926, but does not include an annuity created by a marriage settlement or will;

"the Board" means the Commissioners of Inland Revenue;

"conveyance" includes a mortgage, charge, lease, assent, vesting declaration, vesting instrument, release and every other assurance of property, or of an interest in property, by any instrument except a will, and "convey" has a corresponding meaning;

"court" means the High Court, or the county court in a case where that court has jurisdiction;

"deed of arrangement" has the same meaning as in the Deeds of Arrangement Act 1914;

"estate owner", "legal estate", "equitable interest", [...][44] "charge by way of

[41] Words substituted by the Land Registration Act 2002, s.133, Sched. 11, para. 10(1), (2).
[42] Words substituted by the Land Registration Act 2002, s.133, Sched. 11, para. 10(1), (3).
[43] Words substituted by the Land Registration Act 2002, s.133, Sched. 11, para. 10(1), (3).
[44] Words repealed by the Trusts of Land and Appointment of Trustees Act 1996, s.25(2), Sched. 4.

legal mortgage", [and "will"][45] have the same meanings as in the Law of Property Act 1925;

"judgment" includes any order or decree having the effect of a judgment;

"land" includes land of any tenure and mines and minerals, whether or not severed from the surface, buildings or parts of buildings (whether the division is horizontal, vertical or made in any other way) and other corporeal hereditaments, also a manor, an advowson and a rent and other incorporeal hereditaments, and an easement, right, privilege or benefit in, over or derived from land, but not an undivided share in land, and "hereditament" means real property which, on an intestacy occurring before 1st January 1926, might have devolved on an heir;

"land improvement charge" means any charge under the Improvement of Land Act 1864 or under any special improvement Act within the meaning of the Improvement of Land Act 1899;

"pending land action" means any action or proceeding pending in court relating to land or any interest in or charge on land;

"prescribed" means prescribed by rules made pursuant to this Act;

"purchaser" means any person (including a mortgagee or lessee) who, for valuable consideration, takes any interest in land or in a charge on land, and "purchase" has a corresponding meaning;

"registrar" means the Chief Land Registrar, "registry" means Her Majesty's Land Registry, and "registered land" has the same meaning as in the [Land Registration Act 2002][46];

"tenant for life", "statutory owner", "vesting instrument" and "settlement" have the same meanings as in the Settled Land Act 1925.

(2) For the purposes of any provision in this Act requiring or authorising anything to be done at or delivered or sent to the registry, any reference to the registry shall, if the registrar so direct, be read as a reference to such office of the registry (whether in London or elsewhere) as may be specified in the direction.

(3) Any reference in this Act to any enactment is a reference to it as amended by or under any other enactment, including this Act.

. . . . . .

SCHEDULES

Section 1

SCHEDULE 1

ANNUITIES

1. No further entries shall be made in the register of annuities.

2. An entry of an annuity made in the register of annuities before 1st January 1926 may be vacated in the prescribed manner on the prescribed evidence as to satisfaction, cesser or discharge being furnished.

3. The register shall be closed when all the entries in it have been vacated or the prescribed evidence of the satisfaction, cesser or discharge of all the annuities has been furnished.

4. An annuity which before 1st January 1926 was capable of being registered in the register of annuities shall be void as against a creditor or a purchaser of any interest in the land charged with the

[45] Words substituted by the Finance Act 1975, s.52(1), Sched. 12, para. 18(1), (6).

[46] Words substituted by the Land Registration Act 2002, s.133, Sched. 11, para. 10(1), (4).

annuity unless the annuity is for the time being registered in the register of annuities or in the register of land charges.

Section 2

SCHEDULE 2

CLASS A LAND CHARGES

1. Charges created pursuant to applications under the enactments mentioned in this Schedule may be registered as land charges of Class A by virtue of paragraph (b) of section 2(2) of this Act:—

(a) The Tithe Act 1918 (8 & 9 Geo. 5, c. 54)	Sections 4(2) and 6(1) (charge of consideration money for redemption of tithe rentcharge).
(b) The Tithe Annuities Apportionment Act 1921 (11 & 12 Geo. 5, c. 20)	Section 1 (charge of apportioned part of tithe redemption annuity).
(c) The Landlord and Tenant Act 1927 (17 & 18 Geo. 5, c. 36)	Paragraph (7) of Schedule 1 (charge in respect of improvements to business premises).
(d) [The Land Drainage Act 1991 (c. 60)][47]	[Section 34(2)][48] (charge in respect of sum paid in commutation of certain obligations to repair banks, water-courses etc.).
(e) The Tithe Act 1936 (26 Geo. 5 & 1 Edw. 8, c. 43)	Section 30(1) (charge for redemption of corn rents etc.).
(f) The Civil Defence Act 1939 (2 & 3 Geo. 6, c. 31)	Sections 18(4) and 19(1) (charges in respect of civil defence works).
(g) The Agricultural Holdings Act 1948 (11 & 12 Geo. 6, c. 63)	[Section 74 (charges in respect of sums due to][49] occupier of agricultural holding). [. . .][50]
(h) The Corn Rents Act 1963 (1963 c. 14)	Section 1(5) (charge under a scheme for the apportionment or redemption of corn rents or other payments in lieu of tithes).
[(i) The Agricultural Holdings Act 1986	Section 85 (charges in respect of sums due to tenant of agricultural holding). Section 86 (charges in favour of landlord of agricultural holding in respect of compensation for or cost of certain improvements).][51]

2. The following provisions of paragraph 1 above shall cease to have effect upon the coming into operation of the first scheme under the Corn Rents Act 1963, that is to say:—

(a) in sub-paragraph (a), the words "and 6(1)"; and

(b) sub-paragraph (e).

3. [The reference in paragraph 1(g) above to section 74 of the Agricultural Holdings Act 1948 and the references in paragraph 1(i) above to section 85 and 86 of the Agricultural Holdings Act 1986][52] include references to any previous similar enactment.

---

47 Words substituted by the Water Consolidation (Consequential Provisions) Act 1991, s.2(1), Sched. 1, para. 21.

48 Words substituted by the Water Consolidation (Consequential Provisions) Act 1991, s.2(1), Sched. 1, para. 21.

49 Words substituted by the Agricultural Holdings Act 1986, s.100, Sched. 14, para. 51.

50 Words repealed by the Agricultural Holdings Act 1986, ss.100, 101(1), Sched. 14, para. 51, Sched. 15, Pt. I.

51 Sub-para. (i) added by the Agricultural Holdings Act 1986, s.100, Sched. 14, para. 51.

52 Words substituted by the Agricultural Holdings Act 1986, s.100, Sched. 14, para. 51.

Administration of Justice Act 1973

(1973 c. 15)

Extension of powers of court in action by mortgagee of dwelling-house

8.[1]—(1) Where by a mortgage of land which consists of or includes a dwelling-house, or by any agreement between the mortgagee under such a mortgage and the mortgagor, the mortgagor is entitled or is to be permitted to pay the principal sum secured by instalments or otherwise to defer payment of it in whole or in part, but provision is also made for earlier payment in the event of any default by the mortgagor or of a demand by the mortgagee or otherwise, then for purposes of section 36 of the Administration of Justice Act 1970 (under which a court has power to delay giving a mortgagee possession of the mortgaged property so as to allow the mortgagor a reasonable time to pay any sums due under the mortgage) a court may treat as due under the mortgage on account of the principal sum secured and of interest on it only such amounts as the mortgagor would have expected to be required to pay if there had been no such provision for earlier payment. **32–001**

(2) A court shall not exercise by virtue of subsection (1) above the powers conferred by section 36 of the Administration of Justice Act 1970 unless it appears to the court not only that the mortgagor is likely to be able within a reasonable period to pay any amounts regarded (in accordance with subsection (1) above) as due on account of the principal sum secured, together with the interest on those amounts, but also that he is likely to be able by the end of that period to pay any further amounts that he would have expected to be required to pay by then on account of that sum and of interest on it if there had been no such provision as is referred to in subsection (1) above for earlier payment.

(3) Where subsection (1) above would apply to an action in which a mortgagee only claimed possession of the mortgaged property, and the mortgagee brings an action for foreclosure (with or without also claiming possession of the property), then section 36 of the Administration of Justice Act 1970 together with subsections (1) and (2) above shall apply as they would apply if it were an action in which the mortgagee only claimed possession of the mortgaged property, except that—

(a) section 36(2)(b) shall apply only in relation to any claim for possession; and

(b) section 36(5) shall not apply.

(4) For purposes of this section the expressions "dwelling-house", "mortgage", "mortgagee" and "mortgagor" shall be construed in the same way as for the purposes of Part IV of the Administration of Justice Act 1970.

(5) This section shall have effect in relation to an action begun before the date on which this section comes into force if before that date judgment has not been given, nor an order made, in that action for delivery of possession of the mortgaged property and, where it is a question of subsection (3) above, an order *nisi* for foreclosure has not been made in that action.

[1] See the Administration of Justice Act 1970, s.36, *ante*, para. 28–001.

(6) In the application of this section to Northern Ireland, subsection (3) shall be omitted.

Consumer Credit Act 1974

(1974 c. 39)

PART II

CREDIT AGREEMENTS, HIRE AGREEMENTS AND LINKED TRANSACTIONS

Consumer credit agreements

33–001 **8.**—(1) A personal credit agreement is an agreement between an individual ("the debtor") and any other person ("the creditor") by which the creditor provides the debtor with credit of any amount.

(2) A consumer credit agreement is a personal credit agreement by which the creditor provides the debtor with credit not exceeding [£25,000][1].

(3) A consumer credit agreement is a regulated agreement within the meaning of this Act if it is not an agreement (an "exempt agreement") specified in or under section 16.

Exempt agreements

33–002 **16.**—(1) This Act does not regulate a consumer credit agreement where the creditor is a local authority […][2], or a body specified, or of a description specified, in an order made by the Secretary of State, being—

[(a) an insurer;][3]

(b) a friendly society,

(c) an organisation of employers or organisation of workers,

(d) a charity,

(e) a land improvement company, […][4]

(f) a body corporate named or specifically referred to in any public general Act [, or

[(ff) a body corporate named or specifically referred to in an order made under—

section 156(4), […][5] or 447(2)(a) of the Housing Act 1985, [section 156(4) of that Act as it has effect by virtue of section 17 of the Housing Act 1996 (the right to acquire),][6]

[1] Figure substituted by the Consumer Credit (Increase of Monetary Limits) Order 1983 (S.I. 1983 No. 1878), art. 4, Sched., Pt. II, as amended by the Consumer Credit (Increase of Monetary Limits) (Amendment) Order 1998 (S.I. 1998 No. 996), art. 2.

[2] Words repealed by the Building Societies Act 1986, s.120(1), (2), Sched. 18, Pt. I, para. 10(1), (2), Sched. 19, Pt. I.

[3] Para. (a) substituted by the Financial Services and Markets Act 2000 (Consequential Amendments and Repeals) Order 2001 (S.I. 2001 No. 3649), art. 165(1), (2)(a).

[4] Word repealed by the Building Societies Act 1986, s.120(2), Sched. 19, Pt. I.

[5] Section number repealed by the Housing Act 1996, s.227, Sched. 19, Pt. XIV.

[6] Words inserted by the Housing Act 1996 (Consequential Amendments) (No. 2) Order 1997 (S.I. 1997 No. 627), art. 2, Sched., para. 2.

section 2 of the Home Purchase Assistance and Housing Corporation Guarantee Act 1978 or section 31 of the Tenants' Rights, etc. (Scotland) Act 1980, or

Article 154(1)(a) or 156AA of the Housing (Northern Ireland) Order 1981 or Article 10(6A) of the Housing (Northern Ireland) Order 1983; or][7]

[(g) a building society][8] [, or

[(h) a deposit-taker.][9]][10]

(2) Subsection (1) applies only where the agreement is—

(a) a debtor–creditor–supplier agreement financing—

(i) the purchase of land, or

(ii) the provision of dwellings on any land,

and secured by a land mortgage on that land; or

(b) a debtor–creditor agreement secured by any land mortgage; or

(c) a debtor–creditor–supplier agreement financing a transaction which is a linked transaction in relation to—

(i) an agreement falling within paragraph (a), or

(ii) an agreement falling within paragraph (b) financing—

(aa) the purchase of any land, or

(bb) the provision of dwellings on any land,

and secured by a land mortgage on the land referred to in paragraph (a) or, as the case may be, the land referred to in sub-paragraph (ii).

[(3) Before he makes, varies or revokes an order under subsection (1), the Secretary of state must undertake the necessary consultation.

(3A) The necessary consultation means consultation with the bodies mentioned in the following table in relation to the provision under which the order is to be made, varied or revoked:

TABLE

Provision of subsection (1)	*Consultee*
Paragraph (a) or (b)	The Financial Services Authority
Paragraph (d)	The Charity Commissioners
Paragraph (e), (f), or (ff)	Any Minister of the Crown with responsibilities in relation to the body in question
Paragraph (g) or (h)	The Treasury and the Financial Services Authority.][11]

(4) An order under subsection (1) relating to a body may be limited so as to apply only to agreements by that body of a description specified in the order.

(5) The Secretary of State may by order provide that this Act shall not regulate other consumer credit agreements where—

(a) the number of payments to be made by the debtor does not exceed the number specified for that purpose in the order, or

---

[7] Para. (ff) inserted by the Housing and Planning Act 1986, s.22(2).

[8] Para. (g) added by the Building Societies Act 1986, s.120(1), Sched. 18, Pt. I, para. 10(1), (2).

[9] Para. (h) substituted by the Financial Services and Markets Act 2000 (Consequential Amendments and Repeals) Order 2001 (S.I. 2001 No. 3649), art. 165(1), (2)(b).

[10] Words added by the Banking Act 1987, s.88(2).

[11] subss. (3) and (3A) substituted (for subs. (3) by the Financial Services and Markets Act 2000 (Consequential Amendments and Repeals) Order 2001 (S.I. 2001 No. 3649), art. 165(1), (3).

(b) the rate of the total charge for credit does not exceed the rate so specified, or

(c) an agreement has a connection with a country outside the United Kingdom.

(6) The Secretary of State may by order provide that this Act shall not regulate consumer hire agreements of a description specified in the order where—

(a) the owner is a body corporate authorised by or under any enactment to supply electricity, gas or water, and

(b) the subject of the agreement is a meter or metering equipment,

[or where the owner is a public telecommunications operator specified in the order][12].

[(6A) This Act does not regulate a consumer credit agreement where the creditor is a housing authority and the agreement is secured by a land mortgage of a dwelling.

(6B) In subsection (6A) "housing authority" means—

(a) as regards England and Wales, [the Housing Corporation [...][13] and][14] an authority or body within section 80(1) of the Housing Act 1985 (the landlord condition for secure tenancies), other than a housing association or a housing trust which is a charity;

(b) as regards Scotland, a development corporation established under an order made, or having effect as if made under the New Towns (Scotland) Act 1968, the Scottish Special Housing Association or the Housing Corporation;

(c) as regards Northern Ireland, the Northern Ireland Housing Executive.][15]

[(6C) This Act does not regulate a consumer credit agreement if—

(a) it is secured by a land mortgage; and

(b) entering into that agreement as lender is a regulated activity for the purposes of the Financial Services and Markets Act 2000.

(6D) But section 126, and any other provisions so far as it relates to section 126, applies to an agreement which would (but for subsection (6C)) be a regulated agreement.

(6E) Subsection (6C) must be read with—

(a) section 22 of the Financial Services and Markets Act 2000 (regulated activities: power to specify classes of activity and categories of investment);

(b) any order for the time being in force under that section; and

(c) Schedule 2 to that Act.][16]

(7) Nothing in this section affects the application of sections 137 to 140 (extortionate credit bargains).

[(8) In the application of this section to Scotland, subsection (3A) shall have effect as if the reference to the Charity Commissioners were a reference to the Lord Advocate.][17]

(9) In the application of this section to Northern Ireland [subsection (3A)][18]

[12] Words substituted by the Telecommunications Act 1984, s.109(1), Sched. 4, para. 60(1).

[13] Words repealed by the Government of Wales Act 1998, s.152, Sched. 18, Pt. VI.

[14] Words inserted by the Housing Act 1988, s.140(1), Sched. 17, para. 20.

[15] subss. (6A) and (6B) inserted by the Housing and Planning Act 1986, s.22(3).

[16] subss. (6C)–(6E) inserted by the Financial Services and Markets Act 2000 (Regulated Activities (Order 2001 (S.I. 2001 No 544), art. 90(1), (2).

[17] subs. (8) substituted by the Financial Services and Markets Act 2000 (Consequential Amendments and Repeals) Order 2001 (S.I. 2001 No. 3649), art. 165(1), (4).

[18] Words substituted by the Financial Services and Markets Act 2000 (Consequential Amendments and Repeals) Order 2001 (S.I. 2001 No. 3649), art. 165(1), (5)(a).

shall have effect as if any reference to a Minister of the Crown were a reference to a Northern Ireland department, [...][19], and any reference to the Charity Commissioners were a reference to the Department of Finance for Northern Ireland.

[(10) In this section—

(a) "deposit-taker" means—

(i) a person who has permission under Part 4 of the Financial Services and Markets Act 2000 to accept deposits,

(ii) An EEA firm of the kind in paragraph 5(b) of Schedule 3 to that Act which has permission under paragraph 15 of that Schedule (as a result of qualifying for authorisation under paragraph 12 of that Schedule) to accept deposits,

(iii) Any wholly owned subsidiary (within the meaning of the Companies Act 1985) of a person mentioned in sub-paragraph (i), or

(iv) Any undertaking which, in relation to a person in subparagraph (ii), is a subsidiary undertaking within the meaning of any rule of law in force in the EEA State in question for purposes connected with the implementation of the European Council Seventh Company Law directive of 13 June 1983 on consolidated accounts (No. 83/349/EEC), and which has no members other than that person;

(b) "insurer" means—

(i) a person who has permission under Part 4 of the Financial Services and Markets Act 2000 to effect or carry out contracts of insurance, or

(ii) an EEA firm of the kind mentioned in paragraph 5(d) of Schedule 3 to that Act, which has permission under paragraph 15 of that schedule (as a result of qualifying for authorisation under paragraph 12 of the Schedule) to effect or carry out contracts of insurance;

but does not include a friendly society or an organisation of workers or of employers.

(11) Subsection (10) must be read with—

(a) section 22 of the Financial Services and Markets Act 2000;

(b) any relevant order under that section; and

(c) Schedule 2 to that Act.][20]

. . . . . .

[19] Words repealed by the Financial Services and Markets Act 2000 (Consequential Amendments and Repeals) Order 2001 (S.I. 2001 No. 3649), art. 165(1), (5)(b).

[20] subss. (10) and (11) added by the Financial Services and Markets Act 2000 (Consequential Amendments and Repeals) Order 2001 (S.I. 2001 No. 3649), art. 165(1), (6).

Part V

Entry into Credit or Hire Agreements

Preliminary matters

Opportunity for withdrawal from prospective land mortgage

33–003 **58.**—(1) Before sending to the debtor or hirer, for his signature, an unexecuted agreement in a case where the prospective regulated agreement is to be secured on land (the "mortgaged land"), the creditor or owner shall give the debtor or hirer a copy of the unexecuted agreement which contains a notice in the prescribed form indicating the right of the debtor or hirer to withdraw from the prospective agreement, and how and when the right is exercisable, together with a copy of any other document referred to in the unexecuted agreement.

(2) Subsection (1) does not apply to—

(a) a restricted-use credit agreement to finance the purchase of the mortgaged land, or

(b) an agreement for a bridging loan in connection with the purchase of the mortgaged land or other land.

. . . . . .

Part VII

Default and Termination

Further restriction of remedies for default

Recovery of possession of goods or land

33–004 **92.**—(1) Except under an order of the court, the creditor or owner shall not be entitled to enter any premises to take possession of goods subject to a regulated hire-purchase agreement, regulated conditional sale agreement or regulated consumer hire agreement.

(2) At any time when the debtor is in breach of a regulated conditional sale agreement relating to land, the creditor is entitled to recover possession of the land from the debtor, or any person claiming under him, on an order of the court only.

(3) An entry in contravention of subsection (1) or (2) is actionable as a breach of statutory duty.

. . . . . .

Part VIII

Security

Land mortgages

Enforcement of land mortgages

33–005 **126.** A land mortgage securing a regulated agreement is enforceable (so far as provided in relation to the agreement) on an order of the court only.

. . . . . .

Part IX

Judicial Control

Extortionate credit bargains[21]

Extortionate credit bargains

137.—(1) If the court finds a credit bargain extortionate it may reopen the credit agreement so as to do justice between the parties. **33–006**

(2) In this section and sections 138 to 140,—

(a) "credit agreement" means any agreement [(other than an agreement which is an exempt agreement as a result of section 16(6C))][22] between an individual (the "debtor") and any other person (the "creditor") by which the creditor provides the debtor with credit of any amount, and

(b) "credit bargain"—

(i) where no transaction other than the credit agreement is to be taken into account in computing the total charge for credit, means the credit agreement, or

(ii) where one or more other transactions are to be so taken into account, means the credit agreement and those other transactions, taken together.

When bargains are extortionate

138.—(1) A credit bargain is extortionate if it— **33–007**

(a) requires the debtor or a relative of his to make payments (whether unconditionally, or on certain contingencies) which are grossly exorbitant, or

(b) otherwise grossly contravenes ordinary principles of fair dealing.

(2) In determining whether a credit bargain is extortionate, regard shall be had to such evidence as is adduced concerning—

(a) interest rates prevailing at the time it was made,

(b) the factors mentioned in subsection (3) to (5), and

(c) any other relevant considerations.

(3) Factors applicable under subsection (2) in relation to the debtor include—

(a) his age, experience, business capacity and state of health; and

(b) the degree to which, at the time of making the credit bargain, he was under financial pressure, and the nature of that pressure.

(4) Factors applicable under subsection (2) in relation to the creditor include—

(a) the degree of risk accepted by him, having regard to the value of any security provided;

(b) his relationship to the debtor; and

(c) whether or not a colourable cash price was quoted for any goods or services included in the credit bargain.

[21] See also the Insolvency Act 1986, s.343, *post*, para. 47–014.

[22] Words inserted by the Financial Services and Markets Act 2000 (Regulated Activities) Order 2001 (S.I. 2001 No 544), art. 90(1), (6).

(5) Factors applicable under subsection (2) in relation to a linked transaction include the question how far the transaction was reasonably required for the protection of debtor or creditor, or was in the interest of the debtor.

Reopening of extortionate agreements[23]

33–008 **139.**—(1) A credit agreement may, if the court thinks just, be reopened on the ground that the credit bargain is extortionate—

(a) on an application for the purpose made by the debtor or any surety to the High Court, county court or sheriff court; or
(b) at the instance of the debtor or a surety in any proceedings to which the debtor and creditor are parties, being proceedings to enforce the credit agreement, any security relating to it, or any linked transaction; or
(c) at the instance of the debtor or a surety in other proceedings in any court where the amount paid or payable under the credit agreement is relevant.

(2) In reopening the agreement, the court may, for the purpose of relieving the debtor or a surety from payment of any sum in excess of that fairly due and reasonable, by order—

(a) direct accounts to be taken, or (in Scotland) an accounting to be made, between any persons,
(b) set aside the whole or part of any obligation imposed on the debtor or a surety by the credit bargain or any related agreement,
(c) require the creditor to repay the whole or part of any sum paid under the credit bargain or any related agreement by the debtor or a surety, whether paid to the creditor or any other person,
(d) direct the return to the surety of any property provided for the purposes of the security, or
(e) alter the terms of the credit agreement or any security instrument.

(3) An order may be made under subsection (2) notwithstanding that its effect is to place a burden on the creditor in respect of an advantage unfairly enjoyed by another person who is a party to a linked transaction.

(4) An order under subsection (2) shall not alter the effect of any judgment.

(5) In England and Wales an application under subsection (1)(a) shall be brought only in the county court in the case of—

(a) a regulated agreement, or
(b) an agreement (not being a regulated agreement) under which the creditor provides the debtor with fixed-sum credit […][24] or running-account credit […][25]

(5A) [*Repealed by the High Court and County Courts Jurisdiction Order 1991 (S.I. 1991 No. 724), art. 2(8), Sched.*][26]

. . . . . .

[23] See the Insolvency Act 1986, s.343(6), *post*, para. 47–014.
[24] Words repealed by the High Court and County Courts Jurisdiction Order 1991 (S.I. 1991 No. 724), art. 2(8), Sched.
[25] Words repealed by the High Court and County Courts Jurisdiction Order 1991 (S.I. 1991 No. 724), art. 2(8), Sched.
[26] subs. (5A) originally inserted by the Administration of Justice Act 1982, s.37, Sched. 3, Pt. II, para. 4.

Interpretation of sections 137 to 139

140. Where the credit agreement is not a regulated agreement, expressions used in sections 137 to 139 which, apart from this section, apply only to regulated agreements, shall be construed as nearly as may be as if the credit agreement were a regulated agreement. **33–009**

Inheritance (Provision for Family and Dependants) Act 1975[1]

(1975 c. 63)

Arrangement of Sections

Powers of court to order financial provision from deceased's estate

SECT.

---

[1] All amendments made by the Family Law Act 1996 are prospective amendments and take effect from a day to be appointed: Family Law Act 1996, s.67(3).

Application for financial provision from deceased's estate

34–001 **1.**—(1) Where after the commencement of this Act a person dies domiciled in England and Wales and is survived by any of the following persons:—

(a) the wife or husband of the deceased;
(b) a former wife or former husband of the deceased who has not remarried;
[(ba) any person (not being a person included in paragraph (a) or (b) above) to whom subsection (1A) below applies;][2]
(c) a child of the deceased;
(d) any person (not being a child of the deceased) who, in the case of any marriage to which the deceased was at any time a party, was treated by the deceased as a child of the family in relation to that marriage;
(e) any person (not being a person included in the foregoing paragraphs of this subsection) who immediately before the death of the deceased was being maintained, either wholly or partly, by the deceased;

that person may apply to the court for an order under section 2 of this Act on the ground that the disposition of the deceased's estate effected by his will or the law relating to intestacy, or the combination of his will and that law, is not such as to make reasonable financial provision for the applicant.

[(1A) This subsection applies to a person if the deceased died on or after 1st January 1996 and, during the whole of the period of two years ending immediately before the date when the deceased died, the person was living—

(a) in the same household as the deceased, and
(b) as the husband or wife of the deceased.][3]

(2) In this Act "reasonable financial provision"—

(a) in the case of an application made by virtue of subsection (1)(a) above by the husband or wife of the deceased (except where [, at the date of death, a separation order under the Family Law Act 1996 was in force in relation to the marriage][4] and the separation was continuing), means such financial provision as it would be reasonable in all the circumstances of the case for a husband or wife to receive, whether or not that provision is required for his or her maintenance;
(b) in the case of any other application made by virtue of subsection (1) above, means such financial provision as it would be reasonable in all the circumstances of the case for the applicant to receive for his maintenance.

(3) For the purposes of subsection (1)(e) above, a person shall be treated as being maintained by the deceased, either wholly or partly, as the case may be, if the deceased, otherwise than for full valuable consideration, was making a substantial contribution in money or money's worth towards the reasonable needs of that person.

Powers of court to make orders

34–002 **2.**—(1) Subject to the provisions of this Act, where an application is made for an order under this section, the court may, if it is satisfied that the disposition of

[2] Para. (ba) inserted by the Law Reform (Succession) Act 1995, s.2(1), (2).
[3] subs. (1A) inserted by the Law Reform (Succession) Act 1995, s.2(1), (3).
[4] Words substituted by the Family Law Act 1996, s.66(1), Sched. 8, Pt. I, para. 27(1), (2).

the deceased's estate effected by his will or the law relating to intestacy, or the combination of his will and that law, is not such as to make reasonable financial provision for the applicant, make any one or more of the following orders:—

(a) an order for the making to the applicant out of the net estate of the deceased of such periodical payments and for such term as may be specified in the order;
(b) an order for the payment to the applicant out of that estate of a lump sum of such amount as may be so specified;
(c) an order for the transfer to the applicant of such property comprised in that estate as may be so specified;
(d) an order for the settlement for the benefit of the applicant of such property comprised in that estate as may be so specified;
(e) an order for the acquisition out of property comprised in that estate of such property as may be so specified and for the transfer of the property so acquired to the applicant or for the settlement thereof for his benefit;
(f) an order varying any ante-nuptial or post-nuptial settlement (including such a settlement made by will) made on the parties to a marriage to which the deceased was one of the parties, the variation being for the benefit of the surviving party to that marriage, or any child of that marriage, or any person who was treated by the deceased as a child of the family in relation to that marriage.

(2) An order under subsection (1)(a) above providing for the making out of the net estate of the deceased of periodical payments may provide for—

(a) payments of such amount as may be specified in the order,
(b) payments equal to the whole of the income of the net estate or of such portion thereof as may be so specified,
(c) payments equal to the whole of the income of such part of the net estate as the court may direct to be set aside or appropriated for the making out of the income thereof of payments under this section,

or may provide for the amount of the payments or any of them to be determined in any other way the court thinks fit.

(3) Where an order under subsection (1)(a) above provides for the making of payments of an amount specified in the order, the order may direct that such part of the net estate as may be so specified shall be set aside or appropriated for the making out of the income thereof of those payments; but no larger part of the net estate shall be so set aside or appropriated than is sufficient, at the date of the order, to produce by the income thereof the amount required for the making of those payments.

(4) An order under this section may contain such consequential and supplemental provisions as the court thinks necessary or expedient for the purpose of giving effect to the order or for the purpose of securing that the order operates fairly as between one beneficiary of the estate of the deceased and another and may, in particular, but without prejudice to the generality of this subsection—

(a) order any person who holds any property which forms part of the net estate of the deceased to make such payment or transfer such property as may be specified in the order;
(b) vary the disposition of the deceased's estate effected by the will or the law relating to intestacy, or by both the will and the law relating to intestacy, in such manner as the court thinks fair and reasonable having regard to the provisions of the order and all the circumstances of the case;

(c) confer on the trustees of any property which is the subject of an order under this section such powers as appear to the court to be necessary or expedient.

Matters to which court is to have regard in exercising powers under s.2

34–003 **3.**—(1) Where an application is made for an order under section 2 of this Act, the court shall, in determining whether the disposition of the deceased's estate effected by his will or the law relating to intestacy, or the combination of his will and that law, is such as to make reasonable financial provision for the applicant and, if the court considers that reasonable financial provision has not been made, in determining whether and in what manner it shall exercise its powers under that section, have regard to the following matters, that is to say—

(a) the financial resources and financial needs which the applicant has or is likely to have in the foreseeable future;
(b) the financial resources and financial needs which any other applicant for an order under section 2 of this Act has or is likely to have in the foreseeable future;
(c) the financial resources and financial needs which any beneficiary of the estate of the deceased has or is likely to have in the foreseeable future;
(d) any obligations and responsibilities which the deceased had towards any applicant for an order under the said section 2 or towards any beneficiary of the estate of the deceased;
(e) the size and nature of the net estate of the deceased;
(f) any physical or mental disability of any applicant for an order under the said section 2 or any beneficiary of the estate of the deceased;
(g) any other matter, including the conduct of the applicant or any other person, which in the circumstances of the case the court may consider relevant.

(2) Without prejudice to the generality of paragraph (g) of subsection (1) above, where an application for an order under section 2 of this Act is made by virtue of section 1(1)(a) or 1(1)(b) of this Act, the court shall, in addition to the matters specifically mentioned in paragraphs (a) to (f) of that subsection, have regard to—

(a) the age of the applicant and the duration of the marriage;
(b) the contribution made by the applicant to the welfare of the family of the deceased, including any contribution made by looking after the home or caring for the family;

and, in the case of an application by the wife or husband of the deceased, the court shall also, unless at the date of death a [separation order under the Family Law Act 1996][5] was in force and the separation was continuing, have regard to the provision which the applicant might reasonably have expected to receive if on the day on which the deceased died the marriage, instead of being terminated by death, had been terminated by [a divorce order][6].

[(2A) Without prejudice to the generality of paragraph (g) of subsection (1) above, where an application for an order under section 2 of this Act is made by virtue of section 1(1)(ba) of this Act, the court shall, in addition to the matters specifically mentioned in paragraphs (a) to (f) of that subsection, have regard to—

[5] Words substituted by the Family Law Act 1996, s.66(1), Sched. 8, Pt. I, para. 27(1), (3).
[6] Words substituted by the Family Law Act 1996, s.66(1), Sched. 8, Pt. I, para. 27(1), (3).

(a) the age of the applicant and the length of the period during which the applicant lived as the husband or wife of the deceased and in the same household as the deceased;

(b) the contribution made by the applicant to the welfare of the family of the deceased, including any contribution made by looking after the home or caring for the family.][7]

(3) Without prejudice to the generality of paragraph (g) of subsection (1) above, where an application for an order under section 2 of this Act is made by virtue of section 1(1)(c) or 1(1)(d) of this Act, the court shall, in addition to the matters specifically mentioned in paragraphs (a) to (f) of that subsection, have regard to the manner in which the applicant was being or in which he might expect to be educated or trained, and where the application is made by virtue of section 1(1)(d) the court shall also have regard—

(a) to whether the deceased had assumed any responsibility for the applicant's maintenance and, if so, to the extent to which and the basis upon which the deceased assumed that responsibility and to the length of time for which the deceased discharged that responsibility;

(b) to whether in assuming and discharging that responsibility the deceased did so knowing that the applicant was not his own child;

(c) to the liability of any other person to maintain the applicant.

(4) Without prejudice to the generality of paragraph (g) of subsection (1) above, where an application for an order under section 2 of this Act is made by virtue of section 1(1)(e) of this Act, the court shall, in addition to the matters specifically mentioned in paragraphs (a) to (f) of that subsection, have regard to the extent to which and the basis upon which the deceased assumed responsibility for the maintenance of the applicant and to the length of time for which the deceased discharged that responsibility.

(5) In considering the matters to which the court is required to have regard under this section, the court shall take into account the facts as known to the court at the date of the hearing.

(6) In considering the financial resources of any person for the purposes of this section the court shall take into account his earning capacity and in considering the financial needs of any person for the purposes of this section the court shall take into account his financial obligations and responsibilities.

Time-limit for applications

4. An application for an order under section 2 of this Act shall not, except with the permission of the court, be made after the end of the period of six months from the date on which representation with respect to the estate of the deceased is first taken out. **34–004**

Interim orders

5.—(1) Where on an application for an order under section 2 of this Act it appears to the court— **34–005**

(a) that the applicant is in immediate need of financial assistance, but it is not yet possible to determine what order (if any) should be made under that section; and

(b) that property forming part of the net estate of the deceased is or can be made available to meet the need of the applicant;

[7] subs. (2A) inserted by the Law Reform (Succession) Act 1995, s.2(1), (4).

the court may order that, subject to such conditions or restrictions, if any, as the court may impose and to any further order of the court, there shall be paid to the applicant out of the net estate of the deceased such sum or sums and (if more than one) at such intervals as the court thinks reasonable; and the court may order that, subject to the provisions of this Act, such payments are to be made until such date as the court may specify, not being later than the date on which the court either makes an order under the said section 2 or decides not to exercise its powers under that section.

(2) Subsections (2), (3) and (4) of section 2 of this Act shall apply in relation to an order under this section as they apply in relation to an order under that section.

(3) In determining what order, if any, should be made under this section the court shall, so far as the urgency of the case admits, have regard to the same matters as those to which the court is required to have regard under section 3 of this Act.

(4) An order made under section 2 of this Act may provide that any sum paid to the applicant by virtue of this section shall be treated to such an extent and in such manner as may be provided by that order as having been paid on account of any payment provided for by that order.

Variation, discharge, etc. of orders for periodical payments

34–006 **6.**—(1) Subject to the provisions of this Act, where the court has made an order under section 2(1)(a) of this Act (in this section referred to as "the original order") for the making of periodical payments to any person (in this section referred to as "the original recipient"), the court, on an application under this section, shall have power by order to vary or discharge the original order or to suspend any provision of it temporarily and to revive the operation of any provision so suspended.

(2) Without prejudice to the generality of subsection (1) above, an order made on an application for the variation of the original order may—

(a) provide for the making out of any relevant property of such periodical payments and for such term as may be specified in the order to any person who has applied, or would but for section 4 of this Act be entitled to apply, for an order under section 2 of this Act (whether or not, in the case of any application, an order was made in favour of the applicant);
(b) provide for the payment out of any relevant property of a lump sum of such amount as may be so specified to the original recipient or to any such person as is mentioned in paragraph (a) above;
(c) provide for the transfer of the relevant property, or such part thereof as may be so specified, to the original recipient or to any such person as is so mentioned.

(3) Where the original order provides that any periodical payments payable thereunder to the original recipient are to cease on the occurrence of an event specified in the order (other than the remarriage of a former wife or former husband) or on the expiration of a period so specified, then, if, before the end of the period of six months from the date of the occurrence of that event or of the expiration of that period, an application is made for an order under this section, the court shall have power to make an order which it would have had power to make if the application had been made before that date (whether in favour of the original recipient or any such person as is mentioned in subsection (2)(a) above and whether having effect from that date or from such later date as the court may specify).

(4) Any reference in this section to the original order shall include a reference to an order made under this section and any reference in this section to the original recipient shall include a reference to any person to whom periodical payments are required to be made by virtue of an order under this section.

(5) An application under this section may be made by any of the following persons, that is to say—

(a) any person who by virtue of section 1(1) of this Act has applied, or would but for section 4 of this Act be entitled to apply, for an order under section 2 of this Act,

(b) the personal representatives of the deceased,

(c) the trustees of any relevant property, and

(d) any beneficiary of the estate of the deceased.

(6) An order under this section may only affect—

(a) property the income of which is at the date of the order applicable wholly or in part for the making of periodical payments to any person who has applied for an order under this Act, or

(b) in the case of an application under subsection (3) above in respect of payments which have ceased to be payable on the occurrence of an event or the expiration of a period, property the income of which was so applicable immediately before the occurrence of that event or the expiration of that period, as the case may be,

and any such property as is mentioned in paragraph (a) or (b) above is in subsections (2) and (5) above referred to as "relevant property".

(7) In exercising the powers conferred by this section the court shall have regard to all the circumstances of the case, including any change in any of the matters to which the court was required to have regard when making the order to which the application relates.

(8) Where the court makes an order under this section, it may give such consequential directions as it thinks necessary or expedient having regard to the provisions of the order.

(9) No such order as is mentioned in sections 2(1)(d), (e) or (f), 9, 10 or 11 of this Act shall be made on an application under this section.

(10) For the avoidance of doubt it is hereby declared that, in relation to an order which provides for the making of periodical payments which are to cease on the occurrence of an event specified in the order (other than the remarriage of a former wife or former husband) or on the expiration of a period so specified, the power to vary an order includes power to provide for the making of periodical payments after the expiration of that period or the occurrence of that event.

Payment of lump sums by instalments

7.—(1) An order under section 2(1)(b) or 6(2)(b) of this Act for the payment of a lump sum may provide for the payment of that sum by instalments of such amount as may be specified in the order. **34–007**

(2) Where an order is made by virtue of subsection (1) above, the court shall have power, on an application made by the person to whom the lump sum is payable, by the personal representatives of the deceased or by the trustees of the property out of which the lump sum is payable, to vary that order by varying the number of instalments payable, the amount of any instalment and the date on which any instalment becomes payable.

Property available for financial provision

Property treated as part of "net estate"

34–008 **8.**—(1) Where a deceased person has in accordance with the provisions of any enactment nominated any person to receive any sum of money or other property on his death and that nomination is in force at the time of his death, that sum of money, after deducting therefrom any [inheritance tax][8] payable in respect thereof, or that other property, to the extent of the value thereof at the date of the death of the deceased after deducting therefrom any [inheritance tax][9] so payable, shall be treated for the purposes of this Act as part of the net estate of the deceased; but this subsection shall not render any person liable for having paid that sum or transferred that other property to the person named in the nomination in accordance with the directions given in the nomination.

(2) Where any sum of money or other property is received by any person as a donatio mortis causa made by a deceased person, that sum of money, after deducting therefrom any [inheritance tax][10] payable thereon, or that other property, to the extent of the value thereof at the date of the death of the deceased after deducting therefrom any [inheritance tax][11] so payable, shall be treated for the purposes of this Act as part of the net estate of the deceased; but this subsection shall not render any person liable for having paid that sum or transferred that other property in order to give effect to that donatio mortis causa.

(3) The amount of [inheritance tax][12] to be deducted for the purposes of this section shall not exceed the amount of that tax which has been borne by the person nominated by the deceased or, as the case may be, the person who has received a sum of money or other property as a donatio mortis causa.

Property held on a joint tenancy

34–009 **9.**—(1) Where a deceased person was immediately before his death beneficially entitled to a joint tenancy of any property, then, if, before the end of the period of six months from the date on which representation with respect to the estate of the deceased was first taken out, an application is made for an order under section 2 of this Act, the court for the purpose of facilitating the making of financial provision for the applicant under this Act may order that the deceased's severable share of that property, at the value thereof immediately before his death, shall, to such extent as appears to the court to be just in all the circumstances of the case, be treated for the purposes of this Act as part of the net estate of the deceased.

[8] From July 25, 1986 any reference to capital transfer tax, except where the reference relates to a liability to tax arising before that date, has effect as a reference to inheritance tax: Finance Act 1986, s.100(1)(b), (2).

[9] From July 25, 1986 any reference to capital transfer tax, except where the reference relates to a liability to tax arising before that date, has effect as a reference to inheritance tax: Finance Act 1986, s.100(1)(b), (2).

[10] From July 25, 1986 any reference to capital transfer tax, except where the reference relates to a liability to tax arising before that date, has effect as a reference to inheritance tax: Finance Act 1986, s.100(1)(b), (2).

[11] From July 25, 1986 any reference to capital transfer tax, except where the reference relates to a liability to tax arising before that date, has effect as a reference to inheritance tax: Finance Act 1986, s.100(1)(b), (2).

[12] From July 25, 1986 any reference to capital transfer tax, except where the reference relates to a liability to tax arising before that date, has effect as a reference to inheritance tax: Finance Act 1986, s.100(1)(b), (2).

(2) In determining the extent to which any severable share is to be treated as part of the net estate of the deceased by virtue of an order under subsection (1) above, the court shall have regard to any [inheritance tax][13] payable in respect of that severable share.

(3) Where an order is made under subsection (1) above, the provisions of this section shall not render any person liable for anything done by him before the order was made.

(4) For the avoidance of doubt it is hereby declared that for the purposes of this section there may be a joint tenancy of a chose in action.

Powers of court in relation to transactions intended to defeat applications for financial provision

Dispositions intended to defeat applications for financial provision

10.—(1) Where an application is made to the court for an order under section **34–010** 2 of this Act, the applicant may, in the proceedings on that application, apply to the court for an order under subsection (2) below.

(2) Where on an application under subsection (1) above the court is satisfied—

(a) that, less than six years before the date of the death of the deceased, the deceased with the intention of defeating an application for financial provision under this Act made a disposition, and

(b) that full valuable consideration for that disposition was not given by the person to whom or for the benefit of whom the disposition was made (in this section referred to as "the donee") or by any other person, and

(c) that the exercise of the powers conferred by this section would facilitate the making of financial provision for the applicant under this Act,

then, subject to the provisions of this section and of sections 12 and 13 of this Act, the court may order the donee (whether or not at the date of the order he holds any interest in the property disposed of to him or for his benefit by the deceased) to provide, for the purpose of the making of that financial provision, such sum of money or other property as may be specified in the order.

(3) Where an order is made under subsection (2) above as respects any disposition made by the deceased which consisted of the payment of money to or for the benefit of the donee, the amount of any sum of money or the value of any property ordered to be provided under that subsection shall not exceed the amount of the payment made by the deceased after deducting therefrom any [inheritance tax][14] borne by the donee in respect of that payment.

(4) Where an order is made under subsection (2) above as respects any disposition made by the deceased which consisted of the transfer of property (other than a sum of money) to or for the benefit of the donee, the amount of any sum of money or the value of any property ordered to be provided under that subsection shall not exceed the value at the date of the death of the deceased of the property disposed of by him to or for the benefit of the donee (or if that property has been disposed of by the person to whom it was transferred by the deceased, the value at the date of that disposal thereof) after deducting

[13] From July 25, 1986 any reference to capital transfer tax, except where the reference relates to a liability to tax arising before that date, has effect as a reference to inheritance tax: Finance Act 1986, s.100(1)(b), (2).

[14] From July 25, 1986 any reference to capital transfer tax, except where the reference relates to a liability to tax arising before that date, has effect as a reference to inheritance tax: Finance Act 1986, s.100(1)(b), (2).

therefrom any [inheritance tax][15] borne by the donee in respect of the transfer of that property by the deceased.

(5) Where an application (in this subsection referred to as "the original application") is made for an order under subsection (2) above in relation to any disposition, then, if on an application under this subsection by the donee or by any applicant for an order under section 2 of this Act the court is satisfied—

(a) that, less than six years before the date of the death of the deceased, the deceased with the intention of defeating an application for financial provision under this Act made a disposition other than the disposition which is the subject of the original application, and

(b) that full valuable consideration for that other disposition was not given by the person to whom or for the benefit of whom that other disposition was made or by any other person,

the court may exercise in relation to the person to whom or for the benefit of whom that other disposition was made the powers which the court would have had under subsection (2) above if the original application had been made in respect of that other disposition and the court had been satisfied as to the matters set out in paragraphs (a), (b) and (c) of that subsection; and where any application is made under this subsection, any reference in this section (except in subsection (2)(b)) to the donee shall include a reference to the person to whom or for the benefit of whom that other disposition was made.

(6) In determining whether and in what manner to exercise its powers under this section, the court shall have regard to the circumstances in which any disposition was made and any valuable consideration which was given therefor, the relationship, if any, of the donee to the deceased, the conduct and financial resources of the donee and all the other circumstances of the case.

(7) In this section "disposition" does not include—

(a) any provision in a will, any such nomination as is mentioned in section 8(1) of this Act or any donatio mortis causa, or

(b) any appointment of property made, otherwise than by will, in the exercise of a special power of appointment,

but, subject to these exceptions, includes any payment of money (including the payment of a premium under a policy of assurance) and any conveyance, assurance, appointment or gift of property of any description, whether made by an instrument or otherwise.

(8) The provisions of this section do not apply to any disposition made before the commencement of this Act.

Contracts to leave property by will

34–011 **11.**—(1) Where an application is made to a court for an order under section 2 of this Act, the applicant may, in the proceedings on that application, apply to the court for an order under this section.

(2) Where on an application under subsection (1) above the court is satisfied—

(a) that the deceased made a contract by which he agreed to leave by his will a sum of money or other property to any person or by which he agreed that a sum of money or other property would be paid or transferred to any person out of his estate, and

[15] From July 25, 1986 any reference to capital transfer tax, except where the reference relates to a liability to tax arising before that date, has effect as a reference to inheritance tax: Finance Act 1986, s.100(1)(b), (2).

(b) that the deceased made that contract with the intention of defeating an application for financial provision under this Act, and

(c) that when the contract was made full valuable consideration for that contract was not given or promised by the person with whom or for the benefit of whom the contract was made (in this section referred to as "the donee") or by any other person, and

(d) that the exercise of the powers conferred by this section would facilitate the making of financial provision for the applicant under this Act,

then, subject to the provisions of this section and of sections 12 and 13 of this Act, the court may make any one or more of the following orders, that is to say—

(i) if any money has been paid or any other property has been transferred to or for the benefit of the donee in accordance with the contract, an order directing the donee to provide, for the purpose of the making of that financial provision, such sum of money or other property as may be specified in the order;

(ii) if the money or all the money has not been paid or the property or all the property has not been transferred in accordance with the contract, an order directing the personal representatives not to make any payment or transfer any property, or not to make any further payment or transfer any further property, as the case may be, in accordance therewith or directing the personal representatives only to make such payment or transfer such property as may be specified in the order.

(3) Notwithstanding anything in subsection (2) above, the court may exercise its powers thereunder in relation to any contract made by the deceased only to the extent that the court considers that the amount of any sum of money paid or to be paid or the value of any property transferred or to be transferred in accordance with the contract exceeds the value of any valuable consideration given or to be given for that contract, and for this purpose the court shall have regard to the value of property at the date of the hearing.

(4) In determining whether and in what manner to exercise its powers under this section, the court shall have regard to the circumstances in which the contract was made, the relationship, if any, of the donee to the deceased, the conduct and financial resources of the donee and all the other circumstances of the case.

(5) Where an order has been made under subsection (2) above in relation to any contract, the rights of any person to enforce that contract or to recover damages or to obtain other relief for the breach thereof shall be subject to any adjustment made by the court under section 12(3) of this Act and shall survive to such extent only as is consistent with giving effect to the terms of that order.

(6) The provisions of this section do not apply to a contract made before the commencement of this Act.

Provisions supplementary to ss.10 and 11

12.—(1) Where the exercise of any of the powers conferred by section 10 or 11 **34–012** of this Act is conditional on the court being satisfied that a disposition or contract was made by a deceased person with the intention of defeating an application for financial provision under this Act, that condition shall be fulfilled if the court is of the opinion that, on a balance of probabilities, the intention of the deceased (though not necessarily his sole intention) in making the disposition or contract was to prevent an order for financial provision being made under this Act or to reduce the amount of the provision which might otherwise be granted by an order thereunder.

(2) Where an application is made under section 11 of this Act with respect to any contract made by the deceased and no valuable consideration was given or promised by any person for that contract then, notwithstanding anything in subsection (1) above, it shall be presumed, unless the contrary is shown, that the deceased made that contract with the intention of defeating an application for financial provision under this Act.

(3) Where the court makes an order under section 10 or 11 of this Act it may give such consequential directions as it thinks fit (including directions requiring the making of any payment or the transfer of any property) for giving effect to the order or for securing a fair adjustment of the rights of the persons affected thereby.

(4) Any power conferred on the court by the said section 10 or 11 to order the donee, in relation to any disposition or contract, to provide any sum of money or other property shall be exercisable in like manner in relation to the personal representative of the donee, and—

(a) any reference in section 10(4) to the disposal of property by the donee shall include a reference to disposal by the personal representative of the donee, and

(b) any reference in section 10(5) to an application by the donee under that subsection shall include a reference to an application by the personal representative of the donee;

but the court shall not have power under the said section 10 or 11 to make an order in respect of any property forming part of the estate of the donee which has been distributed by the personal representative; and the personal representative shall not be liable for having distributed any such property before he has notice of the making of an application under the said section 10 or 11 on the ground that he ought to have taken into account the possibility that such an application would be made.

Provisions as to trustees in relation to ss.10 and 11

34–013 **13.**—(1) Where an application is made for—

(a) an order under section 10 of this Act in respect of a disposition made by the deceased to any person as a trustee, or

(b) an order under section 11 of this Act in respect of any payment made or property transferred, in accordance with a contract made by the deceased, to any person as a trustee,

the powers of the court under the said section 10 or 11 to order that trustee to provide a sum of money or other property shall be subject to the following limitation (in addition, in a case of an application under section 10, to any provision regarding the deduction of [inheritance tax][16]) namely, that the amount of any sum of money or the value of any property ordered to be provided—

(i) in the case of an application in respect of a disposition which consisted of the payment of money or an application in respect of the payment of money in accordance with a contract, shall not exceed the aggregate of so much of that money as is at the date of the order in the hands of the trustee and the value at that date of any property which represents that

[16] From July 25, 1986 any reference to capital transfer tax, except where the reference relates to a liability to tax arising before that date, has effect as a reference to inheritance tax: Finance Act 1986, s.100(1)(b), (2).

money or is derived therefrom and is at that date in the hands of the trustee;

(ii) in the case of an application in respect of a disposition which consisted of the transfer of property (other than a sum of money) or an application in respect of the transfer of property (other than a sum of money) in accordance with a contract, shall not exceed the aggregate of the value at the date of the order of so much of that property as is at that date in the hands of the trustee and the value at that date of any property which represents the first-mentioned property or is derived therefrom and is at that date in the hands of the trustee.

(2) Where any such application is made in respect of a disposition made to any person as a trustee or in respect of any payment made or property transferred in pursuance of a contract to any person as a trustee, the trustee shall not be liable for having distributed any money or other property on the ground that he ought to have taken into account the possibility that such an application would be made.

(3) Where any such application is made in respect of a disposition made to any person as a trustee or in respect of any payment made or property transferred in accordance with a contract to any person as a trustee, any reference in the said section 10 or 11 to the donee shall be construed as including a reference to the trustee or trustees for the time being of the trust in question and any reference in subsection (1) or (2) above to a trustee shall be construed in the same way.

Special provisions relating to cases of divorce, separation, etc.

Provision as to cases where no financial relief was granted in divorce proceedings, etc.

14.—(1) Where, within twelve months from the date on which [a divorce order or separation order has been made under the Family Law Act 1996 in relation to a marriage or a decree of nullity of marriage has been made absolute][17], a party to the marriage dies and— **34–014**

(a) an application for a financial provision order under [section 22A or 23][18] of the Matrimonial Causes Act 1973 or a property adjustment order under [section 23A or 24][19] of that Act has not been made by the other party to that marriage, or

(b) such an application has been made but the proceedings thereon have not been determined at the time of the death of the deceased,

then, if an application for an order under section 2 of this Act is made by that other party, the court shall, notwithstanding anything in section 1 or section 3 of this Act, have power, if it thinks it just to do so, to treat that party for the purposes of that application as if [, as the case may be, the divorce order or separation order had not been made or the decree of nullity had not been made absolute][20].

(2) This subsection shall not apply in relation to a [separation order][21] unless at the date of the death of the deceased [the order][22] was in force and the separation was continuing.

[17] Words substituted by the Family Law Act 1996, s.66(1), Sched. 8, Pt. I, para. 27(1), (4).
[18] Words substituted by the Family Law Act 1996, s.66(1), Sched. 8, Pt. I, para. 27(1), (4).
[19] Words substituted by the Family Law Act 1996, s.66(1), Sched. 8, Pt. I, para. 27(1), (4).
[20] Words substituted by the Family Law Act 1996, s.66(1), Sched. 8, Pt. I, para. 27(1), (4).
[21] Words substituted by the Family Law Act 1996, s.66(1), Sched. 8, Pt. I, para. 27(1), (4).
[22] Words substituted by the Family Law Act 1996, s.66(1), Sched. 8, Pt. I, para. 27(1), (4).

Restriction imposed in divorce proceedings, etc. on application under this Act

34–015 **15.**—[(1) [At any time when the court—

(a) has jurisdiction under section 23A or 24 of the Matrimonial Causes Act 1973 to make a property adjustment order in relation to a marriage; or

(b) would have such jurisdiction if either the jurisdiction had not already been exercised or an application for such an order were made with the leave of the court,][23]

the court, if it considers it just to do so, may, on the application of either party to the marriage, order that the other party to the marriage shall not on the death of the applicant be entitled to apply for an order under section 2 of this Act.

In this subsection "the court" means the High Court or, where a county court has jurisdiction by virtue of Part V of the Matrimonial and Family Proceedings Act 1984, a county court.][24]

[(2) An order made under subsection (1) above with respect to any party to a marriage has effect in accordance with subsection (3) below at any time—

(a) after the marriage has been dissolved;

(b) after a decree of nullity has been made absolute in relation to the marriage; and

(c) while a separation order under the Family Law Act 1996 is in force in relation to the marriage and the separation is continuing.

(3) If at any time when an order made under subsection (1) above with respect to any party to a marriage has effect the other party to the marriage dies, the court shall not entertain any application made by the surviving party to the marriage for an order under section 2 of this Act.][25]

[Restriction imposed in proceedings under Matrimonial and Family Proceedings Act 1984 on application under this Act

34–016 **15A.**—(1) On making an order under section 17 of the Matrimonial and Family Proceedings Act 1984 (orders for financial provision and property adjustment following overseas divorces, etc.) the court, if it considers it just to do so, may, on the application of either party to the marriage, order that the other party to the marriage shall not on the death of the applicant be entitled to apply for an order under section 2 of this Act.

In this subsection "the court" means the High Court or, where a county court has jurisdiction by virtue of Part V of the Matrimonial and Family Proceedings Act 1984, a county court.

(2) Where an order under subsection (1) above has been made with respect to a party to a marriage which has been dissolved or annulled, then, on the death of the other party to that marriage, the court shall not entertain an application under section 2 of this Act made by the first-mentioned party.

(3) Where an order under subsection (1) above has been made with respect to a party to a marriage the parties to which have been legally separated, then, if the other party to the marriage dies while the legal separation is in force, the court shall not entertain an application under section 2 of this Act made by the first-mentioned party.][26]

[23] Words substituted by the Family Law Act 1996, s.66(1), Sched. 8, Pt. I, para. 27(1), (5).
[24] subs. (1) substituted by the Matrimonial and Family Proceedings Act 1984, s.8(1).
[25] subss. (2) and (3) substituted (for subss.(2)–(4)) by the Family Law Act 1996, s.66(1), Sched. 8, Pt. I, para. 27(1), (6).
[26] s.15A inserted by the Matrimonial and Family Proceedings Act 1984, s.25(3).

Variation and discharge of secured periodical payments orders made under Matrimonial Causes Act 1973

16.—(1) Where an application for an order under section 2 of this Act is made to the court by any person who was at the time of the death of the deceased entitled to payments from the deceased under a secured periodical payments order made under the Matrimonial Causes Act 1973, then, in the proceedings on that application, the court shall have power, if an application is made under this section by that person or by the personal representative of the deceased, to vary or discharge that periodical payments order or to revive the operation of any provision thereof which has been suspended under section 31 of that Act. **34–017**

(2) In exercising the powers conferred by this section the court shall have regard to all the circumstances of the case, including any order which the court proposes to make under section 2 or section 5 of this Act and any change (whether resulting from the death of the deceased or otherwise) in any of the matters to which the court was required to have regard when making the secured periodical payments order.

(3) The powers exercisable by the court under this section in relation to an order shall be exercisable also in relation to any instrument executed in pursuance of the order.

Variation and revocation of maintenance agreements

17.—(1) Where an application for an order under section 2 of this Act is made to the court by any person who was at the time of the death of the deceased entitled to payments from the deceased under a maintenance agreement which provided for the continuation of payments under the agreement after the death of the deceased, then, in the proceedings on that application, the court shall have power, if an application is made under this section by that person or by the personal representative of the deceased, to vary or revoke that agreement. **34–018**

(2) In exercising the powers conferred by this section the court shall have regard to all the circumstances of the case, including any order which the court proposes to make under section 2 or section 5 of this Act and any change (whether resulting from the death of the deceased or otherwise) in any of the circumstances in the light of which the agreement was made.

(3) If a maintenance agreement is varied by the court under this section the like consequences shall ensue as if the variation had been made immediately before the death of the deceased by agreement between the parties and for valuable consideration.

(4) In this section "maintenance agreement", in relation to a deceased person, means any agreement made, whether in writing or not and whether before or after the commencement of this Act, by the deceased with any person with whom he entered into a marriage, being an agreement which contained provisions governing the rights and liabilities towards one another when living separately of the parties to that marriage (whether or not the marriage has been dissolved or annulled) in respect of the making or securing of payments or the disposition or use of any property, including such rights and liabilities with respect to the maintenance or education of any child, whether or not a child of the deceased or a person who was treated by the deceased as a child of the family in relation to that marriage.

Availability of court's powers under this Act in applications under ss.31 and 36 of the Matrimonial Causes Act 1973

34–019 **18.**—(1) Where—

(a) a person against whom a secured periodical payments order was made under the Matrimonial Causes Act 1973 has died and an application is made under section 31(6) of that Act for the variation or discharge of that order or for the revival of the operation of any provision thereof which has been suspended, or

(b) a party to a maintenance agreement within the meaning of section 34 of that Act has died, the agreement being one which provides for the continuation of payments thereunder after the death of one of the parties, and an application is made under section 36(1) of that Act for the alteration of the agreement under section 35 thereof,

the court shall have power to direct that the application made under the said section 31(6) or 36(1) shall be deemed to have been accompanied by an application for an order under section 2 of this Act.

(2) Where the court gives a direction under subsection (1) above it shall have power, in the proceedings on the application under the said section 31(6) or 36(1), to make any order which the court would have had power to make under the provisions of this Act if the application under the said section 31(6) or 36(1), as the case may be, had been made jointly with an application for an order under the said section 2; and the court shall have power to give such consequential directions as may be necessary for enabling the court to exercise any of the powers available to the court under this Act in the case of an application for an order under section 2.

(3) Where an order made under section 15(1) of this Act is in force with respect to a party to a marriage, the court shall not give a direction under subsection (1) above with respect to any application made under the said section 31(6) or 36(1) by that party on the death of the other party.

Miscellaneous and supplementary provisions

Effect, duration and form of orders

34–020 **19.**—(1) Where an order is made under section 2 of this Act then for all purposes, including the purposes of the enactments relating to [inheritance tax][27], the will or the law relating to intestacy, or both the will and the law relating to intestacy, as the case may be, shall have effect and be deemed to have had effect as from the deceased's death subject to the provisions of the order.

(2) Any order made under section 2 or 5 of this Act in favour of—

(a) an applicant who was the former husband or former wife of the deceased, or

(b) an applicant who was the husband or wife of the deceased in a case where [, at the date of death, a separation order under the Family Law Act 1996 was in force in relation to the marriage with the deceased][28] and the separation was continuing,

shall, in so far as it provides for the making of periodical payments, cease to have effect on the remarriage of the applicant, except in relation to any arrears due under the order on the date of the remarriage.

[27] From July 25, 1986 any reference to capital transfer tax, except where the reference relates to a liability to tax arising before that date, has effect as a reference to inheritance tax: Finance Act 1986, s.100(1)(b), (2).

[28] Words substituted by the Family Law Act 1996, s.66(1), Sched. 8, Pt. I, para. 27(1), (7).

(3) A copy of every order made under this Act [other than an order made under section 15(1) of this Act][29] shall be sent to the principal registry of the Family Division for entry and filing, and a memorandum of the order shall be endorsed on, or permanently annexed to, the probate or letters of administration under which the estate is being administered.

Provisions as to personal representatives

20.—(1) The provisions of this Act shall not render the personal representative of a deceased person liable for having distributed any part of the estate of the deceased, after the end of the period of six months from the date on which representation with respect to the estate of the deceased is first taken out, on the ground that he ought to have taken into account the possibility— **34–021**

(a) that the court might permit the making of an application for an order under section 2 of this Act after the end of that period, or

(b) that, where an order has been made under the said section 2, the court might exercise in relation thereto the powers conferred on it by section 6 of this Act,

but this subsection shall not prejudice any power to recover, by reason of the making of an order under this Act, any part of the estate so distributed.

(2) Where the personal representative of a deceased person pays any sum directed by an order under section 5 of this Act to be paid out of the deceased's net estate, he shall not be under any liability by reason of that estate not being sufficient to make the payment, unless at the time of making the payment he has reasonable cause to believe that the estate is not sufficient.

(3) Where a deceased person entered into a contract by which he agreed to leave by his will any sum of money or other property to any person or by which he agreed that a sum of money or other property would be paid or transferred to any person out of his estate, then, if the personal representative of the deceased has reason to believe that the deceased entered into the contract with the intention of defeating an application for financial provision under this Act, he may, notwithstanding anything in that contract, postpone the payment of that sum of money or the transfer of that property until the expiration of the period of six months from the date on which representation with respect to the estate of the deceased is first taken out or, if during that period an application is made for an order under section 2 of this Act, until the determination of the proceedings on that application.

21. [*Repealed by the Civil Evidence Act 1995, s.15(2), Sched. 2.*]

22. [*Repealed by the Administration of Justice Act 1982, s.75, Sched. 9, Pt. 1.*]

Determination of date on which representation was first taken out

23. In considering for the purposes of this Act when representation with respect to the estate of a deceased person was first taken out, a grant limited to settled land or to trust property shall be left out of account, and a grant limited to real estate or to personal estate shall be left out of account unless a grant limited to the remainder of the estate has previously been made or is made at the same time. **34–022**

---

[29] Words inserted by the Administration of Justice Act 1982, s.52.

Effect of this Act on s.46(1)(vi) of Administration of Estates Act 1925

34–023 **24.** Section 46(1)(vi) of the Administration of Estates Act 1925, in so far as it provides for the devolution of property on the Crown, the Duchy of Lancaster or the Duke of Cornwall as bona vacantia, shall have effect subject to the provisions of this Act.

Interpretation

34–024 **25.**—(1) In this Act—

"beneficiary", in relation to the estate of a deceased person, means—

(a) a person who under the will of the deceased or under the law relating to intestacy is beneficially interested in the estate or would be so interested if an order had not been made under this Act, and

(b) a person who has received any sum of money or other property which by virtue of section 8(1) or 8(2) of this Act is treated as part of the net estate of the deceased or would have received that sum or other property if an order had not been made under this Act;

"child" includes an illegitimate child and a child en ventre sa mere at the death of the deceased;

"the court" means [unless the context otherwise requires][30] the High Court, or where a county court has jurisdiction by virtue of section 22 of this Act[31], a county court;

["former wife" or "former husband" means a person whose marriage with the deceased was during the lifetime of the deceased either—

(a) dissolved or annulled by [an order or decree][32] of divorce or a decree of nullity of marriage granted under the law of any part of the British Islands, or

(b) dissolved or annulled in any country or territory outside the British Islands by a divorce or annulment which is entitled to be recognised as valid by the law of England and Wales;][33]

"net estate", in relation to a deceased person, means:—

(a) all property of which the deceased had power to dispose by his will (otherwise than by virtue of a special power of appointment) less the amount of his funeral, testamentary and administration expenses, debts and liabilities, including any [inheritance tax][34] payable out of his estate on his death;

(b) any property in respect of which the deceased held a general power of appointment (not being a power exercisable by will) which has not been exercised;

(c) any sum of money or other property which is treated for the purposes of this Act as part of the net estate of the deceased by virtue of section 8(1) or (2) of this Act;

---

[30] Words inserted by the Matrimonial and Family Proceedings Act 1984, s.8(2).

[31] See now the County Courts Act 1984, s.25, *post*, para. 42–004.

[32] Words substituted by the Family Law Act 1996, s.66(1), Sched. 8, Pt. I, para. 27(1), (8).

[33] Definition substituted by the Matrimonial and Family Proceedings Act 1984, s.25(2).

[34] From July 25, 1986 any reference to capital transfer tax, except where the reference relates to a liability to tax arising before that date, has effect as a reference to inheritance tax: Finance Act 1986, s.100(1)(b), (2).

(d) any property which is treated for the purposes of this Act as part of the net estate of the deceased by virtue of an order made under section 9 of the Act;

(e) any sum of money or other property which is, by reason of a disposition or contract made by the deceased, ordered under section 10 or 11 of this Act to be provided for the purpose of the making of financial provision under this Act;

"property" includes any chose in action;

"reasonable financial provision" has the meaning assigned to it by section 1 of this Act;

"valuable consideration" does not include marriage or a promise of marriage;

"will" includes codicil.

(2) For the purposes of paragraph (a) of the definition of "net estate" in subsection (1) above a person who is not of full age and capacity shall be treated as having power to dispose by will of all property of which he would have had power to dispose by will if he had been of full age and capacity.

(3) Any reference in this Act to provision out of the net estate of a deceased person includes a reference to provision extending to the whole of that estate.

(4) For the purposes of this Act any reference to a wife or husband will be treated as including a reference to a person who in good faith entered into a void marriage with the deceased unless either—

(a) the marriage of the deceased and that person was dissolved or annulled during the lifetime of the deceased and the dissolution or annulment is recognised by the law of England and Wales, or

(b) that person has during the lifetime of the deceased entered into a later marriage.

(5) Any reference in this Act to remarriage or to a person who has remarried includes a reference to a marriage which is by law void or voidable or to a person who has entered into such a marriage, as the case may be, and a marriage shall be treated for the purposes of this Act as a remarriage, in relation to any party thereto, notwithstanding that the previous marriage of that party was void or voidable.

(6) Any reference in this Act to an order or decree made under the Matrimonial Causes Act 1973 or under any section of that Act shall be construed as including a reference to an order or decree which is deemed to have been made under that Act or under that section thereof, as the case may be.

(7) Any reference in this Act to any enactment is a reference to that enactment as amended by or under any subsequent enactment.

. . . . . .

Local Land Charges Act 1975

(1975 c. 76)

ARRANGEMENT OF SECTIONS

Definition of local land charges

. . . . .

Definition of local land charges

Local land charges

35–001 **1.**—(1) A charge or other matter affecting land is a local land charge if it falls within any of the following descriptions and is not one of the matters set out in section 2 below:—

(a) any charge acquired either before or after the commencement of this Act by a local authority [or National Park authority][1], water authority [sewerage undertaker][2] or new town development corporation under the Public Health Acts 1936 and 1937, [. . .][3] the Public Health Act 1961 or [the Highways Act 1980 (or any Act repealed by that Act)][4] [or the Building Act 1984][5], or any similar charge acquired by a local authority [or National Park authority][6] under any other Act, whether passed before or after this Act, being a charge that is binding on successive owners of the land affected;

(b) any prohibition of or restriction on the use of land—

(i) imposed by a local authority [or National Park authority][7] on or after 1st January 1926 (including any prohibition or restriction embodied in any condition attached to a consent, approval or licence granted by a local authority [or National Park authority][8] on or after that date), or

[1] Words inserted by the Environment Act 1995, s.78, Sched. 10, para. 14.
[2] Words inserted by the Water Act 1989, s.190(1), Sched. 25, para. 52.
[3] Words repealed by the Highways Act 1980, s.343(2), Sched. 24, para. 26.
[4] Words substituted by the Highways Act 1980, s.343(2), Sched. 24, para. 26.
[5] Words inserted by the Building Act 1984, s.133(1), Sched. 6, para. 16.
[6] Words inserted by the Environment Act 1995, s.78, Sched. 10, para. 14.
[7] Words inserted by the Environment Act 1995, s.78, Sched. 10, para. 14.
[8] Words inserted by the Environment Act 1995, s.78, Sched. 10, para. 14.

(ii) enforceable by a local authority [or National Park authority][9] under any covenant or agreement made with them on or after that date, being a prohibition or restriction binding on successive owners of the land affected;

(c) any prohibition of or restriction on the use of land—

(i) imposed by a Minister of the Crown or government department on or after the date of the commencement of this Act (including any prohibition or restriction embodied in any condition attached to a consent, approval or licence granted by such a Minister or department on or after that date), or

(ii) enforceable by such a Minister or department under any covenant or agreement made with him or them on or after that date,

being a prohibition or restriction binding on successive owners of the land affected;

(d) any positive obligation affecting land enforceable by a Minister of the Crown, government department or local authority [or National Park authority][10] under any covenant or agreement made with him or them on or after the date of the commencement of this Act and binding on successive owners of the land affected;

(e) any charge or other matter which is expressly made a local land charge by any statutory provision not contained in this section.

(2) For the purposes of subsection (1)(a) above, any sum which is recoverable from successive owners or occupiers of the land in respect of which the sum is recoverable shall be treated as a charge, whether the sum is expressed to be a charge on the land or not.

[(3) For the purposes of this section and section 2 of this Act, the Broads Authority shall be treated as a local authority [or National Park authority][11].][12]

Matters which are not local land charges

2. The following matters are not local land charges:— **35–002**

(a) a prohibition or restriction enforceable under a covenant or agreement made between a lessor and a lessee;

(b) a positive obligation enforceable under a covenant or agreement made between a lessor and a lessee;

(c) a prohibition or restriction enforceable by a Minister of the Crown, government department or local authority [or National Park authority][13] under any covenant or agreement, being a prohibition or restriction binding on successive owners of the land affected by reason of the fact that the covenant or agreement is made for the benefit of land of the Minister, government department or local authority [or National Park authority][14];

(d) a prohibition or restriction embodied in any bye-laws;

(e) a condition or limitation subject to which planning permission was granted at any time before the commencement of this Act or was or is (at any time) deemed to be granted under any statutory provision relating to town and country planning, whether by a Minister of the Crown,

9 Words inserted by the Environment Act 1995, s.78, Sched. 10, para. 14.
10 Words inserted by the Environment Act 1995, s.78, Sched. 10, para. 14.
11 Words inserted by the Environment Act 1995, s.78, Sched. 10, para. 14.
12 subs. (3) added by the Norfolk and Suffolk Broads Act 1988, s.21, Sched. 6, para. 14.
13 Words inserted by the Environment Act 1995, s.78, Sched. 10, para. 14.
14 Words inserted by the Environment Act 1995, s.78, Sched. 10, para. 14.

government department or local authority [or National Park authority][15];

(f) a prohibition or restriction embodied in a scheme under the Town and Country Planning Act 1932 or any enactment repealed by that Act;

(g) a prohibition or restriction enforceable under a forestry dedication covenant entered into pursuant to section 5 of the Forestry Act 1967;

(h) a prohibition or restriction affecting the whole of any of the following areas:—

(i) England, Wales or England and Wales;

(ii) England, or England and Wales, with the exception of, or of any part of, Greater London;

(iii) Greater London.

Local land charges registers, registration and related matters

Registering authorities, local land charges registers, and indexes

35–003 **3.**—(1) Each of the following local authorities—

(a) the council of any district,

[(aa) a Welsh county council;

(ab) a county borough council;][16]

(b) the council of any London borough, and

(c) the Common Council of the City of London,

shall be a registering authority for the purposes of this Act.

(2) There shall continue to be kept for the area of each registering authority—

(a) a local land charges register, and

(b) an index whereby all entries made in that register can readily be traced,

and as from the commencement of this Act the register and index kept for the area of a registering authority shall be kept by that authority.

[(3) Neither a local land charges register nor an index such as is mentioned in subsection (2)(b) above need be kept in documentary form.][17]

(4) For the purposes of this Act the area of the Common Council of the City of London includes the Inner Temple and the Middle Temple.

The appropriate local land charges register

35–004 **4.** In this Act […][18], unless the context otherwise requires, "the appropriate local land charges register", in relation to any land or to a local land charge, means the local land charges register for the area in which the land or, as the case may be, the land affected by the charge is situated or, if the land in question is situated in two or more areas for which local land charges registers are kept, each of the local land charges registers kept for those areas respectively.

Registration

35–005 **5.**—(1) Subject to subsection (6) below, where the originating authority as respects a local land charge are the registering authority, it shall be their duty to register it in the appropriate local land charges register.

---

[15] Words inserted by the Environment Act 1995, s.78, Sched. 10, para. 14.

[16] Paras (aa) and (ab) inserted by the Local Government (Wales) Act 1994, s.66(6), Sched. 16, para. 49.

[17] subs. (3) substituted by the Local Government (Miscellaneous Provisions) Act 1982, s.34(a).

[18] Words repealed by the Interpretation Act 1978, s.25(1), Sched. 3.

(2) Subject to subsection (6) below, where the originating authority as respects a local land charge are not the registering authority, it shall be the duty of the originating authority to apply to the registering authority for its registration in the appropriate local land charges register and upon any such application being made it shall be the duty of the registering authority to register the charge accordingly.

(3) The registration in a local land charges register of a local land charge, or of any matter which when registered becomes a local land charge, shall be carried out by reference to the land affected or such part of it as is situated in the area for which the register is kept.

(4) In this Act, "the originating authority", as respects a local land charge, means the Minister of the Crown, government department, local authority or other person by whom the charge is brought into existence or by whom, on its coming into existence, the charge is enforceable; and for this purpose—

(a) where a matter that is a local land charge consists of or is embodied in, or is otherwise given effect by, an order, scheme or other instrument made or confirmed by a Minister of the Crown or government department on the application of another authority the charge shall be treated as brought into existence by that other authority; and

(b) a local land charge brought into existence by a Minister of the Crown or government department on an appeal from a decision or determination of another authority or in the exercise of powers ordinarily exercisable by another authority shall be treated as brought into existence by that other authority.

(5) The registration of a local land charge may be cancelled pursuant to an order of the court.

(6) Where a charge or other matter is registrable in a local land charges register and before the commencement of this Act was also registrable in a register kept under the Land Charges Act 1972, then, if before the commencement of this Act it was registered in a register kept under that Act, there shall be no duty to register it, or to apply for its registration, under this Act and section 10 below shall not apply in relation to it.

Local authority's right to register a general charge against land in certain circumstances

6.—(1) Where a local authority have incurred any expenditure in respect of which, when any relevant work is completed and any requisite resolution is passed or order is made, there will arise in their favour a local land charge (in this section referred to as "the specific charge"), the following provisions of this section shall apply. **35–006**

(2) At any time before the specific charge comes into existence, a general charge against the land, without any amount being specified, may be registered in the appropriate local land charges register by the registering authority if they are the originating authority and, if they are not, shall be registered therein by them if the originating authority make an application for that purpose.

(3) A general charge registered under this section shall be a local land charge, but section 5(1) and (2) above shall not apply in relation to such a charge.

(4) If a general charge is registered under this section pursuant to an application by the originating authority, they shall, when the specific charge comes into existence, notify the registering authority of that fact, and any such notification shall be treated as an application (subject to subsection (5) below)

for the cancellation of the general charge and the registration of the specific charge.

(5) Where a general charge is registered under this section its registration shall be cancelled within such period starting with the day on which the specific charge comes into existence, and not being less than 1 year, as may be prescribed, and the specific charge shall not be registered before the general charge is cancelled.

(6) If the registration of the general charge is duly cancelled within the period specified in subsection (5) above and the specific charge is registered forthwith upon the cancellation or was discharged before the cancellation, then, for the purposes of section 10 below, the specific charge shall be treated as having come into existence at the time when the general charge was cancelled.

Effect of registering certain financial charges

35–007 **7.** A local land charge falling within section 1(1)(a) above shall, when registered, take effect as if it had been created by a deed of charge by way of legal mortgage within the meaning of the Law of Property Act 1925, but without prejudice to the priority of the charge.

Searches

Personal searches

35–008 **8.**—(1) Any person may search in any local land charges register on paying the prescribed fee.

[(1A) If a local land charges register is kept otherwise than in documentary form, the entitlement of a person to search in it is satisfied if the registering authority makes the portion of it which he wishes to examine available for inspection in visible and legible form.][19]

(2) Without prejudice to [subsections (1) and (1A)][20] above, a registering authority may provide facilities for enabling persons entitled to search in the authority's local land charges register to see photographic or other images or copies of any portion of the register which they may wish to examine.

Official searches

35–009 **9.**—(1) Where any person requires an official search of the appropriate local land charges register to be made in respect of any land, he may make a requisition in that behalf to the registering authority.

(2) [. . .][21] For the purposes of serving any such requisition on the Common Council of the City of London section 231(1) of the Local Government Act 1972 shall apply in relation to that Council as it applies in relation to a local authority within the meaning of that Act.

(3) The prescribed fee shall be payable in the prescribed manner in respect of every requisition made under this section.

(4) Where a requisition is made to a registering authority under this section and the fee payable in respect of it is paid in accordance with subsection (3)

[19] subs. (1A) inserted by the Local Government (Miscellaneous Provisions) Act 1982, s.34(b).
[20] Words substituted by the Local Government (Miscellaneous Provisions) Act 1982, s.34(c).
[21] Words repealed by the Local Government and Housing Act 1989, ss.158(1), 194(4), Sched. 12, Pt. II.

above, the registering authority shall thereupon make the search required and shall issue an official certificate setting out the result of the search.

Compensation for non-registration or defective official search certificate

Compensation for non-registration or defective official search certificate

10.—(1) Failure to register a local land charge in the appropriate local land charges register shall not affect the enforceability of the charge but where a person has purchased any land affected by a local land charge, then— **35–010**

(a) in a case where a material personal search of the appropriate local land charges register was made in respect of the land in question before the relevant time, if at the time of the search the charge was in existence but not registered in that register; or

[(aa) in a case where the appropriate local land charges register is kept otherwise than in documentary form and a material personal search of that register was made in respect of the land in question before the relevant time, if the entitlement to search in that register conferred by section 8 above was not satisfied as mentioned in subsection (1A) of that section; or][22]

(b) in a case where a material official search of the appropriate local land charges register was made in respect of the land in question before the relevant time, if the charge was in existence at the time of the search but (whether registered or not) was not shown by the official search certificate as registered in that register,

the purchaser shall (subject to section 11(1) below) be entitled to compensation for any loss suffered by him [in consequence][23].

(2) At any time when rules made under this Act make provision for local land charges registers to be divided into parts then, for the purposes of subsection (1) above—

(a) a search (whether personal or official) of a part or parts only of any such register shall not constitute a search of that register in relation to any local land charge registrable in a part of the register not searched; and

(b) a charge shall not be taken to be registered in the appropriate local land charges register unless registered in the appropriate part of the register.

(3) For the purposes of this section—

(a) a person purchases land where, for valuable consideration, he acquires any interest in land or the proceeds of sale of land, and this includes cases where he acquires as lessee or mortgagee and shall be treated as including cases where an interest is conveyed or assigned at his direction to another person;

(b) the relevant time—

(i) where the acquisition of the interest in question was preceded by a contract for its acquisition, other than a qualified liability contract, is the time when that contract was made;

(ii) in any other case, is the time when the purchaser acquired the interest in question or, if he acquired it under a disposition which took effect only when registered [in the register of title kept under the Land Registration Act 2002][24], the time when that disposition was made;

[22] Para. (aa) inserted by the Local Government (Miscellaneous Provisions) Act 1982, s.34(d).
[23] Words substituted by the Local Government (Miscellaneous Provisions) Act 1982, s.34(d).
[24] Words substituted by the Land Registration Act 2002, s.133, Sched. 11, para. 13.

and for the purposes of sub-paragraph (i) above, a qualified liability contract is a contract containing a term the effect of which is to make the liability of the purchaser dependent upon, or avoidable by reference to, the outcome of a search for local land charges affecting the land to be purchased;

(c) a personal search is material if, but only if—
(i) it is made after the commencement of this Act, and
(ii) it is made by or on behalf of the purchaser or, before the relevant time, the purchaser or his agent has knowledge of the result of it;

(d) an official search is material if, but only if—
(i) it is made after the commencement of this Act, and
(ii) it is requisitioned by or on behalf of the purchaser or, before the relevant time, the purchaser or his agent has knowledge of the contents of the official search certificate.

(4) Any compensation for loss under this section shall be paid by the registering authority in whose area the land affected is situated; and where the purchaser has incurred expenditure for the purpose of obtaining compensation under this section, the amount of the compensation shall include the amount of the expenditure reasonably incurred by him for that purpose (so far as that expenditure would not otherwise fall to be treated as loss for which he is entitled to compensation under this section).

(5) Where any compensation for loss under this section is paid by a registering authority in respect of a local land charge as respects which they are not the originating authority, then, unless an application for registration of the charge was made to the registering authority by the originating authority in time for it to be practicable for the registering authority to avoid incurring liability to pay that compensation, an amount equal thereto shall be recoverable from the originating authority by the registering authority.

(6) Where any compensation for loss under this section is paid by a registering authority, no part of the amount paid, or of any corresponding amount paid to that authority by the originating authority under subsection (5) above, shall be recoverable by the registering authority or the originating authority from any other person except as provided by subsection (5) above or under a policy of insurance or on grounds of fraud.

(7) In the case of an action to recover compensation under this section the cause of action shall be deemed for the purposes of the Limitation Act 1939[25] to accrue at the time when the local land charge comes to the notice of the purchaser; and for the purposes of this subsection the question when the charge came to his notice shall be determined without regard to the provisions of section 198 of the Law of Property Act 1925 (under which registration under certain enactments is deemed to constitute actual notice).

[(8) Where the amount claimed by way of compensation under this section does not exceed £5,000, proceedings for the recovery of such compensation may be begun in a county court.][26]

(9) If in any proceedings for the recovery of compensation under this section the court dismisses a claim to compensation, it shall not order the purchaser to pay the registering authority's costs unless it considers that it was unreasonable for the purchaser to commence the proceedings.

---

[25] Now the Limitation Act 1980, *post*, para. 39–001.

[26] subs. (8) substituted (for subss. (8) and (8A), the latter inserted by the County Courts Act 1984, s.148(1), Sched. 2, Pt. V, para. 57) by the High Court and County Courts Jurisdiction Order 1991 (S.I. 1991 No. 724), art. 2(8), Sched.

Mortgages, trusts for sale and settled land

11.—(1) Where there appear to be grounds for a claim under section 10 above in respect of an interest that is subject to a mortgage— **35–011**

(a) the claim may be made by any mortgagee of the interest as if he were the person entitled to that interest but without prejudice to the making of a claim by that person;
(b) no compensation shall be payable under that section in respect of the interest of the mortgagee (as distinct from the interest which is subject to the mortgage);
(c) any compensation payable under that section in respect of the interest that is subject to the mortgage shall be paid to the mortgagee or, if there is more than one mortgagee, to the first mortgagee and shall in either case be applied by him as if it were proceeds of sale.

(2) Where an interest is [subject to a trust of land][27] any compensation payable in respect of it under section 10 above shall be dealt with as if it were proceeds of sale arising under the trust.

(3) Where an interest is settled land for the purposes of the Settled Land Act 1925 any compensation payable in respect of it under section 10 above shall be treated as capital money arising under that Act.

. . . . . .

Rentcharges Act 1977[1]

(1977 c. 30)

Prohibition and extinguishment

Meaning of "rentcharge"

1. For the purposes of this Act "rentcharge" means any annual or other periodic sum charged on or issuing out of land, except— **36–001**

(a) rent reserved by a lease or tenancy, or
(b) any sum payable by way of interest.

Creation of rentcharges prohibited

2.—(1) Subject to this section, no rentcharge may be created whether at law or in equity after the coming into force of this section. **36–002**

(2) Any instrument made after the coming into force of this section shall, to the extent that it purports to create a rentcharge the creation of which is prohibited by this section, be void.

[27] Words substituted by the Trusts of Land and Appointment of Trustees Act 1996, s.25(1), Sched. 3, para. 14.

[1] The functions of the Secretary of State under this Act, in so far as they are exercisable in relation to Wales, are transferred to the National Assembly for Wales: National Assembly for Wales (Transfer of Functions) Order 1999 (S.I. 1999 No. 672), art. 2(a), Sched. 1.

(3) This section does not prohibit the creation of a rentcharge—

[(a) in the case of which paragraph 3 of Schedule 1 to the Trusts of Land and Appointment of Trustees Act 1996 (trust in case of family charge) applies to the land on which the rent is charged;

(b) in the case of which paragraph (a) above would have effect but for the fact that the land on which the rent is charged is settled land or subject to a trust of land;][2]

(c) which is an estate rentcharge;

(d) under any Act of Parliament providing for the creation of rentcharges in connection with the execution of works on land (whether by way of improvements, repairs or otherwise) or the commutation of any obligation to do any such work; or

(e) by, or in accordance with the requirements of, any order of a court.

(4) For the purposes of this section "estate rentcharge" means (subject to subsection (5) below) a rentcharge created for the purpose—

(a) of making covenants to be performed by the owner of the land affected by the rentcharge enforceable by the rent owner against the owner for the time being of the land; or

(b) of meeting, or contributing towards, the cost of the performance by the rent owner of covenants for the provision of services, the carrying out of maintenance or repairs, the effecting of insurance or the making of any payment by him for the benefit of the land affected by the rentcharge or for the benefit of that and other land.

(5) A rentcharge of more than a nominal amount shall not be treated as an estate rentcharge for the purposes of this section unless it represents a payment for the performance by the rent owner of any such covenant as is mentioned in subsection (4)(b) above which is reasonable in relation to that covenant.

Extinguishment of rentcharges

36–003 **3.**—(1) Subject to this section, every rentcharge shall (if it has not then ceased to have effect) be extinguished at the expiry of the period of 60 years beginning—

(a) with the passing of this Act, or

(b) with the date on which the rentcharge first became payable,

whichever is the later; and accordingly the land on which it was charged or out of which it issued shall, at the expiration of that period, be discharged and freed from the rentcharge.

(2) The extinguishment of a rentcharge under this section shall not affect the exercise by any person of any right or remedy for the recovery of any rent which accrues before the rentcharge is so extinguished.

(3) This section shall not have the effect of extinguishing any rentcharge—

(a) which is, by virtue of any enactment or agreement or by custom, charged on or otherwise payable in relation to land wholly or partly in lieu of tithes; or

(b) which is of a kind referred to in subsection (3) of section 2 above (disregarding subsection (5) of that section).

(4) Subsection (1) above shall not apply to a variable rentcharge; but where such a rentcharge ceases to be variable, subsection (1) above shall apply as if the

[2] Paras (a) and (b) substituted by the Trusts of Land and Appointment of Trustees Act 1996, s.25(1), Sched. 3, para. 15(1), (2).

date on which the rentcharge first became payable were the date on which it ceased to be variable.

(5) For the purposes of subsection (4) above, a rentcharge shall (at any time) be treated as variable if at any time thereafter the amount of the rentcharge will, or may, vary in accordance with the provisions of the instrument under which it is payable.

Apportionment

Application for apportionment

4.—(1) The owner of any land which is affected by a rentcharge which also affects land which is not in his ownership may, subject to this section, apply to the Secretary of State for an order apportioning the rentcharge between that land and the remaining land affected by the rentcharge. **36–004**

(2) The owner of any land which is affected by a rentcharge which does not affect land not in his ownership may apply to the Secretary of State for an order apportioning the rentcharge between such parts of his land as may be specified in the application.

(3) No application for apportionment may be made under this section in respect of—

(a) a rentcharge of a kind mentioned in section 2(3)(d) or 3(3)(a) above, or

(b) land affected by a rentcharge which also affects other land, if the whole of that other land is exonerated or indemnified from the whole of the rentcharge by means of a charge on the first mentioned land.

(4) Every application—

(a) under subsection (1) above, shall specify the amount (if any) equitably apportioned to the applicant's land, and

(b) under subsection (2) above, shall specify the applicant's proposal for apportioning the rentcharge between the parts of his land specified in the application.

(5) Subject to subsection (4) above, every application under this section shall be in such form and shall contain such information and be accompanied by such documents as may be prescribed by regulations.

(6) In any case where the Secretary of State considers that any additional document or information ought to be furnished by the applicant he may require the applicant—

(a) to deliver to him such documents (including documents of title and, in the case of registered land, an authority to inspect the register), and

(b) to furnish him with such information,

as the Secretary of State may specify.

(7) Where an applicant's documents of title are in the custody of a mortgagee the mortgagee shall, if requested to do so by the Secretary of State for the purpose of an application made under this section, deliver those documents to the Secretary of State on such terms as to their custody and return as the mortgagee may reasonably require.

Apportionment

5.—(1) Where an application for apportionment is made under section 4 above and the Secretary of State is satisfied that he is in a position to do so, he shall prepare a draft order for apportionment of the rentcharge. **36–005**

(2) If the application is made under section 4(1) above, the amount specified in the draft order as being that part of the rentcharge apportioned to the applicant's land shall be—

(a) the amount specified in the application as the amount equitably apportioned to that land; or

(b) where no amount has been equitably apportioned to that land, such amount as the Secretary of State considers appropriate.

(3) If the application is made under section 4(2) above, the amounts specified in the draft order as apportioned between the parts of the applicant's land specified in the application shall be those proposed in the application.

(4) A copy of the draft order shall be served by the Secretary of State on the person appearing to him to be the rent owner or his agent, and, in a case falling within subsection (2)(b) above, on such persons as appear to him to be the owners of the land affected by the rentcharge.

(5) After service of a draft order on the rent owner or his agent under subsection (4) above, the rent owner may, before the expiry of the period of 21 days beginning with the date on which the draft order is served (or such longer period, not exceeding the period of 42 days beginning with that date, as the Secretary of State may in a particular case allow)—

(a) object to it on the ground that such an apportionment would provide insufficient security for any part of the rentcharge;

(b) make an application to the effect that in the event of the apportionment not exceeding the sum mentioned in section 7(2) below, a condition should be imposed under that section.

(6) Where a draft order is served under subsection (4) above on a person who is the owner of any land affected by the rentcharge, that person may, before the expiry of the period of 21 days beginning with the date on which the draft order is served (or such longer period, not exceeding the period of 42 days beginning with that date, as the Secretary of State may in a particular case allow), make representations to the Secretary of State concerning the apportionment specified in the draft order.

(7) Any objection, application or representations under subsection (5) or (6) above shall be made in writing.

(8) An objection under subsection (5) above shall state what apportionment (if any) would in the opinion of the rent owner provide sufficient security for the rentcharge or, as the case may be, part of the rentcharge.

(9) The Secretary of State shall consider any objection duly made under subsection (5) above and any representations duly made under subsection (6) above and, if he is satisfied that the draft order should be modified—

(a) in the case of an objection, in order to preserve for the rent owner sufficient security for each apportioned part of the rentcharge, or

(b) to take account of any such representations,

he shall make such modifications in the draft order as appear to him to be appropriate.

(10) Where—

(a) the relevant period has expired without any objection or representation having been duly made, or

(b) an objection has, or any representations have, been duly made and the objection has, or, as the case may be, all the representations have, been considered by the Secretary of State,

the Secretary of State shall, if the applicant has not then withdrawn his application and the Secretary of State is satisfied that it is appropriate to do so, make an order (an "apportionment order") in the form of the draft but incorporating—

(i) any modifications made by the Secretary of State in accordance with subsection (9) above, and

(ii) where appropriate, a condition imposed by virtue of section 7(2) below.

(11) Immediately after making an apportionment order the Secretary of State shall serve copies of the order on the applicant and on the person appearing to him to be the rent owner or his agent, and, in a case falling within subsection (2)(b) above, on those other persons on whom copies of the draft order were served under subsection (4) above.

(12) In a case where modifications have been made in a draft order under subsection (9) above, the Secretary of State shall not make an apportionment order without giving the applicant an opportunity to withdraw his application.

Appeal

6.—(1) Where the applicant or the rent owner or, in a case falling within section 5(2)(b) above, any other person who is the owner of any land affected by the rentcharge, is aggrieved by the terms of an apportionment order, he may appeal to the Lands Tribunal. **36–006**

(2) Where an appeal has been duly made to the Lands Tribunal under this section, the Tribunal shall—

(a) confirm the order, or

(b) set it aside, and, subject to section 7(2) below, make such other order apportioning the rentcharge as it thinks fit.

Effect of apportionment order

7.—(1) An apportionment order shall, subject to subsection (2) below, have effect— **36–007**

(a) on the expiry of the period of 28 days beginning with the day on which it is made, or

(b) where an appeal against the order has been duly made under section 6 above, on such day as the Lands Tribunal shall specify.

(2) If—

(a) in the case of an application made under section 4(1) above, the part of the rentcharge apportioned to the applicant's land, or

(b) in the case of an application under section 4(2) above, any apportioned part of the rentcharge,

does not exceed the annual sum of £5, then, subject to subsection (3) below, it shall, where an application has been made under section 5(5)(b) above, be made a condition of the apportionment order that it shall have effect only for the purpose of the redemption of that part of the rentcharge in accordance with the following provisions of this Act.

(3) The Secretary of State shall not impose a condition under subsection (2) above in any case where he considers that, having regard to all the circumstances, to do so would cause the applicant to suffer financial hardship.

(4) In the case of an application under section 4(1) above, the effect of an apportionment order shall (subject to subsection (2) above) be to release the

applicant's land from any part of the rentcharge not apportioned to it and to release the remaining land affected by the rentcharge from such part (if any) of the rentcharge as is apportioned to the applicant's land.

(5) In the case of an application under section 4(2) above, the effect of an apportionment order shall (subject to subsection (2) above) be to release each part of the applicant's land from any part of the rentcharge not apportioned to it.

(6) The Secretary of State may by regulations specify, in substitution for the sum mentioned in subsection (2) above, such other annual sum as he considers appropriate.

Redemption

Application for redemption certificate

36–008 **8.**—(1) The owner of any land affected by a rentcharge may apply to the Secretary of State, in accordance with this section, for a certificate (in this Act referred to as a "redemption certificate") certifying that the rentcharge has been redeemed.

(2) Every application under this section shall be in such form and shall contain such information and be accompanied by such documents as may be prescribed by regulations.

(3) In any case where the Secretary of State considers that any additional document or information ought to be furnished by the applicant he may require the applicant—

(a) to deliver to him such documents (including documents of title and, in the case of registered land, an authority to inspect the register), and
(b) to furnish him with such information,

as the Secretary of State may specify.

(4) No application may be made under this section in respect of a rentcharge of a kind mentioned in section 2(3) or 3(3)(a) above.

(5) An application under this section may only be made—

(a) if the period for which the rentcharge concerned would remain payable if it were not redeemed is ascertainable, and
(b) in the case of a rentcharge which has at any time been a variable rentcharge, if it has ceased to be variable at the time of making the application.

For the purposes of this section a rentcharge shall (at any time) be treated as variable if at any time thereafter the amount of the rentcharge will, or may, vary in accordance with the provisions of the instrument under which it is payable.

(6) Where an applicant's documents of title are in the custody of a mortgagee the mortgagee shall, if requested to do so by the Secretary of State for the purpose of an application made under this section, deliver those documents to the Secretary of State on such terms as to their custody and return as the mortgagee may reasonably require.

Issue of redemption certificate

36–009 **9.**—(1) Where an application for a redemption certificate has been duly made under section 8 above, the Secretary of State shall serve notice of the application ("notice of application") on the person appearing to him to be the rent owner in relation to the rentcharge to which the application relates or his agent.

(2) A notice of application shall require the person on whom it is served to notify the Secretary of State, before the expiry of the period of 21 days

beginning with the date on which the notice of application is served, whether or not he is the rent owner in relation to that rentcharge.

(3) Notification under subsection (2) above shall be given in the form prescribed by regulations and shall contain such information, and be accompanied by such documents, as may be so prescribed.

(4) Where the Secretary of State has been duly notified under subsection (2) above, or the period mentioned in that subsection has expired without his being so notified, he shall serve a notice ("instructions for redemption") on the applicant for the redemption certificate—

(a) specifying the sum required to redeem the rentcharge (the "redemption price") calculated in accordance with section 10(1) below, and

(b) naming the person (determined in accordance with section 10(2) below), if any, appearing to the Secretary of State to be the person to whom the redemption price should be paid by the applicant.

(5) After service of instructions for redemption, the Secretary of State shall issue the applicant with a redemption certificate on proof—

(a) that the applicant has, before the expiry of the period of 28 days beginning with the date on which the instructions are served—

(i) paid the amount specified as the redemption price to the person named in the instructions as the person to whom payment should be made, or

(ii) where no person is so named, paid that amount into court in accordance with section 10(4) below, or

(b) in a case where the applicant has been authorised to do so under subsection (6) below, that he has paid that amount into court in accordance with section 10(4) below before the expiry of that period, (or such longer period as the Secretary of State may allow).

(6) For the purposes of subsection (5)(b) above, the Secretary of State may authorise payment into court in any case where he is satisfied that the applicant is unable to effect payment in accordance with the instructions for redemption or that it would be unreasonable to require him to do so.

Provisions supplemental to section 9

10.—(1) For the purposes of section 9 above, the redemption price shall be calculated by applying the formula:— **36–010**

$$P = £\frac{R}{Y} - \frac{R}{Y(1+Y)^n}$$

where:—

P = the redemption price;
R = the annual amount of the rentcharge to be redeemed;
Y = the yield, expressed as a decimal fraction, from 2½ per cent. Consolidated Stock; and
n = the period, expressed in years (taking any part of a year as a whole year), for which the rentcharge would remain payable if it were not redeemed.

In calculating the yield from 2½ per cent. Consolidated Stock, the price of that stock shall be taken to be the middle market price at the close of business on the last trading day in the week before that in which instructions for redemption are served under section 9(4) above.

(2) For the purposes of section 9(4)(b) above, the person to whom the redemption price should be paid is—

(a) in a case where the rentcharge was subject to a mortgage, the mortgagee or, if there is more than one mortgagee, the first mortgagee;

(b) in a case where the rentcharge was not subject to a mortgage but was settled land or was subject to a [trust of land][3], the trustees;

(c) in any other case, the rent owner.

(3) Where a redemption certificate has been issued under section 9 above—

(a) it shall have the effect of releasing the applicant's land from the rentcharge concerned, but

(b) it shall not affect the exercise by the rent owner of any right or remedy for the recovery of any rent which accrues before the date on which it was issued.

(4) Where a payment is made into court for the purposes of section 9 above, the sum concerned shall—

(a) if it does not exceed [£5,000][4] be paid into the county court, and

(b) in any other case, be paid into the High Court.

[(4A) [*Repealed by the High Court and County Courts Jurisdiction Order 1991 (S.I. 1991 No. 724), art. 2(8), Sched.*][5]

(5) Any person who, in notifying the Secretary of State under section 9(2) above, makes a statement which he knows to be false in a material particular, or recklessly makes any statement which is so false, shall be guilty of an offence punishable on summary conviction by a fine not exceeding [level 5 on the standard scale.][6]

Miscellaneous and general

Implied covenants

36–011 **11.**—(1) Where any land affected by a rentcharge created after the passing of this Act by virtue of section 2(3)(a) or (b) above—

(a) is conveyed for consideration in money or money's worth, and

(b) remains affected by the rentcharge or by any part of it,

the following provisions of this section shall have effect in place of those of section 77 of the Law of Property Act 1925, in respect of the covenants deemed to be included and implied in the conveyance.

(2) In addition to the covenants implied under [Part I of the Law of Property (Miscellaneous Provisions) Act 1994][7], there shall be deemed to be included and implied in the conveyance covenants by the conveying party or joint and several covenants by the conveying parties (if more than one) with the grantee (or with each of the grantees) in the following terms:—

(a) that the conveying party will at all times from the date of the conveyance duly pay the rentcharge (or part of the rentcharge) and keep the grantee and those deriving title under him and their respective estates and effects indemnified against all claims and demands whatsoever in respect of the rentcharge; and

[3] Words substituted by the Trusts of Land and Appointment of Trustees Act 1996, s.25(1), Sched. 3, para. 15(1), (3).
[4] Figure substituted by the High Court and County Courts Jurisdiction Order 1991 (S.I. 1991 No. 724), art. 2(8), Sched.
[5] subs. (4A) originally inserted by the County Courts Act 1984, s.148(1), Sched. 2, Pt. V, para. 63.
[6] Words substituted by virtue of the Criminal Justice Act 1982, s.46.
[7] Words substituted by the Law of Property (Miscellaneous Provisions) Act 1994, s.21(1), Sched. 1, para. 7.

(b) that the conveying party will (at his expense), in the event of the rentcharge (or part of the rentcharge) ceasing to affect the land conveyed, furnish evidence of that fact to the grantee and those deriving title under him.

(3) The benefit of the covenants deemed to be included and implied in a conveyance, by virtue of subsection (2) above, shall be annexed and incident to and shall go with the estate or interest of the implied covenantee and shall be capable of being enforced by every person in whom the estate or interest is from time to time vested.

(4) Any stipulation which is contained in an agreement and which is inconsistent with, or designed to prevent the operation of, the said covenants (or any part of them) shall be void.

. . . . . .

Interpretation

13.—(1) In this Act— **36–012**

"apportionment", in relation to a rentcharge, includes an apportionment which provides for the amount apportioned to any part of the land affected by the rentcharge to be nil;

"apportionment order" means an order made under section 5(10) above or, where appropriate, an order made by the Lands Tribunal under section 6(2)(b) above;

"conveyance" has the same meaning as in section 205(1) of the Law of Property Act 1925;

"land" has the same meaning as in section 205(1) of the Law of Property Act 1925;

"legal apportionment" and "equitable apportionment" in relation to a rentcharge mean, respectively—

(a) any apportionment of the rentcharge which is binding on the rent owner, and

(b) any apportionment or exoneration of the rentcharge which is not binding on the rent owner;

"owner", in relation to any land, means a person, other than a mortgagee not in possession, who is for the time being entitled to dispose of the fee simple of the land, whether in possession or in reversion, and includes a person holding or entitled to the rents and profits of the land under a lease or agreement;

"redemption certificate" has the meaning given in section 8(1) above;

"rent owner", in relation to a rentcharge, means the person entitled to the rentcharge or empowered to dispose of it absolutely or to give an absolute discharge for the capital value thereof.

(2) The provisions of this Act relating to the redemption and apportionment of rentcharges shall apply equally to the redemption and further apportionment of legally apportioned parts of rentcharges.

(3) Subject to section 3(4) above, a rentcharge shall be treated for the purposes of this Act as becoming payable on the first day of the first period in respect of which it is to be paid.

. . . . . .

Protection from Eviction Act 1977[1]

(1977 c. 43)

Part I

Unlawful Eviction and Harassment[2]

Unlawful eviction and harassment of occupier

37–001 **1.**—(1) In this section "residential occupier", in relation to any premises, means a person occupying the premises as a residence, whether under a contract or by virtue of any enactment or rule of law giving him the right to remain in occupation or restricting the right of any other person to recover possession of the premises.

(2) If any person unlawfully deprives the residential occupier of any premises of his occupation of the premises or any part thereof, or attempts to do so, he shall be guilty of an offence unless he proves that he believed, and had reasonable cause to believe, that the residential occupier had ceased to reside in the premises.

(3) If any person with intent to cause the residential occupier of any premises—

(a) to give up the occupation of the premises or any part thereof; or

(b) to refrain from exercising any right or pursuing any remedy in respect of the premises or part therof;

does acts [likely][3] to interfere with the peace or comfort of the residential occupier or members of his household, or persistently withdraws or withholds services reasonably required for the occupation of the premises as a residence, he shall be guilty of an offence.

[(3A) Subject to subsection (3B) below, the landlord of a residential occupier or an agent of the landlord shall be guilty of an offence if—

(a) he does acts likely to interfere with the peace or comfort of the residential occupier or members of his household, or

(b) he persistently withdraws or withholds services reasonably required for the occupation of the premises in question as a residence,

and (in either case) he knows, or has reasonable cause to believe, that that conduct is likely to cause the residential occupier to give up the occupation of the whole or part of the premises or to refrain from exercising any right or pursuing any remedy in respect of the whole or part of the premises.

(3B) A person shall not be guilty of an offence under subsection (3A) above if he proves that he had reasonable grounds for doing the acts or withdrawing or withholding the services in question.

(3C) In subsection (3A) above "landlord", in relation to a residential occupier of any premises, means the person who, but for—

(a) the residential occupier's right to remain in occupation of the premises, or

(b) a restriction on the person's right to recover possession of the premises,

---

[1] The functions of the Secretary of State under this Act, in so far as they are exercisable in relation to Wales, are transferred to the National Assembly for Wales: National Assembly for Wales (Transfer of Functions) Order 1999 (S.I. 1999 No. 672), art. 2(a), Sched. 1.

[2] For damages for unlawful eviction, see the Housing Act 1988, ss.27–28

[3] Word substituted by the Housing Act 1988, s.29(1).

would be entitled to occupation of the premises and any superior landlord under whom that person derives title.][4]

(4) A person guilty of an offence under this section shall be liable—

(a) on summary conviction, to a fine not exceeding [the prescribed sum][5] or to imprisonment for a term not exceeding 6 months or to both;

(b) on conviction on indictment, to a fine or to imprisonment for a term not exceeding 2 years or to both.

(5) Nothing in this section shall be taken to prejudice any liability or remedy to which a person guilty of an offence thereunder may be subject in civil proceedings.

(6) Where an offence under this section committed by a body corporate is proved to have been committed with the consent or connivance of, or to be attributable to any neglect on the part of, any director, manager or secretary or other similar officer of the body corporate or any person who was purporting to act in any such capacity, he as well as the body corporate shall be guilty of that offence and shall be liable to be proceeded against and punished accordingly.

Restriction on re-entry without due process of law

2. Where any premises are let as a dwelling on a lease which is subject to a right of re-entry or forfeiture it shall not be lawful to enforce that right otherwise than by proceedings in the court while any person is lawfully residing in the premises or part of them. **37–002**

Prohibition of eviction without due process of law

3.—(1) Where any premises have been let as a dwelling under a tenancy which is [neither a statutorily protected tenancy nor an excluded tenancy][6] and— **37–003**

(a) the tenancy (in this section referred to as the former tenancy) has come to an end, but

(b) the occupier continues to reside in the premises or part of them,

it shall not be lawful for the owner to enforce against the occupier, otherwise than by proceedings in the court, his right to recover possession of the premises.

(2) In this section "the occupier", in relation to any premises, means any person lawfully residing in the premises or part of them at the termination of the former tenancy.

[(2A) Subsections (1) and (2) above apply in relation to any restricted contract (within the meaning of the Rent Act 1977) which—

(a) creates a licence; and

(b) is entered into after the commencement of section 69 of the Housing Act 1980;

as they apply in relation to a restricted contract which creates a tenancy.][7]

[(2B) Subsections (1) and (2) above apply in relation to any premises occupied as a dwelling under a licence, other than an excluded licence, as they apply in relation to premises let as a dwelling under a tenancy, and in those subsections the expressions "let" and "tenancy" shall be construed accordingly.

(2C) References in the preceding provisions of this section and section 4(2A) below to an excluded tenancy do not apply to—

[4] subss. (3A)–(3C) inserted by the Housing Act 1988, s.29(2).
[5] Words substituted by virtue of the Magistrates' Courts Act 1980, s.32(2).
[6] Words substituted by the Housing Act 1988, s.30(1).
[7] subs. (2A) inserted by the Housing Act 1980, s.69(1).

(a) a tenancy entered into before the date on which the Housing Act 1988 came into force, or

(b) a tenancy entered into on or after that date but pursuant to a contract made before that date,

but, subject to that, "excluded tenancy" and "excluded licence" shall be construed in accordance with section 3A below.][8]

(3) This section shall, with the necessary modifications, apply where the owner's right to recover possession arises on the death of the tenant under a statutory tenancy within the meaning of the Rent Act 1977 or the Rent (Agriculture) Act 1976.

[Excluded tenancies and licences

37–004 **3A.**—(1) Any reference in this Act to an excluded tenancy or an excluded licence is a reference to a tenancy or licence which is excluded by virtue of any of the following provisions of this section.

(2) A tenancy or licence is excluded if—

(a) under its terms the occupier shares any accommodation with the landlord or licensor; and

(b) immediately before the tenancy or licence was granted and also at the time it comes to an end, the landlord or licensor occupied as his only or principal home premises of which the whole or part of the shared accommodation formed part.

(3) A tenancy or licence is also excluded if—

(a) under its terms the occupier shares any accommodation with a member of the family of the landlord or licensor;

(b) immediately before the tenancy or licence was granted and also at the time it comes to an end, the member of the family of the landlord or licensor occupied as his only or principal home premises of which the whole or part of the shared accommodation formed part; and

(c) immediately before the tenancy or licence was granted and also at the time it comes to an end, the landlord or licensor occupied as his only or principal home premises in the same building as the shared accommodation and that building is not a purpose-built block of flats.

(4) For the purposes of subsections (2) and (3) above, an occupier shares accommodation with another person if he has the use of it in common with that person (whether or not also in common with others) and any reference in those subsections to shared accommodation shall be construed accordingly, and if, in relation to any tenancy or licence, there is at any time more than one person who is the landlord or licensor, any reference in those subsections to the landlord or licensor shall be construed as a reference to any one of those persons.

(5) In subsections (2) to (4) above—

(a) "accommodation" includes neither an area used for storage nor a staircase, passage, corridor or other means of access;

(b) "occupier" means, in relation to a tenancy, the tenant and, in relation to a licence, the licensee; and

(c) "purpose-built block of flats" has the same meaning as in Part III of Schedule 1 to the Housing Act 1988;

and section 113 of the Housing Act 1985 shall apply to determine whether a

[8] subss. (2B) and (2C) inserted by the Housing Act 1988, s.30(2).

person is for the purposes of subsection (3) above a member of another's family as it applies for the purposes of Part IV of that Act.

(6) A tenancy or licence is excluded if it was granted as a temporary expedient to a person who entered the premises in question or any other premises as a trespasser (whether or not, before the beginning of that tenancy or licence, another tenancy or licence to occupy the premises or any other premises had been granted to him).

(7) A tenancy or licence is excluded if—

(a) it confers on the tenant or licensee the right to occupy the premises for a holiday only; or

(b) it is granted otherwise than for money or money's worth.

[(7A) A tenancy or licence is excluded if it is granted in order to provide accommodation under Part IV of the Immigration and Asylum Act 1999.][9]

[(7B) Section 32 of the Nationality, Immigration and Asylum Act 2002 (accommodation centre: tenure) provides for a resident's licence to occupy an accommodation centre to be an excluded licence.][10]

(8) A licence is excluded if it confers rights of occupation in a hostel, within the meaning of the Housing Act 1985, which is provided by—

(a) the council of a county, [county borough,][11] district or London Borough, the Common Council of the City of London, the Council of the Isles of Scilly, the Inner London Education Authority, [the London Fire and Emergency Planning Authority,][12] a joint authority within the meaning of the Local Government Act 1985 or a residuary body within the meaning of that Act;

(b) a development corporation within the meaning of the New Towns Act 1981;

(c) the Commission for the New Towns;

(d) an urban development corporation established by an order under section 135 of the Local Government, Planning and Land Act 1980;

(e) a housing action trust established under Part III of the Housing Act 1988; [. . .][13]

(g) the Housing Corporation [. . .][14];

[(ga) the Secretary of State under section 89 of the Housing Associations Act 1985;][15]

[(h) a housing trust (within the meaning of the Housing Associations Act 1985) which is a charity or a registered social landlord (within the meaning of the Housing Act 1985); or][16]

(i) any other person who is, or who belongs to a class of person which is, specified in an order made by the Secretary of State.

(9) The power to make an order under subsection (8)(i) above shall be exercisable by statutory instrument which shall be subject to annulment in pursuance of a resolution of either House of Parliament.][17]

---

[9] subs. (7A) inserted by the Immigration and Asylum Act 1999, s.169(1), Sched. 14, para. 73.
[10] subs. (7B) inserted by the Nationality, Immigration and Asylum Act 2002, s.32(5).
[11] Words inserted by the Local Government (Wales) Act 1994, s.22(2), Sched. 8, para. 4(1).
[12] Words inserted by the Greater London Authority Act 1999, s.328(8), Sched. 29, para. 27.
[13] Para. (f) repealed by the Government of Wales Act 1998, s.152, Sched. 18, Pt. IV.
[14] Words repealed by the Government of Wales Act 1998, ss.140, 152, Sched. 16, para. 2(a), Sched. 18, Pt. VI.
[15] Para. (ga) inserted by the Government of Wales Act 1998, ss.140, Sched. 16, para. 2(b).
[16] Para. (h) substituted by the Housing Act 1996 (Consequential Provisions) Order 1996 (S.I. 1996 No. 2325), art. 5, Sched. 2, para. 7.
[17] s.3A inserted by the Housing Act 1988, s.31.

Special provisions for agricultural employees

37–005 **4.**—(1) This section shall apply where the tenant under the former tenancy (within the meaning of section 3 of this Act) occupied the premises under the terms of his employment as a person employed in agriculture, as defined in section 1 of the Rent (Agriculture) Act 1976, but is not a statutory tenant as defined in that Act.

(2) In this section "the occupier", in relation to any premises, means—

(a) the tenant under the former tenancy; or

(b) the widow or widower of the tenant under the former tenancy residing with him at his death or, if the former tenant leaves no such widow or widower, any member of his family residing with him at his death.

[(2A) In accordance with section 3(2B) above, any reference in subsections (1) and (2) above to the tenant under the former tenancy includes a reference to the licensee under a licence (other than an excluded licence) which has come to an end (being a licence to occupy premises as a dwelling); and in the following provisions of this section the expressions "tenancy" and "rent" and any other expressions referable to a tenancy shall be construed accordingly.][18]

(3) Without prejudice to any power of the court apart from this section to postpone the operation or suspend the execution of an order for possession, if in proceedings by the owner against the occupier the court makes an order for the possession of the premises the court may suspend the execution of the order on such terms and conditions, including conditions as to the payment by the occupier of arrears of rent, mesne profits and otherwise as the court thinks reasonable.

(4) Where the order for possession is made within the period of 6 months beginning with the date when the former tenancy came to an end, then, without prejudice to any powers of the court under the preceding provisions of this section or apart from this section to postpone the operation or suspend the execution of the order for a longer period, the court shall suspend the execution of the order for the remainder of the said period of 6 months unless the court—

(a) is satisfied either—

(i) that other suitable accommodation is, or will within that period be made, available to the occupier; or

(ii) that the efficient management of any agricultural land or the efficient carrying on of any agricultural operations would be seriously prejudiced unless the premises are available for occupation by a person employed or to be employed by the owner; or

(iii) that greater hardship (being hardship in respect of matters other than the carrying on of such a business as aforesaid) would be caused by the suspension of the order until the end of that period than by its execution within that period; or

(iv) that the occupier, or any person residing or lodging with the occupier, has been causing damage to the premises or has been guilty of conduct which is a nuisance or annoyance to persons occupying other premises; and

(b) considers that it would be reasonable not to suspend the execution of the order for the remainder of that period.

(5) Where the court suspends the execution of an order for possession under subsection (4) above it shall do so on such terms and conditions, including

[18] subs. (2A) inserted by the Housing Act 1988, s.30(3).

conditions as to the payment by the occupier of arrears of rent, mesne profits and otherwise as the court thinks reasonable.

(6) A decision of the court not to suspend the execution of the order under subsection (4) above shall not prejudice any other power of the court to postpone the operation or suspend the execution of the order for the whole or part of the period of 6 months mentioned in that subsection.

(7) Where the court has, under the preceding provisions of this section, suspended the execution of an order for possession, it may from time to time vary the period of suspension or terminate it and may vary any terms or conditions imposed by virtue of this section.

(8) In considering whether or how to exercise its powers under subsection (3) above, the court shall have regard to all the circumstances and, in particular, to—

(a) whether other suitable accommodation is or can be made available to the occupier;

(b) whether the efficient management of any agricultural land or the efficient carrying on of any agricultural operations would be seriously prejudiced unless the premises were available for occupation by a person employed or to be employed by the owner; and

(c) whether greater hardship would be caused by the suspension of the execution of the order than by its execution without suspension or further suspension.

(9) Where in proceedings for the recovery of possession of the premises the court makes an order for possession but suspends the execution of the order under this section, it shall make no order for costs, unless it appears to the court, having regard to the conduct of the owner or of the occupier, that there are special reasons for making such an order.

(10) Where, in the case of an order for possession of the premises to which subsection (4) above applies, the execution of the order is not suspended under that subsection or, the execution of the order having been so suspended, the suspension is terminated, then, if it is subsequently made to appear to the court that the failure to suspend the execution of the order or, as the case may be, the termination of the suspension was—

(a) attributable to the provisions of paragraph (a)(ii) of subsection (4), and

(b) due to misrepresentation or concealment of material facts by the owner of the premises,

the court may order the owner to pay to the occupier such sum as appears sufficient as compensation for damage or loss sustained by the occupier as a result of that failure or termination.

Part II

Notice to Quit

Validity of notices to quit

5.—(1) [Subject to subsection (1B) below][19] no notice by a landlord or a tenant to quit any premises let (whether before or after the commencement of this Act) as a dwelling shall be valid unless— **37–006**

(a) it is in writing and contains such information as may be prescribed, and

[19] Words inserted by the Housing Act 1988, s.32(1).

(b) it is given not less than 4 weeks before the date on which it is to take effect.

[(1A) Subject to subsection (1B) below, no notice by a licensor or a licensee to determine a periodic licence to occupy premises as a dwelling (whether the licence was granted before or after the passing of this Act) shall be valid unless—

(a) it is in writing and contains such information as may be prescribed, and
(b) it is given not less than 4 weeks before the date on which it is to take effect.

(1B) Nothing in subsection (1) or subsection (1A) above applies to—

(a) premises let on an excluded tenancy which is entered into on or after the date on which the Housing Act 1988 came into force unless it is entered into pursuant to a contract made before that date; or
(b) premises occupied under an excluded licence.][20]

(2) In this section "prescribed" means prescribed by regulations made by the Secretary of State by statutory instrument, and a statutory instrument containing any such regulations shall be subject to annulment in pursuance of a resolution of either House of Parliament.

(3) Regulations under this section may make different provision in relation to different descriptions of lettings and different circumstances.

PART III

SUPPLEMENTAL PROVISIONS

. . . . . .

Interpretation

37–007 **8.**—(1) In this Act "statutorily protected tenancy" means—

(a) a protected tenancy within the meaning of the Rent Act 1977 or a tenancy to which Part I of the Landlord and Tenant Act 1954 applies;
(b) a protected occupancy or statutory tenancy as defined in the Rent (Agriculture) Act 1976;
(c) a tenancy to which Part II of the Landlord and Tenant Act 1954 applies;
(d) a tenancy of an agricultural holding within the meaning of the [Agricultural Holdings Act 1986][21] [which is a tenancy in relation to which that Act applies][22];
[(e) an assured tenancy or assured agricultural occupancy under Part I of the Housing Act 1988][23];
[(f) a tenancy to which Schedule 10 to the Local Government and Housing Act 1989 applies][24];
[(g) a farm business tenancy within the meaning of the Agricultural Tenancies Act 1995.][25]

(2) For the purposes of Part I of this Act a person who, under the terms of his employment, had exclusive possession of any premises other than as a tenant

[20] subss. (1A) and (1B) inserted by the Housing Act 1988, s.32(2).
[21] Words substituted by the Agricultural Holdings Act 1986, s.100, Sched. 14, para. 61.
[22] Words inserted by the Agricultural Tenancies Act 1995, s.40, Sched., para. 29(a).
[23] Para. (e) added by the Housing Act 1988, s.33(2).
[24] Para. (f) added by the Local Government and Housing Act 1989, s.194(1), Sched. 11, para. 54.
[25] Para. (g) added by the Agricultural Tenancies Act 1995, s.40, Sched., para. 29(b).

shall be deemed to have been a tenant and the expressions "let" and "tenancy" shall be construed accordingly.

(3) In Part I of this Act "the owner", in relation to any premises, means the person who, as against the occupier, is entitled to possession thereof.

[(4) In this Act "excluded tenancy" and "excluded licence" have the meaning assigned by section 3A of this Act.

(5) If, on or after the date on which the Housing Act 1988 came into force, the terms of an excluded tenancy or excluded licence entered into before that date are varied, then—

(a) if the variation affects the amount of the rent which is payable under the tenancy or licence, the tenancy or licence shall be treated for the purposes of sections 3(2C) and 5(1B) above as a new tenancy or licence entered into at the time of the variation; and

(b) if the variation does not affect the amount of the rent which is so payable, nothing in this Act shall affect the determination of the question whether the variation is such as to give rise to a new tenancy or licence.

(6) Any reference in subsection (5) above to a variation affecting the amount of the rent which is payable under a tenancy or licence does not include a reference to—

(a) a reduction or increase effected under Part III or Part VI of the Rent Act 1977 (rents under regulated tenancies and housing association tenancies), section 78 of that Act (power of rent tribunal in relation to restricted contracts) or sections 11 to 14 of the Rent (Agriculture) Act 1976; or

(b) a variation which is made by the parties and has the effect of making the rent expressed to be payable under the tenancy or licence the same as a rent for the dwelling which is entered in the register under Part IV or section 79 of the Rent Act 1977.][26]

. . . . . .

Charging Orders Act 1979

(1979 c. 53)

Charging orders

Charging orders

1.—(1) Where, under a judgment or order of the High Court or a county court, a person (the "debtor") is required to pay a sum of money to another person (the "creditor") then, for the purpose of enforcing that judgment or order, the appropriate court may make an order in accordance with the provisions of this Act imposing on any such property of the debtor as may be specified in the order a charge for securing the payment of any money due or to become due under the judgment or order. **38–001**

[26] subss. (4)–(6) added by the Housing Act 1988, s.33(3).

(2) The appropriate court is—

(a) in a case where the property to be charged is a fund in court, the court in which that fund is lodged;

(b) in a case where paragraph (a) above does not apply and the order to be enforced is a maintenance order of the High Court, the High Court or a county court;

(c) in a case where neither paragraph (a) nor paragraph (b) above applies and the judgment or order to be enforced is a judgment or order of the High Court for a sum exceeding [the county court limit][1], the High Court [or a county court][2]; and

(d) in any other case, a county court.

In this section ["county court limit" means the county court limit for the time being specified in an Order in Council under [section 145 of the County Courts Act 1984][3], as the county court limit for the purposes of this section and][4] "maintenance order" has the same meaning as in section 2(a) of the Attachment of Earnings Act 1971.

(3) An order under subsection (1) above is referred to in this Act as a "charging order".

(4) Where a person applies to the High Court for a charging order to enforce more than one judgment or order, that court shall be the appropriate court in relation to the application if it would be the appropriate court, apart from this subsection, on an application relating to one or more of the judgments or orders concerned.

(5) In deciding whether to make a charging order the court shall consider all the circumstances of the case and, in particular, any evidence before it as to—

(a) the personal circumstances of the debtor, and

(b) whether any other creditor of the debtor would be likely to be unduly prejudiced by the making of the order.

Property which may be charged

38–002 **2.**—(1) Subject to subsection (3) below, a charge may be imposed by a charging order only on—

(a) any interest held by the debtor beneficially—

(i) in any asset of a kind mentioned in subsection (2) below, or

(ii) under any trust; or

(b) any interest held by a person as trustee of a trust ("the trust"), if the interest is in such an asset or is an interest under another trust and—

(i) the judgment or order in respect of which a charge is to be imposed was made against that person as trustee of the trust, or

(ii) the whole beneficial interest under the trust is held by the debtor unencumbered and for his own benefit, or

(iii) in a case where there are two or more debtors all of whom are liable to the creditor for the same debt, they together hold the whole beneficial interest under the trust unencumbered and for their own benefit.

(2) The assets referred to in subsection (1) above are—

(a) land,

[1] Words substituted by the Administration of Justice Act 1982, s.37, Sched. 3, Pt. II, paras 2, 3.
[2] Words inserted by the Administration of Justice Act 1982, s.34(3).
[3] Words substituted by the County Courts Act 1984, s.148(1), Sched. 2, Pt. V, para. 71.
[4] Words inserted by the Administration of Justice Act 1982, s.37, Sched. 3, Pt. II, para. 6.

(b) securities of any of the following kinds—
(i) government stock,
(ii) stock of any body (other than a building society) incorporated within England and Wales,
(iii) stock of any body incorporated outside England and Wales or of any state or territory outside the United Kingdom, being stock registered in a register kept at any place within England and Wales,
(iv) units of any unit trust in respect of which a register of the unit holders is kept at any place within England and Wales, or
(c) funds in court.

(3) In any case where a charge is imposed by a charging order on any interest in an asset of a kind mentioned in paragraph (b) or (c) of subsection (2) above, the court making the order may provide for the charge to extend to any interest or dividend payable in respect of the asset.

Provisions supplementing sections 1 and 2

3.—(1) A charging order may be made either absolutely or subject to conditions as to notifying the debtor or as to the time when the charge is to become enforceable, or as to other matters. **38–003**

(2) The Land Charges Act 1972 and the [Land Registration Act 2002][5] shall apply in relation to charging orders as they apply in relation to other orders or writs issued or made for the purposes of enforcing judgments.

(3) [*Repealed by the Land Registration Act 2002, s.135, Sched. 13.*]

(4) Subject to the provisions of this Act, a charge imposed by a charging order shall have the like effect and shall be enforceable in the same courts and in the same manner as an equitable charge created by the debtor by writing under his hand.

(5) The court by which a charging order was made may at any time, on the application of the debtor or of any person interested in any property to which the order relates, make an order discharging or varying the charging order.

(6) Where a charging order has been protected by an entry registered under the Land Charges Act 1972 or the [Land Registration Act 2002][6] an order under subsection (5) above discharging the charging order may direct that the entry be cancelled.

(7) The Lord Chancellor may by order made by statutory instrument amend section 2(2) of this Act by adding to, or removing from, the kinds of asset for the time being referred to there, any asset of a kind which in his opinion ought to be so added or removed.

(8) Any order under subsection (7) above shall be subject to annulment in pursuance of a resolution of either House of Parliament.

4. [*Repealed by the Insolvency Act 1985, s.235(3), Sched. 10, Pt. III.*]

Stop orders and notices

Stop orders and notices

5.—(1) In this section— **38–004**

"stop order" means an order of the court prohibiting the taking, in respect of

[5] Words substituted by the Land Registration Act 2002, s.133, Sched. 11, para. 15.
[6] Words substituted by the Land Registration Act 2002, s.133, Sched. 11, para. 15.

any of the securities specified in the order, of any of the steps mentioned in subsection (5) below;

"stop notice" means a notice requiring any person or body on whom it is duly served to refrain from taking, in respect of any of the securities specified in the notice, any of those steps without first notifying the person by whom, or on whose behalf, the notice was served; and

"prescribed securities" means securities (including funds in court) of a kind prescribed by rules of court made under this section.

[(2) The power to make rules of court under section 1 of, and Schedule 1 to, the Civil Procedure Act 1997 shall include power by any such rules to make provision—

(a) for the High Court to make a stop order on the application of any person claiming to be entitled to an interest in prescribed securities; and

(b) for the service of a stop notice by any person claiming to be entitled to an interest in prescribed securities.][7]

(3) [*Repealed by the Civil Procedure (Modification of Enactments) Order 2002 (S.I. 2002 No. 439), art. 5(b).*]

(4) Rules of court made by virtue of subsection (2) [. . .][8] above shall prescribe the person or body on whom a copy of any stop order or a stop notice is to be served.

(5) The steps mentioned in subsection (1) above are—

(a) the registration of any transfer of the securities;

(b) in the case of funds in court, the transfer, sale, delivery out, payment or other dealing with the funds, or of the income thereon;

(c) the making of any payment by way of dividend, interest or otherwise in respect of the securities; and

(d) in the case of units of a unit trust, any acquisition of or other dealing with the units by any person or body exercising functions under the trust.

(6) Any rules of court made by virtue of this section may include such incidental, supplemental and consequential provisions as the authority making them consider necessary or expedient, and may make different provision in relation to different cases or classes of case.

Supplemental

Interpretation

38–005 **6.**—(1) In this Act—

"building society" has the same meaning as in the Building Societies Act [1986][9];

"charging order" means an order made under section 1(1) of this Act;

"debtor" and "creditor" have the meanings given by section 1(1) of this Act;

"dividend" includes any distribution in respect of any unit of a unit trust;

"government stock" means any stock issued by Her Majesty's government in the United Kingdom or any funds of, or annuity granted by, that government;

"stock" includes shares, debentures and any securities of the body concerned, whether or not constituting a charge on the assets of that body;

"unit trust" means any trust established for the purpose, or having the effect, of

[7] subs. (2) substituted by the Civil Procedure (Modification of Enactments) Order 2002 (S.I. 2002 No. 439), art. 5(a).

[8] Words repealed by the Civil Procedure (Modification of Enactments) Order 2002 (S.I. 2002 No. 439), art. 5(c).

[9] Year substituted by the Building Societies Act 1986, s.120(1), Sched. 18, Pt. I, para. 14.

providing, for persons having funds available for investment, facilities for the participation by them, as beneficiaries under the trust, in any profits or income arising from the acquisition, holding, management or disposal of any property whatsoever.

(2) For the purposes of section 1 of this Act references to a judgment or order of the High Court or a county court shall be taken to include references to a judgment, order, decree or award (however called) of any court or arbitrator (including any foreign court or arbitrator) which is or has become enforceable (whether wholly or to a limited extent) as if it were a judgment or order of the High Court or a county court.

(3) References in section 2 of this Act to any securities include references to any such securities standing in the name of the Accountant General.

. . . . . .

Limitation Act 1980

(1980 c. 58)

Arrangement of Sections

Part I

Ordinary Time Limits for Different Classes of Action

Actions to recover land and rent

PART I

ORDINARY TIME LIMITS FOR DIFFERENT CLASSES OF ACTION

. . . . . .

Actions to recover land and rent[1]

Time limit for actions to recover land

39–001 **15.**—(1) No action shall be brought by any person to recover any land after the expiration of twelve years from the date on which the right of action accrued to him, or if it first accrued to some person through whom he claims, to that person.

(2) Subject to the following provisions of this section, where—

(a) the estate or interest claimed was an estate or interest in reversion or remainder or any other future estate or interest and the right of action to recover the land accrued on the date on which the estate or interest fell into possession by the determination of the preceding estate or interest; and

(b) the person entitled to the preceding estate or interest (not being a term of years absolute) was not in possession of the land on that date;

no action shall be brought by the person entitled to the succeeding estate or interest after the expiration of twelve years from the date on which the right of action accrued to the person entitled to the preceding estate or interest or six years from the date on which the right of action accrued to the person entitled to the succeeding estate or interest, whichever period last expires.

(3) Subsection (2) above shall not apply to any estate or interest which falls into possession on the determination of an entailed interest and which might have been barred by the person entitled to the entailed interest.

(4) No person shall bring an action to recover any estate or interest in land under an assurance taking effect after the right of action to recover the land had

[1] See the Land Registration Act 2002, s.96, *post*, para. 65–096.

accrued to the person by whom the assurance was made or some person through whom he claimed or some person entitled to a preceding estate or interest, unless the action is brought within the period in which the person by whom the assurance was made could have brought such an action.

(5) Where any person is entitled to any estate or interest in land in possession and, while so entitled, is also entitled to any future estate or interest in that land, and his right to recover the estate or interest in possession is barred under this Act, no action shall be brought by that person, or by any person claiming through him, in respect of the future estate or interest, unless in the meantime possession of the land has been recovered by a person entitled to an intermediate estate or interest.

(6) Part I of Schedule 1 to this Act contains provisions for determining the date of accrual of rights of action to recover land in the cases there mentioned.

(7) Part II of that Schedule contains provisions modifying the provisions of this section in their application to actions brought by, or by a person claiming through, the Crown or any spiritual or eleemosynary corporation sole.

Time limit for redemption actions

16. When a mortgagee of land has been in possession of any of the mortgaged land for a period of twelve years, no action to redeem the land of which the mortgagee has been so in possession shall be brought after the end of that period by the mortgagor or any person claiming through him. **39–002**

Extinction of title to land after expiration of time limit

17. Subject to— **39–003**

(a) section 18 of this Act;

[. . .][2]

at the expiration of the period prescribed by this Act for any person to bring an action to recover land (including a redemption action) the title of that person to the land shall be extinguished.

Settled land and land held on trust

18.—(1) Subject to section 21(1) and (2) of this Act, the provisions of this Act shall apply to equitable interests in land [. . .][3], as they apply to legal estates. **39–004**

Accordingly a right of action to recover the land shall, for the purposes of this Act but not otherwise, be treated as accruing to a person entitled in possession to such an equitable interest in the like manner and circumstances, and on the same date, as it would accrue if his interest were a legal estate in the land (and any relevant provision of Part I of Schedule 1 to this Act shall apply in any such case accordingly).

(2) Where the period prescribed by this Act has expired for the bringing of an action to recover land by a tenant for life or a statutory owner of settled land—

(a) his legal estate shall not be extinguished if and so long as the right of action to recover the land of any person entitled to a beneficial interest in the land either has not accrued or has not been barred by this Act; and

[2] Para. (b) repealed by the Land Registration Act 2002, s.135, Sched. 13.
[3] Words repealed by the Trusts of Land and Appointment of Trustees Act 1996, s.25(2), Sched. 4.

(b) the legal estate shall accordingly remain vested in the tenant for life or statutory owner and shall devolve in accordance with the Settled Land Act 1925;

but if and when every such right of action has been barred by this Act, his legal estate shall be extinguished.

(3) Where any land is held upon trust [. . .][4] and the period prescribed by this Act has expired for the bringing of an action to recover the land by the trustees, the estate of the trustees shall not be extinguished if and so long as the right of action to recover the land of any person entitled to a beneficial interest in the land [. . .][5] either has not accrued or has not been barred by this Act; but if and when every such right of action has been so barred the estate of the trustees shall be extinguished.

(4) Where—

(a) any settled land is vested in a statutory owner; or

(b) any land is held upon trust [. . .][6];

an action to recover the land may be brought by the statutory owner or trustees on behalf of any person entitled to a beneficial interest in possession in the land [. . .][7] whose right of action has not been barred by this Act, notwithstanding that the right of action of the statutory owner or trustees would apart from this provision have been barred by this Act.

Time limit for actions to recover rent

39–005 **19.** No action shall be brought, or distress made, to recover arrears of rent, or damages in respect of arrears of rent, after the expiration of six years from the date on which the arrears become due.

[Commonhold

Actions for breach of commonhold duty

39–006 **19A.** An action in respect of a right or duty of a kind referred in section 37(1) of the Commonhold and Leasehold Reform Act 2002 (enforcement) shall not be brought after the expiration of six years from the date on which the cause accrued.][8]

Actions to recover money secured by a mortgage or charge or to recover proceeds of the sale of land

Time limit for actions to recover money secured by a mortgage or charge or to recover proceeds of the sale of land

39–007 **20.**—(1) No action shall be brought to recover—

(a) any principal sum of money secured by a mortgage or other charge on property (whether real or personal); or

[4] Words repealed by the Trusts of Land and Appointment of Trustees Act 1996, s.25(2), Sched. 4.
[5] Words repealed by the Trusts of Land and Appointment of Trustees Act 1996, s.25(2), Sched. 4.
[6] Words repealed by the Trusts of Land and Appointment of Trustees Act 1996, s.25(2), Sched. 4.
[7] Words repealed by the Trusts of Land and Appointment of Trustees Act 1996, s.25(2), Sched. 4.
[8] s.19A inserted by the Commonhold and Leasehold Reform Act 2002, s.68, Sched. 5, para. 4.

(b) proceeds of the sale of land;

after the expiration of twelve years from the date on which the right to receive the money accrued.

(2) No foreclosure action in respect of mortgaged personal property shall be brought after the expiration of twelve years from the date on which the right to foreclose accrued.

But if the mortgagee was in possession of the mortgaged property after that date, the right to foreclose on the property which was in his possession shall not be treated as having accrued for the purposes of this subsection until the date on which his possession discontinued.

(3) The right to receive any principal sum of money secured by a mortgage or other charge and the right to foreclose on the property subject to the mortgage or charge shall not be treated as accruing so long as that property comprises any future interest or any life insurance policy which has not matured or been determined.

(4) Nothing in this section shall apply to a foreclosure action in respect of mortgaged land, but the provisions of this Act relating to actions to recover land shall apply to such an action.

(5) Subject to subsections (6) and (7) below, no action to recover arrears of interest payable in respect of any sum of money secured by a mortgage or other charge or payable in respect of proceeds of the sale of land, or to recover damages in respect of such arrears shall be brought after the expiration of six years from the date on which the interest became due.

(6) Where—

(a) a prior mortgagee or other incumbrancer has been in possession of the property charged; and

(b) an action is brought within one year of the discontinuance of that possession by the subsequent incumbrancer;

the subsequent incumbrancer may recover by that action all the arrears of interest which fell due during the period of possession by the prior incumbrancer or damages in respect of those arrears, notwithstanding that the period exceeded six years.

(7) Where

(a) the property subject to the mortgage or charge comprises any future interest or life insurance policy; and

(b) it is a term of the mortgage or charge that arrears of interest shall be treated as part of the principal sum of money secured by the mortgage or charge;

interest shall not be treated as becoming due before the right to recover the principal sum of money has accrued or is treated as having accrued.

Actions in respect of trust property or the personal estate of deceased persons

Time limits for actions in respect of trust property

21.—(1) No period of limitation prescribed by this Act shall apply to an action by a beneficiary under a trust, being an action— **39–008**

(a) in respect of any fraud or fraudulent breach of trust to which the trustee was a party or privy; or

(b) to recover from the trustee trust property or the proceeds of trust property in the possession of the trustee, or previously received by the trustee and converted to his use.

(2) Where a trustee who is also a beneficiary under the trust receives or retains

trust property or its proceeds as his share on a distribution of trust property under the trust, his liability in any action brought by virtue of subsection (1)(b) above to recover that property or its proceeds after the expiration of the period of limitation prescribed by this Act for bringing an action to recover trust property shall be limited to the excess over his proper share.

This subsection only applies if the trustee acted honestly and reasonably in making the distribution.

(3) Subject to the preceding provisions of this section, an action by a beneficiary to recover trust property or in respect of any breach of trust, not being an action for which a period of limitation is prescribed by any other provision of this Act, shall not be brought after the expiration of six years from the date on which the right of action accrued.

For the purposes of this subsection, the right of action shall not be treated as having accrued to any beneficiary entitled to a future interest in the trust property until the interest fell into possession.

(4) No beneficiary as against whom there would be a good defence under this Act shall derive any greater or other benefit from a judgment or order obtained by any other beneficiary than he could have obtained if he had brought the action and this Act had been pleaded in defence.

Time limit for actions claiming personal estate of a deceased person

39–009 **22.** Subject to section 21(1) and (2) of this Act—

(a) no action in respect of any claim to the personal estate of a deceased person or to any share or interest in any such estate (whether under a will or on intestacy) shall be brought after the expiration of twelve years from the date on which the right to receive the share or interest accrued; and

(b) no action to recover arrears of interest in respect of any legacy, or damages in respect of such arrears, shall be brought after the expiration of six years from the date on which the interest became due.

Actions for an account

Time limit in respect of actions for an account

39–010 **23.** An action for an account shall not be brought after the expiration of any time limit under this Act which is applicable to the claim which is the basis of the duty to account.

Miscellaneous and supplemental

. . . . . .

Administration to date back to death

39–011 **26.** For the purposes of the provisions of this Act relating to actions for the recovery of land and advowsons an administrator of the estate of a deceased person shall be treated as claiming as if there had been no interval of time between the death of the deceased person and the grant of the letters of administration.

. . . . . .

PART II

EXTENSION OR EXCLUSION OF ORDINARY TIME LIMITS

Disability

Extension of limitation period in case of disability

28.—(1) Subject to the following provisions of this section, if on the date when any right of action accrued for which a period of limitation is prescribed by this Act, the person to whom it accrued was under a disability, the action may be brought at any time before the expiration of six years from the date when he ceased to be under a disability or died (whichever first occurred) notwithstanding that the period of limitation has expired. **39–012**

(2) This section shall not affect any case where the right of action first accrued to some person (not under a disability) through whom the person under a disability claims.

(3) When a right of action which has accrued to a person under a disability accrues, on the death of that person while still under a disability, to another person under a disability, no further extension of time shall be allowed by reason of the disability of the second person.

(4) No action to recover land or money charged on land shall be brought by virtue of this section by any person after the expiration of thirty years from the date on which the right of action accrued to that person or some person through whom he claims.

. . . .

Acknowledgment and part payment

Fresh accrual of action on acknowledgment or part payment

29.—(1) Subsections (2) and (3) below apply where any right of action (including a foreclosure action) to recover land or an advowson or any right of a mortgagee of personal property to bring a foreclosure action in respect of the property has accrued. **39–013**

(2) If the person in possession of the land, benefice or personal property in question acknowledges the title of the person to whom the right of action has accrued—

(a) the right shall be treated as having accrued on and not before the date of the acknowledgment; and

(b) in the case of a right of action to recover land which has accrued to a person entitled to an estate or interest taking effect on the determination of an entailed interest against whom time is running under section 27 of this Act, section 27 shall thereupon cease to apply to the land.

(3) In the case of a foreclosure or other action by a mortgagee, if the person in possession of the land, benefice or personal property in question or the person liable for the mortgage debt makes any payment in respect of the debt (whether of principal or interest) the right shall be treated as having accrued on and not before the date of the payment.

(4) Where a mortgagee is by virtue of the mortgage in possession of any mortgaged land and either—

(a) receives any sum in respect of the principal or interest of the mortgage debt; or

(b) acknowledges the title of the mortgagor, or his equity of redemption;

an action to redeem the land in his possession may be brought at any time before the expiration of twelve years from the date of the payment or acknowledgment.

(5) Subject to subsection (6) below, where any right of action has accrued to recover—

(a) any debt or other liquidated pecuniary claim; or

(b) any claim to the personal estate of a deceased person or to any share or interest in any such estate;

and the person liable or accountable for the claim acknowledges the claim or makes any payment in respect of it the right shall be treated as having accrued on and not before the date of the acknowledgment or payment.

(6) A payment of a part of the rent or interest due at any time shall not extend the period for claiming the remainder then due, but any payment of interest shall be treated as a payment in respect of the principal debt.

(7) Subject to subsection (6) above, a current period of limitation may be repeatedly extended under this section by further acknowledgments or payments, but a right of action, once barred by this Act, shall not be revived by any subsequent acknowledgment or payment.

Formal provisions as to acknowledgments and part payments

39–014 **30.**—(1) To be effective for the purposes of section 29 of this Act, an acknowledgment must be in writing and signed by the person making it.

(2) For the purposes of section 29, any acknowledgment or payment—

(a) may be made by the agent of the person by whom it is required to be made under that section; and

(b) shall be made to the person, or to an agent of the person, whose title or claim is being acknowledged or, as the case may be, in respect of whose claim the payment is being made.

Effect of acknowledgment or part payment on persons other than the maker or recipient

39–015 **31.**—(1) An acknowledgment of the title to any land, benefice, or mortgaged personalty by any person in possession of it shall bind all other persons in possession during the ensuing period of limitation.

(2) A payment in respect of a mortgage debt by the mortgagor or any other person liable for the debt, or by any person in possession of the mortgaged property, shall, so far as any right of the mortgagee to foreclose or otherwise to recover the property is concerned, bind all other persons in possession of the mortgaged property during the ensuing period of limitation.

(3) Where two of more mortgagees are by virtue of the mortgage in possession of the mortgaged land, an acknowledgment of the mortgagor's title or of his equity of redemption by one of the mortgagees shall only bind him and his successors and shall not bind any other mortgagee or his successors.

(4) Where in a case within subsection (3) above the mortgagee by whom the acknowledgment is given is entitled to a part of the mortgaged land and not to any ascertained part of the mortgage debt the mortgagor shall be entitled to

redeem that part of the land on payment, with interest, of the part of the mortgage debt which bears the same proportion to the whole of the debt as the value of the part of the land bears to the whole of the mortgaged land.

(5) Where there are two or more mortgagors, and the title or equity of redemption of one of the mortgagors is acknowledged as mentioned above in this section, the acknowledgment shall be treated as having been made to all the mortgagors.

(6) An acknowledgment of any debt or other liquidated pecuniary claim shall bind the acknowledgor and his successors but not any other person.

(7) A payment made in respect of any debt or other liquidated pecuniary claim shall bind all persons liable in respect of the debt or claim.

(8) An acknowledgment by one of several personal representatives of any claim to the personal estate of a deceased person or to any share or interest in any such estate, or a payment by one of several personal representatives in respect of any such claim, shall bind the estate of the deceased person.

(9) In this section "successor", in relation to any mortgagee or person liable in respect of any debt or claim, means his personal representatives and any other person on whom the rights under the mortgage or, as the case may be, the liability in respect of the debt or claim devolve (whether on death or bankruptcy or the disposition of property or the determination of a limited estate or interest in settled property or otherwise).

Fraud, concealment and mistake

Postponement of limitation period in case of fraud, concealment or mistake

32.—(1) Subject to [subsections (3) and (4A)][9] below, where in the case of any **39–016**
action for which a period of limitation is prescribed by this Act, either—

(a) the action is based upon the fraud of the defendant; or
(b) any fact relevant to the plaintiff's right of action has been deliberately concealed from him by the defendant; or
(c) the action is for relief from the consequences of a mistake;

the period of limitation shall not begin to run until the plaintiff has discovered the fraud, concealment or mistake (as the case may be) or could with reasonable diligence have discovered it.

References in this subsection to the defendant include references to the defendant's agent and to any person through whom the defendant claims and his agent.

(2) For the purposes of subsection (1) above, deliberate commission of a breach of duty in circumstances in which it is unlikely to be discovered for some time amounts to deliberate concealment of the facts involved in that breach of duty.

(3) Nothing in this section shall enable any action—

(a) to recover, or recover the value of, any property; or
(b) to enforce any charge against, or set aside any transaction affecting, any property;

to be brought against the purchaser of the property or any person claiming through him in any case where the property has been purchased for valuable consideration by an innocent third party since the fraud or concealment or (as the case may be) the transaction in which the mistake was made took place.

[9] Words substituted by the Consumer Protection Act 1987, s.6(6), Sched. 1, para. 5.

(4) A purchaser is an innocent third party for the purposes of this section—

(a) in the case of fraud or concealment of any fact relevant to the plaintiff's right of action, if he was not a party to the fraud or (as the case may be) to the concealment of that fact and did not at the time of the purchase know or have reason to believe that the fraud or concealment had taken place; and

(b) in the case of mistake, if he did not at the time of the purchase know or have reason to believe that the mistake had been made.

. . . . . .

PART III

MISCELLANEOUS AND GENERAL

. . . . . .

Interpretation

39–017 **38.**—(1) In this Act, unless the context otherwise requires—

"action" includes any proceedings in a court of law, including an ecclesiastical court;

"land" includes corporeal hereditaments, tithes and rentcharges and any legal or equitable estate or interest therein [. . .][10], but except as provided above in this definition does not include any incorporeal hereditament;

"personal estate" and "personal property" do not include chattels real;

. . . . . .

"rent" includes a rentcharge and a rentservice;

"rentcharge" means any annuity or periodical sum of money charged upon or payable out of land, except a rent service or interest on a mortgage on land;

"settled land", "statutory owner" and "tenant for life" have the same meanings respectively as in the Settled Land Act 1925;

"trust" and "trustee" have the same meanings respectively as in the Trustee Act 1925.

[. . .][11]

(2) For the purposes of this Act a person shall be treated as under a disability while he is an infant, or of unsound mind.

(3) For the purposes of subsection (2) above a person is of unsound mind if he is a person who, by reason of mental disorder [is incapable of managing and administering his property and affairs; and in this section "mental disorder" has the same meaning as in the Mental Health Act 1983][12].

(4) Without prejudice to the generality of subsection (3) above, a person shall be conclusively presumed for the purposes of subsection (2) above to be of unsound mind—

[10] Words repealed by the Trusts of Land and Appointment of Trustees Act 1996, s.25(2), Sched. 4.

[11] Definition of "trust for sale" repealed by the Trusts of Land and Appointment of Trustees Act 1996, s.25(2), Sched. 4.

[12] Words substituted by the Care Standards Act 2000, s.116, Sched. 4, para. 8(a).

(a) while he is liable to be detained or subject to guardianship under [the Mental Health Act 1983 (otherwise than by virtue of section 35 or 89)][13]; and

[(b) while he is receiving treatment [for mental disorder][14] as an in-patient in any hospital within the meaning of the Mental Health Act 1983 [or independent hospital or care home within the meaning of the Care Standards Act 2000][15] without being liable to be detained under the said Act 1983 (otherwise than by virtue of section 35 or 89), being treatment which follows without any interval a period during which he was liable to be detained or subject to guardianship under the Mental Health Act 1959, or the said Act of 1983 (otherwise than by virtue of section 35 or 89) or by virtue of any enactment repealed or excluded by the Mental Health Act 1959.][16]

(5) Subject to subsection (6) below, a person shall be treated as claiming through another person if he became entitled by, through, under, or by the act of that other person to the right claimed, and any person whose estate or interest might have been barred by a person entitled to an entailed interest in possession shall be treated as claiming through the person so entitled.

(6) A person becoming entitled to any estate or interest by virtue of a special power of appointment shall not be treated as claiming through the appointor.

(7) References in this Act to a right of action to recover land shall include references to a right to enter into possession of the land or, in the case of rentcharges and tithes, to distrain for arrears of rent or tithe, and references to the bringing of such an action shall include references to the making of such an entry or distress.

(8) References in this Act to the possession of land shall, in the case of tithes and rentcharges, be construed as references to the receipt of the tithe or rent, and references to the date of dispossession or discontinuance of possession of land shall, in the case of rent charges, be construed as references to the date of the last receipt of rent.

(9) References in Part II of this Act to a right of action shall include references to—

(a) a cause of action;

(b) a right to receive money secured by a mortgage or charge on any property;

(c) a right to recover proceeds of the sale of land; and

(d) a right to receive a share or interest in the personal estate of a deceased person.

(10) References in Part II to the date of the accrual of a right of action shall be construed—

(a) in the case of an action upon a judgment, as references to the date on which the judgment became enforceable; and

(b) in the case of an action to recover arrears of rent or interest, or damages in respect of arrears of rent or interest, as references to the date on which the rent or interest became due.

. . . . . .

[13] Words substituted by the Mental Health Act 1983, s.148(1), Sched. 4, para. 55.
[14] Words inserted by the Care Standards Act 2000, s.116, Sched. 4, para. 8(b).
[15] Words substituted by the Care Standards Act 2000, s.116, Sched. 4, para. 8(b).
[16] Para. (b) substituted by the Mental Health Act 1983, s.148(1), Sched. 4, para. 55.

SCHEDULES

Section 15(6) (7)

SCHEDULE 1

PROVISIONS WITH RESPECT TO ACTIONS TO RECOVER LAND

PART I

ACCRUAL OF RIGHTS OF ACTION TO RECOVER LAND

Accrual of right of action in case of present interests in land

1. Where the person bringing an action to recover land, or some person through whom he claims, has been in possession of the land, and has while entitled to the land been dispossessed or discontinued his possession, the right of action shall be treated as having accrued on the date of the dispossession or discontinuance.

2. Where any person brings an action to recover any land of a deceased person (whether under a will or on intestacy) and the deceased person—

(a) was on the date of his death in possession of the land or, in the case of a rentcharge created by will or taking effect upon his death, in possession of the land charged; and

(b) was the last person entitled to the land to be in possession of it;

the right of action shall be treated as having accrued on the date of his death.

3. Where any person brings an action to recover land, being an estate or interest in possession assured otherwise than by will to him, or to some person through whom he claims, and—

(a) the person making the assurance was on the date when the assurance took effect in possession of the land or, in the case of a rentcharge created by the assurance, in possession of the land charged; and

(b) no person has been in possession of the land by virtue of the assurance;

the right of action shall be treated as having accrued on the date when the assurance took effect.

Accrual of right of action in case of future interests

4. The right of action to recover any land shall, in a case where—

(a) the estate or interest claimed was an estate or interest in reversion or remainder or any other future estate or interest; and

(b) no person has taken possession of the land by virtue of the estate or interest claimed;

be treated as having accrued on the date on which the estate or interest fell into possession by the determination of the preceding estate or interest.

5.—(1) Subject to sub-paragraph (2) below, a tenancy from year to year or other period, without a lease in writing, shall for the purposes of this Act be treated as being determined at the expiration of the first year or other period; and accordingly the right of action of the person entitled to the land subject to the tenancy shall be treated as having accrued at the date on which in accordance with this sub-paragraph the tenancy is determined.

(2) Where any rent has subsequently been received in respect of the tenancy, the right of action shall be treated as having accrued on the date of the last receipt of rent.

6.—(1) Where—

(a) any person is in possession of land by virtue of a lease in writing by which a rent of not less than ten pounds a year is reserved; and

(b) the rent is received by some person wrongfully claiming to be entitled to the land in reversion immediately expectant on the determination of the lease; and

(c) no rent is subsequently received by the person rightfully so entitled;

the right of action to recover the land of the person rightfully so entitled shall be treated as having accrued on the date when the rent was first received by the person wrongfully claiming to be so entitled and not on the date of the determination of the lease.

(2) Sub-paragraph (1) above shall not apply to any lease granted by the Crown.

Accrual of right of action in case of forfeiture or breach of condition

7.—(1) Subject to sub-paragraph (2) below, a right of action to recover land by virtue of a forfeiture or breach of condition shall be treated as having accrued on the date on which the forfeiture was incurred or the condition broken.

(2) If any such right has accrued to a person entitled to an estate or interest in reversion or remainder and the land was not recovered by virtue of that right, the right of action to recover the land shall not be treated as having accrued to that person until his estate or interest fell into possession, as if no such forfeiture or breach of condition had occurred.

Right of action not to accrue or continue unless there is adverse possession

8.—(1) No right of action to recover land shall be treated as accruing unless the land is in the possession of some person in whose favour the period of limitation can run (referred to below in this paragraph as "adverse possession"); and where under the preceding provisions of this Schedule any such right of action is treated as accruing on a certain date and no person is in adverse possession on that date, the right of action shall not be treated as accruing unless and until adverse possession is taken of the land.

(2) Where a right of action land has accrued and after its accrual, before the right is barred, the land ceases to be in adverse possession, the right of action shall no longer be treated as having accrued and no fresh right of action shall be treated as accruing unless and until the land is again taken into adverse possession.

(3) For the purposes of this paragraph—

(a) possession of any land subject to a rentcharge by a person (other than the person entitled to the rentcharge) who does not pay the rent shall be treated as adverse possession of the rentcharge; and

(b) receipt of rent under a lease by a person wrongfully claiming to be entitled to the land in reversion immediately expectant on the determination of the lease shall be treated as adverse possession of the land.

(4) For the purpose of determining whether a person occupying any land is in adverse possession of the land it shall not be assumed by implication of law that his occupation is by permission of the person entitled to the land merely by virtue of the fact that his occupation is not inconsistent with the latter's present or future enjoyment of the land.

This provision shall not be taken as prejudicing a finding to the effect that a person's occupation of any land is by implied permission of the person entitled to the land in any case where such a finding is justified on the actual facts of the case.

Possession of beneficiary not adverse to others interested in settled land or land held on trust for sale

9. Where any settled land or any land [subject to a trust of land][17] is in the possession of a person entitled to a beneficial interest in the land [. . .][18] (not being a person solely or absolutely entitled to the land [. . .][19]), no right of action to recover the land shall be treated for the purposes of this Act as accruing during that possession to any person in whom the land is vested as tenant for life, statutory owner or trustee, or to any other person entitled to a beneficial interest in the land [. . .][20].

---

[17] Words substituted by the Trusts of Land and Appointment of Trustees Act 1996, s.25(1), Sched. 3, para. 18.

[18] Words repealed by the Trusts of Land and Appointment of Trustees Act 1996, s.25(2), Sched. 4.

[19] Words repealed by the Trusts of Land and Appointment of Trustees Act 1996, s.25(2), Sched. 4.

[20] Words repealed by the Trusts of Land and Appointment of Trustees Act 1996, s.25(2), Sched. 4.

Supreme Court Act 1981

(1981 c. 54)

Part II

Jurisdiction

The High Court

Other particular fields of jurisdiction

Probate jurisdiction of High Court

40–001 **25.**—(1) Subject to the provisions of Part V, the High Court shall, in accordance with section 19(2), have the following probate jurisdiction, that is to say all such jurisdiction in relation to probates and letters of administration as it had immediately before the commencement of this Act, and in particular all such contentious and non-contentious jurisdiction as it then had in relation to—

(a) testamentary causes or matters;
(b) the grant, amendment or revocation of probates and letters of administration; and
(c) the real and personal estate of deceased persons.

(2) Subject to the provisions of Part V, the High Court shall, in the exercise of its probate jurisdiction, perform all such duties with respect to the estates of deceased persons as fell to be performed by it immediately before the commencement of this Act.

Powers

Powers of High Court with respect to injunctions and receivers

40–002 **37.**—(1) The High Court may by order (whether interlocutory or final) grant an injunction or appoint a receiver in all cases in which it appears to the court to be just and convenient to do so.

(2) Any such order may be made either unconditionally or on such terms and conditions as the court thinks just.

(3) The power of the High Court under subsection (1) to grant an interlocutory injunction restraining a party to any proceedings from removing from the jurisdiction of the High Court, or otherwise dealing with, assets located within that jurisdiction shall be exercisable in cases where that party is, as well as in cases where he is not, domiciled, resident or present within that jurisdiction.

(4) The power of the High Court to appoint a receiver by way of equitable execution shall operate in relation to all legal estates and interests in land; and that power—

(a) may be exercised in relation to an estate or interest in land whether or not a charge has been imposed on that land under section 1 of the Charging Orders Act 1979 for the purpose of enforcing the judgment, order or award in question; and
(b) shall be in addition to, and not in derogation of, any power of any court to appoint a receiver in proceedings for enforcing such a charge.

(5) Where an order under the said section 1 imposing a charge for the purpose of enforcing a judgment, order or award has been, or has effect as if, registered under section 6 of the Land Charges Act 1972, subsection (4) of the said section 6 (effect of non-registration of writs and orders registrable under that section) shall not apply to an order appointing a receiver made either—

(a) in proceedings for enforcing the charge; or

(b) by way of equitable execution of the judgment, order or award or, as the case may be, of so much of it as requires payment of moneys secured by the charge.

Relief against forfeiture for non-payment of rent

38.[1]—(1) In any action in the High Court for the forfeiture of a lease for non-payment of rent, the court shall have power to grant relief against forfeiture in a summary manner, and may do so subject to the same terms and conditions as to the payment of rent, costs or otherwise as could have been imposed by it in such an action immediately before the commencement of this Act. **40–003**

(2) Where the lessee or a person deriving title under him is granted relief under this section, he shall hold the demised premises in accordance with the terms of the lease without the necessity for a new lease.

GENERAL PROVISIONS

Law and equity

Concurrent administration of law and equity

49.—(1) Subject to the provisions of this or any other Act, every court exercising jurisdiction in England and Wales in any civil cause or matter shall continue to administer law and equity on the basis that, wherever there is any conflict or variance between the rules of equity and the rules of the common law with reference to the same matter, the rules of equity shall prevail. **40–004**

(2) Every such court shall give the same effect as hitherto—

(a) to all equitable estates, titles, rights, reliefs, defences and counter-claims, and to all equitable duties and liabilities; and

(b) subject thereto, to all legal claims and demands and all estates, titles, rights, duties, obligations and liabilities existing by the common law or by any custom or created by any statute,

and, subject to the provisions of this or any other Act, shall so exercise its jurisdiction in every cause or matter before it as to secure that, as far as possible, all matters in dispute between the parties are completely and finally determined, and all multiplicity of legal proceedings with respect to any of those matters is avoided.

(3) Nothing in this Act shall affect the power of the Court of Appeal or the High Court to stay any proceedings before it, where it thinks fit to do so, either of its own motion or on the application of any person, whether or not a party to the proceedings.

[1] See the Common Law Procedure Act 1852, ss.210–212, *ante*, paras 4–001 *et seq*., and the Law of Property Act 1925, s.146(4), *ante*, para. 9–122.

Power to award damages as well as, or in substitution for, injunction or specific performance

40–005 **50.** Where the Court of Appeal or the High Court has jurisdiction to entertain an application for an injunction or specific performance, it may award damages in addition to, or in substitution for, an injunction or specific performance.

PART III

PRACTICE AND PROCEDURE

. . . . . .

THE HIGH COURT

Distribution of business

Distribution of business among Divisions

40–006 **61.**—(1) Subject to any provision made by or under this or any other Act (and in particular to any rules of court made in pursuance of subsection (2) and any order under subsection (3)), business in the High Court of any description mentioned in Schedule 1, as for the time being in force, shall be distributed among the Divisions in accordance with that Schedule.

. . . . . .

PART V

PROBATE CAUSES AND MATTERS

Procedure in probate registries in relation to grants of representation

Applications

40–007 **105.** Applications for grants of probate or administration and for the revocation of grants may be made to—

(a) the Principal Registry of the Family Division (in this Part referred to as "the Principal Registry"); or
(b) a district probate registry.

Grants by district probate registrars

40–008 **106.**—(1) Any grant made by a district probate registrar shall be made in the name of the High Court under the seal used in the registry.

(2)–(4) [*Repealed by the Administration of Justice Act 1985, ss.51(2), 67(2), Sched. 8, Pt. III.*]

No grant where conflicting applications

40–009 **107.** Subject to probate rules, no grant in respect of the estate, or part of the estate, of a deceased person shall be made out of the Principal Registry or any district probate registry on any application if, at any time before the making of a grant, it appears to the registrar concerned that some other application has been made in respect of that estate or, as the case may be, that part of it and has not been either refused or withdrawn.

Caveats

108.—(1) A caveat against a grant of probate or administration may be entered in the Principal Registry or in any district probate registry. **40–010**

(2) On a caveat being entered in a district probate registry, the district probate registrar shall immediately send a copy of it to the Principal Registry to be entered among the caveats in that Registry.

Refusal of grant where inheritance tax unpaid

109.—(1) Subject to subsections (2) and (3), no grant shall be made, and no grant made outside the United Kingdom shall be resealed, except on the production of an account prepared in pursuance of [the Inheritance Tax Act 1984][2] showing by means of such receipt or certification as may be prescribed by the Commissioners of Inland Revenue (in this and the following section referred to as "the Commissioners") either— **40–011**

(a) that the [inheritance tax][3] payable on the delivery of the account has been paid; or

(b) that no such tax is so payable.

(2) Arrangements may be made between the President of the Family Division and the Commissioners providing for the purposes of this section in such cases as may be specified in the arrangements that the receipt or certification of an account may be dispensed with or that some other document may be substituted for the account required by [the Inheritance Tax Act 1984][4].

(3) Nothing in subsection (1) applies in relation to a case where the delivery of the account required by that Part of that Act has for the time being been dispensed with by any regulations under [section 256(1)(a) of the Inheritance Tax Act 1984][5].

Documents to be delivered to Commissioners of Inland Revenue

110. Subject to any arrangements which may from time to time be made between the President of the Family Division and the Commissioners, the Principal Registry and every district probate registry shall, within such period after a grant as the President may direct, deliver to the Commissioners or their proper officer the following documents— **40–012**

(a) in the case of a grant of probate or of administration with the will annexed, a copy of the will;

(b) in every case, such certificate or note of the grant as the Commissioners may require.

---

[2] Words substituted by the Inheritance Tax Act 1984 (formerly the Capital Transfer Tax Act 1984: see the Finance Act 1986, s.100(1)(a)), s.276, Sched. 8, para. 20.

[3] From July 25, 1986, any reference to capital transfer tax, except where the reference relates to a liability to tax arising before that date, has effect as a reference to inheritance tax: Finance Act 1986, s.100(1)(b), (2).

[4] Words substituted by the Inheritance Tax Act 1984 (formerly the Capital Transfer Tax Act 1984: see the Finance Act 1986, s.100(1)(a)), s.276, Sched. 8, para. 20.

[5] Words substituted by the Inheritance Tax Act 1984 (formerly the Capital Transfer Tax Act 1984: see the Finance Act 1986, s.100(1)(a)), s.276, Sched. 8, para. 20.

Records of grant

40–013 **111.**—(1) There shall continue to be kept records of all grants which are made in the Principal Registry or in any district probate registry.

(2) Those records shall be in such form, and shall contain such particulars, as the President of the Family Division may direct.

Powers of court in relation to personal representatives

Summons to executor to prove or renounce

40–014 **112.** The High Court may summon any person named as executor in a will to prove, or renounce probate of, the will, and to do such other things concerning the will as the court had power to order such a person to do immediately before the commencement of this Act.

Power of court to sever grant

40–015 **113.**—(1) Subject to subsection (2), the High Court may grant probate or administration in respect of any part of the estate of a deceased person, limited in any way the court thinks fit.

(2) Where the estate of a deceased person is known to be insolvent, the grant of representation to it shall not be severed under subsection (1) except as regards a trust estate in which he had no beneficial interest.

Number of personal representatives

40–016 **114.**—(1) Probate or administration shall not be granted by the High Court to more than four persons in respect of the same part of the estate of a deceased person.

(2) Where under a will or intestacy any beneficiary is a minor or a life interest arises, any grant of administration by the High Court shall be made either to a trust corporation (with or without an individual) or to not less than two individuals, unless it appears to the court to be expedient in all the circumstances to appoint an individual as sole administrator.

(3) For the purpose of determining whether a minority or life interest arises in a particular case, the court may act on such evidence as may be prescribed.

(4) If at any time during the minority of a beneficiary or the subsistence of a life interest under a will or intestacy there is only one personal representative (not being a trust corporation), the High Court may, on the application of any person interested or the guardian or receiver of any such person, and in accordance with probate rules, appoint one or more additional personal representatives to act while the minority or life interest subsists and until the estate is fully administered.

(5) An appointment of an additional personal representative under subsection (4) to act with an executor shall not have the effect of including him in any chain of representation.

Grants to trust corporations

40–017 **115.**—(1) The High Court may—

(a) where a trust corporation is named in a will as executor, grant probate to the corporation either solely or jointly with any other person named in the will as executor, as the case may require; or

(b) grant administration to a trust corporation, either solely or jointly with another person;

and the corporation may act accordingly as executor or administrator, as the case may be.

(2) Probate or administration shall not be granted to any person as nominee of a trust corporation.

(3) Any officer authorised for the purpose by a trust corporation or its directors or governing body may, on behalf of the corporation, swear affidavits, give security and do any other act which the court may require with a view to the grant to the corporation of probate or administration; and the acts of an officer so authorised shall be binding on the corporation.

[(4) Subsections (1) to (3) shall also apply in relation to any body which is exempt from the provisions of section 23(1) of the Solicitors Act 1974 (unqualified persons not to prepare papers for probate etc.) by virtue of any of paragraphs (e) to (h) of subsection (2) of that section.][6]

Power of court to pass over prior claims to grant

116.—(1) If by reason of any special circumstances it appears to the High Court to be necessary or expedient to appoint as administrator some person other than the person who, but for this section, would in accordance with probate rules have been entitled to the grant, the court may in its discretion appoint as administrator such person as it thinks expedient. **40–018**

(2) Any grant of administration under this section may be limited in any way the court thinks fit.

Administration pending suit

117.—(1) Where any legal proceedings concerning the validity of the will of a deceased person, or for obtaining, recalling or revoking any grant, are pending, the High Court may grant administration of the estate of the deceased person in question to an administrator pending suit, who shall, subject to subsection (2), have all the rights, duties and powers of a general administrator. **40–019**

(2) An administrator pending suit shall be subject to the immediate control of the court and act under its direction; and, except in such circumstances as may be prescribed, no distribution of the estate, or any part of the estate, of the deceased person in question shall be made by such an administrator without the leave of the court.

(3) The court may, out of the estate of the deceased, assign an admin- istrator pending suit such reasonable remuneration as it thinks fit.

Effect of appointment of minor as executor

118. Where a testator by his will appoints a minor to be an executor, the appointment shall not operate to vest in the minor the estate, or any part of the estate, of the testator, or to constitute him a personal representative for any purpose, unless and until probate is granted to him in accordance with probate rules. **40–020**

[6] subs. (4) added by the Courts and Legal Services Act 1990, s.54(2), from a day to be appointed.

Administration with will annexed

40–021 **119.**—(1) Administration with the will annexed shall be granted, subject to and in accordance with probate rules, in every class of case in which the High Court had power to make such a grant immediately before the commencement of this Act.

(2) Where administration with the will annexed is granted, the will of the deceased shall be performed and observed in the same manner as if probate of it had been granted to an executor.

Power to require administrators to produce sureties

40–022 **120.**—(1) As a condition of granting administration to any person the High Court may, subject to the following provisions of this section and subject to and in accordance with probate rules, require one or more sureties to guarantee that they will make good, within any limit imposed by the court on the total liability of the surety or sureties, any loss which any person interested in the administration of the estate of the deceased may suffer in consequence of a breach by the administrator of his duties as such.

(2) A guarantee given in pursuance of any such requirement shall enure for the benefit of every person interested in the administration of the estate of the deceased as if contained in a contract under seal made by the surety or sureties with every such person and, where there are two or more sureties, as if they had bound themselves jointly and severally.

(3) No action shall be brought on any such guarantee without the leave of the High Court.

(4) Stamp duty shall not be chargeable on any such guarantee.

(5) This section does not apply where administration is granted to the Treasury Solicitor, the Official Solicitor, the Public Trustee, the Solicitor for the affairs of the Duchy of Lancaster or the Duchy of Cornwall or the Crown Solicitor for Northern Ireland, or to the consular officer of a foreign state to which section 1 of the Consular Conventions Act 1949 applies, or in such other cases as may be prescribed.

Revocation of grants and cancellation of resealing at instance of court

Revocation of grants and cancellation of resealing at instance of court

40–023 **121.**—(1) Where it appears to the High Court that a grant either ought not to have been made or contains an error, the court may call in the grant and, if satisfied that it would be revoked at the instance of a party interested, may revoke it.

(2) A grant may be revoked under subsection (1) without being called in, if it cannot be called in.

(3) Where it appears to the High Court that a grant resealed under the Colonial Probates Acts 1892 and 1927 ought not to have been resealed, the court may call in the relevant document and, if satisfied that the resealing would be cancelled at the instance of a party interested, may cancel the resealing.

In this and the following subsection "the relevant document" means the original grant or, where some other document was sealed by the court under those Acts, that document.

(4) A resealing may be cancelled under subsection (3) without the relevant document being called in, if it cannot be called in.

Ancillary powers of court

Examination of person with knowledge of testamentary document

122.—(1) Where it appears that there are reasonable grounds for believing that any person has knowledge of any document which is or purports to be a testamentary document, the High Court may, whether or not any legal proceedings are pending, order him to attend for the purpose of being examined in open court. **40–024**

(2) The court may—

(a) require any person who is before it in compliance with an order under subsection (1) to answer any question relating to the document concerned; and

(b) if appropriate, order him to bring in the document in such manner as the court may direct.

(3) Any person who, having been required by the court to do so under this section, fails to attend for examination, answer any question or bring in any document shall be guilty of contempt of court.

Subpoena to bring in testamentary document

123. Where it appears that any person has in his possession, custody or power any document which is or purports to be a testamentary document, the High Court may, whether or not any legal proceedings are pending, issue a subpoena requiring him to bring in the document in such manner as the court may in the subpoena direct. **40–025**

Provisions as to documents

Place for deposit of original wills and other documents

124. All original wills and other documents which are under the control of the High Court in the Principal Registry or in any district probate registry shall be deposited and preserved in such places as the Lord Chancellor may direct; and any wills or other documents so deposited shall, subject to the control of the High Court and to probate rules, be open to inspection. **40–026**

Copies of wills and grants

125. An office copy, or a sealed and certified copy, of any will or part of a will open to inspection under section 124 or of any grant may, on payment of the prescribed fee, be obtained— **40–027**

(a) from the registry in which in accordance with section 124 the will or documents relating to the grant are preserved; or

(b) where in accordance with that section the will or such documents are preserved in some place other than a registry, from the Principal Registry; or

(c) subject to the approval of the Senior Registrar of the Family Division, from the Principal Registry in any case where the will was proved in or the grant was issued from a district probate registry.

Depositories for wills of living persons

40–028 **126.**[7]—(1) There shall be provided, under the control and direction of the High Court, safe and convenient depositories for the custody of the wills of living persons; and any person may deposit his will in such a depository on payment of the prescribed fee and subject to such conditions as may be prescribed by regulations made by the President of the Family Division with the concurrence of the Lord Chancellor.

(2) Any regulations made under this section shall be made by statutory instrument which shall be laid before Parliament after being made; and the Statutory Instruments Act 1946 shall apply to a statutory instrument containing regulations under this section in like manner as if they had been made by a Minister of the Crown.

Probate rules

Probate rules

40–029 **127.**—(1) The President of the Family Division may, with the concurrence of the Lord Chancellor, make rules of court (in this Part referred to as "probate rules") for regulating and prescribing the practice and procedure of the High Court with respect to non-contentious or common form probate business.

(2)[8] Without prejudice to the generality of subsection (1), probate rules may make provision for regulating the classes of persons entitled to grants of probate or administration in particular circumstances and the relative priorities of their claims thereto.

(3) Probate rules shall be made by statutory instrument subject to annulment in pursuance of a resolution of either House of Parliament; and the Statutory Instruments Act 1946 shall apply to a statutory instrument containing probate rules in like manner as if they had been made by a Minister of the Crown.

Interpretation of Part V and other probate provisions

Interpretation of Part V and other probate provisions

40–030 **128.** In this Part, and in the other provisions of this Act relating to probate causes and matters, unless the context otherwise requires—

"administration" includes all letters of administration of the effects of deceased persons, whether with or without a will annexed, and whether granted for general, special or limited purposes;

"estate" means real and personal estate, and "real estate" includes—

(a) chattels real and land in possession, remainder or reversion and every interest in or over land to which the deceased person was entitled at the time of his death, and

(b) real estate held on trust or by way of mortgage or security, but not [. . .][9] money secured or charged on land;

"grant" means a grant of probate or administration;

"non-contentious or common form probate business" means the business of

---

[7] s.126 repealed by the Administration of Justice Act 1982, s.75, Sched. 9, Pt. I, from a day to be appointed.

[8] See the Family Law Reform Act 1987, s.21, *post*, para. 50–004.

[9] Words repealed by the Trusts of Land and Appointment of Trustees Act 1996, s.25(2), Sched. 4.

obtaining probate and administration where there is no contention as to the right thereto, including—

(a) the passing of probates and administrations through the High Court in contentious cases where the contest has been terminated,

(b) all business of a non-contentious nature in matters of testacy and intestacy not being proceedings in any action, and

(c) the business of lodging caveats against the grant of probate or administration;

"Principal Registry" means the Principal Registry of the Family Division;

"probate rules" means rules of court made under section 127;

"trust corporation"[10] means the Public Trustee or a corporation either appointed by the court in any particular case to be a trustee or authorised by rules made under section 4(3) of the Public Trustee Act 1906 to act as a custodian trustee;

"will" includes a nuncupative will and any testamentary document of which probate may be granted.

SCHEDULES

Section 61(1), (3)

SCHEDULE 1

DISTRIBUTION OF BUSINESS IN HIGH COURT

Chancery Division

1. To the Chancery Division are assigned all causes and matters relating to—

(a) the sale, exchange or partition of land, or the raising of charges on land;
(b) the redemption or foreclosure of mortgages;
(c) the execution of trusts;
(d) the administration of the estates of deceased persons;
(e) bankruptcy;
(f) the dissolution of partnerships or the taking of partnership or other accounts;
(g) the rectification, setting aside or cancellation of deeds or other instruments in writing;
(h) probate business, other than non-contentious or common form business;
(i) patents, trade marks, registered designs [, copyright or design right][11];
(j) the appointment of a guardian of a minor's estate,

and all causes and matters involving the exercise of the High Court's jurisdiction under the enactments relating to companies.

Administration of Justice Act 1982

(1982 c. 53)

Part IV

Wills

17–19. [*Amend the Wills Act 1837, ante, para. 2–001.*]

---

[10] Definition of "trust corporation" extended by the Law of Property (Amendment) Act 1926, s.3, *ante*, para. 11–002, and the Charities Act 1993, s.35, *post*, para. 56–034.

[11] Words substituted by the Copyright, Designs and Patents Act 1988, s.303(1), Sched. 7, para. 28(1), (3).

Rectification and interpretation of wills

Rectification

41–001 **20.**—(1) If a court is satisfied that a will is so expressed that it fails to carry out the testator's intentions, in consequence—

(a) of a clerical error; or

(b) of a failure to understand his instructions,

it may order that the will shall be rectified so as to carry out his intentions.

(2) An application for an order under this section shall not, except with the permission of the court, be made after the end of the period of six months from the date on which representation with respect to the estate of the deceased is first taken out.

(3) The provisions of this section shall not render the personal representatives of a deceased person liable for having distributed any part of the estate of the deceased, after the end of the period of six months from the date on which representation with respect to the estate of the deceased is first taken out, on the ground that they ought to have taken into account the possibility that the court might permit the making of an application for an order under this section after the end of that period; but this subsection shall not prejudice any power to recover, by reason of the making of an order under this section, any part of the estate so distributed.

(4) In considering for the purposes of this section when representation with respect to the estate of a deceased person was first taken out, a grant limited to settled land or to trust property shall be left out of account, and a grant limited to real estate or to personal estate shall be left out of account unless a grant limited to the remainder of the estate has previously been made or is made at the same time.

Interpretation of wills—general rules as to evidence

41–002 **21.**—(1) This section applies to a will—

(a) in so far as any part of it is meaningless;

(b) in so far as the language used in any part of it is ambiguous on the face of it;

(c) in so far as evidence, other than evidence of the testator's intention, shows that the language used in any part of it is ambiguous in the light of surrounding circumstances.

(2) In so far as this section applies to a will extrinsic evidence, including evidence of the testator's intention, may be admitted to assist in its interpretation.

Presumption as to effect of gifts to spouses

41–003 **22.** Except where a contrary intention is shown it shall be presumed that if a testator devises or bequeaths property to his spouse in terms which in themselves would give an absolute interest to the spouse, but by the same instrument purports to give his issue an interest in the same property, the gift to the spouse is absolute notwithstanding the purported gift to the issue.

Registration of wills[1]

Deposit and registration of wills of living persons

23.—(1) The following, namely— **41–004**

(a) the Principal Registry of the Family Division of the High Court of Justice;
(b) the Keeper of the Registers of Scotland; and
(c) the Probate and Matrimonial Office of the Supreme Court of Northern Ireland,

shall be registering authorities for the purposes of this section.

(2) Each registering authority shall provide and maintain safe and convenient depositories for the custody of the wills of living persons.

(3) Any person may deposit his will in such a depository in accordance with regulations under section 25 below and on payment of the prescribed fee.

(4) It shall be the duty of a registering authority to register in accordance with regulations under section 25 below—

(a) any will deposited in a depository maintained by the authority; and
(b) any other will whose registration is requested under Article 6 of the Registration Convention.

(5) A will deposited in a depository provided—

(a) under section 172 of the Supreme Court of Judicature (Consolidation) Act 1925 or section 126 of the Supreme Court Act 1981; or
(b) under Article 27 of the Administration of Estates (Northern Ireland) Order 1979,

shall be treated for the purposes of this section as if it had been deposited under this section.

(6) In this section "prescribed" means—

(a) in the application of this section to England and Wales, prescribed by an order under section 130 of the Supreme Court Act 1981;
(b) in its application to Scotland, prescribed by an order under section 26 below; and
(c) in its application to Northern Ireland, prescribed by an order under section 116 of the Judicature (Northern Ireland) Act 1978.

Designation of Principal Registry as national body under Registration Convention

24.—(1) The Principal Registry of the Family Division of the High Court of Justice shall be the national body for the purposes of the Registration Convention, and shall accordingly have the functions assigned to the national body by the Registration Convention including, without prejudice to the general application of the Convention to the Principal Registry by virtue of this section, the functions— **41–005**

(a) of arranging for the registration of wills in other Contracting States as provided for in Article 6 of the Convention;
(b) of receiving and answering requests for information arising from the national bodies of other Contracting States.

(2) In this Part of this Act "the Registration Convention" means the Convention on the Establishment of a Scheme of Registration of Wills concluded at Basle on 16th May 1972.

[1] ss.23–25 not yet in force. See the Supreme Court Act 1981, s.126, *ante*, para. 40–028.

Regulations as to deposit and registration of wills, etc.

41–006 **25.**—(1) Regulations may make provision—

(a) as to the conditions for the deposit of a will;

(b) as to the manner of and procedure for—

(i) the deposit and registration of a will; and

(ii) the withdrawal of a will which has been deposited; and

(iii) the cancellation of the registration of a will; and

(c) as to the manner in which the Principal Registry of the Family Division is to perform its functions as the national body under the Registration Convention.

(2) Regulations under this section may contain such incidental or supplementary provisions as the authority making the regulations considers appropriate.

(3) Any such regulations are to be made—

(a) for England and Wales, by the President of the Family Division of the High Court of Justice, with the concurrence of the Lord Chancellor;

(b) for Scotland, by the Secretary of State after consultation with the Lord President of the Court of Session; and

(c) for Northern Ireland, by the Northern Ireland Supreme Court Rules Committee, with the concurrence of the Lord Chancellor.

(4) Regulations made by virtue of subsection (1)(c) above shall be made by the Lord Chancellor.

(5) Subject to subsection (6) below, regulations under this section shall be made by statutory instrument and shall be laid before Parliament after being made.

(6) Regulations for Northern Ireland shall be statutory rules for the purposes of the Statutory Rules (Northern Ireland) Order 1979; and any such statutory rule shall be laid before Parliament after being made in like manner as a statutory instrument and section 4 of the Statutory Instruments Act 1946 shall apply accordingly.

(7) The Statutory Instruments Act 1946 shall apply to a statutory instrument containing regulations made in accordance with subsection (3)(a) or (c) above as if the regulations had been made by a Minister of the Crown.

(8) Any regulations made under section 172 of the Supreme Court of Judicature (Consolidation) Act 1925 or section 126 of the Supreme Court Act 1981 shall have effect for the purposes of this Part of this Act as they have effect for the purposes of the enactment under which they were made.

County Courts Act 1984

(1984 c. 28)

Part II

Jurisdiction and Transfer of Proceedings

Recovery of land and cases where title in question

Actions for recovery of land and actions where title is in question

21.—(1) A county court shall have jurisdiction to hear and determine any action for the recovery of land [. . .][1] **42–001**

(2) A county court shall have jurisdiction to hear and determine any action in which the title to any hereditament comes in question [. . .][2]

(3) Where a mortgage of land consists of or includes a dwelling-house and no part of the land is situated in Greater London then, subject to subsection (4), if a county court has jurisdiction by virtue of this section to hear and determine an action in which the mortgagee under that mortgage claims possession of the mortgaged property, no court other than a county court shall have jurisdiction to hear and determine that action.

(4) Subsection (3) shall not apply to an action for foreclosure or sale in which a claim for possession of the mortgaged property is also made.

(5), (6) [*Repealed by the High Court and County Courts Jurisdiction Order 1991 (S.I. 1991 No. 724), art. 2(8), Sched.*]

(7) In this section—

"dwelling-house" includes any building or part of a building which is used as a dwelling;

"mortgage" includes a charge and "mortgagor" and "mortgagee" shall be construed accordingly;

"mortgagor" and "mortgagee" includes any person deriving title under the original mortgagor or mortgagee.

(8) The fact that part of the premises comprised in a dwelling-house is used as a shop or office or for business, trade or professional purposes shall not prevent the dwelling-house from being a dwelling-house for the purposes of this section.

(9) This section does not apply to a mortgage securing an agreement which is a regulated agreement within the meaning of the Consumer Credit Act 1974.

22. [*Repealed by the Courts and Legal Services Act 1990, s.125(7), Sched. 20.*]

Equity proceedings

Equity jurisdiction

23. A county court shall have all the jurisdiction of the High Court to hear and determine— **42–002**

[1] Words repealed by the High Court and County Courts Jurisdiction Order 1991 (S.I. 1991 No. 724), art. 2(8), Sched.

[2] Words repealed by the High Court and County Courts Jurisdiction Order 1991 (S.I. 1991 No. 724), art. 2(8), Sched.

(a) proceedings for the administration of the estate of a deceased person, where the estate does not exceed in amount or value the county court limit;
(b) proceedings—
(i) for the execution of any trust, or
(ii) for a declaration that a trust subsists, or
(iii) under section 1 of the Variation of Trusts Act 1958,
where the estate or fund subject, or alleged to be subject, to the trust does not exceed in amount or value the county court limit;
(c) proceedings for foreclosure or redemption of any mortgage or for enforcing any charge or lien, where the amount owing in respect of the mortgage, charge or lien does not exceed the county court limit;
(d) proceedings for the specific performance, or for the rectification, delivery up or cancellation, of any agreement for the sale, purchase or lease of any property, where, in the case of a sale or purchase, the purchase money, or in the case of a lease, the value of the property, does not exceed the county court limit;
(e) proceedings relating to the maintenance or advancement of a minor, where the property of the minor does not exceed in amount or value the county court limit;
(f) proceedings for the dissolution or winding-up of any partnership (whether or not the existence of the partnerships is in dispute), where the whole assets of the partnership do not exceed in amount or value the county court limit;
(g) proceedings for relief against fraud or mistake, where the damage sustained or the estate or fund in respect of which relief is sought does not exceed in amount or value the county court limit.

Jurisdiction by agreement in certain equity proceedings

42–003 **24.**—(1) If, as respects any proceedings to which this section applies, the parties agree, by a memorandum signed by them or by their respective [legal representatives][3] or agents, that a county court specified in the memorandum shall have jurisdiction in the proceedings, that court shall, notwithstanding anything in any enactment, have jurisdiction to hear and determine the proceedings accordingly.

(2) Subject to subsection (3), this section applies to any proceedings in which a county court would have jurisdiction by virtue of—
(a) section 113(3) of the Settled Land Act 1925,
(b) section 63A of the Trustee Act 1925,
(c) sections 3(7), [. . .][4] 49(4), 66(4), 89(7), 90(3), 91(8), 92(2), 136(3), [. . .][5] 181(2), 188(2) of, and paragraph 3A of Part III and paragraph 1(3A) and (4A) of Part IV of Schedule I to, the Law of Property Act 1925,
(d) sections 17(2), 38(4), 41(1A), and 43(4) of the Administration of Estates Act 1925,
(e) section 6(1) of the Leasehold Property (Repairs) Act 1938,
(f) sections 1(6A) and 5(11) of the Land Charges Act 1972, and

[3] Words substituted by the Courts and Legal Services Act 1990, s.125(3), Sched. 18, para. 49(3).
[4] Subsection number repealed by the High Court and County Courts Jurisdiction Order 1991 (S.I. 1991 No. 724), art. 2(8), Sched.
[5] Subsection numbers repealed by the High Court and County Courts Jurisdiction Order 1991 (S.I. 1991 No. 724), art. 2(8), Sched.

(g) sections 23 and 25 of this Act,

but for the limits of the jurisdiction of the court provided in those enactments.

(3) This section does not apply to proceedings under section 1 of the Variation of Trusts Act 1958.

Family provision proceedings

Jurisdiction under Inheritance (Provision for Family and Dependants) Act 1975

25. A county court shall have jurisdiction to hear and determine any application for an order under section 2 of the Inheritance (Provision for Family and Dependants) Act 1975 (including any application for permission to apply for such an order and any application made, in the proceedings on an application for such an order, for an order under any other provision of that Act) [. . .][6] **42–004**

. . . . . .

Probate proceedings

[Contentious probate jurisdiction

32.—(1) Where— **42–005**

(a) an application for the grant or revocation of probate or administration has been made through the principal registry of the Family Division or a district probate registry under section 105 of the Supreme Court Act 1981; and

(b) it is shown to the satisfaction of a county court that the value at the date of the death of the deceased of his net estate does not exceed the county court limit,

the county court shall have the jurisdiction of the High Court in respect of any contentious matter arising in connection with the grant or revocation.

(2) In subsection (1) "net estate", in relation to a deceased person, means the estate of that person exclusive of any property he was possessed of or entitled to as a trustee and not beneficially, and after making allowances for funeral expenses and for debts and liabilities.][7]

Effect of order of judge in probate proceedings

33.—Where an order is made by [. . .][8] a county court for the grant or revocation of probate or administration, in pursuance of any jurisdiction conferred upon [the court][9] by section 32— **42–006**

(a) the registrar of the county court shall transmit to the principal registry of the Family Division or a district probate registry, as he thinks convenient, a certificate under the seal of the court certifying that the order has been made; and

[6] Words repealed by the High Court and County Courts Jurisdiction Order 1991 (S.I. 1991 No. 724), art. 2(8), Sched.

[7] s.32 substituted by the Administration of Justice Act 1985, s.51(1).

[8] Words repealed by the Administration of Justice Act 1985, s.67(1), (2), Sched. 7, para. 7(a), Sched. 8, Pt. III.

[9] Words substituted by the Administration of Justice Act 1985, s.67(1), Sched. 7, para. 7(b).

(b) on the application of a party in favour of whom the order has been made, probate or administration in compliance with the order shall be issued from the registry to which the certificate was sent or, as the case may require, the probate or letters of administration previously granted shall be recalled or varied by, as the case may be, a registrar of the principal registry of the Family Division or the district probate registrar according to the effect of the order.

. . . . . .

PART IX

MISCELLANEOUS AND GENERAL

Forfeiture for non-payment of rent

Provisions as to forfeiture for non-payment of rent

42–007 **138.**—(1) This section has effect where a lessor is proceeding by action in a county court (being an action in which the county court has jurisdiction) to enforce against a lessee a right of re-entry or forfeiture in respect of any land for non-payment of rent.

(2) If the lessee pays into court [or to the lessor][10] not less than 5 clear days before the return day all the rent in arrear and the costs of the action, the action shall cease, and the lessee shall hold the land according to the lease without any new lease.

(3) If—

(a) the action does not cease under subsection (2); and

(b) the court at the trial is satisfied that the lessor is entitled to enforce the right of re-entry or forfeiture,

the court shall order possession of the land to be given to the lessor at the expiration of such period, not being less than 4 weeks from the date of the order, as the court thinks fit, unless within that period the lessee pays into court [or to the lessor][11] all the rent in arrear and the costs of the action.

(4) The court may extend the period specified under subsection (3) at any time before possession of the land is recovered in pursuance of the order under that subsection.

(5) [. . .][12] If—

(a) within the period specified in the order; or

(b) within that period as extended under subsection (4),

the lessee pays into court [or to the lessor][13]—

(i) all the rent in arrear; and

(ii) the costs of the action,

he shall hold the land according to the lease without any new lease.

(6) Subsection (2) shall not apply where the lessor is proceeding in the same action to enforce a right of re-entry or forfeiture on any other ground as well as for non-payment of rent, or to enforce any other claim as well as the right of re-entry or forfeiture and the claim for arrears of rent.

(7) If the lessee does not—

---

[10] Words inserted by the Courts and Legal Services Act 1990, s.125(2), Sched. 17, para. 17.
[11] Words inserted by the Courts and Legal Services Act 1990, s.125(2), Sched. 17, para. 17.
[12] Words repealed by the Administration of Justice Act 1985, ss.55(1), (2), 67(2), Sched. 8, Pt. III.
[13] Words inserted by the Courts and Legal Services Act 1990, s.125(2), Sched. 17, para. 17.

(a) within the period specified in the order; or
(b) within that period as extended under subsection (4),

pay into court [or to the lessor][14]—

(i) all the rent in arrear; and
(ii) the costs of the action,

the order shall be [enforceable][15] in the prescribed manner and so long as the order remains unreversed the lessee shall [, subject to subsections (8) and (9A),][16] be barred from all relief.

(8) The extension under subsection (4) of a period fixed by a court shall not be treated as relief from which the lessee is barred by subsection (7) if he fails to pay into court [or to the lessor][17] all the rent in arrear and the costs of the action within that period.

(9) Where the court extends a period under subsection (4) at a time when—

(a) that period has expired; and
(b) a warrant has been issued for the possession of the land,

the court shall suspend the warrant for the extended period; and, if, before the expiration of the extended period, the lessee pays into court [or to the lessor][18] all the rent in arrear and all the costs of the action, the court shall cancel the warrant.

[(9A) Where the lessor recovers possession of the land at any time after the making of the order under subsection (3) (whether as a result of the enforcement of the order or otherwise) the lessee may, at any time within six months from the date on which the lessor recovers possession, apply to the court for relief; and on any such application the court may, if it thinks fit, grant to the lessee such relief, subject to such terms and conditions, as it thinks fit.

(9B) Where the lessee is granted relief on an application under subsection (9A) he shall hold the land according to the lease without any new lease.

(9C) An application under subsection (9A) may be made by a person with an interest under a lease of the land derived (whether immediately or otherwise) from the lessee's interest therein in like manner as if he were the lessee; and on any such application the court may make an order which (subject to such terms and conditions as the court thinks fit) vests the land in such a person, as lessee of the lessor, for the remainder of the term of the lease under which he has any such interest as aforesaid, or for any lesser term.

In this subsection any reference to the land includes a reference to a part of the land.][19]

(10) Nothing in this section or section 139 shall be taken to affect—

(a) the power of the court to make any order which it would otherwise have power to make as respects a right of re-entry or forfeiture on any ground other than non-payment of rent; or
(b) section 146(4) of the Law of Property Act 1925 (relief against forfeiture).

Service of summons and re-entry

139.—(1) In a case where section 138 has effect, if— **42–008**

(a) one-half-year's rent is in arrear at the time of the commencement of the action; and

[14] Words inserted by the Courts and Legal Services Act 1990, s.125(2), Sched. 17, para. 17.
[15] Word substituted by the Administration of Justice Act 1985, s.55(1), (3).
[16] Words inserted by the Administration of Justice Act 1985, s.55(1), (3).
[17] Words inserted by the Courts and Legal Services Act 1990, s.125(2), Sched. 17, para. 17.
[18] Words inserted by the Courts and Legal Services Act 1990, s.125(2), Sched. 17, para. 17.
[19] subss. (9A)–(9C) inserted by the Administration of Justice Act 1985, s.55(1), (4).

(b) the lessor has a right to re-enter for non-payment of that rent; and
(c) no sufficient distress is to be found on the premises countervailing the arrears then due,

the service of the summons in the action in the prescribed manner shall stand in lieu of a demand and re-entry.

(2) Where a lessor has enforced against a lessee, by re-entry without action, a right of re-entry or forfeiture as respects any land for non-payment of rent, the lessee may […][20] at any time within six months from the date on which the lessor re-entered apply to the county court for relief, and on any such application the court may, if it thinks fit, grant to the lessee such relief as the High Court could have granted.

[(3) Subsections (9B) and (9C) of section 138 shall have effect in relation to an application under subsection (2) of this section as they have effect in relation to an application under subsection (9A) of that section.][21]

Interpretation of sections 138 and 139

42–009 **140.** For the purposes of sections 138 and 139—

"lease" includes—
(a) an original or derivative under-lease;
(b) an agreement for a lease where the lessee has become entitled to have his lease granted; and
(c) a grant at a fee farm rent, or under a grant securing a rent by condition;

"lessee" includes—
(a) an original or derivative under-lessee;
(b) the persons deriving title under a lessee;
(c) a grantee under a grant at a fee farm rent, or under a grant securing a rent by condition; and
(d) the persons deriving title under such a grantee;

"lessor" includes—
(a) an original or derivative under-lessor;
(b) the persons deriving title under a lessor;
(c) a person making a grant at a fee farm rent, or a grant securing a rent by condition; and
(d) the persons deriving title under such a grantor;

"under-lease" includes an agreement for an under-lease where the under-lessee has become entitled to have his under-lease granted; and

"under-lessee" includes any person deriving title under an under-lessee.

[20] Words repealed by the High Court and County Courts Jurisdiction Order 1991 (S.I. 1991 No. 724), art. 2(8), Sched.

[21] subs. (3) added by the Administration of Justice Act 1985, s.55(1), (5).

Enduring Powers of Attorney Act 1985

(1985 c. 29)

Enduring powers of attorney

Enduring power of attorney to survive mental incapacity of donor

1.—(1) Where an individual creates a power of attorney which is an enduring power within the meaning of this Act then— **43–001**

(a) the power shall not be revoked by any subsequent mental incapacity of his; but

(b) upon such incapacity supervening the donee of the power may not do anything under the authority of the power except as provided by subsection (2) below or as directed or authorised by the court under section 5 unless or, as the case may be, until the instrument creating the power is registered by the court under section 6; and

(c) section 5 of the Powers of Attorney Act 1971 (protection of donee and third persons) so far as applicable shall apply if and so long as paragraph (b) above operates to suspend the donee's authority to act under the power as if the power had been revoked by the donor's mental incapacity.

(2) Notwithstanding subsection (1)(b) above, where the attorney has made an application for registration of the instrument then, until the application has been initially determined, the attorney may take action under the power—

(a) to maintain the donor or prevent loss to his estate; or

(b) to maintain himself or other persons in so far as section 3(4) permits him to do so.

(3) Where the attorney purports to act as provided by subsection (2) above then, in favour of a person who deals with him without knowledge that the attorney is acting otherwise than in accordance with paragraph (a) or (b) of that subsection, the transaction between them shall be as valid as if the attorney were acting in accordance with paragraph (a) or (b).

Characteristics of an enduring power

2.—(1) Subject to subsections (7) to (9) below and section 11, a power of attorney is an enduring power within the meaning of this Act if the instrument which creates the power— **43–002**

(a) is in the prescribed form; and

(b) was executed in the prescribed manner by the donor and the attorney; and

(c) incorporated at the time of execution by the donor the prescribed explanatory information.

(2) The Lord Chancellor shall make regulations as to the form and execution of instruments creating enduring powers and the regulations shall contain such provisions as appear to him to be appropriate for securing—

(a) that no document is used to create an enduring power which does not incorporate such information explaining the general effect of creating or accepting the power as may be prescribed; and

(b) that such instruments include statements to the following effect—

(i) by the donor, that he intends the power to continue in spite of any supervening mental incapacity of his;

(ii) by the donor, that he read or had read to him the information explaining the effect of creating the power;

(iii) by the attorney, that he understands the duty of registration imposed by this Act.

(3) Regulations under subsection (2) above—

(a) may include different provision for cases where more than one attorney is to be appointed by the instrument than for cases where only one attorney is to be appointed; and

(b) may, if they amend or revoke any regulations previously made under that subsection, include saving and transitional provisions.

(4) Regulations under subsection (2) above shall be made by statutory instrument which shall be subject to annulment in pursuance of a resolution of either House of Parliament.

(5) An instrument in the prescribed form purporting to have been executed in the prescribed manner shall be taken, in the absence of evidence to the contrary, to be a document which incorporated at the time of execution by the donor the prescribed explanatory information.

(6) Where an instrument differs in an immaterial respect in form or mode of expression from the prescribed form the instrument shall be treated as sufficient in point of form and expression.

(7) A power of attorney cannot be an enduring power unless, when he executes the instrument creating it, the attorney is—

(a) an individual who has attained eighteen years and is not bankrupt; or

(b) a trust corporation.

(8) [*Repealed by the Trustee Delegation Act 1999, ss.6, 12, Sched.*]

(9) A power of attorney which gives the attorney a right to appoint a substitute or successor cannot be an enduring power.

(10) An enduring power shall be revoked by the bankruptcy of the attorney whatever the circumstances of the bankruptcy.

(11) An enduring power shall be revoked on the exercise by the court of any of its powers under Part VII of the Mental Health Act 1983 if, but only if, the court so directs.

(12) No disclaimer of an enduring power, whether by deed or otherwise, shall be valid unless and until the attorney gives notice of it to the donor or, where section 4(6) or 7(1) applies, to the court.

(13) In this section "prescribed" means prescribed under subsection (2) above.

Scope of authority, etc. of attorney under enduring power

43–003 **3.**—(1) An enduring power may confer general authority (as defined in subsection (2) below) on the attorney to act on the donor's behalf in relation to all or a specified part of the property and affairs of the donor or may confer on him authority to do specified things on the donor's behalf and the authority may, in either case, be conferred subject to conditions and restrictions.

(2) When an instrument is expressed to confer general authority on the attorney it operates to confer, subject to the restriction imposed by subsection (5) below and to any conditions or restrictions contained in the instrument, authority to do on behalf of the donor anything which the donor can lawfully do by an attorney.

(3) [*Repealed by the Trustee Delegation Act 1999, ss.4(1), 12, Sched.*][1]

(4) Subject to any conditions or restrictions contained in the instrument, an attorney under an enduring power, whether general or limited, may (without obtaining any consent) act under the power so as to benefit himself or other persons than the donor to the following extent but no further, that is to say—

(a) he may so act in relation to himself or in relation to any other person if the donor might be expected to provide for his or that person's needs respectively; and

(b) he may do whatever the donor might be expected to do to meet those needs.

(5) Without prejudice to subsection (4) above but subject to any conditions or restrictions contained in the instrument, an attorney under an enduring power, whether general or limited, may (without obtaining any consent) dispose of the property of the donor by way of gift to the following extent but no further, that is to say—

(a) he may make gifts of a seasonal nature or at a time, or on an anniversary, of a birth or marriage, to persons (including himself) who are related to or connected with the donor, and

(b) he may make gifts to any charity to whom the donor made or might be expected to make gifts,

provided that the value of each such gift is not unreasonable having regard to all the circumstances and in particular the size of the donor's estate.

Action on actual or impending incapacity of donor

Duties of attorney in event of actual or impending incapacity of donor

4.—(1) If the attorney under an enduring power has reason to believe that the donor is or is becoming mentally incapable subsections (2) to (6) below shall apply. **43–004**

(2) The attorney shall, as soon as practicable, make an application to the court for the registration of the instrument creating the power.

(3) Before making an application for registration the attorney shall comply with the provisions as to notice set out in Schedule 1.

(4) An application for registration shall be made in the prescribed form and shall contain such statements as may be prescribed.

(5) The attorney may, before making an application for the registration of the instrument, refer to the court for its determination any question as to the validity of the power and he shall comply with any direction given to him by the court on that determination.

(6) No disclaimer of the power shall be valid unless and until the attorney gives notice of it to the court.

(7) Any person who, in an application for registration, makes a statement which he knows to be false in a material particular shall be liable—

(a) on conviction on indictment, to imprisonment for a term not exceeding two years or to a fine, or both; and

(b) on summary conviction, to imprisonment for a term not exceeding six months or to a fine not exceeding the statutory maximum, or both.

(8) In this section and Schedule 1 "prescribed" means prescribed by rules of the court.

[1] See the Trustee Delegation Act 1999, s.4, *post*, para. 62B–003.

Functions of court prior to registration

43–005 **5.** Where the court has reason to believe that the donor of an enduring power may be, or may be becoming, mentally incapable and the court is of the opinion that it is necessary, before the instrument creating the power is registered, to exercise any power with respect to the power of attorney or the attorney appointed to act under it which would become exercisable under section 8(2) on its registration, the court may exercise that power under this section and may do so whether the attorney has or has not made an application to the court for the registration of the instrument.

Functions of court on application for registration

43–006 **6.**—(1) In any case where—

(a) an application for registration is made in accordance with section 4(3) and (4), and

(b) neither subsection (2) nor subsection (4) below applies,

the court shall register the instrument to which the application relates.

(2) Where it appears to the court that there is in force under Part VII of the Mental Health Act 1983 an order appointing a receiver for the donor but the power has not also been revoked then, unless it directs otherwise, the court shall not exercise or further exercise its functions under this section but shall refuse the application for registration.

(3) Where it appears from an application for registration that notice of it has not been given under Schedule 1 to some person entitled to receive it (other than a person in respect of whom the attorney has been dispensed or is otherwise exempt from the requirement to give notice) the court shall direct that the application be treated for the purposes of this Act as having been made in accordance with section 4(3), if the court is satisfied that, as regards each such person—

(a) it was undesirable or impracticable for the attorney to give him notice; or

(b) no useful purpose is likely to be served by giving him notice.

(4) If, in the case of an application for registration—

a valid notice of objection to the registration is received by the courtbefore the expiry of the period of five weeks beginning with the date or, as the case may be, the latest date on which the attorney gave notice to any person under Schedule 1, or

(b) it appears from the application that there is no one to whom notice has been given under paragraph 1 of that Schedule, or

(c) the court has reason to believe that appropriate inquiries might bring to light evidence on which the court could be satisfied that one of the grounds of objection set out in subsection (5) below was established,

the court shall neither register the instrument nor refuse the application until it has made or caused to be made such inquiries (if any) as it thinks appropriate in the circumstances of the case.

(5) For the purposes of this Act a notice of objection to the registration of an instrument is valid if the objection is made on one or more of the following grounds, namely—

(a) that the power purported to have been created by the instrument was not valid as an enduring power of attorney;

(b) that the power created by the instrument no longer subsists;
(c) that the application is premature because the donor is not yet becoming mentally incapable;
(d) that fraud or undue pressure was used to induce the donor to create the power;
(e) that, having regard to all the circumstances and in particular the attorney's relationship to or connection with the donor, the attorney is unsuitable to be the donor's attorney.

(6) If, in a case where subsection (4) above applies, any of the grounds of objection in subsection (5) above is established to the satisfaction of the court, the court shall refuse the application but if, in such a case, it is not so satisfied, the court shall register the instrument to which the application relates.

(7) Where the court refuses an application for registration on ground (d) or (e) in subsection (5) above it shall by order revoke the power created by the instrument.

(8) Where the court refuses an application for registration on any ground other than that specified in subsection (5)(c) above the instrument shall be delivered up to be cancelled, unless the court otherwise directs.

Legal position after registration

Effect and proof of registration, etc.

7.—(1) The effect of the registration of an instrument under section 6 is that— **43–007**
(a) no revocation of the power by the donor shall be valid unless and until the court confirms the revocation under section 8(3);
(b) no disclaimer of the power shall be valid unless and until the attorney gives notice of it to the court;
(c) the donor may not extend or restrict the scope of the authority conferred by the instrument and no instruction or consent given by him after registration shall, in the case of a consent, confer any right and, in the case of an instruction, impose or confer any obligation or right on or create any liability of the attorney or other persons having notice of the instruction or consent.

(2) Subsection (1) above applies for so long as the instrument is registered under section 6 whether or not the donor is for the time being mentally incapable.

(3) A document purporting to be an office copy of an instrument registered under this Act [or under the Enduring Powers of Attorney (Northern Ireland) Order 1987][2] shall, in any part of the United Kingdom, be evidence of the contents of the instrument and of the fact that it has been so registered.

(4) Subsection (3) above is without prejudice to section 3 of the Powers of Attorney Act 1971 (proof by certified copies) and to any other method of proof authorised by law.

Functions of court with respect to registered power

8.—(1) Where an instrument has been registered under section 6, the court shall have the following functions with respect to the power and the donor of and the attorney appointed to act under the power. **43–008**

[2] Words inserted by the Enduring Powers of Attorney (Northern Ireland Consequential Amendment) Order 1987 (S.I. 1987 No. 1628), art. 2.

(2) The court may—

(a) determine any question as to the meaning or effect of the instrument;

(b) gave directions with respect to—

(i) the management or disposal by the attorney of the property and affairs of the donor;

(ii) the rendering of accounts by the attorney and the production of the records kept by him for the purpose;

(iii) the remuneration or expenses of the attorney, whether or not in default of or in accordance with any provision made by the instrument, including directions for the repayment of excessive or the payment of additional remuneration;

(c) require the attorney to furnish information or produce documents or things in his possession as attorney;

(d) give any consent or authorisation to act which the attorney would have to obtain from a mentally capable donor;

(e) authorise the attorney to act so as to benefit himself or other persons than the donor otherwise than in accordance with section 3(4) and (5) (but subject to any conditions or restrictions contained in the instrument);

(f) relieve the attorney wholly or partly from any liability which he has or may have incurred on account of a breach of his duties as attorney.

(3) On application made for the purpose by or on behalf of the donor, the court shall confirm the revocation of the power if satisfied that the donor has done whatever is necessary in law to effect an express revocation of the power and was mentally capable of revoking a power of attorney when he did so (whether or not he is so when the court considers the application).

(4) The court shall cancel the registration of an instrument registered under section 6 in any of the following circumstances, that is to say—

(a) on confirming the revocation of the power under subsection (3) above or receiving notice of disclaimer under section 7(1)(b);

(b) on giving a direction revoking the power on exercising any of its powers under Part VII of the Mental Health Act 1983;

(c) on being satisfied that the donor is and is likely to remain mentally capable;

(d) on being satisfied that the power has expired or has been revoked by the death or bankruptcy of the donor or the death, mental incapacity or bankruptcy of the attorney or, if the attorney is a body corporate, its winding up or dissolution;

(e) on being satisfied that the power was not a valid and subsisting enduring power when registration was effected;

(f) on being satisfied that fraud or undue pressure was used to induce the donor to create the power; or

(g) on being satisfied that, having regard to all the circumstances and in particular, the attorney's relationship to or connection with the donor, the attorney is unsuitable to be the donor's attorney.

(5) Where the court cancels the registration of an instrument on being satisfied of the matters specified in paragraph (f) or (g) of subsection (4) above it shall by order revoke the power created by the instrument.

(6) On the cancellation of the registration of an instrument under subsection (4) above except paragraph (c) the instrument shall be delivered up to be cancelled, unless the court otherwise directs.

Protection of attorney and third parties

Protection of attorney and third persons where power invalid or revoked

9.—(1) Subsections (2) and (3) below apply where an instrument which did not create a valid power of attorney has been registered under section 6 (whether or not the registration has been cancelled at the time of the act or transaction in question). **43–009**

(2) An attorney who acts in pursuance of the power shall not incur any liability (either to the donor or to any other person) by reason of the non-existence of the power unless at the time of acting he knows—

(a) that the instrument did not create a valid enduring power; or

(b) that an event has occurred which, if the instrument had created a valid enduring power, would have had the effect of revoking the power; or

(c) that, if the instrument had created a valid enduring power, the power would have expired before that time.

(3) Any transaction between the attorney and another person shall, in favour of that person, be as valid as if the power had then been in existence, unless at the time of the transaction that person has knowledge of any of the matters mentioned in subsection (2) above.

(4) Where the interest of a purchaser depends on whether a transaction between the attorney and another person was valid by virtue of subsection (3) above, it shall be conclusively presumed in favour of the purchaser that the transaction was valid if—

(a) the transaction between that person and the attorney was completed within twelve months of the date on which the instrument was registered; or

(b) that person makes a statutory declaration, before or within three months after the completion of the purchase, that he had no reason at the time of the transaction to doubt that the attorney had authority to dispose of the property which was the subject of the transaction.

(5) For the purposes of section 5 of the Powers of Attorney Act 1971 (protection of attorney and third persons where action is taken under the power of attorney in ignorance of its having been revoked) in its application to an enduring power the revocation of which by the donor is by virtue of section 7(1)(a) above invalid unless and until confirmed by the court under section 8(3) above, knowledge of the confirmation of the revocation is, but knowledge of the unconfirmed revocation is not, knowledge of the revocation of the power.

(6) Schedule 2 shall have effect to confer protection in cases where the instrument failed to create a valid enduring power and the power has been revoked by the donor's mental incapacity.

(7) In this section "purchaser" and "purchase" have the meanings specified in section 205(1) of the Law of Property Act 1925.

Supplementary

Application of Mental Health Act provisions relating to the court

10.—(1) The provisions of Part VII of the Mental Health Act 1983 (relating to the Court of Protection) specified below shall apply to persons within and proceedings under this Act in accordance with the following paragraphs of this subsection and subsection (2) below, that is to say— **43–010**

(a) section 103 (functions of Visitors) shall apply to persons within this Act as it applies to the persons mentioned in that section;
(b) section 104 (powers of judge) shall apply to proceedings under this Act with respect to persons within this Act as it applies to the proceedings mentioned in subsection (1) of that section;
(c) section 105(1) (appeals to nominated judge) shall apply to any decision of the Master of the Court of Protection or any nominated officer in proceedings under this Act as it applies to any decision to which that subsection applies and an appeal shall lie to the Court of Appeal from any decision of a nominated judge whether given in the exercise of his original jurisdiction or on the hearing of an appeal under section 105(1) as extended by this paragraph;
(d) section 106 except subsection (4) (rules of procedure) shall apply to proceedings under this Act and persons within this Act as it applies to the proceedings and persons mentioned in that section.

(2) Any functions conferred or imposed by the provisions of the said Part VII applied by subsection (1) above shall be exercisable also for the purposes of this Act and the persons who are "within this Act" are the donors of and attorneys under enduring powers of attorney whether or not they would be patients for the purposes of the said Part VII.

(3) In this section "nominated judge" and "nominated officer" have the same meaning as in Part VII of the Mental Health Act 1983.

Application to joint and joint and several attorneys

43–011 **11.**—(1) An instrument which appoints more than one person to be an attorney cannot create an enduring power unless the attorneys are appointed to act jointly or jointly and severally.

(2) This Act, in its application to joint attorneys, applies to them collectively as it applies to a single attorney but subject to the modifications specified in Part I of Schedule 3.

(3) This Act, in its application to joint and several attorneys, applies with the modifications specified in subsections (4) to (7) below and in Part II of Schedule 3.

(4) A failure, as respects any one attorney, to comply with the requirements for the creation of enduring powers, shall prevent the instrument from creating such a power in his case without however affecting its efficacy for that purpose as respects the other or others or its efficacy in his case for the purpose of creating a power of attorney which is not an enduring power.

(5) Where one or more but not both or all the attorneys makes or joins in making an application for registration of the instrument then—
(a) an attorney who is not an applicant as well as one who is may act pending the initial determination of the application as provided in section 1(2) (or under section 5);
(b) notice of the application shall also be given under Schedule 1 to the other attorney or attorneys; and
(c) objection may validly be taken to the registration on a ground relating to an attorney or to the power of an attorney who is not an applicant as well as to one or the power of one who is an applicant.

(6) The court shall not refuse under section 6(6) to register an instrument because a ground of objection to an attorney or power is established if an enduring power subsists as respects some attorney who is not affected thereby but shall give effect to it by the prescribed qualification of the registration.

(7) The court shall not cancel the registration of an instrument under section 8(4) for any of the causes vitiating registration specified in that subsection if an enduring power subsists as respects some attorney who is not affected thereby but shall give effect to it by the prescribed qualification of the registration.

(8) In this section—

"prescribed" means prescribed by rules of the court; and

"the requirements for the creation of enduring powers" means the provisions of section 2 other than subsections (10) to (12) and of regulations under subsection (2) of that section.

Power of Lord Chancellor to modify pre-registration requirements in certain cases

12.—(1) The Lord Chancellor may by order exempt attorneys of such descriptions as he thinks fit from the requirements of this Act to give notice to relatives prior to registration. **43–012**

(2) Subject to subsection (3) below, where an order is made under this section with respect to attorneys of a specified description then, during the currency of the order, this Act shall have effect in relation to any attorney of that description with the omission of so much of section 4(3) and Schedule 1 as requires notice of an application for registration to be given to relatives.

(3) Notwithstanding that an attorney under a joint or joint and several power is of a description specified in a current order under this section, subsection (2) above shall not apply in relation to him if any of the other attorneys under the power is not of a description specified in that or another current order under this section.

(4) The power to make an order under this section shall be exercisable by statutory instrument which shall be subject to annulment in pursuance of a resolution of either House of Parliament.

Interpretation

13.—(1) In this Act— **43–013**

"the court", in relation to any functions under this Act, means the authority having jurisdiction under Part VII of the Mental Health Act 1983;

"enduring power" is to be construed in accordance with section 2;

"mentally incapable" or "mental incapacity", except where it refers to revocation at common law, means, in relation to any person, that he is incapable by reason of mental disorder of managing and administering his property and affairs and "mentally capable" and "mental capacity" shall be construed accordingly;

"mental disorder" has the same meaning as it has in the Mental Health Act 1983;

"notice" means notice in writing;

"rules of the court" means rules under Part VII of the Mental Health Act 1983 as applied by section 10;

[. . .][3]

"trust corporation" means the Public Trustee or a corporation either appointed by the High Court or a county court (according to their respective jurisdictions) in any particular case to be a trustee or entitled by rules under section 4(3) of the Public Trustee Act 1906 to act as custodian trustee.

[3] Definition of "statutory maximum" repealed by the Statute Law (Repeals) Act 1993, s.1(1), Sched. 1, Pt. XIV.

(2) Any question arising under or for the purposes of this Act as to what the donor of the power might at any time be expected to do shall be determined by assuming that he had full mental capacity at the time but otherwise by reference to the circumstances existing at that time.

SCHEDULES

Section 4(3)

SCHEDULE 1

NOTIFICATION PRIOR TO REGISTRATION

PART I

DUTY TO GIVE NOTICE TO RELATIVES AND DONOR

Duty to give notice to relatives

1. Subject to paragraph 3 below, before making an application for registration the attorney shall give notice of his intention to do so to all those persons (if any) who are entitled to receive notice by virtue of paragraph 2 below.

2.—(1) Subject to the limitations contained in sub-paragraphs (2) to (4) below, persons of the following classes (referred to in this Act as "relatives") are entitled to receive notice under paragraph 1 above—

(a) the donor's husband or wife;
(b) the donor's children;
(c) the donor's parents;
(d) the donor's brothers and sisters, whether of the whole or half blood;
(e) the widow or widower of a child of the donor;
(f) the donor's grandchildren;
(g) the children of the donor's brothers and sisters of the whole blood;
(h) the children of the donor's brothers and sisters of the half blood;
(i) the donor's uncles and aunts of the whole blood; and
(j) the children of the donor's uncles and aunts of the whole blood.

(2) A person is not entitled to receive notice under paragraph 1 above if—

(a) his name or address is not known to the attorney and cannot be reasonably ascertained by him; or
(b) the attorney has reason to believe that he has not attained eighteen years or is mentally incapable.

(3) Except where sub-paragraph (4) below applies, no more than three persons are entitled to receive notice under paragraph 1 above and, in determining the persons who are so entitled, persons falling within class (a) of sub-paragraph (1) above are to be preferred to persons falling within class (b) of that sub-paragraph, persons falling within class (b) are to be preferred to persons falling within class (c) of that sub-paragraph; and so on.

(4) Notwithstanding the limit of three specified in sub-paragraph (3) above, where—

(a) there is more than one person falling within any of classes (a) to (j) of sub-paragraph (1) above, and
(b) at least one of those persons would be entitled to receive notice under paragraph 1 above,

then, subject to sub-paragraph (2) above, all the persons falling within that class are entitled to receive notice under paragraph 1 above.

3.—(1) An attorney shall not be required to give notice under paragraph 1 above to himself or to any other attorney under the power who is joining in making the application, notwithstanding that he or, as the case may be, the other attorney is entitled to receive notice by virtue of paragraph 2 above.

(2) In the case of any person who is entitled to receive notice under paragraph 1 above, the attorney, before applying for registration, may make an application to the court to be dispensed from the requirement to give him notice; and the court shall grant the application if it is satisfied—

(a) that it would be undesirable or impracticable for the attorney to give him notice; or
(b) that no useful purpose is likely to be served by giving him notice.

Duty to give notice to donor

4.—(1) Subject to sub-paragraph (2) below, before making an application for registration the attorney shall give notice of his intention to do so to the donor.

(2) Paragraph 3(2) above shall apply in relation to the donor as it applies in relation to a person who is entitled to receive notice under paragraph 1 above.

PART II

CONTENTS OF NOTICES

5. A notice to relatives under this Schedule—
(a) shall be in the prescribed form;
(b) shall state that the attorney proposes to make an application to the Court of Protection for the registration of the instrument creating the enduring power in question;
(c) shall inform the person to whom it is given that he may object to the proposed registration by notice in writing to the Court of Protection before the expiry of the period of four weeks beginning with the day on which the notice under this Schedule was given to him;
(d) shall specify, as the grounds on which an objection to registration may be made, the grounds set out in section 6(5).

6. A notice to the donor under this Schedule—
(a) shall be in the prescribed form;
(b) shall contain the statement mentioned in paragraph 5(b) above; and
(c) shall inform the donor that, whilst the instrument remains registered, any revocation of the power by him will be ineffective unless and until the revocation is confirmed by the Court of Protection.

PART III

DUTY TO GIVE NOTICE TO OTHER ATTORNEYS

7.—(1) Subject to sub-paragraph (2) below, before making an application for registration an attorney under a joint and several power shall give notice of his intention to do so to any other attorney under the power who is not joining in making the application; and paragraphs 3(2) and 5 above shall apply in relation to attorneys entitled to receive notice by virtue of this paragraph as they apply in relation to persons entitled to receive notice by virtue of paragraph 2 above.

(2) An attorney is not entitled to receive notice by virtue of this paragraph if—
(a) his address is not known to the applying attorney and cannot reasonably be ascertained by him; or
(b) the applying attorney has reason to believe that he has not attained eighteen years or is mentally incapable.

PART IV

SUPPLEMENTARY

8.—(1) For the purposes of this Schedule an illegitimate child shall be treated as if he were the legitimate child of his mother and father.

(2) Notwithstanding anything in section 7 of the Interpretation Act 1978 (construction of references to service by post), for the purposes of this Schedule a notice given by post shall be regarded as given on the date on which it was posted.

Section 9(6) SCHEDULE 2

FURTHER PROTECTION OF ATTORNEY AND THIRD PERSONS

1. Where—
(a) an instrument framed in a form prescribed under section 2(2) creates a power which is not a valid enduring power; and
(b) the power is revoked by the mental incapacity of the donor,

paragraphs 2 and 3 below shall apply, whether or not the instrument has been registered.

2. An attorney who acts in pursuance of the power shall not, by reason of the revocation, incur any liability (either to the donor or to any other person) unless at the time of acting he knows—
(a) that the instrument did not create a valid enduring power; and
(b) that the donor has become mentally incapable.

3. Any transaction between the attorney and another person shall, in favour of that person, be as valid as if the power had then been in existence, unless at the time of the transaction that person knows—

(a) that the instrument did not create a valid enduring power; and
(b) that the donor has become mentally incapable.

4. Section 9(4) shall apply for the purpose of determining whether a transaction was valid by virtue of paragraph 3 above as it applies for the purpose of determining whether a transaction was valid by virtue of section 9(3).

Section 11(2) (3) SCHEDULE 3

JOINT AND JOINT AND SEVERAL ATTORNEYS

PART I

JOINT ATTORNEYS

1. In section 2(7), the reference to the time when the attorney executes the instrument shall be read as a reference to the time when the second or last attorney executes the instrument.
2. In section 2(9) and (10), the reference to the attorney shall be read as a reference to any attorney under the power.
3. In section 5, references to the attorney shall be read as including references to any attorney under the power.
4. Section 6 shall have effect as if the ground of objection to the registration of the instrument specified in subsection (5)(e) applied to any attorney under the power.
5. In section 8(2), references to the attorney shall be read as including references to any attorney under the power.
6. In section 8(4), references to the attorney shall be read as including references to any attorney under the power.

PART II

JOINT AND SEVERAL ATTORNEYS

7. In section 2(10), the reference to the bankruptcy of the attorney shall be construed as a reference to the bankruptcy of the last remaining attorney under the power; and the bankruptcy of any other attorney under the power shall cause that person to cease to be attorney, whatever the circumstances of the bankruptcy.
8. The restriction upon disclaimer imposed by section 4(6) applies only to those attorneys who have reason to believe that the donor is or is becoming mentally incapable.

Administration of Justice Act 1985

(1985 C. 61)

PART IV

THE SUPREME COURT AND COUNTY COURTS

Proceedings relating to estates of deceased persons and trusts

Power of High Court to make judgments binding on persons who are not parties

44–001 **47.**—(1) This section applies to actions in the High Court relating to the estates of deceased persons or to trusts and falling within any description specified in rules of court.

(2) Rules of court may make provision for enabling any judgment given in an action to which this section applies to be made binding on persons who—

(a) are or may be affected by the judgment and would not otherwise be bound by it; but

(b) have in accordance with the rules been given notice of the action and of such matters connected with it as the rules may require.

(3) Different provision may be made under this section in relation to actions of different descriptions.

Power of High Court to authorise action to be taken in reliance on counsel's opinion

48.—(1) Where— **44–002**

(a) any question of construction has arisen out of the terms of a will or a trust; and

(b) an opinion in writing given by a [person who has a 10 year High Court qualification, within the meaning of section 71 of the Courts and Legal Services Act 1990][1] has been obtained on that question by the personal representatives or trustees under the will or trust,

the High Court may, on the application of the personal representatives or trustees and without hearing argument, make an order authorising those persons to take such steps in reliance on the said opinion as are specified in the order.

(2) The High Court shall not make an order under subsection (1) if it appears to the court that a dispute exists which would make it inappropriate for the court to make the order without hearing argument.

Power of High Court on compromise of probate action

49.—(1) Where on a compromise of a probate action in the High Court— **44–003**

(a) the court is invited to pronounce for the validity of one or more wills, or against the validity of one or more wills, or for the validity of one or more wills and against the validity of one or more other wills; and

(b) the court is satisfied that consent to the making of the pronouncement or, as the case may be, each of the pronouncements in question has been given by or on behalf of every relevant beneficiary,

the court may without more pronounce accordingly.

(2) In this section—

"probate action" means an action for the grant of probate of the will, or letters of administration of the estate, of a deceased person or for the revocation of such a grant or for a decree pronouncing for or against the validity of an alleged will, not being an action which is non-contentious or common form probate business; and

"relevant beneficiary", in relation to a pronouncement relating to any will or wills of a deceased person, means—

(a) a person who under any such will is beneficially interested in the deceased's estate; and

(b) where the effect of the pronouncement would be to cause the estate to devolve as on an intestacy (or partial intestacy), or to

[1] Words substituted by the Courts and Legal Services Act 1990, s.71(2), Sched. 10, para. 63.

prevent it from so devolving, a person who under the law relating to intestacy is beneficially interested in the estate.

Power of High Court to appoint substitute for, or to remove, personal representative

44–004 **50.**—(1) Where an application relating to the estate of a deceased person is made to the High Court under this subsection by or on behalf of a personal representative of the deceased or a beneficiary of the estate, the court may in its discretion—

(a) appoint a person (in this section called a substituted personal representative) to act as personal representative of the deceased in place of the existing personal representative or representatives of the deceased or any of them; or

(b) if there are two or more existing personal representatives of the deceased, terminate the appointment of one or more, but not all, of those persons.

(2) Where the court appoints a person to act as a substituted personal representative of a deceased person, then—

(a) if that person is appointed to act with an executor or executors the appointment shall (except for the purpose of including him in any chain of representation) constitute him executor of the deceased as from the date of the appointment; and

(b) in any other case the appointment shall constitute that person administrator of the deceased's estate as from the date of the appointment.

(3) The court may authorise a person appointed as a substituted personal representative to charge remuneration for his services as such, on such terms (whether or not involving the submission of bills of charges for taxation by the court) as the court may think fit.

(4) Where an application relating to the estate of a deceased person is made to the court under subsection (1), the court may if it thinks fit, proceed as if the application were, or included, an application for the appointment under the Judicial Trustees Act 1896 of a judicial trustee in relation to that estate.

(5) In this section "beneficiary", in relation to the estate of a deceased person, means a person who under the will of the deceased or under the law relating to intestacy is beneficially interested in the estate.

(6) [*Amends the Judicial Trustees Act 1896, s.1.*]

Landlord and Tenant Act 1985

(1985 c. 70)

Implied terms as to fitness for human habitation

Implied terms as to fitness for human habitation

45–001 **8.**—(1) In a contract to which this section applies for the letting of a house for human habitation there is implied, notwithstanding any stipulation to the contrary—

(a) a condition that the house is fit for human habitation at the commencement of the tenancy, and
(b) an undertaking that the house will be kept by the landlord fit for human habitation during the tenancy.

(2) The landlord, or a person authorised by him in writing, may at reasonable times of the day, on giving 24 hours' notice in writing to the tenant or occupier, enter premises to which this section applies for the purpose of viewing their state and condition.

(3) This section applies to a contract if—
(a) the rent does not exceed the figure applicable in accordance with subsection (4), and
(b) the letting is not on such terms as to the tenant's responsibility as are mentioned in subsection (5).

(4) The rent limit for the application of this section is shown by the following Table, by reference to the date of making of the contract and the situation of the premises:

TABLE

Date of making of contract	*Rent limit*
Before 31st July 1923.	In London: £40. Elsewhere: £26 or £16 (see Note 1).
On or after 31st July 1923 and before 6th July 1957.	In London: £40. Elsewhere: £26.
On or after 6th July 1957.	In London: £80. Elsewhere: £52.

NOTES

1. The applicable figure for contracts made before 31st July 1923 is £26 in the case of premises situated in a borough or urban district which at the date of the contract had according to the last published census a population of 50,000 or more. In the case of a house situated elsewhere, the figure is £16.

2. The references to "London" are, in relation to contracts made before 1st April 1965, to the administrative county of London and, in relation to contracts made on or after that date, to Greater London exclusive of the outer London boroughs.

(5) This section does not apply where a house is let for a term of three years or more (the lease not being determinable at the option of either party before the expiration of three years) upon terms that the tenant puts the premises into a condition reasonably fit for human habitation.

(6) In this section "house" includes—
(a) a part of a house, and
(b) any yard, garden, outhouses and appurtenances belonging to the house or usually enjoyed with it.

. . . .

Fitness for human habitation

10. In determining for the purposes of this Act whether a house is unfit for **45–002**
human habitation, regard shall be had to its condition in respect of the following matters—

repair,
stability,
freedom from damp,
internal arrangement,
natural lighting,
ventilation,
water supply,
drainage and sanitary conveniences,
facilities for preparation and cooking of food and for the disposal of waste water;

and the house shall be regarded as unfit for human habitation if, and only if, it is so far defective in one or more of those matters that it is not reasonably suitable for occupation in that condition.

Repairing obligations

Repairing obligations in short leases

45–003 **11.**—(1) In a lease to which this section applies (as to which, see sections 13 and 14) there is implied a covenant by the lessor—

(a) to keep in repair the structure and exterior of the dwelling-house (including drains, gutters and external pipes),

(b) to keep in repair and proper working order the installations in the dwelling-house for the supply of water, gas and electricity and for sanitation (including basins, sinks, baths and sanitary conveniences, but not other fixtures, fittings and appliances for making use of the supply of water, gas or electricity), and

(c) to keep in repair and proper working order the installations in the dwelling-house for space heating and heating water.

[(1A) If a lease to which this section applies is a lease of a dwelling-house which forms part only of a building, then, subject to subsection (1B), the covenant implied by subsection (1) shall have effect as if—

(a) the reference in paragraph (a) of that subsection to the dwelling-house included a reference to any part of the building in which the lessor has an estate or interest; and

(b) any reference in paragraphs (b) and (c) of that subsection to an installation in the dwelling-house included a reference to an installation which, directly or indirectly, serves the dwelling-house and which either—

(i) forms part of any part of a building in which the lessor has an estate or interest; or

(ii) is owned by the lessor or under his control.

(1B) Nothing in subsection (1A) shall be construed as requiring the lessor to carry out any works or repairs unless the disrepair (or failure to maintain in working order) is such as to affect the lessee's enjoyment of the dwelling-house or of any common parts, as defined in section 60(1) of the Landlord and Tenant Act 1987, which the lessee, as such, is entitled to use.][1]

(2) The covenant implied by subsection (1) ("the lessor's repairing covenant") shall not be construed as requiring the lessor—

(a) to carry out works or repairs for which the lessee is liable by virtue of his

[1] subss. (1A) and (1B) inserted by the Housing Act 1988, s.116(1).

duty to use the premises in a tenant-like manner, or would be so liable but for an express covenant on his part,

(b) to rebuild or reinstate the premises in the case of destruction or damage by fire, or by tempest, flood or other inevitable accident, or

(c) to keep in repair or maintain anything which the lessee is entitled to remove from the dwelling-house.

(3) In determining the standard of repair required by the lessor's repairing covenant, regard shall be had to the age, character and prospective life of the dwelling-house and the locality in which it is situated.

[(3A) In any case where—

(a) the lessor's repairing covenant has effect as mentioned in subsection (1A), and

(b) in order to comply with the covenant the lessor needs to carry out works or repairs otherwise than in, or to an installation in, the dwelling-house, and

(c) the lessor does not have a sufficient right in the part of the building or the installation concerned to enable him to carry out the required works or repairs,

then, in any proceedings relating to a failure to comply with the lessor's repairing covenant, so far as it requires the lessor to carry out the works or repairs in question, it shall be a defence for the lessor to prove that he used all reasonable endeavours to obtain, but was unable to obtain, such rights as would be adequate to enable him to carry out the works or repairs.][2]

(4) A covenant by the lessee for the repair of the premises is of no effect so far as it relates to the matters mentioned in subsection (1)(a) to (c), except so far as it imposes on the lessee any of the requirements mentioned in subsection (2)(a) or (c).

(5) The reference in subsection (4) to a covenant by the lessee for the repair of the premises includes a covenant—

(a) to put in repair or deliver up in repair,

(b) to paint, point or render,

(c) to pay money in lieu of repairs by the lessee, or

(d) to pay money on account of repairs by the lessor.

(6) In a lease in which the lessor's repairing covenant is implied there is also implied a covenant by the lessee that the lessor, or any person authorised by him in writing, may at reasonable times of the day and on giving 24 hours' notice in writing to the occupier, enter the premises comprised in the lease for the purpose of viewing their condition and state of repair.

Restriction on contracting out of s.11

12.—(1) A covenant or agreement, whether contained in a lease to which section 11 applies or in an agreement collateral to such a lease, is void in so far as it purports— **45–004**

(a) to exclude or limit the obligations of the lessor or the immunities of the lessee under that section, or

(b) to authorise any forfeiture or impose on the lessee any penalty, disability or obligation in the event of his enforcing or relying upon those obligations or immunities,

unless the inclusion of the provision was authorised by the county court.

[2] subs. (3A) inserted by the Housing Act 1988, s.116(2).

(2) The county court may, by order made with the consent of the parties, authorise the inclusion in a lease, or in an agreement collateral to a lease, of provisions excluding or modifying in relation to the lease, the provisions of section 11 with respect to the repairing obligations of the parties if it appears to the court that it is reasonable to do so, having regard to all the circumstances of the case, including the other terms and conditions of the lease.

Leases to which s.11 applies: general rule

45–005 **13.**—(1) Section 11 (repairing obligations) applies to a lease of a dwelling-house granted on or after 24th October 1961 for a term of less than seven years.

(2) In determining whether a lease is one to which section 11 applies—

(a) any part of the term which falls before the grant shall be left out of account and the lease shall be treated as a lease for a term commencing with the grant,

(b) a lease which is determinable at the option of the lessor before the expiration of seven years from the commencement of the term shall be treated as a lease for a term of less than seven years, and

(c) a lease (other than a lease to which paragraph (b) applies) shall not be treated as a lease for a term of less than seven years if it confers on the lessee an option for renewal for a term which, together with the original term, amounts to seven years or more.

(3) This section has effect subject to—

section 14 (leases to which section 11 applies: exceptions), and

section 32(2) (provisions not applying to tenancies within Part II of the Landlord and Tenant Act 1954).

Leases to which s.11 applies: exceptions

45–006 **14.**—(1) Section 11 (repairing obligations) does not apply to a new lease granted to an existing tenant, or to a former tenant still in possession, if the previous lease was not a lease to which section 11 applied (and, in the case of a lease granted before 24th October 1961, would not have been if it had been granted on or after that date).

(2) In subsection (1)—

"existing tenant" means a person who is when, or immediately before, the new lease is granted, the lessee under another lease of the dwelling-house;

"former tenant still in possession" means a person who—

(a) was the lessee under another lease of the dwelling-house which terminated at some time before the new lease was granted, and

(b) between the termination of that other lease and the grant of the new lease was continuously in possession of the dwelling-house or of the rents and profits of the dwelling-house; and

"the previous lease" means the other lease referred to in the above definitions.

(3) Section 11 does not apply to a lease of a dwelling-house which is a tenancy of an agricultural holding within the meaning of the [Agricultural Holdings Act 1986][3] [and in relation to which that Act applies or to a farm business tenancy within the meaning of the Agricultural Tenancies Act 1995][4].

---

[3] Words substituted by the Agricultural Holdings Act 1986, s.100, Sched. 14, para. 64.
[4] Words added by the Agricultural Tenancies Act 1995, s.40, Sched., para. 31.

(4) Section 11 does not apply to a lease granted on or after 3rd October 1980 to—

a local authority,
[a National Park authority][5],
a new town corporation,
an urban development corporation,
the Development Board for Rural Wales,
a [registered social landlord][6],
a co-operative housing association, or
an educational institution or other body specified, or of a class specified, by regulations under section 8 of the Rent Act 1977 [or paragraph 8 of Schedule 1 to the Housing Act 1988][7] (bodies making student lettings),
[a housing action trust established under Part III of the Housing Act 1988][8].

(5) Section 11 does not apply to a lease granted on or after 3rd October 1980 to—

(a) Her Majesty in right of the Crown (unless the lease is under the management of the Crown Estate Commissioners), or
(b) a government department or a person holding in trust for Her Majesty for the purposes of a government department.

Jurisdiction of county court

15. The county court has jurisdiction to make a declaration that section 11 (repairing obligations) applies, or does not apply, to a lease— **45–007**

(a) whatever the net annual value of the property in question, and
(b) notwithstanding that no other relief is sought than a declaration.

Meaning of "lease" and related expressions

16. In sections 11 to 15 (repairing obligations in short leases)— **45–008**

(a) "lease" does not include a mortgage term;
(b) "lease of a dwelling-house" means a lease by which a building or part of a building is let wholly or mainly as a private residence, and "dwelling-house" means that building or part of a building;
(c) "lessee" and "lessor" mean, respectively, the person for the time being entitled to the term of a lease and to the reversion expectant on it.

Specific performance of landlord's repairing obligations

17.—(1) In proceedings in which a tenant of a dwelling alleges a breach on the part of his landlord of a repairing covenant relating to any part of the premises in which the dwelling is comprised, the court may order specific performance of the covenant whether or not the breach relates to a part of the premises let to the tenant and notwithstanding any equitable rule restricting the scope of the remedy, whether on the basis of a lack of mutuality or otherwise. **45–009**

---

[5] Words inserted by the Environment Act 1995, s.78, Sched. 10, para. 25(1).
[6] Words substituted by the Housing Act 1996 (Consequential Provisions) Order 1996 (S.I. 1996 No. 2325), art. 5, Sched. 2, para. 16(1), (2).
[7] Words inserted by the Local Government and Housing Act 1989, s.194(1), Sched. 11, para. 89.
[8] Words added by the Housing Act 1988, s.116(3).

(2) In this section—
(a) "tenant" includes a statutory tenant,
(b) in relation to a statutory tenant the reference to the premises let to him is to the premises of which he is a statutory tenant,
(c) "landlord", in relation to a tenant, includes any person against whom the tenant has a right to enforce a repairing covenant, and
(d) "repairing covenant" means a covenant to repair, maintain, renew, construct or replace any property.

Land Registration Act 1986

(1986 c. 26)

1–4. [*Repealed by the Land Registration Act 2002, s.135, Sched. 13.*]

Abolition of Minor Interests Index

46–001 **5.**—(1) In section 102 of the 1925 Act, subsection (2) (under which priorities between certain dealings with equitable interests are regulated by the order of lodging of priority cautions and inhibitions) is repealed, and accordingly—
(a) the index maintained for the purposes of that subsection and known as the Minor Interests Index shall cease to be kept, and
(b) any question of priority which would have fallen to be determined in accordance with that subsection shall be determined in accordance with the rule of law referred to in section 137(1) of the Law of Property Act 1925 (which applies to dealings with equitable interests in land the rule commonly known as the rule in *Dearle v. Hall*).

(2) The following provisions have effect for the purposes of the application of the rule in *Dearle v. Hall*, and of sections 137 and 138 of the Law of Property Act 1925, to dealings in respect of which a priority caution or inhibition was entered in the Minor Interests Index—
(a) the notice of the making of the entry which was given under the Land Registration Rules 1925 before the commencement of this Act to the proprietor or, in the case of settled land, to the trustees of the settlement, shall be treated for those purposes as a notice of the dealing to which the entry relates given (at the time it was issued by the registrar) by the person on whose behalf the entry was made to the trustees or other persons appropriate to receive it for the purposes of establishing priority under the rule in *Dearle v. Hall*;
(b) where a trust corporation has been nominated to receive notices of dealings in accordance with section 138, subsection (4) of that section (under which the notice does not affect priority until received by the corporation) does not apply but the trustees shall, if the notice has not already been transmitted to the corporation, deliver it or send it by post to the corporation as soon as practicable after the commencement of this Act.

(3) A person who suffers loss as a result of the operation of this section is entitled to be indemnified in the same way as a person suffering loss by reason of

an error or omission in the register, except that in relation to a claim under this subsection the reference in [section 83(8)(a)][1] of the 1925 Act (restriction on amount of indemnity in certain cases) to the value of the relevant estate, interest or charge at the time when the error or omission was made shall be construed as a reference to its value immediately before the commencement of this Act.

(4) For the purposes of subsection (3) above, a loss resulting from trustees failing to comply with their duty under subsection (2)(b) above shall be treated as a loss resulting from the operation of this section; but this is without prejudice to the liability of the trustees for breach of that duty or to the registrar's right of recourse against them under [section 83(10)(b)(i)][2] of the 1925 Act (under which the registrar may enforce a right which a person indemnified would have been entitled to enforce in relation to a matter in respect of which an indemnity has been paid).

Insolvency Act 1986

(1986 c. 45)

Part IX

Bankruptcy

Chapter II

Protection of Bankrupt's Estate and Investigation of his Affairs

Definition of bankrupt's estate

283.—(1) Subject as follows, a bankrupt's estate for the purposes of any of this Group of Parts comprises— **47–001**

(a) all property belonging to or vested in the bankrupt at the commencement of the bankruptcy, and

(b) any property which by virtue of any of the following provisions of this Part is comprised in that estate or is treated as falling within the preceding paragraph.

(2) Subsection (1) does not apply to—

(a) such tools, books, vehicles and other items of equipment as are necessary to the bankrupt for use personally by him in his employment, business or vocation;

(b) such clothing, bedding, furniture, household equipment and provisions as are necessary for satisfying the basic domestic needs of the bankrupt and his family.

This subsection is subject to section 308 in Chapter IV (certain excluded property reclaimable by trustee).

(3) Subsection (1) does not apply to—

(a) property held by the bankrupt on trust for any other person, or

---

[1] Words substituted by the Land Registration Act 1997, s.4(1), Sched. 1, Pt. II, para. 8.
[2] Words substituted by the Land Registration Act 1997, s.4(1), Sched. 1, Pt. II, para. 8.

(b) the right of nomination to a vacant ecclesiastical benefice.

[(3A) Subject to section 308A in Chapter IV, subsection (1) does not apply to—

(a) a tenancy which is an assured tenancy or an assured agricultural occupancy, within the meaning of Part I of the Housing Act 1988, and the terms of which inhibit an assignment as mentioned in section 127(5) of the Rent Act 1977, or

(b) a protected tenancy, within the meaning of the Rent Act 1977, in respect of which, by virtue of any provision of Part IX of that Act, no premium can lawfully be required as a condition of assignment, or

(c) a tenancy of a dwelling-house by virtue of which the bankrupt is, within the meaning of the Rent (Agriculture) Act 1976, a protected occupier of the dwelling-house, and the terms of which inhibit an assignment as mentioned in section 127(5) of the Rent Act 1977, or

(d) a secure tenancy, within the meaning of Part IV of the Housing Act 1985, which is not capable of being assigned, except in the cases mentioned in section 91(3) of that Act.][1]

(4) References in any of this Group of Parts to property, in relation to a bankrupt, include references to any power exercisable by him over or in respect of property except in so far as the power is exercisable over or in respect of property not for the time being comprised in the bankrupt's estate and—

(a) is so exercisable at a time after either the official receiver has had his release in respect of that estate under section 299(2) in Chapter III or a meeting summoned by the trustee of that estate under section 331 in Chapter IV has been held, or

(b) cannot be so exercised for the benefit of the bankrupt;

and a power exercisable over or in respect of property is deemed for the purposes of any of this Group of Parts to vest in the person entitled to exercise it at the time of the transaction or event by virtue of which it is exercisable by that person (whether or not it becomes so exercisable at that time).

(5) For the purposes of any such provision in this Group of Parts, property comprised in a bankrupt's estate is so comprised subject to the rights of any person other than the bankrupt (whether as a secured creditor of the bankrupt or otherwise) in relation thereto, but disregarding—

(a) any rights in relation to which a statement such as is required by section 269(1)(a) was made in the petition on which the bankrupt was adjudged bankrupt, and

(b) any rights which have been otherwise given up in accordance with the rules.

(6) This section has effect subject to the provisions of any enactment not contained in this Act under which any property is to be excluded from a bankrupt's estate.

[Bankrupt's home ceasing to form part of estate

47–002 **283A.**—(1) This section applies where property comprised in the bankrupt's estate consists of an interest in a dwelling-house which at the date of the bankruptcy was the sole or principal residence of—

(a) the bankrupt,

(b) the bankrupt's spouse, or

[1] subs. (3A) inserted by the Housing Act 1988, s.117(1).

(c) a former spouse of the bankrupt.

(2) At the end of the period of three years beginning with the date of the bankruptcy the interest mentioned in subsection (1) shall—

(a) cease to be comprised in the bankrupt's estate, and

(b) vest in the bankrupt (without conveyance, assignment or transfer).

(3) Subsection (2) shall not apply if during the period mentioned in that subsection—

(a) the trustee realises the interest mentioned in subsection (1),

(b) the trustee applies for an order for sale in respect of the dwelling-house,

(c) the trustee applies for an order for possession of the dwelling-house,

(d) the trustee applies for an order under section 313 in Chapter IV in respect of that interest, or

(e) the trustee and the bankrupt agree that the bankrupt shall incur a specified liability to his estate (with or without the addition of interest from the date of the agreement) in consideration of which the interest mentioned in subsection (1) shall cease to form part of the estate.

(4) Where an application of a kind described in subsection (3)(b) to (d) is made during the period mentioned in subsection (2) and is dismissed, unless the court orders otherwise the interest to which the application relates shall on the dismissal of the application—

(a) cease to be comprised in the bankrupt's estate, and

(b) vest in the bankrupt (without conveyance, assignment or transfer).

(5) If the bankrupt does not inform the trustee or the official receiver of his interest in a property before the end of the period of three months beginning with the date of the bankruptcy, the period of three years mentioned in subsection (2)—

(a) shall not begin with the date of the bankruptcy, but

(b) shall begin with the date on which the trustee or official receiver becomes aware of the bankrupt's interest.

(6) The court may substitute for the period of three years mentioned in subsection (2) a longer period—

(a) in prescribed circumstances, and

(b) in such other circumstances as the court thinks appropriate.

(7) The rules may make provision for this section to have effect with the substitution of a shorter period for the period of three years mentioned in subsection (2) in specified circumstances (which may be described by reference to action to be taken by a trustee in bankruptcy).

(8)The rules may also, in particular, make provision—

(a) requiring or enabling the trustee of a bankrupt's estate to give notice that this section applies or does not apply;

(b) about the effect of a notice under paragraph (a);

(c) requiring the trustee of a bankrupt's estate to make an application to the Chief Land Registrar.

(9) Rules under subsection (8)(b) may, in particular—

(a) disapply this section;

(b) enable a court to disapply this section;

(c) make provision in consequence of a disapplication of this section;

(d) enable a court to make provision in consequence of a disapplication of this section;

(e) make provision (which may include provision conferring jurisdiction on a court or tribunal) about compensation.][2]

[2] s.283A inserted by the Enterprise Act 2002, s.261(1).

Restrictions on dispositions of property

47–003 **284.**—(1) Where a person is adjudged bankrupt, any disposition of property made by that person in the period to which this section applies is void except to the extent that it is or was made with the consent of the court, or is or was subsequently ratified by the court.

(2) Subsection (1) applies to a payment (whether in cash or otherwise) as it applies to a disposition of property and, accordingly, where any payment is void by virtue of that subsection, the person paid shall hold the sum paid for the bankrupt as part of his estate.

(3) This section applies to the period beginning with the day of the presentation of the petition for the bankruptcy order and ending with the vesting, under Chapter IV of this Part, of the bankrupt's estate in a trustee.

(4) The preceding provisions of this section do not give a remedy against any person—

(a) in respect of any property or payment which he received before the commencement of the bankruptcy in good faith, for value and without notice that the petition had been presented, or

(b) in respect of any interest in property which derives from an interest in respect of which there is, by virtue of this subsection, no remedy.

(5) Where after the commencement of his bankruptcy the bankrupt has incurred a debt to a banker or other person by reason of the making of a payment which is void under this section, that debt is deemed for the purposes of any of this Group of Parts to have been incurred before the commencement of the bankruptcy unless—

(a) that banker or person had notice of the bankruptcy before the debt was incurred, or

(b) it is not reasonably practicable for the amount of the payment to be recovered from the person to whom it was made.

(6) A disposition of property is void under this section notwithstanding that the property is not or, as the case may be, would not be comprised in the bankrupt's estate; but nothing in this section affects any disposition made by a person of property held by him on trust for any other person.

. . . . .

Chapter IV

Administration by Trustee

Acquisition, control and realisation of bankrupt's estate

. . . . .

Charge on bankrupt's home

47–004 **313.**—(1) Where any property consisting of an interest in a dwelling house which is occupied by the bankrupt or by his spouse or former spouse is comprised in the bankrupt's estate and the trustee is, for any reason, unable for the time being to realise that property, the trustee may apply to the court for an order imposing a charge on the property for the benefit of the bankrupt's estate.

(2) If on an application under this section the court imposes a charge on any property, the benefit of that charge shall be comprised in the bankrupt's estate

and is enforceable [, up to the charged value from time to time,][3] for the payment of any amount which is payable otherwise than to the bankrupt out of the estate and of interest on that amount at the prescribed rate.

[(2A) In subsection (2) the charged value means—

(a) the amount specified in the charging order as the value of the bankrupt's interest in the property at the date of the order, plus

(b) interest on that amount from the date of the charging order at the prescribed rate.

(2B) In determining the value of an interest for the purposes of this section the court shall disregard any matter which it is required to disregard by the rules.][4]

(3) An order under this section made in respect of property vested in the trustee shall provide, in accordance with the rules, for the property to cease to be comprised in the bankrupt's estate and, subject to the charge (and any prior charge), to vest in the bankrupt.

(4) Subsections (1) and (2) and (4) to (6) of section 3 of the Charging Orders Act 1979 (supplemental provisions with respect to charging orders) have effect in relation to orders under this section as in relation to charging orders under that Act.

[(5) But an order under section 3(5) of that Act may not vary a charged value.][5]

[Low value home: application for sale, possession or charge

313A.—(1) This section applies where— **47–005**

(a) property comprised in the bankrupt's estate consists of an interest in a dwelling-house which at the date of the bankruptcy was the sole or principal residence of—

(i) the bankrupt,

(ii) the bankrupt's spouse, or

(iii) a former spouse of the bankrupt, and

(b) the trustee applies for an order for the sale of the property, for an order for possession of the property or for an order under section 313 in respect of the property.

(2) The court shall dismiss the application if the value of the interest is below the amount prescribed for the purposes of this subsection.

(3) In determining the value of an interest for the purposes of this section the court shall disregard any matter which it is required to disregard by the order which prescribes the amount for the purposes of subsection (2).][6]

---

[3] Words substituted by the Enterprise Act 2002, s.261(2)(a).
[4] subss. (2A) and (2B) inserted by the Enterprise Act 2002, s.261(2)(b).
[5] subs. (5) added by the Enterprise Act 2002, s.261(2)(c).
[6] s.313A inserted by the Enterprise Act 2002, s.261(3).

Chapter V

Effect of Bankruptcy on Certain Rights, Transactions, Etc.

[*Rights under trusts of land*

Rights under trusts of land

47–006 **335A.**—(1) Any application by a trustee of a bankrupt's estate under section 14 of the Trusts of Land and Appointment of Trustees Act 1996 (powers of court in relation to trusts of land) for an order under that section for the sale of land shall be made to the court having jurisdiction in relation to the bankruptcy.

(2) On such an application the court shall make such order as it thinks just and reasonable having regard to—

(a) the interests of the bankrupt's creditors;

(b) where the application is made in respect of land which includes a dwelling house which is or has been the home of the bankrupt or the bankrupt's spouse or former spouse—

(i) the conduct of the spouse or former spouse, so far as contributing to the bankruptcy,

(ii) the needs and financial resources of the spouse or former spouse, and

(iii) the needs of any children; and

(c) all the circumstances of the case other than the needs of the bankrupt.

(3) Where such an application is made after the end of the period of one year beginning with the first vesting under Chapter IV of this Part of the bankrupt's estate in a trustee, the court shall assume, unless the circumstances of the case are exceptional, that the interests of the bankrupt's creditors outweigh all other considerations.

(4) The powers conferred on the court by this section are exercisable on an application whether it is made before or after the commencement of this section.][7]

Rights of occupation[8]

Rights of occupation, etc. of bankrupt's spouse

47–007 **336.**—(1) Nothing occurring in the initial period of the bankruptcy (that is to say, the period beginning with the day of the presentation of the petition for the bankruptcy order and ending with the vesting of the bankrupt's estate in a trustee) is to be taken as having given rise to any [matrimonial home rights under Part IV of the Family Law Act 1996][9] in relation to a dwelling house comprised in the bankrupt's estate.

(2) Where a spouse's [matrimonial home rights under the Act of 1996][10] are a charge on the estate or interest of the other spouse, or of trustees for the other spouse, and the other spouse is adjudged bankrupt—

[7] s.335A inserted by the Trusts of Land and Appointment of Trustees Act 1996, s.25(1), Sched. 3, para. 23.
[8] See the Family Law Act 1996, Pt. IV, *post*, para. 60–001.
[9] Words substituted by the Family Law Act 1996, s.66(1), Sched. 8, Pt. III, para. 57(1), (2).
[10] Words substituted by the Family Law Act 1996, s.66(1), Sched. 8, Pt. III, para. 57(1), (3).

(a) the charge continues to subsist notwithstanding the bankruptcy and, subject to the provisions of that Act, binds the trustee of the bankrupt's estate and persons deriving title under that trustee, and
(b) any application for an order [under section 33 of that Act][11] shall be made to the court having jurisdiction in relation to the bankruptcy.

(3) [*Repealed by the Trusts of Land and Appointment of Trustees Act 1996, s.25(2), Sched. 4.*]

(4) On such an application as is mentioned in subsection (2) [. . .][12] the court shall make such order under [section 33 of the Act of 1996][13] [. . .][14] as it thinks just and reasonable having regard to—
(a) the interests of the bankrupt's creditors,
(b) the conduct of the spouse or former spouse, so far as contributing to the bankruptcy,
(c) the needs and financial resources of the spouse or former spouse,
(d) the needs of any children, and
(e) all the circumstances of the case other than the needs of the bankrupt.

(5) Where such an application is made after the end of the period of one year beginning with the first vesting under Chapter IV of this Part of the bankrupt's estate in a trustee, the court shall assume, unless the circumstances of the case are exceptional, that the interests of the bankrupt's creditors outweigh all other considerations.

Rights of occupation of bankrupt

337.—(1) This section applies where— **47–008**
(a) a person who is entitled to occupy a dwelling house by virtue of a beneficial estate or interest is adjudged bankrupt, and
(b) any persons under the age of 18 with whom that person had at some time occupied that dwelling house had their home with that person at the time when the bankruptcy petition was presented and at the commencement of the bankruptcy.

(2) Whether or not the bankrupt's spouse (if any) has [matrimonial home rights under Part IV of the Family Law Act 1996][15]—
(a) the bankrupt has the following rights as against the trustee of his estate—
(i) if in occupation, a right not to be evicted or excluded from the dwelling house or any part of it, except with the leave of the court,
(ii) if not in occupation, a right with the leave of the court to enter into and occupy the dwelling house, and
(b) the bankrupt's rights are a charge, having the like priority as an equitable interest created immediately before the commencement of the bankruptcy, on so much of his estate or interest in the dwelling house as vests in the trustee.

[(3) The Act of 1996 has effect, with the necessary modifications, as if—
(a) the rights conferred by paragraph (a) of subsection (2) were matrimonial home rights under that Act,
(b) any application for leave such as is mentioned in that paragraph were an application for an order under section 33 of that Act, and

[11] Words substituted by the Family Law Act 1996, s.66(1), Sched. 8, Pt. III, para. 57(1), (3).
[12] Words repealed by the Trusts of Land and Appointment of Trustees Act 1996, s.25(2), Sched. 4.
[13] Words substituted by the Family Law Act 1996, s.66(1), Sched. 8, Pt. III, para. 57(1), (4).
[14] Words repealed by the Trusts of Land and Appointment of Trustees Act 1996, s.25(2), Sched. 4.
[15] Words substituted by the Family Law Act 1996, s.66(1), Sched. 8, Pt. III, para. 58(1), (2).

(c) any charge under paragraph (b) of that subsection on the estate or interest of the trustee were a charge under that Act on the estate or interest of a spouse.][16]

(4) Any application for leave such as is mentioned in subsection (2)(a) or otherwise by virtue of this section for an order under [section 33 of the Act of 1996][17] shall be made to the court having jurisdiction in relation to the bankruptcy.

(5) On such an application the court shall make such order under [section 33 of the Act of 1996][18] as it thinks just and reasonable having regard to the interests of the creditors, to the bankrupt's financial resources, to the needs of the children and to all the circumstances of the case other than the needs of the bankrupt.

(6) Where such an application is made after the end of the period of one year beginning with the first vesting (under Chapter IV of this Part) of the bankrupt's estate in a trustee, the court shall assume, unless the circumstances of the case are exceptional, that the interests of the bankrupt's creditors outweigh all other considerations.

Payments in respect of premises occupied by bankrupt

47–009 **338.** Where any premises comprised in a bankrupt's estate are occupied by him (whether by virtue of the preceding section or otherwise) on condition that he makes payments towards satisfying any liability arising under a mortgage of the premises or otherwise towards the outgoings of the premises, the bankrupt does not, by virtue of those payments, acquire any interest in the premises.

Adjustment of prior transactions, etc.

Transactions at an undervalue

47–010 **339.**[19]—(1) Subject as follows in this section and sections 341 and 342, where an individual is adjudged bankrupt and he has at a relevant time (defined in section 341) entered into a transaction with any person at an undervalue, the trustee of the bankrupt's estate may apply to the court for an order under this section.

(2) The court shall, on such an application, make such order as it thinks fit for restoring the position to what it would have been if that individual had not entered into that transaction.

(3) For the purposes of this section and sections 341 and 342, an individual enters into a transaction with a person at an undervalue if—

(a) he makes a gift to that person or he otherwise enters into a transaction with that person on terms that provide for him to receive no consideration,

(b) he enters into a transaction with that person in consideration of marriage, or

(c) he enters into a transaction with that person for a consideration the value of which, in money or money's worth, is significantly less than the value,

[16] subs. (3) substituted by the Family Law Act 1996, s.66(1), Sched. 8, Pt. III, para. 58(1), (3).
[17] Words substituted by the Family Law Act 1996, s.66(1), Sched. 8, Pt. III, para. 58(1), (4).
[18] Words substituted by the Family Law Act 1996, s.66(1), Sched. 8, Pt. III, para. 58(1), (4).
[19] See also ss.343, 423, *post*, paras 47–014—47–015.

in money or money's worth, of the consideration provided by the individual.

Preferences

340.—(1) Subject as follows in this and the next two sections, where an individual is adjudged bankrupt and he has at a relevant time (defined in section 341) given a preference to any person, the trustee of the bankrupt's estate may apply to the court for an order under this section. **47–011**

(2) The court shall, on such an application, make such order as it thinks fit for restoring the position to what it would have been if that individual had not given that preference.

(3) For the purposes of this and the next two sections, an individual gives a preference to a person if—

(a) that person is one of the individual's creditors or a surety or guarantor for any of his debts or other liabilities, and

(b) the individual does anything or suffers anything to be done which (in either case) has the effect of putting that person into a position which, in the event of the individual's bankruptcy, will be better than the position he would have been in if that thing had not been done.

(4) The court shall not make an order under this section in respect of a preference given to any person unless the individual who gave the preference was influenced in deciding to give it by a desire to produce in relation to that person the effect mentioned in subsection (3)(b) above.

(5) An individual who has given a preference to a person who, at the time the preference was given, was an associate of his (otherwise than by reason only of being his employee) is presumed, unless the contrary is shown, to have been influenced in deciding to give it by such a desire as is mentioned in subsection (4).

(6) The fact that something has been done in pursuance of the order of a court does not, without more, prevent the doing or suffering of that thing from constituting the giving of a preference.

"Relevant time" under ss.339, 340

341.—(1) Subject as follows, the time at which an individual enters into a transaction at an undervalue or gives a preference is a relevant time if the transaction is entered into or the preference given— **47–012**

(a) in the case of a transaction at an undervalue, at a time in the period of 5 years ending with the day of the presentation of the bankruptcy petition on which the individual is adjudged bankrupt,

(b) in the case of a preference which is not a transaction at an undervalue and is given to a person who is an associate of the individual (otherwise than by reason only of being his employee), at a time in the period of 2 years ending with that day, and

(c) in any other case of a preference which is not a transaction at an undervalue, at a time in the period of 6 months ending with that day.

(2) Where an individual enters into a transaction at an undervalue or gives a preference at a time mentioned in paragraph (a), (b) or (c) of subsection (1) (not being, in the case of a transaction at an undervalue, a time less than 2 years before the end of the period mentioned in paragraph (a)), that time is not a relevant time for the purposes of sections 339 and 340 unless the individual—

(a) is insolvent at that time, or
(b) becomes insolvent in consequence of the transaction or preference;

but the requirements of this subsection are presumed to be satisfied, unless the contrary is shown, in relation to any transaction at an undervalue which is entered into by an individual with a person who is an associate of his (otherwise than by reason only of being his employee).

(3) For the purposes of subsection (2), an individual is insolvent if—

(a) he is unable to pay his debts as they fall due, or
(b) the value of his assets is less than the amount of his liabilities, taking into account his contingent and prospective liabilities.

(4), (5) [*Repealed by the Criminal Justice Act 1988, s.170(2), Sched. 16.*][20]

Orders under ss.339, 340

47–013 **342.**—(1) Without prejudice to the generality of section 339(2) or 340(2), an order under either of those sections with respect to a transaction or preference entered into or given by an individual who is subsequently adjudged bankrupt may (subject as follows)—

(a) require any property transferred as part of the transaction, or in connection with the giving of the preference, to be vested in the trustee of the bankrupt's estate as part of that estate;
(b) require any property to be so vested if it represents in any person's hands the application either of the proceeds of sale of property so transferred or of money so transferred;
(c) release or discharge (in whole or in part) any security given by the individual;
(d) require any person to pay, in respect of benefits received by him from the individual, such sums to the trustee of his estate as the court may direct;
(e) provide for any surety or guarantor whose obligations to any persons were released or discharged (in whole or in part) under the transaction or by the giving of the preference to be under such new or revived obligations to that person as the court thinks appropriate;
(f) provide for security to be provided for the discharge of any obligation imposed by or arising under the order, for such an obligation to be charged on any property and for the security or charge to have the same priority as a security or charge released or discharged (in whole or in part) under the transaction or by the giving of the preference; and
(g) provide for the extent to which any person whose property is vested by the order in the trustee of the bankrupt's estate, or on whom obligations are imposed by the order, is to be able to prove in the bankruptcy for debts or other liabilities which arose from, or were released or discharged (in whole or in part) under or by, the transaction or the giving of the preference.

(2) An order under section 339 or 340 may affect the property of, or impose any obligation on, any person whether or not he is the person with whom the individual in question entered into the transaction or, as the case may be, the person to whom the preference was given; but such an order—

(a) shall not prejudice any interest in property which was acquired from a person other than that individual and was acquired [in good faith and for value][21] or prejudice any interest deriving from such an interest, and

[20] The repeal of subss. (4) and (5) is prospective and takes effect from a day to be appointed.
[21] Words substituted by the Insolvency (No. 2) Act 1994, s.2(1).

(b) shall not require a person who received a benefit from the transaction or preference [in good faith and for value][22] to pay a sum to the trustee of the bankrupt's estate, except where he was a party to the transaction or the payment is to be in respect of a preference given to that person at a time when he was a creditor of that individual.

[(2A) Where a person has acquired an interest in property from a person other than the individual in question, or has received a benefit from the transaction or preference, and at the time of that acquisition or receipt—

(a) he had notice of the relevant surrounding circumstances and of the relevant proceedings, or

(b) he was an associate of, or was connected with, either the individual in question or the person with whom that individual entered into the transaction or to whom that individual gave the preference,

then, unless the contrary is shown, it shall be presumed for the purposes of paragraph (a) or (as the case may be) paragraph (b) of subsection (2) that the interest was acquired or the benefit was received otherwise than in good faith.][23]

(3) Any sums required to be paid to the trustee in accordance with an order under section 339 or 340 shall be comprised in the bankrupt's estate.

[(4) For the purposes of subsection (2A)(a), the relevant surrounding circumstances are (as the case may require)—

(a) the fact that the individual in question entered into the transaction at an undervalue; or

(b) the circumstances which amounted to the giving of the preference by the individual in question.

(5) For the purposes of subsection (2A)(a), a person has notice of the relevant proceedings if he has notice—

(a) of the fact that the petition on which the individual in question is adjudged bankrupt has been presented; or

(b) of the fact that the individual in question has been adjudged bankrupt.

(6) Section 249 in Part VII of this Act shall apply for the purposes of subsection (2A)(b) as it applies for the purposes of the first Group of Parts.][24]

. . . . . .

Extortionate credit transactions

343.[25]—(1) This section applies where a person is adjudged bankrupt who is or **47–014**
has been a party to a transaction for, or involving, the provision to him of credit.

(2) The court may, on the application of the trustee of the bankrupt's estate, make an order with respect to the transaction if the transaction is or was extortionate and was not entered into more than 3 years before the commencement of the bankruptcy.

(3) For the purposes of this section a transaction is extortionate if, having regard to the risk accepted by the person providing the credit—

(a) the terms of it are or were such as to require grossly exorbitant payments to be made (whether unconditionally or in certain contingencies) in respect of the provision of the credit, or

(b) it otherwise grossly contravened ordinary principles of fair dealing;

[22] Words substituted by the Insolvency (No. 2) Act 1994, s.2(1).
[23] subs. (2A) inserted by the Insolvency (No. 2) Act 1994, s.2(2).
[24] subss. (4)–(6) substituted (for subs. (4)) by the Insolvency (No. 2) Act 1994, s.2(3).
[25] See also the Consumer Credit Act 1974, ss.137–140, *ante*, paras 33–006 *et seq.*

and it shall be presumed, unless the contrary is proved, that a transaction with respect to which an application is made under this section is or, as the case may be, was extortionate.

(4) An order under this section with respect to any transaction may contain such one or more of the following as the court thinks fit, that is to say—

(a) provision setting aside the whole or part of any obligation created by the transaction;

(b) provision otherwise varying the terms of the transaction or varying the terms on which any security for the purposes of the transaction is held;

(c) provision requiring any person who is or was party to the transaction to pay to the trustee any sums paid to that person, by virtue of the transaction, by the bankrupt;

(d) provision requiring any person to surrender to the trustee any property held by him as security for the purposes of the transaction;

(e) provision directing accounts to be taken between any persons.

(5) Any sums or property required to be paid or surrendered to the trustee in accordance with an order under this section shall be comprised in the bankrupt's estate.

(6) Neither the trustee of a bankrupt's estate not an undischarged bankrupt is entitled to make an application under section 139(1)(a) of the Consumer Credit Act 1974 (re-opening of extortionate credit agreements) for any agreement by which credit is or has been provided to the bankrupt to be re-opened.

But the powers conferred by this section are exercisable in relation to any transaction concurrently with any powers exercisable under this Act in relation to that transaction as a transaction at an undervalue.

. . . .

PART XVI

PROVISIONS AGAINST DEBT AVOIDANCE (ENGLAND AND WALES ONLY)

Transactions defrauding creditors

47–015 **423.**—(1) This section relates to transactions entered into at an undervalue; and a person enters into such a transaction with another person if—

(a) he makes a gift to the other person or he otherwise enters into a transaction with the other on terms that provide for him to receive no consideration;

(b) he enters into a transaction with the other in consideration of marriage; or

(c) he enters into a transaction with the other for a consideration the value of which, in money or money's worth, is significantly less than the value, in money or money's worth, of the consideration provided by himself.

(2) Where a person has entered into such a transaction, the court may, if satisfied under the next subsection, make such order as it thinks fit for—

(a) restoring the position to what it would have been if the transaction had not been entered into, and

(b) protecting the interests of persons who are victims of the transaction.

(3) In the case of a person entering into such a transaction, an order shall only be made if the court is satisfied that it was entered into by him for the purpose—

(a) of putting assets beyond the reach of a person who is making, or may at some time make, a claim against him, or

(b) of otherwise prejudicing the interests of such a person in relation to the claim which he is making or may make.

(4) In this section "the court" means the High Court or—

(a) if the person entering into the transaction is an individual, any other court which would have jurisdiction in relation to a bankruptcy petition relating to him;

(b) if that person is a body capable of being wound up under Part IV or V of this Act, any other court having jurisdiction to wind it up.

(5) In relation to a transaction at an undervalue, references here and below to a victim of the transaction are to a person who is, or is capable of being, prejudiced by it; and in the following two sections the person entering into the transaction is referred to as "the debtor".

Those who may apply for an order under s.423

424.—(1) An application for an order under section 423 shall not be made in relation to a transaction except— **47–016**

(a) in a case where the debtor has been adjudged bankrupt or is a body corporate which is being wound up or [is in administration][26], by the official receiver, by the trustee of the bankrupt's estate or the liquidator or administrator of the body corporate or (with the leave of the court) by a victim of the transaction;

(b) in a case where a victim of the transaction is bound by a voluntary arrangement approved under Part I or Part VIII of this Act, by the supervisor of the voluntary arrangement or by any person who (whether or not so bound) is such a victim; or

(c) in any other case, by a victim of the transaction.

(2) An application made under any of the paragraphs of subsection (1) is to be treated as made on behalf of every victim of the transaction.

Provision which may be made by order under s.423

425.—(1) Without prejudice to the generality of section 423, an order made under that section with respect to a transaction may (subject as follows)— **47–017**

(a) require any property transferred as part of the transaction to be vested in any person, either absolutely or for the benefit of all the persons on whose behalf the application for the order is treated as made;

(b) require any property to be so vested if it represents, in any person's hands, the application either of the proceeds of sale of property so transferred or of money so transferred;

(c) release or discharge (in whole or in part) any security given by the debtor;

(d) require any person to pay to any other person in respect of benefits received from the debtor such sums as the court may direct;

(e) provide for any surety or guarantor whose obligations to any person were released or discharged (in whole or in part) under the transaction to be under such new or revived obligations as the court thinks appropriate;

[26] Words substituted by the Enterprise Act 2002, s.248(3), Sched. 17, paras 9, 36.

(f) provide for security to be provided for the discharge of any obligation imposed by or arising under the order, for such an obligation to be charged on any property and for such security or charge to have the same priority as a security or charge released or discharged (in whole or in part) under the transaction.

(2) An order under section 423 may affect the property of, or impose any obligation on, any person whether or not he is the person with whom the debtor entered into the transaction; but such an order—

(a) shall not prejudice any interest in property which was acquired from a person other than the debtor and was acquired in good faith, for value and without notice of the relevant circumstances, or prejudice any interest deriving from such an interest, and

(b) shall not require a person who received a benefit from the transaction in good faith, for value and without notice of the relevant circumstances to pay any sum unless he was a party to the transaction.

(3) For the purposes of this section the relevant circumstances in relation to a transaction are the circumstances by virtue of which an order under section 423 may be made in respect of the transaction.

(4) In this section "security" means any mortgage, charge, lien or other security.

Recognition of Trusts Act 1987

(1987 c. 14)

Applicable law and recognition of trusts

48–001 **1.**—(1) The provisions of the Convention set out in the Schedule to this Act shall have the force of law in the United Kingdom.

(2) Those provisions shall, so far as applicable, have effect not only in relation to the trusts described in Articles 2 and 3 of the Convention but also in relation to any other trusts of property arising under the law of any part of the United Kingdom or by virtue of a judicial decision whether in the United Kingdom or elsewhere.

(3) In accordance with Articles 15 and 16 such provisions of the law as are there mentioned shall, to the extent there specified, apply to the exclusion of the other provisions of the Convention.

(4) In Article 17 the reference to a State includes a reference to any country or territory (whether or not a party to the Convention and whether or not forming part of the United Kingdom) which has its own system of law.

(5) Article 22 shall not be construed as affecting the law to be applied in relation to anything done or omitted before the coming into force of this Act.

Section 1 SCHEDULE

CONVENTION ON THE LAW APPLICABLE TO TRUSTS AND ON THEIR RECOGNITION

CHAPTER I—SCOPE

Article 1

This Convention specifies the law applicable to trusts and governs their recognition.

Article 2

For the purposes of this Convention, the term "trust" refers to the legal relationship created—inter vivos or on death—by a person, the settlor, when assets have been placed under the control of a trustee for the benefit of a beneficiary or for a specified purpose.

A trust has the following characteristics—

(a) the assets constitute a separate fund and are not a part of the trustee's own estate;

(b) title to the trust assets stands in the name of the trustee or in the name of another person on behalf of the trustee;

(c) the trustee has the power and the duty, in respect of which he is accountable, to manage, employ or dispose of the assets in accordance with the terms of the trust and the special duties imposed upon him by law.

The reservation by the settlor of certain rights and powers, and the fact that the trustee may himself have rights as a beneficiary, are not necessarily inconsistent with the existence of a trust.

Article 3

The Convention applies only to trusts created voluntarily and evidenced in writing.

Article 4

The Convention does not apply to preliminary issues relating to the validity of wills or of other acts by virtue of which assets are transferred to the trustee.

Article 5

The Convention does not apply to the extent that the law specified by Chapter II does not provide for trusts or the category of trusts involved.

Chapter II—Applicable Law

Article 6

A trust shall be governed by the law chosen by the settlor. The choice must be express or be implied in the terms of the instrument creating or the writing evidencing the trust, interpreted, if necessary, in the light of the circumstances of the case.

Where the law chosen under the previous paragraph does not provide for trusts or the category of trust involved, the choice shall not be effective and the law specified in Article 7 shall apply.

Article 7

Where no applicable law has been chosen, a trust shall be governed by the law with which it is most closely connected.

In ascertaining the law with which a trust is most closely connected reference shall be made in particular to—

(a) the place of administration of the trust designated by the settlor;

(b) the situs of the assets of the trust;

(c) the place of residence or business of the trustee;

(d) the objects of the trust and the places where they are to be fulfilled.

Article 8

The law specified by Article 6 or 7 shall govern the validity of the trust, its construction, its effects and the administration of the trust. In particular that law shall govern—

(a) the appointment, resignation and removal of trustees, the capacity to act as a trustee, and the devolution of the office of trustee;

(b) the rights and duties of trustees among themselves;

(c) the right of trustees to delegate in whole or in part the discharge of their duties or the exercise of their powers;

(d) the power of trustees to administer or to dispose of trust assets, to create security interests in the trust assets, or to acquire new assets;

(e) the powers of investment of trustees;

(f) restrictions upon the duration of the trust, and upon the power to accumulate the income of the trust;

(g) the relationships between the trustees and the beneficiaries including the personal liability of the trustees to the beneficiaries;

(h) the variation or termination of the trust;

(i) the distribution of the trust assets;

(j) the duty of trustees to account for their administration.

Article 9

In applying this Chapter a severable aspect of the trust, particularly matters of administration, may be governed by a different law.

Article 10

The law applicable to the validity of the trust shall determine whether that law or the law governing a severable aspect of the trust may be replaced by another law.

CHAPTER III—RECOGNITION

Article 11

A trust created in accordance with the law specified by the preceding Chapter shall be recognised as a trust.

Such recognition shall imply, as a minimum, that the trust property constitutes a separate fund, that the trustee may sue and be sued in his capacity as trustee, and that he may appear or act in this capacity before a notary or any person acting in an official capacity.

In so far as the law applicable to the trust requires or provides, such recognition shall imply in particular—

(a) that personal creditors of the trustee shall have no recourse against the trust assets;
(b) that the trust assets shall not form part of the trustee's estate upon his insolvency or bankruptcy;
(c) that the trust assets shall not form part of the matrimonial property of the trustee or his spouse nor part of the trustee's estate upon his death;
(d) that the trust assets may be recovered when the trustee, in breach of trust, has mingled trust assets with his own property or has alienated trust assets. However, the rights and obligations of any third party holder of the assets shall remain subject to the law determined by the choice of law rules of the forum.

Article 12

Where the trustee desires to register assets, movable or immovable, or documents of title to them, he shall be entitled, in so far as this is not prohibited by or inconsistent with the law of the State where registration is sought, to do so in his capacity as trustee or in such other way that the existence of the trust is disclosed.

Article 14

The Convention shall not prevent the application of rules of law more favourable to the recognition of trusts.

CHAPTER IV—GENERAL CLAUSES

Article 15

The Convention does not prevent the application of provisions of the law designated by the conflicts rules of the forum, in so far as those provisions cannot be derogated from by voluntary act, relating in particular to the following matters—

(a) the protection of minors and incapable parties;
(b) the personal and proprietary effects of marriage;
(c) succession rights, testate and intestate, especially the indefeasible shares of spouses and relatives;
(d) the transfer of title to property and security interests in property;
(e) the protection of creditors in matters of insolvency;
(f) the protection, in other respects, of third parties acting in good faith.

If recognition of a trust is prevented by application of the preceding paragraph, the court shall try to give effect to the objects of the trust by other means.

Article 16

The Convention does not prevent the application of those provisions of the law of the forum which must be applied even to international situations, irrespective of rules of conflict of laws.

Article 17

In the Convention the word "law" means the rules of law in force in a State other than its rules of conflict of laws.

Article 18

The provisions of the Convention may be disregarded when their application would be manifestly incompatible with public policy.

Article 22

The Convention applies to trusts regardless of the date on which they were created.

Reverter of Sites Act 1987[1]

(1987 c. 15)

Right of reverter replaced by [trust][2]

1.—(1) Where any relevant enactment provides for land to revert to the ownership of any person at any time, being a time when the land ceases, or has ceased for a specified period, to be used for particular purposes, that enactment shall have effect, and (subject to subsection (4) below) shall be deemed always to have had effect, as if it provided (instead of for the reverter) for the land to be vested after that time, on the trust arising under this section, in the persons in whom it was vested immediately before that time. **49–001**

(2) Subject to the following provisions of this Act, the trust arising under this section in relation to any land is a trust [for the persons who (but for this Act) would from time to time be entitled to the ownership of the land by virtue of its reverter with a power, without consulting them,][3] to sell the land and to stand possessed of the net proceeds of sale (after payment of costs and expenses) and of the net rents and profits until sale (after payment of rates, taxes, costs of insurance, repairs and other outgoings) [in trust for those persons; but they shall not be entitled by reason of their interest to occupy the land.][4]

(3) Where—

(a) a trust in relation to any land has arisen or is treated as having arisen under this section at such a time as is mentioned in subsection (1) above; and

(b) immediately before that time the land was vested in any persons in their capacity as the minister and churchwardens of any parish,

those persons shall be treated as having become [trustees][5] under this section in

---

[1] The functions of the Secretary of State under this Act, in so far as they are exercisable in relation to Wales, are transferred to the National Assembly for Wales: National Assembly for Wales (Transfer of Functions) Order 1999 (S.I. 1999 No. 672), art. 2(a), Sched. 1.

[2] Word substituted by the Trusts of Land and Appointment of Trustees Act 1996, s.5(1), Sched. 2, para. 6(1), (5).

[3] Words inserted by the Trusts of Land and Appointment of Trustees Act 1996, s.5(1), Sched. 2, para. 6(1), (2)(a).

[4] Words substituted by the Trusts of Land and Appointment of Trustees Act 1996, s.5(1), Sched. 2, para. 6(1), (2)(b).

[5] Word substituted by the Trusts of Land and Appointment of Trustees Act 1996, s.5(1), Sched. 2, para. 6(1), (3).

that capacity and, accordingly, their interest in the land shall pass and, if the case so requires, be treated as having passed to their successors from time to time.

(4) This section shall not confer any right on any person as a beneficiary—

(a) in relation to any property in respect of which that person's claim was statute-barred before the commencement of this Act, or in relation to any property derived from any such property; or

(b) in relation to any rents or profits received, or breach of trust committed, before the commencement of this Act;

and anything validly done before the commencement of this Act in relation to any land which by virtue of this section is deemed to have been held at the time [in trust][6] shall, if done by the beneficiaries, be deemed, so far as necessary for preserving its validity, to have been done by the trustees.

(5) Where any property is held by any persons as trustees of a trust which has arisen under this section and, in consequence of subsection (4) above, there are no beneficiaries of that trust, the trustees shall have no power to act in relation to that property except—

(a) for the purposes for which they could have acted in relation to that property if this Act had not been passed; or

(b) for the purpose of securing the establishment of a scheme under section 2 below or the making of an order under [section 554 of the Education Act 1996][7] (special powers as to trusts for religious education).

(6) In this section—

"churchwardens" includes chapel wardens;

"minister" includes a rector, vicar or perpetual curate; and

"parish" includes a parish of the Church of Wales;

and the reference to a person's claim being statute-barred is a reference to the Limitation Act 1980 providing that no proceedings shall be brought by that person to recover the property in respect of which the claim subsists.

Charity Commissioners' schemes

49–002 **2.**—(1) Subject to the following provisions of this section and to sections 3 and 4 below, where any persons hold any property as trustees of a trust which has arisen under section 1 above, the Charity Commissioners may, on the application of the trustees, by order establish a scheme which—

(a) extinguishes the rights of beneficiaries under the trust; and

(b) requires the trustees to hold the property on trust for such charitable purposes as may be specified in the order.

(2) Subject to subsections (3) and (4) below, an order made under this section—

(a) may contain any such provision as may be contained in an order made by the High Court for establishing a scheme for the administration of a charity; and

(b) shall have the same effect as an order so made.

(3) The charitable purposes specified in an order made under this section on an application with respect to any trust shall be as similar in character as the Charity Commissioners think is practicable in all the circumstances to the purposes (whether charitable or not) for which the trustees held the relevant

---

[6] Words substituted by the Trusts of Land and Appointment of Trustees Act 1996, s.5(1), Sched. 2, para. 6(1), (4).

[7] Words substituted by the Education Act 1996, s.582(1), Sched. 37, Pt. I, para. 67(1), (2).

land before the cesser of use in consequence of which the trust arose; but in determining the character of the last-mentioned purposes the Commissioners, if they think it appropriate to do so, may give greater weight to the persons or locality benefited by the purposes than to the nature of the benefit.

(4) An order made under this section on an application with respect to any trust shall be so framed as to secure that if a person who—

(a) but for the making of the order would have been a beneficiary under the trust; and

(b) has not consented to the establishment of a scheme under this section,

notifies a claim to the trustees within the period of five years after the date of the making of the order, that person shall be paid an amount equal to the value of his rights at the time of their extinguishment.

(5) The Charity Commissioners shall not make any order under this section establishing a scheme unless—

(a) the requirements of section 3 below with respect to the making of the application for the order are satisfied or, by virtue of subsection (4) of that section, do not apply;

(b) one of the conditions specified in subsection (6) below is fulfilled;

(c) public notice of the Commissioners' proposals has been given inviting representations to be made to them within a period specified in the notice, being a period ending not less than one month after the date of the giving of the notice; and

(d) that period has ended and the Commissioners have taken into consideration any representations which have been made within that period and not withdrawn.

(6) The conditions mentioned in subsection (5)(b) above are—

(a) that there is no claim by any person to be a beneficiary in respect of rights proposed to be extinguished—

(i) which is outstanding; or

(ii) which has at any time been accepted as valid by the trustees or by persons whose acceptance binds the trustees; or

(iii) which has been upheld in proceedings that have been concluded;

(b) that consent to the establishment of a scheme under this section has been given by every person whose claim to be a beneficiary in respect of those rights is outstanding or has been so accepted or upheld.

(7) The Charity Commissioners shall refuse to consider an application under this section unless it is accompanied by a statutory declaration by the applicants—

(a) that the requirements of section 3 below are satisfied with respect to the making of the application or, if the declaration so declares, do not apply; and

(b) that a condition specified in subsection (6) above and identified in the declaration is fulfilled;

and the declaration shall be conclusive for the purposes of this section of the matters declared therein.

(8) A notice given for the purposes of subsection (5)(c) above shall contain such particulars of the Commissioners' proposals, or such directions for obtaining information about them, and shall be given in such manner, as they think sufficient and appropriate; and a further such notice shall not be required where the Commissioners decide, before proceeding with any proposals of which notice has been so given, to modify them.

Applications for schemes

49–003 **3.**—(1) Where an application is made under section 2 above by the trustees of any trust that has arisen under section 1 above, the requirements of this section are satisfied with respect to the making of that application if, before the application is made—

(a) notices under subsection (2) below have been published in two national newspapers and in a local newspaper circulating in the locality where the relevant land is situated;

(b) each of those notices specified a period for the notification to the trustees of claims by beneficiaries, being a period ending not less than three months after the date of publication of the last of those notices to be published;

(c) that period has ended;

(d) for a period of not less than twenty-one days during the first month of that period, a copy of one of those notices was affixed to some object on the relevant land in such a position and manner as, so far as practicable, to make the notice easy for members of the public to see and read without going on to the land; and

(e) the trustees have considered what other steps could be taken to trace the persons who are or may be beneficiaries and to inform those persons of the application to be made under section 2 above and have taken such of the steps considered by them as it was reasonably practicable for them to take.

(2) A notice under this subsection shall—

(a) set out the circumstances that have resulted in a trust having arisen under section 1 above;

(b) state that an application is to be made for the establishment of a scheme with respect to the property subject to the trust; and

(c) contain a warning to every beneficiary that, if he wishes to oppose the extinguishment of his rights, he should notify his claim to the trustees in the manner, and within the period, specified in the notice.

(3) Where at the time when the trustees publish a notice for the purposes of subsection (2) above—

(a) the relevant land is not under their control; and

(b) it is not reasonably practicable for them to arrange for a copy of the notice to be affixed as required by paragraph (d) of subsection (1) above to some object on the land,

that paragraph shall be disregarded for the purposes of this section.

(4) The requirements of this section shall not apply in the case of an application made in respect of any trust if—

(a) the time when that trust is treated as having arisen was before the commencement of this Act; and

(b) more than twelve years have elapsed since that time.

Provisions supplemental to ss.2 and 3

49–004 **4.**—(1) Where an order is made under section 2 above—

(a) public notice of the order shall be given in such manner as the Charity Commissioners think sufficient and appropriate; and

(b) a copy of the order shall, for not less than one month after the date of the giving of the notice, be available for public inspection at all reasonable times at the Commissioners' office and at some convenient place in the locality where the relevant land is situated;

and a notice given for the purposes of paragraph (a) above shall contain such particulars of the order, or such directions for obtaining information about it, as the Commissioners think sufficient and appropriate.

(2) Subject to subsection (3) below, an appeal against an order made under section 2 above may be brought in the High Court by any of the following, that is to say—

(a) the Attorney General;
(b) the trustees of the trust established under the order;
(c) a beneficiary of, or the trustees of, the trust in respect of which the application for the order had been made;
(d) any person interested in the purposes for which the last-mentioned trustees or any of their predecessors held the relevant land before the cesser of use in consequence of which the trust arose under section 1 above;
(e) any two or more inhabitants of the locality where that land is situated.

(3) An appeal shall not be brought under subsection (2) above against any order—

(a) after the end of the period of three months beginning with the day following the date on which public notice of the order is given; or
(b) without either a certificate by the Charity Commissioners that it is a proper case for an appeal or the leave of the High Court,

unless it is brought by the Attorney General.

(4) [Sections 89, 91 and 92 of the Charities Act 1993][8] (supplemental provisions with respect to orders and appeals) shall apply in relation to, and to appeals against, orders under section 2 above as they apply in relation to, and to appeals against, orders under that Act.

(5) Trustees of a trust which has arisen under section 1 above may pay or apply capital money for any of the purposes of section 2 or 3 above or of this section.

Orders under the Education Act 1973

5.—(1) An order made under [section 554 of the Education Act 1996][9] (special powers as to certain trusts for religious education) with respect to so much of any endowment as consists of— **49–005**

(a) land in relation to which a trust under section 1 above has arisen or will arise after the land ceased or ceases to be used for particular purposes; or
(b) any other property subject to a trust under that section,

may extinguish any rights to which a person is or may become entitled as a beneficiary under the trust.

(2) The Secretary of State shall not by an order under [section 554 of the 1996 Act][10] extinguish any such rights unless he is satisfied that all reasonably practicable steps to trace the persons who are or may become entitled to any of those rights have been taken and either—

(a) that there is no claim by any person to be a person who is or may become so entitled—
 (i) which is outstanding; or

[8] Words substituted by the Charities Act 1993, s.98(1), Sched. 6, para. 24.
[9] Words substituted by the Education Act 1996, s.582(1), Sched. 37, Pt. I, para. 67(1), (3).
[10] Words substituted by the Education Act 1996, s.582(1), Sched. 37, Pt. I, para. 67(1), (3).

(ii) which has at any time been accepted as valid by the trustees or by persons whose acceptance binds or will bind the trustees; or

(iii) which has been upheld in proceedings that have been concluded; or

(b) that consent to the making of an order under [section 554 of the 1996 Act][11] has been given by every person whose claim to be such a person is outstanding or has been so accepted or upheld.

(3) Where applications for the extinguishment of the rights of any beneficiaries are made with respect to the same trust property both to the Secretary of State under [section 554 of the 1996 Act][12] and to the Charity Commissioners under section 2 above, the Commissioners shall not consider, or further consider, the application made to them, unless the Secretary of State either—

(a) consents to the application made to the Charity Commissioners being considered before the application made to him; or

(b) disposes of the application made to him without extinguishing the rights of one or more of the beneficiaries.

(4) Trustees of a trust which has arisen under section 1 above may pay or apply capital money for the purposes of any provision of this section or [section 554 of the 1996 Act][13].

Clarification of status, etc. of land before reverter

49–006 **6.**—(1) Nothing in this Act shall require any land which is or has been the subject of any grant, conveyance or other assurance under any relevant enactment to be treated as or as having been settled land.

(2) It is hereby declared—

(a) that the power conferred by section 14 of the Schools Sites Act 1841 (power of sale etc.) is exercisable at any time in relation to land in relation to which (but for the exercise of the power) a trust might subsequently arise under section 1 above; and

(b) that the exercise of that power in respect of any land prevents any trust from arising under section 1 above in relation to that land or any land representing the proceeds of sale of that land.

Construction

49–007 **7.**—(1) In this Act—

"relevant enactment" means any enactment contained in—

(a) the School Sites Acts;

(b) the Literary and Scientific Institutions Act 1854; or

(c) the Places of Worship Sites Act 1873;

"relevant land", in relation to a trust which has arisen under section 1 above, means the land which but for this Act would have reverted to the persons who are the first beneficiaries under the trust.

(2) In this Act references to land include references to—

(a) any part of any land which has been the subject of a grant, conveyance or other assurance under any relevant enactment; and

[11] Words substituted by the Education Act 1996, s.582(1), Sched. 37, Pt. I, para. 67(1), (3).
[12] Words substituted by the Education Act 1996, s.582(1), Sched. 37, Pt. I, para. 67(1), (3).
[13] Words substituted by the Education Act 1996, s.582(1), Sched. 37, Pt. I, para. 67(1), (3).

(b) any land an interest in which (including any future or contingent interest arising under any such enactment) belongs to the Crown, the Duchy of Lancaster or the Duchy of Cornwall.

(3) For the purposes of this Act a claim by any person to be a beneficiary under a trust is outstanding if—

(a) it has been notified to the trustees;

(b) it has not been withdrawn; and

(c) proceedings for determining whether it should be upheld have not been commenced or (if commenced) have not been concluded.

(4) For the purposes of this Act proceedings shall not, in relation to any person's claim, be treated as concluded where the time for appealing is unexpired or an appeal is pending unless that person has indicated his intention not to appeal or, as the case may be, not to continue with the appeal.

Family Law Reform Act 1987

(1987 c. 42)

Part 1

General Principle

General principle

1.—(1) In this Act and enactments passed and instruments made after the coming into force of this section, references (however expressed) to any relationship between two persons shall, unless the contrary intention appears, be construed without regard to whether or not the father and mother of either of them, or the father and mother of any person through whom the relationship is deduced, have or had been married to each other at any time. **50–001**

(2) In this Act and enactments passed after the coming into force of this section, unless the contrary intention appears—

(a) references to a person whose father and mother were married to each other at the time of his birth include; and

(b) references to a person whose father and mother were not married to each other at the time of his birth do not include,

references to any person to whom subsection (3) below applies, and cognate references shall be construed accordingly.

(3) This subsection applies to any person who—

(a) is treated as legitimate by virtue of section 1 of the Legitimacy Act 1976;

(b) is a legitimated person within the meaning of section 10 of that Act;

[(c) is an adopted person within the meaning of Chapter 4 of Part I of the Adoption and Children Act 2002][1]; or

(d) is otherwise treated in law as legitimate.

(4) For the purpose of construing references falling within subsection (2) above, the time of a person's birth shall be taken to include any time during the period beginning with—

(a) the insemination resulting in his birth; or

---

[1] Paragraph (c) substituted by the Adoption and Children Act 2002, s.139, Sched. 3, paras 50, 51.

(b) where there was no such insemination, his conception,
and (in either case) ending with his birth.

PART III

PROPERTY RIGHTS

Succession on intestacy

50–002 **18.**—(1) In Part IV of the Administration of Estates Act 1925 (which deals with the distribution of the estate of an intestate), references (however expressed) to any relationship between two persons shall be construed in accordance with section 1 above.

(2) For the purposes of subsection (1) above and that Part of that Act, a person whose father and mother were not married to each other at the time of his birth shall be presumed not to have been survived by his father, or by any person related to him only through his father, unless the contrary is shown.

(3) In section 50(1) of that Act (which relates to the construction of documents), the reference to Part IV of that Act, or to the foregoing provisions of that Part, shall in relation to an instrument inter vivos made, or a will or codicil coming into operation, after the coming into force of this section (but not in relation to instruments inter vivos made or wills or codicils coming into operation earlier) be construed as including references to this section.

(4) This section does not affect any rights under the intestacy of a person dying before the coming into force of this section.

Dispositions of property

50–003 **19.**—(1) In the following dispositions, namely—

(a) dispositions inter vivos made on or after the date on which this section comes into force; and
(b) dispositions by will or codicil where the will or codicil is made on or after that date,

references (whether express or implied) to any relationship between two persons shall be construed in accordance with section 1 above.

(2) It is hereby declared that the use, without more, of the word "heir" or "heirs" or any expression [purporting to create][2] an entailed interest in real or personal property does not show a contrary intention for the purposes of section 1 as applied by subsection (1) above.

(3) In relation to the dispositions mentioned in subsection (1) above, section 33 of the Trustee Act 1925 (which specifies the trust implied by a direction that income is to be held on protective trusts for the benefit of any person) shall have effect as if any reference (however expressed) to any relationship between two persons were construed in accordance with section 1 above.

(4) Where under any disposition of real or personal property, any interest in such property is limited (whether subject to any preceding limitation or charge or not) in such a way that it would, apart from this section, devolve (as nearly as the law permits) along with a dignity or title of honour, then—

(a) whether or not the disposition contains an express reference to the dignity or title of honour; and

[2] Words substituted by the Trusts of Land and Appointment of Trustees Act 1996, s.25(1), Sched. 3, para. 25.

(b) whether or not the property or some interest in the property may in some event become severed from it,

nothing in this section shall operate to sever the property or any interest in it from the dignity or title, but the property or interest shall devolve in all respects as if this section had not been enacted.

(5) This section is without prejudice to section 42 of the Adoption Act 1976 [or section 69 of the Adoption and Children Act 2002][3] (construction of dispositions in cases of adoption).

(6) In this section "disposition" means a disposition, including an oral disposition, of real or personal property whether inter vivos or by will or codicil.

(7) Notwithstanding any rule of law, a disposition made by will or codicil executed before the date on which this section comes into force shall not be treated for the purposes of this section as made on or after that date by reason only that the will or codicil is confirmed by a codicil executed on or after that date.

. . . . . .

Entitlement to grant of probate, etc.

21.—(1) For the purpose of determining the person or persons who would in accordance with probate rules be entitled to a grant of probate or administration in respect of the estate of a deceased person, the deceased shall be presumed, unless the contrary is shown, not to have been survived— **50–004**

(a) by any person related to him whose father and mother were not married to each other at the time of his birth; or

(b) by any person whose relationship with him is deduced through such a person as is mentioned in paragraph (a) above.

(2) In this section "probate rules" means rules of court made under section 127 of the Supreme Court Act 1981.

(3) This section does not apply in relation to the estate of a person dying before the coming into force of this section.

Landlord and Tenant Act 1988

(1988 c. 26)

Qualified duty to consent to assigning, underletting, etc. of premises

1.[1]—(1) This section applies in any case where— **51–001**

(a) a tenancy includes a covenant on the part of the tenant not to enter into one or more of the following transactions, that is—

(i) assigning,
(ii) underletting,
(iii) charging, or
(iv) parting with the possession of,

---

[3] Words inserted by the Adoption and Children Act 2002, s.139, Sched. 3, paras 50, 52.

[1] See the Landlord and Tenant Act 1927, s.19(1A), *ante*, para. 12–002.

the premises comprised in the tenancy or any part of the premises without the consent of the landlord or some other person, but

(b) the covenant is subject to the qualification that the consent is not to be unreasonably withheld (whether or not it is also subject to any other qualification).

(2) In this section and section 2 of this Act—

(a) references to a proposed transaction are to any assignment, underletting, charging or parting with possession to which the covenant relates, and

(b) references to the person who may consent to such a transaction are to the person who under the covenant may consent to the tenant entering into the proposed transaction.

(3) Where there is served on the person who may consent to a proposed transaction a written application by the tenant for consent to the transaction, he owes a duty to the tenant within a reasonable time—

(a) to give consent, except in a case where it is reasonable not to give consent,

(b) to serve on the tenant written notice of his decision whether or not to give consent specifying in addition—

(i) if the consent is given subject to conditions, the conditions,

(ii) if the consent is withheld, the reasons for withholding it.

(4) Giving consent subject to any condition that is not a reasonable condition does not satisfy the duty under subsection (3)(a) above.

(5) For the purposes of this Act it is reasonable for a person not to give consent to a proposed transaction only in a case where, if he withheld consent and the tenant completed the transaction, the tenant would be in breach of a covenant.

(6) It is for the person who owed any duty under subsection (3) above—

(a) if he gave consent and the question arises whether he gave it within a reasonable time, to show that he did,

(b) if he gave consent subject to any condition and the question arises whether the condition was a reasonable condition, to show that it was,

(c) if he did not give consent and the question arises whether it was reasonable for him not to do so, to show that it was reasonable,

and, if the question arises whether he served notice under that subsection within a reasonable time, to show that he did.

Duty to pass on applications

51–002 **2.**—(1) If, in a case where section 1 of this Act applies, any person receives a written application by the tenant for consent to a proposed transaction and that person—

(a) is a person who may consent to the transaction or (though not such a person) is the landlord, and

(b) believes that another person, other than a person who he believes has received the application or a copy of it, is a person who may consent to the transaction,

he owes a duty to the tenant (whether or not he owes him any duty under section 1 of this Act) to take such steps as are reasonable to secure the receipt within a reasonable time by the other person of a copy of the application.

(2) The reference in section 1(3) of this Act to the service of an application on a person who may consent to a proposed transaction includes a reference to the

receipt by him of an application or a copy of an application (whether it is for his consent or that of another).

Qualified duty to approve consent by another

3.—(1) This section applies in any case where— **51–003**

(a) a tenancy includes a covenant on the part of the tenant not without the approval of the landlord to consent to the sub-tenant—
  (i) assigning.
  (ii) underletting,
  (iii) charging, or
  (iv) parting with the possession of,

the premises comprised in the sub-tenancy or any part of the premises, but

(b) the covenant is subject to the qualification that the approval is not to be unreasonably withheld (whether or not it is also subject to any other qualification).

(2) Where there is served on the landlord a written application by the tenant for approval or a copy of a written application to the tenant by the sub-tenant for consent to a transaction to which the covenant relates the landlord owes a duty to the sub-tenant within a reasonable time—

(a) to give approval, except in a case where it is reasonable not to give approval,
(b) to serve on the tenant and the sub-tenant written notice of his decision whether or not to give approval specifying in addition—
  (i) if approval is given subject to conditions, the conditions,
  (ii) if approval is withheld, the reasons for withholding it.

(3) Giving approval subject to any condition that is not a reasonable condition does not satisfy the duty under subsection (2)(a) above.

(4) For the purposes of this section it is reasonable for the landlord not to give approval only in a case where, if he withheld approval and the tenant gave his consent, the tenant would be in breach of covenant.

(5) It is for a landlord who owed any duty under subsection (2) above—

(a) if he gave approval and the question arises whether he gave it within a reasonable time, to show that he did,
(b) if he gave approval subject to any condition and the question arises whether the condition was a reasonable condition, to show that it was,
(c) if he did not give approval and the question arises whether it was reasonable for him not to do so, to show that it was reasonable,

and, if the question arises whether he served notice under that subsection within a reasonable time, to show that he did.

Breach of duty

4. A claim that a person has broken any duty under this Act may be made the subject of civil proceedings in like manner as any other claim in tort for breach of statutory duty. **51–004**

Interpretation

5.—(1) In this Act— **51–005**

"covenant" includes condition and agreement,

"consent" includes licence,
"landlord" includes any superior landlord from whom the tenant's immediate landlord directly or indirectly holds,
"tenancy", subject to subsection (3) below, means any lease or other tenancy (whether made before or after the coming into force of this Act) and includes—
(a) a sub-tenancy, and
(b) an agreement for a tenancy
and references in this Act to the landlord and to the tenant are to be interpreted accordingly, and
"tenant", where the tenancy is affected by a mortgage (within the meaning of the Law of Property Act 1925) and the mortgagee proposes to exercise his statutory or express power of sale, includes the mortgagee.

(2) An application or notice is to be treated as served for the purposes of this Act if—
(a) served in any manner provided in the tenancy, and
(b) in respect of any matter for which the tenancy makes no provision, served in any manner provided by section 23 of the Landlord and Tenant Act 1927.

(3) This Act does not apply to a secure tenancy (defined in section 79 of the Housing Act 1985) [or to an introductory tenancy (within the meaning of Chapter I of Part V of the Housing Act 1996)][2].

(4) This Act applies only to applications for consent or approval served after its coming into force.

Common Land (Rectification of Registers) Act 1989

(1989 c. 18)

Removal from registers

52–001 **1.**—(1) Within three years of the passing of this Act any person may, by notice in writing given to the registration authority maintaining a register of common land and of town and village greens under the Commons Registration Act 1965, object to the inclusion on either of the registers of the whole or part of any land in respect of which the requirements specified in subsection (2) below are satisfied.

(2) Those requirements are—
(a) that—
(i) there is a dwellinghouse on the land and, if and so far as the land is not the site of that dwellinghouse, it is ancillary to that dwellinghouse; or
(ii) the land is ancillary to a dwellinghouse which is not on the land; and
(b) that the requirements of paragraph (a) above have been satisfied at all times since 5th August 1945.

---

[2] Words added by the Housing Act 1996 (Consequential Amendments) Order 1997 (S.I. 1997 No. 74), art. 2, Sched., para. 5.

(3) For the purposes of subsection (2) above land ancillary to a dwellinghouse means a garden, private garage or outbuildings used and enjoyed with the dwellinghouse; and in that subsection "dwellinghouse" includes a building consisting of two or more separate dwellings.

(4) On the receipt of a notice under subsection (1) of this section the registration authority shall refer the matter to a Commons Commissioner who shall inquire into the matter and, if he considers that the requirements specified in subsection (2) above are satisfied in the case of the land to which the objection relates or in the case of any part of it, he shall give notice of his decision to the registration authority who shall modify the register so as to exclude that land or, as the case may be, that part of it.

(5) Where a register is modified under this section so as to exclude any land the registration authority shall also cancel the registration of any person as the owner of that land.

(6) Section 17(2) of the said Act of 1965 (procedure of Commons Commissioners) shall apply to a matter referred to a Commissioner under this section as it applies to a matter referred under that Act.

Regulations

2. Section 19(1), (4) and (5) of the said Act of 1965 (regulations) shall have effect as if this Act were included in that Act; and regulations under that section may also— **52–002**

(a) prescribe the payment of a fee not exceeding £100 on the making of an objection under this Act;

(b) require any notice of such an objection to be accompanied by such documents, statements or declarations as the regulations may prescribe; and

(c) require a registration authority, on receiving such a notice, to take such steps as the regulations may prescribe for informing the public of the objection.

Law of Property (Miscellaneous Provisions) Act 1989

(1989 c. 34)

Deeds and their execution

1.—(1) Any rule of law which— **53–001**

(a) restricts the substances on which a deed may be written;

(b) requires a seal for the valid execution of an instrument as a deed by an individual; or

(c) requires authority by one person to another to deliver an instrument as a deed on his behalf to be given by deed,

is abolished.

(2) An instrument shall not be a deed unless—

(a) it makes it clear on its face that it is intended to be a deed by the person making it or, as the case may be, by the parties to it (whether by describing itself as a deed or expressing itself to be executed or signed as a deed or otherwise); and

(b) it is validly executed as a deed by that person or, as the case may be, one or more of those parties.

(3) An instrument is validly executed as a deed by an individual if, and only if—

(a) it is signed—

(i) by him in the presence of a witness who attests the signature; or

(ii) at his direction and in his presence and the presence of two witnesses who each attest the signature; and

(b) it is delivered as a deed by him or a person authorised to do so on his behalf.

(4) In subsections (2) and (3) above "sign", in relation to an instrument, includes making one's mark on the instrument and "signature" is to be construed accordingly.

(5) Where a solicitor [, duly certificated notary public][1] or licensed conveyancer, or an agent or employee of a solicitor [, duly certificated notary public][2] or licensed conveyancer, in the course of or in connection with a transaction involving the disposition or creation of an interest in land, purports to deliver an instrument as a deed on behalf of a party to the instrument, it shall be conclusively presumed in favour of a purchaser that he is authorised so to deliver the instrument.

(6) In subsection (5) above—

"disposition" and "purchaser" have the same meanings as in the Law of Property Act 1925;

["duly certificated notary public" has the same meaning as it has in the Solicitors Act 1974 by virtue of section 87(1) of that Act;][3] and

"interest in land" means any estate, interest or charge in or over land [. . .][4].

(7) Where an instrument under seal that constitutes a deed is required for the purposes of an Act passed before this section comes into force, this section shall have effect as to signing, sealing or delivery of an instrument by an individual in place of any provision of that Act as to signing, sealing or delivery.

(8) The enactments mentioned in Schedule 1 to this Act (which in consequence of this section require amendments other than those provided by subsection (7) above) shall have effect with the amendments specified in that Schedule.

(9) Nothing in subsection (1)(b), (2), (3), (7) or (8) above applies in relation to deeds required or authorised to be made under—

(a) the seal of the county palatine of Lancaster;

(b) the seal of the Duchy of Lancaster; or

(c) the seal of the Duchy of Cornwall.

(10) The references in this section to the execution of a deed by an individual do not include execution by a corporation sole and the reference in subsection (7) above to signing, sealing or delivery by an individual does not include signing, sealing or delivery by such a corporation.

(11) Nothing in this section applies in relation to instruments delivered as deeds before this section comes into force.

[1] Words inserted by the Courts and Legal Services Act 1990, s.125(2), Sched. 17, para. 20(1).
[2] Words inserted by the Courts and Legal Services Act 1990, s.125(2), Sched. 17, para. 20(1).
[3] Definition inserted by the Courts and Legal Services Act 1990, s.125(2), Sched. 17, para. 20(2).
[4] Words repealed by the Trusts of Land and Appointment of Trustees Act 1996, s.25(2), Sched. 4.

Contracts for sale, etc. of land to be made by signed writing

2.—(1) A contract for the sale or other disposition of an interest in land can only be made in writing and only by incorporating all the terms which the parties have expressly agreed in one document or, where contracts are exchanged, in each. **53–002**

(2) The terms may be incorporated in a document either by being set out in it or by reference to some other document.

(3) The document incorporating the terms or, where contracts are exchanged, one of the documents incorporating them (but not necessarily the same one) must be signed by or on behalf of each party to the contract.

(4) Where a contract for the sale or other disposition of an interest in land satisfies the conditions of this section by reason only of the rectification of one or more documents in pursuance of an order of a court, the contract shall come into being, or be deemed to have come into being, at such time as may be specified in the order.

(5) This section does not apply in relation to—

(a) a contract to grant such a lease as is mentioned in section 54(2) of the Law of Property Act 1925 (short leases);

(b) a contract made in the course of a public auction; or

[(c) a contract regulated under the Financial Services and Markets Act 2000, other than a regulated mortgage contract;][5]

and nothing in this section affects the creation or operation of resulting, implied or constructive trusts.

(6) In this section—

"disposition" has the same meaning as in the Law of Property Act 1925;

"interest in land" means any estate, interest or charge in or over land [. . .][6].

["regulated mortgage contract" must be read with—

(a) section 22 of the Financial Services and Markets Act 2000,

(b) any relevant order under that section, and

(c) Schedule 2 to that Act.][7]

(7) Nothing in this section shall apply in relation to contracts made before this section comes into force.

(8) [*Repeals the Law of Property Act* 1925, *s*.40.]

Abolition of rule in Bain v. Fothergill

3. The rule of law known as the rule in Bain v. Fothergill is abolished in relation to contracts made after this section comes into force. **53–003**

. . . . . .

---

[5] Para. (c) substituted by the Financial Services and Markets Act 2000 (Consequential Amendments and Repeals) Order 2001 (S.I. 2001 No. 3649), art. 317(1), (2).

[6] Words repealed by the Trusts of Land and Appointment of Trustees Act 1996, s.25(2), Sched. 4.

[7] Definition added by the Financial Services and Markets Act 2000 (Consequential Amendments and Repeals) Order 2001 (S.I. 2001 No. 3649), art. 317(1), (3).

Access to Neighbouring Land Act 1992

(1992 c. 23)

Access orders

54–001 **1.**—(1) A person—

(a) who, for the purpose of carrying out works to any land (the "dominant land"), desires to enter upon any adjoining or adjacent land (the "servient land"), and

(b) who needs, but does not have, the consent of some other person to that entry,

may make an application to the court for an order under this section ("an access order") against that other person.

(2) On an application under this section, the court shall make an access order if, and only if, it is satisfied—

(a) that the works are reasonably necessary for the preservation of the whole or any part of the dominant land; and

(b) that they cannot be carried out, or would be substantially more difficult to carry out, without entry upon the servient land;

but this subsection is subject to subsection (3) below.

(3) The court shall not make an access order in any case where it is satisfied that, were it to make such an order—

(a) the respondent or any other person would suffer interference with, or disturbance of, his use or enjoyment of the servient land, or

(b) the respondent, or any other person (whether of full age or capacity or not) in occupation of the whole or any part of the servient land, would suffer hardship,

to such a degree by reason of the entry (notwithstanding any requirement of this Act or any term or condition that may be imposed under it) that it would be unreasonable to make the order.

(4) Where the court is satisfied on an application under this section that it is reasonably necessary to carry out any basic preservation works to the dominant land, those works shall be taken for the purposes of this Act to be reasonably necessary for the preservation of the land; and in this subsection "basic preservation works" means any of the following, that is to say—

(a) the maintenance, repair or renewal of any part of a building or other structure comprised in, or situate on, the dominant land;

(b) the clearance, repair or renewal of any drain, sewer, pipe or cable so comprised or situate;

(c) the treatment, cutting back, felling, removal or replacement of any hedge, tree, shrub or other growing thing which is so comprised and which is, or is in danger of becoming, damaged, diseased, dangerous, insecurely rooted or dead;

(d) the filling in, or clearance, of any ditch so comprised;

but this subsection is without prejudice to the generality of the works which may, apart from it, be regarded by the court as reasonably necessary for the preservation of any land.

(5) If the court considers it fair and reasonable in all the circumstances of the case, works may be regarded for the purposes of this Act as being reasonably necessary for the preservation of any land (or, for the purposes of subsection (4) above, as being basic preservation works which it is reasonably necessary to carry out to any land) notwithstanding that the works incidentally involve—

(a) the making of some alteration, adjustment or improvement to the land, or

(b) the demolition of the whole or any part of a building or structure comprised in or situate upon the land.

(6) Where any works are reasonably necessary for the preservation of the whole or any part of the dominant land, the doing to the dominant land of anything which is requisite for, incidental to, or consequential on, the carrying out of those works shall be treated for the purposes of this Act as the carrying out of works which are reasonably necessary for the preservation of that land; and references in this Act to works, or to the carrying out of works, shall be construed accordingly.

(7) Without prejudice to the generality of subsection (6) above, if it is reasonably necessary for a person to inspect the dominant land—

(a) for the purpose of ascertaining whether any works may be reasonably necessary for the preservation of the whole or any part of that land,

(b) for the purpose of making any map or plan, or ascertaining the course of any drain, sewer, pipe or cable, in preparation for, or otherwise in connection with, the carrying out of works which are so reasonably necessary, or

(c) otherwise in connection with the carrying out of any such works,

the making of such an inspection shall be taken for the purposes of this Act to be the carrying out to the dominant land of works which are reasonably necessary for the preservation of that land; and references in this Act to works, or to the carrying out of works, shall be construed accordingly.

Terms and conditions of access orders

2.—(1) An access order shall specify— **54–002**

(a) the works to the dominant land that may be carried out by entering upon the servient land in pursuance of the order;

(b) the particular area of servient land that may be entered upon by virtue of the order for the purpose of carrying out those works to the dominant land; and

(c) the date on which, or the period during which, the land may be so entered upon;

and in the following provisions of this Act any reference to the servient land is a reference to the area specified in the order in pursuance of paragraph (b) above.

(2) An access order may impose upon the applicant or the respondent such terms and conditions as appear to the court to be reasonably necessary for the purpose of avoiding or restricting—

(a) any loss, damage, or injury which might otherwise be caused to the respondent or any other person by reason of the entry authorised by the order; or

(b) any inconvenience or loss of privacy that might otherwise be so caused to the respondent or any other person.

(3) Without prejudice to the generality of subsection (2) above, the terms and conditions which may be imposed under that subsection include provisions with respect to—

(a) the manner in which the specified works are to be carried out;

(b) the days on which, and the hours between which, the work involved may be executed;

(c) the persons who may undertake the carrying out of the specified works or enter upon the servient land under or by virtue of the order;

(d) the taking of any such precautions by the applicant as may be specified in the order.

(4) An access order may also impose terms and conditions—

(a) requiring the applicant to pay, or to secure that such person connected with him as may be specified in the order pays, compensation for—

(i) any loss, damage or injury, or

(ii) any substantial loss of privacy or other substantial inconvenience,

which will, or might, be caused to the respondent or any other person by reason of the entry authorised by the order;

(b) requiring the applicant to secure that he, or such person connected with him as may be specified in the order, is insured against any such risks as may be so specified; or

(c) requiring such a record to be made of the condition of the servient land, or of such part of it as may be so specified, as the court may consider expedient with a view to facilitating the determination of any question that may arise concerning damage to that land.

(5) An access order may include provision requiring the applicant to pay the respondent such sum by way of consideration for the privilege of entering the servient land in pursuance of the order as appears to the court to be fair and reasonable having regard to all the circumstances of the case, including, in particular—

(a) the likely financial advantage of the order to the applicant and any persons connected with him; and

(b) the degree of inconvenience likely to be caused to the respondent or any other person by the entry;

but no payment shall be ordered under this subsection if and to the extent that the works which the applicant desires to carry out by means of the entry are works to residential land.

(6) For the purposes of subsection (5)(a) above, the likely financial advantage of an access order to the applicant and any persons connected with him shall in all cases be taken to be a sum of money equal to the greater of the following amounts, that is to say—

(a) the amount (if any) by which so much of any likely increase in the value of any land—

(i) which consists of or includes the dominant land, and

(ii) which is owned or occupied by the same person as the dominant land,

as may reasonably be regarded as attributable to the carrying out of the specified works exceeds the likely cost of carrying out those works with the benefit of the access order; and

(b) the difference (if it would have been possible to carry out the specified works without entering upon the servient land) between—

(i) the likely cost of carrying out those works without entering upon the servient land; and

(ii) the likely cost of carrying them out with the benefit of the access order.

(7) For the purposes of subsection (5) above, "residential land" means so much of any land as consists of—

(a) a dwelling or part of a dwelling;

(b) a garden, yard, private garage or outbuilding which is used and enjoyed wholly or mainly with a dwelling; or

(c) in the case of a building which includes one or more dwellings, any part of the building which is used and enjoyed wholly or mainly with those dwellings or any of them.

(8) The persons who are to be regarded for the purposes of this section as "connected with" the applicant are—

(a) the owner of any estate or interest in, or right over, the whole or any part of the dominant land;

(b) the occupier of the whole or any part of the dominant land; and

(c) any person whom the applicant may authorise under section 3(7) below to exercise the power of entry conferred by the access order.

(9) The court may make provision—

(a) for the reimbursement by the applicant of any expenses reasonably incurred by the respondent in connection with the application which are not otherwise recoverable as costs;

(b) for the giving of security by the applicant for any sum that might become payable to the respondent or any other person by virtue of this section or section 3 below.

Effect of access order

3.—(1) An access order requires the respondent, so far as he has power to do **54–003**
so, to permit the applicant or any of his associates to do anything which the applicant or associate is authorised or required to do under or by virtue of the order or this section.

(2) Except as otherwise provided by or under this Act, an access order authorises the applicant or any of his associates, without the consent of the respondent,—

(a) to enter upon the servient land for the purpose of carrying out the specified works;

(b) to bring on to that land, leave there during the period permitted by the order and, before the end of that period, remove, such materials, plant and equipment as are reasonably necessary for the carrying out of those works; and

(c) to bring on to that land any waste arising from the carrying out of those works, if it is reasonably necessary to do so in the course of removing it from the dominant land;

but nothing in this Act or in any access order shall authorise the applicant or any of his associates to leave anything in, on or over the servient land (otherwise than in discharge of their duty to make good that land) after their entry for the purpose of carrying out works to the dominant land ceases to be authorised under or by virtue of the order.

(3) An access order requires the applicant—

(a) to secure that any waste arising from the carrying out of the specified works is removed from the servient land forthwith;

(b) to secure that, before the entry ceases to be authorised under or by virtue of the order, the servient land is, so far as reasonably practicable, made good; and

(c) to indemnify the respondent against any damage which may be caused to the servient land or any goods by the applicant or any of his associates which would not have been so caused had the order not been made;

but this subsection is subject to subsections (4) and (5) below.

(4) In making an access order, the court may vary or exclude, in whole or in part,—

(a) any authorisation that would otherwise be conferred by subsection (2)(b) or (c) above; or
(b) any requirement that would otherwise be imposed by subsection (3) above.

(5) Without prejudice to the generality of subsection (4) above, if the court is satisfied that it is reasonably necessary for any such waste as may arise from the carrying out of the specified works to be left on the servient land for some period before removal, the access order may, in place of subsection (3)(a) above, include provision—
(a) authorising the waste to be left on that land for such period as may be permitted by the order; and
(b) requiring the applicant to secure that the waste is removed before the end of that period.

(6) Where the applicant or any of his associates is authorised or required under or by virtue of an access order or this section to enter, or do any other thing, upon the servient land, he shall not (as respects that access order) be taken to be a trespasser from the beginning on account of his, or any other person's, subsequent conduct.

(7) For the purposes of this section, the applicant's "associates" are such number of persons (whether or not servants or agents of his) whom he may reasonably authorise under this subsection to exercise the power of entry conferred by the access order as may be reasonably necessary for carrying out the specified works.

Persons bound by access order, unidentified persons and bar on contracting out

54–004 **4.**—(1) In addition to the respondent, an access order shall, subject to the provisions of the Land Charges Act 1972 and the [Land Registration Act 2002][1], be binding on—
(a) any of his successors in title to the servient land; and
(b) any person who has an estate or interest in, or right over, the whole or any part of the servient land which was created after the making of the order and who derives his title to that estate, interest or right under the respondent;

and references to the respondent shall be construed accordingly.

(2) If and to the extent that the court considers it just and equitable to allow him to do so, a person on whom an access order becomes binding by virtue of subsection (1)(a) or (b) above shall be entitled, as respects anything falling to be done after the order becomes binding on him, to enforce the order or any of its terms or conditions as if he were the respondent, and references to the respondent shall be construed accordingly.

(3) Rules of court may—
(a) provide a procedure which may be followed where the applicant does not know, and cannot reasonably ascertain, the name of any person whom he desires to make respondent to the application; and
(b) make provision enabling such an applicant to make such a person respondent by description instead of by name;

and in this subsection "applicant" includes a person who proposes to make an application for an access order.

(4) Any agreement, whenever made, shall be void if and to the extent that it

[1] Words substituted by the Land Registration Act 2002, s.133, Sched. 11, para. 26(1), (2).

would, apart from this subsection, prevent a person from applying for an access order or restrict his right to do so.

Registration of access orders and of applications for such orders

5.—(1) [*Amends the Land Charges Act 1972, s.6(1), ante, para. 31–006.*] **54–005**

(2), (3) [*Repealed by the Land Registration Act 2002, s.135, Sched. 13.*]

(4) In any case where—

(a) an access order is discharged under section 6(1)(a) below, and

(b) the order has been protected by an entry registered under the Land Charges Act 1972 or by a [notice under the Land Registration Act 2002][2],

the court may by order direct that the [entry or notice][3] shall be cancelled.

[(5) The rights conferred on a person by or under an access order shall not be capable of falling within paragraph 2 of Schedule 1 or 3 to the Land Registration Act 2002 (overriding status of interest of person in actual occupation).][4]

(6) An application for an access order shall be regarded as a pending land action for the purposes of the Land Charges Act 1972 and the [Land Registration Act 2002][5].

Variation of orders and damages for breach

6.—(1) Where an access order or an order under this subsection has been made, the court may, on the application of any party to the proceedings in which the order was made or of any other person on whom the order is binding— **54–006**

(a) discharge or vary the order or any of its terms or conditions;

(b) suspend any of its terms or conditions; or

(c) revive any term or condition suspended under paragraph (b) above;

and in the application of subsections (1) and (2) of section 4 above in relation to an access order, any order under this subsection which relates to the access order shall be treated for the purposes of those subsections as included in the access order.

(2) If any person contravenes or fails to comply with any requirement, term or condition imposed upon him by or under this Act, the court may, without prejudice to any other remedy available, make an order for the payment of damages by him to any other person affected by the contravention or failure who makes an application for relief under this subsection.

Jurisdiction over, and allocation of, proceedings

7.—(1) The High Court and the county courts shall both have jurisdiction under this Act. **54–007**

. . . . . .

Interpretation and application

8.—(1) Any reference in this Act to an "entry" upon any servient land includes a reference to the doing on that land of anything necessary for carrying **54–008**

[2] Words substituted by the Land Registration Act 2002, s.133, Sched. 11, para. 26(1), (2).
[3] Words substituted by the Land Registration Act 2002, s.133, Sched. 11, para. 26(1), (3).
[4] subs. (5) substituted by the Land Registration Act 2002, s.133, Sched. 11, para. 26(1), (4).
[5] Words substituted by the Land Registration Act 2002, s.133, Sched. 11, para. 26(1), (5).

out the works to the dominant land which are reasonably necessary for its preservation; and "enter" shall be construed accordingly.

(2) This Act applies in relation to any obstruction of, or other interference with, a right over, or interest in, any land as it applies in relation to an entry upon that land; and "enter" and "entry" shall be construed accordingly.

(3) In this Act—

"access order" has the meaning giving by section 1(1) above;

"applicant" means a person making an application for an access order and, subject to section 4 above, "the respondent" means the respondent, or any of the respondents, to such an application;

"the court" means the High Court or a county court;

"the dominant land" and "the servient land" respectively have the meanings given by section 1(1) above, but subject, in the case of servient land, to section 2(1) above;

"land" does not include a highway;

"the specified works" means the works specified in the access order in pursuance of section 2(1)(a) above.

Charities Act 1992

(1992 c. 41)

PART I

CHARITIES

Preliminary

Interpretation of Part I, etc.

55–001 **1.**—(1) In this Part—

"the 1960 Act" means the Charities Act 1960;

"financial year"—

(a) in relation to a charity which is a company, shall be construed in accordance with section 223 of the Companies Act 1985; and

(b) in relation to any other charity, shall be construed in accordance with regulations made by virtue of section 20(2);

"gross income", in relation to a charity, means its gross recorded income from all sources, including special trusts;

"independent examiner", in relation to a charity, means such a person as is mentioned in section 21(3)(a);

"the official custodian" means the official custodian for charities;

"the register" (unless the context otherwise requires) means the register of charities kept under section 4 of the 1960 Act, and "registered" shall be construed accordingly;

"special trust" means property which is held and administered by or on behalf of a charity for any special purposes of the charity, and is so held and administered on separate trusts relating only to that property.

(2), (3) [*Repealed by the Charities Act* 1993, s.98(2), *Sched.* 7.]

(4) No vesting or transfer of any property in pursuance of any provision of this Part, or of any provision of the 1960 Act as amended by this Part, shall operate as a breach of a covenant or condition against alienation or give rise to a forfeiture.

Charity property

Divestment of charity property held by official custodian for charities

29.—(1) The official custodian shall, in accordance with this section, divest himself of all property to which this subsection applies. **55–002**

(2) Subsection (1) applies to any property held by the official custodian in his capacity as such, with the exception of—

(a) any land; and

(b) any property (other than land) which is vested in him by virtue of an order of the Commissioners under section 20 of the 1960 Act [or section 18 of the Charities Act 1993][1] (power to act for protection of charities).

(3) Where property to which subsection (1) applies is held by the official custodian in trust for particular charities, he shall (subject to subsection (7)) divest himself of that property in such manner as the Commissioners may direct.

(4) Without prejudice to the generality of subsection (3), directions given by the Commissioners under that subsection may make different provision in relation to different property held by the official custodian or in relation to different classes or descriptions or property held by him, including (in particular)—

(a) provision designed to secure that the divestment required by subsection (1) is effected in stages or by means of transfers or other disposals taking place at different times;

(b) provision requiring the official custodian to transfer any specified investments, or any specified class or description of investments, held by him in trust for a charity—

(i) to the charity trustees or any trustee for the charity, or

(ii) to a person nominated by the charity trustees to hold any such investments in trust for the charity;

(c) provision requiring the official custodian to sell or call in any specified investments, or any specified class or description of investments, so held by him and to pay any proceeds of sale or other money accruing therefrom—

(i) to the charity trustees or any trustees for the charity, or

(ii) into any bank account kept in its name.

(5) The charity trustees of a charity may, in the case of any property falling to be transferred by the official custodian in accordance with a direction under subsection (3), nominate a person to hold any such property in trust for the charity; but a person shall not be so nominated unless—

(a) if an individual, he resides in England and Wales; or

(b) if a body corporate, it has a place of business there.

(6) Directions under subsection (3) shall, in the case of any property vested in the official custodian by virtue of section 22(6) of the 1960 Act (common investment funds), provide for any such property to be transferred—

(a) to the trustees appointed to manage the common investment fund concerned; or

[1] Words inserted by the Charities Act 1993, s.98(1), Sched. 6, para. 29(1), (2).

(b) to any person nominated by those trustees who is authorised by or under the common investment scheme concerned to hold that fund or any part of it.

(7) Where the official custodian—

(a) holds any relevant property in trust for a charity, but

(b) after making reasonable inquiries is unable to locate the charity or any of its trustees,

he shall—

(i) unless the relevant property is money, sell the property and hold the proceeds of sale pending the giving by the Commissioners of a direction under subsection (8);

(ii) if the relevant property is money, hold it pending the giving of any such direction;

and for this purpose "relevant property" means any property to which subsection (1) applies or any proceeds of sale or other money accruing to the official custodian in consequence of a direction under subsection (3).

(8) Where subsection (7) applies in relation to a charity ("the dormant charity"), the Commissioners may direct the official custodian—

(a) to pay such amount as is held by him in accordance with that subsection to such other charity as is specified in the direction in accordance with subsection (9), or

(b) to pay to each of two or more other charities so specified in the direction such part of that amount as is there specified in relation to that charity.

(9) The Commissioners may specify in a direction under subsection (8) such charity or charities as they consider appropriate, being in each case a charity whose purposes are, in the opinion of the Commissioners, as similar in character to those of the dormant charity as is reasonably practicable; but the Commissioners shall not so specify any charity unless they have received from the charity trustees written confirmation that they are willing to accept the amount proposed to be paid to the charity.

(10) Any amount received by a charity by virtue of subsection (8) shall be received by the charity on terms that—

(a) it shall be held and applied by the charity for the purposes of the charity, but

(b) it shall, as property of the charity, nevertheless be subject to any restrictions on expenditure to which it, or (as the case may be) the property which it represents, was subject as property of the dormant charity.

(11) At such time as the Commissioners are satisfied that the official custodian has divested himself of all property held by him in trust for particular charities, all remaining funds held by him as official custodian shall be paid by him into the Consolidated Fund.

(12) Nothing in subsection (11) applies in relation to any property held by the official custodian which falls within subsection (2)(a) or (b).

(13) In this section "land" does not include any interest in land by way of mortgage or other security.

Provisions supplementary to s.29

55–003 **30.**—(1) Any directions of the Commissioners under section 29 above shall have effect notwithstanding anything—

(a) in the trusts of a charity, or

(b) in section 17(1) of the 1960 Act [or section 22(1) of the Charities Act 1993][2] (supplementary provisions as to property vested in official custodian).

(2) Subject to subsection (3), any provision—

(a) of the trusts of a charity, or

(b) of any directions given by an order of the Commissioners made in connection with a transaction requiring the sanction of an order under section 29(1) of the 1960 Act (restrictions on dealing with charity property),

shall cease to have effect if and to the extent that it requires or authorises personal property of the charity to be transferred to or held by the official custodian; and for this purpose "personal property" extends to any mortgage or other real security, but does not include any interest in land other than such an interest by way of mortgage or other security.

(3) Subsection (2) does not apply to—

(a) any provision of an order made under section 20 of the 1960 Act [or section 18 of the Charities Act 1993][3] (power to act for protection of charities); or

(b) any provision of any other order, or of any scheme, of the Commissioners if the provision requires trustees of a charity to make payments into an account maintained by the official custodian with a view to the accumulation of a sum as capital of the charity (whether or not by way of recoupment of a sum expended out of the charity's permanent endowment);

but any such provision as is mentioned in paragraph (b) shall have effect as if, instead of requiring the trustees to make such payments into an account maintained by the official custodian, it required the trustees to make such payments into an account maintained by them or by any other person (apart from the official custodian) who is either a trustee for the charity or a person nominated by them to hold such payments in trust for the charity.

(4) The disposal of any property by the official custodian in accordance with section 29 above shall operate to discharge him from his trusteeship of that property.

(5) Where any instrument issued by the official custodian in connection with any such disposal contains a printed reproduction of his official seal, that instrument shall have the same effect as if it were duly sealed with his official seal.

Removal of requirements under statutory provisions for consent to dealings with charity land

36.—(1) Any provision— **55–004**

(a) establishing or regulating a particular charity and contained in, or having effect under, any Act of Parliament, or

(b) contained in the trusts of a charity,

shall cease to have effect if and to the extent that it provides for dispositions of, or other dealings with, land held by or in trust for the charity to require the consent of the Commissioners (whether signified by order or otherwise).

(2) Any provision of an order or scheme under the Education Act 1944 or the

[2] Words inserted by the Charities Act 1993, s.98(1). Sched. 6, para. 29(1), (3).
[3] Words inserted by the Charities Act 1993, s.98(1), Sched. 6, para. 29(1), (4).

Education Act 1973 relating to a charity shall cease to have effect if and to the extent that it requires, in relation to any sale, lease or other disposition of land held by or in trust for the charity, approval by the Commissioners or the Secretary of State of the amount for which the land is to be sold, leased or otherwise disposed of.

(3) In this section "land" means land in England or Wales.

Charities Act 1993

(1993 c. 10)

Arrangement of Sections

Part I

The Charity Commissioners and the Official Custodian for Charities

Part II

Registration and Names of Charities

Registration of charities

Charity names

Part III

Commissioners' Information Powers

Part IV

Application of Property Cy-près and Assistance and Supervision of Charities by Court and Commissioners

Extended powers of court and variation of charters

Powers of Commissioners to make schemes and act for protection of charities etc.

18. Power to act for protection of charities.
19. Supplementary provisions relating to receiver and manager appointed for a charity.
20. Publicity for proceedings under ss.16 to 18.

Property vested in official custodian

21. Entrusting charity property to official custodian, and termination of trust.
22. Supplementary provisions as to property vested in official custodian.
23. Divestment in the case of land subject to Reverter of Sites Act 1987.

Establishment of common investment or deposit funds

24. Schemes to establish common investment funds.
25. Schemes to establish common deposit funds.

Additional powers of Commissioners

26. Power to authorise dealings with charity property etc.
27. Power to authorise ex gratia payments etc.
28. Power to give directions about dormant bank accounts of charities.
29. Power to advise charity trustees.
30. Powers for preservation of charity documents.
31. Power to order taxation of solicitor's bill.

Legal proceedings relating to charities

32. Proceedings by Commissioners.
33. Proceedings by other persons.
34. Report of s.8 inquiry to be evidence in certain proceedings.

Meaning of "trust corporation"

35. Application of provisions to trust corporations appointed under s.16 or 18.

PART V

CHARITY LAND

36. Restrictions on dispositions.
37. Supplementary provisions relating to dispositions.
38. Restrictions on mortgaging.
39. Supplementary provisions relating to mortgaging.
40. Release of charity rentcharges.

PART VI

CHARITY ACCOUNTS, REPORTS AND RETURNS

41. Duty to keep accounting records.
42. Annual statements of accounts.
43. Annual audit or examination of charity accounts.
44. Supplementary provisions relating to audits etc.
45. Annual reports.
46. Special provision as respects accounts and annual reports of exempt and other excepted charities.
47. Public inspection of annual reports etc.
48. Annual returns by registered charities.
49. Offences.

PART VII

INCORPORATION OF CHARITY TRUSTEES

50. Incorporation of trustees of a charity.
51. Estate to vest in body corporate.
52. Applications for incorporation.
53. Nomination of trustees, and filling up vacancies.

PART I

THE CHARITY COMMISSIONERS AND THE OFFICIAL CUSTODIAN FOR CHARITIES

The Charity Commissioners

56–001 **1.**—(1) There shall continue to be a body of Charity Commissioners for England and Wales, and they shall have such functions as are conferred on them by this Act in addition to any functions under any other enactment for the time being in force.

(2) The provisions of Schedule 1 to this Act shall have effect with respect to the constitution and proceedings of the Commissioners and other matters relating to the Commissioners and their officers and employees.

(3) The Commissioners shall (without prejudice to their specific powers and duties under other enactments) have the general function of promoting the effective use of charitable resources by encouraging the development of better methods of administration, by giving charity trustees information or advice on any matter affecting the charity and by investigating and checking abuses.

(4) It shall be the general object of the Commissioners so to act in the case of any charity (unless it is a matter of altering its purposes) as best to promote and make effective the work of the charity in meeting the needs designated by its trusts; but the Commissioners shall not themselves have power to act in the administration of a charity.

(5) The Commissioners shall, as soon as possible after the end of every year, make to the Secretary of State a report on their operations during that year, and he shall lay a copy of the report before each House of Parliament.

The official custodian for charities

2.—(1) There shall continue to be an officer known as the official custodian **56–002** for charities (in this Act referred to as "the official custodian") whose function it shall be to act as trustee for charities in the cases provided for by this Act; and the official custodian shall be by that name a corporation sole having perpetual succession and using an official seal which shall be officially and judicially noticed.

(2) Such officer of the Commissioners as they may from time to time designate shall be the official custodian.

(3) The official custodian shall perform his duties in accordance with such general or special directions as may be given him by the Commissioners, and his expenses (except those re-imbursed to him or recovered by him as trustee for any charity) shall be defrayed by the Commissioners.

(4) Anything which is required to or may be done by, to or before the official custodian may be done by, to or before any officer of the Commissioners generally or specially authorised by them to act for him during a vacancy in his office or otherwise.

(5) The official custodian shall not be liable as trustee for any charity in respect of any loss or of the mis-application of any property unless it is occasioned by or through the wilful neglect or default of the custodian or of any person acting for him; but the Consolidated Fund shall be liable to make good to a charity any sums for which the custodian may be liable by reason of any such neglect or default.

(6) The official custodian shall keep such books of account and such records in relation thereto as may be directed by the Treasury and shall prepare accounts in such form, in such manner and at such times as may be so directed.

(7) The accounts so prepared shall be examined and certified by the Comptroller and Auditor General, and the report to be made by the Commissioners to the Secretary of State for any year shall include a copy of the accounts so prepared for any period ending in or with the year and of the certificate and report of the Comptroller and Auditor General with respect to those accounts.

PART II

REGISTRATION AND NAMES OF CHARITIES

Registration of charities

The register of charities

56–003 **3.**—(1) The Commissioners shall continue to keep a register of charities, which shall be kept by them in such manner as they think fit.

(2) There shall be entered in the register every charity not excepted by subsection (5) below; and a charity so excepted (other than one excepted by paragraph (a) of that subsection) may be entered in the register at the request of the charity, but (whether or not it was excepted at the time of registration) may at any time, and shall at the request of the charity, be removed from the register.

(3) The register shall contain—

(a) the name of every registered charity; and

(b) such other particulars of, and such other information relating to, every such charity as the Commissioners think fit.

(4) Any institution which no longer appears to the Commissioners to be a charity shall be removed from the register, with effect, where the removal is due to any change in its purposes or trusts, from the date of that change; and there shall also be removed from the register any charity which ceases to exist or does not operate.

(5) The following charities are not required to be registered—

(a) any charity comprised in Schedule 2 to this Act (in this Act referred to as an "exempt charity");

(b) any charity which is excepted by order or regulations;

(c) any charity which has neither—

(i) any permanent endowment, nor

(ii) the use or occupation of any land,

and whose income from all sources does not in aggregate amount to more than £1,000 a year;

and no charity is required to be registered in respect of any registered place of worship.

[(5A) In subsection (5) above, paragraph (a) shall be read as referring also to—

(a) any higher education corporation within the meaning of the Education Reform Act 1988, and

(b) any further education corporation within the meaning of the Further and Higher Education Act 1992.][1]

[(5B) In addition, in subsection (5) above—

(a) paragraph (a) shall be read as referring also to—

(i) any body to which section 23(1)(a) or (b) of the School Standards and Framework Act 1998 applies, and

(ii) any Education Action Forum established by virtue of section 10(1) of that Act; and

(b) paragraph (b) shall read as referring also to any foundation to which section 23(3) of that Act applies;

but an order of the Commissioners, or regulations made by the Secretary of State, may provide that section 23(3) of that Act shall cease to apply to any such

[1] subs. (5A) inserted by the Teaching and Higher Education Act 1998, s.44(1), Sched. 3, para. 9.

foundation as is mentioned in that provision or to any such foundation of a description specified in the order or regulations.][2]

(6) With any application for a charity to be registered there shall be supplied to the Commissioners copies of its trusts (or, if they are not set out in any extant document, particulars of them), and such other documents or information as may be prescribed by regulations made by the Secretary of State or as the Commissioners may require for the purpose of the application.

(7) It shall be the duty—

(a) of the charity trustees of any charity which is not registered nor excepted from registration to apply for it to be registered, and to supply the documents and information required by subsection (6) above; and

(b) of the charity trustees (or last charity trustees) of any institution which is for the time being registered to notify the Commissioners if it ceases to exist, or if there is any change in its trusts or in the particulars of it entered in the register, and to supply to the Commissioners particulars of any such change and copies of any new trusts or alterations of the trusts.

(8) The register (including the entries cancelled when institutions are removed from the register) shall be open to public inspection at all reasonable times; and copies (or particulars) of the trusts of any registered charity as supplied to the Commissioners under this section shall, so long as it remains on the register, be kept by them and be open to public inspection at all reasonable times, except in so far as regulations made by the Secretary of State otherwise provide.

(9) Where any information contained in the register is not in documentary form, subsection (8) above shall be construed as requiring the information to be available for public inspection in legible form at all reasonable times.

(10) If the Commissioners so determine, subsection (8) above shall not apply to any particular information contained in the register and specified in their determination.

(11) Nothing in the foregoing subsections shall require any person to supply the Commissioners with copies of schemes for the administration of a charity made otherwise than by the court, or to notify the Commissioners of any change made with respect to a registered charity by such a scheme, or require a person, if he refers the Commissioners to a document or copy already in the possession of the Commissioners, to supply a further copy of the document; but where by virtue of this subsection a copy of any document need not be supplied to the Commissioners, a copy of it, if it relates to a registered charity, shall be open to inspection under subsection (8) above as if supplied to the Commissioners under this section.

(12) If the Secretary of State thinks it expedient to do so—

(a) in consequence of changes in the value of money, or

(b) with a view to extending the scope of the exception provided for by subsection (5)(c) above,

he may by order amend subsection (5)(c) by substituting a different sum for the sum for the time being specified there.

(13) The reference in subsection (5)(b) above to a charity which is excepted by order or regulations is to a charity which—

(a) is for the time being permanently or temporarily excepted by order of the Commissioners; or

(b) is of a description permanently or temporarily excepted by regulations made by the Secretary of State,

and which complies with any conditions of the exception.

[2] subs. (5B) inserted by the School Standards and Framework Act 1998, s.140(1), Sched. 30, para. 48.

(14) In this section "registered place of worship" means any land or building falling within section 9 of the Places of Worship Registration Act 1855 (that is to say, the land and buildings which if the Charities Act 1960 had not been passed, would by virtue of that section as amended by subsequent enactments be partially exempted from the operation of the Charitable Trusts Act 1853), and for the purposes of this subsection "building" includes part of a building.

Effect of, and claims and objections to, registration

56–004 **4.**—(1) An institution shall for all purposes other than rectification of the register be conclusively presumed to be or to have been a charity at any time when it is or was on the register of charities.

(2) Any person who is or may be affected by the registration of an institution as a charity may, on the ground that it is not a charity, object to its being entered by the Commissioners in the register, or apply to them for it to be removed from the register; and provision may be made by regulations made by the Secretary of State as to the manner in which any such objection or application is to be made, prosecuted or dealt with.

(3) An appeal against any decision of the Commissioners to enter or not to enter an institution in the register of charities, or to remove or not to remove an institution from the register, may be brought in the High Court by the Attorney-General, or by the persons who are or claim to be the charity trustees of the institution, or by any person whose objection or application under subsection (2) above is disallowed by the decision.

(4) If there is an appeal to the High Court against any decision of the Commissioners to enter an institution in the register, or not to remove an institution from the register, then until the Commissioners are satisfied whether the decision of the Commissioners is or is not to stand, the entry in the register shall be maintained, but shall be in suspense and marked to indicate that it is in suspense; and for the purposes of subsection (1) above an institution shall be deemed not to be on the register during any period when the entry relating to it is in suspense under this subsection.

(5) Any question affecting the registration or removal from the register of an institution may, notwithstanding that it has been determined by a decision on appeal under subsection (3) above, be considered afresh by the Commissioners and shall not be concluded by that decision, if it appears to the Commissioners that there has been a change of circumstances or that the decision is inconsistent with a later judicial decision, whether given on such an appeal or not.

Status of registered charity (other than small charity) to appear on official publications etc.

56–005 **5.**—(1) This section applies to a registered charity if its gross income in its last financial year exceeded [£10,000][3].

(2) Where this section applies to a registered charity, the fact that it is a registered charity shall be stated [...][4] in legible characters—

[3] Figure substituted by the Charities Act 1993 (Substitution of Sums) Order 1995 (S.I. 1995 No. 2696), art. 2(1), (2).
[4] Words repealed by the Welsh Language Act 1993, ss.32(1), (2), 35(1), Sched. 2.

(a) in all notices, advertisements and other documents issued by or on behalf of the charity and soliciting money or other property for the benefit of the charity;
(b) in all bills of exchange, promissory notes, endorsements, cheques and orders for money or goods purporting to be signed on behalf of the charity; and
(c) in all bills rendered by it and in all its invoices, receipts and letters of credit.

[(2A) The statement required by subsection (2) above shall be in English, except that, in the case of a document which is otherwise wholly in Welsh, the statement may be in Welsh if it consists of or includes the words "elusen cofrestredig" (the Welsh equivalent of "registered charity").][5]

(3) Subsection (2)(a) above has effect whether the solicitation is express or implied, and whether the money or other property is to be given for any consideration or not.

(4) If, in the case of a registered charity to which this section applies, any person issues or authorises the issue of any document falling within paragraph (a) or (c) of subsection (2) above [which does not contain the statement][6] required by that subsection, he shall be guilty of an offence and liable on summary conviction to a fine not exceeding level 3 on the standard scale.

(5) If, in the case of any such registered charity, any person signs any document falling within paragraph (b) of subsection (2) above [which does not contain the statement][7] required by that subsection, he shall be guilty of an offence and liable on summary conviction to a fine not exceeding level 3 on the standard scale.

(6) The Secretary of State may by order amend subsection (1) above by substituting a different sum for the sum for the time being specified there.

Charity names

Power of Commissioners to require charity's name to be changed

6.—(1) Where this subsection applies to a charity, the Commissioners may give a direction requiring the name of the charity to be changed, within such period as is specified in the direction, to such other name as the charity trustees may determine with the approval of the Commissioners. **56–006**

(2) Subsection (1) above applies to a charity if—
(a) it is a registered charity and its name ("the registered name")—
(i) is the same as, or
(ii) is in the opinion of the Commissioners too like,
the name, at the time when the registered name was entered in the register in respect of the charity, of any other charity (whether registered or not);
(b) the name of the charity is in the opinion of the Commissioners likely to mislead the public as to the true nature—
(i) of the purposes of the charity as set out in its trusts, or
(ii) of the activities which the charity carries on under its trusts in pursuit of those purposes;
(c) the name of the charity includes any word or expression for the time being specified in regulations made by the Secretary of State and the

[5] subs. (2A) inserted by the Welsh Language Act 1993, ss.32(1), (3).
[6] Words substituted by the Welsh Language Act 1993, ss.32(1), (4).
[7] Words substituted by the Welsh Language Act 1993, ss.32(1), (5).

inclusion in its name of that word or expression is in the opinion of the Commissioners likely to mislead the public in any respect as to the status of the charity;

(d) the name of the charity is in the opinion of the Commissioners likely to give the impression that the charity is connected in some way with Her Majesty's Government or any local authority, or with any other body of persons or any individual, when it is not so connected; or

(e) the name of the charity is in the opinion of the Commissioners offensive;

and in this subsection any reference to the name of a charity is, in relation to a registered charity, a reference to the name by which it is registered.

(3) Any direction given by virtue of subsection (2)(a) above must be given within twelve months of the time when the registered name was entered in the register in respect of the charity.

(4) Any direction given under this section with respect to a charity shall be given to the charity trustees; and on receiving any such direction the charity trustees shall give effect to it notwithstanding anything in the trusts of the charity.

(5) Where the name of any charity is changed under this section, then (without prejudice to section 3(7)(b) above) it shall be the duty of the charity trustees forthwith to notify the Commissioners of the charity's new name and of the date on which the change occurred.

(6) A change of name by a charity under this section does not affect any rights or obligations of the charity; and any legal proceedings that might have been continued or commenced by or against it in its former name may be continued or commenced by or against it in its new name.

(7) Section 26(3) of the Companies Act 1985 (minor variations in names to be disregarded) shall apply for the purposes of this section as if the reference to section 26(1)(c) of that Act were a reference to subsection (2)(a) above.

(8) Any reference in this section to the charity trustee of a charity shall, in relation to a charity which is a company, be read as a reference to the directors of the company.

(9) Nothing in this section applies to any exempt charity.

Effect of direction under s.6 where charity is a company

56–007 **7.**—(1) Where any direction is given under section 6 above with respect to a charity which is a company, the direction shall be taken to require the name of the charity to be changed by resolution of the directors of the company.

(2) Section 380 of the Companies Act 1985 (registration etc. of resolutions and agreements) shall apply to any resolution passed by the directors in compliance with any such direction.

(3) Where the name of such a charity is changed in compliance with any such direction, the registrar of companies—

(a) shall, subject to section 26 of the Companies Act 1985 (prohibition on registration of certain names), enter the new name on the register of companies in place of the former name, and

(b) shall issue a certificate of incorporation altered to meet the circumstances of the case;

and the change of name has effect from the date on which the altered certificate is issued.

Part III

Commissioners' Information Powers

General power to institute inquiries

8.—(1) The Commissioners may from time to time institute inquiries with regard to charities or a particular charity or class of charities, either generally or for particular purposes, but no such inquiry shall extend to any exempt charity. **56–008**

(2) The Commissioners may either conduct such an inquiry themselves or appoint a person to conduct it and make a report to them.

(3) For the purposes of any such inquiry the Commissioners, or a person appointed by them to conduct it, may direct any person (subject to the provisions of this section)—

(a) to furnish accounts and statements in writing with respect to any matter in question at the inquiry, being a matter on which he has or can reasonably obtain information, or to return answers in writing to any questions or inquiries addressed to him on any such matter, and to verify any such accounts, statements or answers by statutory declaration;

(b) to furnish copies of documents in his custody or under his control which relate to any matter in question at the inquiry, and to verify any such copies by statutory declaration;

(c) to attend at a specified time and place and give evidence or produce any such documents.

(4) For the purposes of any such inquiry evidence may be taken on oath, and the person conducting the inquiry may for that purpose administer oaths, or may instead of administering an oath require the person examined to make and subscribe a declaration of the truth of the matters about which he is examined.

(5) The Commissioners may pay to any person the necessary expenses of his attendance to give evidence or produce documents for the purpose of an inquiry under this section, and a person shall not be required in obedience to a direction under paragraph (c) of subsection (3) above to go more than ten miles from his place of residence unless those expenses are paid or tendered to him.

(6) Where an inquiry has been held under this section, the Commissioners may either—

(a) cause the report of the person conducting the inquiry, or such other statement of the results of the inquiry as they think fit, to be printed and published, or

(b) publish any such report or statement in some other way which is calculated in their opinion to bring it to the attention of persons who may wish to make representations to them about the action to be taken.

(7) The council of a county or district, the Common Council of the City of London and the council of a London borough may contribute to the expenses of the Commissioners in connection with inquiries under this section into local charities in the council's area.

Power to call for documents and search records

9.—(1) The Commissioners may by order— **56–009**

(a) require any person to furnish them with any information in his possession which relates to any charity and is relevant to the discharge of their functions or of the functions of the official custodian;

(b) require any person who has in his custody or under his control any document which relates to any charity and is relevant to the discharge of their functions or of the functions of the official custodian—

(i) to furnish them with a copy of or extract from the document, or

(ii) (unless the document forms part of the records or other documents of a court or of a public or local authority) to transmit the document itself to them for their inspection.

(2) Any officer of the Commissioners, if so authorised by them, shall be entitled without payment to inspect and take copies of or extracts from the records or other documents of any court, or of any public registry or office of records, for any purpose connected with the discharge of the functions of the Commissioners or of the official custodian.

(3) The Commissioners shall be entitled without payment to keep any copy or extract furnished to them under subsection (1) above; and where a document transmitted to them under that subsection for their inspection relates only to one or more charities and is not held by any person entitled as trustee or otherwise to the custody of it, the Commissioners may keep it or may deliver it to the charity trustees or to any other person who may be so entitled.

(4) No person properly having the custody of documents relating only to an exempt charity shall be required under subsection (1) above to transmit to the Commissioners any of those documents, or to furnish any copy of or extract from any of them.

(5) The rights conferred by subsection (2) above shall, in relation to information recorded otherwise than in legible form, include the right to require the information to be made available in legible form for inspection or for a copy or extract to be made of or from it.

Disclosure of information to and by Commissioners

56–010 **10.**—(1) Subject to subsection (2) below and to any express restriction imposed by or under any other enactment, a body or person to whom this section applies may disclose to the Charity Commissioners any information received by that body or person under or for the purposes of any enactment, where the disclosure is made by the body or person for the purpose of enabling or assisting the Commissioners to discharge any of their functions.

(2) Subsection (1) above shall not have effect in relation to the Commissioners of Customs and Excise or the Commissioners of Inland Revenue; but either of those bodies of Commissioners ("the relevant body") may disclose to the Charity Commissioners the following information—

(a) the name and address of any institution which has for any purpose been treated by the relevant body as established for charitable purposes;

(b) information as to the purposes of an institution and the trusts under which it is established or regulated, where the disclosure is made by the relevant body in order to give or obtain assistance in determining whether the institution ought for any purpose to be treated as established for charitable purposes; and

(c) information with respect to an institution which has for any purpose been treated as so established but which appears to the relevant body—

(i) to be, or to have been, carrying on activities which are not charitable, or

(ii) to be, or to have been, applying any of its funds for purposes which are not charitable.

(3) In subsection (2) above, any reference to an institution shall, in relation to

the Commissioners of Inland Revenue, be construed as a reference to an institution in England and Wales.

(4) Subject to subsection (5) below, the Charity Commissioners may disclose to a body or person to whom this section applies any information received by them under or for the purposes of any enactment, where the disclosure is made by the Commissioners—

(a) for any purpose connected with the discharge of their functions, and

(b) for the purpose of enabling or assisting that body or person to discharge any of its or his functions.

(5) Where any information disclosed to the Charity Commissioners under subsection (1) or (2) above is so disclosed subject to any express restriction on the disclosure of the information by the Commissioners, the Commissioners' power of disclosure under subsection (4) above shall, in relation to the information, be exercisable by them subject to any such restriction.

(6) This section applies to the following bodies and persons—

(a) any government department (including a Northern Ireland department);

(b) any local authority;

(c) any constable; and

(d) any other body or person discharging functions of a public nature (including a body or person discharging regulatory functions in relation to any description of activities).

(7) In subsection (6)(d) above the reference to any such body or person as is there mentioned shall, in relation to a disclosure by the Charity Commissioners under subsection (4) above, be construed as including a reference to any such body or person in a country or territory outside the United Kingdom.

(8) Nothing in this section shall be construed as affecting any power of disclosure exercisable apart from this section.

(9) In this section "enactment" includes an enactment comprised in subordinate legislation (within the meaning of the Interpretation Act 1978).

Supply of false or misleading information to Commissioners, etc.

11.—(1) Any person who knowingly or recklessly provides the **56–011**
Commissioners with information which is false or misleading in a material particular shall be guilty of an offence if the information—

(a) is provided in purported compliance with a requirement imposed by or under this Act; or

(b) is provided otherwise than as mentioned in paragraph (a) above but in circumstances in which the person providing the information intends, or could reasonably be expected to know, that it would be used by the Commissioners for the purpose of discharging their functions under this Act.

(2) Any person who wilfully alters, suppresses, conceals or destroys any document which he is or is liable to be required, by or under this Act, to produce to the Commissioners shall be guilty of an offence.

(3) Any person guilty of an offence under this section shall be liable—

(a) on summary conviction, to a fine not exceeding the statutory maximum;

(b) on conviction on indictment, to imprisonment for a term not exceeding two years or to a fine, or both.

(4) In this section references to the Commissioners include references to any person conducting an inquiry under section 8 above.

12. [*Repealed by the Data Protection Act 1998, s.74(2), Sched. 16, Pt. I.*]

PART IV

APPLICATION OF PROPERTY CY-PRÈS AND ASSISTANCE AND SUPERVISION OF CHARITIES BY COURT AND COMMISSIONERS

Extended powers of court and variation of charters

Occasions for applying property cy-près

56–012 **13.**—(1) Subject to subsection (2) below, the circumstances in which the original purposes of a charitable gift can be altered to allow the property given or part of it to be applied cy-près shall be as follows—

(a) where the original purposes, in whole or in part—

(i) have been as far as may be fulfilled; or

(ii) cannot be carried out, or not according to the directions given and to the spirit of the gift; or

(b) where the original purposes provide a use for part only of the property available by virtue of the gift; or

(c) where the property available by virtue of the gift and other property applicable for similar purposes can be more effectively used in conjunction, and to that end can suitably, regard being had to the spirit of the gift, be made applicable to common purposes; or

(d) where the original purposes were laid down by reference to an area which then was but has since ceased to be a unit for some other purpose, or by reference to a class of persons or to an area which has for any reason since ceased to be suitable, regard being had to the spirit of the gift, or to be practical in administering the gift; or

(e) where the original purposes, in whole or in part, have, since they were laid down,—

(i) been adequately provided for by other means; or

(ii) ceased, as being useless or harmful to the community or for other reasons, to be in law charitable; or

(iii) ceased in any other way to provide a suitable and effective method of using the property available by virtue of the gift, regard being had to the spirit of the gift.

(2) Subsection (1) above shall not affect the conditions which must be satisfied in order that property given for charitable purposes may be applied cy-près except in so far as those conditions require a failure of the original purposes.

(3) References in the foregoing subsections to the original purposes of a gift shall be construed, where the application of the property given has been altered or regulated by a scheme or otherwise, as referring to the purposes for which the property is for the time being applicable.

(4) Without prejudice to the power to make schemes in circumstances falling within subsection (1) above, the court may by scheme made under the court's jurisdiction with respect to charities, in any case where the purposes for which the property is held are laid down by reference to any such area as is mentioned in the first column in Schedule 3 to this Act, provide for enlarging the area to any such area as is mentioned in the second column in the same entry in that Schedule.

(5) It is hereby declared that a trust for charitable purposes places a trustee

under a duty, where the case permits and requires the property or some part of it to be applied cy-près, to secure its effective use for charity by taking steps to enable it to be so applied.

Application cy-près of gifts of donors unknown or disclaiming

14.—(1) Property given for specific charitable purposes which fail shall be applicable cy-près as if given for charitable purposes generally, where it belongs— **56–013**

(a) to a donor who after—

(i) the prescribed advertisements and inquiries have been published and made, and

(ii) the prescribed period beginning with the publication of those advertisements has expired,

cannot be identified or cannot be found; or

(b) to a donor who has executed a disclaimer in the prescribed form of his right to have the property returned.

(2) Where the prescribed advertisements and inquiries have been published and made by or on behalf of trustees with respect to any such property, the trustees shall not be liable to any person in respect of the property if no claim by him to be interested in it is received by them before the expiry of the period mentioned in subsection (1)(a)(ii) above.

(3) For the purposes of this section property shall be conclusively presumed (without any advertisement or inquiry) to belong to donors who cannot be identified, in so far as it consists—

(a) of the proceeds of cash collections made by means of collecting boxes or by other means not adapted for distinguishing one gift from another; or

(b) of the proceeds of any lottery, competition, entertainment, sale or similar money-raising activity, after allowing for property given to provide prizes or articles for sale or otherwise to enable the activity to be undertaken.

(4) The court may by order direct that property not falling within subsection (3) above shall for the purposes of this section be treated (without any advertisement or inquiry) as belonging to donors who cannot be identified where it appears to the court either—

(a) that it would be unreasonable, having regard to the amounts likely to be returned to the donors, to incur expense with a view to returning the property; or

(b) that it would be unreasonable, having regard to the nature, circumstances and amounts of the gifts, and to the lapse of time since the gifts were made, for the donors to expect the property to be returned.

(5) Where property is applied cy-près by virtue of this section, the donor shall be deemed to have parted with all his interest at the time when the gift was made; but where property is so applied as belonging to donors who cannot be identified or cannot be found, and is not so applied by virtue of subsection (3) or (4) above—

(a) the scheme shall specify the total amount of that property; and

(b) the donor of any part of that amount shall be entitled, if he makes a claim not later than six months after the date on which the scheme is made, to recover from the charity for which the property is applied a sum equal to that part, less any expenses properly incurred by the charity trustees after that date in connection with claims relating to his gift; and

(c) the scheme may include directions as to the provision to be made for meeting any such claim.

(6) Where—

(a) any sum is, in accordance with any such directions, set aside for meeting any such claims, but

(b) the aggregate amount of any such claims actually made exceeds the relevant amount,

then, if the Commissioners so direct, each of the donors in question shall be entitled only to such proportion of the relevant amount as the amount of his claim bears to the aggregate amount referred to in paragraph (b) above; and for this purpose "the relevant amount" means the amount of the sum so set aside after deduction of any expenses properly incurred by the charity trustees in connection with claims relating to the donors' gifts.

(7) For the purposes of this section, charitable purposes shall be deemed to "fail" where any difficulty in applying property to those purposes makes that property or the part not applicable cy-près available to be returned to the donors.

(8) In this section "prescribed" means prescribed by regulations made by the Commissioners; and such regulations may, as respects the advertisements which are to be published for the purposes of subsection (1)(a) above, make provision as to the form and content of such advertisements as well as the manner in which they are to be published.

(9) Any regulations made by the Commissioners under this section shall be published by the Commissioners in such manner as they think fit.

(10) In this section, except in so far as the context otherwise requires, references to a donor include persons claiming through or under the original donor, and references to property given include the property for the time being representing the property originally given or property derived from it.

(11) This section shall apply to property given for charitable purposes, notwithstanding that it was so given before the commencement of this Act.

Charities governed by charter, or by or under statute

56–014 **15.**—(1) Where a Royal charter establishing or regulating a body corporate is amendable by the grant and acceptance of a further charter, a scheme relating to the body corporate or to the administration of property held by the body (including a scheme for the cy-près application of any such property) may be made by the court under the court's jurisdiction with respect to charities notwithstanding that the scheme cannot take effect without the alteration of the charter, but shall be so framed that the scheme, or such part of it as cannot take effect without the alteration of the charter, does not purport to come into operation unless or until Her Majesty thinks fit to amend the charter in such manner as will permit the scheme or that part of it to have effect.

(2) Where under the court's jurisdiction with respect to charities or the corresponding jurisdiction of a court in Northern Ireland, or under powers conferred by this Act or by any Northern Ireland legislation relating to charities, a scheme is made with respect to a body corporate, and it appears to Her Majesty expedient, having regard to the scheme, to amend any Royal charter relating to that body, Her Majesty may, on the application of that body, amend the charter accordingly by Order in Council in any way in which the charter could be amended by the grant and acceptance of a further charter; and any such Order in Council may be revoked or varied in like manner as the charter it amends.

(3) The jurisdiction of the court with respect to charities shall not be excluded or restricted in the case of a charity of any description mentioned in Schedule 4 to this Act by the operation of the enactments or instruments there mentioned in relation to that description, and a scheme established for any such charity may modify or supersede in relation to it the provision made by any such enactment or instrument as if made by a scheme of the court, and may also make any such provision as is authorised by that Schedule.

Powers of Commissioners to make schemes and act for protection of charities etc.

Concurrent jurisdiction with High Court for certain purposes

16.—(1) Subject to the provisions of this Act, the Commissioners may by order exercise the same jurisdiction and powers as are exercisable by the High Court in charity proceedings for the following purposes— **56–015**

(a) establishing a scheme for the administration of a charity;
(b) appointing, discharging or removing a charity trustee or trustee for a charity, or removing an officer or employee;
(c) vesting or transferring property, or requiring or entitling any person to call for or make any transfer of property or any payment.

(2) Where the court directs a scheme for the administration of a charity to be established, the court may by order refer the matter to the Commissioners for them to prepare or settle a scheme in accordance with such directions (if any) as the court sees fit to give, and any such order may provide for the scheme to be put into effect by order of the Commissioners as if prepared under subsection (1) above and without any further order of the court.

(3) The Commissioners shall not have jurisdiction under this section to try or determine the title at law or in equity to any property as between a charity or trustee for a charity and a person holding or claiming the property or an interest in it adversely to the charity, or to try or determine any question as to the existence or extent of any charge or trust.

(4) Subject to the following subsections the Commissioners shall not exercise their jurisdiction under this section as respects any charity, except—

(a) on the application of the charity; or
(b) on an order of the court under subsection (2) above; or
(c) in the case of a charity other than an exempt charity, on the application of the Attorney-General.

(5) In the case of a charity which is not an exempt charity and whose income from all sources does not in aggregate exceed £500 a year, the Commissioners may exercise their jurisdiction under this section on the application—

(a) of any one or more of the charity trustees; or
(b) of any person interested in the charity; or
(c) of any two or more inhabitants of the area of the charity if it is a local charity.

(6) Where in the case of a charity, other than an exempt charity, the Commissioners are satisfied that the charity trustees ought in the interests of the charity to apply for a scheme, but have unreasonably refused or neglected to do so and the Commissioners have given the charity trustees an opportunity to make representations to them, the Commissioners may proceed as if an

application for a scheme had been made by the charity but the Commissioners shall not have power in a case where they act by virtue of this subsection to alter the purposes of a charity, unless 40 years have elapsed from the date of its foundation.

(7) Where—

(a) a charity cannot apply to the Commissioners for a scheme by reason of any vacancy among the charity trustees or the absence or incapacity of any of them, but

(b) such an application is made by such number of the charity trustees as the Commissioners consider appropriate in the circumstances of the case,

the Commissioners may nevertheless proceed as if the application were an application made by the charity.

(8) The Commissioners may on the application of any charity trustee or trustee for a charity exercise their jurisdiction under this section for the purpose of discharging him from his trusteeship.

(9) Before exercising any jurisdiction under this section otherwise than on an order of the court, the Commissioners shall give notice of their intention to do so to each of the charity trustees, except any that cannot be found or has no known address in the United Kingdom or who is party or privy to an application for the exercise of the jurisdiction; and any such notice may be given by post, and, if given by post, may be addressed to the recipient's last known address in the United Kingdom.

(10) The Commissioners shall not exercise their jurisdiction under this section in any case (not referred to them by order of the court) which, by reason of its contentious character, or of any special question of law or of fact which it may involve, or for other reasons, the Commissioners may consider more fit to be adjudicated on by the court.

(11) An appeal against any order of the Commissioners under this section may be brought in the High Court by the Attorney-General.

(12) An appeal against any order of the Commissioners under this section may also, at any time within the three months beginning with the day following that on which the order is published, be brought in the High Court by the charity or any of the charity trustees, or by any person removed from any office or employment by the order (unless he is removed with the concurrence of the charity trustees or with the approval of the special visitor, if any, of the charity).

(13) No appeal shall be brought under subsection (12) above except with a certificate of the Commissioners that it is a proper case for an appeal or with the leave of one of the judges of the High Court attached to the Chancery Division.

(14) Where an order of the Commissioners under this section establishes a scheme for the administration of a charity, any person interested in the charity shall have the like right of appeal under subsection (12) above as a charity trustee, and so also, in the case of a charity which is a local charity in any area, shall any two or more inhabitants of the area and the council of any parish or (in Wales) any community comprising the area or any part of it.

(15) If the Secretary of State thinks it expedient to do so—

(a) in consequence of changes in the value of money, or

(b) with a view to increasing the number of charities in respect of which the Commissioners may exercise their jurisdiction under this section in accordance with subsection (5) above,

he may by order amend that subsection by substituting a different sum for the sum for the time being specified there.

Further powers to make schemes or alter application of charitable property

17.—(1) Where it appears to the Commissioners that a scheme should be established for the administration of a charity, but also that it is necessary or desirable for the scheme to alter the provision made by an Act of Parliament establishing or regulating the charity or to make any other provision which goes or might go beyond the powers exercisable by them apart from this section, or that it is for any reason proper for the scheme to be subject to parliamentary review, then (subject to subsection (6) below) the Commissioners may settle a scheme accordingly with a view to its being given effect under this section. **56–016**

(2) A scheme settled by the Commissioners under this section may be given effect by order of the Secretary of State, and a draft of the order shall be laid before Parliament.

(3) Without prejudice to the operation of section 6 of the Statutory Instruments Act 1946 in other cases, in the case of a scheme which goes beyond the powers exercisable apart from this section in altering a statutory provision contained in or having effect under any public general Act of Parliament, the order shall not be made unless the draft has been approved by resolution of each House of Parliament.

(4) Subject to subsection (5) below, any provision of a scheme brought into effect under this section may be modified or superseded by the court or the Commissioners as if it were a scheme brought into effect by order of the Commissioners under section 16 above.

(5) Where subsection (3) above applies to a scheme, the order giving effect to it may direct that the scheme shall not be modified or superseded by a scheme brought into effect otherwise than under this section, and may also direct that that subsection shall apply to any scheme modifying or superseding the scheme to which the order gives effect.

(6) The Commissioners shall not proceed under this section without the like application and the like notice to the charity trustees, as would be required if they were proceeding (without an order of the court) under section 16 above; but on any application for a scheme, or in a case where they act by virtue of subsection (6) or (7) of that section, the Commissioners may proceed under this section or that section as appears to them appropriate.

(7) Notwithstanding anything in the trusts of a charity, no expenditure incurred in preparing or promoting a Bill in Parliament shall without the consent of the court or the Commissioners be defrayed out of any moneys applicable for the purposes of a charity but this subsection shall not apply in the case of an exempt charity.

(8) Where the Commissioners are satisfied—

(a) that the whole of the income of a charity cannot in existing circumstances be effectively applied for the purposes of the charity; and

(b) that, if those circumstances continue, a scheme might be made for applying the surplus cy-près; and

(c) that it is for any reason not yet desirable to make such a scheme;

then the Commissioners may by order authorise the charity trustees at their discretion (but subject to any conditions imposed by the order) to apply any accrued or accruing income for any purposes for which it might be made applicable by such a scheme, and any application authorised by the order shall be deemed to be within the purposes of the charity.

(9) An order under subsection (8) above shall not extend to more than £300

out of income accrued before the date of the order, nor to income accruing more than three years after that date, nor to more than £100 out of the income accruing in any of those three years.

Power to act for protection of charities

56–017 **18.**—(1) Where, at any time after they have instituted an inquiry under section 8 above with respect to any charity, the Commissioners are satisfied—

(a) that there is or has been any misconduct or mismanagement in the administration of the charity; or

(b) that it is necessary or desirable to act for the purpose of protecting the property of the charity or securing a proper application for the purposes of the charity of that property or of property coming to the charity,

the Commissioners may of their own motion do one or more of the following things—

(i) by order suspend any trustee, charity trustee, officer, agent or employee of the charity from the exercise of his office or employment pending consideration being given to his removal (whether under this section or otherwise);

(ii) by order appoint such number of additional charity trustees as they consider necessary for the proper administration of the charity;

(iii) by order vest any property held by or in trust for the charity in the official custodian, or require the persons in whom any such property is vested to transfer it to him, or appoint any person to transfer any such property to him;

(iv) order any person who holds any property on behalf of the charity, or of any trustee for it, not to part with the property without the approval of the Commissioners;

(v) order any debtor of the charity not to make any payment in or towards the discharge of his liability to the charity without the approval of the Commissioners;

(vi) by order restrict (notwithstanding anything in the trusts of the charity) the transactions which may be entered into, or the nature or amount of the payments which may be made, in the administration of the charity without the approval of the Commissioners;

(vii) by order appoint (in accordance with section 19 below) a receiver and manager in respect of the property and affairs of the charity.

(2) Where, at any time after they have instituted an inquiry under section 8 above with respect to any charity, the Commissioners are satisfied—

(a) that there is or has been any misconduct or mismanagement in the administration of the charity; and

(b) that it is necessary or desirable to act for the purpose of protecting the property of the charity or securing a proper application for the purposes of the charity of that property or of property coming to the charity,

the Commissioners may of their own motion do either or both of the following things—

(i) by order remove any trustee, charity trustee, officer, agent or employee of the charity trustee, officer, agent or employee of the charity who has been responsible for a privy to the misconduct or mismanagement or has by his conduct contributed to it or facilitated it;

(ii) by order establish a scheme for the administration of the charity.

(3) The references in subsection (1) or (2) above to misconduct or mismanagement shall (notwithstanding anything in the trusts of the charity)

extend to the employment for the remuneration or reward of persons acting in the affairs of the charity, or for other administrative purposes, of sums which are excessive in relation to the property which is or is likely to be applied or applicable for the purposes of the charity.

(4) The Commissioners may also remove a charity trustee by order made of their own motion—

(a) where, within the last five years, the trustee—

(i) having previously been adjudged bankrupt or had his estate sequestrated, has been discharged, or

(ii) having previously made a composition or arrangement with, or granted a trust deed for, his creditors, has been discharged in respect of it;

(b) where the trustee is a corporation in liquidation;

(c) where the trustee is incapable of acting by reason of mental disorder within the meaning of the Mental Health Act 1983;

(d) where the trustee has not acted, and will not declare his willingness or unwillingness to act;

(e) where the trustee is outside England and Wales or cannot be found or does not act, and his absence or failure to act impedes the proper administration of the charity.

(5) The Commissioners may by order made of their own motion appoint a person to be a charity trustee—

(a) in place of a charity trustee removed by them under this section or otherwise;

(b) where there are no charity trustees, or where by reason of vacancies in their number or the absence or incapacity of any of their number the charity cannot apply for the appointment;

(c) where there is a single charity trustee, not being a corporation aggregate, and the Commissioners are of opinion that it is necessary to increase the number for the proper administration of the charity;

(d) where the Commissioners are of opinion that it is necessary for the proper administration of the charity to have an additional charity trustee because one of the existing charity trustees who ought nevertheless to remain a charity trustee either cannot be found or does not act or is outside England and Wales.

(6) The powers of the Commissioners under this section to remove or appoint charity trustees of their own motion shall include power to make any such order with respect to the vesting in or transfer to the charity trustees of any property as the Commissioners could make on the removal or appointment of a charity trustee by them under section 16 above.

(7) Any order under this section for the removal or appointment of a charity trustee or trustee for a charity, or for the vesting or transfer of any property, shall be of the like effect as an order made under section 16 above.

(8) Subject to subsection (9) below, subsections (11) to (13) of section 16 above shall apply to orders under this section as they apply to orders under that section.

(9) The requirement to obtain any such certificate or leave as is mentioned in section 16(13) above shall not apply to—

(a) an appeal by a charity or any of the charity trustees of a charity against an order under subsection (1)(vii) above appointing a receiver and manager in respect of the charity's property and affairs, or

(b) an appeal by a person against an order under subsection (2)(i) or (4)(a) above removing him from his office or employment.

(10) Subsection (14) of section 16 above shall apply to an order under this section which establishes a scheme for the administration of a charity as it applies to such an order under that section.

(11) The power of the Commissioners to make an order under subsection (1)(i) above shall not be exercisable so as to suspend any person from the exercise of his office or employment for a period of more than 12 months; but (without prejudice to the generality of section 89(1) below), any such order made in the case of any person may make provision as respects the period of his suspension for matters arising out of it, and in particular for enabling any person to execute any instrument in his name or otherwise act for him and, in the case of a charity trustee, for adjusting any rules governing the proceedings of the charity trustees to take account of the reduction in the number capable of acting.

(12) Before exercising any jurisdiction under this section otherwise than by virtue of subsection (1) above, the Commissioners shall give notice of their intention to do so to each of the charity trustees, except any that cannot be found or has no known address in the United Kingdom; and any such notice may be given by post and, if given by post, may be addressed to the recipient's last known address in the United Kingdom.

(13) The Commissioners shall, at such intervals as they think fit, review any order made by them under paragraph (i), or any of the paragraphs (iii) to (vii), of subsection (1) above; and, if on any such review it appears to them that it would be appropriate to discharge the order in whole or in part, they shall so discharge it (whether subject to any savings or other transitional provisions or not).

(14) If any person contravenes an order under subsection (1)(iv), (v) or (vi) above, he shall be guilty of an offence and liable on summary conviction to a fine not exceeding level 5 on the standard scale.

(15) Subsection (14) above shall not be taken to preclude the bringing of proceedings for breach of trust against any charity trustee or trustee for a charity in respect of a contravention of an order under subsection (1)(iv) or (vi) above (whether proceedings in respect of the contravention are brought against him under subsection (14) above or not).

(16) This section shall not apply to an exempt charity.

Supplementary provisions relating to receiver and manager appointed for a charity

56–018 **19.**—(1) The Commissioners may under section 18(1)(vii) above appoint to be receiver and manager in respect of the property and affairs of a charity such person (other than an officer or employee of theirs) as they think fit.

(2) Without prejudice to the generality of section 89(1) below, any order made by the Commissioners under section 18(1)(vii) above may make provision with respect to the functions to be discharged by the receiver and manager appointed by the order; and those functions shall be discharged by him under the supervision of the Commissioners.

(3) In connection with the discharge of those functions any such order may provide—

(a) for the receiver and manager appointed by the order to have such powers and duties of the charity trustees of the charity concerned (whether arising under this Act or otherwise) as are specified in the order;

(b) for any powers or duties exercisable or falling to be performed by the receiver and manager by virtue of paragraph (a) above to be exercisable or performed by him to the exclusion of those trustees.

(4) Where a person has been appointed receiver and manager by any such order—

(a) section 29 below shall apply to him and to his functions as a person so appointed as it applies to a charity trustee of the charity concerned and to his duties as such; and

(b) the Commissioners may apply to the High Court for directions in relation to any particular matter arising in connection with the discharge of those functions.

(5) The High Court may on an application under subsection (4)(b) above—

(a) give such directions, or

(b) make such orders declaring the rights of any persons (whether before the court or not),

as it thinks just; and the costs of any such application shall be paid by the charity concerned.

(6) Regulations made by the Secretary of State may make provision with respect to—

(a) the appointment and removal of persons appointed in accordance with this section;

(b) the remuneration of such persons out of the income of the charities concerned;

(c) the making of reports to the Commissioners by such persons.

(7) Regulations under subsection (6) above may, in particular, authorise the Commissioners—

(a) to require security for the due discharge of his functions to be given by a person so appointed;

(b) to determine the amount of such a person's remuneration;

(c) to disallow any amount of remuneration in such circumstances as are prescribed by the regulations.

Publicity for proceedings under ss.16 to 18

20.—(1) The Commissioners shall not make any order under this Act to establish a scheme for the administration of a charity, or submit such a scheme to the court or the Secretary of State for an order giving it effect, unless not less than one month previously there has been given public notice of their proposals, inviting representations to be made to them within a time specified in the notice, being not less than one month from the date of such notice, and, in the case of a scheme relating to a local charity, other than an ecclesiastical charity, in a parish or (in Wales) a community, a draft of the scheme has been communicated to the parish or community council or, in the case of a parish not having a council, to the chairman of the parish meeting. **56–019**

(2) The Commissioners shall not make any order under this Act to appoint, discharge or remove a charity trustee or trustee for a charity (other than the official custodian), unless not less than one month previously there has been given the like public notice as is required by subsection (1) above for an order establishing a scheme but this subsection shall not apply in the case of—

(a) an order under section 18(1)(ii) above; or

(b) an order discharging or removing a trustee if the Commissioners are of opinion that it is unnecessary and not in his interest to give publicity to the proposal to discharge or remove him.

(3) Before the Commissioners make an order under this Act to remove without his consent a charity trustee or trustee for a charity, or an officer, agent or employee of a charity, the Commissioners shall, unless he cannot be found or has no known address in the United Kingdom, give him not less than one month's notice of their proposal, inviting representations to be made to them within a time specified in the notice.

(4) Where notice is given of any proposals as required by subsections (1) to (3) above, the Commissioners shall take into consideration any representations made to them about the proposals within the time specified in the notice, and may (without further notice) proceed with the proposals either without modification or with such modifications as appear to them to be desirable.

(5) Where the Commissioners make an order which is subject to appeal under subsection (12) of section 16 above the order shall be published either by giving public notice of it or by giving notice of it to all persons entitled to appeal against it under that subsection, as the Commissioners think fit.

(6) Where the Commissioners make an order under this Act to establish a scheme for the administration of a charity, a copy of the order shall, for not less than one month after the order is published, be available for public inspection at all reasonable times at the Commissioners' office and also at some convenient place in the area of the charity, if it is a local charity.

(7) Any notice to be given under this section of any proposals or order shall give such particulars of the proposals or order, or such directions for obtaining information about them, as the Commissioners think sufficient and appropriate, and any public notice shall be given in such manner as they think sufficient and appropriate.

(8) Any notice to be given under this section, other than a public notice, may be given by post and, if given by post, may be addressed to the recipient's last known address in the United Kingdom.

Property vested in official custodian

Entrusting charity property to official custodian, and termination of trust

56–020 **21.**—(1) The court may by order—

(a) vest in the official custodian any land held by or in trust for a charity;

(b) authorise or require the persons in whom any such land is vested to transfer it to him; or

(c) appoint any person to transfer any such land to him;

but this section does not apply to any interest in land by way of mortgage or other security.

(2) Where property is vested in the official custodian in trust for a charity, the court may make an order discharging him from the trusteeship as respects all or any of that property.

(3) Where the official custodian is discharged from his trusteeship of any property, or the trusts on which he holds any property come to an end, the court may make such vesting orders and give such directions as may seem to the court to be necessary or expedient in consequence.

(4) No person shall be liable for any loss occasioned by his acting in conformity with an order under this section or by his giving effect to anything done in pursuance of such an order, or be excused from so doing by reason of the order having been in any respect improperly obtained.

Supplementary provisions as to property vested in official custodian

22.—(1) Subject to the provisions of this Act, where property is vested in the official custodian in trust for a charity, he shall not exercise any powers of management, but he shall as trustee of any property have all the same powers, duties and liabilities, and be entitled to the same rights and immunities, and be subject to the control and orders of the court, as a corporation appointed custodian trustee under section 4 of the Public Trustee Act 1906 except that he shall have no power to charge fees. **56–021**

(2) Subject to subsection (3) below, where any land is vested in the official custodian in trust for a charity, the charity trustees shall have power in his name and on his behalf to execute and do all assurances and things which they could properly execute or do in their own name and on their own behalf if the land were vested in them.

(3) If any land is so vested in the official custodian by virtue of an order under section 18 above, the power conferred on the charity trustees by subsection (2) above shall not be exercisable by them in relation to any transaction affecting the land, unless the transaction is authorised by order of the court or of the Commissioners.

(4) Where any land is vested in the official custodian in trust for a charity, the charity trustees shall have the like power to make obligations entered into by them binding on the land as if it were vested in them; and any covenant, agreement or condition which is enforceable by or against the custodian by reason of the land being vested in him shall be enforceable by or against the charity trustees as if the land were vested in them.

(5) In relation to a corporate charity, subsections (2), (3) and (4) above shall apply with the substitution of references to the charity for references to the charity trustees.

(6) Subsections (2), (3) and (4) above shall not authorise any charity trustees or charity to impose any personal liability on the official custodian.

(7) Where the official custodian is entitled as trustee for a charity to the custody of securities or documents of title relating to the trust property, he may permit them to be in the possession or under the control of the charity trustees without thereby incurring any liability.

Divestment in the case of land subject to Reverter of Sites Act 1987

23.—(1) Where— **56–022**

(a) any land is vested in the official custodian in trust for a charity, and
(b) it appears to the Commissioners that section 1 of the Reverter of Sites Act 1987 (right of reverter replaced by [trust][8]) will, or is likely to, operate in relation to the land at a particular time or in particular circumstances,

the jurisdiction which, under section 16 above, is exercisable by the Commissioners for the purpose of discharging a trustee for a charity may, at any time before section 1 of that Act ("the 1987 Act") operates in relation to the land, be exercised by them of their own motion for the purpose of—

(i) making an order discharging the official custodian from his trusteeship of the land, and

[8] Word substituted by the Trusts of Land and Appointment of Trustees Act 1996, s.25(1), Sched. 3, para. 26.

(ii) making such vesting orders and giving such directions as appear to them to be necessary or expedient in consequence.

(2) Where—

(a) section 1 of the 1987 Act has operated in relation to any land which, immediately before the time when that section so operated, was vested in the official custodian in trust for a charity, and

(b) the land remains vested in him but on the trust arising under that section,

the court or the Commissioners (of their own motion) may—

(i) make an order discharging the official custodian from his trusteeship of the land, and

(ii) (subject to the following provisions of this section) make such vesting orders and give such directions as appear to it or them to be necessary or expedient in consequence.

(3) Where any order discharging the official custodian from his trusteeship of any land—

(a) is made by the court under section 21(2) above, or by the Commissioners under section 16 above, on the grounds that section 1 of the 1987 Act will, or is likely to, operate in relation to the land, or

(b) is made by the court or the Commissioners under subsection (2) above,

the persons in whom the land is to be vested on the discharge of the official custodian shall be the relevant charity trustees (as defined in subsection (4) below), unless the court or (as the case may be) the Commissioners is or are satisfied that it would be appropriate for it to be vested in some other persons.

(4) In subsection (3) above "the relevant charity trustees" means—

(a) in relation to an order made as mentioned in paragraph (a) of that subsection, the charity trustees of the charity in trust for which the land is vested in the official custodian immediately before the time when the order takes effect, or

(b) in relation to an order made under subsection (2) above, the charity trustees of the charity in trust for which the land was vested in the official custodian immediately before the time when section 1 of the 1987 Act operated in relation to the land.

(5) Where—

(a) section 1 of the 1987 Act has operated in relation to any such land as is mentioned in subsection (2)(a) above, and

(b) the land remains vested in the official custodian as mentioned in subsection (2)(b) above,

then (subject to subsection (6) below), all the powers, duties and liabilities that would, apart from this section, be those of the official custodian as [trustee][9] of the land shall instead be those of the charity trustees of the charity concerned; and those trustees shall have power in his name and on his behalf to execute and do all assurances and things which they could properly execute or do in their own name and on their own behalf if the land were vested in them.

(6) Subsection (5) above shall not be taken to require or authorise those trustees to sell the land at a time when it remains vested in the official custodian.

(7) Where—

(a) the official custodian has been discharged from his trusteeship of any land by an order under subsection (2) above, and

[9] Word substituted by the Trusts of Land and Appointment of Trustees Act 1996, s.25(1), Sched. 3, para. 26.

(b) the land has, in accordance with subsection (3) above, been vested in the charity trustees concerned or (as the case may be) in any persons other than those trustees,

the land shall be held by those trustees, or (as the case may be) by those persons, as [trustees][10] on the terms of the trust arising under section 1 of the 1987 Act.

(8) The official custodian shall not be liable to any person in respect of any loss or misapplication of any land vested in him in accordance with that section unless it is occasioned by or through any wilful neglect or default of his or of any person acting for him; but the Consolidated Fund shall be liable to make good to any person any sums for which the official custodian may be liable by reason of any such neglect or default.

(9) In this section any reference to section 1 of the 1987 Act operating in relation to any land is a reference to a [trust][11] arising in relation to the land under that section.

Establishment of common investment or deposit funds

Schemes to establish common investment funds

24.—(1) The court or the Commissioners may by order make and bring into effect schemes (in this section referred to as "common investment schemes") for the establishment of common investment funds under trusts which provide— **56–023**

(a) for property transferred to the fund by or on behalf of a charity participating in the scheme to be invested under the control of trustees appointed to manage the fund; and

(b) for the participating charities to be entitled (subject to the provisions of the scheme) to the capital and income of the fund in shares determined by reference to the amount or value of the property transferred to it by or on behalf of each of them and to the value of the fund at the time of the transfers.

(2) The court or the Commissioners may make a common investment scheme on the application of any two or more charities.

(3) A common investment scheme may be made in terms admitting any charity to participate, or the scheme may restrict the right to participate in any manner.

(4) A common investment scheme may make provision for, and for all matters connected with, the establishment, investment, management and winding up of the common investment fund, and may in particular include provision—

(a) for remunerating persons appointed trustees to hold or manage thefund or any part of it, with or without provision authorising a person to receive the remuneration notwithstanding that he is also a charity trustee of or trustee for a participating charity;

(b) for restricting the size of the fund, and for regulating as to time, amount or otherwise the right to transfer property to or withdraw it from the fund, and for enabling sums to be advanced out of the fund by way of loan to a participating charity pending the withdrawal of property from the fund by the charity;

[10] Word substituted by the Trusts of Land and Appointment of Trustees Act 1996, s.25(1), Sched. 3, para. 26.

[11] Word substituted by the Trusts of Land and Appointment of Trustees Act 1996, s.25(1), Sched. 3, para. 26.

(c) for enabling income to be withheld from distribution with a view to avoiding fluctuations in the amounts distributed, and generally for regulating distributions of income;

(d) for enabling money to be borrowed temporarily for the purpose of meeting payments to be made out of the funds;

(e) for enabling questions arising under the scheme as to the right of a charity to participate, or as to the rights of participating charities, or as to any other matter, to be conclusively determined by the decision of the trustees managing the fund or in any other manner;

(f) for regulating the accounts and information to be supplied to participating charities.

(5) A common investment scheme, in addition to the provision for property to be transferred to the fund on the basis that the charity shall be entitled to a share in the capital and income of the fund, may include provisions for enabling sums to be deposited by or on behalf of a charity on the basis that (subject to the provisions of the scheme) the charity shall be entitled to repayment of the sums deposited and to interest thereon at a rate determined by or under the scheme; and where a scheme makes any such provision it shall also provide for excluding from the amount of capital and income to be shared between charities participating otherwise than by way of deposit such amounts (not exceeding the amounts properly attributable to the making of deposits) as are from time to time reasonably required in respect of the liabilities of the fund for the repayment of deposits and for the interest on deposits, including amounts required by way of reserve.

(6) Except in so far as common investment scheme provides to the contrary, the rights under it of a participating charity shall not be capable of being assigned or charged, nor shall any trustee or other person concerned in the management of the common investment fund be required or entitled to take account of any trust or other equity affecting a participating charity or its property or rights.

(7) The powers of investment of every charity shall include power to participate in common investment schemes unless the power is excluded by a provision specifically referring to common investment schemes in the trusts of the charity.

(8) A common investment fund shall be deemed for all purposes to be a charity; and if the scheme admits only exempt charities, the fund shall be an exempt charity for the purposes of this Act.

(9) Subsection (8) above shall apply not only to common investment funds established under the powers of this section, but also to any similar fund established for the exclusive benefit of charities by or under any enactment relating to any particular charities or class of charity.

Schemes to establish common deposit funds

56–024 **25.**—(1) The court or the Commissioners may by order make and bring into effect schemes (in this section referred to as "common deposit schemes") for the establishment of common deposit funds under trusts which provide—

(a) for sums to be deposited by or on behalf of a charity participating in the scheme and invested under the control of trustees appointed to manage the fund; and

(b) for any such charity to be entitled (subject to the provisions of the scheme) to repayment of any sums so deposited and to interest thereon at a rate determined under the scheme.

(2) Subject to subsection (3) below, the following provisions of section 24 above, namely—

(a) subsections (2) to (4), and

(b) subsections (6) to (9),

shall have effect in relation to common deposit schemes and common deposit funds as they have effect in relation to common investment schemes and common investment funds.

(3) In its application in accordance with subsection (2) above, subsection (4) of that section shall have effect with the substitution for paragraphs (b) and (c) of the following paragraphs—

"(b) for regulating as to time, amount or otherwise the right to repayment of sums deposited in the fund;

(c) for authorising a part of the income for any year to be credited to a reserve account maintained for the purpose of counteracting any losses accruing to the fund, and generally for regulating the manner in which the rate of interest on deposits is to be determined from time to time;".

Additional powers of Commissioners

Power to authorise dealings with charity property etc.

26.—(1) Subject to the provisions of this section, where it appears to the Commissioners that any action proposed or contemplated in the administration of a charity is expedient in the interests of the charity, they may by order sanction that action, whether or not it would otherwise be within the powers exercisable by the charity trustees in the administration of the charity; and anything done under the authority of such an order shall be deemed to be properly done in the exercise of those powers. **56–025**

(2) An order under this section may be made so as to authorise a particular transaction, compromise or the like, or a particular application of property, or so as to give a more general authority, and (without prejudice to the generality of subsection (1) above) may authorise a charity to use common premises, or employ a common staff, or otherwise combine for any purpose of administration, with any other charity.

(3) An order under this section may give directions as to the manner in which any expenditure is to be borne and as to other matters connected with or arising out of the action thereby authorised; and where anything is done in pursuance of an authority given by any such order, any directions given in connection therewith shall be binding on the charity trustees for the time being as if contained in the trusts of the charity; but any such directions may on the application of the charity be modified or superseded by a further order.

(4) Without prejudice to the generality of subsection (3) above, the directions which may be given by an order under this section shall in particular include directions for meeting any expenditure out of a specified fund, for charging any expenditure to capital or to income, for requiring expenditure charged to capital to be recouped out of income within a specified period, for restricting the costs to be incurred at the expense of the charity, or for the investment of moneys arising from any transaction.

(5) An order under this section may authorise any act notwithstanding that it is prohibited by any of the disabling Acts mentioned in subsection (6) below or that the trusts of the charity provide for the act to be done by or under the

authority of the court; but no such order shall authorise the doing of any act expressly prohibited by Act of Parliament other than the disabling Acts or by the trusts of the charity or shall extend or alter the purposes of the charity.

(6) The Acts referred to in subsection (5) above as the disabling Acts are the Ecclesiastical Leases Act 1571, the Ecclesiastical Leases Act 1572, the Ecclesiastical Leases Act 1575 and the Ecclesiastical Leases Act 1836.

(7) An order under this section shall not confer any authority in relation to a building which has been consecrated and of which the use or disposal is regulated, and can be further regulated, by a scheme having effect under the Union of Benefices Measures 1923 to 1952, the Reorganisation Areas Measures 1944 and 1954, the Pastoral Measure 1968 or the Pastoral Measure 1983, the reference to a building being taken to include part of a building and any land which under such a scheme is to be used or disposed of with a building to which the scheme applies.

Power to authorise ex gratia payments etc.

56–026 **27.**—(1) Subject to subsection (3) below, the Commissioners may by order exercise the same power as is exercisable by the Attorney-General to authorise the charity trustees of a charity—

(a) to make any application of property of the charity, or
(b) to waive to any extent, on behalf of the charity, its entitlement to receive any property,

in a case where the charity trustees—

(i) (apart from this section) have no power to do so, but
(ii) in all the circumstances regard themselves as being under a moral obligation to do so.

(2) The power conferred on the Commissioners by subsection (1) above shall be exercisable by them under the supervision of, and in accordance with such directions as may be given by, the Attorney-General; and any such directions may in particular require the Commissioners, in such circumstances as are specified in the directions—

(a) to refrain from exercising that power; or
(b) to consult the Attorney-General before exercising it.

(3) Where—

(a) an application is made to the Commissioners for them to exercise that power in a case where they are not precluded from doing so by any such directions, but
(b) they consider that it would nevertheless be desirable for the application to be entertained by the Attorney-General rather than by them,

they shall refer the application to the Attorney-General.

(4) It is hereby declared that where, in the case of any application made to them as mentioned in subsection (3)(a) above, the Commissioners determine the application by refusing to authorise charity trustees to take any action falling within subsection (1)(a) or (b) above, that refusal shall not preclude the Attorney-General, on an application subsequently made to him by the trustees, from authorising the trustees to take that action.

Power to give directions about dormant bank accounts of charities

56–027 **28.**—(1) Where the Commissioners—

(a) are informed by a relevant institution—

(i) that it holds one or more accounts in the name of or on behalf of a particular charity ("the relevant charity"), and

(ii) that the account, or (if it so holds two or more accounts) each of the accounts, is dormant, and

(b) are unable, after making reasonable inquiries, to locate that charity or any of its trustees,

they may give a direction under subsection (2) below.

(2) A direction under this subsection is a direction which—

(a) requires the institution concerned to transfer the amount, or (as the case may be) the aggregate amount, standing to the credit of the relevant charity in the account or accounts in question to such other charity as is specified in the direction in accordance with subsection (3) below; or

(b) requires the institution concerned to transfer to each of two or more other charities so specified in the direction such part of that amount or aggregate amount as is there specified in relation to that charity.

(3) The Commissioners may specify in a direction under subsection (2) above such other charity or charities as they consider appropriate, having regard, in a case where the purposes of the relevant charity are known to them, to those purposes and to the purposes of the other charity or charities; but the Commissioners shall not so specify any charity unless they have received from the charity trustees written confirmation that those trustees are willing to accept the amount proposed to be transferred to the charity.

(4) Any amount received by a charity by virtue of this section shall be received by the charity on terms that—

(a) it shall be held and applied by the charity for the purposes of the charity, but

(b) it shall, as property of the charity, nevertheless be subject to any restrictions on expenditure to which it was subject as property of the relevant charity.

(5) Where—

(a) the Commissioners have been informed as mentioned in subsection (1)(a) above by any relevant institution, and

(b) before any transfer is made by the institution in pursuance of a direction under subsection (2) above, the institution has, by reason of any circumstances, cause to believe that the account, or (as the case may be) any of the accounts, held by it in the name of or on behalf of the relevant charity is no longer dormant,

the institution shall forthwith notify those circumstances in writing to the Commissioners; and, if it appears to the Commissioners that the account or accounts in question is or are no longer dormant, they shall revoke any direction under subsection (2) above which has previously been given by them to the institution with respect to the relevant charity.

(6) The receipt of any charity trustees or trustee for a charity in respect of any amount received from a relevant institution by virtue of this section shall be a complete discharge of the institution in respect of that amount.

(7) No obligation as to secrecy or other restriction on disclosure (however imposed) shall preclude a relevant institution from disclosing any information to the Commissioners for the purpose of enabling them to discharge their functions under this section.

(8) For the purposes of this section—

(a) an account is dormant if no transaction, other than—

(i) a transaction consisting in a payment into the account, or

(ii) a transaction which the institution holding the account has itself caused to be effected,

has been effected in relation to the account within the period of five years immediately preceding the date when the Commissioners are informed as mentioned in paragraph (a) of subsection (1) above;

(b) a "relevant institution" means—

(i) the Bank of England;

[(ii) a person who has permission under Part 4 of the Financial Services and Markets Act 2000 to accept deposits;

(iii) an EEA firm of the kind mentioned in paragraph 5(b) of Schedule 3 to that Act which has permission under paragraph 15 of that Schedule (as a result of qualifying for authorisation under paragraph 12(1) of that Schedule) to accept deposits; or

(iv) such other person who may lawfully accept deposits in the United Kingdom as may be prescribed by the Secretary of State.][12]

(c) references to the transfer of any amount to a charity are references to its transfer—

(i) to the charity trustees, or

(ii) to any trustee for the charity,

as the charity trustees may determine (and any reference to any amount received by a charity shall be construed accordingly).

[(8A) Sub-paragraphs (ii) to (iv) of the definition of "relevant institution" in subsection (8)(b) must be read with—

(a) section 22 of the Financial Services and Markets Act 2000;

(b) any relevant order under that section; and

(c) Schedule 2 to that Act.][13]

(9) For the purpose of determining the matters in respect of which any of the powers conferred by section 8 or 9 above may be exercised it shall be assumed that the Commissioners have no functions under this section in relation to accounts to which this subsection applies (with the result that, for example, a relevant institution shall not, in connection with the functions of the Commissioners under this section, be required under section 8(3)(a) above to furnish any statements, or answer any questions or inquiries, with respect to any such accounts held by the institution).

This subsection applies to accounts which are dormant accounts by virtue of subsection (8)(a) above but would not be such accounts if sub-paragraph (i) of that provision were omitted.

(10) Subsection (1) above shall not apply to any account held in the name of or on behalf of an exempt charity.

Power to advise charity trustees

56–028 **29.**—(1) The Commissioners may on the written application of any charity trustee give him their opinion or advice on any matter affecting the performance of his duties as such.

(2) A charity trustee or trustee for a charity acting in accordance with the opinion or advice of the Commissioners given under this section with respect to

[12] Sub-paras (ii)–(iv) substituted (for sub-paras (ii)–(v)) by the Financial Services and Markets Act 2000 (Consequential Amendments and Repeals) Order 2001 (S.I. 2001 No. 3649), art. 339(1), (2).

[13] subs. (8A) inserted by the Financial Services and Markets Act 2000 (Consequential Amendments and Repeals) Order 2001 (S.I. 2001 No. 3649), art. 339(1), (3).

the charity shall be deemed, as regards his responsibility for so acting, to have acted in accordance with his trust, unless, when he does so, either—

(a) he knows or has reasonable cause to suspect that the opinion or advice was given in ignorance of material facts; or

(b) the decision of the court has been obtained on the matter or proceedings are pending to obtain one.

Powers for preservation of charity documents

30.—(1) The Commissioners may provide books in which any deed, will or other document relating to a charity may be enrolled. **56–029**

(2) The Commissioners may accept for safe keeping any document of or relating to a charity, and the charity trustees or other persons having the custody of documents of or relating to a charity (including a charity which has ceased to exist) may with the consent of the Commissioners deposit them with the Commissioners for safe keeping, except in the case of documents required by some other enactment to be kept elsewhere.

(3) Where a document is enrolled by the Commissioners or is for the time being deposited with them under this section, evidence of its contents may be given by means of a copy certified by any officer of the Commissioners generally or specially authorised by them to act for this purpose; and a document purporting to be such a copy shall be received in evidence without proof of the official position, authority or handwriting of the person certifying it or of the original document being enrolled or deposited as aforesaid.

(4) Regulations made by the Secretary of State may make provision for such documents deposited with the Commissioners under this section as may be prescribed by the regulations to be destroyed or otherwise disposed of after such period or in such circumstances as may be so prescribed.

(5) Subsections (3) and (4) above shall apply to any document transmitted to the Commissioners under section 9 above and kept by them under subsection (3) of that section, as if the document had been deposited with them for safe keeping under this section.

Power to order taxation of solicitor's bill

31.—(1) The Commissioners may order that a solicitor's bill of costs for business done for a charity, or for charity trustees or trustees for a charity, shall be taxed, together with the costs of the taxation, by a taxing officer in such division of the High Court as may be specified in the order, or by the taxing officer of any other court having jurisdiction to order the taxation of the bill. **56–030**

(2) On any order under this section for the taxation of a solicitor's bill the taxation shall proceed, and the taxing officer shall have the same powers and duties, and the costs of the taxation shall be borne, as if the order had been made, on the application of the person chargeable with the bill, by the court in which the costs are taxed.

(3) No order under this section for the taxation of a solicitor's bill shall be made after payment of the bill unless the Commissioners are of opinion that it contains exorbitant charges; and no such order shall in any case be made where the solicitor's costs are not subject to taxation on an order of the High Court by reason either of an agreement as to his remuneration or the lapse of time since payment of the bill.

Legal proceedings relating to charities

Proceedings by Commissioners

56–031 **32.**—(1) Subject to subsection (2) below, the Commissioners may exercise the same powers with respect to—

(a) the taking of legal proceedings with reference to charities or the property or affairs of charities, or

(b) the compromise of claims with a view to avoiding or ending such proceedings,

as are exercisable by the Attorney-General acting ex officio.

(2) Subsection (1) above does not apply to the power of the Attorney-General under section 63(1) below to present a petition for the winding up of a charity.

(3) The practice and procedure to be followed in relation to any proceedings taken by the Commissioners under subsection (1) above shall be the same in all respects (and in particular as regards costs) as if they were proceedings taken by the Attorney-General acting ex officio.

(4) No rule of law or practice shall be taken to require the Attorney- General to be a party to any such proceedings.

(5) The powers exercisable by the Commissioners by virtue of this section shall be exercisable by them of their own motion, but shall be exercisable only with the agreement of the Attorney-General on each occasion.

Proceedings by other persons

56–032 **33.**—(1) Charity proceedings may be taken with reference to a charity either by the charity, or by any of the charity trustees, or by any person interested in the charity, or by any two or more inhabitants of the area of the charity if it is a local charity, but not by any other person.

(2) Subject to the following provisions of this section, no charity proceedings relating to a charity (other than an exempt charity) shall be entertained or proceeded with in any court unless the taking of the proceedings is authorised by order of the Commissioners.

(3) The Commissioners shall not, without special reasons, authorise the taking of charity proceedings where in their opinion the case can be dealt with by them under the powers of this Act other than those conferred by section 32 above.

(4) This section shall not require any order for the taking of proceedings in a pending cause or matter or for the bringing of any appeal.

(5) Where the foregoing provisions of this section require the taking of charity proceedings to be authorised by an order of the Commissioners, the proceedings may nevertheless be entertained or proceeded with if, after the order had been applied for and refused, leave to take the proceedings was obtained from one of the judges of the High Court attached to the Chancery Division.

(6) Nothing in the foregoing subsections shall apply to the taking of proceedings by the Attorney-General, with or without a relator, or to the taking of proceedings by the Commissioners in accordance with section 32 above.

(7) Where it appears to the Commissioners, on an application for an order under this section or otherwise, that it is desirable for legal proceedings to be taken with reference to any charity (other than an exempt charity) or its property or affairs, and for the proceedings to be taken by the Attorney-

General, the Commissioners shall so inform the Attorney-General, and send him such statements and particulars as they think necessary to explain the matter.

(8) In this section "charity proceedings" means proceedings in any court in England or Wales brought under the court's jurisdiction with respect to charities, or brought under the court's jurisdiction with respect to trusts in relation to the administration of a trust for charitable purposes.

Report of s.8 inquiry to be evidence in certain proceedings

34.—(1) A copy of the report of the person conducting an inquiry under section 8 above shall, if certified by the Commissioners to be a true copy, be admissible in any proceedings to which this section applies— **56–033**

(a) as evidence of any fact stated in the report; and

(b) as evidence of the opinion of that person as to any matter referred to in it.

(2) This section applies to—

(a) any legal proceedings instituted by the Commissioners under this Part of this Act; and

(b) any legal proceedings instituted by the Attorney-General in respect of a charity.

(3) A document purporting to be a certificate issued for the purposes of subsection (1) above shall be received in evidence and be deemed to be such a certificate, unless the contrary is proved.

Meaning of "trust corporation"

Application of provisions to trust corporations appointed under s.16 or 18

35.—(1) In the definition of "trust corporation" contained in the following provisions— **56–034**

(a) section 117(xxx) of the Settled Land Act 1925,

(b) section 68(18) of the Trustee Act 1925,

(c) section 205(xxviii) of the Law of Property Act 1925,

(d) section 55(xxvi) of the Administration of Estates Act 1925, and

(e) section 128 of the Supreme Court Act 1981,

the reference to a corporation appointed by the court in any particular case to be a trustee includes a reference to a corporation appointed by the Commissioners under this Act to be a trustee.

(2) This section shall be deemed always to have had effect; but the reference to section 128 of the Supreme Court Act 1981 shall, in relation to any time before 1st January 1982, be construed as a reference to section 175(1) of the Supreme Court of Judicature (Consolidation) Act 1925.

PART V

CHARITY LAND

Restrictions on dispositions

36.—(1) Subject to the following provisions of this section and section 40 below, no land held by or in trust for a charity shall be sold, leased or otherwise disposed of without an order of the court or of the Commissioners. **56–035**

(2) Subsection (1) above shall not apply to a disposition of such land if—

(a) the disposition is made to a person who is not—

(i) a connected person (as defined in Schedule 5 to this Act), or

(ii) a trustee for, or nominee of, a connected person; and

(b) the requirements of subsection (3) or (5) below have been complied with in relation to it.

(3) Except where the proposed disposition is the granting of such a lease as is mentioned in subsection (5) below, the charity trustees must, before entering into an agreement for the sale, or (as the case may be) for a lease or other disposition, of the land—

(a) obtain and consider a written report on the proposed disposition from a qualified surveyor instructed by the trustees and acting exclusively for the charity;

(b) advertise the proposed disposition for such period and in such manner as the surveyor has advised in his report (unless he has there advised that it would not be in the best interests of the charity to advertise the proposed disposition); and

(c) decide that they are satisfied, having considered the surveyor's report, that the terms on which the disposition is proposed to be made are the best that can reasonably be obtained for the charity.

(4) For the purposes of subsection (3) above a person is a qualified surveyor if—

(a) he is a fellow or professional associate of the Royal Institution of Chartered Surveyors or of the Incorporated Society of Valuers and Auctioneers or satisfies such other requirement or requirements as may be prescribed by regulations made by the Secretary of State; and

(b) he is reasonably believed by the charity trustees to have ability in, and experience of, the valuation of land of the particular kind, and in the particular area, in question;

and any report prepared for the purposes of that subsection shall contain such information, and deal with such matters, as may be prescribed by regulations so made.

(5) Where the proposed disposition is the granting of a lease for a term ending not more than seven years after it is granted (other than one granted wholly or partly in consideration of a fine), the charity trustees must, before entering into an agreement for the lease—

(a) obtain and consider the advice on the proposed disposition of a person who is reasonably believed by the trustees to have the requisite ability and practical experience to provide them with competent advice on the proposed disposition; and

(b) decide that they are satisfied, having considered that person's advice, that the terms on which the disposition is proposed to be made are the best that can reasonably be obtained for the charity.

(6) Where—

(a) any land is held by or in trust for a charity, and

(b) the trusts on which it is so held stipulate that it is to be used for the purposes, or any particular purposes, of the charity,

then (subject to subsections (7) and (8) below and without prejudice to the operation of the preceding provisions of this section) the land shall not be sold, leased or otherwise disposed of unless the charity trustees have previously—

(i) given public notice of the proposed disposition, inviting representations to be made to them within a time specified in the notice, being not less than one month from the date of the notice; and

(ii) taken into consideration any representations made to them within that time about the proposed disposition.

(7) Subsection (6) above shall not apply to any such disposition of land as is there mentioned if—

(a) the disposition is to be effected with a view to acquiring by way of replacement other property which is to be held on the trusts referred to in paragraph (b) of that subsection; or

(b) the disposition is the granting of a lease for a term ending not more than two years after it is granted (other than one granted wholly or partly in consideration of a fine).

(8) The Commissioners may direct—

(a) that subsection (6) above shall not apply to dispositions of land held by or in trust for a charity or class of charities (whether generally or only in the case of a specified class of dispositions of land, or otherwise as may be provided in the direction), or

(b) that that subsection shall not apply to a particular disposition of land held by or in trust for a charity,

if, on the application made to them in writing by or on behalf of the charity or charities in question, the Commissioners are satisfied that it would be in the interests of the charity or charities for them to give the direction.

(9) The restrictions on disposition imposed by this section apply notwithstanding anything in the trusts of a charity; but nothing in this section applies—

(a) to any disposition for which general or special authority is expressly given (without the authority being made subject to the sanction of an order of the court) by any statutory provision contained in or having effect under an Act of Parliament or by any scheme legally established; or

(b) to any disposition of land held by or in trust for a charity which—

(i) is made to another charity otherwise than for the best price that can reasonably be obtained, and

(ii) is authorised to be so made by the trusts of the first-mentioned charity; or

(c) to the granting, by or on behalf of a charity and in accordance with its trusts, of a lease to any beneficiary under those trusts where the lease—

(i) is granted otherwise than for the best rent that can reasonably be obtained; and

(ii) is intended to enable the demised premises to be occupied for the purposes, or any particular purposes, of the charity.

(10) Nothing in this section applies—

(a) to any disposition of land held by or in trust for an exempt charity;

(b) to any disposition of land by way of mortgage or other security; or

(c) to any disposition of an advowson.

(11) In this section "land" means land in England or Wales.

Supplementary provisions relating to dispositions

37.—(1) Any of the following instruments, namely— **56–036**

(a) any contract for the sale, or for a lease or other disposition, of land which is held by or in trust for a charity, and

(b) any conveyance, transfer, lease or other instrument effecting a disposition of such land,

shall state—

(i) that the land is held by or in trust for a charity,
(ii) whether the charity is an exempt charity and whether the disposition is one falling within paragraph (a), (b) or (c) of subsection (9) of section 36 above, and
(iii) if it is not an exempt charity and the disposition is not one falling within any of those paragraphs, that the land is land to which the restrictions on disposition imposed by that section apply.

(2) Where any land held by or in trust for a charity is sold, leased or otherwise disposed of by a disposition to which subsection (1) or (2) of section 36 above applies, the charity trustees shall certify in the instrument by which the disposition is effected—
(a) (where subsection (1) of that section applies) that the disposition has been sanctioned by an order of the court or of the Commissioners (as the case may be), or
(b) (where subsection (2) of that section applies) that the charity trustees have power under the trusts of the charity to effect the disposition, and that they have complied with the provisions of that section so far as applicable to it.

(3) Where subsection (2) above has been complied with in relation to any disposition of land, then in favour of a person who (whether under the disposition or afterwards) acquires an interest in the land for money or money's worth, it shall be conclusively presumed that the facts were as stated in the certificate.

(4) Where—
(a) any land held by or in trust for a charity is sold, leased or otherwise disposed of by a disposition to which subsection (1) or (2) of section 36 above applies, but
(b) subsection (2) above has not been complied with in relation to the disposition,

then in favour of a person who (whether under the disposition or afterwards) in good faith acquires an interest in the land for money or money's worth, the disposition shall be valid whether or not—
(i) the disposition has been sanctioned by an order of the court or of the Commissioners, or
(ii) the charity trustees have power under the trusts of the charity to effect the disposition and have complied with the provisions of that section so far as applicable to it.

(5) Any of the following instruments, namely—
(a) any contract for the sale, or for a lease or other disposition, of land which will, as a result of the disposition, be held by or in trust for a charity, and
(b) any conveyance, transfer, lease or other instrument effecting a disposition of such land,

shall state—
(i) that the land will, as a result of the disposition, be held by or in trust for a charity,
(ii) whether the charity is an exempt charity, and
(iii) if it is not an exempt charity, that the restrictions on disposition imposed by section 36 above will apply to the land (subject to subsection (9) of that section).

(6) [*Repealed by the Trusts of Land and Appointment of Trustees Act 1996, s.25(2), Sched. 4.*]

[(7) Where the disposition to be effected by any such instrument as is mentioned in subsection (1)(b) or (5)(b) above will be—

(a) a registrable disposition, or

(b) a disposition which triggers the requirement of registration

the statement which, by virtue of subsection (1) or (5) above, is to be contained in the instrument shall be in such form as may be prescribed by land registration rules.

(8) Where the registrar approved an application for registration of—

(a) a disposition of registered land, or

(b) a person's title under a disposition of unregistered land,

and the instrument effecting the disposition contains a statement complying with subsections (5) and (7) above, he shall enter in the register a restriction reflecting the limitation under section 36 above on subsequent disposal.][14]

(9) Where—

(a) any such restriction is entered in the register in respect of any land, and

(b) the charity by or in trust for which the land is held becomes an exempt charity,

the charity trustees shall apply to the registrar for [the removal of the entry][15]; and on receiving any application duly made under this subsection the registrar shall [remove the entry].[16]

(10) Where—

(a) any registered land is held by or in trust for an exempt charity and the charity ceases to be an exempt charity, or

(b) any registered land becomes, as a result of a declaration of trust by the registered proprietor, land held in trust for a charity (other than an exempt charity),

the charity trustees shall apply to the registrar for such a restriction as is mentioned in subsection (8) above to be entered in the register in respect of the land; and on receiving any application duly made under this subsection the registrar shall enter such a restriction in the register in respect of the land.

(11) In this section—

(a) references to a disposition of land do not include references to—

(i) a disposition of land by way of mortgage or other security,

(ii) any disposition of an advowson, or

(iii) any release of a rentcharge falling within section 40(1) below; and

(b) "land" means land in England or Wales;

and subsections (7) to (10) above shall be construed as one with the [Land Registration Act 2002].[17]

Restrictions on mortgaging

38.—(1) Subject to subsection (2) below, no mortgage of land held by or in trust for a charity shall be granted without an order of the court or of the Commissioners. **56–037**

(2) Subsection (1) above shall not apply to a mortgage of any such land by way of security for the repayment of a loan where the charity trustees have, before executing the mortgage, obtained and considered proper advice, given to them in writing, on the matters mentioned in subsection (3) below.

(3) Those matters are—

(a) whether the proposed loan is necessary in order for the charity trustees

[14] subss. (7) and (8) substituted by the Land Registration Act 2002, s.133, Sched. 11, para. 29(1), (2).
[15] Words substituted by the Land Registration Act 2002, s.133, Sched. 11, para. 29(1), (3).
[16] Words substituted by the Land Registration Act 2002, s.133, Sched. 11, para. 29(1), (3).
[17] Words substituted by the Land Registration Act 2002, s.133, Sched. 11, para. 29(1), (4).

to be able to pursue the particular course of action in connection with which the loan is sought by them;

(b) whether the terms of the proposed loan are reasonable having regard to the status of the charity as a prospective borrower; and

(c) the ability of the charity to repay on those terms the sum proposed to be borrowed.

(4) For the purposes of subsection (2) above proper advice is the advice of a person—

(a) who is reasonably believed by the charity trustees to be qualified by his ability in and practical experience of financial matters; and

(b) who has no financial interest in the making of the loan in question;

and such advice may constitute proper advice for those purposes notwithstanding that the person giving it does so in the course of his employment as an officer or employee of the charity or of the charity trustees.

(5) This section applies notwithstanding anything in the trusts of a charity; but nothing in this section applies to any mortgage for which general or special authority is given as mentioned in section 36(9)(a) above.

(6) In this section—

"land" means land in England or Wales;

"mortgage" includes a charge.

Supplementary provisions relating to mortgaging

56–038 **39.**—(1) Any mortgage of land held by or in trust for a charity shall state—

(a) that the land is held by or in trust for a charity,

(b) whether the charity is an exempt charity and whether the mortgage is one falling within subsection (5) of section 38 above, and

(c) if it is not an exempt charity and the mortgage is not one falling within that subsection, that the mortgage is one to which the restrictions imposed by that section apply;

and where the mortgage will be a registered disposition any such statement shall be in such form as may be prescribed [by land registration rules].[18]

[(1A) Where any such mortgage will be one to which section 4(1)(g) of the Land Registration Act 2002 applies—

(a) the statement required by subsection (1) above shall be in such form as may be prescribed by land registration rules; and

(b) if the charity is not an exempt charity, the mortgage shall also contain a statement, in such form as may be prescribed by land registration rules, that the restrictions on disposition imposed by section 36 above apply to the land (subject to subsection (9) of that section).

(1B) Where—

(a) the registrar approves an application for registration of a person's title to land in connection with such a mortgage as is mentioned in subsection (1A) above,

(b) the mortgage contains statements complying with subsection (1) and (1A) above, and

(c) the charity is not an exempt charity,

the registrar shall enter in the register a restriction reflecting the limitation under section 36 above on subsequent disposal.

(1C) Section 37(9) above shall apply in relation to any restriction entered

[18] Words added by the Land Registration Act 2002, s.133, Sched. 11, para. 29(1), (5).

under subsection (1B) as it applies in relation to any restriction entered under section 37(8).][19]

(2) Where subsection (1) or (2) of section 38 above applies to any mortgage of land held by or in trust for a charity, the charity trustees shall certify in the mortgage—

(a) (where subsection (1) of that section applies) that the mortgage has been sanctioned by an order of the court or of the Commissioners (as the case may be), or

(b) (where subsection (2) of that section applies) that the charity trustees have power under the trusts of the charity to grant the mortgage, and that they have obtained and considered such advice as is mentioned in that subsection.

(3) Where subsection (2) above has been complied with in relation to any mortgage, then in favour of the person who (whether under the mortgage or afterwards) acquires an interest in the land in question for money or money's worth, it shall be conclusively presumed that the facts were as stated in the certificate.

(4) Where—

(a) subsection (1) or (2) of section 38 above applies to any mortgage of land held by or in trust for a charity, but

(b) subsection (2) above has not been complied with in relation to the mortgage,

then in favour of a person who (whether under the mortgage or afterwards) in good faith acquires an interest in the land for money or money's worth, the mortgage shall be valid whether or not—

(i) the mortgage has been sanctioned by an order of the court or of the Commissioners, or

(ii) the charity trustees have power under the trusts of the charity to grant the mortgage and have obtained and considered such advice as is mentioned in subsection (2) of that section.

(5) [*Repealed by the Trusts of Land and Appointment of Trustees Act 1996, s.25(2), Sched. 4.*]

(6) In this section—

"mortgage" includes a charge, and "mortgagee" shall be construed accordingly;

"land" means land in England or Wales;

[and subsections (1) to (1B) above shall be construed as one with the Land Registration Act 2002.][20]

Release of charity rentcharges

40.—(1) Section 36(1) above shall not apply to the release by a charity of a rentcharge which it is entitled to receive if the release is given in consideration of the payment of an amount which is not less than ten times the annual amount of the rentcharge. **56–039**

(2) Where a charity which is entitled to receive a rentcharge releases it in consideration of the payment of an amount not exceeding £500, any costs incurred by the charity in connection with proving its title to the rentcharge shall

[19] subss. (1A)–(1C) substituted (for subss. (1A) and (1B), inserted by the Land Registration Act 1997, s.4(1), Sched. 1, Pt. I, para. 6(2)) by the Land Registration Act 2002, s.133, Sched. 11, para. 29(1), (6).

[20] Words substituted by the Land Registration Act 2002, s.133, Sched. 11, para. 29(1), (7).

be recoverable by the charity from the person or persons in whose favour the rentcharge is being released.

(3) Neither section 36(1) nor subsection (2) above applies where a rentcharge which a charity is entitled to receive is redeemed under sections 8 to 10 of the Rentcharges Act 1977.

(4) The Secretary of State may by order amend subsection (2) above by substituting a different sum for the sum for the time being specified there.

PART VI

CHARITY ACCOUNTS, REPORTS AND RETURNS

Duty to keep accounting records

56–040 **41.**—(1) The charity trustees of a charity shall ensure that accounting records are kept in respect of the charity which are sufficient to show and explain all the charity's transactions, and which are such as to—

(a) disclose at any time, with reasonable accuracy, the financial position of the charity at that time, and

(b) enable the trustees to ensure that, where any statements of accounts are prepared by them under section 42(1) below, those statements of accounts comply with the requirements of regulations under that provision.

(2) The accounting records shall in particular contain—

(a) entries showing from day to day all sums of money received and expended by the charity, and the matters in respect of which the receipt and expenditure takes place; and

(b) a record of the assets and liabilities of the charity.

(3) The charity trustees of a charity shall preserve any accounting records made for the purposes of this section in respect of the charity for at least six years from the end of the financial year of the charity in which they are made.

(4) Where a charity ceases to exist within the period of six years mentioned in subsection (3) above as it applies to any accounting records, the obligation to preserve those records in accordance with that subsection shall continue to be discharged by the last charity trustees of the charity, unless the Commissioners consent in writing to the records being destroyed or otherwise disposed of.

(5) Nothing in this section applies to a charity which is a company.

Annual statements of accounts

56–041 **42.**—(1) The charity trustees of a charity shall (subject to subsection (3) below) prepare in respect of each financial year of the charity a statement of accounts complying with such requirements as to its form and contents as may be prescribed by regulations made by the Secretary of State.

(2) Without prejudice to the generality of subsection (1) above, regulations under that subsection may make provision—

(a) for any such statement to be prepared in accordance with such methods and principles as are specified or referred to in the regulations;

(b) as to any information to be provided by way of notes to the accounts;

and regulations under that subsection may also make provision for determining the financial years of a charity for the purposes of this Act and any regulations made under it.

(3) Where a charity's gross income in any financial year does not exceed

[£100,000][21], the charity trustees may, in respect of that year, elect to prepare the following, namely—

(a) a receipts and payments account, and

(b) a statement of assets and liabilities,

instead of a statement of accounts under subsection (1) above.

(4) The charity trustees of a charity shall preserve—

(a) any statement of accounts prepared by them under subsection (1) above, or

(b) any account and statement prepared by them under subsection (3) above,

for at least six years from the end of the financial year to which any such statement relates or (as the case may be) to which any such account and statement relate.

(5) Subsection (4) of section 41 above shall apply in relation to the preservation of any such statement or account and statement as it applies in relation to the preservation of any accounting records (the references to subsection (3) of that section being read as references to subsection (4) above).

(6) The Secretary of State may by order amend subsection (3) above by substituting a different sum for the sum for the time being specified there.

(7) Nothing in this section applies to a charity which is a company.

Annual audit or examination of charity accounts

43.—(1) Subsection (2) below applies to a financial year of a charity ("the relevant year") if the charity's gross income or total expenditure in any of the following, namely— **56–042**

(a) the relevant year,

(b) the financial year of the charity immediately preceding the relevant year (if any), and

(c) the financial year of the charity immediately preceding the year specified in paragraph (b) above (if any),

exceeds [£250,000][22].

(2) If this subsection applies to a financial year of a charity, the accounts of the charity for that year shall be audited by a person who—

(a) is, in accordance with section 25 of the Companies Act 1989 (eligibility for appointment), eligible for appointment as a company auditor, or

(b) is a member of a body for the time being specified in regulations under section 44 below and is under the rules of that body eligible for appointment as auditor of the charity.

(3) If subsection (2) above does not apply to a financial year for a charity [and its gross income or total expenditure in that year exceeds £10,000][23], then (subject to subsection (4) below) the accounts of the charity for that year shall, at the election of the charity trustees, either—

(a) be examined by an independent examiner, that is to say an independent person who is reasonably believed by the trustees to have the requisite ability and practical experience to carry out a competent examination of the accounts, or

(b) be audited by such a person as is mentioned in subsection (2) above.

[21] Figure substituted by the Charities Act 1993 (Substitution of Sums) Order 1995 (S.I. 1995 No. 2696), art. 2(1), (3).
[22] Figure substituted by the Charities Act 1993 (Substitution of Sums) Order 1995 (S.I. 1995 No. 2696), art. 2(1), (4).
[23] Words inserted by the Deregulation and Contracting Out Act 1994, s.28(1), (2).

(4) Where it appears to the Commissioners—

(a) that subsection (2), or (as the case may be) subsection (3) above, has not been complied with in relation to the financial year of a charity within ten months from the end of that year, or

(b) that, although subsection (2) above does not apply to a financial year of a charity, it would nevertheless be desirable for the accounts of the charity for that year to be audited by such a person as is mentioned in that subsection,

the Commissioners may by order require the accounts of the charity for that year to be audited by such a person as is mentioned in that subsection.

(5) If the Commissioners make an order under subsection (4) above with respect to a charity, then unless—

(a) the order is made by virtue of paragraph (b) of that subsection, and

(b) the charity trustees themselves appoint an auditor in accordance with the order,

the auditor shall be a person appointed by the Commissioners.

(6) The expenses of any audit carried out by an auditor appointed by the Commissioners under subsection (5) above, including the auditor's remuneration, shall be recoverable by the Commissioners—

(a) from the charity trustees of the charity concerned, who shall be personally liable, jointly and severally, for those expenses; or

(b) to the extent that it appears to the Commissioners not to be practical to seek recovery of those expenses in accordance with paragraph (a) above, from the funds of the charity.

(7) The Commissioners may—

(a) give guidance to charity trustees in connection with the selection of a person for appointment as an independent examiner;

(b) give such directions as they think appropriate with respect to the carrying out of an examination in pursuance of subsection (3)(a) above;

and any such guidance or directions may either be of general application or apply to a particular charity only.

(8) The Secretary of State may by order amend subsection (1) [or (3)][24] above by substituting a different sum for the sum for the time being specified there.

(9) Nothing in this section applies to a charity which is a company.

Supplementary provisions relating to audits etc.

56–043 **44.**—(1) The Secretary of State may by regulations make provision—

(a) specifying one or more bodies for the purposes of section 43(2)(b) above;

(b) with respect to the duties of an auditor carrying out an audit under section 43 above, including provision with respect to the making by him of a report on—

(i) the statement of accounts prepared for the financial year in question under section 42(1) above, or

(ii) the account and statement so prepared under section 42(3) above, as the case may be;

(c) with respect to the making by an independent examiner of a report in respect of an examination carried out by him under section 43 above;

(d) conferring on such an auditor or on an independent examiner a right of

[24] Words inserted by the Deregulation and Contracting Out Act 1994, s.28(1), (3).

access with respect to books, documents and other records (however kept) which relate to the charity concerned;

(e) entitling such an auditor or an independent examiner to require, in the case of a charity, information and explanations from past or present charity trustees or trustees for the charity, or from past or present officers or employees of the charity;

(f) enabling the Commissioners, in circumstances specified in the regulations, to dispense with the requirements of section 43(2) or (3) above in the case of a particular charity or in the case of any particular financial year of a charity.

(2) If any person fails to afford an auditor or an independent examiner any facility to which he is entitled by virtue of subsection (1)(d) or (e) above, the Commissioners may by order give—

(a) to that person, or

(b) to the charity trustees for the time being of the charity concerned,

such directions as the Commissioners think appropriate for securing that the default is made good.

(3) Section 727 of the Companies Act 1985 (power of court to grant relief in certain cases) shall have effect in relation to an auditor or independent examiner appointed by a charity in pursuance of section 43 above as it has effect in relation to a person employed as auditor by a company within the meaning of that Act.

Annual reports

45.—(1) The charity trustees of a charity shall prepare in respect of each financial year of the charity an annual report containing— **56–044**

(a) such a report by the trustees on the activities of the charity during that year, and

(b) such other information relating to the charity or to its trustees or officers,

as may be prescribed by regulations made by the Secretary of State.

(2) Without prejudice to the generality of subsection (1) above, regulations under that subsection may make provision—

(a) for any such report as is mentioned in paragraph (a) of that subsection to be prepared in accordance with such principles as are specified or referred to in the regulations;

(b) enabling the Commissioners to dispense with any requirement prescribed by virtue of subsection (1)(b) above in the case of a particular charity or a particular class of charities, or in the case of a particular financial year of a charity or of any class of charities.

(3) [Where in any financial year of a charity its gross income or total expenditure exceeds £10,000, the annual report required to be prepared under this section in respect of that year][25] shall be transmitted to the Commissioners by the charity trustees—

(a) within ten months from the end of that year, or

(b) within such longer period as the Commissioners may for any special reason allow in the case of that report.

[(3A) Where in any financial year of a charity neither its gross income nor its total expenditure exceeds £10,000, the annual report required to be prepared under this section in respect of that year shall, if the Commissioners so request, be transmitted to them by the charity trustees—

[25] Words substituted by the Deregulation and Contracting Out Act 1994, s.29(1).

(a) in the case of a request made before the end of seven months from the end of the financial year to which the report relates, within ten months from the end of that year, and

(b) in the case of a request not so made, within three months from the date of the request,

or, in either case, within such longer period as the Commissioners may for any special reason allow in the case of that report.][26]

(4) Subject to subsection (5) below, [any annual report transmitted to the Commissioners under this section][27] shall have attached to it the statement of accounts prepared for the financial year in question under section 42(1) above or (as the case may be) the account and statement so prepared under section 42(3) above, together with—

(a) where the accounts of the charity for that year have been audited under section 43 above, a copy of the report made by the auditor on that statement of accounts or (as the case may be) on that account and statement;

(b) where the accounts of the charity for that year have been examined under section 43 above, a copy of the report made by the independent examiner in respect of the examination carried out by him under that section.

(5) Subsection (4) above does not apply to a charity which is a company, and any annual report transmitted by the charity trustees of such a charity under [this section][28] shall instead have attached to it a copy of the charity's annual accounts prepared for the financial year in question under Part VII of the Companies Act 1985, together with a copy of [any auditors' report or report made for the purposes of section 249A(2) of that Act][29] on those accounts.

(6) Any annual report transmitted to the Commissioners under [this section][30], together with the documents attached to it, shall be kept by the Commissioners for such period as they think fit.

[(7) The charity trustees of a charity shall preserve, for at least six years from the end of the financial year to which it relates, any annual report prepared by them under subsection (1) above which they have not been required to transmit to the Commissioners.

(8) Subsection (4) of section 41 above shall apply in relation to the preservation of any such annual report as it applies in relation to the preservation of any accounting records (the references in subsection (3) of that section being read as references to subsection (7) above).

(9) The Secretary of State may by order amend subsection (3) or (3A) above by substituting a different sum for the sum for the time being specified there.][31]

Special provision as respects accounts and annual reports of exempt and other excepted charities

56–045 **46.**—(1) Nothing in sections 41 to 45 above applies to any exempt charity; but the charity trustees of an exempt charity shall keep proper books of account with respect to the affairs of the charity, and if not required by or under the

[26] subs. (3A) inserted by the Deregulation and Contracting Out Act 1994, s.29(2).
[27] Words substituted by the Deregulation and Contracting Out Act 1994, s.29(3).
[28] Words substituted by the Deregulation and Contracting Out Act 1994, s.29(4).
[29] Words substituted by the Companies Act 1985 (Audit Exemption) Regulations 1994 (S.I. 1994 No. 1935), reg. 4, Sched. 1, Pt. II, para. 6.
[30] Words substituted by the Deregulation and Contracting Out Act 1994, s.29(5).
[31] subss. (7)–(9) added by the Deregulation and Contracting Out Act 1994, s.29(6).

authority of any other Act to prepare periodical statements of account shall prepare consecutive statements of account consisting on each occasion of an income and expenditure account relating to a period of not more than fifteen months and a balance sheet relating to the end of that period.

(2) The books of accounts and statements of account relating to an exempt charity shall be preserved for a period of six years at least unless the charity ceases to exist and the Commissioners consent in writing to their being destroyed or otherwise disposed of.

(3) Nothing in sections 43 to 45 above applies to any charity which—

(a) falls within section 3(5)(c) above, and

(b) is not registered.

(4) Except in accordance with subsection (7) below, nothing in section 45 above applies to any charity (other than an exempt charity or a charity which falls within section 3(5)(c) above) which—

(a) is excepted by section 3(5) above, and

(b) is not registered.

(5) If requested to do so by the Commissioners, the charity trustees of any such charity as is mentioned in subsection (4) above shall prepare an annual report in respect of such financial year of the charity as is specified in the Commissioners' request.

(6) Any report prepared under subsection (5) above shall contain—

(a) such a report by the charity trustees on the activities of the charity during the year in question, and

(b) such other information relating to the charity or to its trustees or officers,

as may be prescribed by regulations made under section 45(1) above in relation to annual reports prepared under that provision.

(7) Subsections (3) to (6) of section 45 [(as originally enacted)][32] above shall apply to any report required to be prepared under subsection (5) above as if it were an annual report required to be prepared under subsection (1) of that section.

(8) Any reference in this section to a charity which falls within section 3(5)(c) above includes a reference to a charity which falls within that provision but is also excepted from registration by section 3(5)(b) above.

Public inspection of annual reports etc.

47.—(1) Any annual report or other document kept by the Commissioners in pursuance of section 45(6) above shall be open to public inspection at all reasonable times— **56–046**

(a) during the period for which it is so kept; or

(b) if the Commissioners so determine, during such lesser period as they may specify.

(2) Where any person—

(a) requests the charity trustees of a charity in writing to provide him with a copy of the charity's most recent accounts, and

(b) pays them such reasonable fee (if any) as they may require in respect of the costs of complying with the request,

those trustees shall comply with the request within the period of two months beginning with the date on which it is made.

[32] Words inserted by the Deregulation and Contracting Out Act 1994, s.29(7).

(3) In subsection (2) above the reference to a charity's most recent accounts is—

[...][33]

(b) in the case of [a charity other than one falling within paragraph (c) or (d) below][34] a reference to the statement of accounts or account and statement prepared in pursuance of section 42(1) or (3) above in respect of the last financial year of the charity in respect of which a statement of accounts or account and statement has or have been so prepared;

[(c) in the case of a charity which is a company, a reference to the most recent annual accounts of the company prepared under Part VII of the Companies Act 1985 in relation to which any of the following conditions is satisfied—

(i) they have been audited;

(ii) a report required for the purposes of section 249A(2) of that Act has been made in respect of them; or

(iii) they relate to a year in respect of which the company is exempt from audit by virtue of section 249A(1) of that Act; and][35]

(d) in the case of an exempt charity, a reference to the accounts of the charity most recently audited in pursuance of any statutory or other requirement or, if its accounts are not required to be audited, the accounts most recently prepared in respect of the charity.

Annual returns by registered charities

56–047 **48.**—(1) [Subject to subsection (1A) below,][36] every registered charity shall prepare in respect of each of its financial years an annual return in such form, and containing such information, as may be prescribed by regulations made by the Commissioners.

[(1A) Subsection (1) above shall not apply in relation to any financial years of a charity in which neither the gross income nor the total expenditure of the charity exceeds £10,000.][37]

(2) Any such return shall be transmitted to the Commissioners by the date by which the charity trustee are, by virtue of section 45(3) above, required to transmit to them the annual report required to be prepared in respect of the financial year in question.

(3) The Commissioners may dispense with the requirements of subsection (1) above in the case of a particular charity or a particular class of charities, or in the case of a particular financial year of a charity or of any class of charities.

[(4) The Secretary of State may by order amend subsection (1A) above by substituting a different sum for the sum for the time being specified there.][38]

Offences

56–048 **49.** Any person who, without reasonable excuse, is persistently in default in relation to any requirement imposed—

---

[33] Para. (a) repealed by the Deregulation and Contracting Out Act 1994, ss.39, 81(1), Sched. 11, para. 12(a), Sched. 17.
[34] Words substituted by the Deregulation and Contracting Out Act 1994, s.39, Sched. 11, para. 12(b).
[35] Para. (c) substituted by the Companies Act 1985 (Audit Exemption) Regulations 1994 (S.I. 1994 No. 1935), reg. 4, Sched. 1, Pt. II, para. 7.
[36] Words inserted by the Deregulation and Contracting Out Act 1994, s.30(1), (2).
[37] subs. (1A) inserted by the Deregulation and Contracting Out Act 1994, s.30(1), (3).
[38] subs. (4) added by the Deregulation and Contracting Out Act 1994, s.30(1), (4).

(a) by section 45(3) [or (3A)][39] above (taken with section 45(4) or (5), as the case may require), or
(b) by section 47(2) or 48(2) above,
shall be guilty of an offence and liable on summary conviction to a fine not exceeding level 4 on the standard scale.

PART VII

INCORPORATION OF CHARITY TRUSTEES

Incorporation of trustees of a charity

50.—(1) Where— **56–049**
(a) the trustees of a charity, in accordance with section 52 below, apply to the Commissioners for a certificate of incorporation of the trustees as a body corporate, and
(b) the Commissioners consider that the incorporation of the trustees would be in the interests of the charity,
the Commissioners may grant such a certificate, subject to such conditions or directions as they think fit to insert in it.

(2) The Commissioners shall not, however, grant such a certificate in a case where the charity appears to them to be required to be registered under section 3 above but is not so registered.

(3) On the grant of such a certificate—
(a) the trustees of the charity shall become a body corporate by such name as is specified in the certificate; and
(b) (without prejudice to the operation of section 54 below) any relevant rights or liabilities of those trustees shall become rights or liabilities of that body.

(4) After their incorporation the trustees—
(a) may sue and be sued in their corporate name; and
(b) shall have the same powers, and be subject to the same restrictions and limitations, as respects the holding, acquisition and disposal of property for or in connection with the purposes of the charity as they had or were subject to while unincorporated;
and any relevant legal proceedings that might have been continued or commenced by or against the trustees may be continued or commenced by or against them in their corporate name.

(5) A body incorporated under this section need not have a common seal.

(6) In this section—
"relevant rights or liabilities" means rights or liabilities in connection with any property vesting in the body in question under section 51 below; and
"relevant legal proceedings" means legal proceedings in connection with any such property.

Estate to vest in body corporate

51. The certificate of incorporation shall vest in the body corporate all real and personal estate, of whatever nature or tenure, belonging to or held by any person or persons in trust for the charity, and thereupon any person or persons in whose name or names any stocks, funds or securities are standing in trust for **56–050**

[39] Words inserted by the Deregulation and Contracting Out Act 1994, s.29(8).

the charity, shall transfer them into the name of the body corporate, except that the foregoing provisions shall not apply to property vested in the official custodian.

Applications for incorporation

56–051 **52.**—(1) Every application to the Commissioners for a certificate of incorporation under this Part of this Act shall—

(a) be in writing and signed by the trustees of the charity concerned; and

(b) be accompanied by such documents or information as the Commissioners may require for the purpose of the application.

(2) The Commissioners may require—

(a) any statement contained in any such application, or

(b) any document or information supplied under subsection (1)(b) above,

to be verified in such manner as they may specify.

Nomination of trustees, and filling up vacancies

56–052 **53.**—(1) Before a certificate of incorporation is granted under this Part of this Act, trustees of the charity must have been effectively appointed to the satisfaction of the Commissioners.

(2) Where a certificate of incorporation is granted vacancies in the number of the trustees of the charity shall from time to time be filled up so far as required by the constitution or settlement of the charity, or by any conditions or directions in the certificate, by such legal means as would have been available for the appointment of new trustees of the charity if no certificate of incorporation had been granted, or otherwise as required by such conditions or directions.

Liability of trustees and others, notwithstanding incorporation

56–053 **54.** After a certificate of incorporation has been granted under this Part of this Act all trustees of the charity, notwithstanding their incorporation, shall be chargeable for such property as shall come into their hands, and shall be answerable and accountable for their own acts, receipts, neglects, and defaults, and for the due administration of the charity and its property, in the same manner and to the same extent as if no such incorporation had been effected.

Certificate to be evidence of compliance with requirements for incorporation

56–054 **55.** A certificate of incorporation granted under this Part of this Act shall be conclusive evidence that all the preliminary requirements for incorporation under this Part of this Act have been complied with, and the date of incorporation mentioned in the certificate shall be deemed to be the date at which incorporation has taken place.

Power of Commissioners to amend certificate of incorporation

56–055 **56.**—(1) The Commissioners may amend a certificate of incorporation either on the application of the incorporated body to which it relates or of their own motion.

(2) Before making any such amendment of their own motion, the Commissioners shall by notice in writing—

(a) inform the trustees of the relevant charity of their proposals, and

(b) invite those trustees to make representations to them within a time specified in the notice, being not less than one month from the date of the notice.

(3) The Commissioners shall take into consideration any representations made by those trustees within the time so specified, and may then (without further notice) proceed with their proposals either without modification or with such modifications as appear to them to be desirable.

(4) The Commissioners may amend a certificate of incorporation either—

(a) by making an order specifying the amendment; or

(b) by issuing a new certificate of incorporation taking account of the amendment.

Records of applications and certificates

57.—(1) The Commissioners shall keep a record of all applications for, and certificates of, incorporation under this Part of this Act and shall preserve all documents sent to them under this Part of this Act. **56–056**

(2) Any person may inspect such documents, under the direction of the Commissioners, and any person may require a copy or extract of any such document to be certified by a certificate signed by the secretary of the Commissioners.

Enforcement of orders and directions

58. All conditions and directions inserted in any certificate of incorporation shall be binding upon and performed or observed by the trustees as trusts of the charity, and section 88 below shall apply to any trustee who fails to perform or observe any such condition or direction as it applies to a person guilty of disobedience to any such order of the Commissioners as is mentioned in that section. **56–057**

Gifts to charity before incorporation to have same effect afterwards

59. After the incorporation of the trustees of any charity under this Part of this Act every donation, gift and disposition of property, real or personal, lawfully made before the incorporation but not having actually taken effect, or thereafter lawfully made, by deed, will or otherwise to or in favour of the charity, or the trustees of the charity, or otherwise for the purposes of the charity, shall take effect as if made to or in favour of the incorporated body or otherwise for the like purposes. **56–058**

Execution of documents by incorporated body

60.—(1) This section has effect as respects the execution of documents by an incorporated body. **56–059**

(2) If an incorporated body has a common seal, a document may be executed by the body by the affixing of its common seal.

(3) Whether or not it has a common seal, a document may be executed by an incorporated body either—

(a) by being signed by a majority of the trustees of the relevant charity and expressed (in whatever form of words) to be executed by the body; or

(b) by being executed in pursuance of an authority given under subsection (4) below.

(4) For the purposes of subsection (3)(b) above the trustees of the relevant charity in the case of an incorporated body may, subject to the trusts of the charity, confer on any two or more of their number—

(a) a general authority, or

(b) an authority limited in such manner as the trustees think fit,

to execute in the name and on behalf of the body documents for giving effect to transactions to which the body is a party.

(5) An authority under subsection (4) above—

(a) shall suffice for any document if it is given in writing or by resolution of a meeting of the trustees of the relevant charity, notwithstanding the want of any formality that would be required in giving an authority apart from that subsection;

(b) may be given so as to make the powers conferred exercisable by any of the trustees, or may be restricted to named persons or in any other way;

(c) subject to any restriction, and until it is revoked, shall, notwithstanding any change in the trustees of the relevant charity, have effect as a continuing authority given by the trustees from time to time of the charity and exercisable by such trustees.

(6) In any authority under subsection (4) above to execute a document in the name and on behalf of an incorporated body there shall, unless the contrary intention appears, be implied authority also to execute it for the body in the name and on behalf of the official custodian or of any other person, in any case in which the trustees could do so.

(7) A document duly executed by an incorporated body which makes it clear on its face that it is intended by the person or persons making it to be a deed has effect, upon delivery, as a deed; and it shall be presumed, unless a contrary intention is proved, to be delivered upon its being so executed.

(8) In favour of a purchaser a document shall be deemed to have been duly executed by such a body if it purports to be signed—

(a) by a majority of the trustees of the relevant charity, or

(b) by such of the trustees of the relevant charity as are authorised by the trustees of that charity to execute it in the name and on behalf of the body,

and, where the document makes it clear on its face that it is intended by the person or persons making it to be a deed, it shall be deemed to have been delivered upon its being executed.

For this purpose "purchaser" means a purchaser in good faith for valuable consideration and includes a lessee, mortgagee or other person who for valuable consideration acquires an interest in property.

Power of Commissioners to dissolve incorporated body

56–060 **61.**—(1) Where the Commissioners are satisfied—

(a) that an incorporated body has no assets or does not operate, or

(b) that the relevant charity in the case of an incorporated body has ceased to exist, or

(c) that the institution previously constituting, or treated by them as constituting, any such charity has ceased to be, or (as the case may be) was not at the time of the body's incorporation, a charity, or

(d) that the purposes of the relevant charity in the case of an incorporated body have been achieved so far as is possible or are in practice incapable of being achieved,

they may of their own motion make an order dissolving the body as from such date as is specified in the order.

(2) Where the Commissioners are satisfied, on the application of the trustees of the relevant charity in the case of an incorporated body, that it would be in the interests of the charity for that body to be dissolved, the Commissioners may make an order dissolving the body as from such date as is specified in the order.

(3) Subject to subsection (4) below, an order made under this section with respect to an incorporated body shall have the effect of vesting in the trustees of the relevant charity, in trust for that charity, all property for the time being vested—

(a) in the body, or

(b) in any other person (apart from the official custodian),

in trust for that charity.

(4) If the Commissioners so direct in the order—

(a) all or any specified part of that property shall, instead of vesting in the trustees of the relevant charity, vest—

(i) in a specified person as trustee for, or nominee of, that charity, or

(ii) in such persons (other than the trustees of the relevant charity as may be specified;

(b) any specified investments, or any specified class or description of investments, held by any person in trust for the relevant charity, shall be transferred—

(i) to the trustees of that charity, or

(ii) to any such person or persons as is or are mentioned in paragraph (a)(i) or (ii) above;

and for this purpose "specified" means specified by the Commissioners in the order.

(5) Where an order to which this subsection applies is made with respect to an incorporated body—

(a) any rights or liabilities of the body shall become rights or liabilities of the trustees of the relevant charity; and

(b) any legal proceedings that might have been continued or commenced by or against the body may be continued or commenced by or against those trustees.

(6) Subsection (5) above applies to any order under this section by virtue of which—

(a) any property vested as mentioned in subsection (3) above is vested—

(i) in the trustees of the relevant charity, or

(ii) in any person as trustee for, or nominee of, that charity; or

(b) any investments held by any person in trust for the relevant charity are required to be transferred—

(i) to the trustees of that charity, or

(ii) to any person as trustee for, or nominee of, that charity.

(7) Any order made by the Commissioners under this section may be varied or revoked by a further order so made.

Interpretation of Part VII

62. In this Part of this Act— **56–061**

"incorporated body" means a body incorporated under section 50 above;

"the relevant charity", in relation to an incorporated body, means the charity the trustees of which have been incorporated as that body;
"the trustees", in relation to a charity, means the charity trustees.

PART VIII

CHARITABLE COMPANIES

Winding up

56–062 **63.**—(1) Where a charity may be wound up by the High Court under the Insolvency Act 1986, a petition for it to be wound up under that Act by any court in England or Wales having jurisdiction may be presented by the Attorney-General, as well as by any person authorised by that Act.

(2) Where a charity may be so wound up by the High Court, such a petition may also be presented by the Commissioners if, at any time after they have instituted an inquiry under section 8 above with respect to the charity, they are satisfied as mentioned in section 18(1)(a) or (b) above.

(3) Where a charitable company is dissolved, the Commissioners may make an application under section 651 of the Companies Act 1985 (power of court to declare dissolution of company void) for an order to be made under that section with respect to the company; and for this purpose subsection (1) of that section shall have effect in relation to a charitable company as if the reference to the liquidator of the company included a reference to the Commissioners.

(4) Where a charitable company's name has been struck off the register of companies under section 652 of the Companies Act 1985 (power of registrar to strike defunct company off register), the Commissioners may make an application under section 653(2) of that Act (objection to striking off by person aggrieved) for an order restoring the company's name to that register; and for this purpose section 653(2) shall have effect in relation to a charitable company as if the reference to any such person aggrieved as is there mentioned included a reference to the Commissioners.

(5) The powers exercisable by the Commissioners by virtue of this section shall be exercisable by them of their own motion, but shall be exercisable only with the agreement of the Attorney-General on each occasion.

(6) In this section "charitable company" means a company which is a charity.

Alteration of objects clause

56–063 **64.**—(1) Where a charity is a company or other body corporate having power to alter the instruments establishing or regulating it as a body corporate, no exercise of that power which has the effect of the body ceasing to be a charity shall be valid so as to affect the application of—

(a) any property acquired under any disposition or agreement previously made otherwise than for full consideration in money or money's worth, or any property representing property so acquired,
(b) any property representing income which has accrued before the alteration is made, or
(c) the income from any such property as aforesaid.

(2) Where a charity is a company, any alteration by it—
(a) of the objects clause in its memorandum of association, or
(b) of any other provision in its memorandum of association, or any provision in its articles of association, which is a provision directing or restricting the manner in which property of the company may be used or applied,

is ineffective without the prior written consent of the Commissioners.

(3) Where a company has made any such alteration in accordance with subsection (2) above and—
(a) in connection with the alteration is required by virtue of—
(i) section 6(1) of the Companies Act 1985 (delivery of documents following alteration of objects), or
(ii) that provision as applied by section 17(3) of that Act (alteration of condition in memorandum which could have been contained in articles),
to deliver to the registrar of companies a printed copy of its memorandum, as altered, or
(b) is required by virtue of section 380(1) of that Act (registration etc. of resolutions and agreements) to forward to the registrar a printed or other copy of the special resolution effecting the alteration,

the copy so delivered or forwarded by the company shall be accompanied by a copy of the Commissioners' consent.

(4) Section 6(3) of that Act (offences) shall apply to any default by a company in complying with subsection (3) above as it applies to any such default as is mentioned in that provision.

Invalidity of certain transactions

65.—(1) Sections 35 and 35A of the Companies Act 1985 (capacity of company not limited by its memorandum; power of directors to bind company) do not apply to the acts of a company which is a charity except in favour of a person who— **56–064**
(a) gives full consideration in money or money's worth in relation to the act in question, and
(b) does not know that the act is not permitted by the company's memorandum or, as the case may be, is beyond the powers of the directors,

or who does not know at the time the act is done that the company is a charity.

(2) However, where such a company purports to transfer or grant an interest in property, the fact that the act was not permitted by the company's memorandum or, as the case may be, that the directors in connection with the act exceeded any limitation on their powers under the company's constitution, does not affect the title of a person who subsequently acquires the property or any interest in it for full consideration without actual notice of any such circumstances affecting the validity of the company's act.

(3) In any proceedings arising out of subsection (1) above the burden of proving—
(a) that a person knew that an act was not permitted by the company's memorandum or was beyond the powers of the directors, or
(b) that a person knew that the company was a charity,

lies on the person making that allegation.

(4) Where a company is a charity, the ratification of an act under section 35(3) of the Companies Act 1985, or the ratification of a transaction to which section 322A of that Act applies (invalidity of certain transactions to which directors or

their associates are parties), is ineffective without the prior written consent of the Commissioners.

Requirement of consent of Commissioners to certain acts

56–065 **66.**—(1) Where a company is a charity—

(a) any approval given by the company for the purposes of any of the provisions of the Companies Act 1985 specified in subsection (2) below, and

(b) any affirmation by it for the purposes of section 322(2)(c) of that Act (affirmation of voidable arrangements under which assets are acquired by or from a director or person connected with him),

is ineffective without the prior written consent of the Commissioners.

(2) The provisions of the Companies Act 1985 referred to in subsection (1)(a) above are—

(a) section 312 (payment to director in respect of loss of office or retirement);

(b) section 313(1) (payment to director in respect of loss of office or retirement made in connection with transfer of undertaking or property of company);

(c) section 319(3) (incorporation in director's service contract of term whereby his employment will or may continue for a period of more than five years);

(d) section 320(1) (arrangement whereby assets are acquired by or from director or person connected with him);

(e) section 337(3)(a) (provision of funds to meet certain expenses incurred by director).

Name to appear on correspondence etc.

56–066 **67.** Section 30(7) of the Companies Act 1985 (exemption from requirements relating to publication of name etc.) shall not, in its application to any company which is a charity, have the effect of exempting the company from the requirements of section 349(1) of that Act (company's name to appear in its correspondence etc.).

Status to appear on correspondence etc.

56–067 **68.**—(1) Where a company is a charity and its name does not include the word "charity" or the word "charitable" [then, subject to subsection (1A)][40], the fact that the company is a charity shall be stated […][41] in legible characters—

(a) in all business letters of the company,

(b) in all its notices and other official publications,

(c) in all bills of exchange, promissory notes, endorsements, cheques and orders for money or goods purporting to be signed on behalf of the company,

(d) in all conveyances purporting to be executed by the company, and

(e) in all bills rendered by it and in all its invoices, receipts, and letters of credit.

[40] Words inserted by the Welsh Language Act 1993, s.33(1), (2)(a).
[41] Words repealed by the Welsh Language Act 1993, ss.33(1), (2)(b), 35, Sched. 2.

[(1A) Where a company's name includes the word "elusen" or the word "elusennol" (the Welsh equivalents of the words "charity" and "charitable"), subsection (1) above shall not apply in relation to any document which is wholly in Welsh.

(1B) The statement required by subsection (1) above shall be in English, except that, in the case of a document which is otherwise wholly in Welsh, the statement may be in Welsh if it consists of or includes the word "elusen" or the word "elusennol".][42]

(2) In subsection (1)(d) above "conveyance" means any instrument creating, transferring, varying or extinguishing an interest in land.

(3) Subsections (2) to (4) of section 349 of the Companies Act 1985 (offences in connection with failure to include required particulars in business letters etc.) shall apply in relation to a contravention of subsection (1) above, taking the reference in subsection (3)(b) of that section to a bill of parcels as a reference to any such bill as is mentioned in subsection (1)(e) above.

Investigation of accounts

69.—(1) In the case of a charity which is a company the Commissioners may by order require that the condition and accounts of the charity for such period as they think fit shall be investigated and audited by an auditor appointed by them, being a person eligible for appointment as a company auditor under section 25 of the Companies Act 1989. **56–068**

(2) An auditor acting under subsection (1) above—

(a) shall have a right of access to all books, accounts and documents relating to the charity which are in the possession or control of the charity trustees or to which the charity trustees have access;

(b) shall be entitled to require from any charity trustee, past or present, and from any past or present officer or employee of the charity such information and explanation as he thinks necessary for the perfomance of his duties;

(c) shall at the conclusion or during the progress of the audit make such reports to the Commissioners about the audit or about the accounts or affairs of the charity as he thinks the case requires, and shall send a copy of any such report to the charity trustees.

(3) The expenses of any audit under subsection (1) above, including the remuneration of the auditor, shall be paid by the Commissioners.

(4) If any person fails to afford an auditor any facility to which he is entitled under subsection (2) above the Commissioners may by order give to that person or to the charity trustees for the time being such directions as the Commissioners think appropriate for securing that the default is made good.

Part IX

Miscellaneous

70–71. [*Repealed by the Trustee Act 2000, s.40(1), (3), Sched. 2, Pt. I, para. 2(1), Sched. 4, Pt. I.*]

[42] subss. (1A) and (1B) inserted by the Welsh Language Act 1993, s.33(1), (3).

Disqualification for acting as charity trustee

Persons disqualified for being trustees of a charity

56–069 **72.**—(1) Subject to the following provisions of this section, a person shall be disqualified for being a charity trustee or trustee for a charity if—

(a) he has been convicted of any offence involving dishonesty or deception;

(b) he has been adjudged bankrupt or sequestration of his estate has been awarded and (in either case) he has not been discharged;

(c) he has made a composition or arrangement with, or granted a trust deed for, his creditors and has not been discharged in respect of it;

(d) he has been removed from the office of charity trustee or trustee for a charity by an order made—

(i) by the Commissioners under section 18(2)(i) above, or

(ii) by the Commissioners under section 20(1A)(i) of the Charities Act 1960 (power to act for protection of charities) or under section 20(1)(i) of that Act (as in force before the commencement of section 8 of the Charities Act 1992), or

(iii) by the High Court,

on the grounds of any misconduct or mismanagement in the administration of the charity for which he was responsible or to which he was privy, or which he by his conduct contributed to or facilitated;

(e) he has been removed, under section 7 of the Law Reform (Miscellaneous Provisions) (Scotland) Act 1990 (powers of Court of Session to deal with management of charities), from being concerned in the management or control of any body;

(f) he is subject to a disqualification order [or disqualification undertaking][43] under the Company Directors Disqualification Act 1986 [to a disqualification order under Part II of the Companies (Northern Ireland) Order 1989][44] or to an order made under section 429(2)(b) of the Insolvency Act 1986 (failure to pay under county court administration order).

(2) In subsection (1) above—

(a) paragraph (a) applies whether the conviction occurred before or after the commencement of that subsection, but does not apply in relation to any conviction which is a spent conviction for the purposes of the Rehabilitation of Offenders Act 1974;

(b) paragraph (b) applies whether the adjudication of bankruptcy or the sequestration occurred before or after the commencement of that subsection;

(c) paragraph (c) applies whether the composition or arrangement was made, or the trust deed was granted, before or after the commencement of that subsection; and

(d) paragraphs (d) to (f) apply in relation to orders made and removals effected before or after the commencement of that subsection.

(3) Where (apart from this subsection) a person is disqualified under subsection (1)(b) above for being a charity trustee or trustee for any charity which is a company, he shall not be so disqualified if leave has been granted under section 11 of the Company Directors Disqualification Act 1986 (undischarged bankrupts) for him to act as director of the charity; and similarly

[43] Words inserted by the Insolvency Act 2000, s.8, Sched. 4, Pt. II, para. 18(a).
[44] Words inserted by the Insolvency Act 2000, s.8, Sched. 4, Pt. II, para. 18(a).

a person shall not be disqualified under subsection (1)(f) above for being a charity trustee or trustee for such a charity if—

[(a) in the case of a person subject to a disqualification order or disqualification undertaking under the Company Directors Disqualification Act 1986, leave for the purposes of section 1(1)(a) or 1A(1)(a) of that Act has been granted for him to act as director of the charity,

(aa) in the case of a person subject to a disqualification order under Part II of the Companies (Northern Ireland) Order 1989, leave has been granted by the High Court in Northern Ireland for him to act as director of the charity][45]

(b) in the case of a person subject to an order under section 429(2)(b) of the Insolvency Act 1986, leave has been granted by the court which made the order for him to so act.

(4) The Commissioners may, on the application of any person disqualified under subsection (1) above, waive his disqualification either generally or in relation to a particular charity or a particular class of charities; but no such waiver may be granted in relation to any charity which is a company if—

(a) the person concerned is for the time being prohibited, by virtue of—

(i) a disqualification order [or disqualification undertaking][46] under the Company Directors Disqualification Act 1986, or

(ii) section 11(1) [12(2) or 12A][47] of that Act (undischarged bankrupts; failure to pay under county court administration order [Northern Irish disqualification orders][48]),

from acting as director of the charity; and

(b) leave has not been granted for him to act as director of any other company.

(5) Any waiver under subsection (4) above shall be notified in writing to the person concerned.

(6) For the purposes of this section the Commissioners shall keep, in such manner as they think fit, a register of all persons who have been removed from office as mentioned in subsection (1)(d) above either—

(a) by an order of the Commissioners made before or after the commencement of subsection (1) above, or

(b) by an order of the High Court made after the commencement of section 45(1) of the Charities Act 1992;

and, where any person is so removed from office by an order of the High Court, the court shall notify the Commissioners of his removal.

(7) The entries in the register kept under subsection (6) above shall be available for public inspection in legible form at all reasonable times.

Person acting as charity trustee while disqualified

73.—(1) Subject to subsection (2) below, any person who acts as a charity trustee or trustee for a charity while he is disqualified for being such a trustee by virtue of section 72 above shall be guilty of an offence and liable— **56–070**

[45] Paras (a) and (aa) substituted (for para. (a)) by the Insolvency Act 2000, s.8, Sched. 4, Pt. II, para. 18(b).
[46] Words inserted by the Insolvency Act 2000, s.8, Sched. 4, Pt. II, para. 18(c)(i).
[47] Words substituted by the Insolvency Act 2000, s.8, Sched. 4, Pt. II, para. 18(c)(ii).
[48] Words inserted by the Insolvency Act 2000, s.8, Sched. 4, Pt. II, para. 18(c)(ii).

(a) on summary conviction, to imprisonment for a term not exceeding six months or to a fine not exceeding the statutory maximum, or both;
(b) on conviction on indictment, to imprisonment for a term not exceeding two years or to a fine, or both.

(2) Subsection (1) above shall not apply where—
(a) the charity concerned is a company; and
(b) the disqualified person is disqualified by virtue only of paragraph (b) or (f) of section 72(1) above.

(3) Any acts done as charity trustee or trustee for a charity by a person disqualified for being such a trustee by virtue of section 72 above shall not be invalid by reason only of that disqualification.

(4) Where the Commissioners are satisfied—
(a) that any person has acted as charity trustee or trustee for a charity (other than an exempt charity) while disqualified for being such a trustee by virtue of section 72 above, and
(b) that, while so acting, he has received from the charity any sums by way of remuneration or expenses, or any benefit in kind, in connection with his acting as charity trustee or trustee for the charity,

they may by order direct him to repay to the charity the whole or part of any such sums, or (as the case may be) to pay to the charity the whole or part of the monetary value (as determined by them) of any such benefit.

(5) Subsection (4) above does not apply to any sums received by way of remuneration or expenses in respect of any time when the person concerned was not disqualified for being a charity trustee or trustee for the charity.

Small charities

Power to transfer all property, modify objects etc.

56–071 **74.**—(1) This section applies to a charity if—
(a) its gross income in its last financial year did not exceed £5,000, and
(b) it does not hold any land on trusts which stipulate that the land is to be used for the purposes, or any particular purposes, of the charity,

and it is neither an exempt charity nor a charitable company.

(2) Subject to the following provisions of this section, the charity trustees of a charity to which this section applies may resolve for the purposes of this section—
(a) that all the property of the charity should be transferred to such other charity as is specified in the resolution, being either a registered charity or a charity which is not required to be registered;
(b) that all the property of the charity should be divided, in such manner as is specified in the resolution, between such two or more other charities as are so specified, being in each case either a registered charity or a charity which is not required to be registered;
(c) that the trusts of the charity should be modified by replacing all or any of the purposes of the charity with such other purposes, being in law charitable, as are specified in the resolution;
(d) that any provision of the trusts of the charity—
  (i) relating to any of the powers exercisable by the charity trustees in the administration of the charity, or
  (ii) regulating the procedure to be followed in any respect in connection with its administration,

should be modified in such manner as is specified in the resolution.

(3) Any resolution passed under subsection (2) above must be passed by a majority of not less than two-thirds of such charity trustees as vote on the resolution.

(4) The charity trustees of a charity to which this section applies ("the transferor charity") shall not have power to pass a resolution under subsection (2)(a) or (b) above unless they are satisfied—

(a) that the existing purposes of the transferor charity have ceased to be conducive to a suitable and effective application of the charity's resources; and

(b) that the purposes of the charity or charities specified in the resolution are as similar in character to the purposes of the transferor charity as is reasonably practicable;

and before passing the resolution they must have received from the charity trustees of the charity, or (as the case may be) of each of the charities, specified in the resolution written confirmation that those trustees are willing to accept a transfer of property under this section.

(5) The charity trustees of any such charity shall not have power to pass a resolution under subsection (2)(c) above unless they are satisfied—

(a) that the existing purposes of the charity (or, as the case may be, such of them as it is proposed to replace) have ceased to be conducive to a suitable and effective application of the charity's resources; and

(b) that the purposes specified in the resolution are as similar in character to those existing purposes as is practical in the circumstances.

(6) Where charity trustees have passed a resolution under subsection (2) above, they shall—

(a) give public notice of the resolution in such manner as they think reasonable in the circumstances; and

(b) send a copy of the resolution to the Commissioners, together with a statement of their reasons for passing it.

(7) The Commissioners may, when considering the resolution, require the charity trustees to provide additional information or explanation—

(a) as to the circumstances in and by reference to which they have determined to act under this section, or

(b) relating to their compliance with this section in connection with the resolution;

and the Commissioners shall take into account any representations made to them by persons appearing to them to be interested in the charity where those representations are made within the period of six weeks beginning with the date when the Commissioners receive a copy of the resolution by virtue of subsection (6)(b) above.

(8) Where the Commissioners have so received a copy of a resolution from any charity trustees and it appears to them that the trustees have complied with this section in connection with the resolution, the Commissioners shall, within the period of three months beginning with the date when they receive the copy of the resolution, notify the trustees in writing either—

(a) that the Commissioners concur with the resolution; or

(b) that they do not concur with it.

(9) Where the Commissioners so notify their concurrence with the resolution, then—

(a) if the resolution was passed under subsection (2)(a) or (b) above, the charity trustees shall arrange for all the property of the transferor charity to be transferred in accordance with the resolution and on terms that any property so transferred—

(i) shall be held and applied by the charity to which it is transferred ("the transferee charity") for the purposes of that charity, but

(ii) shall, as property of the transferee charity, nevertheless be subject to any restrictions on expenditure to which it is subject as property of the transferor charity,

and those trustees shall arrange for it to be so transferred by such date as may be specified in the notification; and

(b) if the resolution was passed under subsection (2)(c) or (d) above, the trusts of the charity shall be deemed, as from such date as may be specified in the notification, to have been modified in accordance with the terms of the resolution.

(10) For the purpose of enabling any property to be transferred to a charity under this section, the Commissioners shall have power, at the request of the charity trustees of that charity, to make orders vesting any property of the transferor charity—

(a) in the charity trustees of the first mentioned charity or in any trustee for that charity, or

(b) in any other person nominated by those charity trustees to hold the property in trust for that charity.

(11) The Secretary of State may by order amend subsection (1) above by substituting a different sum for the sum for the time being specified there.

(12) In this section—

(a) "charitable company" means a charity which is a company or other body corporate; and

(b) references to the transfer of property to a charity are references to its transfer—

(i) to the charity trustees, or

(ii) to any trustee for the charity, or

(iii) to a person nominated by the charity trustees to hold it in trust for the charity,

as the charity trustees may determine.

Power to spend capital

56–072 **75.**—(1) This section applies to a charity if—

(a) it has a permanent endowment which does not consist of or comprise any land, and

(b) its gross income in its last financial year did not exceed £1,000,

and it is neither an exempt charity nor a charitable company.

(2) Where the charity trustees of a charity to which this section applies are of the opinion that the property of the charity is too small, in relation to its purposes, for any useful purpose to be achieved by the expenditure of income alone, they may resolve for the purposes of this section that the charity ought to be freed from the restrictions with respect to expenditure of capital to which its permanent endowment is subject.

(3) Any resolution passed under subsection (2) above must be passed by a majority of not less than two-thirds of such charity trustees as vote on the resolution.

(4) Before passing such a resolution the charity trustees must consider whether any reasonable possibility exists of effecting a transfer or division of all the charity's property under section 74 above (disregarding any such transfer or

division as would, in their opinion, impose on the charity an unacceptable burden of costs).

(5) Where charity trustees have passed a resolution under subsection (2) above, they shall—

(a) give public notice of the resolution in such manner as they think reasonable in the circumstances; and

(b) send a copy of the resolution to the Commissioners, together with a statement of their reasons for passing it.

(6) The Commissioners may, when considering the resolution, require the charity trustees to provide additional information or explanation—

(a) as to the circumstances in and by reference to which they have determined to act under this section, or

(b) relating to their compliance with this section in connection with the resolution;

and the Commissioners shall take into account any representations made to them by persons appearing to them to be interested in the charity where those representations are made within the period of six weeks beginning with the date when the Commissioners receive a copy of the resolution by virtue of subsection (5)(b) above.

(7) Where the Commissioners have so received a copy of a resolution from any charity trustees and it appears to them that the trustees have complied with this section in connection with the resolution, the Commissioners shall, within the period of three months beginning with the date when they receive the copy of the resolution, notify the trustees in writing either—

(a) that the Commissioners concur with the resolution; or

(b) that they do not concur with it.

(8) Where the Commissioners so notify their concurrence with the resolution, the charity trustees shall have, as from such date as may be specified in the notification, power by virtue of this section to expend any property of the charity without regard to any such restrictions as are mentioned in subsection (2) above.

(9) The Secretary of State may by order amend subsection (1) above by substituting a different sum for the sum for the time being specified there.

(10) In this section "charitable company" means a charity which is a company or other body corporate.

. . . . . .

Part X

Supplementary

Construction of references to a "charity" or to particular classes of charity

96.—(1) In this Act, except in so far as the context otherwise requires— **56–073**

"charity" means any institution, corporate or not, which is established for charitable purposes and is subject to the control of the High Court in the exercise of the court's jurisdiction with respect to charities;

"ecclesiastical charity" has the same meaning as in the Local Government Act 1894;

"exempt charity" means (subject to section 24(8) above) a charity comprised in Schedule 2 to this Act;

"local charity" means, in relation to any area, a charity established for purposes which are by their nature or by the trusts of the charity directed wholly or mainly to the benefit of that area or of part of it;

"parochial charity" means, in relation to any parish or (in Wales) community, a charity the benefits of which are, or the separate distribution of the benefits of which is, confined to inhabitants of the parish or community, or of a single ancient ecclesiastical parish which included that parish or community or part of it, or of an area consisting of that parish or community with not more than four neighbouring parishes or communities.

(2) The expression "charity" is not in this Act applicable—

(a) to any ecclesiastical corporation (that is to say, any corporation in the Church of England, whether sole or aggregate, which is established for spiritual purposes) in respect of the corporate property of the corporation, except to a corporation aggregate having some purposes which are not ecclesiastical in respect of its corporate property held for those purposes; or

(b) to any Diocesan Board of Finance [(or any subsidiary thereof)][49] within the meaning of the Endowments and Glebe Measure 1976 for any diocese in respect of the diocesan glebe land of that diocese within the meaning of that Measure; or

(c) to any trust of property for purposes for which the property has been consecrated.

(3) A charity shall be deemed for the purposes of this Act to have a permanent endowment unless all property held for the purposes of the charity may be expended for those purposes without distinction between capital and income, and in this Act "permanent endowment" means, in relation to any charity, property held subject to a restriction on its being expended for the purposes of the charity.

(4) References in this Act to a charity whose income from all sources does not in aggregate amount to more than a specified amount shall be construed—

(a) by reference to the gross revenues of the charity, or

(b) if the Commissioners so determine, by reference to the amount which they estimate to be the likely amount of those revenues,

but without (in either case) bringing into account anything for the yearly value of land occupied by the charity apart from the pecuniary income (if any) received from that land; and any question as to the application of any such reference to a charity shall be determined by the Commissioners, whose decision shall be final.

(5) The Commissioners may direct that for all or any of the purposes of this Act an institution established for any special purposes of or in connection with a charity (being charitable purposes) shall be treated as forming part of that charity or as forming a distinct charity.

[(6) The Commissioners may direct that for all or any of the purposes of this Act two or more charities having the same charity trustees shall be treated as a single charity.][50]

[49] Words inserted by the Church of England (Miscellaneous Provisions) Measure 2000, s.11.
[50] subs. (6) added by the Charities (Amendment) Act 1995, s.1.

General interpretation

97.—(1) In this Act, except in so far as the context otherwise requires— **56–074**

"charitable purposes" means purposes which are exclusively charitable according to the law of England and Wales;

"charity trustees" means the persons having the general control and management of the administration of a charity;

"the Commissioners" means the Charity Commissioners for England and Wales;

"company" means a company formed and registered under the Companies Act 1985 or to which the provisions of that Act apply as they apply to such a company;

"the court" means the High Court and, within the limits of its jurisdiction, any other court in England and Wales having a jurisdiction in respect of charities concurrent (within any limit of area or amount) with that of the High Court, and includes any judge or officer of the court exercising the jurisdiction of the court;

"financial year"—

(a) in relation to a charity which is a company, shall be construed in accordance with section 223 of the Companies Act 1985; and

(b) in relation to any other charity, shall be construed in accordance with regulations made by virtue of section 42(2) above;

but this definition is subject to the transitional provisions in section 99(4) below and Part II of Schedule 8 to this Act;

"gross income", in relation to charity, means its gross recorded income from all sources including special trusts;

"independent examiner", in relation to a charity, means such a person as is mentioned in section 43(3)(a) above;

"institution" includes any trust or undertaking;

"the official custodian" means the official custodian for charities;

"permanent endowment" shall be construed in accordance with section 96(3) above;

"the register" means the register of charities kept under section 3 above and "registered" shall be construed accordingly;

"special trust" means property which is held and administered by or on behalf of a charity for any special purposes of the charity, and is so held and administered on separate trusts relating only to that property but a special trust shall not, by itself, constitute a charity for the purposes of Part VI of this Act;

"trusts" in relation to a charity, means the provisions establishing it as a charity and regulating its purposes and administration, whether those provisions take effect by way of trust or not, and in relation to other institutions has a corresponding meaning.

(2) In this Act, except in so far as the context otherwise requires, "document" includes information recorded in any form, and, in relation to information recorded otherwise than in legible form—

(a) any reference to its production shall be construed as a reference to the furnishing of a copy of it in legible form; and

(b) any reference to the furnishing of a copy of, or extract from, it shall accordingly be construed as a reference to the furnishing of a copy of, or extract from, it in legible form.

(3) No vesting or transfer of any property in pursuance of any provision of Part IV or IX of this Act shall operate as a breach of a covenant or condition against alienation or give rise to a forfeiture.

SCHEDULES

. . . .

Sections 3 and 96

SCHEDULE 2

Exempt Charities

The following institutions, so far as they are charities, are exempt charities within the meaning of this Act, that is to say—

(a) any institution which, if the Charities Act 1960 had not been passed, would be exempted from the powers and jurisdiction, under the Charitable Trusts Acts 1853 to 1939, of the Commissioners or Minister of Education (apart from any power of the Commissioners or Minister to apply those Acts in whole or in part to charities otherwise exempt) by the terms of any enactment not contained in those Acts other than section 9 of the Places of Worship Registration Act 1855;

(b) the universities of Oxford, Cambridge, London, Durham and Newcastle, the colleges and halls in the universities of Oxford, Cambridge, Durham and Newcastle, Queen Mary and Westfield College in the University of London and the colleges of Winchester and Eton;

(c) any university, university college, or institution connected with a university or university college, which Her Majesty declares by Order in Council to be an exempt charity for the purposes of this Act;

[. . .][51]

[(da) the Qualifications and Curriculum Authority;][52]

[. . .][53]

[(f) the Qualifications, Curriculum and Assessment Authority for Wales;][54]

[. . .][55]

[. . .][56]

(i) a successor company to a higher education corporation (within the meaning of section 129(5) of the Education Reform Act 1988) at a time when an institution conducted by the company is for the time being designated under that section;

[. . .][57]

(k) the Board of Trustees of the Victoria and Albert Museum;

(l) the Board of Trustees of the Science Museum;

(m) the Board of Trustees of the Armouries;

(n) the Board of Trustees of the Royal Botanic Gardens, Kew;

(o) the Board of Trustees of the National Museums and Galleries on Merseyside;

(p) the trustees of the British Museum and the trustees of the Natural History Museum;

(q) the Board of Trustees of the National Gallery;

(r) the Board of Trustees of the Tate Gallery;

(s) the Board of Trustees of the National Portrait Gallery;

(t) the Board of Trustees of the Wallace Collection;

(u) the Trustees of the Imperial War Museum;

(v) the Trustees of the National Maritime Museum;

---

[51] Para. (d) repealed by the School Standards and Framework Act 1998, s.140(3), Sched. 31.

[52] Para. (da) substituted (for that inserted by the Education Act 1993, s.307(1), Sched. 19, para. 175 and the Education Act 1996, s.582(1), Sched. 37, para. 120(1), (2)) by the Education Act 1997, s.57(1), Sched. 7, para. 7(a).

[53] Para. (e) repealed by the Education Act 1993, s.307(3), Sched. 21, Pt. II and the Education Act 1996, s.582(2), Sched. 38, Pt. I.

[54] Para. (f) substituted by the Education Act 1997, s.57(1), Sched. 7, para. 7(b).

[55] Para. (g) repealed by the Education Act 1993, s.307(3), Sched. 21, Pt. II and the Education Act 1996, s.582(2), Sched. 38, Pt. I.

[56] Para. (h) repealed by the Teaching and Higher Education Act 1998, s.44(2), Sched. 4.

[57] Para. (j) repealed by the Teaching and Higher Education Act 1998, s.44(2), Sched. 4.

(w) any institution which is administered by or on behalf of an institution included above and is established for the general purposes of, or for any special purpose of or in connection with, the last-mentioned institution;
(x) the Church Commissioners and any institution which is administered by them;
(y) any registered society within the meaning of the Industrial and Provident Societies Act 1965 and any registered society or branch within the meaning of the Friendly Societies Act 1974;
(z) the Board of Governors of the Museum of London;
(za) the British Library Board.
[(zb) the National Lottery Charities Board.][58]

Law of Property (Miscellaneous Provisions) Act 1994

(1994 c. 36)

ARRANGEMENT OF SECTIONS

PART I

IMPLIED COVENANTS FOR TITLE

The covenants

[58] Para. (zb) added by the National Lottery Act 1993, s.37(2), Sched. 5, para. 12.

Part I

Implied covenants for title

The covenants

Covenants to be implied on a disposition of property

57–001 **1.**—(1) In an instrument effecting or purporting to effect a disposition of property there shall be implied on the part of the person making the disposition, whether or not the disposition is for valuable consideration, such of the covenants specified in sections 2 to 5 as are applicable to the disposition.

(2) Of those sections—

(a) sections 2, 3(1) and (2), 4 and 5 apply where dispositions are expressed to be made with full title guarantee; and

(b) sections 2, 3(3), 4 and 5 apply where dispositions are expressed to be made with limited title guarantee.

(3) Sections 2 to 4 have effect subject to section 6 (no liability under covenants in certain cases); and sections 2 to 5 have effect subject to section 8(1) (limitation or extension of covenants by instrument effecting the disposition).

(4) In this Part—

"disposition" includes the creation of a term of years;

"instrument" includes an instrument which is not a deed; and

"property" includes a thing in action, and any interest in real or personal property.

Right to dispose and further assurance

57–002 **2.**—(1) If the disposition is expressed to be made with full title guarantee or with limited title guarantee there shall be implied the following covenants—

(a) that the person making the disposition has the right (with the concurrence of any other person conveying the property) to dispose of the property as he purports to, and

(b) that that person will at his own cost do all that he reasonably can to give the person to whom he disposes of the property the title he purports to give.

(2) The latter obligation includes—

(a) in relation to a disposition of an interest in land the title to which is registered, doing all that he reasonably can to ensure that the person to whom the disposition is made is entitled to be registered as proprietor with at least the class of title registered immediately before the disposition; and

(b) in relation to a disposition of an interest in land the title to which is required to be registered by virtue of the disposition, giving all reasonable assistance fully to establish to the satisfaction of the Chief Land Registrar the right of the person to whom the disposition is made to registration as proprietor.

(3) In the case of a disposition of an existing legal interest in land, the following presumptions apply, subject to the terms of the instrument, in

ascertaining for the purposes of the covenants implied by this section what the person making the disposition purports to dispose of—

(a) where the title to the interest is registered, it shall be presumed that the disposition is of the whole of that interest;

(b) where the title to the interest is not registered, then—

(i) if it appears from the instrument that the interest is a leasehold interest, it shall be presumed that the disposition is of the property for the unexpired portion of the term of years created by the lease; and

(ii) in any other case, it shall be presumed that what is disposed of is the fee simple.

Charges, incumbrances and third party rights

3.—(1) If the disposition is expressed to be made with full title guarantee there shall be implied a covenant that the person making the disposition is disposing of the property free— **57–003**

(a) from all charges and incumbrances (whether monetary or not), and

(b) from all other rights exercisable by third parties,

other than any charges, incumbrances or rights which that person does not and could not reasonably be expected to know about.

(2) In its application to charges, incumbrances and other third party rights subsection (1) extends to liabilities imposed and rights conferred by or under any enactment, except to the extent that such liabilities and rights are, by reason of—

(a) being, at the time of the disposition, only potential liabilities and rights in relation to the property, or

(b) being liabilities and rights imposed or conferred in relation to property generally,

not such as to constitute defects in title.

(3) If the disposition is expressed to be made with limited title guarantee there shall be implied a covenant that the person making the disposition has not since the last disposition for value—

(a) charged or incumbered the property by means of any charge or incumbrance which subsists at the time when the disposition is made, or granted third party rights in relation to the property which so subsist, or

(b) suffered the property to be so charged or incumbered or subjected to any such rights,

and that he is not aware that anyone else has done so since the last disposition for value.

Validity of lease

4.—(1) Where the disposition is of leasehold land and is expressed to be made with full title guarantee or with limited title guarantee, the following covenants shall also be implied— **57–004**

(a) that the lease is subsisting at the time of the disposition, and

(b) that there is no subsisting breach of a condition or tenant's obligation, and nothing which at that time would render the lease liable to forfeiture.

(2) If the disposition is the grant of an underlease, the references to "the lease" in subsection (1) are references to the lease out of which the underlease is created.

Discharge of obligations where property subject to rentcharge or leasehold land

57–005 **5.**—(1) Where the disposition is a mortgage of property subject to a rentcharge, [of leasehold land or of a commonhold unit][1], and is expressed to be made with full title guarantee or with limited title guarantee, the following covenants shall also be implied.

(2) If the property is subject to a rentcharge, there shall be implied a covenant that the mortgagor will fully and promptly observe and perform all the obligations under the instrument creating the rentcharge that are for the time being enforceable with respect to the property by the owner of the rentcharge in his capacity as such.

(3) If the property is leasehold land, there shall be implied a covenant that the mortgagor will fully and promptly observe and perform all the obligations under the lease subject to the mortgage that are for the time being imposed on him in his capacity as tenant under the lease.

[(3A) If the property is a commonhold unit, there shall be implied a covenant that the mortgagor will fully and promptly observe and perform all the obligations under the commonhold community statement that are fir the time being imposed on him in his capacity as a unit-holder or as a joint unit-holder.][2]

[(4) In this section—

(a) "commonhold community statement", "commonhold unit", "joint unit-holder" and "unit-holder" have the same meanings as in the Commonhold and Leasehold Reform Act 2001, and

(b) "mortgage" includes charge, and "mortgagor" shall be construed accordingly.][3]

Effect of covenants

No liability under covenants in certain cases

57–006 **6.**—(1) The person making the disposition is not liable under the covenants implied by virtue of—

(a) section 2(1)(a) (right to dispose),

(b) section 3 (charges, incumbrances and third party rights), or

(c) section 4 (validity of lease),

in respect of any particular matter to which the disposition is expressly made subject.

(2) Furthermore that person is not liable under any of those covenants for anything (not falling within subsection (1))—

(a) which at the time of the disposition is within the actual knowledge, or

(b) which is a necessary consequence of facts that are then within the actual knowledge,

of the person to whom the disposition is made.

(3) For this purpose section 198 of the Law of Property Act 1925 (deemed notice by virtue of registration) shall be disregarded.

[(4) Moreover, where the disposition is of an interest the title to which is registered under the Land Registration Act 2002, that person is not liable under

[1] Words substituted by the Commonhold and Leasehold Reform Act 2002, s.68, Sched. 5, para. 7(1), (2).

[2] subs. (3A) inserted by the Commonhold and Leasehold Reform Act 2002, s.68, Sched. 5, para. 7(1), (3).

[3] subs. (4) substituted by the Commonhold and Leasehold Reform Act 2002, s.68, Sched. 5, para. 7(1), (4).

any of those covenants for anything (not falling within subsection (1) or (2)) which at the time of the disposition was entered in relation to that interest in the register of title under that Act.][4]

Annexation of benefit of covenants

7. The benefit of a covenant implied by virtue of this Part shall be annexed and incident to, and shall go with, the estate or interest of the person to whom the disposition is made, and shall be capable of being enforced by every person in whom that estate or interest is (in whole or in part) for the time being vested. **57–007**

Supplementary provisions

8.—(1) The operation of any covenant implied in an instrument by virtue of this Part may be limited or extended by a term of that instrument. **57–008**

(2) Sections 81 and 83 of the Law of Property Act 1925 (effect of covenant with two or more jointly; construction of implied covenants) apply to a covenant implied by virtue of this Part as they apply to a covenant implied by virtue of that Act.

(3) Where in an instrument effecting or purporting to effect a disposition of property a person is expressed to direct the disposition, this Part applies to him as if he were the person making the disposition.

(4) This Part has effect—

(a) where "gyda gwarant teitl llawn" is used instead of "with full title guarantee", and

(b) where "gyda gwarant teitl cyfyngedig" is used instead of "with limited title guarantee",

as it has effect where the English words are used.

Modifications of statutory forms

9.—(1) Where a form set out in an enactment, or in an instrument made under an enactment, includes words which (in an appropriate case) would have resulted in the implication of a covenant by virtue of section 76 of the Law of Property Act 1925, the form shall be taken to authorise instead the use of the words "with full title guarantee" or "with limited title guarantee" or their Welsh equivalent given in section 8(4). **57–009**

(2) This applies in particular to the forms set out in Schedule 1 to the Settled Land Act 1925 and Schedules 4 and 5 to the Law of Property Act 1925.

Transitional provisions

General saving for covenants in old form

10.—(1) Except as provided by section 11 below (cases in which covenants in old form implied on disposition after commencement), the following provisions, namely— **57–010**

(a) section 76 of the Law of Property Act 1925, and

[4] subs. (4) added by the Land Registration Act 2002, s.133, Sched. 11, para. 31(1), (2).

(b) section 24(1)(a) of the Land Registration Act 1925,

are repealed as regards dispositions of property made after the commencement of this Part.

(2) The repeal of those provisions by this Act accordingly does not affect the enforcement of a covenant implied by virtue of either of them on a disposition before the commencement of this Part.

Covenants in old form implied in certain cases

57–011 **11.**—(1) Section 76 of the Law of Property Act 1925 applies in relation to a disposition of property made after the commencement of this Part in pursuance of a contract entered into before commencement where—

(a) the contract contains a term providing for a disposition to which that section would have applied if the disposition had been made before commencement, and

(b) the existence of the contract and of that term is apparent on the face of the instrument effecting the disposition,

unless there has been an intervening disposition of the property expressed, in accordance with this Part, to be made with full title guarantee.

(2) Section 24(1)(a) of the Land Registration Act 1925 applies in relation to a disposition of a leasehold interest in land made after the commencement of this Part in pursuance of a contract entered into before commencement where—

(a) the covenant specified in that provision would have been implied on the disposition if it had been made before commencement, and

(b) the existence of the contract is apparent on the face of the instrument effecting the disposition,

unless there has been an intervening disposition of the leasehold interest expressed, in accordance with this Part, to be made with full title guarantee.

(3) In subsections (1) and (2) an "intervening disposition" means a disposition after the commencement of this Part to, or to a predecessor in title of, the person by whom the disposition in question is made.

(4) Where in order for subsection (1) or (2) to apply it is necessary for certain matters to be apparent on the face of the instrument effecting the disposition, the contract shall be deemed to contain an implied term that they should so appear.

Covenants in new form to be implied in other cases

57–012 **12.**—(1) This section applies to a contract for the disposition of property entered into before the commencement of this Part where the disposition is made after commencement and section 11 (cases in which covenants in old form to be implied) does not apply because there has been an intervening disposition expressed, in accordance with this Part, to be with full title guarantee.

(2) A contract which contains a term that the person making the disposition shall do so as beneficial owner shall be construed as requiring that person to do so by an instrument expressed to be made with full title guarantee.

(3) A contract which contains a term that the person making the disposition shall do so—

(a) as settlor, or

(b) as trustee or mortgagee or personal representative,

shall be construed as requiring that person to do so by an instrument expressed to be made with limited title guarantee.

(4) A contract for the disposition of a leasehold interest in land entered into at a date when the title to the leasehold interest was registered shall be construed as requiring the person making the disposition for which it provides to do so by an instrument expressed to be made with full title guarantee.

(5) Where this section applies and the contract provides that any of the covenants to be implied by virtue of section 76 of the Law of Property Act 1925 or section 24(1)(a) of the Land Registration Act 1925 shall be implied in a modified form, the contract shall be construed as requiring a corresponding modification of the covenants implied by virtue of this Part.

Application of transitional provisions in relation to options

13. For the purposes of sections 11 and 12 (transitional provisions: implication of covenants in old form in certain cases and new form in others) as they apply in relation to a disposition of property in accordance with an option granted before the commencement of this Part and exercised after commencement, the contract for the disposition shall be deemed to have been entered into on the grant of the option. **57–013**

PART II

MATTERS ARISING IN CONNECTION WITH DEATH

14. [*Substitutes the Administration of Estates Act 1925, s.9, ante, para. 10–008.*]

15. [*Amends the Land Charges Act 1972, ante, para. 31–001.*]

16. [*Amends the Administration of Estates Act 1925, s.2(2), ante, para. 10–002.*]

Notices affecting land: absence of knowledge of intended recipient's death

17.—(1) Service of a notice affecting land which would be effective but for the death of the intended recipient is effective despite his death if the person serving the notice has no reason to believe that he has died. **57–014**

(2) Where the person serving a notice affecting land has no reason to believe that the intended recipient has died, the proper address for the purposes of section 7 of the Interpretation Act 1978 (service of documents by post) shall be what would be the proper address apart from his death.

(3) The above provisions do not apply to a notice authorised or required to be served for the purposes of proceedings before—

(a) any court,
(b) any tribunal specified in Schedule 1 to the Tribunals and Inquiries Act 1992 (tribunals within general supervision of Council on Tribunals), or
(c) the Chief Land Registrar or [the Adjudicator to Her Majesty's Land Registry][5];

but this is without prejudice to the power to make provision in relation to such proceedings by rules of court, procedural rules within the meaning of section 8 of the Tribunals and Inquiries Act 1992 or rules under [the Land Registration Act 2002][6].

[5] Words substituted by the Land Registration Act 2002, s.133, Sched. 11. para. 31(1), (3).
[6] Words substituted by the Land Registration Act 2002, s.133, Sched. 11. para. 31(1), (3).

Notices affecting land: service on personal representatives before filing of grant

57–015 **18.**—(1) A notice affecting land which would have been authorised or required to be served on a person but for his death shall be sufficiently served before a grant of representation has been filed if—

(a) it is addressed to "The Personal Representatives of" the deceased (naming him) and left at or sent by post to his last known place of residence or business in the United Kingdom, and

(b) a copy of it, similarly addressed, is served on the Public Trustee.

(2) The reference in subsection (1) to the filing of a grant of representation is to the filing at the Principal Registry of the Family Division of the High Court of a copy of a grant of representation in respect of the deceased's estate or, as the case may be, the part of his estate which includes the land in question.

(3) The method of service provided for by this section is not available where provision is made—

(a) by or under any enactment, or

(b) by an agreement in writing,

requiring a different method of service, or expressly prohibiting the method of service provided for by this section, in the circumstances.

Functions of Public Trustee in relation to notices, etc.

57–016 **19.**—(1) The Public Trustee may give directions as to the office or offices at which documents may be served on him—

(a) by virtue of section 9 of the Administration of Estates Act 1925 (as substituted by section 14(1) above), or

(b) in pursuance of section 18(1)(b) above (service on Public Trustee of copy of certain notices affecting land);

and he shall publish such directions in such manner as he considers appropriate.

(2) The Lord Chancellor may by regulations make provision with respect to the functions of the Public Trustee in relation to such documents; and the regulations may make different provision in relation to different descriptions of document or different circumstances.

(3) The regulations may, in particular, make provision requiring the Public Trustee—

(a) to keep such documents for a specified period and thereafter to keep a copy or record of their contents in such form as may be specified;

(b) to keep such documents, copies and records available for inspection at such reasonable hours as may be specified; and

(c) to supply copies to any person on request.

In this subsection "specified" means specified by or under the regulations.

(4) Regulations under this section shall be made by statutory instrument which shall be subject to annulment in pursuance of a resolution of either House of Parliament.

(5) The following provisions of the Public Trustee Act 1906, namely—

(a) section 8(5) (payment of expenses out of money provided by Parliament), and

(b) section 9(1) [and (3)][7] (provisions as to fees),

apply in relation to the functions of the Public Trustee in relation to documents to which this section applies as in relation to his functions under that Act.

---

[7] Words substituted by the Public Trustee (Liability and Fees) Act 2002, s.2(4).

Landlord and Tenant (Covenants) Act 1995

(1995 c. 30)

Arrangement of Sections

Supplemental

Preliminary

Tenancies to which the Act applies

58–001 **1.**—(1) Sections 3 to 16 and 21 apply only to new tenancies.

(2) Sections 17 to 20 apply to both new and other tenancies.

(3) For the purposes of this section a tenancy is a new tenancy if it is granted on or after the date on which this Act comes into force otherwise than in pursuance of—

(a) an agreement entered into before that date, or

(b) an order of a court made before that date.

(4) Subsection (3) has effect subject to section 20(1) in the case of overriding leases granted under section 19.

(5) Without prejudice to the generality of subsection (3), that subsection applies to the grant of a tenancy where by virtue of any variation of a tenancy there is a deemed surrender and regrant as it applies to any other grant of a tenancy.

(6) Where a tenancy granted on or after the date on which this Act comes into force is so granted in pursuance of an option granted before that date, the tenancy shall be regarded for the purposes of subsection (3) as granted in pursuance of an agreement entered into before that date (and accordingly is not a new tenancy), whether or not the option was exercised before that date.

(7) In subsection (6) "option" includes right of first refusal.

Covenants to which the Act applies

58–002 **2.**—(1) This Act applies to a landlord covenant or a tenant covenant of a tenancy—

(a) whether or not the covenant has reference to the subject matter of tenancy, and

(b) whether the covenant is express, implied or imposed by law,

but does not apply to a covenant falling within subsection (2).

(2) Nothing in this Act affects any covenant imposed in pursuance of—

(a) section 35 or 155 of the Housing Act 1985 (covenants for repayment of discount on early disposals);

(b) paragraph 1 of Schedule 6A to that Act (covenants requiring redemption of landlord's share); or

(c) [section 11 or 13 of the Housing Act 1996 or][1] paragraph 1 or 3 of Schedule 2 to the Housing Associations Act 1985 (covenants for repaying of discount on early disposals or for restricting disposals).

[1] Words inserted by the Housing Act 1996 (Consequential Provisions) Order 1996 (S.I. 1996 No. 2325), art. 5, Sched. 2, para. 22.

Transmission of covenants

Transmission of benefit and burden of covenants

3.—(1) The benefit and burden of all landlord and tenant covenants of a tenancy— **58–003**

(a) shall be annexed and incident to the whole, and to each and every part, of the premises demised by the tenancy and of the reversion in them, and

(b) shall in accordance with this section pass on an assignment of the whole or any part of those premises or of the reversion in them.

(2) Where the assignment is by the tenant under the tenancy, then as from the assignment the assignee—

(a) becomes bound by the tenant covenants of the tenancy except to the extent that—

(i) immediately before the assignment they did not bind the assignor, or

(ii) they fall to be complied with in relation to any demised premises not comprised in the assignment; and

(b) becomes entitled to the benefit of the landlord covenants of the tenancy except to the extent that they fall to be complied with in relation to any such premises.

(3) Where the assignment is by the landlord under the tenancy, then as from the assignment the assignee—

(a) becomes bound by the landlord covenants of the tenancy except to the extent that—

(i) immediately before the assignment they did not bind the assignor, or

(ii) they fall to be complied with in relation to any demised premises not comprised in the assignment; and

(b) becomes entitled to the benefit of the tenant covenants of the tenancy except to the extent that they fall to be complied with in relation to any such premises.

(4) In determining for the purposes of subsection (2) or (3), whether any covenant bound the assignor immediately before the assignment, any waiver or release of the covenant which (in whatever terms) is expressed to be personal to the assignor shall be disregarded.

(5) Any landlord or tenant covenant of a tenancy which is restrictive of the user of land shall, as well as being capable of enforcement against an assignee, be capable of being enforced against any other person who is the owner or occupier of any demised premises to which the covenant relates, even though there is no express provision in the tenancy to that effect.

(6) Nothing in this section shall operate—

(a) in the case of a covenant which (in whatever terms) is expressed to be personal to any person, to make the covenant enforceable by or (as the case may be) against any other person; or

(b) to make a covenant enforceable against any person if, apart from this section, it would not be enforceable against him by reason of its not having been registered under the [Land Registration Act 2002][2] or the Land Charges Act 1972.

(7) To the extent that there remains in force any rule of law by virtue of which the burden of a covenant whose subject matter is not in existence at the time

[2] Words substituted by the Land Registration Act 2002, s.133, Sched. 11, para. 33(1), (2).

when it is made does not run with the land affected unless the covenantor covenants on behalf of himself and his assigns, that rule of law is hereby abolished in relation to tenancies.

Transmission of rights of re-entry

58–004 **4.** The benefit of a landlord's right of re-entry under a tenancy—

(a) shall be annexed and incident to the whole, and to each and every part, of the reversion in the premises demised by the tenancy, and

(b) shall pass on an assignment of the whole or any part of the reversion in those premises.

Release of covenants on assignment

Tenant released from covenants on assignment of tenancy

58–005 **5.**—(1) This section applies where a tenant assigns premises demised to him under a tenancy.

(2) If the tenant assigns the whole of the premises demised to him, he—

(a) is released from the tenant covenants of the tenancy, and

(b) ceases to be entitled to the benefit of the landlord covenants of the tenancy,

as from the assignment.

(3) If the tenant assigns part only of the premises demised to him, then as from the assignment he—

(a) is released from the tenant covenants of the tenancy, and

(b) ceases to be entitled to the benefit of the landlord covenants of the tenancy,

only to the extent that those covenants fall to be complied with in relation to that part of the demised premises.

(4) This section applies as mentioned in subsection (1) whether or not the tenant is tenant of the whole of the premises comprised in the tenancy.

Landlord may be released from covenants on assignment of reversion

58–006 **6.**—(1) This section applies where a landlord assigns the reversion in premises of which he is the landlord under a tenancy.

(2) If the landlord assigns the reversion in the whole of the premises of which he is the landlord—

(a) he may apply to be released from the landlord covenants of the tenancy in accordance with section 8; and

(b) if he is so released from all of those covenants, he ceases to be entitled to the benefit of the tenant covenants of the tenancy as from the assignment.

(3) If the landlord assigns the reversion in part only of the premises of which he is the landlord—

(a) he may apply to be so released from the landlord covenants of the tenancy to the extent that they fall to be complied with in relation to that part of those premises; and

(b) if he is, to that extent, so released from all of those covenants, then as from the assignment he ceases to be entitled to the benefit of the tenant covenants only to the extent that they fall to be complied with in relation to that part of those premises.

(4) This section applies as mentioned in subsection (1) whether or not the landlord is landlord of the whole of the premises comprised in the tenancy.

Former landlord may be released from covenants on assignment of reversion

7.—(1) This section applies where— **58–007**

(a) a landlord assigns the reversion in premises of which he is the landlord under a tenancy, and

(b) immediately before the assignment a former landlord of the premises remains bound by a landlord covenant of the tenancy ("the relevant covenant").

(2) If immediately before the assignment the former landlord does not remain the landlord of any other premises demised by the tenancy, he may apply to be released from the relevant covenant in accordance with section 8.

(3) In any other case the former landlord may apply to be so released from the relevant covenant to the extent that it falls to be complied with in relation to any premises comprised in the assignment.

(4) If the former landlord is so released from every landlord covenant by which he remained bound immediately before the assignment, he ceases to be entitled to the benefit of the tenant covenants of the tenancy.

(5) If the former landlord is so released from every such landlord covenant to the extent that it falls to be complied with in relation to any premises comprised in the assignment, he ceases to be entitled to the benefit of the tenant covenants of the tenancy to the extent that they fall to be so complied with.

(6) This section applies as mentioned in subsection (1)—

(a) whether or not the landlord making the assignment is landlord of the whole of the premises comprised in the tenancy; and

(b) whether or not the former landlord has previously applied (whether under section 6 or this section) to be released from the relevant covenant.

Procedure for seeking release from a covenant under section 6 or 7

8.—(1) For the purposes of section 6 or 7 an application for the release of a covenant to any extent is made by serving on the tenant, either before or within the period of four weeks beginning with the date of the assignment in question, a notice informing him of— **58–008**

(a) the proposed assignment or (as the case may be) the fact that the assignment has taken place, and

(b) the request for the covenant to be released to that extent.

(2) Where an application for the release of a covenant is made in accordance with subsection (1), the covenant is released to the extent mentioned in the notice if—

(a) the tenant does not, within the period of four weeks beginning with the day on which the notice is served, serve on the landlord or former landlord a notice in writing objecting to the release, or

(b) the tenant does so serve such a notice but the court, on the application of the landlord or former landlord, makes a declaration that it is reasonable for the covenant to be so released, or

(c) the tenant serves on the landlord or former landlord a notice in writing consenting to the release and, if he has previously served a notice objecting to it, stating that that notice is withdrawn.

(3) Any release from a covenant in accordance with this section shall be regarded as occurring at the time when the assignment in question takes place.

(4) In this section—

(a) "the tenant" means the tenant of the premises comprised in the assignment in question (or, if different parts of those premises are held under the tenancy by different tenants, each of those tenants);

(b) any reference to the landlord or the former landlord is a reference to the landlord referred to in section 6 or the former landlord referred to in section 7, as the case may be; and

(c) "the court" means a county court.

Apportionment of liability between assignor and assignee

Apportionment of liability under covenants binding both assignor and assignee of tenancy or reversion

58–009 **9.**—(1) This section applies where—

(a) a tenant assigns part only of the premises demised to him by a tenancy;

(b) after the assignment both the tenant and his assignee are to be bound by a non-attributable tenant covenant of the tenancy; and

(c) the tenant and his assignee agree that as from the assignment liability under the covenant is to be apportioned between them in such manner as is specified in the agreement.

(2) This section also applies where—

(a) a landlord assigns the reversion in part only of the premises of which he is the landlord under a tenancy;

(b) after the assignment both the landlord and his assignee are to be bound by a non-attributable landlord covenant of the tenancy; and

(c) the landlord and his assignee agree that as from the assignment liability under the covenant is to be apportioned between them in such manner as is specified in the agreement.

(3) Any such agreement as is mentioned in subsection (1) or (2) may apportion liability in such a way that a party to the agreement is exonerated from all liability under a covenant.

(4) In any case falling within subsection (1) or (2) the parties to the agreement may apply for the apportionment to become binding on the appropriate person in accordance with section 10.

(5) In any such case the parties to the agreement may also apply for the apportionment to become binding on any person (other than the appropriate person) who is for the time being entitled to enforce the covenant in question; and section 10 shall apply in relation to such an application as it applies in relation to an application made with respect to the appropriate person.

(6) For the purposes of this section a covenant is, in relation to an assignment, a "non-attributable" covenant if it does not fall to be complied with in relation to any premises comprised in the assignment.

(7) In this section "the appropriate person" means either—

(a) the landlord of the entire premises referred to in subsection (1)(a) (or, if different parts of those premises are held under the tenancy by different landlords, each of those landlords), or

(b) the tenant of the entire premises referred to in subsection (2)(a) (or, if different parts of those premises are held under the tenancy by different tenants, each of those tenants),

depending on whether the agreement in question falls within subsection (1) or subsection (2).

Procedure for making apportionment bind other party to lease

10.—(1) For the purposes of section 9 the parties to an agreement falling within subsection (1) or (2) of that section apply for an apportionment to become binding on the appropriate person if, either before or within the period of four weeks beginning with the date of the assignment in question, they serve on that person a notice informing him of— **58–010**

(a) the proposed assignment or (as the case may be) the fact that the assignment has taken place;
(b) the prescribed particulars of the agreement; and
(c) their request that the apportionment should become binding on him.

(2) Where an application for an apportionment to become binding has been made in accordance with subsection (1), the apportionment becomes binding on the appropriate person if—

(a) he does not, within the period of four weeks beginning with the day on which the notice is served under subsection (1) serve on the parties to the agreement a notice in writing objecting to the apportionment becoming binding on him, or
(b) he does so serve such a notice but the court, on the application of the parties to the agreement, makes a declaration that it is reasonable for the apportionment to become binding on him, or
(c) he serves on the parties to the agreement a notice in writing consenting to the apportionment becoming binding on him and, if he has previously served a notice objecting thereto, stating that the notice is withdrawn.

(3) Where any apportionment becomes binding in accordance with this section, this shall be regarded as occurring at the time when the assignment in question takes place.

(4) In this section—

"the appropriate persons" has the same meaning as in section 9;
"the court" means a county court;
"prescribed" means prescribed by virtue of section 27.

Excluded assignments

Assignments in breach of covenant or by operation of law

11.—(1) This section provides for the operation of sections 5 to 10 in relation to assignments in breach of a covenant of a tenancy or assignments by operation of law ("excluded assignments"). **58–011**

(2) In the case of an excluded assignment subsection (2) or (3) of section 5—

(a) shall not have the effect mentioned in that subsection in relation to the tenant as from that assignment, but
(b) shall have that effect as from the next assignment (if any) of the premises assigned by him which is not an excluded assignment.

(3) In the case of an excluded assignment subsection (2) or (3) of section 6 or 7—

(a) shall not enable the landlord or former landlord to apply for such a release as is mentioned in that subsection as from that assignment, but

(b) shall apply on the next assignment (if any) of the reversion assigned by the landlord which is not an excluded assignment so as to enable the landlord or former landlord to apply for any such release as from that subsequent assignment.

(4) Where subsection (2) or (3) of section 6 or 7 does so apply—

(a) any reference in that section to the assignment (except where it relates to the time as from which the release takes effect) is a reference to the excluded assignment; but

(b) in that excepted case and in section 8 as it applies in relation to any application under that section made by virtue of subsection (3) above, any reference to the assignment or proposed assignment is a reference to any such subsequent assignment as is mentioned in that subsection.

(5) In the case of an excluded assignment section 9—

(a) shall not enable the tenant or landlord and his assignee to apply for an agreed apportionment to become binding in accordance with section 10 as from that assignment, but

(b) shall apply on the next assignment (if any) of the premises or reversion assigned by the tenant or landlord which is not an excluded assignment so as to enable him and his assignee to apply for such an apportionment to become binding in accordance with section 10 as from that subsequent assignment.

(6) Where section 9 does so apply—

(a) any reference in that section to the assignment or the assignee under it is a reference to the excluded assignment and the assignee under that assignment; but

(b) in section 10 as it applies in relation to any application under section 9 made by virtue of subsection (5) above, any reference to the assignment or proposed assignment is a reference to any such subsequent assignment as is mentioned in that subsection.

(7) If any such subsequent assignment as is mentioned in subsection (2), (3) or (5) above comprises only part of the premises assigned by the tenant or (as the case may be) only part of the premises the reversion in which was assigned by the landlord on the excluded assignment—

(a) the relevant provision or provisions of section 5, 6, 7 or 9 shall only have the effect mentioned in that subsection to the extent that the covenants or covenant in question fall or falls to be complied with in relation to that part of those premises; and

(b) that subsection may accordingly apply on different occasions in relation to different parts of those premises.

Third party covenants

Covenants with management companies etc.

58–012 **12.**—(1) This section applies where—

(a) a person other than the landlord or tenant ("the third party") is under a covenant of a tenancy liable (as principal) to discharge any function with respect to all or any of the demised premises ("the relevant function"); and

(b) that liability is not the liability of a guarantor or any other financial liability referable to the performance or otherwise of a covenant of the tenancy by another party to it.

(2) To the extent that any covenant of the tenancy confers any rights against the third party with respect to the relevant function, then for the purposes of the transmission of the benefit of the covenant in accordance with this Act it shall be treated as if it were—

(a) a tenant covenant of the tenancy to the extent that those rights are exercisable by the landlord; and

(b) a landlord covenant of the tenancy to the extent that those rights are exercisable by the tenant.

(3) To the extent that any covenant of the tenancy confers any rights exercisable by the third party with respect to the relevant functions, then for the purposes mentioned in subsection (4), it shall be treated as if it were—

(a) a tenant covenant of the tenancy to the extent that those rights are exercisable against the tenant; and

(b) a landlord covenant of the tenancy to the extent that those rights are exercisable against the landlord.

(4) The purposes mentioned in subsection (3) are—

(a) the transmission of the burden of the covenant in accordance with this Act; and

(b) any release from, or apportionment of liability in respect of, the covenant in accordance with this Act.

(5) In relation to the release of the landlord from any covenant which is to be treated as a landlord covenant by virtue of subsection (3), section 8 shall apply as if any reference to the tenant were a reference to the third party.

Joint liability under covenants

Covenants binding two or more persons

13.—(1) Where in consequence of this Act two or more persons are bound by the same covenant, they are so bound both jointly and severally. **58–013**

(2) Subject to section 24(2), where by virtue of this Act—

(a) two or more persons are bound jointly and severally by the same covenant, and

(b) any of the persons so bound is released from the covenant,

the release does not extend to any other of those persons.

(3) For the purpose of providing for contribution between persons who, by virtue of this Act, are bound jointly and severally by a covenant, the Civil Liability (Contribution) Act 1978 shall have effect as if—

(a) liability to a person under a covenant were liability in respect of damage suffered by that person;

(b) references to damage accordingly included a breach of a covenant of a tenancy; and

(c) section 7(2) of that Act were omitted.

Abolition of indemnity covenants implied by statute

14. The following provisions (by virtue of which indemnity covenants are implied on the assignment of a tenancy) shall cease to have effect— **58–014**

(a) subsections (1)(C) and (D) of section 77 of the Law of Property Act 1925; and
(b) subsections (1)(b) and (2) of section 24 of the Land Registration Act 1925.

Enforcement of covenants

Enforcement of covenants

58–015 **15.**—(1) Where any tenant covenant of a tenancy, or any right of re-entry contained in a tenancy, is enforceable by the reversioner in respect of any premises demised by the tenancy, it shall also be so enforceable by—
(a) any person (other than the reversioner) who, as the holder of the immediate reversion in those premises, is for the time being entitled to the rents and profits under the tenancy in respect of those premises, or
(b) any mortgagee in possession of the reversion in those premises who is so entitled.

(2) Where any landlord covenant of a tenancy is enforceable against the reversioner in respect of any premises demised by the tenancy, it shall also be enforceable against any person falling within subsection (1)(a) or (b).

(3) Where any landlord covenant of a tenancy is enforceable by the tenant in respect of any premises demised by the tenancy, it shall also be so enforceable by any mortgagee in possession of those premises under a mortgage granted by the tenant.

(4) Where any tenant covenant of a tenancy, or any right of re-entry contained in a tenancy, is enforceable against the tenant in respect of any premises demised by the tenancy, it shall also be so enforceable against any such mortgagee.

(5) Nothing in this section shall operate—
(a) in the case of a covenant which (in whatever terms) is expressed to be personal to any person to make the covenant enforceable by or (as the case may be) against any other person; or
(b) to make a covenant enforceable against any person if, apart from this section, it would not be enforceable against him by reason of its not having been registered under the [Land Registration Act 2002][3] or the Land Charges Act 1972.

(6) In this section—
"mortgagee" and "mortgage" include "chargee" and "charge" respectively;
"the reversioner", in relation to a tenancy, means the holder for the time being of the interest of the landlord under the tenancy.

Liability of former tenant etc. in respect of covenants

Tenant guaranteeing performance of covenant by assignee

58–016 **16.**—(1) Where on an assignment a tenant is to any extent released from a tenant covenant of a tenancy by virtue of this Act ("the relevant covenant"), nothing in this Act (and in particular section 25) shall preclude him from entering into an authorised guarantee agreement with respect to the performance of that covenant by the assignee.

[3] Words substituted by the Land Registration Act 2002, s.133, Sched. 11, para. 33(1), (2).

(2) For the purposes of this section an agreement is an authorised guarantee agreement if—

(a) under it the tenant guarantees the performance of the relevant covenant to any extent by the assignee; and

(b) it is entered into in the circumstances set out in subsection (3); and

(c) its provisions conform with subsections (4) and (5).

(3) Those circumstances are as follows—

(a) by virtue of a covenant against assignment (whether absolute or qualified) the assignment cannot be effected without the consent of the landlord under the tenancy or some other person;

(b) any such consent is given subject to a condition (lawfully imposed) that the tenant is to enter into an agreement guaranteeing the performance of the covenant by the assignee; and

(c) the agreement is entered into by the tenant in pursuance of that condition.

(4) An agreement is not an authorised guarantee agreement to the extent that it purports—

(a) to impose on the tenant any requirement to guarantee in any way the performance of the relevant covenant by any person other than the assignee; or

(b) to impose on the tenant any liability, restriction or other requirement (of whatever nature) in relation to any time after the assignee is released from that covenant by virtue of this Act.

(5) Subject to subsection (4), an authorised guarantee agreement may—

(a) impose on the tenant any liability as sole or principal debtor in respect of any obligation owed by the assignee under the relevant covenant;

(b) impose on the tenant liabilities as guarantor in respect of the assignee's performance of that covenant which are no more onerous than those to which he would be subject in the event of his being liable as sole or principal debtor in respect of any obligation owed by the assignee under that covenant;

(c) require the tenant, in the event of the tenancy assigned by him being disclaimed, to enter into a new tenancy of the premises comprised in the assignment—

(i) whose term expires not later than the term of the tenancy assigned by the tenant, and

(ii) whose tenant covenants are no more onerous than those of that tenancy;

(d) make provision incidental or supplementary to any provision made by virtue of any of paragraphs (a) to (c).

(6) Where a person ("the former tenant") is to any extent released from a covenant of a tenancy by virtue of section 11(2) as from an assignment and the assignor under the assignment enters into an authorised guarantee agreement with the landlord with respect to the performance of that covenant by the assignee under the assignment—

(a) the landlord may require the former tenant to enter into an agreement under which he guarantees, on terms corresponding to those of that authorised guarantee agreement, the performance of that covenant by the assignee under the assignment; and

(b) if its provisions conform with subsections (4) and (5), any such agreement shall be an authorised guarantee agreement for the purposes of this section; and

(c) in the application of this section in relation to any such agreement—

(i) subsections (2)(b) and (c) and (3) shall be omitted, and

(ii) any reference to the tenant or to the assignee shall be read as a reference to the former tenant or to the assignee under the assignment.

(7) For the purposes of subsection (1) it is immaterial that—

(a) the tenant has already made an authorised guarantee agreement in respect of a previous assignment by him of the tenancy referred to in that subsection, it having been subsequently revested in him following a disclaimer on behalf of the previous assignee, or

(b) the tenancy referred to in that subsection is a new tenancy entered into by the tenant in pursuance of an authorised guarantee agreement;

and in any such case subsections (2) to (5) shall apply accordingly.

(8) It is hereby declared that the rules of law relating to guarantees (and in particular those relating to the release of sureties) are, subject to its terms, applicable in relation to any authorised guarantee agreement as in relation to any other guarantee agreement.

Restriction on liability of former tenant or his guarantor for rent or service charge etc

58–017 **17.**—(1) This section applies where a person ("the former tenant") is as a result of an assignment no longer a tenant under a tenancy but—

(a) (in the case of a tenancy which is a new tenancy) he has under an authorised guarantee agreement guaranteed the performance by his assignee of a tenant covenant of the tenancy under which any fixed charge is payable; or

(b) (in the case of any tenancy) he remains bound by such a covenant.

(2) The former tenant shall not be liable under that agreement or (as the case may be) the covenant to pay any amount in respect of any fixed charge payable under the covenant unless, within the period of six months beginning with the date when the charge becomes due, the landlord serves on the former tenant a notice informing him—

(a) that the charge is now due; and

(b) that in respect of the charge the landlord intends to recover from the former tenant such amount as is specified in the notice and (where payable) interest calculated on such basis as is so specified.

(3) Where a person ("the guarantor") has agreed to guarantee the performance by the former tenant of such a covenant as is mentioned in subsection (1), the guarantor shall not be liable under the agreement to pay any amount in respect of any fixed charge payable under the covenant unless, within the period of six months beginning with the date when the charge becomes due, the landlord serves on the guarantor a notice informing him—

(a) that the charge is now due; and

(b) that in respect of the charge the landlord intends to recover from the guarantor such amount as is specified in the notice and (where payable) interest calculated on such basis as is so specified.

(4) Where the landlord has duly served a notice under subsection (2) or (3), the amount (exclusive of interest) which the former tenant or (as the case may be) the guarantor is liable to pay in respect of the fixed charge in question shall not exceed the amount specified in the notice unless—

(a) his liability in respect of the charge is subsequently determined to be for a greater amount,

(b) the notice informed him of the possibility that that liability would be so determined, and

(c) within the period of three months beginning with the date of the determination, the landlord serves on him a further notice informing him that the landlord intends to recover that greater amount from him (plus interest, where payable).

(5) For the purposes of subsection (2) or (3) any fixed charge which has become due before the date on which this Act comes into force shall be treated as becoming due on that date; but neither of those subsections applies to any such charge if before that date proceedings have been instituted by the landlord for the recovery from the former tenant of any amount in respect of it.

(6) In this section—

"fixed charge", in relation to a tenancy, means—

(a) rent,

(b) any service charge as defined by section 18 of the Landlord and Tenant Act 1985 (the words "of a dwelling" being disregarded for this purpose), and

(c) any amount payable under a tenant covenant of the tenancy providing for the payment of a liquidated sum in the event of a failure to comply with any such covenant;

"landlord", in relation to a fixed charge, includes any person who has a right to enforce payment of the charge.

Restriction of liability of former tenant or his guarantor where tenancy subsequently varied

18.—(1) This section applies where a person ("the former tenant") is as a result of an assignment no longer a tenant under a tenancy but— **58–018**

(a) (in the case of a new tenancy) he has under an authorised guarantee agreement guaranteed the performance by his assignee of any tenant covenant of the tenancy; or

(b) (in the case of any tenancy) he remains bound by such a covenant.

(2) The former tenant shall not be liable under the agreement or (as the case may be) the covenant to pay any amount in respect of the covenant to the extent that the amount is referable to any relevant variation of the tenant covenants of the tenancy effected after the assignment.

(3) Where a person ("the guarantor") has agreed to guarantee the performance by the former tenant of a tenant covenant of the tenancy, the guarantor (where his liability to do so is not wholly discharged by any such variation of the tenant covenants of the tenancy) shall not be liable under the agreement to pay any amount in respect of the covenant to the extent that the amount is referable to any such variation.

(4) For the purposes of this section a variation of the tenant covenants of a tenancy is a "relevant variation" if either—

(a) the landlord has, at the time of the variation, an absolute right to refuse to allow it; or

(b) the landlord would have had such a right if the variation had been sought by the former tenant immediately before the assignment by him but, between the time of that assignment and the time of the variation, the tenant covenants of the tenancy have been so varied as to deprive the landlord of such a right.

(5) In determining whether the landlord has or would have had such a right at any particular time regard shall be had to all the circumstances (including the effect of any provision made by or under any enactment).

(6) Nothing in this section applies to any variation of the tenant covenants of a tenancy effected before the date on which this Act comes into force.

(7) In this section "variation" means a variation whether effected by deed or otherwise.

Overriding leases

Right of former tenant or his guarantor to overriding lease

58–019 **19.**—(1) Where in respect of any tenancy ("the relevant tenancy") any person ("the claimant") makes full payment of an amount which he has been duly required to pay in accordance with section 17, together with any interest payable, he shall be entitled (subject to and in accordance with this section) to have the landlord under that tenancy grant him an overriding lease of the premises demised by the tenancy.

(2) For the purposes of this section "overriding lease" means a tenancy of the reversion expectant on the relevant tenancy which—

- (a) is granted for a term equal to the remainder of the term of the relevant tenancy plus three days or the longest period (less than three days) that will not wholly displace the landlord's reversionary interest expectant on the relevant tenancy, as the case may require; and
- (b) (subject to subsections (3) and (4) and to any modifications agreed to by the claimant and the landlord) otherwise contains the same covenants as the relevant tenancy, as they have effect immediately before the grant of the lease.

(3) An overriding lease shall not be required to reproduce any covenant of the relevant tenancy to the extent that the covenant is (in whatever terms) expressed to be a personal covenant between the landlord and the tenant under that tenancy.

(4) If any right, liability or other matter arising under a covenant of the relevant tenancy falls to be determined or otherwise operates (whether expressly or otherwise) by reference to the commencement of that tenancy—

- (a) the corresponding covenant of the overriding lease shall be so framed that that right, liability or matter falls to be determined or otherwise operates by reference to the commencement of that tenancy; but
- (b) the overriding lease shall not be required to reproduce any covenant of that tenancy to the extent that it has become spent by the time that that lease is granted.

(5) A claim to exercise the right to an overriding lease under this section is made by the claimant making a request for such a lease to the landlord; and any such request—

- (a) must be made to the landlord in writing and specify the payment by virtue of which the claimant claims to be entitled to the lease ("the qualifying payment"); and
- (b) must be so made at the time of making the qualifying payment or within the period of 12 months beginning with the date of that payment.

(6) Where the claimant duly makes such a request—

(a) the landlord shall (subject to subsection (7)) grant and deliver to the claimant an overriding lease of the demised premises within a reasonable time of the request being received by the landlord; and

(b) the claimant—

(i) shall thereupon deliver to the landlord a counterpart of the lease duly executed by the claimant, and

(ii) shall be liable for the landlord's reasonable costs of and incidental to the grant of the lease.

(7) The landlord shall not be under any obligation to grant an overriding lease of the demised premises under this section at a time when the relevant tenancy has been determined; and a claimant shall not be entitled to the grant of such a lease if at the time when he makes his request—

(a) the landlord has already granted such a lease and that lease remains in force; or

(b) another person has already duly made a request for such a lease to the landlord and that request has been neither withdrawn nor abandoned by that person.

(8) Where two or more requests are duly made on the same day, then for the purposes of subsection (7)—

(a) a request made by a person who was liable for the qualifying payment as a former tenant shall be treated as made before a request made by a person who was so liable as a guarantor; and

(b) a request made by a person whose liability in respect of the covenant in question commenced earlier than any such liability of another person shall be treated as made before a request made by that other person.

(9) Where a claimant who has duly made a request for an overriding lease under this section subsequently withdraws or abandons the request before he is granted such a lease by the landlord, the claimant shall be liable for the landlord's reasonable costs incurred in pursuance of the request down to the time of its withdrawal or abandonment; and for the purposes of this section—

(a) a claimant's request is withdrawn by the claimant notifying the landlord in writing that he is withdrawing his request; and

(b) a claimant is to be regarded as having abandoned his request if—

(i) the landlord has requested the claimant in writing to take, within such reasonable period as is specified in the landlord's request, all or any of the remaining steps required to be taken by the claimant before the lease can be granted, and

(ii) the claimant fails to comply with the landlord's request,

and is accordingly to be regarded as having abandoned it at the time when that period expires.

(10) Any request or notification under this section may be sent by post.

(11) The preceding provisions of this section shall apply where the landlord is the tenant under an overriding lease granted under this section as they apply where no such lease has been granted; and accordingly there may be two or more such leases interposed between the first such lease and the relevant tenancy.

Overriding leases: supplementary provisions

20.—(1) For the purposes of section 1 an overriding lease shall be a new tenancy only if the relevant tenancy is a new tenancy. **58–020**

(2) Every overriding lease shall state—

(a) that it is a lease granted under section 19, and

(b) whether it is or is not a new tenancy for the purposes of section 1;

and any such statement shall comply with such requirements as may be prescribed by [land registration rules under the Land Registration Act 2002][4].

(3) A claim that the landlord has failed to comply with subsection (6)(a) of section 19 may be made the subject of civil proceedings in like manner as any other claim in tort for breach of statutory duty; and if the claimant under that section fails to comply with subsection (6)(b)(i) of that section he shall not be entitled to exercise any of the rights otherwise exercisable by him under the overriding lease.

(4) An overriding lease—

(a) shall be deemed to be authorised as against the persons interested in any mortgage of the landlord's interest (however created or arising); and

(b) shall be binding on any such persons;

and if any such person is by virtue of such a mortgage entitled to possession of the documents of title relating to the landlord's interest—

(i) the landlord shall within one month of the execution of the lease deliver to that person the counterpart executed in pursuance of section 19(6)(b)(i); and

(ii) if he fails to do so, the instrument creating or evidencing the mortgage shall apply as if the obligation to deliver a counterpart were included in the terms of the mortgage as set out in that instrument.

(5) It is hereby declared—

(a) that the fact that an overriding lease takes effect subject to the relevant tenancy shall not consititute a breach of any covenant of the lease against subletting or parting with possession of the premises demised by the lease or any part of them; and

(b) that each of sections 16, 17 and 18 applies where the tenancy referred to in subsection (1) of that section is an overriding lease as it applies in other cases falling within that subsection.

(6) No tenancy shall be registrable under the Land Charges Act 1972 or be taken to be an estate contract within the meaning of that Act by reason of any right or obligation that may arise under section 19, and any right arising from a request made under that section shall not be [capable of falling within paragraph 2 of Schedule 1 or 3 to the Land Registration Act 2002][5]; but any such request shall be registrable under the Land Charges Act 1972, or may be the subject of a notice [under the Land Registration Act 2002][6], as if it were an estate contract.

(7) In this section—

(a) "mortgage" includes "charge"; and

(b) any expression which is also used in section 19 has the same meaning as in that section.

Forfeiture and disclaimer

Forfeiture or disclaimer limited to part only of demised premises

58–021 **21.**—(1) Where—

(a) as a result of one or more assignments a person is the tenant of part only of the premises demised by a tenancy, and

(b) under a proviso or stipulation in the tenancy there is a right of re-entry or forfeiture for a breach of a tenant covenant of the tenancy, and

[4] Words substituted by the Land Registration Act 2002, s.133, Sched. 11, para. 33(1), (3).
[5] Words substituted by the Land Registration Act 2002, s.133, Sched. 11, para. 33(1), (4).
[6] Words substituted by the Land Registration Act 2002, s.133, Sched. 11, para. 33(1), (4).

(c) the right is (apart from this subsection) exercisable in relation to that part and other land demised by the tenancy,

the right shall nevertheless, in connection with a breach of any such covenant by that person, be taken to be a right exercisable only in relation to that part.

(2) Where—

(a) a company which is being wound up, or a trustee in bankruptcy, is as a result of one or more assignments the tenant of part only of the premises demised by a tenancy, and

(b) the liquidator of the company exercises his power under section 178 of the Insolvency Act 1986, or the trustee in bankruptcy exercises his power under section 315 of that Act, to disclaim property demised by the tenancy,

the power is exercisable only in relation to the part of the premises referred to in paragraph (a).

22. [*Amends the Landlord and Tenant Act 1927, s.19, ante, para. 12–002.*]

Supplemental

Effects of becoming subject to liability under, or entitled to benefit of, covenant etc.

23.—(1) Where as a result of an assignment a person becomes by virtue of this Act, bound by or entitled to the benefit of a covenant, he shall not by virtue of this Act have any liability or rights under the covenant in relation to any time falling before the assignment. **58–022**

(2) Subsection (1) does not preclude any such rights being expressly assigned to the person in question.

(3) Where as a result of an assignment a person becomes, by virtue of this Act, entitled to a right of re-entry contained in a tenancy, that right shall be exercisable in relation to any breach of a covenant of the tenancy occurring before the assignment as in relation to one occurring thereafter, unless by reason of any waiver or release it was not so exercisable immediately before the assignment.

Effects of release from liability under, or loss of benefit of, covenant

24.—(1) Any release of a person from a covenant by virtue of this Act does not affect any liability of his arising from a breach of the covenant occurring before the release. **58–023**

(2) Where—

(a) by virtue of this Act a tenant is released from a tenant covenant of a tenancy, and

(b) immediately before the release another person is bound by a covenant of the tenancy imposing any liability or penalty in the event of a failure to comply with that tenant covenant,

then, as from the release of the tenant, that other person is released from the covenant mentioned in paragraph (b) to the same extent as the tenant is released from that tenant covenant.

(3) Where a person bound by a landlord or tenant covenant of a tenancy—

(a) assigns the whole or part of his interest in the premises demised by the tenancy, but

(b) is not released by virtue of this Act from the covenant (with the result that subsection (1) does not apply),

the assignment does not affect any liability of his arising from a breach of the covenant occurring before the assignment.

(4) Where by virtue of this Act a person ceases to be entitled to the benefit of a covenant, this does not affect any rights of his arising from a breach of the covenant occurring before he ceases to be so entitled.

Agreement void if it restricts operation of the Act

58–024 **25.**—(1) Any agreement relating to a tenancy is void to the extent that—

(a) it would apart from this section have effect to exclude, modify or otherwise frustrate the operation of any provision of this Act, or

(b) it provides for—

(i) the termination or surrender of the tenancy, or

(ii) the imposition on the tenant of any penalty, disability or liability,

in the event of the operation of any provision of this Act, or

(c) it provides for any of the matters referred to in paragraph (b)(i) or (ii) and does so (whether expressly or otherwise) in connection with, or in consequence of, the operation of any provision of this Act.

(2) To the extent that an agreement relating to a tenancy constitutes a covenant (whether absolute or qualified) against the assignment, or parting with the possession, of the premises demised by the tenancy or any part of them—

(a) the agreement is not void by virtue of subsection (1) by reason only of the fact that as such the covenant prohibits or restricts any such assignment or parting with possession; but

(b) paragraph (a) above does not otherwise affect the operation of that subsection in relation to the agreement (and in particular does not preclude its application to the agreement to the extent that it purports to regulate the giving of, or the making of any application for, consent to any such assignment or parting with possession).

(3) In accordance with section 16(1) nothing in this section applies to any agreement to the extent that it is an authorised guarantee agreement; but (without prejudice to the generality of subsection (1) above) an agreement is void to the extent that it is one falling within section 16(4)(a) or (b).

(4) This section applies to an agreement relating to a tenancy whether or not the agreement is—

(a) contained in the instrument creating the tenancy; or

(b) made before the creation of the tenancy.

Miscellaneous savings etc.

58–025 **26.**—(1) Nothing in this Act is to be read as preventing—

(a) a party to a tenancy from releasing a person from a landlord covenant or a tenant covenant of the tenancy; or

(b) the parties to a tenancy from agreeing to an apportionment of liability under such a covenant.

(2) Nothing in this Act affects the operation of section 3(3A) of the Landlord and Tenant Act 1985 (preservation of former landlord's liability until tenant notified of new landlord).

(3) No apportionment which has become binding in accordance with section 10 shall be affected by any order or decision made under or by virtue of any enactment not contained in this Act which relates to apportionment.

Notices for the purposes of the Act

27.—(1) The form of any notice to be served for the purposes of section 8, 10, or 17 shall be prescribed by regulations made by the Lord Chancellor by statutory instrument. **58–026**

(2) The regulations shall require any notice served for the purposes of section 8(1) or 10(1) ("the initial notice") to include—

(a) an explanation of the significance of the notice and the options available to the person on whom it is served;

(b) a statement that any objections to the proposed release, or (as the case may be) to the proposed effect of the apportionment, must be made by notice in writing served on the person or persons by whom the initial notice is served within the period of four weeks beginning with the day on which the initial notice is served; and

(c) an address in England and Wales to which any such objections may be sent.

(3) The regulations shall require any notice served for the purposes of section 17 to include an explanation of the significance of the notice.

(4) If any notice purporting to be served for the purposes of section 8(1), 10(1) or 17 is not in the prescribed form, or in a form substantially to the same effect, the notice shall not be effective for the purposes of section 8, section 10 or section 17 (as the case may be).

(5) Section 23 of the Landlord and Tenant Act 1927 shall apply in relation to the service of notices for the purposes of section 8, 10 or 17.

(6) Any statutory instrument made under this section shall be subject to annulment in pursuance of a resolution of either House of Parliament.

Interpretation

28.—(1) In this Act (unless the context otherwise requires)— **58–027**

"assignment" includes equitable assignment and in addition (subject to section 11) assignment in breach of a covenant of a tenancy or by operation of law;

"authorised guarantee agreement" means an agreement which is an authorised guarantee agreement for the purposes of section 16;

"collateral agreement", in relation to a tenancy, means any agreement collateral to the tenancy, whether made before or after its creation;

"consent" includes licence;

"covenant" includes term, condition and obligation, and references to a covenant (or any description of covenant) of a tenancy include a covenant (or a covenant of that description) contained in a collateral agreement;

"landlord" and "tenant", in relation to a tenancy, mean the person for the time being entitled to the reversion expectant on the term of the tenancy and the person so entitled to that term respectively;

"landlord covenant", in relation to a tenancy, means a covenant falling to be complied with by the landlord of premises demised by the tenancy;

"new tenancy" means a tenancy which is a new tenancy for the purposes of section 1;

"reversion" means the interest expectant on the termination of a tenancy;
"tenancy" means any lease or other tenancy and includes—
(a) a sub-tenancy, and
(b) an agreement for a tenancy,
but does not include a mortgage term;
"tenant covenant", in relation to a tenancy, means a covenant falling to be complied with by the tenant of premises demised by the tenancy.

(2) For the purposes of any reference in this Act to a covenant falling to be complied with in relation to a particular part of the premises demised by a tenancy, a covenant falls to be so complied with if—
(a) it in terms applies to that part of the premises, or
(b) in its practical application it can be attributed to that part of the premises (whether or not it can also be so attributed to other individual parts of those premises).

(3) Subsection (2) does not apply in relation to covenants to pay money; and, for the purposes of any reference in this Act to a covenant falling to be complied with in relation to a particular part of the premises demised by a tenancy, a covenant of a tenancy which is a covenant to pay money falls to be so complied with if—
(a) the covenant in terms applies to that part; or
(b) the amount of the payment is determinable specifically by reference—
(i) to that part, or
(ii) to anything falling to be done by or for a person as tenant or occupier of that part (if it is a tenant covenant), or
(iii) to anything falling to be done by or for a person as landlord of that part (if it is a landlord covenant).

(4) Where two or more persons jointly constitute either the landlord or the tenant in relation to a tenancy, any reference in this Act to the landlord or the tenant is a reference to both or all of the persons who jointly constitute the landlord or the tenant, as the case may be (and accordingly nothing in section 13 applies in relation to the rights and liabilities of such persons between themselves).

(5) References in this Act to the assignment by a landlord of the reversion in the whole or part of the premises demised by a tenancy are to the assignment by him of the whole of his interest (as owner of the reversion) in the whole or part of those premises.

(6) For the purposes of this Act—
(a) any assignment (however effected) consisting in the transfer of the whole of the landlord's interest (as owner of the reversion) in any premises demised by a tenancy shall be treated as an assignment by the landlord of the reversion in those premises even if it is not effected by him; and
(b) any assignment (however effected) consisting in the transfer of the whole of the tenant's interest in any premises demised by a tenancy shall be treated as an assignment by the tenant of those premises even if it is not effected by him.

Treasure Act 1996

(1996 c. 24)

Meaning of "treasure"

Meaning of "treasure"

1.—(1) Treasure is— **59–001**
(a) any object at least 300 years old when found which—
(i) is not a coin but has metallic content of which at least 10 per cent by weight is precious metal;
(ii) when found, is one of at least two coins in the same find which are at least 300 years old at that time and have that percentage of precious metal; or
(iii) when found, is one of at least ten coins in the same find which are at least 300 years old at that time;
(b) any object at least 200 years old when found which belongs to a class designated under section 2(1);
(c) any object which would have been treasure trove if found before the commencement of section 4;
(d) any object which, when found, is part of the same find as—
(i) an object within paragraph (a), (b) or (c) found at the same time or earlier; or
(ii) an object found earlier which would be within paragraph (a) or (b) if it had been found at the same time.

(2) Treasure does not include objects which are—
(a) unworked natural objects, or
(b) minerals as extracted from a natural deposit
or which belong to a class designated under section 2(2).

Power to alter meaning

2.—(1) The Secretary of State may by order, for the purposes of section 1(1)(b), designate any class of object which he considers to be of outstanding historical, archaeological or cultural importance. **59–002**

(2) The Secretary of State may by order, for the purposes of section 1(2), designate any class of object which (apart from the order) would be treasure.

(3) An order under this section shall be made by statutory instrument.

(4) No order is to be made under this section unless a draft of the order has been laid before Parliament and approved by a resolution of each House.

Supplementary

3.—(1) This section supplements section 1. **59–003**

(2) "Coin" includes any metal token which was, or can reasonably be assumed to have been, used or intended for use as or instead of money.

(3) "Precious metal" means gold or silver.

(4) When an object is found, it is part of the same find as another object if—
(a) they are found together,
(b) the other object was found earlier in the same place where they had been left together,

(c) the other object was found earlier in a different place, but they had been left together and had become separated before being found.

(5) If the circumstances in which objects are found can reasonably be taken to indicate that they were together at some time before being found, the objects are to be presumed to have been left together, unless shown not to have been.

(6) An object which can reasonably be taken to be at least a particular age is to be presumed to be at least that age, unless shown not to be.

(7) An object is not treasure if it is wreck within the meaning of Part IX of the Merchant Shipping Act 1995.

Ownership of treasure

Ownership of treasure which is found

59–004 **4.**—(1) When treasure is found, it vests, subject to prior interests and rights—

(a) in the franchisee, if there is one;

(b) otherwise, in the Crown.

(2) Prior interests and rights are any which, or which derive from any which—

(a) were held when the treasure was left where it was found, or

(b) if the treasure had been moved before being found, were held when it was left where it was before being moved.

(3) If the treasure would have been treasure trove if found before the commencement of this section, neither the Crown nor any franchisee has any interest in it or right over it except in accordance with this Act.

(4) This section applies—

(a) whatever the nature of the place where the treasure was found, and

(b) whatever the circumstances in which it was left (including being lost or being left with no intention of recovery).

Meaning of "franchisee"

59–005 **5.**—(1) The franchisee for any treasure is the person who—

(a) was, immediately before the commencement of section 4, or

(b) apart from this Act, as successor in title, would have been, the franchisee of the Crown in right of treasure trove for the place where the treasure was found.

(2) It is as franchisees in right of treasure trove that Her Majesty and the Duke of Cornwall are to be treated as having enjoyed the rights to treasure trove which belonged respectively to the Duchy of Lancaster and the Duchy of Cornwall immediately before the commencement of section 4.

Treasure vesting in the Crown

59–006 **6.**—(1) Treasure vesting in the Crown under this Act is to be treated as part of the hereditary revenues of the Crown to which section 1 of the Civil List Act 1952 applies (surrender of hereditary revenues to the Exchequer).

(2) Any such treasure may be transferred, or otherwise disposed of, in accordance with directions given by the Secretary of State.

(3) The Crown's title to any such treasure may be disclaimed at any time by the Secretary of State.

(4) If the Crown's title is disclaimed, the treasure—

(a) is deemed not to have vested in the Crown under this Act, and

(b) without prejudice to the interests or rights of others, may be delivered to any person in accordance with the code published under section 11.

Coroners' jurisdiction

Jurisdiction of coroners

7.—(1) The jurisdiction of coroners which is referred to in section 30 of the Coroners Act 1988 (treasure) is exercisable in relation to anything which is treasure for the purposes of this Act. **59–007**

(2) That jurisdiction is not exercisable for the purposes of the law relating to treasure trove in relation to anything found after the commencement of section 4.

(3) The Act of 1988 and anything saved by virtue of section 36(5) of that Act (saving for existing law and practice etc.) has effect subject to this section.

(4) An inquest held by virtue of this section is to be held without a jury, unless the coroner orders otherwise.

Duty of finder to notify coroner

8.—(1) A person who finds an object which he believes or has reasonable grounds for believing is treasure must notify the coroner for the district in which the object was found before the end of the notice period. **59–008**

(2) The notice period is fourteen days beginning with—

(a) the day after the find; or

(b) if later, the day on which the finder first believes or has reason to believe the object is treasure.

(3) Any person who fails to comply with subsection (1) is guilty of an offence and liable on summary conviction to—

(a) imprisonment for a term not exceeding three months;

(b) a fine of an amount not exceeding level 5 on the standard scale; or

(c) both.

(4) In proceedings for an offence under this section, it is a defence for the defendant to show that he had, and has continued to have, a reasonable excuse for failing to notify the coroner.

(5) If the office of coroner for a district is vacant, the person acting as coroner for that district is the coroner for the purposes of subsection (1).

Procedure for inquests

9.—(1) In this section, "inquest" means an inquest held under section 7. **59–009**

(2) A coroner proposing to conduct an inquest must notify—

(a) the British Museum, if his district is in England; or

(b) the National Museum of Wales, if it is in Wales.

(3) Before conducting the inquest, the coroner must take reasonable steps to notify—

(a) any person who it appears to him may have found the treasure; and

(b) any person who, at the time the treasure was found, occupied land which it appears to him may be where it was found.

(4) During the inquest the coroner must take reasonable steps to notify any such person not already notified.

(5) Before or during the inquest, the coroner must take reasonable steps—

(a) to obtain from any person notified under subsection (3) or (4) the names and addresses of interested persons; and

(b) to notify any interested person whose name and address he obtains.

(6) The coroner must take reasonable steps to give any interested person notified under subsection (3), (4) or (5) an opportunity to examine witnesses at the inquest.

(7) In subsections (5) and (6), "interested person" means a person who appears to the coroner to be likely to be concerned with the inquest—
(a) as the finder of the treasure or otherwise involved in the find;
(b) as the occupier, at the time the treasure was found, of the land where it was found, or
(c) as having had an interest in that land at that time or since.

Rewards, codes of practice and report

Rewards

59–010 **10.**—(1) This section applies if treasure—
(a) has vested in the Crown under section 4; and
(b) is to be transferred to a museum.

(2) The Secretary of State must determine whether a reward is to be paid by the museum before the transfer.

(3) If the Secretary of State determines that a reward is to be paid, he must also determine, in whatever way he thinks fit—
(a) the treasure's market value;
(b) the amount of the reward;
(c) to whom the reward is to be payable; and
(d) if it is to be payable to more than one person, how much each is to receive.

(4) The total reward must not exceed the treasure's market value.

(5) The reward may be payable to—
(a) the finder or any other person involved in the find;
(b) the occupier of the land at the time of the find;
(c) any person who had an interest in the land at that time, or has had such an interest at any time since then.

(6) Payment of the reward is not enforceable against a museum or the Secretary of State.

(7) In a determination under this section, the Secretary of State must take into account anything relevant in the code of practice issued under section 11.

(8) This section also applies in relation to treasure which has vested in a franchisee under section 4, if the franchisee makes a request to the Secretary of State that it should.

Codes of practice

59–011 **11.**—(1) The Secretary of State must—
(a) prepare a code of practice relating to treasure;
(b) keep the code under review; and
(c) revise it when appropriate.

(2) The code must, in particular, set out the principles and practice to be followed by the Secretary of State—
(a) when considering to whom treasure should be offered;
(b) when making a determination under section 10; and
(c) where the Crown's title to treasure is disclaimed.

(3) The code may include guidance for—

(a) those who search for or find treasure; and

(b) museums and others who exercise functions in relation to treasure.

(4) Before preparing the code or revising it, the Secretary of State must consult such persons appearing to him to be interested as he thinks appropriate.

(5) A copy of the code and of any proposed revision of the code shall be laid before Parliament.

(6) Neither the code nor any revision shall come into force until approved by a resolution of each House of Parliament.

(7) The Secretary of State must publish the code in whatever way he considers appropriate for bringing it to the attention of those interested.

(8) If the Secretary of State considers that different provision should be made for—

(a) England and Wales, and

(b) Northern Ireland,

or that different provision should otherwise be made for treasure found in different areas, he may prepare two or more separate codes.

Family Law Act 1996

(1996 c. 27)

FAMILY HOMES AND DOMESTIC VIOLENCE

Rights to occupy matrimonial home[1]

Rights concerning matrimonial home where one spouse has no estate, etc.

30.—(1) This section applies if— **60–001**

(a) one spouse is entitled to occupy a dwelling-house by virtue of

(i) a beneficial estate or interest or contract; or

(ii) any enactment giving that spouse the right to remain in occupation; and

(b) the other spouse is not so entitled.

(2) Subject to the provisions of this Part, the spouse not so entitled has the following rights ("matrimonial home rights")—

(a) if in occupation, a right not to be evicted or excluded from the dwelling-house or any part of it by the other spouse except with the leave of the court given by an order under section 33;

(b) if not in occupation, a right with the leave of the court so given to enter into and occupy the dwelling-house.

(3) If a spouse is entitled under this section to occupy a dwelling-house or any part of a dwelling-house, any payment or tender made or other thing done by that spouse in or towards satisfaction of any liability of the other spouse in respect of rent, mortgage payments or other outgoings affecting the dwelling-

---

[1] See also the Insolvency Act 1986, ss.336–338, *ante*, paras 47–007—47–009.

house is, whether or not it is made or done in pursuance of an order under section 40, as good as if made or done by the other spouse.

(4) A spouse's occupation by virtue of this section—

(a) is to be treated, for the purposes of the Rent (Agriculture) Act 1976 and the Rent Act 1977 (other than Part V and sections 103 to 106 of that Act), as occupation by the other spouse as the other spouse's residence, and

(b) if the spouse occupies the dwelling-house as that spouse's only or principal home, is to be treated, for the purposes of the Housing Act 1985 [, Part I of the Housing Act 1988 and Chapter I of Part V of the Housing Act 1996][2], as occupation by the other spouse as the other spouse's only or principal home.

(5) If a spouse ("the first spouse")—

(a) is entitled under this section to occupy a dwelling-house or any part of a dwelling-house, and

(b) makes any payment in or towards satisfaction of any liability of the other spouse ("the second spouse") in respect of mortgage payments affecting the dwelling-house,

the person to whom the payment is made may treat it as having been made by the second spouse, but the fact that that person has treated any such payment as having been so made does not affect any claim of the first spouse against the second spouse to an interest in the dwelling-house by virtue of the payment.

(6) If a spouse is entitled under this section to occupy a dwelling-house or part of a dwelling-house by reason of an interest of the other spouse under a trust, all the provisions of subsections (3) to (5) apply in relation to the trustees as they apply in relation to the other spouse.

(7) This section does not apply to a dwelling-house which has at no time been, and which was at no time intended by the spouses to be, a matrimonial home of theirs.

(8) A spouse's matrimonial home rights continue—

(a) only so long as the marriage subsists, except to the extent that an order under section 33(5) otherwise provides; and

(b) only so long as the other spouse is entitled as mentioned in subsection (1) to occupy the dwelling-house, except where provision is made by section 31 for those rights to be a charge on an estate or interest in the dwelling-house.

(9) It is hereby declared that a spouse—

(a) who has an equitable interest in a dwelling-house or in its proceeds of sale, but

(b) is not a spouse in whom there is vested (whether solely or as joint tenant) a legal estate in fee simple or a legal term of years absolute in the dwelling-house,

is to be treated, only for the purpose of determining whether he has matrimonial home rights, as not being entitled to occupy the dwelling-house by virtue of that interest.

Effect of matrimonial home rights as charge on dwelling-house

60–002 **31.**—(1) Subsections (2) and (3) apply if, at any time during a marriage, one spouse is entitled to occupy a dwelling-house by virtue of a beneficial estate or interest.

[2] Words inserted by the Housing Act 1996 (Consequential Amendments) Order 1997 (S.I. 1997 No. 74), art. 2, Sched., para. 10(a).

(2) The other spouse's matrimonial home rights are a charge on the estate or interest.

(3) The charge created by subsection (2) has the same priority as if it were an equitable interest created at whichever is the latest of the following dates—

(a) the date on which the spouse so entitled acquires the estate or interest;
(b) the date of the marriage; and
(c) 1st January 1968 (the commencement date of the Matrimonial Homes Act 1967).

(4) Subsections (5) and (6) apply if, at any time when a spouse's matrimonial home rights are a charge on an interest of the other spouse under a trust, there are, apart from either of the spouses, no persons, living or unborn, who are or could become beneficiaries under the trust.

(5) The rights are a charge also on the estate or interest of the trustees for the other spouse.

(6) The charge created by subsection (5) has the same priority as if it were an equitable interest created (under powers overriding the trusts) on the date when it arises.

(7) In determining for the purposes of subsection (4) whether there are any persons who are not, but could become, beneficiaries under the trust, there is to be disregarded any potential exercise of a general power of appointment exercisable by either or both the spouses alone (whether or not the exercise of it requires the consent of another person).

(8) Even though a spouse's matrimonial home rights are a charge on an estate or interest in the dwelling-house, those rights are brought to an end by—

(a) the death of the other spouse, or
(b) the termination (otherwise than by death) of the marriage,

unless the court directs otherwise by an order made under section 33(5).

(9) If—

(a) a spouse's matrimonial home rights are a charge on an estate or interest in the dwelling-house, and
(b) that estate or interest is surrendered to merge in some other estate or interest expectant on it in such circumstances that, but for the merger, the person taking the estate or interest would be bound by the charge,

the surrender has effect subject to the charge and the persons thereafter entitled to the other estate or interest are, for so long as the estate or interest surrendered would have endured if not so surrendered, to be treated for all purposes of this Part as deriving title to the other estate or interest under the other spouse or, as the case may be, under the trustees for the other spouse, by virtue of the surrender.

(10) If the title to the legal estate by virtue of which a spouse is entitled to occupy a dwelling-house (including any legal estate held by trustees for that spouse) is registered under the [Land Registration Act 2002][3] or any enactment replaced by that Act—

(a) registration of a land charge affecting the dwelling-house by virtue of this Part is to be effected by registering a notice under that Act; and
[(b) a spouse's matrimonial home rights are not to be capable of falling within paragraph 2 of Schedule 1 or 3 to that Act.][4]

(11) [*Repealed by the Land Registration Act 2002, s.135, Sched. 13.*]

[3] Words substituted by the Land Registration Act 2002, s.133, Sched. 11, para. 34(1), (2)(a).
[4] Para. (b) substituted by the Land Registration Act 2002, s.133, Sched. 11, para. 34(1), (2)(b).

(12) If—

(a) a spouse's matrimonial home rights are a charge on the estate of the other spouse or of trustees of the other spouse, and

(b) that estate is the subject of a mortgage,

then if, after the date of the creation of the mortgage ("the first mortgage"), the charge is registered under section 2 of the Land Charges Act 1972, the charge is, for the purposes of section 94 of the Law of Property Act 1925 (which regulates the rights of mortgagees to make further advances ranking in priority to subsequent mortgages), to be deemed to be a mortgage subsequent in date to the first mortgage.

(13) It is hereby declared that a charge under subsection (2) or (5) is not registrable under subsection (10) or under section 2 of the Land Charges Act 1972 unless it is a charge on a legal estate.

Further provisions relating to matrimonial home rights

60–003 **32.** Schedule 4 re-enacts with consequential amendments and minor modifications provisions of the Matrimonial Homes Act 1983.

Occupation orders

Occupation orders where applicant has estate or interest etc. or has matrimonial home rights

60–004 **33.**—(1) If—

(a) a person ("the person entitled")—

(i) is entitled to occupy a dwelling-house by virtue of a beneficial estate or interest or contract or by virtue of any enactment giving him the right to remain in occupation, or

(ii) has matrimonial home rights in relation to a dwelling-house, and

(b) the dwelling-house—

(i) is or at any time has been the home of the person entitled and of another person with whom he is associated, or

(ii) was at any time intended by the person entitled and any such other person to be their home,

the person entitled may apply to the court for an order containing any of the provisions specified in subsections (3), (4) and (5).

(2) If an agreement to marry is terminated, no application under this section may be made by virtue of section 62(3)(e) by reference to that agreement after the end of the period of three years beginning with the day on which it is terminated.

(3) An order under this section may—

(a) enforce the applicant's entitlement to remain in occupation as against the other person ("the respondent");

(b) require the respondent to permit the applicant to enter and remain in the dwelling-house or part of the dwelling-house;

(c) regulate the occupation of the dwelling-house by either or both parties;

(d) if the respondent is entitled as mentioned in subsection (1)(a)(i), prohibit, suspend or restrict the exercise by him of his right to occupy the dwelling-house;

(e) if the respondent has matrimonial home rights in relation to the dwelling-house and the applicant is the other spouse, restrict or terminate those rights;

(f) require the respondent to leave the dwelling-house or part of the dwelling-house; or
(g) exclude the respondent from a defined area in which the dwelling-house is included.

(4) An order under this section may declare that the applicant is entitled as mentioned in subsection (1)(a)(i) or has matrimonial home rights.

(5) If the applicant has matrimonial home rights and the respondent is the other spouse, an order under this section made during the marriage may provide that those rights are not brought to an end by—
(a) the death of the other spouse; or
(b) the termination (otherwise than by death) of the marriage.

(6) In deciding whether to exercise its powers under subsection (3) and (if so) in what manner, the court shall have regard to all the circumstances including—
(a) the housing needs and housing resources of each of the parties and of any relevant child;
(b) the financial resources of each of the parties;
(c) the likely effect of any order, or of any decision by the court not to exercise its powers under subsection (3), on the health, safety or well-being of the parties and of any relevant child; and
(d) the conduct of the parties in relation to each other and otherwise.

(7) If it appears to the court that the applicant or any relevant child is likely to suffer significant harm attributable to conduct of the respondent if an order under this section containing one or more of the provisions mentioned in subsection (3) is not made, the court shall make the order unless it appears to it that—
(a) the respondent or any relevant child is likely to suffer significant harm if the order is made; and
(b) the harm likely to be suffered by the respondent or child in that event is as great as, or greater than, the harm attributable to conduct of the respondent which is likely to be suffered by the applicant or child if the order is not made.

(8) The court may exercise its powers under subsection (5) in any case where it considers that in all the circumstances it is just and reasonable to do so.

(9) An order under this section—
(a) may not be made after the death of either of the parties mentioned in subsection (1); and
(b) except in the case of an order made by virtue of subsection (5)(a), ceases to have effect on the death of either party.

(10) An order under this section may, in so far as it has continuing effect, be made for a specified period, until the occurrence of a specified event or until further order.

. . . . . .

Dwelling-house subject to mortgage

Dwelling-house subject to mortgage

54.—(1) In determining for the purposes of this Part whether a person is entitled to occupy a dwelling-house by virtue of an estate or interest, any right to **60–005**

possession of the dwelling-house conferred on a mortgagee of the dwelling-house under or by virtue of his mortgage is to be disregarded.

(2) Subsection (1) applies whether or not the mortgagee is in possession.

(3) Where a person ("A") is entitled to occupy a dwelling-house by virtue of an estate or interest, a connected person does not by virtue of—

(a) any matrimonial home rights conferred by section 30, or

(b) any rights conferred by an order under section 35 or 36,

have any larger right against the mortgagee to occupy the dwelling-house than A has by virtue of his estate or interest and of any contract with the mortgagee.

(4) Subsection (3) does not apply, in the case of matrimonial home rights, if under section 31 those rights are a charge, affecting the mortgagee, on the estate or interest mortgaged.

(5) In this section "connected person", in relation to any person, means that person's spouse, former spouse, cohabitant or former cohabitant.

Actions by mortgagees: joining connected persons as parties

60–006 **55.**—(1) This section applies if a mortgagee of land which consists of or includes a dwelling-house brings an action in any court for the enforcement of his security.

(2) A connected person who is not already a party to the action is entitled to be made a party in the circumstances mentioned in subsection (3).

(3) The circumstances are that—

(a) the connected person is enabled by section 30(3) or (6) (or by section 30(3) or (6) as applied by section 35(13) or 36(13)), to meet the mortgagor's liabilities under the mortgage;

(b) he has applied to the court before the action is finally disposed of in that court; and

(c) the court sees no special reason against his being made a party to the action and is satisfied—

(i) that he may be expected to make such payments or do such other things in or towards satisfaction of the mortgagor's liabilities or obligations as might affect the outcome of the proceedings; or

(ii) that the expectation of it should be considered under section 36 of the Administration of Justice Act 1970.

(4) In this section "connected person" has the same meaning as in section 54.

Actions by mortgagees: service of notice on certain persons

60–007 **56.**—(1) This section applies if a mortgagee of land which consists, or substantially consists, of a dwelling-house brings an action for the enforcement of his security, and at the relevant time there is—

(a) in the case of unregistered land, a land charge of Class F registered against the person who is the estate owner at the relevant time or any person who, where the estate owner is a trustee, preceded him as trustee during the subsistence of the mortgage; or

(b) in the case of registered land, a subsisting registration of—

(i) a notice under section 31(10);

(ii) a notice under section 2(8) of the Matrimonial Homes Act 1983; or

(iii) a notice or caution under section 2(7) of the Matrimonial Homes Act 1967.

(2) If the person on whose behalf—

(a) the land charge is registered, or
(b) the notice or caution is entered,

is not a party to the action, the mortgagee must serve notice of the action on him.

(3) If—

(a) an official search has been made on behalf of the mortgagee which would disclose any land charge of Class F, notice or caution within subsection (1)(a) or (b),
(b) a certificate of the result of the search has been issued, and
(c) the action is commenced within the priority period,

the relevant time is the date of the certificate.

(4) In any other case the relevant time is the time when the action is commenced.

(5) The priority period is, for both registered and unregistered land, the period for which, in accordance with section 11(5) and (6) of the Land Charges Act 1972, a certificate on an official search operates in favour of a purchaser.

. . . . . .

SCHEDULE 4

Section 32

PROVISIONS SUPPLEMENTARY TO SECTIONS 30 AND 31

Interpretation

1.—(1) In this Schedule—

(a) any reference to a solicitor includes a reference to a licensed conveyancer or a recognised body, and
(b) any reference to a person's solicitor includes a reference to a licensed conveyancer or recognised body acting for that person,

(2) In sub-paragraph (1)—

"licensed conveyancer" has the meaning given by section 11(2) of the Administration of Justice Act 1985;

"recognised body" means a body corporate for the time being recognised under section 9 (incorporated practices) or section 32 (provision of conveyancing by recognised bodies) of that Act.

Restriction on registration where spouse entitled to more than one charge

2. Where one spouse is entitled by virtue of section 31 to a registrable charge in respect of each of two or more dwelling-houses, only one of the charges to which that spouse is so entitled shall be registered under section 31(10) or under section 2 of the Land Charges Act 1972 at any one time, and if any of those charges is registered under either of those provisions the Chief Land Registrar, on being satisfied that any other of them is so registered, shall cancel the registration of the charge first registered.

Contract for sale of house affected by registered charge to include term requiring cancellation of registration before completion

3.—(1) Where one spouse is entitled by virtue of section 31 to a charge on an estate in a dwelling-house and the charge is registered under section 31(10) or section 2 of the Land Charges Act 1972, it shall be a term of any contract for the sale of that estate whereby the vendor agrees to give vacant possession of the dwelling-house on completion of the contract that the vendor will before such completion procure the cancellation of the registration of the charge at his expense.

(2) Sub-paragraph (1) shall not apply to any such contract made by a vendor who is entitled to sell the estate in the dwelling-house freed from any such charge.

(3) If, on the completion of such a contract as is referred to in sub-paragraph (1), there is delivered to the purchaser or his solicitor an application by the spouse entitled to the charge for the

cancellation of the registration of that charge, the term of the contract for which sub-paragraph (1) provides shall be deemed to have been performed.

(4) This paragraph applies only if and so far as a contrary intention is not expressed in the contract.

(5) This paragraph shall apply to a contract for exchange as it applies to a contract for sale.

(6) This paragraph shall, with the necessary modifications, apply to a contract for the grant of a lease or underlease of a dwelling-house as it applies to a contract for the sale of an estate in a dwelling-house.

Cancellation of registration after termination of marriage, etc.

4.—(1) Where a spouse's matrimonial home rights are a charge on an estate in the dwelling-house and the charge is registered under section 31(10) or under section 2 of the Land Charges Act 1972, the Chief Land Registrar shall, subject to sub-paragraph (2), cancel the registration of the charge if he is satisfied—

(a) by the production of a certificate or other sufficient evidence, that either spouse is dead, or

(b) by the production of an official copy of a decree or order of a court, that the marriage in question has been terminated otherwise than by death, or

(c) by the production of an order of the court, that the spouse's matrimonial home rights constituting the charge have been terminated by the order.

(2) Where—

(a) the marriage in question has been terminated by the death of the spouse entitled to an estate in the dwelling-house or otherwise than by death, and

(b) an order affecting the charge of the spouse not so entitled had been made under section 33(5),

then if, after the making of the order, registration of the charge was renewed or the charge registered in pursuance of sub-paragraph (3), the Chief Land Registrar shall not cancel the registration of the charge in accordance with sub-paragraph (1) unless he is also satisfied that the order has ceased to have effect.

(3) Where such an order has been made, then, for the purposes of sub-paragraph (2), the spouse entitled to the charge affected by the order may—

(a) if before the date of the order the charge was registered under section 31(10) or under section 2 of the Land Charges Act 1972, renew the registration of the charge, and

(b) if before the said date the charge was not so registered, register the charge under section 31(10) or under section 2 of the Land Charges Act 1972.

(4) Renewal of the registration of a charge in pursuance of sub-paragraph (3) shall be effected in such manner as may be prescribed, and an application for such renewal or for registration of a charge in pursuance of that sub-paragraph shall contain such particulars of any order affecting the charge made under section 33(5) as may be prescribed.

(5) The renewal in pursuance of sub-paragraph (3) of the registration of a charge shall not affect the priority of the charge.

(6) In this paragraph "prescribed" means prescribed by rules made under section 16 of the Land Charges Act 1972 or [by land registration rules under the Land Registration Act 2002][5], as the circumstances of the case require.

Release of matrimonial home rights

5.—(1) A spouse entitled to matrimonial home rights may by a release in writing release those rights or release them as respects part only of the dwelling-house affected by them.

(2) Where a contract is made for the sale of an estate or interest in a dwelling-house, or for the grant of a lease or underlease of a dwelling-house, being (in either case) a dwelling-house affected by a charge registered under section 31(10) or under section 2 of the Land Charges Act 1972, then, without prejudice to sub-paragraph (1), the matrimonial home rights constituting the charge shall be deemed to have been released on the happening of whichever of the following events first occurs—

(a) the delivery to the purchaser or lessee, as the case may be, or his solicitor on completion of the contract of an application by the spouse entitled to the charge for the cancellation of the registration of the charge; or

(b) the lodging of such an application at Her Majesty's Land Registry.

Postponement of priority of charge

6. A spouse entitled by virtue of section 31 to a charge on an estate or interest may agree in writing that any other charge on, or interest in, that estate or interest shall rank in priority to the charge to which that spouse is so entitled.

---

[5] Words substituted by the Land Registration Act 2002, s.133, Sched. 11, para. 34(1), (3).

Party Wall Etc. Act 1996

(1996 c. 40)

Construction and repair of walls on line of junction

New building on line of junction

1.—(1) This section shall have effect where lands of different owners adjoin and— **61–001**

(a) are not built on at the line of junction; or

(b) are built on at the line of junction only to the extent of a boundary wall (not being a party fence wall or the external wall of a building),

and either owner is about to build on any part of the line of junction.

(2) If a building owner desires to build a party wall or party fence wall on the line of junction he shall, at least one month before he intends the building work to start, serve on any adjoining owner a notice which indicates his desire to build and describes the intended wall.

(3) If, having been served with notice described in subsection (2), an adjoining owner serves on the building owner a notice indicating his consent to the building of a party wall or party fence wall—

(a) the wall shall be built half on the land of each of the two owners or in such other position as may be agreed between the two owners; and

(b) the expense of building the wall shall be from time to time defrayed by the two owners in such proportion as has regard to the use made or to be made of the wall by each of them and to the cost of labour and materials prevailing at the time when that use is made by each owner respectively.

(4) If, having been served with notice described in subsection (2), an adjoining owner does not consent under this subsection to the building of a party wall or party fence wall, the building owner may only build the wall—

(a) at his own expense; and

(b) as an external wall or a fence wall, as the case may be, placed wholly on his own land,

and consent under this subsection is consent by a notice served within the period of fourteen days beginning with the day on which the notice described in subsection (2) is served.

(5) If the building owner desires to build on the line of junction a wall placed wholly on his own land he shall, at least one month before he intends the building work to start, serve on any adjoining owner a notice which indicates his desire to build and describes the intended wall.

(6) Where the building owner builds a wall wholly on his own land in accordance with subsection (4) or (5) he shall have the right, at any time in the period which—

(a) begins one month after the day on which the notice mentioned in the subsection concerned was served, and

(b) ends twelve months after that day,

to place below the level of the land of the adjoining owner such projecting footings and foundations as are necessary for the construction of the wall.

(7) Where the building owner builds a wall wholly on his own land in accordance with subsection (4) or (5) he shall do so at his own expense and shall

compensate any adjoining owner and any adjoining occupier for any damage to his property occasioned by—

(a) the building of the wall;

(b) the placing of any footings or foundations placed in accordance with subsection (6).

(8) Where any dispute arises under this section between the building owner and any adjoining owner or occupier it is to be determined in accordance with section 10.

Repair etc. of party wall: rights of owner

61–002 **2.**—(1) This section applies where lands of different owners adjoin and at the line of junction the said lands are built on or a boundary wall, being a party fence wall or the external wall of a building, has been erected.

(2) A building owner shall have the following rights—

(a) to underpin, thicken or raise a party structure, a party fence wall, or an external wall which belongs to the building owner and is built against a party structure or party fence wall;

(b) to make good, repair, or demolish and rebuild, a party structure or party fence wall in a case where such work is necessary on account of defect or want of repair of the structure or wall;

(c) to demolish a partition which separates buildings belonging to different owners but does not conform with statutory requirements and to build instead a party wall which does so conform;

(d) in the case of buildings connected by arches or structures over public ways or over passages belonging to other persons, to demolish the whole or part of such buildings, arches or structures which do not conform with statutory requirements and to rebuild them so that they do so conform;

(e) to demolish a party structure which is of insufficient strength or height for the purposes of any intended building of the building owner and to rebuild it of sufficient strength or height for the said purposes (including rebuilding to a lesser height or thickness where the rebuilt structure is of sufficient strength and height for the purposes of any adjoining owner);

(f) to cut into a party structure for any purpose (which may be or include the purpose of inserting a damp proof course);

(g) to cut away from a party wall, party fence wall, external wall or boundary wall any footing or any projecting chimney breast, jamb or flue, or other projection on or over the land of the building owner in order to erect, raise or underpin any such wall or for any other purpose;

(h) to cut away or demolish parts of any wall or building of an adjoining owner overhanging the land of the building owner or overhanging a party wall, to the extent that it is necessary to cut away or demolish the parts to enable a vertical wall to be erected or raised against the wall or building of the adjoining owner;

(j) to cut into the wall of an adjoining owner's building in order to insert a flashing or other weather-proofing of a wall erected against that wall;

(k) to execute any other necessary works incidental to the connection of a party structure with the premises adjoining it;

(l) to raise a party fence wall, or to raise such a wall for use as a party wall, and to demolish a party fence wall and rebuild it as a party fence wall or as a party wall;

(m) subject to the provisions of section 11(7), to reduce, or to demolish and rebuild, a party wall or party fence wall to—

(i) a height of not less than two metres where the wall is not used by an adjoining owner to any greater extent than a boundary wall; or

(ii) a height currently enclosed upon by the building of an adjoining owner;

(n) to expose a party wall or party structure hitherto enclosed subject to providing adequate weathering.

(3) Where work mentioned in paragraph (a) of subsection (2) is not necessary on account of defect or want of repair of the structure or wall concerned, the right falling within that paragraph is exercisable—

(a) subject to making good all damage occasioned by the work to the adjoining premises or to their internal furnishings and decorations; and

(b) where the work is to a party structure or external wall, subject to carrying any relevant flues and chimney stacks up to such a height and in such materials as may be agreed between the building owner and the adjoining owner concerned or, in the event of dispute, determined in accordance with section 10;

and relevant flues and chimney stacks are those which belong to an adjoining owner and either form part of or rest on or against the party structure or external wall.

(4) The right falling within subsection (2)(e) is exercisable subject to—

(a) making good all damage occasioned by the work to the adjoining premises or to their internal furnishings and decorations; and

(b) carrying any relevant flues and chimney stacks up to such a height and in such materials as may be agreed between the building owner and the adjoining owner concerned or, in the event of dispute, determined in accordance with section 10;

and relevant flues and chimney stacks are those which belong to an adjoining owner and either form part of or rest on or against the party structure.

(5) Any right falling within subsection (2)(f), (g) or (h) is exercisable subject to making good all damage occasioned by the work to the adjoining premises or to their internal furnishings and decorations.

(6) The right falling within subsection (2)(j) is exercisable subject to making good all damage occasioned by the work to the wall of the adjoining owner's building.

(7) The right falling within subsection (2)(m) is exercisable subject to—

(a) reconstructing any parapet or replacing an existing parapet with another one; or

(b) constructing a parapet where one is needed but did not exist before.

(8) For the purposes of this section a building or structure which was erected before the day on which this Act was passed shall be deemed to conform with statutory requirements if it conforms with the statutes regulating buildings or structures on the date on which it was erected.

Party structure notices

3.—(1) Before exercising any right conferred on him by section 2 a building owner shall serve on any adjoining owner a notice (in this Act referred to as a "party structure notice") stating— **61–003**

(a) the name and address of the building owner;
(b) the nature and particulars of the proposed work including, in cases where the building owner proposes to construct special foundations, plans, sections and details of construction of the special foundations together with reasonable particulars of the loads to be carried thereby; and
(c) the date on which the proposed work will begin.

(2) A party structure notice shall—
(a) be served at least two months before the date on which the proposed work will begin;
(b) cease to have effect if the work to which it relates—
(i) has not begun within the period of twelve months beginning with the day on which the notice is served; and
(ii) is not prosecuted with due diligence.

(3) Nothing in this section shall—
(a) prevent a building owner from exercising with the consent in writing of the adjoining owners and of the adjoining occupiers any right conferred on him by section 2; or
(b) require a building owner to serve any party structure notice before complying with any notice served under any statutory provisions relating to dangerous or neglected structures.

Counter notices

61–004 **4.**—(1) An adjoining owner may, having been served with a party structure notice serve on the building owner a notice (in this Act referred to as a "counter notice") setting out—
(a) in respect of a party fence wall or party structure, a requirement that the building owner build in or on the wall or structure to which the notice relates such chimney copings, breasts, jambs or flues, or such piers or recesses or other like works, as may reasonably be required for the convenience of the adjoining owner;
(b) in respect of special foundations to which the adjoining owner consents under section 7(4) below, a requirement that the special foundations—
(i) be placed at a specified greater depth than that proposed by the building owner; or
(ii) be constructed of sufficient strength to bear the load to be carried by columns of any intended building of the adjoining owner,

or both.

(2) A counter notice shall—
(a) specify the works required by the notice to be executed and shall be accompanied by plans, sections and particulars of such works; and
(b) be served within the period of one month beginning with the day on which the party structure notice is served.

(3) A building owner on whom a counter notice has been served shall comply with the requirements of the counter notice unless the execution of the works required by the counter notice would—
(a) be injurious to him;
(b) cause unnecessary inconvenience to him; or
(c) cause unnecessary delay in the execution of the works pursuant to the party structure notice.

Disputes arising under sections 3 and 4

5. If an owner on whom a party structure notice or a counter notice has been served does not serve a notice indicating his consent to it within the period of fourteen days beginning with the day on which the party structure notice or counter notice was served, he shall be deemed to have dissented from the notice and a dispute shall be deemed to have arisen between the parties. **61–005**

Adjacent excavation and construction

Adjacent excavation and construction

6.—(1) This section applies where— **61–006**

(a) a building owner proposes to excavate, or excavate for and erect a building or structure, within a distance of three metres measured horizontally from any part of a building or structure of an adjoining owner; and

(b) any part of the proposed excavation, building or structure will within those three metres extend to a lower level than the level of the bottom of the foundations of the building or structure of the adjoining owner.

(2) This section also applies where—

(a) a building owner proposes to excavate, or excavate for and erect a building or structure, within a distance of six metres measured horizontally from any part of a building or structure of an adjoining owner; and

(b) any part of the proposed excavation, building or structure will within those six metres meet a plane drawn downwards in the direction of the excavation, building or structure of the building owner at an angle of forty-five degrees to the horizontal from the line formed by the intersection of the plane of the level of the bottom of the foundations of the building or structure of the adjoining owner with the plane of the external face of the external wall of the building or structure of the adjoining owner.

(3) The building owner may, and if required by the adjoining owner shall, at his own expense underpin or otherwise strengthen or safeguard the foundations of the building or structure of the adjoining owner so far as may be necessary.

(4) Where the buildings or structures of different owners are within the respective distances mentioned in subsections (1) and (2) the owners of those buildings or structures shall be deemed to be adjoining owners for the purposes of this section.

(5) In any case where this section applies the building owner shall, at least one month before beginning to excavate, or excavate for and erect a building or structure, serve on the adjoining owner a notice indicating his proposals and stating whether he proposes to underpin or otherwise strengthen or safeguard the foundations of the building or structure of the adjoining owner.

(6) The notice referred to in subsection (5) shall be accompanied by plans and sections showing—

(a) the site and depth of any excavation the building owner proposes to make;

(b) if he proposes to erect a building or structure, its site.

(7) If an owner on whom a notice referred to in subsection (5) has been served does not serve a notice indicating his consent to it within the period of fourteen days beginning with the day on which the notice referred to in subsection (5) was

served, he shall be deemed to have dissented from the notice and a dispute shall be deemed to have arisen between the parties.

(8) The notice referred to in subsection (5) shall cease to have effect if the work to which the notice relates—

(a) has not begun within the period of twelve months beginning with the day on which the notice was served; and

(b) is not prosecuted with due diligence.

(9) On completion of any work executed in pursuance of this section the building owner shall if so requested by the adjoining owner supply him with particulars including plans and sections of the work.

(10) Nothing in this section shall relieve the building owner from any liability to which he would otherwise be subject for injury to any adjoining owner or any adjoining occupier by reason of work executed by him.

Rights etc.

Compensation etc.

61–007 **7.**—(1) A building owner shall not exercise any right conferred on him by this Act in such a manner or at such time as to cause unnecessary inconvenience to any adjoining owner or to any adjoining occupier.

(2) The building owner shall compensate any adjoining owner and any adjoining occupier for any loss or damage which may result to any of them by reason of any work executed in pursuance of this Act.

(3) Where a building owner in exercising any right conferred on him by this Act lays open any part of the adjoining land or building he shall at his own expense make and maintain so long as may be necessary a proper hoarding, shoring or fans or temporary construction for the protection of the adjoining land or building and the security of any adjoining occupier.

(4) Nothing in this Act shall authorise the building owner to place special foundations on land of an adjoining owner without his previous consent in writing.

(5) Any works executed in pursuance of this Act shall—

(a) comply with the provisions of statutory requirements; and

(b) be executed in accordance with such plans, sections and particulars as may be agreed between the owners or in the event of dispute determined in accordance with section 10;

and no deviation shall be made from those plans, sections and particulars except such as may be agreed between the owners (or surveyors acting on their behalf) or in the event of dispute determined in accordance with section 10.

Rights of entry

61–008 **8.**—(1) A building owner, his servants, agents and workmen may during usual working hours enter and remain on any land or premises for the purpose of executing any work in pursuance of this Act and may remove any furniture or fittings or take any other action necessary for that purpose.

(2) If the premises are closed, the building owner, his agents and workmen may, if accompanied by a constable or other police officer, break open any fences or doors in order to enter the premises.

(3) No land or premises may be entered by any person under subsection (1) unless the building owner serves on the owner and the occupier of the land or premises—

(a) in case of emergency, such notice of the intention to enter as may be reasonably practicable;

(b) in any other case, such notice of the intention to enter as complies with subsection (4).

(4) Notice complies with this subsection if it is served in a period of not less than fourteen days ending with the day of the proposed entry.

(5) A surveyor appointed or selected under section 10 may during usual working hours enter and remain on any land or premises for the purpose of carrying out the object for which he is appointed or selected.

(6) No land or premises may be entered by a surveyor under subsection (5) unless the building owner who is a party to the dispute concerned serves on the owner and the occupier of the land or premises—

(a) in case of emergency, such notice of the intention to enter as may be reasonably practicable;

(b) in any other case, such notice of the intention to enter as complies with subsection (4).

Easements

9. Nothing in this Act shall— **61–009**

(a) authorise any interference with an easement of light or other easements in or relating to a party wall; or

(b) prejudicially affect any right of any person to preserve or restore any right or other thing in or connected with a party wall in case of the party wall being pulled down or rebuilt.

. . . . . .

Interpretation

20. In this Act, unless the context otherwise requires, the following expressions have the meanings hereby respectively assigned to them— **61–010**

"adjoining owner" and "adjoining occupier" respectively mean any owner and any occupier of land, buildings, storeys or rooms adjoining those of the building owner and for the purposes only of section 6 within the distances specified in that section;

"appointing officer" means the person appointed under this Act by the local authority to make such appointments as are required under section 10(8);

"building owner" means an owner of land who is desirous of exercising rights under this Act;

"foundation", in relation to a wall, means the solid ground or artificially formed support resting on solid ground on which the wall rests;

"owner" includes—

(a) a person in receipt of, or entitled to receive, the whole or part of the rents or profits of land;

(b) a person in possession of land, otherwise than as a mortgagee or as a tenant from year to year or for a lesser term or as a tenant at will;

(c) a purchaser of an interest in land under a contract for purchase or under an agreement for a lease, otherwise than under an agreement for a tenancy from year to year or for a lesser term;

"party fence wall" means a wall (not being part of a building) which stands on lands of different owners and is used or constructed to be used for separating such adjoining lands, but does not include a wall constructed on the land of one owner the artificially formed support of which projects into the land of another owner;

"party structure" means a party wall and also a floor partition or other structure separating buildings or parts of buildings approached solely by separate staircases or separate entrances;

"party wall" means—

(a) a wall which forms part of a building and stands on lands of different owners to a greater extent than the projection of any artificially formed support on which the wall rests; and

(b) so much of a wall not being a wall referred to in paragraph (a) above as separates buildings belonging to different owners;

"special foundations" means foundations in which an assemblage of beams or rods is employed for the purpose of distributing any load; and

"surveyor" means any person not being a party to the matter appointed or selected under section 10 to determine disputes in accordance with the procedures set out in this Act.

Trusts of Land and Appointment of Trustees Act 1996

(1996 c. 47)

ARRANGEMENT OF SECTIONS

PART I

TRUSTS OF LAND

Introductory

SECT.

PART I

TRUSTS OF LAND

Introductory

Meaning of "trust of land"

1.—(1) In this Act— **62–001**

(a) "trust of land" means (subject to subsection (3)) any trust of property which consists of or includes land, and

(b) "trustees of land" means trustees of a trust of land.

(2) The reference in subsection (1)(a) to a trust—

(a) is to any description of trust (whether express, implied, resulting or constructive), including a trust for sale and a bare trust, and

(b) includes a trust created, or arising, before the commencement of this Act.

(3) The reference to land in subsection (1)(a) does not include land which (despite section 2) is settled land or which is land to which the Universities and College Estates Act 1925 applies.

Settlements and trusts for sale as trusts of land

Trusts in place of settlements

62–002 **2.**—(1) No settlement created after the commencement of this Act is a settlement for the purposes of the Settled Land Act 1925; and no settlement shall be deemed to be made under that Act after that commencement.

(2) Subsection (1) does not apply to a settlement created on the occasion of an alteration in any interest in, or of a person becoming entitled under, a settlement which—

(a) is in existence at the commencement of this Act, or

(b) derives from a settlement within paragraph (a) or this paragraph.

(3) But a settlement created as mentioned in subsection (2) is not a settlement for the purposes of the Settled Land Act 1925 if provision to the effect that it is not is made in the instrument, or any of the instruments, by which it is created.

(4) Where at any time after the commencement of this Act there is in the case of any settlement which is a settlement for the purposes of the Settled Land Act 1925 no relevant property which is, or is deemed to be, subject to the settlement, the settlement permanently ceases at that time to be a settlement for the purposes of that Act.

In this subsection "relevant property" means land and personal chattels to which section 67(1) of the Settled Land Act 1925 (heirlooms) applies.

(5) No land held on charitable, ecclesiastical or public trusts shall be or be deemed to be settled land after the commencement of this Act, even if it was or was deemed to be settled land before that commencement.

(6) Schedule 1 has effect to make provision consequential on this section (including provision to impose a trust in circumstances in which, apart from this section, there would be a settlement for the purposes of the Settled Land Act 1925 (and there would not otherwise be a trust)).

Abolition of doctrine of conversion

62–003 **3.**—(1) Where land is held by trustees subject to a trust for sale, the land is not to be regarded as personal property; and where personal property is subject to a trust for sale in order that the trustees may acquire land, the personal property is not to be regarded as land.

(2) Subsection (1) does not apply to a trust created by a will if the testator died before the commencement of this Act.

(3) Subject to that, subsection (1) applies to a trust whether it is created, or arises, before or after that commencement.

Express trusts for sale as trusts of land

62–004 **4.**—(1) In the case of every trust for sale of land created by a disposition there is to be implied, despite any provision to the contrary made by the disposition, a power for the trustees to postpone sale of the land; and the trustees are not liable in any way for postponing sale of the land, in the exercise of their discretion, for an indefinite period.

(2) Subsection (1) applies to a trust whether it is created, or arises, before or after the commencement of this Act.

(3) Subsection (1) does not affect any liability incurred by trustees before that commencement.

Implied trusts for sale as trusts of land

5.—(1) Schedule 2 has effect in relation to statutory provisions which impose a trust for sale of land in certain circumstances so that in those circumstances there is instead a trust of the land (without a duty to sell). **62–005**

(2) Section 1 of the Settled Land Act 1925 does not apply to land held on any trust arising by virtue of that Schedule (so that any such land is subject to a trust of land).

Functions of trustees of land

General powers of trustees

6.—(1) For the purpose of exercising their functions as trustees, the trustees of land have in relation to the land subject to the trust all the powers of an absolute owner. **62–006**

(2) Where in the case of any land subject to a trust of land each of the beneficiaries interested in the land is a person of full age and capacity who is absolutely entitled to the land, the powers conferred on the trustees by subsection (1) include the power to convey the land to the beneficiaries even though they have not required the trustees to do so; and where land is conveyed by virtue of this subsection—

(a) the beneficiaries shall do whatever is necessary to secure that it vests in them, and

(b) if they fail to do so, the court may make an order requiring them to do so.

(3) The trustees of land have power to [acquire land under the power conferred by section 8 of the Trustee Act 2000.][1]

(4) [*Repealed by the Trustee Act 2000, s.40(1), (3), Sched. 2, Pt. II, para. 45(2), Sched. 4, Pt. II.*]

(5) In exercising the powers conferred by this section trustees shall have regard to the rights of the beneficiaries.

(6) The powers conferred by this section shall not be exercised in contravention of, or of any order made in pursuance of, any other enactment or any rule of law or equity.

(7) The reference in subsection (6) to an order includes an order of any court or of the Charity Commissioners.

(8) Where any enactment other than this section confers on trustees authority to act subject to any restriction, limitation or condition, trustees of land may not exercise the powers conferred by this section to do any act which they are prevented from doing under the other enactment by reason of the restriction, limitation or condition.

[(9) The duty of care under section 1 of the Trustee Act 2000 applies to trustees of land when exercising the powers conferred by this section.][2]

[1] Words substituted by the Trustee Act 2000, s.40(1), Sched. 2, Pt. II, para. 45(1).
[2] subs. (9) added by the Trustee Act 2000, s.40(1), Sched. 2, Pt. II, para. 45(3).

Partition by trustees

62–007 **7.**—(1) The trustees of land may, where beneficiaries of full age are absolutely entitled in undivided shares to land subject to the trust, partition the land, or any part of it, and provide (by way of mortgage or otherwise) for the payment of any equality money.

(2) The trustees shall give effect to any such partition by conveying the partitioned land in severalty (whether or not subject to any legal mortgage created for raising equality money), either absolutely or in trust, in accordance with the rights of those beneficiaries.

(3) Before exercising their powers under subsection (2) the trustees shall obtain the consent of each of those beneficiaries.

(4) Where a share in the land is affected by an incumbrance, the trustees may either give effect to it or provide for its discharge from the property allotted to that share as they think fit.

(5) If a share in the land is absolutely vested in a minor, subsections (1) to (4) apply as if he were of full age, except that the trustees may act on his behalf and retain land or other property representing his share in trust for him.

[(6) Subsection (1) is subject to sections 21 (part-unit: interests) and 22 (part-unit: charging) of the Commonhold and Leasehold Reform Act 2002.][3]

Exclusion and restriction of powers

62–008 **8.**—(1) Sections 6 and 7 do not apply in the case of a trust of land created by a disposition in so far as provision to the effect that they do not apply is made by the disposition.

(2) If the disposition creating such a trust makes provision requiring any consent to be obtained to the exercise of any power conferred by section 6 or 7, the power may not be exercised without that consent.

(3) Subsection (1) does not apply in the case of charitable, ecclesiastical or public trusts.

(4) Subsections (1) and (2) have effect subject to any enactment which prohibits or restricts the effect of provision of the description mentioned in them.

Delegation by trustees

62–009 **9.**—(1) The trustees of land may, by power of attorney, delegate to any beneficiary or beneficiaries of full age and beneficially entitled to an interest in possession in land subject to the trust any of their functions as trustees which relate to the land.

(2) Where trustees purport to delegate to a person by a power of attorney under subsection (1) functions relating to any land and another person in good faith deals with him in relation to the land, he shall be presumed in favour of that other person to have been a person to whom the functions could be delegated unless that other person has knowledge at the time of the transaction that he was not such a person.

And it shall be conclusively presumed in favour of any purchaser whose interest depends on the validity of that transaction that that other person dealt

[3] subs. (6) added by the Commonhold and Leasehold Reform Act 2002, s.68, Sched. 5, para. 8.

in good faith and did not have such knowledge if that other person makes a statutory declaration to that effect before or within three months after the completion of the purchase.

(3) A power of attorney under subsection (1) shall be given by all the trustees jointly and (unless expressed to be irrevocable and to be given by way of security) may be revoked by any one or more of them; and such a power is revoked by the appointment as a trustee of a person other than those by whom it is given (though not by any of those persons dying or otherwise ceasing to be a trustee).

(4) Where a beneficiary to whom functions are delegated by a power of attorney under subsection (1) ceases to be a person beneficially entitled to an interest in possession in land subject to the trust—

(a) if the functions are delegated to him alone, the power is revoked,

(b) if the functions are delegated to him and to other beneficiaries to be exercised by them jointly (but not separately), the power is revoked if each of the other beneficiaries ceases to be so entitled (but otherwise functions exercisable in accordance with the power are so exercisable by the remaining beneficiary or beneficiaries), and

(c) if the functions are delegated to him and to other beneficiaries to be exercised by them separately (or either separately or jointly), the power is revoked in so far as it relates to him.

(5) A delegation under subsection (1) may be for any period or indefinite.

(6) A power of attorney under subsection (1) cannot be an enduring power within the meaning of the Enduring Powers of Attorney Act 1985.

(7) Beneficiaries to whom functions have been delegated under subsection (1) are, in relation to the exercise of the functions, in the same position as trustees (with the same duties and liabilities); but such beneficiaries shall not be regarded as trustees for any other purposes (including, in particular, the purposes of any enactment permitting the delegation of functions by trustees or imposing requirements relating to the payment of capital money).

(8) [*Repealed by the Trustee Act 2000, s.40(1), (3), Sched. 2, Pt. II, para. 46, Sched. 4, Pt. II.*]

(9) Neither this section nor the repeal by this Act of section 29 of the Law of Property Act 1925 (which is superseded by this section) affects the operation after the commencement of this Act of any delegation effected before that commencement.

[**Duties of trustees in connection with delegation etc.**

9A.—(1) the duty of care under section 1 of the Trustee Act 2000 applies to trustees of land in deciding whether to delegate any of their functions under section 9. **62–010**

(2) Subsection (3) applies if the trustees of land—

(a) delegate any of their functions under section 9, and

(b) the delegation is not irrevocable.

(3) While the delegation continues, the trustees—

(a) must keep the delegation under review,

(b) if circumstances make it appropriate to do so, must consider whether there is a need to exercise any power of intervention that they have, and

(c) if they consider that there is a need to exercise such a power, must do so.

(4) "Power of intervention" includes—

(a) a power to give directions to the beneficiary;

(b) a power to revoke the delegation.

(5) The duty of care under section 1 of the 2000 Act applies to trustees in carrying out any duty under subsection (3).

(6) A trustee of land is not liable for any act or default of the beneficiary, or beneficiaries, unless the trustee fails to comply with the duty of care in deciding to delegate any of the trustee's functions under section 9 or in carrying out any duty under subsection (3).

(7) Neither this section nor the repeal of section 9(8) by the Trustee Act 2000 affects the operation after the commencement of this section of any delegation effected before that commencement.][4]

Consents and consultation

Consents

62–011 **10.**—(1) If a disposition creating a trust of land requires the consent of more than two persons to the exercise by the trustees of any function relating to the land, the consent of any two of them to the exercise of the function is sufficient in favour of a purchaser.

(2) Subsection (1) does not apply to the exercise of a function by trustees of land held on charitable, ecclesiastical or public trusts.

(3) Where at any time a person whose consent is expressed by a disposition creating a trust of land to be required to the exercise by the trustees of any function relating to the land is not of full age—

(a) his consent is not, in favour of a purchaser, required to the exercise of the function, but

(b) the trustees shall obtain the consent of a parent who has parental responsibility for him (within the meaning of the Children Act 1989) or of a guardian of his.

Consultation with beneficiaries

62–012 **11.**—(1) The trustees of land shall in the exercise of any function relating to land subject to the trust—

(a) so far as practicable, consult the beneficiaries of full age and beneficially entitled to an interest in possession in the land, and

(b) so far as consistent with the general interest of the trust, give effect to the wishes of those beneficiaries, or (in case of dispute) of the majority (according to the value of their combined interests).

(2) Subsection (1) does not apply—

(a) in relation to a trust created by a disposition in so far as provision that it does not apply is made by the disposition,

(b) in relation to a trust created or arising under a will made before the commencement of this Act, or

(c) in relation to the exercise of the power mentioned in section 6(2).

(3) Subsection (1) does not apply to a trust created before the commencement of this Act by a disposition, or a trust created after that commencement by reference to such a trust, unless provision to the effect that it is to apply is made by a deed executed—

(a) in a case in which the trust was created by one person and he is of full capacity, by that person, or

[4] s.9A inserted by the Trustee Act 2000, s.40(1), Sched. 2, Pt. II, para. 47.

(b) in a case in which the trust was created by more than one person, by such of the persons who created the trust as are alive and of full capacity.

(4) A deed executed for the purposes of subsection (3) is irrevocable.

Right of beneficiaries to occupy trust land

The right to occupy

12.—(1) A beneficiary who is beneficially entitled to an interest in possession in land subject to a trust of land is entitled by reason of his interest to occupy the land at any time if at that time— **62–013**

(a) the purposes of the trust include making the land available for his occupation (or for the occupation of beneficiaries of a class of which he is a member or of beneficiaries in general), or

(b) the land is held by the trustees so as to be so available.

(2) Subsection (1) does not confer on a beneficiary a right to occupy land if it is either unavailable or unsuitable for occupation by him.

(3) This section is subject to section 13.

Exclusion and restriction of right to occupy

13.—(1) Where two or more beneficiaries are (or apart from this subsection would be) entitled under section 12 to occupy land, the trustees of land may exclude or restrict the entitlement of any one or more (but not all) of them. **62–014**

(2) Trustees may not under subsection (1)—

(a) unreasonably exclude any beneficiary's entitlement to occupy land, or

(b) restrict any such entitlement to an unreasonable extent.

(3) The trustees of land may from time to time impose reasonable conditions on any beneficiary in relation to his occupation of land by reason of his entitlement under section 12.

(4) The matters to which trustees are to have regard in exercising the powers conferred by this section include—

(a) the intentions of the person or persons (if any) who created the trust,

(b) the purposes for which the land is held, and

(c) the circumstances and wishes of each of the beneficiaries who is (or apart from any previous exercise by the trustees of those powers would be) entitled to occupy the land under section 12.

(5) The conditions which may be imposed on a beneficiary under subsection (3) include, in particular, conditions requiring him—

(a) to pay any outgoings or expenses in respect of the land, or

(b) to assume any other obligation in relation to the land or to any activity which is or is proposed to be conducted there.

(6) Where the entitlement of any beneficiary to occupy land under section 12 has been excluded or restricted, the conditions which may be imposed on any other beneficiary under subsection (3) include, in particular, conditions requiring him to—

(a) make payments by way of compensation to the beneficiary whose entitlement has been excluded or restricted, or

(b) forgo any payment or other benefit to which he would otherwise be entitled under the trust so as to benefit that beneficiary.

(7) The powers conferred on trustees by this section may not be exercised—

(a) so as prevent any person who is in occupation of land (whether or not by reason of an entitlement under section 12) from continuing to occupy the land, or

(b) in a manner likely to result in any such person ceasing to occupy the land,

unless he consents or the court has given approval.

(8) The matters to which the court is to have regard in determining whether to give approval under subsection (7) include the matters mentioned in subsection (4)(a) to (c).

Powers of court

Applications for order

62–015 **14.**—(1) Any person who is a trustee of land or has an interest in property subject to a trust of land may make an application to the court for an order under this section.

(2) On an application for an order under this section the court may make any such order—

(a) relating to the exercise by the trustees of any of their functions (including an order relieving them of any obligation to obtain the consent of, or to consult, any person in connection with the exercise of any of their functions), or

(b) declaring the nature or extent of a person's interest in property subject to the trust,

as the court thinks fit.

(3) The court may not under this section make any order as to the appointment or removal of trustees.

(4) The powers conferred on the court by this section are exercisable on an application whether it is made before or after the commencement of this Act.

Matters relevant in determining applications

62–016 **15.**—(1) The matters to which the court is to have regard in determining an application for an order under section 14 include—

(a) the intentions of the person or persons (if any) who created the trust,

(b) the purposes for which the property subject to the trust is held,

(c) the welfare of any minor who occupies or might reasonably be expected to occupy any land subject to the trust as his home, and

(d) the interests of any secured creditor of any beneficiary.

(2) In the case of an application relating to the exercise in relation to any land of the powers conferred on the trustees by section 13, the matters to which the court is to have regard also include the circumstances and wishes of each of the beneficiaries who is (or apart from any previous exercise by the trustees of those powers would be) entitled to occupy the land under section 12.

(3) In the case of any other application, other than one relating to the exercise of the power mentioned in section 6(2), the matters to which the court is to have regard also include the circumstances and wishes of any beneficiaries of full age and entitled to an interest in possession in property subject to the trust or (in case of dispute) of the majority (according to the value of their combined interests).

(4) This section does not apply to an application if section 335A of the Insolvency Act 1986 (which is inserted by Schedule 3 and relates to applications by a trustee of a bankrupt) applies to it.

Purchaser protection

Protection of purchasers

16.—(1) A purchaser of land which is or has been subject to a trust need not be concerned to see that any requirement imposed on the trustees by section 6(5), 7(3) or 11(1) has been complied with. **62–017**

(2) Where—

(a) trustees of land who convey land which (immediately before it is conveyed) is subject to the trust contravene section 6(6) or (8), but

(b) the purchaser of the land from the trustees has no actual notice of the contravention,

the contravention does not invalidate the conveyance.

(3) Where the powers of trustees of land are limited by virtue of section 8—

(a) the trustees shall take all reasonable steps to bring the limitation to the notice of any purchaser of the land from them, but

(b) the limitation does not invalidate any conveyance by the trustees to a purchaser who has no actual notice of the limitation.

(4) Where trustees of land convey land which (immediately before it is conveyed) is subject to the trust to persons believed by them to be beneficiaries absolutely entitled to the land under the trust and of full age and capacity—

(a) the trustees shall execute a deed declaring that they are discharged from the trust in relation to that land, and

(b) if they fail to do so, the court may make an order requiring them to do so.

(5) A purchaser of land to which a deed under subsection (4) relates is entitled to assume that, as from the date of the deed, the land is not subject to the trust unless he has actual notice that the trustees were mistaken in their belief that the land was conveyed to beneficiaries absolutely entitled to the land under the trust and of full age and capacity.

(6) Subsections (2) and (3) do not apply to land held on charitable, ecclesiastical or public trusts.

(7) This section does not apply to registered land.

Supplementary

Application of provisions to trusts of proceeds of sale

17.—(1) [*Repealed by the Trustee Act 2000, s.40(1), (3), Sched. 2, Pt. II, para. 48, Sched. 4, Pt. II.*] **62–018**

(2) Section 14 applies in relation to a trust of proceeds of sale of land and trustees of such a trust as in relation to a trust of land and trustees of land.

(3) In this section "trust of proceeds of sale of land" means (subject to subsection (5)) any trust of property (other than a trust of land) which consists of or includes—

(a) any proceeds of a disposition of land held in trust (including settled land), or

(b) any property representing any such proceeds.

(4) The references in subsection (3) to a trust—

(a) are to any description of trust (whether express, implied, resulting or constructive), including a trust for sale and a bare trust, and

(b) include a trust created, or arising, before the commencement of this Act.

(5) A trust which (despite section 2) is a settlement for the purposes of the Settled Land Act 1925 cannot be a trust of proceeds of sale of land.

(6) In subsection (3)—

(a) "disposition" includes any disposition made, or coming into operation, before the commencement of this Act, and

(b) the reference to settled land includes personal chattels to which section 67(1) of the Settled Land Act 1925 (heirlooms) applies.

Application of Part to personal representatives

62–019 **18.**—(1) The provisions of this Part relating to trustees, other than sections 10, 11 and 14, apply to personal representatives, but with appropriate modifications and without prejudice to the functions of personal representatives for the purposes of administration.

(2) The appropriate modifications include—

(a) the substitution of references to persons interested in the due administration of the estate for references to beneficiaries, and

(b) the substitution of references to the will for references to the disposition creating the trust.

(3) Section 3(1) does not apply to personal representatives if the death occurs before the commencement of this Act.

PART II

APPOINTMENT AND RETIREMENT OF TRUSTEES[5]

Appointment and retirement of trustee at instance of beneficiaries

62–020 **19.**—(1) This section applies in the case of a trust where—

(a) there is no person nominated for the purpose of appointing new trustees by the instrument, if any, creating the trust, and

(b) the beneficiaries under the trust are of full age and capacity and (taken together) are absolutely entitled to the property subject to the trust.

(2) The beneficiaries may give a direction or directions of either or both of the following descriptions—

(a) a written direction to a trustee or trustees to retire from the trust, and

(b) a written direction to the trustees or trustee for the time being (or, if there are none, to the personal representative of the last person who was a trustee) to appoint by writing to be a trustee or trustees the person or persons specified in the direction.

(3) Where—

(a) a trustee has been given a direction under subsection (2)(a),

(b) reasonable arrangements have been made for the protection of any rights of his in connection with the trust,

(c) after he has retired there will be either a trust corporation or at least two persons to act as trustees to perform the trust, and

[5] See also the Trustee Act 1925, ss.34–43, *ante*, paras 8–019 *et seq.*

(d) either another person is to be appointed to be a new trustee on his retirement (whether in compliance with a direction under subsection (2)(b) or otherwise) or the continuing trustees by deed consent to his retirement,

he shall make a deed declaring his retirement and shall be deemed to have retired and be discharged from the trust.

(4) Where a trustee retires under subsection (3) he and the continuing trustees (together with any new trustee) shall (subject to any arrangements for the protection of his rights) do anything necessary to vest the trust property in the continuing trustees (or the continuing and new trustees).

(5) This section has effect subject to the restrictions imposed by the Trustee Act 1925 on the number of trustees.

Appointment of substitute for incapable trustee

20.—(1) This section applies where— **62–021**

(a) a trustee is incapable by reason of mental disorder of exercising his functions as trustee,

(b) there is no person who is both entitled and willing and able to appoint a trustee in place of him under section 36(1) of the Trustee Act 1925, and

(c) the beneficiaries under the trust are of full age and capacity and (taken together) are absolutely entitled to the property subject to the trust.

(2) The beneficiaries may give to—

(a) a receiver of the trustee,

(b) an attorney acting for him under the authority of a power of attorney created by an instrument which is registered under section 6 of the Enduring Powers of Attorney Act 1985, or

(c) a person authorised for the purpose by the authority having jurisdiction under Part VII of the Mental Health Act 1983,

a written direction to appoint by writing the person or persons specified in the direction to be a trustee or trustees in place of the incapable trustee.

Supplementary

21.—(1) For the purposes of section 19 or 20 a direction is given by beneficiaries if— **62–022**

(a) a single direction is jointly given by all of them, or

(b) (subject to subsection (2)) a direction is given by each of them (whether solely or jointly with one or more, but not all, of the others),

and none of them by writing withdraws the direction given by him before it has been complied with.

(2) Where more than one direction is given each must specify for appointment or retirement the same person or persons.

(3) Subsection (7) of section 36 of the Trustee Act 1925 (powers of trustees appointed under that section) applies to a trustee appointed under section 19 or 20 as if he were appointed under that section.

(4) A direction under section 19 or 20 must not specify a person or persons for appointment if the appointment of that person or those persons would be in contravention of section 35(1) of the Trustee Act 1925 or section 24(1) of the Law of Property Act 1925 (requirements as to identity of trustees).

(5) Sections 19 and 20 do not apply in relation to a trust created by a disposition in so far as provision that they do not apply is made by the disposition.

(6) Sections 19 and 20 do not apply in relation to a trust created before the commencement of this Act by a disposition in so far as provision to the effect that they do not apply is made by a deed executed—

(a) in a case in which the trust was created by one person and he is of full capacity, by that person, or

(b) in a case in which the trust was created by more than one person, by such of the persons who created the trust as are alive and of full capacity.

(7) A deed executed for the purposes of subsection (6) is irrevocable.

(8) Where a deed is executed for the purposes of subsection (6)—

(a) it does not affect anything done before its execution to comply with a direction under section 19 or 20, but

(b) a direction under section 19 or 20 which has been given but not complied with before its execution shall cease to have effect.

PART III

SUPPLEMENTARY

Meaning of "beneficiary"

62–023 **22.**—(1) In this Act "beneficiary", in relation to a trust, means any person who under the trust has an interest in property subject to the trust (including a person who has such an interest as a trustee or a personal representative).

(2) In this Act references to a beneficiary who is beneficially entitled do not include a beneficiary who has an interest in property subject to the trust only by reason of being a trustee or personal representative.

(3) For the purposes of this Act a person who is a beneficiary only by reason of being an annuitant is not to be regarded as entitled to an interest in possession in land subject to the trust.

Other interpretation provisions

62–024 **23.**—(1) In this Act "purchaser" has the same meaning as in Part I of the Law of Property Act 1925.

(2) Subject to that, where an expression used in this Act is given a meaning by the Law of Property Act 1925 it has the same meaning as in that Act unless the context otherwise requires.

(3) In this Act "the court" means—

(a) the High Court, or

(b) a county court.

. . . . . .

SCHEDULES

Section 2 SCHEDULE 1

PROVISIONS CONSEQUENTIAL ON SECTION 2

Minors

1.—(1) Where after the commencement of this Act a person purports to convey a legal estate in land to a minor, or two or more minors, alone, the conveyance—

(a) is not effective to pass the legal estate, but
(b) operates as a declaration that the land is held in trust for the minor or minors (or if he purports to convey it to the minor or minors in trust for any persons, for those persons).

(2) Where after the commencement of this Act a person purports to convey a legal estate in land to—

(a) a minor or two or more minors, and
(b) another person who is, or other persons who are, of full age,

the conveyance operates to vest the land in the other person or persons in trust for the minor or minors and the other person or persons (or if he purports to convey it to them in trust for any persons, for those persons).

(3) Where immediately before the commencement of this Act a conveyance is operating (by virtue of section 27 of the Settled Land Act 1925) as an agreement to execute a settlement in favour of a minor or minors—

(a) the agreement ceases to have effect on the commencement of this Act, and
(b) the conveyance subsequently operates instead as a declaration that the land is held in trust for the minor or minors.

2. Where after the commencement of this Act a legal estate in land would, by reason of intestacy or in any other circumstances not dealt with in paragraph 1, vest in a person who is a minor if he were a person of full age, the land is held in trust for the minor.

3. Where, by virtue of an instrument coming into operation after the commencement of this Act, land becomes charged voluntarily (or in consideration of marriage) or by way of family arrangement, whether immediately or after an interval, with the payment of—

(a) a rentcharge for the life of a person or a shorter period, or
(b) capital, annual or periodical sums for the benefit of a person,

the instrument operates as a declaration that the land is held in trust for giving effect to the charge.

Charitable, ecclesiastical and public trusts

4.—(1) This paragrah applies in the case of land held on charitable, ecclesiastical or public trusts (other than land to which the Universities and College Estates Act 1925 applies).

(2) Where there is a conveyance of such land—

(a) if neither section 37(1) nor section 39(1) of the Charities Act 1993 applies to the conveyance, it shall state that the land is held on such trusts, and
(b) if neither section 37(2) nor section 39(2) of that Act has been complied with in relation to the conveyance and a purchaser has notice that the land is held on such trusts, he must see that any consents or orders necessary to authorise the transaction have been obtained.

(3) Where any trustees or the majority of any set of trustees have power to transfer or create any legal estate in the land, the estate shall be transferred or created by them in the names and on behalf of the persons in whom it is vested.

Entailed interests

5.—(1) Where a person purports by an instrument coming into operation after the commencement of this Act to grant to another person an entailed interest in real or personal property, the instrument—

(a) is not effective to grant an entailed interest, but
(b) operates instead as a declaration that the property is held in trust absolutely for the person to whom an entailed interest in the property was purportedly granted.

(2) Where a person purports by an instrument coming into operation after the commencement of this Act to declare himself a tenant in tail of real or personal property, the instrument is not effective to create an entailed interest.

Property held on settlement ceasing to exist

6. Where a settlement ceases to be a settlement for the purposes of the Settled Land Act 1925 because no relevant property (within the meaning of section 2(4)) is, or is deemed to be, subject to the settlement, any property which is or later becomes subject to the settlement is held in trust for the persons interested under the settlement.

Human Rights Act 1998

(1998 c. 42)

Introduction

The Convention Rights

62A–001 **1.**—(1) In this Act "the Convention rights" means the rights and fundamental freedoms set out in—

(a) Articles 2 to 12 and 14 of the Convention,
(b) Articles 1 to 3 of the First Protocol, and
(c) Articles 1 to 2 of the Sixth Protocol,

as read with Articles 16 to 18 of the Convention.

(2) Those Articles are to have effect for the purposes of this Act subject to any designated derogation or reservation (as to which see sections 14 and 15).

(3) The Articles are set out in Schedule 1.

(4) The Secretary of State may by order make such amendments to this Act as he considers appropriate to reflect the effect, in relation to the United Kingdom, of a protocol.

(5) In subsection (4) "protocol" means a protocol to the Convention—

(a) which the United Kingdom has ratified; or
(b) which the United Kingdom has signed with a view to ratification.

(6) No amendment may be made by an order under subsection (4) so as to come into force before the protocol concerned is in force in relation to the United Kingdom.

Interpretation of Convention rights

62A–002 **2.**—(1) A court or tribunal determining a question which has arisen in connection with a Convention right must take into account any—

(a) judgment, decision, declaration or advisory opinion of the European Court of Human Rights,
(b) opinion of the Commission given in a report adopted under Article 31 of the Convention,
(c) decision of the Commission in connection with Article 26 or 27(2) of the Convention, or
(d) decision of the Committee of Ministers taken under Article 46 of the Convention,

whenever made or given, so far as, in the opinion of the court or tribunal, it is relevant to the proceedings in which that question has arisen.

(2) Evidence of any judgment, decision, declaration or opinion of which account may have to be taken under this section is to be given in proceedings before any court or tribunal in such manner as may be provided by rules.

(3) In this section "rules" means rules of court or, in the case of proceedings before a tribunal, rules made for the purposes of this section—

(a) by the Lord Chancellor or the Secretary of State, in relation to any proceedings outside Scotland;
(b) by the Secretary of State, in relation to proceedings in Scotland; or
(c) by a Northern Ireland department, in relation to proceedings before a tribunal in Northern Ireland—

(i) which deals with transferred matters; and
(ii) for which no rules made under paragraph (a) are in force.

Legislation

Interpretation of legislation

3.—(1) So far as it is possible to do so, primary legislation and subordinate legislation must be read and given effect in a way which is compatible with Convention rights. **62A–003**

(2) This section—

(a) applies to primary legislation and subordinate legislation whenever enacted;
(b) does not affect the validity, continuing operation or enforcement of any incompatible primary legislation; and
(c) does not affect the validity, continuing operation or enforcement of any incompatible subordinate legislation if (disregarding any possibility of revocation) primary legislation prevents removal of the incompatibility.

SCHEDULES

Section 1(3)

SCHEDULE 1

THE ARTICLES

PART I

THE CONVENTION

RIGHTS AND FREEDOMS

Article 8

Right to respect for private and family life

1. Everyone has the right to respect for his private and family life, his home and his correspondence.

2. There shall be no interference by a public authority with the exercise of this right except such as is in accordance with the law and is necessary in a democratic society in the interests of national security, public safety or the economic well-being of the country, for the prevention of disorder or crime, for the protection of health or morals, or for the protection of the rights and freedoms of others.

PART II

THE FIRST PROTOCOL

Article 1

Protection of property

Every natural or legal person is entitled to the peaceful enjoyment of his possessions. No one shall be deprived of his possessions except in the public interest and subject to the conditions provided for by law and by the general principles of international law.

The preceding provisions shall not, however, in any way impair the right of a State to enforce such laws as it deems necessary to control the use of property in accordance with the general interest or to secure the payment of taxes or other contributions or penalties.

Trustee Delegation Act 1999

(1999 c. 15)

ARRANGEMENT OF SECTIONS

Attorney of trustee with beneficial interest in land

Exercise of trustee functions by attorney

62B–001 **1.**—(1) The donee of a power of attorney is not prevented from doing an act in relation to—
(a) land,
(b) capital proceeds of a conveyance of land, or
(c) income from land,
by reason only that the act involves the exercise of a trustee function of the donor if, at the time when the act is done, the donor has a beneficial interest in the land, proceeds or income.

(2) In this section—
(a) "conveyance" has the same meaning as in the Law of Property Act 1925, and
(b) references to a trustee function of the donor are to a function which the donor has as trustee (either alone or jointly with any other person or persons).

(3) Subsection (1) above—
(a) applies only if and so far as a contrary intention is not expressed in the instrument creating the power of attorney, and
(b) has effect subject to the terms of that instrument.

(4) The donor of the power of attorney—

(a) is liable for the acts or defaults of the donee in exercising any function by virtue of subsection (1) above in the same manner as if they were acts or defaults of the donor, but

(b) is not liable by reason only that a function is exercised by the donee by virtue of that subsection.

(5) Subsections (1) and (4) above—

(a) apply only if and so far as a contrary intention is not expressed in the instrument (if any) creating the trust, and

(b) have effect subject to the terms of such an instrument.

(6) The fact that it appears that, in dealing with any shares or stock, the donee of the power of attorney is exercising a function by virtue of subsection (1) above does not effect with any notice of any trust a person in whose books the shares are, or stock is, registered or inscribed.

(7) In any case where (by way of exception to section 3(1) of the Trusts of Land and Appointment of Trustees Act 1996) the doctrine of conversion continues to operate, any person who, by reason of the continuing operation of that doctrine, has a beneficial interest in the proceeds of sale of land shall be treated for the purposes of this section and section 2 below as having a beneficial interest in the land.

(8) The donee of a power of attorney is not to be regarded as exercising a trustee function by virtue of subsection (1) above if he is acting under a trustee delegation power; and for this purpose a trustee delegation power is a power of attorney given under—

(a) a statutory provision, or

(b) a provision of the instrument (if any) creating a trust,

under which the donor of the power is expressly authorised to delegate the exercise of all or any of his trustee functions by power of attorney.

(9) Subject to section 4(6) below, this section applies only to powers of attorney created after the commencement of this Act.

Evidence of beneficial interest

2.—(1) This section applies where the interest of a purchaser depends on the donee of a power of attorney having power to do an act in relation to any property by virtue of section 1(1) above. In this subsection "purchaser" has the same meaning as in Part I of the Law of Property Act 1925. **62B–002**

(2) Where this section applies an appropriate statement is, in favour of the purchaser, conclusive evidence of the donor of the power having a beneficial interest in the property at the time of the doing of the act.

(3) In this section "an appropriate statement" means a signed statement made by the donee—

(a) when doing the act in question, or

(b) at any other time within the period of three months beginning with the day on which the act is done,

that the donor has a beneficial interest in the property at the time of the donee doing the act.

(4) If an appropriate statement is false, the donee is liable in the same way as he would be if the statement were contained in a statutory declaration.

3. [*Amends the Powers of Attorney Act 1971, s.10(2).*]

4.—(1) [*Repeals the Enduring Powers of Attorney Act 1985, s.3(3).*][1] **62B–003**

[1] See the Trustee Act 1925, s.25, *ante*, para. 8–012.

(2) Section 3(3) of the Enduring Powers of Attorney Act 1985 ceases to apply to enduring powers created before the commencement of this Act—

(a) where subsection (3) below applies, in accordance with that subsection, and

(b) otherwise, at the end of the period of one year from that commencement.

(3) Where an application for the registration of the instrument creating such an enduring power is made before the commencement of this Act, or during the period of one year from that commencement, section 3(3) of the Enduring Powers of Attorney Act 1985 ceases to apply to the power—

(a) if the instrument is registered pursuant to the application (whether before commencement or during or after that period), when the registration of the instrument is cancelled, and

(b) if the application is finally refused during or after that period, when the application is finally refused.

(4) In subsection (3) above—

(a) "registration" and "registered" mean registration and registered under section 6 of the Enduring Powers of Attorney Act 1985, and

(b) "cancelled" means cancelled under section 8(4) of that Act.

(5) For the purposes of subsection (3)(b) above an application is finally refused—

(a) if the application is withdrawn or any appeal is abandoned, when the application is withdrawn or the appeal is abandoned, and

(b) otherwise, when proceedings on the application (including any proceedings on, or in consequence of, an appeal) have been determined and any time for appealing or further appealing has expired.

(6) Section 1 above applies to an enduring power created before the commencement of this Act from the time when (in accordance with subsections (2) to (5) above) section 3(3) of the Enduring Powers of Attorney Act 1985 ceases to apply to it.

Trustee delegation under section 25 of the Trustee Act 1925

5. [*Substitutes the Trustee Act 1925, s.25.*]

6. [*Repeals the Enduring Powers of Attorney Act 1985, s.2(8).*][2]

Miscellaneous provisions about attorney acting for trustee

Two-trustee rules

62B–004 **7.**—(1) A requirement imposed by an enactment—

(a) that capital money be paid to, or dealt with as directed by, at least two trustees or that a valid receipt for capital money be given otherwise than by a sole trustee, or

(b) that, in order for an interest or power to be overreached, a conveyance or deed be executed by at least two trustees,

is not satisfied by money being paid to or dealt with as directed by, or a receipt for money being given by, a relevant attorney or by a conveyance or deed being executed by such an attorney.

(2) In this section "relevant attorney" means a person (other than a trust corporation within the meaning of the Trustee Act 1925) who is acting either—

[2] See the Trustee Act 1925, s.25, *ante*, para. 8–012.

(a) both as a trustee and as attorney for one or more other trustees, or
(b) as attorney for two or more trustees,

and who is not acting together with any other person or persons.

(3) This section applies whether a relevant attorney is acting under a power created before or after the commencement of this Act (but in the case of such an attorney acting under an enduring power created before that commencement is without prejudice to any continuing application of section 3(3) of the Enduring Powers of Attorney Act 1985 to the enduring power after the commencement in accordance with section 4 above).

8. [*Amends the Trustee Act 1925, s.36.*]

9. [*Amends the Law of Property Act 1925, s.22.*]

Authority of attorney to act in relation to land

Extent of attorney's authority to act in relation to land

10.—(1) Where the donee of a power of attorney is authorised by the power to do an act of any description in relation to any land, his authority to do an act of that description at any time includes authority to do it with respect to any estate or interest in the land which is held at that time by the donor (whether alone or jointly with any other person or persons). **62B–005**

(2) Subsection (1) above—

(a) applies only if and so far as a contrary intention is not expressed in the instrument creating the power of attorney, and
(b) has effect subject to the terms of that instrument.

(3) This section applies only to powers of attorney created after the commencement of this Act.

Supplementary

Interpretation

11.—(1) In this Act— **62B–006**

"land" has the same meaning as in the Trustee Act 1925, and

"enduring power" has the same meaning as in the Enduring Powers of Attorney Act 1985.

(2) References in this Act to the creation of a power of attorney are to the execution by the donor of the instrument creating it.

Contracts (Rights of Third Parties) Act 1999

(1999 c. 31)

ARRANGEMENT OF SECTIONS

SECT.

Right of third party to enforce contractual term

63–001 **1.**—(1) Subject to the provisions of this Act, a person who is not a party to a contract (a "third party") may in his own right enforce a term of the contract if—

(a) the contract expressly provides that he may, or

(b) subject to subsection (2), the term purports to confer a benefit on him.

(2) Subsection (1)(b) does not apply if on a proper construction of the contract it appears that the parties did not intend the term to be enforceable by the third party.

(3) The third party must be expressly identified in the contract by name, as a member of a class or as answering a particular description but need not be in existence when the contract is entered into.

(4) This section does not confer a right on a third party to enforce a term of a contract otherwise than subject to and in accordance with any other relevant terms of the contract.

(5) For the purpose of exercising his right to enforce a term of contract, there shall be available to the third party any remedy that would have been available to him in an action for breach of contract if he had been a party to the contract (and the rules relating to damages, injunctions, specific performance and other relief shall apply accordingly).

(6) Where a term of a contract excludes or limits liability in relation to any matter references in this Act to the third party enforcing the term shall be construed as references to his availing himself of the exclusion or limitation.

(7) In this Act, in relation to a term of contract which is enforceable by a third party—

"the promisor" means the party to the contract against whom the term is enforceable by the third party, and

"the promisee" means the party to the contract by whom the term is enforceable against the promisor.

Variation and rescission of contract

63–002 **2.**—(1) Subject to the provisions of this section, where a third party has a right under section 1 to enforce a term of the contract, the parties to the contract may not, by agreement, rescind the contract, or vary it in such a way as to extinguish or alter his entitlement under that right, without his consent if—

(a) the third party has communicated his assent to the term to the promisor,

(b) the promisor is aware that the third party has relied on the term, or

(c) the promisor can reasonably be expected to have foreseen that the third party would rely on the term and the third party has in fact relied on it.

(2) assent referred to in subsection (1)(a)—
(a) may be by words or conduct, and
(b) if sent to the promisor by post or other means, shall not be regarded as communicated to the promisor until received by him.

(3) Subsection (1) is subject to any express term of the contract under which—
(a) the parties to the contract may by agreement rescind or vary the contract without the consent of the third party, or
(b) the consent of the third party is required in circumstances specified in the contract instead of those set out in subsection (1)(a) to (c).

(4) Where the consent of a third party is required under subsection (1) or (3), the court or arbitral tribunal may, on the application of the parties to the contract, dispense with his consent if satisfied—
(a) that his consent cannot be obtained because his whereabouts cannot reasonably be ascertained, or
(b) that he is mentally incapable of giving his consent.

(5) The court or arbitral tribunal may, on the application of the parties to a contract, dispense with any consent that may be required under subsection (1)(c) if satisfied that it cannot reasonably be ascertained whether or not the third party has in fact relied on the term.

(6) If the court or arbitral tribunal dispenses with a third party's consent, it may impose such conditions as it thinks fit, including a condition requiring the payment of compensation to the third party.

(7) The jurisdiction conferred on the court by subsections (4) to (6) is exercisable by both the High Court and a county court.

Defences etc. available to promisor

3.—(1) Subsections (2) to (5) apply where, in reliance on section 1, proceedings for the enforcement of a term of a contract are brought by a third party. **63–003**

(2) The promisor shall have available to him by way of defence or set-off any matter that—
(a) arises from or in connection with the contract and is relevant to the term, and
(b) would have been available to him by way of defence or set-off if the proceedings had been brought by the promisee.

(3) The promisor shall also have available to him by way of defence or set-off any matter if—
(a) an express term of the contract provides for it to be available to him in proceedings brought by the third party, and
(b) it would have been available to him by way of defence or set-off if the proceedings had been brought by the promisee.

(4) The promisor shall also have available to him—
(a) by way of defence or set-off any matter, and
(b) by way of counterclaim any matter not arising from the contract,

that would have been available to him by way of defence or set-off or, as the case may be, by way of counterclaim against the third party if the third party had been a party to the contract.

(5) Subsections (2) and (4) are subject to any express term of the contract as to the matters that are not to be available to the promisor by way of defence, set-off or counterclaim.

(6) Where in any proceedings brought against him a third party seeks in reliance on section 1 to enforce a term of a contract (including, in particular, a

term purporting to exclude or limit liability), he may not do so if he could not have done so (whether by reason of any particular circumstances relating to him or otherwise) had he been a party to the contract.

Enforcement of contract by promisee

63–004 **4.** Section 1 does not affect any right of the promisee to enforce any term of the contract.

Protection of promisor from double liability

63–005 **5.** Where under section 1 a term of a contract is enforceable by a third party, and the promisee has recovered from the promisor a sum in respect of—

(a) the third party's loss in respect of the term, or
(b) the expense to the promisee of making good to the third party the default of the promisor,

then, in any proceedings brought in reliance on that section by the third party, the court or arbitral tribunal shall reduce any award to the third party to such extent as it things appropriate to take account of the sum recovered by the promisee.

. . . .

Supplementary provisions relating to third party

63–006 **7.**—(1) Section 1 does not affect any right or remedy of a third party that exists or is available apart from this Act.

(2) Section (2)(2) of the Unfair Contract Terms Act 1977 (restriction on exclusion etc. of liability for negligence) shall not apply where the negligence consists of the breach of an obligation arising from a term of a contract and the person seeking to enforce it is a third party acting in reliance on section 1.

(3) In sections 5 and 8 of the Limitation Act 1980 the references to an action founded on a simple contract and an action upon a specialty shall respectively include references to an action brought in reliance on section 1 relating to a simple contract and an action brought in reliance on that section relating to a specialty.

(4) A third party shall not, by virtue of section 1(5) or 3(4) or (6), be treated as a party to the contract for the purposes of any other Act (or any instrument made under any other Act).

Trustee Act 2000

(2000 c. 29)

ARRANGEMENT OF SECTIONS

PART I

THE DUTY OF CARE

PART II

INVESTMENT

PART III

ACQUISITION OF LAND

PART IV

AGENTS, NOMINEES AND CUSTODIANS

Agents

Nominees and custodians

Review of and liability for agents, nominees and custodians etc.

Supplementary

PART I

THE DUTY OF CARE

The duty of care

64–001 **1.**—(1) Whenever the duty under this subsection applies to a trustee, he must exercise such care and skill as is reasonable in the circumstances, having regard in particular—

(a) to any special knowledge or experience that he has or holds himself out as having, and
(b) if he acts as trustee in the course of a business or profession, to any special knowledge or experience that it is reasonable to expect of a person acting in the course of that kind of business or profession.

(2) In this Act the duty under subsection (1) is called "the duty of care".

Application of duty of care

64–002 **2.**—Schedule 1 makes provision about when the duty of care applies to a trustee.

PART II

INVESTMENT

General power of investment

64–003 **3.**—(1) Subject to the provisions of this Part, a trustee may make any kind of investment that he could make if he were absolutely entitled to the assets of the trust.

(2) In this Act the power under subsection (1) is called "the general power of investment".

(3) The general power of investment does not permit a trustee to make investments in land other than in loans secured on land (but see also section 8).

(4) A person invests in a loan secured on land if he has rights under any contract under which—

(a) one person provides another with credit, and
(b) the obligation of the borrower to repay is secured on land.

(5) "Credit" includes any cash loan or other financial accommodation.

(6) "Cash" includes money in any form.

Standard investment criteria

4.—(1) In exercising any power of investment, whether arising under this Part or otherwise, a trustee must have regard to the standard investment criteria. **64–004**

(2) A trustee must from time to time review the investments of the trust and consider whether, having regard to the standard investment criteria, they should be varied.

(3) The standard investment criteria, in relation to a trust, are—

(a) the suitability to the trust of investments of the same kind as any particular investment proposed to be made or retained and of that particular investment as an investment of that kind, and
(b) the need for diversification of investments of the trust, in so far as is appropriate to the circumstances of the trust.

Advice

5.—(1) Before exercising any power of investment, whether arising under this Part or otherwise, a trustee must (unless the exception applies) obtain and consider proper advice about the way in which, having regard to the standard investment criteria, the power should be exercised. **64–005**

(2) When reviewing the investments of the trust, a trustee must (unless the exception applies) obtain and consider proper advice about whether, having regard to the standard investment criteria, the investments should be varied.

(3) The exception is that a trustee need not obtain such advice if he reasonably concludes that in all the circumstances it is unnecessary or inappropriate to do so.

(4) Proper advice is the advice of a person who is reasonably believed by the trustee to be qualified to give it by his ability in and practical experience of financial and other matters relating to the proposed investment.

Restriction or exclusion of this Part etc.

6.—(1) The general power of investment is— **64–006**

(a) in addition to powers conferred on trustees otherwise than by this Act, but
(b) subject to any restriction or exclusion imposed by the trust instrument or by any enactment or any provision of subordinate legislation.

(2) For the purposes of this Act, an enactment or a provision of subordinate legislation is not to be regarded as being, or as being part of, a trust instrument.

(3) In this Act "subordinate legislation" has the same meaning as in the Interpretation Act 1978.

Existing trusts

64–007 **7.**—(1) This Part applies in relation to trusts whether created before or after its commencement.

(2) No provision relating to the powers of a trustee contained in a trust instrument made before 3rd August 1961 is to be treated (for the purposes of section 6(1)(b)) as restricting or excluding the general power of investment.

(3) A provision contained in a trust instrument made before the commencement of this Part which—

(a) has effect under section 3(2) of the Trustee Investments Act 1961 as a power to invest under that Act, or

(b) confers power to invest under that Act,

is to be treated as conferring the general power of investment on a trustee.

PART III

ACQUISITION OF LAND

Power to acquire freehold and leasehold land

64–008 **8.**—(1) A trustee may acquire freehold or leasehold land in the United Kingdom—

(a) as an investment,

(b) for occupation by a beneficiary, or

(c) for any other reason.

(2) "Freehold or leasehold land" means—

(a) in relation to England and Wales, a legal estate in land,

(b) in relation to Scotland—

(i) the estate or interest of the proprietor of the dominium utile or, in the case of land not held on feudal tenure, the estate or interest of the owner, or

(ii) a tenancy, and

(c) in relation to Northern Ireland, a legal estate in land, including land held under a fee farm grant.

(3) For the purpose of exercising his functions as a trustee, a trustee who acquires land under this section has all the powers of an absolute owner in relation to the land:

Restriction or exclusion of this Part etc.

64–009 **9.** The powers conferred by this Part are—

(a) in addition to powers conferred on trustees otherwise than by this Part, but

(b) subject to any restriction or exclusion imposed by the trust instrument or by any enactment or any provision of subordinate legislation.

Existing trusts

64–010 **10.**—(1) This Part does not apply in relation to—

(a) a trust of property which consists of or includes land which (despite section 2 of the Trusts of Land and Appointment of Trustees Act 1996) is settled land, or

(b) a trust to which the Universities and College Estates Act 1925 applies.

(2) Subject to subsection (1), this Part applies in relation to trusts whether created before or after its commencement.

PART IV[1]

AGENTS, NOMINEES AND CUSTODIANS

Agents

Power to employ agents

11.—(1) Subject to the provisions of this Part, the trustees of a trust may authorise any person to exercise any or all of their delegable functions as their agent. **64–011**

(2) In the case of a trust other than a charitable trust, the trustees' delegable functions consist of any function other than—

(a) any function relating to whether or in what way any assets of the trust should be distributed,

(b) any power to decide whether any fees or other payment due to be made out of the trust funds should be made out of income or capital,

(c) any power to appoint a person to be a trustee of the trust, or

(d) any power conferred by any other enactment or the trust instrument which permits the trustees to delegate any of their functions or to appoint a person to act as a nominee or custodian.

(3) In the case of a charitable trust, the trustees' delegable functions are—

(a) any function consisting of carrying out a decision that the trustees have taken;

(b) any function relating to the investment of assets subject to the trust (including, in the case of land held as an investment, managing the land and creating or disposing of an interest in the land);

(c) any function relating to the raising of funds for the trust otherwise than by means of profits of a trade which is an integral part of carrying out the trust's charitable purpose;

(d) any other function prescribed by an order made by the Secretary of State.

(4) For the purposes of subsection (3)(c) a trade is an integral part of carrying out a trust's charitable purpose if, whether carried on in the United Kingdom or elsewhere, the profits are applied solely to the purposes of the trust and either—

(a) the trade is exercised in the course of the actual carrying out of a primary purpose of the trust, or

(b) the work in connection with the trade is mainly carried out by beneficiaries of the trust.

(5) The power to make an order under subsection (3)(d) is exercisable by statutory instrument which shall be subject to annulment in pursuance of a resolution of either House of Parliament.

Persons who may act as agents

12.—(1) Subject to subsection (2), the persons whom the trustees may under section 11 authorise to exercise functions as their agent include one or more of their number. **64–012**

[1] For delegation by individual trustees, see the Trustees Act 1925, s.25, *ante*, para. 8–012.

(2) The trustees may not authorise two (or more) persons to exercise the same function unless they are to exercise the function jointly.

(3) The trustees may not under section 11 authorise a beneficiary to exercise any function as their agent (even if the beneficiary is also a trustee).

(4) The trustees may under section 11 authorise a person to exercise functions as their agent even though he is also appointed to act as their nominee or custodian (whether under section 16, 17 or 18 or any other power).

Linked functions etc.

64–013 **13.**—(1) Subject to subsections (2) and (5), a person who is authorised under section 11 to exercise a function is (whatever the terms of the agency) subject to any specific duties or restrictions attached to the function.
For example, a person who is authorised under section 11 to exercise the general power of investment is subject to the duties under section 4 in relation to that power.

(2) A person who is authorised under section 11 to exercise a power which is subject to a requirement to obtain advice is not subject to the requirement if he is the kind of person from whom it would have been proper for the trustees, in compliance with the requirement, to obtain advice.

(3) Subsections (4) and (5) apply to a trust to which section 11(1) of the Trusts of Land and Appointment of Trustees Act 1996 (duties to consult beneficiaries and give effect to their wishes) applies.

(4) The trustees may not under section 11 authorise a person to exercise any of their functions on terms that prevent them from complying with section 11(1) of the 1996 Act.

(5) A person who is authorised under section 11 to exercise any function relating to land subject to the trust is not subject to section 11(1) of the 1996 Act.

Terms of agency

64–014 **14.**—(1) Subject to subsection (2) and sections 15(2) and 29 to 32, the trustees may authorise a person to exercise functions as their agent on such terms as to remuneration and other matters as they may determine.

(2) The trustees may not authorise a person to exercise functions as their agent on any of the terms mentioned in subsection (3) unless it is reasonably necessary for them to do so.

(3) The terms are—

(a) a term permitting the agent to appoint a substitute;
(b) a term restricting the liability of the agent or his substitute to the trustees or any beneficiary;
(c) a term permitting the agent to act in circumstances capable of giving rise to a conflict of interest.

Asset management: special restrictions

64–015 **15.**—(1) The trustees may not authorise a person to exercise any of their asset management functions as their agent except by an agreement which is in or evidenced in writing.

(2) The trustees may not authorise a person to exercise any of their asset management functions as their agent unless—

(a) they have prepared a statement that gives guidance as to how the functions should be exercised ("a policy statement"), and
(b) the agreement under which the agent is to act includes a term to the effect that he will secure compliance with—
(i) the policy statement, or
(ii) if the policy statement is revised or replaced under section 22, the revised or replacement policy statement.

(3) The trustees must formulate any guidance given in the policy statement with a view to ensuring that the functions will be exercised in the best interests of the trust.

(4) The policy statement must be in or evidenced in writing.

(5) The asset management functions of trustees are their functions relating to—
(a) the investment of assets subject to the trust,
(b) the acquisition of property which is to be subject to the trust, and
(c) managing property which is subject to the trust and disposing of, or creating or disposing of an interest in, such property.

Nominees and custodians

Power to appoint nominees

16.—(1) Subject to the provisions of this Part, the trustees of a trust may— **64–016**
(a) appoint a person to act as their nominee in relation to such of the assets of the trust as they determine (other than settled land), and
(b) take such steps as are necessary to secure that those assets are vested in a person so appointed.

(2) An appointment under this section must be in or evidenced in writing.

(3) This section does not apply to any trust having a custodian trustee or in relation to any assets vested in the official custodian for charities.

Power to appoint custodians

17.—(1) Subject to the provisions of this Part, the trustees of a trust may appoint a person to act as a custodian in relation to such of the assets of the trust as they may determine. **64–017**

(2) For the purposes of this Act a person is a custodian in relation to assets if he undertakes the safe custody of the assets or of any documents or records concerning the assets.

(3) An appointment under this section must be in or evidenced in writing.

(4) This section does not apply to any trust having a custodian trustee or in relation to any assets vested in the official custodian for charities.

Investment in bearer securities

18.—(1) If trustees retain or invest in securities payable to bearer, they must appoint a person to act as a custodian of the securities. **64–018**

(2) Subsection (1) does not apply if the trust instrument or any enactment or provision of subordinate legislation contains provision which (however expressed) permits the trustees to retain or invest in securities payable to bearer without appointing a person to act as a custodian.

(3) An appointment under this section must be in or evidenced in writing.

(4) This section does not apply to any trust having a custodian trustee or in relation to any securities vested in the official custodian for charities.

Persons who may be appointed as nominees or custodians

64–019 **19.**—(1) A person may not be appointed under section 16, 17 or 18 as a nominee or custodian unless one of the relevant conditions is satisfied.

(2) The relevant conditions are that—

(a) the person carries on a business which consists of or includes acting as a nominee or custodian;

(b) the person is a body corporate which is controlled by the trustees;

(c) the person is a body corporate recognised under section 9 of the Administration of Justice Act 1985.

(3) The question whether a body corporate is controlled by trustees is to be determined in accordance with section 840 of the Income and Corporation Taxes Act 1988.

(4) The trustees of a charitable trust which is not an exempt charity must act in accordance with any guidance given by the Charity Commissioners concerning the selection of a person for appointment as a nominee or custodian under section 16, 17 or 18.

(5) Subject to subsections (1) and (4), the persons whom the trustees may under section 16, 17, or 18 appoint as a nominee or custodian include—

(a) one of their number, if that one is a trust corporation, or

(b) two (or more) of their number, if they are to act as joint nominees or joint custodians.

(6) The trustees may under section 16 appoint a person to act as their nominee even though he is also—

(a) appointed to act as their custodian (whether under section 17 or 18 or any other power), or

(b) authorised to exercise functions as their agent (whether under section 11 or any other power).

(7) Likewise, the trustees may under section 17 or 18 appoint a person to act as their custodian even though he is also—

(a) appointed to act as their nominee (whether under section 16 or any other power), or

(b) authorised to exercise functions as their agent (whether under section 11 or any other power).

Terms of appointment of nominees and custodians

64–020 **20.**—(1) Subject to subsection (2) and sections 29 to 32, the trustees may under section 16, 17 or 18 appoint a person to act as a nominee or custodian on such terms as to remuneration and other matters as they may determine.

(2) The trustees may not under section 16, 17 or 18 appoint a person to act as a nominee or custodian on any of the terms mentioned in subsection (3) unless it is reasonably necessary for them to do so.

(3) The terms are—

(a) a term permitting the nominee or custodian to appoint a substitute;

(b) a term restricting the liability of the nominee or custodian or his substitute to the trustees or to any beneficiary;

(c) a term permitting the nominee or custodian to act in circumstances capable of giving rise to a conflict of interest.

Review of and liability for agents, nominees and custodians etc.

Application of sections 22 and 23

21.—(1) Sections 22 and 23 apply in a case where trustees have, under section 11, 16, 17 or 18— **64–021**

(a) authorised a person to exercise functions as their agent, or
(b) appointed a person to act as a nominee or custodian.

(2) Subject to subsection (3), sections 22 and 23 also apply in a case where trustees have, under any power conferred on them by the trust instrument or by any enactment or any provision of subordinate legislation—

(a) authorised a person to exercise functions as their agent, or
(b) appointed a person to act as a nominee or custodian.

(3) If the application of section 22 or 23 is inconsistent with the terms of the trust instrument or the enactment or provision of subordinate legislation, the section in question does not apply.

Review of agents, nominees and custodians etc.

22.—(1) While the agent, nominee or custodian continues to act for the trust, the trustees— **64–022**

(a) must keep under review the arrangements under which the agent, nominee or custodian acts and how those arrangements are being put into effect,
(b) if circumstances make it appropriate to do so, must consider whether there is a need to exercise any power of intervention that they have, and
(c) if they consider that there is a need to exercise such a power, must do so.

(2) If the agent has been authorised to exercise asset management functions, the duty under subsection (1) includes, in particular—

(a) a duty to consider whether there is any need to revise or replace the policy statement made for the purposes of section 15,
(b) if they consider that there is a need to revise or replace the policy statement, a duty to do so, and
(c) a duty to assess whether the policy statement (as it has effect for the time being) is being complied with.

(3) Subsections (3) and (4) of section 15 apply to the revision or replacement of a policy statement under this section as they apply to the making of a policy statement under that section.

(4)

"Power of intervention" includes—

(a) a power to give directions to the agent, nominee or custodian;
(b) a power to revoke the authorisation or appointment.

Liability for agents, nominees and custodians etc.

23.—(1) A trustee is not liable for any act or default of the agent, nominee or custodian unless he has failed to comply with the duty of care applicable to him, under paragraph 3 of Schedule 1— **64–023**

(a) when entering into the arrangements under which the person acts as agent, nominee or custodian, or
(b) when carrying out his duties under section 22.

(2) If a trustee has agreed a term under which the agent, nominee or custodian is permitted to appoint a substitute, the trustee is not liable for any act or default of the substitute unless he has failed to comply with the duty of care applicable to him, under paragraph 3 of Schedule 1—

(a) when agreeing that term, or

(b) when carrying out his duties under section 22 in so far as they relate to the use of the substitute.

Supplementary

Effect of trustees exceeding their powers

64–024 **24.**—A failure by the trustees to act within the limits of the powers conferred by this Part—

(a) in authorising a person to exercise a function of theirs as an agent, or

(b) in appointing a person to act as a nominee or custodian,

does not invalidate the authorisation or appointment.

Sole trustees

64–025 **25.**—(1) Subject to subsection (2), this Part applies in relation to a trust having a sole trustee as it applies in relation to other trusts (and references in this Part to trustees—except in sections 12(1) and (3) and 19(5)—are to be read accordingly).

(2) Section 18 does not impose a duty on a sole trustee if that trustee is a trust corporation.

Restriction or exclusion of this Part etc.

64–026 **26.** The powers conferred by this Part are—

(a) in addition to powers conferred on trustees otherwise than by this Act, but

(b) subject to any restriction or exclusion imposed by the trust instrument or by any enactment or any provision of subordinate legislation.

Existing trusts

64–027 **27.** This Part applies in relation to trusts whether created before or after its commencement.

PART V

REMUNERATION

Trustee's entitlement to payment under trust instrument

64–028 **28.**—(1) Except to the extent (if any) to which the trust instrument makes inconsistent provision, subsections (2) to (4) apply to a trustee if—

(a) there is a provision in the trust instrument entitling him to receive payment out of trust funds in respect of services provided by him to or on behalf of the trust, and

(b) the trustee is a trust corporation or is acting in a professional capacity.

(2) The trustee is to be treated as entitled under the trust instrument to receive payment in respect of services even if they are services which are capable of being provided by a lay trustee.

(3) Subsection (2) applies to a trustee of a charitable trust who is not a trust corporation only—

(a) if he is not a sole trustee, and

(b) to the extent that a majority of the other trustees have agreed that it should apply to him.

(4) Any payments to which the trustee is entitled in respect of services are to be treated as remuneration for services (and not as a gift) for the purposes of—

(a) section 15 of the Wills Act 1837 (gifts to an attesting witness to be void), and

(b) section 34(3) of the Administration of Estates Act 1925 (order in which estate to be paid out).

(5) For the purposes of this Part, a trustee acts in a professional capacity if he acts in the course of a profession or business which consists of or includes the provision of services in connection with—

(a) the management or administration of trusts generally or a particular kind of trust, or

(b) any particular aspect of the management or administration of trusts generally or a particular kind of trust,

and the services he provides to or on behalf of the trust fall within that description.

(6) For the purposes of this Part, a person acts as a lay trustee if he—

(a) is not a trust corporation, and

(b) does not act in a professional capacity.

Remuneration of certain trustees

29.—(1) Subject to subsection (5), a trustee who— **64–029**

(a) is a trust corporation, but

(b) is not a trustee of a charitable trust,

is entitled to receive reasonable remuneration out of the trust funds for any services that the trust corporation provides to or on behalf of the trust.

(2) Subject to subsection (5), a trustee who—

(a) acts in a professional capacity, but

(b) is not a trust corporation, a trustee of a charitable trust or a sole trustee,

is entitled to receive reasonable remuneration out of the trust funds for any services that he provides to or on behalf of the trust if each other trustee has agreed in writing that he may be remunerated for the services.

(3) "Reasonable remuneration" means, in relation to the provision of services by a trustee, such remuneration as is reasonable in the circumstances for the provision of those services to or on behalf of that trust by that trustee and for the purposes of subsection (1) includes, in relation to the provision of services by a trustee who is an authorised institution under the Banking Act 1987 and provides the services in that capacity, the institution's reasonable charges for the provision of such services.

(4) A trustee is entitled to remuneration under this section even if the services in question are capable of being provided by a lay trustee.

(5) A trustee is not entitled to remuneration under this section if any provision about his entitlement to remuneration has been made—

(a) by the trust instrument, or

(b) by any enactment or any provision of subordinate legislation.

(6) This section applies to a trustee who has been authorised under a power conferred by Part IV or the trust instrument—

(a) to exercise functions as an agent of the trustees, or

(b) to act as a nominee or custodian,

as it applies to any other trustee.

Remuneration of trustees of charitable trusts

64–030 **30.**—(1) The Secretary of State may by regulations make provision for the remuneration of trustees of charitable trusts who are trust corporations or act in a professional capacity.

(2) The power under subsection (1) includes power to make provision for the remuneration of a trustee who has been authorised under a power conferred by Part IV or any other enactment or any provision of subordinate legislation, or by the trust instrument—

(a) to exercise functions as an agent of the trustees, or

(b) to act as a nominee or custodian.

(3) Regulations under this section may—

(a) make different provision for different cases;

(b) contain such supplemental, incidental, consequential and transitional provision as the Secretary of State considers appropriate.

(4) The power to make regulations under this section is exercisable by statutory instrument, but no such instrument shall be made unless a draft of it has been laid before Parliament and approved by a resolution of each House of Parliament.

Trustees' expenses

64–031 **31.**—(1) A trustee—

(a) is entitled to be reimbursed from the trust funds, or

(b) may pay out of the trust funds,

expenses properly incurred by him when acting on behalf of the trust.

(2) This section applies to a trustee who has been authorised under a power conferred by Part IV or any other enactment or any provision of subordinate legislation, or by the trust instrument—

(a) to exercise functions as an agent of the trustees, or

(b) to act as a nominee or custodian,

as it applies to any other trustee.

Remuneration and expenses of agents, nominees and custodians

64–032 **32.**—(1) This section applies if, under a power conferred by Part IV or any other enactment or any provision of subordinate legislation, or by the trust instrument, a person other than a trustee has been—

(a) authorised to exercise functions as an agent of the trustees, or

(b) appointed to act as a nominee or custodian.

(2) The trustees may remunerate the agent, nominee or custodian out of the trust funds for services if—

(a) he is engaged on terms entitling him to be remunerated for those services, and

(b) the amount does not exceed such remuneration as is reasonable in the circumstances for the provision of those services by him to or on behalf of that trust.

(3) The trustees may reimburse the agent, nominee or custodian out of the trust funds for any expenses properly incurred by him in exercising functions as an agent, nominee or custodian.

Application

33.—(1) Subject to subsection (2), sections 28, 29, 31 and 32 apply in relation to services provided to or on behalf of, or (as the case may be) expenses incurred on or after their commencement on behalf of, trusts whenever created. **64–033**

(2) Nothing in section 28 or 29 is to be treated as affecting the operation of—

(a) section 15 of the Wills Act 1837, or

(b) section 34(3) of the Administration of Estates Act 1925,

in relation to any death occurring before the commencement of section 28 or (as the case may be) section 29.

PART VI

MISCELLANEOUS AND SUPPLEMENTARY

34.—(1) [*Substitutes the Trustee Act 1925, s.19.*]

(2) [*Amends the Trustee Act 1925, s.20(1).*]

Personal representatives

35.—(1) Subject to the following provisions of this section, this Act applies in relation to a personal representative administering an estate according to the law as it applies to a trustee carrying out a trust for beneficiaries. **64–034**

(2) For this purpose this Act is to be read with the appropriate modifications and in particular—

(a) references to the trust instrument are to be read as references to the will,

(b) references to a beneficiary or to beneficiaries, apart from the reference to a beneficiary in section 8(1)(b), are to be read as references to a person or the persons interested in the due administration of the estate, and

(c) the reference to a beneficiary in section 8(1)(b) is to be read as a reference to a person who under the will of the deceased or under the law relating to intestacy is beneficially interested in the estate.

(3) Remuneration to which a personal representative is entitled under section 28 or 29 is to be treated as an administration expense for the purposes of—

(a) section 34(3) of the Administration of Estates Act 1925 (order in which estate to be paid out), and

(b) any provision giving reasonable administration expenses priority over the preferential debts listed in Schedule 6 to the Insolvency Act 1986.

(4) Nothing in subsection (3) is to be treated as affecting the operation of the provisions mentioned in paragraphs (a) and (b) of that subsection in relation to any death occurring before the commencement of this section.

Pension schemes

36.—(1) In this section "pension scheme" means an occupational pension scheme (within the meaning of the Pension Schemes Act 1993) established under a trust and subject to the law of England and Wales. **64–035**

(2) Part I does not apply in so far as it imposes a duty of care in relation to—
(a) the functions described in paragraphs 1 and 2 of Schedule 1, or
(b) the functions described in paragraph 3 of that Schedule to the extent that they relate to trustees—
(i) authorising a person to exercise their functions with respect to investment, or
(ii) appointing a person to act as their nominee or custodian.

(3) Nothing in Part II or III applies to the trustees of any pension scheme.

(4) Part IV applies to the trustees of a pension scheme subject to the restrictions in subsections (5) to (8).

(5) The trustees of a pension scheme may not under Part IV authorise any person to exercise any functions relating to investment as their agent.

(6) The trustees of a pension scheme may not under Part IV authorise a person who is—
(a) an employer in relation to the scheme, or
(b) connected with or an associate of such an employer,
to exercise any of their functions as their agent.

(7) For the purposes of subsection (6)—
(a) "employer", in relation to a scheme, has the same meaning as in the Pensions Act 1995;
(b) sections 249 and 435 of the Insolvency Act 1986 apply for the purpose of determining whether a person is connected with or an associate of an employer.

(8) Sections 16 to 20 (powers to appoint nominees and custodians) do not apply to the trustees of a pension scheme.

Authorised unit trusts

64–036 **37.**—(1) Parts II to IV do not apply to trustees of authorised unit trusts.

(2) "Authorised unit trust" means a unit trust scheme in the case of which an order under section 78 of the Financial Services Act 1986 is in force.

Common investment schemes for charities etc.

64–037 **38.** Parts II to IV do not apply to—
(a) trustees managing a fund under a common investment scheme made, or having effect as if made, under section 24 of the Charities Act 1993, other than such a fund the trusts of which provide that property is not to be transferred to the fund except by or on behalf of a charity the trustees of which are the trustees appointed to manage the fund, or
(b) trustees managing a fund under a common deposit scheme made, or having effect as if made, under section 25 of that Act.

Interpretation

64–038 **39.**—(1) In this Act—

"asset" includes any right or interest;

"charitable trust" means a trust under which property is held for charitable purposes and "charitable purposes" has the same meaning as in the Charities Act 1993;

"custodian trustee" has the same meaning as in the Public Trustee Act 1906;

"enactment" includes any provision of a Measure of the Church Assembly or of the General Synod of the Church of England;
"exempt charity" has the same meaning as in the Charities Act 1993;
"functions" includes powers and duties;
"legal mortgage" has the same meaning as in the Law of Property Act 1925;
"personal representative" has the same meaning as in the Trustee Act 1925;
"settled land" has the same meaning as in the Settled Land Act 1925;
"trust corporation" has the same meaning as in the Trustee Act 1925;
"trust funds" means income or capital funds of the trust.

(2) In this Act the expressions listed below are defined or otherwise explained by the provisions indicated—

asset management functions	section 15(5)
custodian	section 17(2)
the duty of care	section 1(2)
the general power of investment	section 3(2)
lay trustee	section 28(6)
power of intervention	section 22(4)
the standard investment criteria	section 4(3)
subordinate legislation	section 6(3)
trustee acting in a professional capacity	section 28(5)
trust instrument	section 6(2) and 35(2)(a)

. . . . . .

Power to amend other Acts

41.—(1) A Minister of the Crown may by order make such amendments of any Act, including an Act extending to places outside England and Wales, as appear to him appropriate in consequence of or in connection with Part II or III. **64–039**

. . . . . .

SCHEDULES

Section 2

SCHEDULE 1

APPLICATION OF DUTY OF CARE

Investment

1. The duty of care applies to a trustee—
(a) when exercising the general power of investment or any other power of investment, however conferred;
(b) when carrying out a duty to which he is subject under section 4 or 5 (duties relating to the exercise of a power of investment or to the review of investments).

Acquisition of land

The duty of care applies to a trustee—
(a) when exercising the power under section 8 to acquire land;
(b) when exercising any other power to acquire land, however conferred;
(c) when exercising any power in relation to land acquired under a power mentioned in sub-paragraph (a) or (b).

Agents, nominees and custodians

3.—(1) The duty of care applies to a trustee—

(a) when entering into arrangements under which a person is authorised under section 11 to exercise functions as an agent;

(b) when entering into arrangements under which a person is appointed under section 16 to act as a nominee;

(c) when entering into arrangements under which a person is appointed under section 17 or 18 to act as a custodian;

(d) when entering into arrangements under which, under any other power, however conferred, a person is authorised to exercise functions as an agent or is appointed to act as a nominee or custodian;

(e) when carrying out his duties under section 22 (review of agent, nominee or custodian, etc.).

(2) For the purposes of sub-paragraph (1), entering into arrangements under which a person is authorised to exercise functions or is appointed to act as a nominee or custodian includes, in particular—

(a) selecting the person who is to act,

(b) determining any terms on which he is to act, and

(c) if the person is being authorised to exercise asset management functions, the preparation of a policy statement under section 15.

Compounding of liabilities

4. The duty of care applies to a trustee—

(a) when exercising the power under section 15 of the Trustee Act 1925 to do any of the things referred to in that section;

(b) when exercising any corresponding power, however conferred.

Insurance

5. The duty of care applies to a trustee—

(a) when exercising the power under section 19 of the Trustee Act 1925 to insure property;

(b) when exercising any corresponding power, however conferred.

Reversionary interests, valuations and audit

6. The duty of care applies to a trustee—

(a) when exercising the power under section 22(1) or (3) of the Trustee Act 1925 to do any of the things referred to there;

(b) when exercising any corresponding power, however conferred.

Exclusion of duty of care

7. The duty of care does not apply if or in so far as it appears from the trust instrument that the duty is not meant to apply.

. . . . .

Land Registration Act 2002

(2002 c. 9)

CONTENTS

PART 1

PRELIMINARY

SECT.

PART 2

FIRST REGISTRATION OF TITLE

CHAPTER 1

FIRST REGISTRATION

Voluntary registration

Compulsory registration

Classes of title

Effect of first registration

Dependent estates

Supplementary

CHAPTER 2

CAUTIONS AGAINST FIRST REGISTRATION

PART 3

DISPOSITIONS OF REGISTERED LAND

Powers of disposition

Registrable dispositions

Effect of dispositions on priority

PART 4

NOTICES AND RESTRICTIONS

Notices

Restrictions

PART 5

CHARGES

Relative priority

Powers as chargee

Realisation of security

Miscellaneous

PART 6

REGISTRATION: GENERAL

Registration as proprietor

Boundaries

PART 9

ADVERSE POSSESSION

PART 10

LAND REGISTRY

Administration

Fees and indemnities

Miscellaneous

PART 11

ADJUDICATION

PART 12

MISCELLANEOUS AND GENERAL

Miscellaneous

. . . . . .

Land Registration rules

. . . . . .

Supplementary

. . . . . .

. . . . . .

SCHEDULES:

Schedule 1—Unregistered interests which override first registration
Schedule 2—Registrable dispositions: registration requirements
Schedule 3—Unregistered interests which override registered dispositions
Schedule 4—Alteration of the register
Schedule 5—Land registry network
Schedule 6—Registration of adverse possessor

. . . .

Schedule 8—Indemnities

. . . .

Schedule 10—Miscellaneous and general powers

. . . .

Schedule 12—Transition

. . . .

PART 1

PRELIMINARY

Register of title

1.—(1) There is to continue to be a register of title kept by the registrar. **65–001**

(2) Rules may make provision about how the register is to be kept and may, in particular, make provision about—

(a) the information to be included in the register,
(b) the form in which information included in the register is to be kept, and
(c) the arrangement of that information.

Scope of title registration

2. This Act makes provision about the registration of title to— **65–002**

(a) unregistered legal estates which are interests of any of the following kinds—
  (i) an estate in land,
  (ii) a rentcharge,
  (iii) a franchise,
  (iv) a profit a prendre in gross, and
  (v) any other interest or charge which subsists for the benefit of, or is a charge on, an interest the title to which is registered; and
(b) interests capable of subsisting at law which are created by a disposition of an interest the title to which is registered.

PART 2

FIRST REGISTRATION OF TITLE

CHAPTER 1

FIRST REGISTRATION

Voluntary registration

When title may be registered

3.—(1) This section applies to any unregistered legal estate which is an interest of any of the following kinds— **65–003**

(a) an estate in land,
(b) a rentcharge,
(c) a franchise, and
(d) a profit a prendre in gross.

(2) Subject to the following provisions, a person may apply to the registrar to be registered as the proprietor of an unregistered legal estate to which this section applies if—

(a) the estate is vested in him, or
(b) he is entitled to require the estate to be vested in him.

(3) Subject to subsection (4), an application under subsection (2) in respect of a leasehold estate may only be made if the estate was granted for a term of which more than seven years are unexpired.

(4) In the case of an estate in land, subsection (3) does not apply if the right to possession under the lease is discontinuous.

(5) A person may not make an application under subsection (2)(a) in respect of a leasehold estate vested in him as a mortgagee where there is a subsisting right of redemption.

(6) A person may not make an application under subsection (2)(b) if his entitlement is as a person who has contracted to buy under a contract.

(7) If a person holds in the same right both—

(a) a lease in possession, and
(b) a lease to take effect in possession on, or within a month of, the end of the lease in possession,

then, to the extent that they relate to the same land, they are to be treated for the purposes of this section as creating one continuous term.

Compulsory registration

When title must be registered

65–004 **4.**—(1) The requirement of registration applies on the occurrence of any of the following events—

(a) the transfer of a qualifying estate—
  (i) for valuable or other consideration, by way of gift or in pursuance of an order of any court, or
  (ii) by means of an assent (including a vesting assent);
(b) the transfer of an unregistered legal estate in land in circumstances where section 171A of the Housing Act 1985 (c. 68) applies (disposal by landlord which leads to a person no longer being a secure tenant);
(c) the grant out of a qualifying estate of an estate in land—
  (i) for a term of years absolute of more than seven years from the date of the grant, and
  (ii) for valuable or other consideration, by way of gift or in pursuance of an order of any court;
(d) the grant out of a qualifying estate of an estate in land for a term of years absolute to take effect in possession after the end of the period of three months beginning with the date of the grant;
(e) the grant of a lease in pursuance of Part 5 of the Housing Act 1985 (the right to buy) out of an unregistered legal estate in land;
(f) the grant of a lease out of an unregistered legal estate in land in such circumstances as are mentioned in paragraph (b);

(g) the creation of a protected first legal mortgage of a qualifying estate.

(2) For the purposes of subsection (1), a qualifying estate is an unregistered legal estate which is—

(a) a freehold estate in land, or

(b) a leasehold estate in land for a term which, at the time of the transfer, grant or creation, has more than seven years to run.

(3) In subsection (1)(a), the reference to transfer does not include transfer by operation of law.

(4) Subsection (1)(a) does not apply to—

(a) the assignment of a mortgage term, or

(b) the assignment or surrender of a lease to the owner of the immediate reversion where the term is to merge in that reversion.

(5) Subsection (1)(c) does not apply to the grant of an estate to a person as a mortgagee.

(6) For the purposes of subsection (1)(a) and (c), if the estate transferred or granted has a negative value, it is to be regarded as transferred or granted for valuable or other consideration.

(7) In subsection (1)(a) and (c), references to transfer or grant by way of gift include transfer or grant for the purpose of—

(a) constituting a trust under which the settlor does not retain the whole of the beneficial interest, or

(b) uniting the bare legal title and the beneficial interest in property held under a trust under which the settlor did not, on constitution, retain the whole of the beneficial interest.

(8) For the purposes of subsection (1)(g)—

(a) a legal mortgage is protected if it takes effect on its creation as a mortgage to be protected by the deposit of documents relating to the mortgaged estate, and

(b) a first legal mortgage is one which, on its creation, ranks in priority ahead of any other mortgages then affecting the mortgaged estate.

(9) In this section—

"land" does not include mines and minerals held apart from the surface;

"vesting assent" has the same meaning as in the Settled Land Act 1925 (c. 18).

Power to extend section 4

5.—(1) The Lord Chancellor may by order— **65–005**

(a) amend section 4 so as to add to the events on the occurrence of which the requirement of registration applies such relevant event as he may specify in the order, and

(b) make such consequential amendments of any provision of, or having effect under, any Act as he thinks appropriate.

(2) For the purposes of subsection (1)(a), a relevant event is an event relating to an unregistered legal estate which is an interest of any of the following kinds—

(a) an estate in land,

(b) a rentcharge,

(c) a franchise, and

(d) a profit a prendre in gross.

(3) The power conferred by subsection (1) may not be exercised so as to require the title to an estate granted to a person as a mortgagee to be registered.
(4) Before making an order under this section the Lord Chancellor must consult such persons as he considers appropriate.

Duty to apply for registration of title

65–006 **6.**—(1) If the requirement of registration applies, the responsible estate owner, or his successor in title, must, before the end of the period for registration, apply to the registrar to be registered as the proprietor of the registrable estate.
(2) If the requirement of registration applies because of section 4(1)(g)—
(a) the registrable estate is the estate charged by the mortgage, and
(b) the responsible estate owner is the owner of that estate.
(3) If the requirement of registration applies otherwise than because of section 4(1)(g)—
(a) the registrable estate is the estate which is transferred or granted, and
(b) the responsible estate owner is the transferee or grantee of that estate.
(4) The period for registration is 2 months beginning with the date on which the relevant event occurs, or such longer period as the registrar may provide under subsection (5).
(5) If on the application of any interested person the registrar is satisfied that there is good reason for doing so, he may by order provide that the period for registration ends on such later date as he may specify in the order.
(6) Rules may make provision enabling the mortgagee under any mortgage falling within section 4(1)(g) to require the estate charged by the mortgage to be registered whether or not the mortgagor consents.

Effect of non-compliance with section 6

65–007 **7.**—(1) If the requirement of registration is not complied with, the transfer, grant or creation becomes void as regards the transfer, grant or creation of a legal estate.
(2) On the application of subsection (1)—
(a) in a case falling within section 4(1)(a) or (b), the title to the legal estate reverts to the transferor who holds it on a bare trust for the transferee, and
(b) in a case falling within section 4(1)(c) to (g), the grant or creation has effect as a contract made for valuable consideration to grant or create the legal estate concerned.
(3) If an order under section 6(5) is made in a case where subsection (1) has already applied, that application of the subsection is to be treated as not having occurred.
(4) The possibility of reverter under subsection (1) is to be disregarded for the purposes of determining whether a fee simple is a fee simple absolute.

Liability for making good void transfers etc

65–008 **8.** If a legal estate is retransferred, regranted or recreated because of a failure to comply with the requirement of registration, the transferee, grantee or, as the case may be, the mortgagor—

(a) is liable to the other party for all the proper costs of an incidental to the retransfer, regrant or recreation of the legal estate, and
(b) is liable to indemnify the other party in respect of any other liability reasonably incurred by him because of the failure to comply with the requirement of registration.

Classes of title

Titles to freehold estates

9.—(1) In the case of an application for registration under this Chapter of a freehold estate, the classes of title with which the applicant may be registered as proprietor are— **65–009**
(a) absolute title,
(b) qualified title, and
(c) possessory title;
and the following provisions deal with when each of the classes of title is available.

(2) A person may be registered with absolute title if the registrar is of the opinion that the person's title to the estate is such as a willing buyer could properly be advised by a competent professional adviser to accept.

(3) In applying subsection (2), the registrar may disregard the fact that a person's title appears to him to be open to objection if he is of the opinion that the defect will not cause the holding under the title to be disturbed.

(4) A person may be registered with qualified title if the registrar is of the opinion that the person's title to the estate has been established only for a limited period or subject to certain reservations which cannot be disregarded under subsection (3).

(5) A person may be registered with possessory title if the registrar is of the opinion—
(a) that the person is in actual possession of the land, or in receipt of the rents and profits of the land, by virtue of the estate, and
(b) that there is no other class of title with which he may be registered.

Titles to leasehold estates

10.—(1) In the case of an application for registration under this Chapter of a leasehold estate, the classes of title with which the applicant may be registered as proprietor are— **65–010**
(a) absolute title,
(b) good leasehold title,
(c) qualified title, and
(d) possessory title;
and the following provisions deal with when each of the classes of title is available.

(2) A person may be registered with absolute title if—
(a) the registrar is of the opinion that the person's title to the estate is such as a willing buyer could properly be advised by a competent professional adviser to accept, and
(b) the registrar approves the lessor's title to grant the lease.

(3) A person may be registered with good leasehold title if the registrar is of the opinion that the person's title to the estate is such as a willing buyer could properly be advised by a competent professional adviser to accept.

(4) In applying subsection (2) or (3), the registrar may disregard the fact that a person's title appears to him to be open to objection if he is of the opinion that the defect will not cause the holding under the title to be disturbed.

(5) A person may be registered with qualified title if the registrar is of the opinion that the person's title to the estate, or the lessor's title to the reversion, has been established only for a limited period or subject to certain reservations which cannot be disregarded under subsection (4).

(6) A person may be registered with possessory title if the registrar is of the opinion—

(a) that the person is in actual possession of the land, or in receipt of the rents and profits of the land, by virtue of the estate, and

(b) that there is no other class of title with which he may be registered.

Effect of first registration

Freehold estates

65–011 **11.**—(1) This section is concerned with the registration of a person under this Chapter as the proprietor of a freehold estate.

(2) Registration with absolute title has the effect described in subsections (3) to (5).

(3) The estate is vested in the proprietor together with all interests subsisting for the benefit of the estate.

(4) The estate is vested in the proprietor subject only to the following interests affecting the estate at the time of registration—

(a) interests which are the subject of an entry in the register in relation to the estate,

(b) unregistered interests which fall within any of the paragraphs of Schedule 1, and

(c) interests acquired under the Limitation Act 1980 (c. 58) of which the proprietor has notice.

(5) If the proprietor is not entitled to the estate for his own benefit, or not entitled solely for his own benefit, then, as between himself and the persons beneficially entitled to the estate, the estate is vested in him subject to such of their interests as he has notice of.

(6) Registration with qualified title has the same effect as registration with absolute title, except that it does not affect the enforcement of any estate, right or interest which appears from the register to be excepted from the effect of registration.

(7) Registration with possessory title has the same effect as registration with absolute title, except that it does not affect the enforcement of any estate, right or interest adverse to, or in derogation of, the proprietor's title subsisting at the time of registration or then capable of arising.

Leasehold estates

65–012 **12.**—(1) This section is concerned with the registration of a person under this Chapter as the proprietor of a leasehold estate.

(2) Registration with absolute title has the effect described in subsections (3) to (5).

(3) The estate is vested in the proprietor together with all interests subsisting for the benefit of the estate.

(4) The estate is vested subject only to the following interests affecting the estate at the time of registration—

(a) implied and express covenants, obligations and liabilities incident to the estate,

(b) interests which are the subject of an entry in the register in relation to the estate,

(c) unregistered interests which fall within any of the paragraphs of Schedule 1, and

(d) interests acquired under the Limitation Act 1980 (c. 58) of which the proprietor has notice.

(5) If the proprietor is not entitled to the estate for his own benefit, or not entitled solely for his own benefit, then, as between himself and the persons beneficially entitled to the estate, the estate is vested in him subject to such of their interests as he has notice of.

(6) Registration with good leasehold title has the same effect as registration with absolute title, except that it does not affect the enforcement of any estate, right or interest affecting, or in derogation of, the title of the lessor to grant the lease.

(7) Registration with qualified title has the same effect as registration with absolute title except that it does not affect the enforcement of any estate, right or interest which appears from the register to be excepted from the effect of registration.

(8) Registration with possessory title has the same effect as registration with absolute title, except that it does not affect the enforcement of any estate, right or interest adverse to, or in derogation of, the proprietor's title subsisting at the time of registration or then capable of arising.

Dependent estates

Appurtenant rights and charges

13. Rules may— **65–013**

(a) make provision for the registration of the proprietor of a registered estate as the proprietor of an unregistered legal estate which subsists for the benefit of the registered estate;

(b) make provision for the registration of a person as the proprietor of an unregistered legal estate which is a charge on a registered estate.

Supplementary

Rules about first registration

14. Rules may— **65–014**

(a) make provision about the making of applications for registration under this Chapter;

(b) make provision about the functions of the registrar following the making of such an application, including provision about—

  (i) the examination of title, and

  (ii) the entries to be made in the register where such an application is approved;

(c) make provision about the effect of any entry made in the register in pursuance of such an application.

CHAPTER 2

CAUTIONS AGAINST FIRST REGISTRATION

Right to lodge

65–015 **15.**—(1) Subject to subsection (3), a person may lodge a caution against the registration of title to an unregistered legal estate if he claims to be—

(a) the owner of a qualifying estate, or
(b) entitled to an interest affecting a qualifying estate.

(2) For the purposes of subsection (1), a qualifying estate is a legal estate which—

(a) relates to land to which the caution relates, and
(b) is an interest of any of the following kinds—
  (i) an estate in land,
  (ii) a rentcharge,
  (iii) a franchise, and
  (iv) a profit a prendre in gross.

(3) No caution may be lodged under subsection (1)—

(a) in the case of paragraph (a), by virtue of ownership of—
  (i) a freehold estate in land, or
  (ii) a leasehold estate in land granted for a term of which more than seven years are unexpired;
(b) in the case of paragraph (b), by virtue of entitlement to such a leasehold estate as is mentioned in paragraph (a)(ii) of this subsection.

(4) The right under subsection (1) is exercisable by application to the registrar.

Effect

65–016 **16.**—(1) Where an application for registration under this Part relates to a legal estate which is the subject of a caution against first registration, the registrar must give the cautioner notice of the application and of his right to object to it.

(2) The registrar may not determine an application to which subsection (1) applies before the end of such period as rules may provide, unless the cautioner has exercised his right to object to the application or given the registrar notice that he does not intend to do so.

(3) Except as provided by this section, a caution against first registration has no effect and, in particular, has no effect on the validity or priority of any interest of the cautioner in the legal estate to which the caution relates.

(4) For the purposes of subsection (1), notice given by a person acting on behalf of an applicant for registration under this Part is to be treated as given by the registrar if—

(a) the person is of a description provided by rules, and
(b) notice is given in such circumstances as rules may provide.

Withdrawal

65–017 **17.** The cautioner may withdraw a caution against first registration by application to the registrar.

Cancellation

18.—(1) A person may apply to the registrar for cancellation of a caution against first registration if he is— **65–018**

(a) the owner of the legal estate to which the caution relates, or
(b) a person of such other description as rules may provide.

(2) Subject to rules, no application under subsection (1)(a) may be made by a person who—

(a) consented in such manner as rules may provide to the lodging of the caution, or
(b) derives title to the legal estate by operation of law from a person who did so.

(3) Where an application is made under subsection (1), the registrar must give the cautioner notice of the application and of the effect of subsection (4).

(4) If the cautioner does not exercise his right to object to the application before the end of such period as rules may provide, the registrar must cancel the caution.

Cautions register

19.—(1) The registrar must keep a register of cautions against first registration. **65–019**

(2) Rules may make provision about how the cautions register is to be kept and may, in particular, make provision about—

(a) the information to be included in the register,
(b) the form in which information included in the register is to be kept, and
(c) the arrangement of that information.

Alteration of register by court

20.—(1) The court may make an order for alteration of the cautions register for the purpose of— **65–020**

(a) correcting a mistake, or
(b) bringing the register up to date.

(2) An order under subsection (1) has effect when served on the registrar to impose a duty on him to give effect to it.

(3) Rules may make provision about—

(a) the circumstances in which there is a duty to exercise the power under subsection (1),
(b) the form of an order under that subsection, and
(c) service of such an order.

Alteration of register by registrar

21.—(1) The registrar may alter the cautions register for the purpose of— **65–021**

(a) correcting a mistake, or
(b) bringing the register up to date.

(2) Rules may make provision about—

(a) the circumstances in which there is a duty to exercise the power under subsection (1),
(b) how the cautions register is to be altered in exercise of that power,

(c) applications for the exercise of that power, and
(d) procedure in relation to the exercise of that power, whether on application or otherwise.

(3) Where an alteration is made under this section, the registrar may pay such amount as he thinks fit in respect of any costs reasonably incurred by a person in connection with the alteration.

Supplementary

65–022 **22.** In this Chapter, "the cautioner", in relation to a caution against first registration, means the person who lodged the caution, or such other person as rules may provide.

Part 3

Dispositions of Registered Land

Powers of disposition

Owner's powers

65–023 **23.**—(1) Owner's powers in relation to a registered estate consist of—
(a) power to make a disposition of any kind permitted by the general law in relation to an interest of that description, other than a mortgage by demise or sub-demise, and
(b) power to charge the estate at law with the payment of money.

(2) Owner's powers in relation to a registered charge consist of—
(a) power to make a disposition of any kind permitted by the general law in relation to an interest of that description, other than a legal sub-mortgage, and
(b) power to charge at law with the payment of money indebtedness secured by the registered charge.

(3) In subsection (2)(a), "legal sub-mortgage" means—
(a) a transfer by way of mortgage,
(b) a sub-mortgage by sub-demise, and
(c) a charge by way of legal mortgage.

Right to exercise owner's powers

65–024 **24.** A person is entitled to exercise owner's powers in relation to a registered estate or charge if he is—
(a) the registered proprietor, or
(b) entitled to be registered as the proprietor.

Mode of exercise

65–025 **25.**—(1) A registrable disposition of a registered estate or charge only has effect if it complies with such requirements as to form and content as rules may provide.

(2) Rules may apply subsection (1) to any other kind of dispositi depends for its effect on registration.

Protection of disponees

26.—(1) Subject to subsection (2), a person's right to exercise owner's powers in relation to a registered estate or charge is to be taken to be free from any limitation affecting the validity of a disposition.

(2) Subsection (1) does not apply to a limitation—

(a) reflected by an entry in the register, or

(b) imposed by, or under, this Act.

(3) This section has effect only for the purpose of preventing the title of a disponee being questioned (and so does not affect the lawfulness of a disposition).

Registrable dispositions

Dispositions required to be registered

27.—(1) If a disposition of a registered estate or registered charge is required **65–027** to be completed by registration, it does not operate at law until the relevant registration requirements are met.

(2) In the case of a registered estate, the following are the dispositions which are required to be completed by registration—

(a) a transfer,

(b) where the registered estate is an estate in land, the grant of a term of years absolute—

(i) for a term of more than seven years from the date of the grant,

(ii) to take effect in possession after the end of the period of three months beginning with the date of the grant,

(iii) under which the right to possession is discontinuous,

(iv) in pursuance of Part 5 of the Housing Act 1985 (c. 68) (the right to buy), or

(v) in circumstances where section 171A of that Act applies (disposal by landlord which leads to a person no longer being a secure tenant),

(c) where the registered estate is a franchise or manor, the grant of a lease,

(d) the express grant or reservation of an interest of a kind falling within section 1(2)(a) of the Law of Property Act 1925 (c. 20), other than one which is capable of being registered under the Commons Registration Act 1965 (c. 64),

(e) the express grant or reservation of an interest of a kind falling within section 1(2)(b) or (e) of the Law of Property Act 1925, and

(f) the grant of a legal charge.

(3) In the case of a registered charge, the following are the dispositions which are required to be completed by registration—

(a) a transfer, and

(b) the grant of a sub-charge.

(4) Schedule 2 to this Act (which deals with the relevant registration requirements) has effect.

(5) This section applies to dispositions by operation of law as it applies to other dispositions, but with the exception of the following—

(a) a transfer on the death or bankruptcy of an individual proprietor,

(b) a transfer on the dissolution of a corporate proprietor, and
(c) the creation of a legal charge which is a local land charge.

(6) Rules may make provision about applications to the registrar for the purpose of meeting registration requirements under this section.

(7) In subsection (2)(d), the reference to express grant does not include grant as a result of the operation of section 62 of the Law of Property Act 1925 (c. 20).

Effect of dispositions on priority

Basic rule

65–028 **28.**—(1) Except as provided by sections 29 and 30, the priority of an interest affecting a registered estate or charge is not affected by a disposition of the estate or charge.

(2) It makes no difference for the purposes of this section whether the interest or disposition is registered.

Effect of registered dispositions: estates

65–029 **29.**—(1) If a registrable disposition of a registered estate is made for valuable consideration, completion of the disposition by registration has the effect of postponing to the interest under the disposition any interest affecting the estate immediately before the disposition whose priority is not protected at the time of registration.

(2) For the purposes of subsection (1), the priority of an interest is protected—

(a) in any case, if the interest—
   (i) is a registered charge or the subject of a notice in the register,
   (ii) falls within any of the paragraphs of Schedule 3, or
   (iii) appears from the register to be excepted from the effect of registration, and

(b) in the case of a disposition of a leasehold estate, if the burden of the interest is incident to the estate.

(3) Subsection (2)(a)(ii) does not apply to an interest which has been the subject of a notice in the register at any time since the coming into force of this section.

(4) Where the grant of a leasehold estate in land out of a registered estate does not involve a registrable disposition, this section has effect as if—

(a) the grant involved such a disposition, and
(b) the disposition were registered at the time of the grant.

Effect of registered dispositions: charges

65–030 **30.**—(1) If a registrable disposition of a registered charge is made for valuable consideration, completion of the disposition by registration has the effect of postponing to the interest under the disposition any interest affecting the charge immediately before the disposition whose priority is not protected at the time of registration.

(2) For the purposes of subsection (1), the priority of an interest is protected—

(a) in any case, if the interest—

(i) is a registered charge or the subject of a notice in the register,
(ii) falls within any of the paragraphs of Schedule 3, or
(iii) appears from the register to be excepted from the effect of registration, and

(b) in the case of a disposition of a charge which relates to a leasehold estate, if the burden of the interest is incident to the estate.

(3) Subsection (2)(a)(ii) does not apply to an interest which has been the subject of a notice in the register at any time since the coming into force of this section.

Inland Revenue charges

31. The effect of a disposition of a registered estate or charge on a charge under section 237 of the Inheritance Tax Act 1984 (c. 51) (charge for unpaid tax) is to be determined, not in accordance with sections 28 to 30 above, but in accordance with sections 237(6) and 238 of that Act (under which a purchaser in good faith for money or money's worth takes free from the charge in the absence of registration). **65–031**

PART 4

NOTICES AND RESTRICTIONS

Notices

Nature and effect

32.—(1) A notice is an entry in the register in respect of the burden of an interest affecting a registered estate or charge. **65–032**

(2) The entry of a notice is to be made in relation to the registered estate or charge affected by the interest concerned.

(3) The fact that an interest is the subject of a notice does not necessarily mean that the interest is valid, but does mean that the priority of the interest, if valid, is protected for the purposes of sections 29 and 30.

Excluded interests

33. No notice may be entered in the register in respect of any of the following— **65–033**

(a) an interest under—
(i) a trust of land, or
(ii) a settlement under the Settled Land Act 1925 (c. 18),

(b) a leasehold estate in land which—
(i) is granted for a term of years of three years or less from the date of the grant, and
(ii) is not required to be registered,

(c) a restrictive covenant made between a lessor and lessee, so far as relating to the demised premises,

(d) an interest which is capable of being registered under the Commons Registration Act 1965 (c. 64), and

(e) an interest in any coal or coal mine, the rights attached to any such interest and the rights of any person under section 38, 49 or 51 of the Coal Industry Act 1994 (c. 21).

Entry on application

65–034 **34.**—(1) A person who claims to be entitled to the benefit of an interest affecting a registered estate or charge may, if the interest is not excluded by section 33, apply to the registrar for the entry in the register of a notice in respect of the interest.

(2) Subject to rules, an application under this section may be for—

(a) an agreed notice, or
(b) a unilateral notice.

(3) The registrar may only approve an application for an agreed notice if—

(a) the applicant is the relevant registered proprietor, or a person entitled to be registered as such proprietor,
(b) the relevant registered proprietor, or a person entitled to be registered as such proprietor, consents to the entry of the notice, or
(c) the registrar is satisfied as to the validity of the applicant's claim.

(4) In subsection (3), references to the relevant registered proprietor are to the proprietor of the registered estate or charge affected by the interest to which the application relates.

Unilateral notices

65–035 **35.**—(1) If the registrar enters a notice in the register in pursuance of an application under section 34(2)(b) ("a unilateral notice"), he must give notice of the entry to—

(a) the proprietor of the registered estate or charge to which it relates, and
(b) such other persons as rules may provide.

(2) A unilateral notice must—

(a) indicate that it is such a notice, and
(b) identify who is the beneficiary of the notice.

(3) The person shown in the register as the beneficiary of a unilateral notice, or such other person as rules may provide, may apply to the registrar for the removal of the notice from the register.

Cancellation of unilateral notices

65–036 **36.**—(1) A person may apply to the registrar for the cancellation of a unilateral notice if he is—

(a) the registered proprietor of the estate or charge to which the notice relates, or
(b) a person entitled to be registered as the proprietor of that estate or charge.

(2) Where an application is made under subsection (1), the registrar must give the beneficiary of the notice notice of the application and of the effect of subsection (3).

(3) If the beneficiary of the notice does not exercise his right to object to the application before the end of such period as rules may provide, the registrar must cancel the notice.

(4) In this section—

"beneficiary", in relation to a unilateral notice, means the person shown in the register as the beneficiary of the notice, or such other person as rules may provide;

"unilateral notice" means a notice entered in the register in pursuance of an application under section 34(2)(b).

Unregistered interests

37.—(1) If it appears to the registrar that a registered estate is subject to an unregistered interest which— **65–037**

(a) falls within any of the paragraphs of Schedule 1, and
(b) is not excluded by section 33,

he may enter a notice in the register in respect of the interest.

(2) The registrar must give notice of an entry under this section to such persons as rules may provide.

Registrable dispositions

38. Where a person is entered in the register as the proprietor of an interest under a disposition falling within section 27(2)(b) to (e), the registrar must also enter a notice in the register in respect of that interest. **65–038**

Supplementary

39. Rules may make provision about the form and content of notices in the register. **65–039**

Restrictions

Nature

40.—(1) A restriction is an entry in the register regulating the circumstances in which a disposition of a registered estate or charge may be the subject of an entry in the register. **65–040**

(2) A restriction may, in particular—

(a) prohibit the making of an entry in respect of any disposition, or a disposition of a kind specified in the restriction;
(b) prohibit the making of an entry—
  (i) indefinitely,
  (ii) for a period specified in the restriction, or
  (iii) until the occurrence of an event so specified.

(3) Without prejudice to the generality of subsection (2)(b)(iii), the events which may be specified include—

(a) the giving of notice,
(b) the obtaining of consent, and
(c) the making of an order by the court or registrar.

(4) The entry of a restriction is to be made in relation to the registered estate or charge to which it relates.

Effect

41.—(1) Where a restriction is entered in the register, no entry in respect of a disposition to which the restriction applies may be made in the register otherwise than in accordance with the terms of the restriction, subject to any order under subsection (2). **65–041**

(2) The registrar may by order—
(a) disapply a restriction in relation to a disposition specified in the order or dispositions of a kind so specified, or
(b) provide that a restriction has effect, in relation to a disposition specified in the order or dispositions of a kind so specified, with modifications so specified.

(3) The power under subsection (2) is exercisable only on the application of a person who appears to the registrar to have a sufficient interest in the restriction.

Power of registrar to enter

65–042 **42.**—(1) The registrar may enter a restriction in the register if it appears to him that it is necessary or desirable to do so for the purpose of—
(a) preventing invalidity or unlawfulness in relation to dispositions of a registered estate or charge,
(b) securing that interests which are capable of being overreached on a disposition of a registered estate or charge are overreached, or
(c) protecting a right or claim in relation to a registered estate or charge.

(2) No restriction may be entered under subsection (1)(c) for the purpose of protecting the priority of an interest which is, or could be, the subject of a notice.

(3) The registrar must give notice of any entry made under this section to the proprietor of the registered estate or charge concerned, except where the entry is made in pursuance of an application under section 43.

(4) For the purposes of subsection (1)(c), a person entitled to the benefit of a charging order relating to an interest under a trust shall be treated as having a right or claim in relation to the trust property.

Applications

65–043 **43.**—(1) A person may apply to the registrar for the entry of a restriction under section 42(1) if—
(a) he is the relevant registered proprietor, or a person entitled to be registered as such proprietor,
(b) the relevant registered proprietor, or a person entitled to be registered as such proprietor, consents to the application, or
(c) he otherwise has a sufficient interest in the making of the entry.

(2) Rules may—
(a) require the making of an application under subsection (1) in such circumstances, and by such person, as the rules may provide;
(b) make provision about the form of consent for the purposes of subsection (1)(b);
(c) provide for classes of person to be regarded as included in subsection (1)(c);
(d) specify standard forms of restriction.

(3) If an application under subsection (1) is made for the entry of a restriction which is not in a form specified under subsection (2)(d), the registrar may only approve the application if it appears to him—
(a) that the terms of the proposed restriction are reasonable, and
(b) that applying the proposed restriction would—
(i) be straightforward, and
(ii) not place an unreasonable burden on him.

(4) In subsection (1), references to the relevant registered proprietor are to the proprietor of the registered estate or charge to which the application relates.

Obligatory restrictions

44.—(1) If the registrar enters two or more persons in the register as the proprietor of a registered estate in land, he must also enter in the register such restrictions as rules may provide for the purpose of securing that interests which are capable of being overreached on a disposition of the estate are overreached. **65–044**

(2) Where under any enactment the registrar is required to enter a restriction without application, the form of the restriction shall be such as rules may provide.

Notifiable applications

45.—(1) Where an application under section 43(1) is notifiable, the registrar must give notice of the application, and of the right to object to it, to— **65–045**

(a) the proprietor of the registered estate or charge to which it relates, and

(b) such other persons as rules may provide.

(2) The registrar may not determine an application to which subsection (1) applies before the end of such period as rules may provide, unless the person, or each of the persons, notified under that subsection has exercised his right to object to the application or given the registrar notice that he does not intend to do so.

(3) For the purposes of this section, an application under section 43(1) is notifiable unless it is—

(a) made by or with the consent of the proprietor of the registered estate or charge to which the application relates, or a person entitled to be registered as such proprietor,

(b) made in pursuance of rules under section 43(2)(a), or

(c) an application for the entry of a restriction reflecting a limitation under an order of the court or registrar, or an undertaking given in place of such an order.

Power of court to order entry

46.—(1) If it appears to the court that it is necessary or desirable to do so for the purpose of protecting a right or claim in relation to a registered estate or charge, it may make an order requiring the registrar to enter a restriction in the register. **65–046**

(2) No order under this section may be made for the purpose of protecting the priority of an interest which is, or could be, the subject of a notice.

(3) The court may include in an order under this section a direction that an entry made in pursuance of the order is to have overriding priority.

(4) If an order under this section includes a direction under subsection (3), the registrar must make such entry in the register as rules may provide.

(5) The court may make the exercise of its power under subsection (3) subject to such terms and conditions as it thinks fit.

Withdrawal

47. A person may apply to the registrar for the withdrawal of a restriction if— **65–047**

(a) the restriction was entered in such circumstances as rules may provide, and

(b) he is of such a description as rules may provide.

PART 5

CHARGES

Relative priority

Registered charges

65–048 **48.**—(1) Registered charges on the same registered estate, or on the same registered charge, are to be taken to rank as between themselves in the order shown in the register.

(2) Rules may make provision about—

(a) how the priority of registered charges as between themselves is to be shown in the register, and

(b) applications for registration of the priority of registered charges as between themselves.

Tacking and further advances

65–049 **49.**—(1) The proprietor of a registered charge may make a further advance on the security of the charge ranking in priority to a subsequent charge if he has not received from the subsequent chargee notice of the creation of the subsequent charge.

(2) Notice given for the purposes of subsection (1) shall be treated as received at the time when, in accordance with rules, it ought to have been received.

(3) The proprietor of a registered charge may also make a further advance on the security of the charge ranking in priority to a subsequent charge if—

(a) the advance is made in pursuance of an obligation, and

(b) at the time of the creation of the subsequent charge the obligation was entered in the register in accordance with rules.

(4) The proprietor of a registered charge may also make a further advance on the security of the charge ranking in priority to a subsequent charge if—

(a) the parties to the prior charge have agreed a maximum amount for which the charge is security, and

(b) at the time of the creation of the subsequent charge the agreement was entered in the register in accordance with rules.

(5) Rules may—

(a) disapply subsection (4) in relation to charges of a description specified in the rules, or

(b) provide for the application of that subsection to be subject, in the case of charges of a description so specified, to compliance with such conditions as may be so specified.

(6) Except as provided by this section, tacking in relation to a charge over registered land is only possible with the agreement of the subsequent chargee.

Overriding statutory charges: duty of notification

65–050 **50.** If the registrar enters a person in the register as the proprietor of a charge which—

(a) is created by or under an enactment, and
(b) has effect to postpone a charge which at the time of registration of the statutory charge is—
(i) entered in the register, or
(ii) the basis for an entry in the register,
he must in accordance with rules give notice of the creation of the statutory charge to such person as rules may provide.

Powers as chargee

Effect of completion by registration

51. On completion of the relevant registration requirements, a charge created by means of a registrable disposition of a registered estate has effect, if it would not otherwise do so, as a charge by deed by way of legal mortgage. **65–051**

Protection of disponees

52.—(1) Subject to any entry in the register to the contrary, the proprietor of a registered charge is to be taken to have, in relation to the property subject to the charge, the powers of disposition conferred by law on the owner of a legal mortgage. **65–052**

(2) Subsection (1) has effect only for the purpose of preventing the title of a disponee being questioned (and so does not affect the lawfulness of a disposition).

Powers as sub-chargee

53. The registered proprietor of a sub-charge has, in relation to the property subject to the principal charge or any intermediate charge, the same powers as the sub-chargor. **65–053**

Realisation of security

Proceeds of sale: chargee's duty

54. For the purposes of section 105 of the Law of Property Act 1925 (c. 20) (mortgagee's duties in relation to application of proceeds of sale), in its application to the proceeds of sale of registered land, a person shall be taken to have notice of anything in the register immediately before the disposition on sale. **65–054**

Local land charges

55. A charge over registered land which is a local land charge may only be realised if the title to the charge is registered. **65–055**

Miscellaneous

Receipt in case of joint proprietors

56. Where a charge is registered in the name of two or more proprietors, a valid receipt for the money secured by the charge may be given by— **65–056**

(a) the registered proprietors,
(b) the survivors or survivor of the registered proprietors, or
(c) the personal representative of the last survivor of the registered proprietors.

Entry of right of consolidation

65–057 **57.** Rules may make provision about entry in the register of a right of consolidation in relation to a registered charge.

PART 6

REGISTRATION: GENERAL

Registration as proprietor

Conclusiveness

65–058 **58.**—(1) If, on the entry of a person in the register as the proprietor of a legal estate, the legal estate would not otherwise be vested in him, it shall be deemed to be vested in him as a result of the registration.

(2) Subsection (1) does not apply where the entry is made in pursuance of a registrable disposition in relation to which some other registration requirement remains to be met.

Dependent estates

65–059 **59.**—(1) The entry of a person in the register as the proprietor of a legal estate which subsists for the benefit of a registered estate must be made in relation to the registered estate.

(2) The entry of a person in the register as the proprietor of a charge on a registered estate must be made in relation to that estate.

(3) The entry of a person in the register as the proprietor of a sub-charge on a registered charge must be made in relation to that charge.

Boundaries

Boundaries

65–060 **60.**—(1) The boundary of a registered estate as shown for the purposes of the register is a general boundary, unless shown as determined under this section.

(2) A general boundary does not determine the exact line of the boundary.

(3) Rules may make provision enabling or requiring the exact line of the boundary of a registered estate to be determined and may, in particular, make provision about—

(a) the circumstances in which the exact line of a boundary may or must be determined,
(b) how the exact line of a boundary may be determined,
(c) procedure in relation to applications for determination, and
(d) the recording of the fact of determination in the register or the index maintained under section 68.

(4) Rules under this section must provide for applications for determination to be made to the registrar.

Accretion and diluvion

61.—(1) The fact that a registered estate in land is shown in the register as having a particular boundary does not affect the operation of accretion or diluvion. **65–061**

(2) An agreement about the operation of accretion or diluvion in relation to a registered estate in land has effect only if registered in accordance with rules.

Quality of title

Power to upgrade title

62.—(1) Where the title to a freehold estate is entered in the register as possessory or qualified, the registrar may enter it as absolute if he is satisfied as to the title to the estate. **65–062**

(2) Where the title to a leasehold estate is entered in the register as good leasehold, the registrar may enter it as absolute if he is satisfied as to the superior title.

(3) Where the title to a leasehold estate is entered in the register as possessory or qualified the registrar may—

(a) enter it as good leasehold if he is satisfied as to the title to the estate, and
(b) enter it as absolute if he is satisfied both as to the title to the estate and as to the superior title.

(4) Where the title to a freehold estate in land has been entered in the register as possessory for at least twelve years, the registrar may enter it as absolute if he is satisfied that the proprietor is in possession of the land.

(5) Where the title to a leasehold estate in land has been entered in the register as possessory for at least twelve years, the registrar may enter it as good leasehold if he is satisfied that the proprietor is in possession of the land.

(6) None of the powers under subsections (1) to (5) is exercisable if there is outstanding any claim adverse to the title of the registered proprietor which is made by virtue of an estate, right or interest whose enforceability is preserved by virtue of the existing entry about the class of title.

(7) The only persons who may apply to the registrar for the exercise of any of the powers under subsections (1) to (5) are—

(a) the proprietor of the estate to which the application relates,
(b) a person entitled to be registered as the proprietor of that estate,
(c) the proprietor of a registered charge affecting that estate, and
(d) a person interested in a registered estate which derives from that estate.

(8) In determining for the purposes of this section whether he is satisfied as to any title, the registrar is to apply the same standards as those which apply under section 9 or 10 to first registration of title.

(9) The Lord Chancellor may by order amend subsection (4) or (5) by substituting for the number of years for the time being specified in that subsection such number of years as the order may provide.

Effect of upgrading title

63.—(1) On the title to a registered freehold or leasehold estate being entered under section 62 as absolute, the proprietor ceases to hold the estate subject to any estate, right or interest whose enforceability was preserved by virtue of the previous entry about the class of title. **65–063**

(2) Subsection (1) also applies on the title to a registered leasehold estate

being entered under section 62 as good leasehold, except that the entry does not affect or prejudice the enforcement of any estate, right or interest affecting, or in derogation of, the title of the lessor to grant the lease.

Use of register to record defects in title

65–064 **64.**—(1) If it appears to the registrar that a right to determine a registered estate in land is exercisable, he may enter the fact in the register.

(2) Rules may make provision about entries under subsection (1) and may, in particular, make provision about—

(a) the circumstances in which there is a duty to exercise the power conferred by that subsection,

(b) how entries under that subsection are to be made, and

(c) the removal of such entries.

Alteration of register

Alteration of register

65–065 **65.** Schedule 4 (which makes provision about alteration of the register) has effect.

Information etc.

Inspection of the registers etc

65–066 **66.**—(1) Any person may inspect and make copies of, or of any part of—

(a) the register of title,

(b) any document kept by the registrar which is referred to in the register of title,

(c) any other document kept by the registrar which relates to an application to him, or

(d) the register of cautions against first registration.

(2) The right under subsection (1) is subject to rules which may, in particular—

(a) provide for exceptions to the right, and

(b) impose conditions on its exercise, including conditions requiring the payment of fees.

Official copies of the registers etc

65–067 **67.**—(1) An official copy of, or of a part of—

(a) the register of title,

(b) any document which is referred to in the register of title and kept by the registrar,

(c) any other document kept by the registrar which relates to an application to him, or

(d) the register of cautions against first registration,

is admissible in evidence to the same extent as the original.

(2) A person who relies on an official copy in which there is a mistake is not liable for loss suffered by another by reason of the mistake.

(3) Rules may make provision for the issue of official copies and may, in particular, make provision about—

(a) the form of official copies,
(b) who may issue official copies,
(c) applications for official copies, and
(d) the conditions to be met by applicants for official copies, including conditions requiring the payment of fees.

Index

68.—(1) The registrar must keep an index for the purpose of enabling the following matters to be ascertained in relation to any parcel of land— **65–068**

(a) whether any registered estate relates to the land,
(b) how any registered estate which relates to the land is identified for the purposes of the register,
(c) whether the land is affected by any, and, if so what, caution against first registration, and
(d) such other matters as rules may provide.

(2) Rules may—

(a) make provision about how the index is to be kept and may, in particular, make provision about—
  (i) the information to be included in the index,
  (ii) the form in which information included in the index is to be kept, and
  (iii) the arrangement of that information;
(b) make provision about official searches of the index.

Historical information

69.—(1) The registrar may on application provide information about the history of a registered title. **65–069**

(2) Rules may make provision about applications for the exercise of the power conferred by subsection (1).

(3) The registrar may—

(a) arrange for the provision of information about the history of registered titles, and
(b) authorise anyone who has the function of providing information under paragraph (a) to have access on such terms as the registrar thinks fit to any relevant information kept by him.

Official searches

70. Rules may make provision for official searches of the register, including searches of pending applications for first registration, and may, in particular, make provision about— **65–070**

(a) the form of applications for searches,
(b) the manner in which such applications may be made,
(c) the form of official search certificates, and
(d) the manner in which such certificates may be issued.

Applications

Duty to disclose unregistered interests

71. Where rules so provide— **65–071**

(a) a person applying for registration under Chapter 1 of Part 2 must provide to the registrar such information as the rules may provide about any interest affecting the estate to which the application relates which—
   (i) falls within any of the paragraphs of Schedule 1, and
   (ii) is of a description specified by the rules;

(b) a person applying to register a registrable disposition of a registered estate must provide to the registrar such information as the rules may provide about any unregistered interest affecting the estate which—
   (i) falls within any of the paragraphs of Schedule 3, and
   (ii) is of description specified by the rules.

Priority protection

65–072 **72.**—(1) For the purposes of this section, an application for an entry in the register is protected if—

(a) it is one to which a priority period relates, and
(b) it is made before the end of that period.

(2) Where an application for an entry in the register is protected, any entry made in the register during the priority period relating to the application is postponed to any entry made in pursuance of it.

(3) Subsection (2) does not apply if—

(a) the earlier entry was made in pursuance of a protected application, and
(b) the priority period relating to that application ranks ahead of the one relating to the application for the other entry.

(4) Subsection (2) does not apply if the earlier entry is one to which a direction under section 46(3) applies.

(5) The registrar may defer dealing with an application for an entry in the register if it appears to him that subsection (2) might apply to the entry were he to make it.

(6) Rules may—

(a) make provision for priority periods in connection with—
   (i) official searches of the register, including searches of pending applications for first registration, or
   (ii) the noting in the register of a contract for the making of a registrable disposition of a registered estate or charge;
(b) make provision for the keeping of records in relation to priority periods and the inspection of such records.

(7) Rules under subsection (6)(a) may, in particular, make provision about—

(a) the commencement and length of a priority period,
(b) the applications for registration to which such a period relates,
(c) the order in which competing priority periods rank, and
(d) the application of subsections (2) and (3) in cases where more than one priority period relates to the same application.

Objections

65–073 **73.**—(1) Subject to subsections (2) and (3), anyone may object to an application to the registrar.

(2) In the case of an application under section 18, only the person who lodged the caution to which the application relates, or such other person as rules may provide, may object.

(3) In the case of an application under section 36, only the person shown in the

register as the beneficiary of the notice to which the application relates, or such other person as rules may provide, may object.

(4) The right to object under this section is subject to rules.

(5) Where an objection is made under this section, the registrar—

(a) must give notice of the objection to the applicant, and

(b) may not determine the application until the objection has been disposed of.

(6) Subsection (5) does not apply if the objection is one which the registrar is satisfied is groundless.

(7) If it is not possible to dispose by agreement of an objection to which subsection (5) applies, the registrar must refer the matter to the adjudicator.

(8) Rules may make provision about references under subsection (7).

Effective date of registration

74 An entry made in the register in pursuance of— **65–074**

(a) an application for registration of an unregistered legal estate, or

(b) an application for registration in relation to a disposition required to be completed by registration,

has effect from the time of the making of the application.

Proceedings before the registrar

Production of documents

75.—(1) The registrar may require a person to produce a document for the purposes of proceedings before him. **65–075**

(2) The power under subsection (1) is subject to rules.

(3) A requirement under subsection (1) shall be enforceable as an order of the court.

(4) A person aggrieved by a requirement under subsection (1) may appeal to a county court, which may make any order which appears appropriate.

Costs

76.—(1) The registrar may make orders about costs in relation to proceedings before him. **65–076**

(2) The power under subsection (1) is subject to rules which may, in particular, make provision about—

(a) who may be required to pay costs,

(b) whose costs a person may be required to pay,

(c) the kind of costs which a person may be required to pay, and

(d) the assessment of costs.

(3) Without prejudice to the generality of subsection (2), rules under that subsection may include provision about—

(a) costs of the registrar, and

(b) liability for costs thrown away as the result of neglect or delay by a legal representative of a party to proceedings.

(4) An order under subsection (1) shall be enforceable as an order of the court.

(5) A person aggrieved by an order under subsection (1) may appeal to a county court, which may make any order which appears appropriate.

Miscellaneous

Duty to act reasonably

65–077 **77.**—(1) A person must not exercise any of the following rights without reasonable cause—

(a) the right to lodge a caution under section 15,

(b) the right to apply for the entry of a notice or restriction, and

(c) the right to object to an application to the registrar.

(2) The duty under this section is owed to any person who suffers damage in consequence of its breach.

Notice of trust not to affect registrar

65–078 **78.** The registrar shall not be affected with notice of a trust.

PART 7

SPECIAL CASES

The Crown

Voluntary registration of demesne land

65–079 **79.**—(1) Her Majesty may grant an estate in fee simple absolute in possession out of demesne land to Herself.

(2) The grant of an estate under subsection (1) is to be regarded as not having been made unless an application under section 3 is made in respect of the estate before the end of the period for registration.

(3) The period for registration is two months beginning with the date of the grant, or such longer period as the registrar may provide under subsection (4).

(4) If on the application of Her Majesty the registrar is satisfied that there is a good reason for doing so, he may by order provide that the period for registration ends on such later date as he may specify in the order.

(5) If an order under subsection (4) is made in a case where subsection (2) has already applied, that application of the subsection is to be treated as not having occurred.

Compulsory registration of grants out of demesne land

65–080 **80.**—(1) Section 4(1) shall apply as if the following were included among the events listed—

(a) the grant by Her Majesty out of demesne land of an estate in fee simple absolute in possession, otherwise than under section 79;

(b) the grant by Her Majesty out of demesne land of an estate in land—

  (i) for a term of years absolute of more than seven years from the date of the grant, and

  (ii) for valuable or other consideration, by way of gift or in pursuance of an order of any court.

(2) In subsection (1)(b)(ii), the reference to grant by way of gift includes grant for the purpose of constituting a trust under which Her Majesty does not retain the whole of the beneficial interest.

(3) Subsection (1) does not apply to the grant of an estate in mines and minerals held apart from the surface.

(4) The Lord Chancellor may by order—

(a) amend this section so as to add to the events in subsection (1) such events relating to demesne land as he may specify in the order, and

(b) make such consequential amendments of any provision of, or having effect under, any Act as he thinks appropriate.

(5) In its application by virtue of subsection (1), section 7 has effect with the substitution for subsection (2) of—

"(2) On the application of subsection (1), the grant has effect as a contract made for valuable consideration to grant the legal estate concerned".

Demesne land: cautions against first registration

81.—(1) Section 15 shall apply as if demesne land were held by Her Majesty for an unregistered estate in fee simple absolute in possession. **65–081**

(2) The provisions of this Act relating to cautions against first registration shall, in relation to cautions lodged by virtue of subsection (1), have effect subject to such modifications as rules may provide.

Escheat etc.

82.—(1) Rules may make provision about— **65–082**

(a) the determination of a registered freehold estate in land, and

(b) the registration of an unregistered freehold legal estate in land in respect of land to which a former registered freehold estate in land related.

(2) Rules under this section may, in particular—

(a) make provision for determination to be dependent on the meeting of such registration requirements as the rules may specify;

(b) make provision for entries relating to a freehold estate in land to continue in the register, notwithstanding determination, for such time as the rules may provide;

(c) make provision for the making in the register in relation to a former freehold estate in land of such entries as the rules may provide;

(d) make provision imposing requirements to be met in connection with an application for the registration of such an unregistered estate as is mentioned in subsection (1)(b).

Crown and Duchy land: representation

83.—(1) With respect to a Crown or Duchy interest, the appropriate authority— **65–083**

(a) may represent the owner of the interest for all purposes of this Act,

(b) is entitled to receive such notice as that person is entitled to receive under this Act, and

(c) may make such applications and do such other acts as that person is entitled to make or do under this Act.

(2) In this section—

"the appropriate authority" means—

(a) in relation to an interest belonging to Her Majesty in right of the Crown and forming part of the Crown Estate, the Crown Estate Commissioners;

(b) in relation to any other interest belonging to Her Majesty in right of the Crown, the government department having the management of the interest or, if there is no such department, such person as Her Majesty may appoint in writing under the Royal Sign Manual;

(c) in relation to an interest belonging to Her Majesty in right of the Duchy of Lancaster, the Chancellor of the Duchy;

(d) in relation to an interest belonging to the Duchy of Cornwall, such person as the Duke of Cornwall, or the possessor for the time being of the Duchy of Cornwall, appoints;

(e) in relation to an interest belonging to a government department, or held in trust for Her Majesty for the purposes of a government department, that department;

"Crown interest" means an interest belonging to Her Majesty in right of the Crown, or belonging to a government department, or held in trust for Her Majesty for the purposes of a government department;

"Duchy interest" means an interest belonging to Her Majesty in right of the Duchy of Lancaster, or belonging to the Duchy of Cornwall;

"interest" means any estate, interest or charge in or over land and any right or claim in relation to land.

Disapplication of requirements relating to Duchy land

65–084 **84.** Nothing in any enactment relating to the Duchy of Lancaster or the Duchy of Cornwall shall have effect to impose any requirement with respect to formalities or enrolment in relation to a disposition by a registered proprietor.

Bona vacantia

65–085 **85.** Rules may make provision about how the passing of a registered estate or charge as bona vacantia is to be dealt with for the purposes of this Act.

Pending actions etc.

Bankruptcy

65–086 **86.**—(1) In this Act, references to an interest affecting an estate or charge do not include a petition in bankruptcy or bankruptcy order.

(2) As soon as practicable after registration of a petition in bankruptcy as a pending action under the Land Charges Act 1972 (c. 61), the registrar must enter in the register in relation to any registered estate or charge which appears to him to be affected a notice in respect of the pending action.

(3) Unless cancelled by the registrar in such manner as rules may provide, a notice entered under subsection (2) continues in force until—

(a) a restriction is entered in the register under subsection (4), or

(b) the trustee in bankruptcy is registered as proprietor.

(4) As soon as practicable after registration of a bankruptcy order under the Land Charges Act 1972, the registrar must, in relation to any registered estate or charge which appears to him to be affected by the order, enter in the register a restriction reflecting the effect of the Insolvency Act 1986 (c. 45).

(5) Where the proprietor of a registered estate or charge is adjudged bankrupt, the title of his trustee in bankruptcy is void as against a person to whom a registrable disposition of the estate or charge is made if—

(a) the disposition is made for valuable consideration,
(b) the person to whom the disposition is made acts in good faith, and
(c) at the time of the disposition—
(i) no notice or restriction is entered under this section in relation to the registered estate or charge, and
(ii) the person to whom the disposition is made has no notice of the bankruptcy petition or the adjudication.

(6) Subsection (5) only applies if the relevant registration requirements are met in relation to the disposition, but, when they are met, has effect as from the date of the disposition.

(7) Nothing in this section requires a person to whom a registrable disposition is made to make any search under the Land Charges Act 1972.

Pending land actions, writs, orders and deeds of arrangement

87.—(1) Subject to the following provisions, references in this Act to an interest affecting an estate or charge include— **65–087**
(a) a pending land action within the meaning of the Land Charges Act 1972,
(b) a writ or order of the kind mentioned in section 6(1)(a) of that Act (writ or order affecting land issued or made by any court for the purposes of enforcing a judgment or recognisance),
(c) an order appointing a receiver or sequestrator, and
(d) a deed of arrangement.

(2) No notice may be entered in the register in respect of—
(a) an order appointing a receiver or sequestrator, or
(b) a deed of arrangement.

(3) None of the matters mentioned in subsection (1) shall be capable of falling within paragraph 2 of Schedule 1 or 3.

(4) In its application to any of the matters mentioned in subsection (1), this Act shall have effect subject to such modifications as rules may provide.

(5) In this section, "deed of arrangement" has the same meaning as in the Deeds of Arrangement Act 1914 (c. 47).

Miscellaneous

Incorporeal hereditaments

88. In its application to— **65–088**
(a) rentcharges,
(b) franchises,
(c) profits a prendre in gross, or
(d) manors,

this Act shall have effect subject to such modification as rules may provide.

Settlements

89.—(1) Rules may make provision for the purposes of this Act in relation to the application to registered land of the enactments relating to settlements under the Settled Land Act 1925 (c. 18). **65–089**

(2) Rules under this section may include provision modifying any of those enactments in its application to registered land.

(3) In this section, "registered land" means an interest the title to which is, or is required to be, registered.

PPP leases relating to transport in London

65–090 **90.**—(1) No application for registration under section 3 may be made in respect of a leasehold estate in land under a PPP lease.

(2) The requirement of registration does not apply on the grant or transfer of a leasehold estate in land under a PPP lease.

(3) For the purposes of section 27, the following are not dispositions requiring to be completed by registration—

(a) the grant of a term of years absolute under a PPP lease;
(b) the express grant of an interest falling within section 1(2) of the Law of Property Act 1925 (c. 20), where the interest is created for the benefit of a leasehold estate in land under a PPP lease.

(4) No notice may be entered in the register in respect of an interest under a PPP lease.

(5) Schedules 1 and 3 have effect as if they included a paragraph referring to a PPP lease.

(6) In this section, "PPP lease" has the meaning given by section 218 of the Greater London Authority Act 1999 (c. 29) (which makes provision about leases created for public-private partnerships relating to transport in London).

PART 8

ELECTRONIC CONVEYANCING

Electronic dispositions: formalities

65–091 **91.**—(1) This section applies to a document in electronic form where—

(a) the document purports to effect a disposition which falls within subsection (2), and
(b) the conditions in subsection (3) are met.

(2) A disposition falls within this subsection if it is—

(a) a disposition of a registered estate or charge,
(b) a disposition of an interest which is the subject of a notice in the register, or
(c) a disposition which triggers the requirement of registration,

which is of a kind specified by rules.

(3) The conditions referred to above are that—

(a) the document makes provision for the time and date when it takes effect,
(b) the document has the electronic signature of each person by whom it purports to be authenticated,
(c) each electronic signature is certified, and
(d) such other conditions as rules may provide are met.

(4) A document to which this section applies is to be regarded as—

(a) in writing, and
(b) signed by each individual, and sealed by each corporation, whose electronic signature it has.

(5) A document to which this section applies is to be regarded for the purposes of any enactment as a deed.

(6) If a document to which this section applies is authenticated by a person as agent, it is to be regarded for the purposes of any enactment as authenticated by him under the written authority of his principal.

(7) If notice of an assignment made by means of a document to which this section applies is given in electronic form in accordance with rules, it is to be regarded for the purposes of any enactment as given in writing.

(8) The right conferred by section 75 of the Law of Property Act 1925 (c. 20) (purchaser's right to have the execution of a conveyance attested) does not apply to a document to which this section applies.

(9) If subsection (4) of section 36A of the Companies Act 1985 (c. 6) (execution of documents) applies to a document because of subsection (4) above, subsection (6) of that section (presumption of due execution) shall have effect in relation to the document with the substitution of "authenticated" for "signed".

(10) In this section, references to an electronic signature and to the certification of such a signature are to be read in accordance with section 7(2) and (3) of the Electronic Communications Act 2000 (c. 7).

Land registry network

92.—(1) The registrar may provide, or arrange for the provision of, an electronic communications network for use for such purposes as he thinks fit relating to registration or the carrying on of transactions which— **65–092**

(a) involve registration, and
(b) are capable of being effected electronically.

(2) Schedule 5 (which makes provision in connection with a network provided under subsection (1) and transactions carried on by means of such a network) has effect.

Power to require simultaneous registration

93.—(1) This section applies to a disposition of— **65–093**

(a) a registered estate or charge, or
(b) an interest which is the subject of a notice in the register,

where the disposition is of a description specified by rules.

(2) A disposition to which this section applies, or a contract to make such a disposition, only has effect if it is made by means of a document in electronic form and if, when the document purports to take effect—

(a) it is electronically communicated to the registrar, and
(b) the relevant registration requirements are met.

(3) For the purposes of subsection (2)(b), the relevant registration requirements are—

(a) in the case of a registrable disposition, the requirements under Schedule 2, and
(b) in the case of any other disposition, or a contract, such requirements as rules may provide.

(4) Section 27(1) does not apply to a disposition to which this section applies.

(5) Before making rules under this section the Lord Chancellor must consult such persons as he considers appropriate.

(6) In this section, "disposition", in relation to a registered charge, includes postponement.

Electronic settlement

65–094 **94.** The registrar may take such steps as he thinks fit for the purpose of securing the provision of a system of electronic settlement in relation to transactions involving registration.

Supplementary

65–095 **95.** Rules may—

(a) make provision about the communication of documents in electronic form to the registrar;

(b) make provision about the electronic storage of documents communicated to the registrar in electronic form.

PART 9

ADVERSE POSSESSION

Disapplication of periods of limitation

65–096 **96.**—(1) No period of limitation under section 15 of the Limitation Act 1980 (c. 58) (time limits in relation to recovery of land) shall run against any person, other than a chargee, in relation to an estate in land or rentcharge the title to which is registered.

(2) No period of limitation under section 16 of that Act (time limits in relation to redemption of land) shall run against any person in relation to such an estate in land or rentcharge.

(3) Accordingly, section 17 of that Act (extinction of title on expiry of time limit) does not operate to extinguish the title of any person where, by virtue of this section, a period of limitation does not run against him.

Registration of adverse possessor

65–097 **97.** Schedule 6 (which makes provision about the registration of an adverse possessor of an estate in land or rentcharge) has effect.

Defences

65–098 **98.**—(1) A person has a defence to an action for possession of land if—

(a) on the day immediately preceding that on which the action was brought he was entitled to make an application under paragraph 1 of Schedule 6 to be registered as the proprietor of an estate in the land, and

(b) had he made such an application on that day, the condition in paragraph 5(4) of that Schedule would have been satisfied.

(2) A judgment for possession of land ceases to be enforceable at the end of the period of two years beginning with the date of the judgment if the proceedings in which the judgment is given were commenced against a person who was at that time entitled to make an application under paragraph 1 of Schedule 6.

(3) A person has a defence to an action for possession of land if on the day immediately preceding that on which the action was brought he was entitled to make an application under paragraph 6 of Schedule 6 to be registered as the proprietor of an estate in the land.

(4) A judgment for possession of land ceases to be enforceable at the end of the period of two years beginning with the date of the judgment if, at the end of that period, the person against whom the judgment was given is entitled to make an application under paragraph 6 of Schedule 6 to be registered as the proprietor of an estate in the land.

(5) Where in any proceedings a court determines that—

(a) a person is entitled to a defence under this section, or

(b) a judgment for possession has ceased to be enforceable against a person by virtue of subsection (4),

the court must order the registrar to register him as the proprietor of the estate in relation to which he is entitled to make an application under Schedule 6.

(6) The defences under this section are additional to any other defences a person may have.

(7) Rules may make provision to prohibit the recovery of rent due under a rentcharge from a person who has been in adverse possession of the rentcharge.

PART 10

LAND REGISTRY

Administration

The land registry

99.—(1) There is to continue to be an office called Her Majesty's Land Registry which is to deal with the business of registration under this Act. **65–099**

(2) The land registry is to consist of—

(a) the Chief Land Registrar, who is its head, and

(b) the staff appointed by him;

and references in this Act to a member of the land registry are to be read accordingly.

(3) The Lord Chancellor shall appoint a person to be the Chief Land Registrar.

(4) Schedule 7 (which makes further provision about the land registry) has effect.

Conduct of business

100.—(1) Any function of the registrar may be carried out by any member of the land registry who is authorised for the purpose by the registrar. **65–100**

(2) The Lord Chancellor may by regulations make provision about the carrying out of functions during any vacancy in the office of registrar.

(3) The Lord Chancellor may by order designate a particular office of the land registry as the proper office for the receipt of applications or a specified description of application.

(4) The registrar may prepare and publish such forms and directions as he considers necessary or desirable for facilitating the conduct of the business of registration under this Act.

Annual report

101.—(1) The registrar must make an annual report on the business of the land registry to the Lord Chancellor. **65–101**

(2) The registrar must publish every report under this section and may do so in such manner as he thinks fit.

(3) The Lord Chancellor must lay copies of every report under this section before Parliament.

Fees and indemnities

Fee orders

65–102 **102.** The Lord Chancellor may with the advice and assistance of the body referred to in section 127(2) (the Rule Committee), and the consent of the Treasury, by order—

(a) prescribe fees to be paid in respect of dealings with the land registry, except under section 69(3)(b) or 105;

(b) make provision about the payment of prescribed fees.

Indemnities

65–103 **103.** Schedule 8 (which makes provision for the payment of indemnities by the registrar) has effect.

Miscellaneous

General information about land

65–104 **104.** The registrar may publish information about land in England and Wales if it appears to him to be information in which there is legitimate public interest.

Consultancy and advisory services

65–105 **105.**—(1) The registrar may provide, or arrange for the provision of, consultancy or advisory services about the registration of land in England and Wales or elsewhere.

(2) The terms on which services are provided under this section by the registrar, in particular terms as to payment, shall be such as he thinks fit.

Incidental powers: companies

65–106 **106.**—(1) If the registrar considers it expedient to do so in connection with his functions under section 69(3)(a), 92(1), 94 or 105(1) or paragraph 10 of Schedule 5, he may—

(a) form, or participate in the formation of, a company, or

(b) purchase, or invest in, a company.

(2) In this section—

"company" means a company within the meaning of the Companies Act 1985 (c. 6);

"invest" means invest in any way (whether by acquiring assets, securities or rights or otherwise).

(3) This section is without prejudice to any powers of the registrar exercisable otherwise than by virtue of this section.

PART 11

ADJUDICATION

The adjudicator

107.—(1) The Lord Chancellor shall appoint a person to be the Adjudicator to Her Majesty's Land Registry. **65–107**

(2) To be qualified for appointment under subsection (1), a person must have a 10 year general qualification (within the meaning of section 71 of the Courts and Legal Services Act 1990 (c. 41)).

(3) Schedule 9 (which makes further provision about the adjudicator) has effect.

Jurisdiction

108.—(1) The adjudicator has the following functions— **65–108**

(a) determining matters referred to him under section 73(7), and

(b) determining appeals under paragraph 4 of Schedule 5.

(2) Also, the adjudicator may, on application, make any order which the High Court could make for the rectification or setting aside of a document which—

(a) effects a qualifying disposition of a registered estate or charge,

(b) is a contract to make such a disposition, or

(c) effects a transfer of an interest which is the subject of a notice in the register.

(3) For the purposes of subsection (2)(a), a qualifying disposition is—

(a) a registrable disposition, or

(b) a disposition which creates an interest which may be the subject of a notice in the register.

(4) The general law about the effect of an order of the High Court for the rectification or setting aside of a document shall apply to an order under this section.

Procedure

109.—(1) Hearings before the adjudicator shall be held in public, except where he is satisfied that exclusion of the public is just and reasonable. **65–109**

(2) Subject to that, rules may regulate the practice and procedure to be followed with respect to proceedings before the adjudicator and matters incidental to or consequential on such proceedings.

(3) Rules under subsection (2) may, in particular, make provision about—

(a) when hearings are to be held,

(b) requiring persons to attend hearings to give evidence or to produce documents,

(c) the form in which any decision of the adjudicator is to be given,

(d) payment of costs of a party to proceedings by another party to the proceedings, and

(e) liability for costs thrown away as the result of neglect or delay by a legal representative of a party to proceedings.

Functions in relation to disputes

65–110 **110.**—(1) In proceedings on a reference under section 73(7), the adjudicator may, instead of deciding a matter himself, direct a party to the proceedings to commence proceedings within a specified time in the court for the purpose of obtaining the court's decision on the matter.

(2) Rules may make provision about the reference under subsection (1) of matters to the court and may, in particular, make provision about—

(a) adjournment of the proceedings before the adjudicator pending the outcome of the proceedings before the court, and

(b) the powers of the adjudicator in the event of failure to comply with a direction under subsection (1).

(3) Rules may make provision about the functions of the adjudicator in consequence of a decision on a reference under section 73(7) and may, in particular, make provision enabling the adjudicator to determine, or give directions about the determination of—

(a) the application to which the reference relates, or

(b) such other present or future application to the registrar as the rules may provide.

(4) If, in the case of a reference under section 73(7) relating to an application under paragraph 1 of Schedule 6, the adjudicator determines that it would be unconscionable because of an equity by estoppel for the registered proprietor to seek to dispossess the applicant, but that the circumstances are not such that the applicant ought to be registered as proprietor, the adjudicator—

(a) must determine how the equity due to the applicant is to be satisfied, and

(b) may for that purpose make any order that the High Court could make in the exercise of its equitable jurisdiction.

Appeals

65–111 **111.**—(1) Subject to subsection (2), a person aggrieved by a decision of the adjudicator may appeal to the High Court.

(2) In the case of a decision on an appeal under paragraph 4 of Schedule 5, only appeal on a point of law is possible.

(3) If on an appeal under this section relating to an application under paragraph 1 of Schedule 6 the court determines that it would be unconscionable because of an equity by estoppel for the registered proprietor to seek to dispossess the applicant, but that the circumstances are not such that the applicant ought to be registered as proprietor, the court must determine how the equity due to the applicant is to be satisfied.

Enforcement of orders etc

65–112 **112.** A requirement of the adjudicator shall be enforceable as an order of the court.

Fees

65–113 **113.** The Lord Chancellor may by order—

(a) prescribe fees to be paid in respect of proceedings before the adjudicator;

(b) make provision about the payment of prescribed fees.

Supplementary

114. Power to make rules under this Part is exercisable by the Lord Chancellor. **65–114**

PART 12

MISCELLANEOUS AND GENERAL

Miscellaneous

Rights of pre-emption

115.—(1) A right of pre-emption in relation to registered land has effect from the time of creation as an interest capable of binding successors in title (subject to the rules about the effect of dispositions on priority). **65–115**

(2) This section has effect in relation to rights of pre-emption created on or after the day on which this section comes into force.

Proprietary estoppel and mere equities

116. It is hereby declared for the avoidance of doubt that, in relation to registered land, each of the following— **65–116**

(a) an equity by estoppel, and

(b) a mere equity,

has effect from the time the equity arises as an interest capable of binding successors in title (subject to the rules about the effect of dispositions on priority).

Reduction in unregistered interests with automatic protection

117.—(1) Paragraphs 10 to 14 of Schedules 1 and 3 shall cease to have effect at the end of the period of ten years beginning with the day on which those come into force. **65–117**

(2) If made before the end of the period mentioned in subsection (1), no fee may be charged for—

(a) an application to lodge a caution against first registration by virtue of an interest falling within any of paragraphs 10 to 14 of Schedule 1, or

(b) an application for the entry in the register of a notice in respect of an interest falling within any of paragraphs 10 to 14 of Schedule 3.

Power to reduce qualifying term

118.—(1) The Lord Chancellor may by order substitute for the term specified in any of the following provisions— **65–118**

(a) section 3(3),

(b) section 4(1)(c)(i) and (2)(b),

(c) section 15(3)(a)(ii),
(d) section 27(2)(b)(i),
(e) section 80(1)(b)(i),
(f) paragraph 1 of Schedule 1,
(g) paragraphs 4(1), 5(1) and 6(1) of Schedule 2, and
(h) paragraph 1 of Schedule 3,

such shorter term as he thinks fit.

(2) An order under this section may contain such transitional provision as the Lord Chancellor thinks fit.

(3) Before making an order under this section, the Lord Chancellor must consult such persons as he considers appropriate.

. . . . . .

Land registration rules

Miscellaneous and general powers

65–119 **119.** Schedule 10 (which contains miscellaneous and general land registration rule-making powers) has effect.

. . . . . .

Supplementary

. . . . . .

"Proprietor in possession"

65–120 **131.**—(1) For the purposes of this Act, land is in the possession of the proprietor of a registered estate in land if it is physically in his possession, or in that of a person who is entitled to be registered as the proprietor of the registered estate.

(2) In the case of the following relationships, land which is (or is treated as being) in the possession of the second-mentioned person is to be treated for the purposes of subsection (1) as in the possession of the first-mentioned person—

(a) landlord and tenant;
(b) mortgagor and mortgagee;
(c) licensor and licensee;
(d) trustee and beneficiary.

(3) In subsection (1), the reference to entitlement does not include entitlement under Schedule 6.

General interpretation

65–121 **132.**—(1) In this Act—

"adjudicator" means the Adjudicator to Her Majesty's Land Registry;

"caution against first registration" means a caution lodged under section 15;

"cautions register" means the register kept under section 19(1);

"charge" means any mortgage, charge or lien for securing money or money's worth;

"demesne land" means land belonging to Her Majesty in right of the Crown which is not held for an estate in fee simple absolute in possession;

"land" includes—

(a) buildings and other structures,

(b) land covered with water, and

(c) mines and minerals, whether or not held with the surface;

"land registration rules" means any rules under this Act, other than rules under section 93, Part 11, section 121 or paragraph 1, 2 or 3 of Schedule 5;

"legal estate" has the same meaning as in the Law of Property Act 1925 (c. 20);

"legal mortgage" has the same meaning as in the Law of Property Act 1925;

"mines and minerals" includes any strata or seam of minerals or substances in or under any land, and powers of working and getting any such minerals or substances;

"registrar" means the Chief Land Registrar;

"register" means the register of title, except in the context of cautions against first registration;

"registered" means entered in the register;

"registered charge" means a charge the title to which is entered in the register;

"registered estate" means a legal estate the title to which is entered in the register, other than a registered charge;

"registered land" means a registered estate or registered charge;

"registrable disposition" means a disposition which is required to be completed by registration under section 27;

"requirement of registration" means the requirement of registration under section 4;

"sub-charge" means a charge under section 23(2)(b);

"term of years absolute" has the same meaning as in the Law of Property Act 1925 (c. 20);

"valuable consideration" does not include marriage consideration or a nominal consideration in money.

(2) In subsection (1), in the definition of "demesne land", the reference to land belonging to Her Majesty does not include land in relation to which a freehold estate in land has determined, but in relation to which there has been no act of entry or management by the Crown.

(3) In this Act—

(a) references to the court are to the High Court or a county court,

(b) references to an interest affecting an estate or charge are to an adverse right affecting the title to the estate or charge, and

(c) references to the right to object to an application to the registrar are to the right under section 73.

. . . .

SCHEDULES

Sections 11 and 12 SCHEDULE 1

UNREGISTERED INTERESTS WHICH OVERRIDE FIRST REGISTRATION

Leasehold estates in land

1. A leasehold estate in land granted for a term not exceeding seven years from the date of the grant, except for a lease the grant of which falls within section 4(1)(d), (e) or (f).

Interests of persons in actual occupation

2. An interest belonging to a person in actual occupation, so far as relating to land of which he is in actual occupation, except for an interest under a settlement under the Settled Land Act 1925 (c. 18).

Easements and profits a prendre

3. A legal easement or profit a prendre.

Customary and public rights

4. A customary right.

5. A public right.

Local land charges

6. A local land charge.

Mines and minerals

7. An interest in any coal or coal mine, the rights attached to any such interest and the rights of any person under section 38, 49 or 51 of the Coal Industry Act 1994 (c. 21).

8. In the case of land to which title was registered before 1898, rights to mines and minerals (and incidental rights) created before 1898.

9. In the case of land to which title was registered between 1898 and 1925 inclusive, rights to mines and minerals (and incidental rights) created before the date of registration of the title.

Miscellaneous

10. A franchise.

11. A manorial right.

12. A right to rent which was reserved to the Crown on the granting of any freehold estate (whether or not the right is still vested in the Crown).

13. A non-statutory right in respect of an embankment or sea or river wall.

14. A right to payment in lieu of tithe.

Section 27

SCHEDULE 2

REGISTRABLE DISPOSITIONS: REGISTRATION REQUIREMENTS

PART 1

REGISTERED ESTATES

Introductory

1. This Part deals with the registration requirements relating to those dispositions of registered estates which are required to be completed by registration.

Transfer

2.— (1) In the case of a transfer of whole or part, the transferee, or his successor in title, must be entered in the register as the proprietor.

(2) In the case of a transfer of part, such details of the transfer as rules may provide must be entered in the register in relation to the registered estate out of which the transfer is made.

Lease of estate in land

3.—(1) This paragraph applies to a disposition consisting of the grant out of an estate in land of a term of years absolute.

(2) In the case of a disposition to which this paragraph applies—

(a) the grantee, or his successor in title, must be entered in the register as the proprietor of the lease, and

(b) a notice in respect of the lease must be entered in the register.

Lease of franchise or manor

4.—(1) This paragraph applies to a disposition consisting of the grant out of a franchise or manor of a lease for a term of more than seven years from the date of the grant.

(2) In the case of a disposition to which this paragraph applies—

(a) the grantee, or his successor in title, must be entered in the register as the proprietor of the lease, and

(b) a notice in respect of the lease must be entered in the register.

5.—(1) This paragraph applies to a disposition consisting of the grant out of a franc
of a lease for a term not exceeding seven years from the date of the grant.

(2) In the case of a disposition to which this paragraph applies, a notice in respect
be entered in the register.

Creation of independently registrable legal interest

6.—(1) This paragraph applies to a disposition consisting of the creation of a legal rentcharge or profit a prendre in gross, other than one created for, or for an interest equivalent to, a term of years absolute not exceeding seven years from the date of creation.

(2) In the case of a disposition to which this paragraph applies—

(a) the grantee, or his successor in title, must be entered in the register as the proprietor of the interest created, and

(b) a notice in respect of the interest created must be entered in the register.

(3) In sub-paragraph (1), the reference to a legal rentcharge or profit a prendre in gross is to one falling within section 1(2) of the Law of Property Act 1925 (c. 20).

Creation of other legal interest

7.—(1) This paragraph applies to a disposition which—

(a) consists of the creation of an interest of a kind falling within section 1(2)(a), (b) or (e) of the Law of Property Act 1925, and

(b) is not a disposition to which paragraph 4, 5 or 6 applies.

(2) In the case of a disposition to which this paragraph applies—

(a) a notice in respect of the interest created must be entered in the register, and

(b) if the interest is created for the benefit of a registered estate, the proprietor of the registered estate must be entered in the register as its proprietor.

(3) Rules may provide for sub-paragraph (2) to have effect with modifications in relation to a right of entry over or in respect of a term of years absolute.

Creation of legal charge

8. In the case of the creation of a charge, the chargee, or his successor in title, must be entered in the register as the proprietor of the charge.

PART 2

REGISTERED CHARGES

Introductory

9. This Part deals with the registration requirements relating to those dispositions of registered charges which are required to be completed by registration.

Transfer

10. In the case of a transfer, the transferee, or his successor in title, must be entered in the register as the proprietor.

Creation of sub-charge

11. In the case of the creation of a sub-charge, the sub-chargee, or his successor in title, must be entered in the register as the proprietor of the sub-charge.

Sections 29 and 30

SCHEDULE 3

UNREGISTERED INTERESTS WHICH OVERRIDE REGISTERED DISPOSITIONS

Leasehold estates in land

1. A leasehold estate in land granted for a term not exceeding seven years from the date of the grant, except for—

(a) a lease the grant of which falls within section 4(1)(d), (e) or (f);

(b) a lease the grant of which constitutes a registrable disposition.

Interests of persons in actual occupation

2. An interest belonging at the time of the disposition to a person in actual occupation, so far as relating to land of which he is in actual occupation, except for—

(a) an interest under a settlement under the Settled Land Act 1925 (c. 18);

(b) an interest of a person of whom inquiry was made before the disposition and who failed to disclose the right when he could reasonably have been expected to do so;

(c) an interest—
(i) which belongs to a person whose occupation would not have been obvious on a reasonably careful inspection of the land at the time of the disposition, and
(ii) of which the person to whom the disposition is made does not have actual knowledge at that time;

(d) a leasehold estate in land granted to take effect in possession after the end of the period of three months beginning with the date of the grant and which has not taken effect in possession at the time of the disposition.

Easements and profits a prendre

3.—(1) A legal easement or profit a prendre, except for an easement, or a profit a prendre which is not registered under the Commons Registration Act 1965 (c. 64), which at the time of the disposition—

(a) is not within the actual knowledge of the person to whom the disposition is made, and
(b) would not have been obvious on a reasonably careful inspection of the land over which the easement or profit is exercisable.

(2) The exception in sub-paragraph (1) does not apply if the person entitled to the easement or profit proves that it has been exercised in the period of one year ending with the day of the disposition.

Customary and public rights

4. A customary right.
5. A public right.

Local land charges

6. A local land charge.

Mines and minerals

7. An interest in any coal or coal mine, the rights attached to any such interest and the rights of any person under section 38, 49 or 51 of the Coal Industry Act 1994 (c. 21).

8. In the case of land to which title was registered before 1898, rights to mines and minerals (and incidental rights) created before 1898.

9. In the case of land to which title was registered between 1898 and 1925 inclusive, rights to mines and minerals (and incidental rights) created before the date of registration of the title.

Miscellaneous

10. A franchise.
11. A manorial right.
12. A right to rent which was reserved to the Crown on the granting of any freehold estate (whether or not the right is still vested in the Crown).
13. A non-statutory right in respect of an embankment or sea or river wall.
14. A right to payment in lieu of tithe.

Section 65 SCHEDULE 4

ALTERATION OF THE REGISTER

Introductory

1. In this Schedule, references to rectification, in relation to alteration of the register, are to alteration which—

(a) involves the correction of a mistake, and
(b) prejudicially affects the title of a registered proprietor.

Alteration pursuant to a court order

2.—(1) The court may make an order for alteration of the register for the purpose of—

(a) correcting a mistake,
(b) bringing the register up to date, or
(c) giving effect to any estate, right or interest excepted from the effect of registration.

(2) An order under this paragraph has effect when served on the registrar to impose a duty on him to give effect to it.

3.—(1) This paragraph applies to the power under paragraph 2, so far as relating to rectification.

(2) If alteration affects the title of the proprietor of a registered estate in land, no order may be

made under paragraph 2 without the proprietor's consent in relation to land in his possession unless—

(a) he has by fraud or lack of proper care caused or substantially contributed to the mistake, or

(b) it would for any other reason be unjust for the alteration not to be made.

(3) If in any proceedings the court has power to make an order under paragraph 2, it must do so, unless there are exceptional circumstances which justify its not doing so.

(4) In sub-paragraph (2), the reference to the title of the proprietor of a registered estate in land includes his title to any registered estate which subsists for the benefit of the estate in land.

4. Rules may—

(a) make provision about the circumstances in which there is a duty to exercise the power under paragraph 2, so far as not relating to rectification;

(b) make provision about the form of an order under paragraph 2;

(c) make provision about service of such an order.

Alteration otherwise than pursuant to a court order

5. The registrar may alter the register for the purpose of—

(a) correcting a mistake,

(b) bringing the register up to date,

(c) giving effect to any estate, right or interest excepted from the effect of registration, or

(d) removing a superfluous entry.

6.—(1) This paragraph applies to the power under paragraph 5, so far as relating to rectification.

(2) No alteration affecting the title of the proprietor of a registered estate in land may be made under paragraph 5 without the proprietor's consent in relation to land in his possession unless—

(a) he has by fraud or lack of proper care caused or substantially contributed to the mistake, or

(b) it would for any other reason be unjust for the alteration not to be made.

(3) If on an application for alteration under paragraph 5 the registrar has power to make the alteration, the application must be approved, unless there are exceptional circumstances which justify not making the alteration.

(4) In sub-paragraph (2), the reference to the title of the proprietor of a registered estate in land includes his title to any registered estate which subsists for the benefit of the estate in land.

7. Rules may—

(a) make provision about the circumstances in which there is a duty to exercise the power under paragraph 5, so far as not relating to rectification;

(b) make provision about how the register is to be altered in exercise of that power;

(c) make provision about applications for alteration under that paragraph, including provision requiring the making of such applications;

(d) make provision about procedure in relation to the exercise of that power, whether on application or otherwise.

Rectification and derivative interests

8. The powers under this Schedule to alter the register, so far as relating to rectification, extend to changing for the future the priority of any interest affecting the registered estate or charge concerned.

Costs in non-rectification cases

9.—(1) If the register is altered under this Schedule in a case not involving rectification, the registrar may pay such amount as he thinks fit in respect of any costs or expenses reasonably incurred by a person in connection with the alteration which have been incurred with the consent of the registrar.

(2) The registrar may make a payment under sub-paragraph (1) notwithstanding the absence of consent if—

(a) it appears to him—

(i) that the costs or expenses had to be incurred urgently, and

(ii) that it was not reasonably practicable to apply for his consent, or

(b) he has subsequently approved the incurring of the costs or expenses.

Section 92 SCHEDULE 5

LAND REGISTRY NETWORK

Access to network

1.—(1) A person who is not a member of the land registry may only have access to a land registry network under authority conferred by means of an agreement with the registrar.

(2) An agreement for the purposes of sub-paragraph (1) ("network access agreement") may authorise access for—

(a) the communication, posting or retrieval of information,
(b) the making of changes to the register of title or cautions register,
(c) the issue of official search certificates,
(d) the issue of official copies, or
(e) such other conveyancing purposes as the registrar thinks fit.

(3) Rules may regulate the use of network access agreements to confer authority to carry out functions of the registrar.

(4) The registrar must, on application, enter into a network access agreement with the applicant if the applicant meets such criteria as rules may provide.

Terms of access

2.—(1) The terms on which access to a land registry network is authorised shall be such as the registrar thinks fit, subject to sub-paragraphs (3) and (4), and may, in particular, include charges for access.

(2) The power under sub-paragraph (1) may be used, not only for the purpose of regulating the use of the network, but also for—

(a) securing that the person granted access uses the network to carry on such qualifying transactions as may be specified in, or under, the agreement,
(b) such other purpose relating to the carrying on of qualifying transactions as rules may provide, or
(c) enabling network transactions to be monitored.

(3) It shall be a condition of a network access agreement which enables the person granted access to use the network to carry on qualifying transactions that he must comply with any rules for the time being in force under paragraph 5.

(4) Rules may regulate the terms on which access to a land registry network is authorised.

. . . . . .

Network transaction rules

5.—(1) Rules may make provision about how to go about network transactions.

(2) Rules under sub-paragraph (1) may, in particular, make provision about dealings with the land registry, including provision about—

(a) the procedure to be followed, and
(b) the supply of information (including information about unregistered interests).

. . . .

Do-it-yourself conveyancing

7.—(1) If there is a land registry network, the registrar has a duty to provide such assistance as he thinks appropriate for the purpose of enabling persons engaged in qualifying transactions who wish to do their own conveyancing to do so by means of the network.

(2) The duty under sub-paragraph (1) does not extend to the provision of legal advice.

. . . . . .

12. In this Schedule—

"land registry network" means a network provided under section 92(1);
"network access agreement" has the meaning given by paragraph 1(2);
"network transaction" means a transaction carried on by means of a land registry network;
"qualifying transaction" means a transaction which—

(a) involves registration, and
(b) is capable of being effected electronically.

Section 97

SCHEDULE 6

REGISTRATION OF ADVERSE POSSESSOR

Right to apply for registration

1.—(1) A person may apply to the registrar to be registered as the proprietor of a registered estate in land if he has been in adverse possession of the estate for the period of ten years ending on the date of the application.

(2) A person may also apply to the registrar to be registered as the proprietor of a registered estate in land if—

(a) he has in the period of six months ending on the date of the application ceased to be in adverse possession of the estate because of eviction by the registered proprietor, or a person claiming under the registered proprietor,

(b) on the day before his eviction he was entitled to make an application under sub-paragraph (1), and

(c) the eviction was not pursuant to a judgment for possession.

(3) However, a person may not make an application under this paragraph if—

(a) he is a defendant in proceedings which involve asserting a right to possession of the land, or

(b) judgment for possession of the land has been given against him in the last two years.

(4) For the purposes of sub-paragraph (1), the estate need not have been registered throughout the period of adverse possession.

Notification of application

2.—(1) The registrar must give notice of an application under paragraph 1 to—

(a) the proprietor of the estate to which the application relates,

(b) the proprietor of any registered charge on the estate,

(c) where the estate is leasehold, the proprietor of any superior registered estate,

(d) any person who is registered in accordance with rules as a person to be notified under this paragraph, and

(e) such other persons as rules may provide.

(2) Notice under this paragraph shall include notice of the effect of paragraph 4.

Treatment of application

3.—(1) A person given notice under paragraph 2 may require that the application to which the notice relates be dealt with under paragraph 5.

(2) The right under this paragraph is exercisable by notice to the registrar given before the end of such period as rules may provide.

4. If an application under paragraph 1 is not required to be dealt with under paragraph 5, the applicant is entitled to be entered in the register as the new proprietor of the estate.

5.—(1) If an application under paragraph 1 is required to be dealt with under this paragraph, the applicant is only entitled to be registered as the new proprietor of the estate if any of the following conditions is met.

(2) The first condition is that—

(a) it would be unconscionable because of an equity by estoppel for the registered proprietor to seek to dispossess the applicant, and

(b) the circumstances are such that the applicant ought to be registered as the proprietor.

(3) The second condition is that the applicant is for some other reason entitled to be registered as the proprietor of the estate.

(4) The third condition is that—

(a) the land to which the application relates is adjacent to land belonging to the applicant,

(b) the exact line of the boundary between the two has not been determined under rules under section 60,

(c) for at least ten years of the period of adverse possession ending on the date of the application, the applicant (or any predecessor in title) reasonably believed that the land to which the application relates belonged to him, and

(d) the estate to which the application relates was registered more than one year prior to the date of the application.

(5) In relation to an application under paragraph 1(2), this paragraph has effect as if the reference in sub-paragraph (4)(c) to the date of the application were to the day before the date of the applicant's eviction.

Right to make further application for registration

6.—(1) Where a person's application under paragraph 1 is rejected, he may make a further application to be registered as the proprietor of the estate if he is in adverse possession of the estate from the date of the application until the last day of the period of two years beginning with the date of its rejection.

(2) However, a person may not make an application under this paragraph if—

(a) he is a defendant in proceedings which involve asserting a right to possession of the land,

(b) judgment for possession of the land has been given against him in the last two years, or

(c) he has been evicted from the land pursuant to a judgment for possession.

7. If a person makes an application under paragraph 6, he is entitled to be entered in the register as the new proprietor of the estate.

Restriction on applications

8.—(1) No one may apply under this Schedule to be registered as the proprietor of an estate in land during, or before the end of twelve months after the end of, any period in which the existing registered proprietor is for the purposes of the Limitation (Enemies and War Prisoners) Act 1945 (8 & 9 Geo. 6 c. 16)—

(a) an enemy, or

(b) detained in enemy territory.

(2) No-one may apply under this Schedule to be registered as the proprietor of an estate in land during any period in which the existing registered proprietor is—

(a) unable because of mental disability to make decisions about issues of the kind to which such an application would give rise, or

(b) unable to communicate such decisions because of mental disability or physical impairment.

(3) For the purposes of sub-paragraph (2), "mental disability" means a disability or disorder of the mind or brain, whether permanent or temporary, which results in an impairment or disturbance of mental functioning.

(4) Where it appears to the registrar that sub-paragraph (1) or (2) applies in relation to an estate in land, he may include a note to that effect in the register.

Effect of registration

9.—(1) Where a person is registered as the proprietor of an estate in land in pursuance of an application under this Schedule, the title by virtue of adverse possession which he had at the time of the application is extinguished.

(2) Subject to sub-paragraph (3), the registration of a person under this Schedule as the proprietor of an estate in land does not affect the priority of any interest affecting the estate.

(3) Subject to sub-paragraph (4), where a person is registered under this Schedule as the proprietor of an estate, the estate is vested in him free of any registered charge affecting the estate immediately before his registration.

(4) Sub-paragraph (3) does not apply where registration as proprietor is in pursuance of an application determined by reference to whether any of the conditions in paragraph 5 applies.

Apportionment and discharge of charges

10.—(1) Where—

(a) a registered estate continues to be subject to a charge notwithstanding the registration of a person under this Schedule as the proprietor, and

(b) the charge affects property other than the estate,

the proprietor of the estate may require the chargee to apportion the amount secured by the charge at that time between the estate and the other property on the basis of their respective values.

(2) The person requiring the apportionment is entitled to a discharge of his estate from the charge on payment of—

(a) the amount apportioned to the estate, and

(b) the costs incurred by the chargee as a result of the apportionment.

(3) On a discharge under this paragraph, the liability of the chargor to the chargee is reduced by the amount apportioned to the estate.

(4) Rules may make provision about apportionment under this paragraph, in particular, provision about—

(a) procedure,

(b) valuation,

(c) calculation of costs payable under sub-paragraph (2)(b), and

(d) payment of the costs of the chargor.

Meaning of "adverse possession"

11.—(1) A person is in adverse possession of an estate in land for the purposes of this Schedule if, but for section 96, a period of limitation under section 15 of the Limitation Act 1980 (c. 58) would run in his favour in relation to the estate.

(2) A person is also to be regarded for those purposes as having been in adverse possession of an estate in land—

(a) where he is the successor in title to an estate in the land, during any period of adverse possession by a predecessor in title to that estate, or

(b) during any period of adverse possession by another person which comes between, and is continuous with, periods of adverse possession of his own.

(3) In determining whether for the purposes of this paragraph a period of limitation would run under section 15 of the Limitation Act 1980, there are to be disregarded—

(a) the commencement of any legal proceedings, and

(b) paragraph 6 of Schedule 1 to that Act.

Trusts

12. A person is not to be regarded as being in adverse possession of an estate for the purposes of this Schedule at any time when the estate is subject to a trust, unless the interest of each of the beneficiaries in the estate is an interest in possession.

Crown foreshore

13.—(1) Where—

(a) a person is in adverse possession of an estate in land,

(b) the estate belongs to Her Majesty in right of the Crown or the Duchy of Lancaster or to the Duchy of Cornwall, and

(c) the land consists of foreshore,

paragraph 1(1) is to have effect as if the reference to ten years were to sixty years.

(2) For the purposes of sub-paragraph (1), land is to be treated as foreshore if it has been foreshore at any time in the previous ten years.

(3) In this paragraph, "foreshore" means the shore and bed of the sea and of any tidal water, below the line of the medium high tide between the spring and neap tides.

Rentcharges

14. Rules must make provision to apply the preceding provisions of this Schedule to registered rentcharges, subject to such modifications and exceptions as the rules may provide.

Procedure

15. Rules may make provision about the procedure to be followed pursuant to an application under this Schedule.

. . . . . .

Section 103

SCHEDULE 8

INDEMNITIES

Entitlement

1.—(1) A person is entitled to be indemnified by the registrar if he suffers loss by reason of—

(a) rectification of the register,

(b) a mistake whose correction would involve rectification of the register,

(c) a mistake in an official search,

(d) a mistake in an official copy,

(e) a mistake in a document kept by the registrar which is not an original and is referred to in the register,

(f) the loss or destruction of a document lodged at the registry for inspection or safe custody,

(g) a mistake in the cautions register, or

(h) failure by the registrar to perform his duty under section 50.

(2) For the purposes of sub-paragraph (1)(a)—

(a) any person who suffers loss by reason of the change of title under section 62 is to be regarded as having suffered loss by reason of rectification of the register, and

(b) the proprietor of a registered estate or charge claiming in good faith under a forged disposition is, where the register is rectified, to be regarded as having suffered loss by reason of such rectification as if the disposition had not been forged.

(3) No indemnity under sub-paragraph (1)(b) is payable until a decision has been made about whether to alter the register for the purpose of correcting the mistake; and the loss suffered by reason of the mistake is to be determined in the light of that decision.

Mines and minerals

2. No indemnity is payable under this Schedule on account of—

(a) any mines or minerals, or

(b) the existence of any right to work or get mines or minerals,

unless it is noted in the register that the title to the registered estate concerned includes the mines or minerals.

Costs

3.—(1) In respect of loss consisting of costs or expenses incurred by the claimant in relation to the matter, an indemnity under this Schedule is payable only on account of costs or expenses reasonably incurred by the claimant with the consent of the registrar.

(2) The requirement of consent does not apply where—

(a) the costs or expenses must be incurred by the claimant urgently, and

(b) it is not reasonably practicable to apply for the registrar's consent.

(3) If the registrar approves the incurring of costs or expenses after they have been incurred, they shall be treated for the purposes of this paragraph as having been incurred with his consent.

4.—(1) If no indemnity is payable to a claimant under this Schedule, the registrar may pay such amount as he thinks fit in respect of any costs or expenses reasonably incurred by the claimant in connection with the claim which have been incurred with the consent of the registrar.

(2) The registrar may make a payment under sub-paragraph (1) notwithstanding the absence of consent if—

(a) it appears to him—

(i) that the costs or expenses had to be incurred urgently, and

(ii) that it was not reasonably practicable to apply for his consent, or

(b) he has subsequently approved the incurring of the costs or expenses.

Claimant's fraud or lack of care

5.—(1) No indemnity is payable under this Schedule on account of any loss suffered by a claimant—

(a) wholly or partly as a result of his own fraud, or

(b) wholly as a result of his own lack of proper care.

(2) Where any loss is suffered by a claimant partly as a result of his own lack of proper care, any indemnity payable to him is to be reduced to such extent as is fair having regard to his share in the responsibility for the loss.

(3) For the purposes of this paragraph any fraud or lack of care on the part of a person from whom the claimant derives title (otherwise than under a disposition for valuable consideration which is registered or protected by an entry in the register) is to be treated as if it were fraud or lack of care on the part of the claimant.

Valuation of estates etc.

6. Where an indemnity is payable in respect of the loss of an estate, interest or charge, the value of the estate, interest or charge for the purposes of the indemnity is to be regarded as not exceeding—

(a) in the case of an indemnity under paragraph 1(1)(a), its value immediately before rectification of the register (but as if there were to be no rectification), and

(b) in the case of an indemnity under paragraph 1(1)(b), its value at the time when the mistake which caused the loss was made.

Determination of indemnity by court

7.—(1) A person may apply to the court for the determination of any question as to—

(a) whether he is entitled to an indemnity under this Schedule, or

(b) the amount of such an indemnity.

(2) Paragraph 3(1) does not apply to the costs of an application to the court under this paragraph or of any legal proceedings arising out of such an application.

Time limits

8. For the purposes of the Limitation Act 1980 (c. 58)—

(a) a liability to pay an indemnity under this Schedule is a simple contract debt, and

(b) the cause of action arises at the time when the claimant knows, or but for his own default might have known, of the existence of his claim.

Interest

9. Rules may make provision about the payment of interest on an indemnity under this Schedule, including—

(a) the circumstances in which interest is payable, and

(b) the periods for and rates at which it is payable.

Recovery of indemnity by registrar

10.—(1) Where an indemnity under this Schedule is paid to a claimant in respect of any loss, the registrar is entitled (without prejudice to any other rights he may have)—

(a) to recover the amount paid from any person who caused or substantially contributed to the loss by his fraud, or

(b) for the purpose of recovering the amount paid, to enforce the rights of action referred to in sub-paragraph (2).

(2) Those rights of action are—

(a) any right of action (of whatever nature and however arising) which the claimant would have been entitled to enforce had the indemnity not been paid, and

(b) where the register has been rectified, any right of action (of whatever nature and however arising) which the person in whose favour the register has been rectified would have been entitled to enforce had it not been rectified.

(3) References in this paragraph to an indemnity include interest paid on an indemnity under rules under paragraph 9.

Interpretation

11.—(1) For the purposes of this Schedule, references to a mistake in something include anything mistakenly omitted from it as well as anything mistakenly included in it.

(2) In this Schedule, references to rectification of the register are to alteration of the register which—

(a) involves the correction of a mistake, and

(b) prejudicially affects the title of a registered proprietor.

. . . . . .

Section 126

SCHEDULE 10

MISCELLANEOUS AND GENERAL POWERS

PART 1

MISCELLANEOUS

Dealings with estates subject to compulsory first registration

1.—(1) Rules may make provision—

(a) applying this Act to a pre-registration dealing with a registrable legal estate as if the dealing had taken place after the date of first registration of the estate, and

(b) about the date on which registration of the dealing is effective.

(2) For the purposes of sub-paragraph (1)—

(a) a legal estate is registrable if a person is subject to a duty under section 6 to make an application to be registered as the proprietor of it, and

(b) a pre-registration dealing is one which takes place before the making of such an application.

Regulation of title matters between sellers and buyers

2.—(1) Rules may make provision about the obligations with respect to—

(a) proof of title, or

(b) perfection of title,

of the seller under a contract for the transfer, or other disposition, for valuable consideration of a registered estate or charge.

(2) Rules under this paragraph may be expressed to have effect notwithstanding any stipulation to the contrary.

Implied covenants

3. Rules may—

(a) make provision about the form of provisions extending or limiting any covenant implied by virtue of Part 1 of the Law of Property (Miscellaneous Provisions) Act 1994 (c. 36) (implied covenants for title) on a registrable disposition;

(b) make provision about the application of section 77 of the Law of Property Act 1925 (c. 20) (implied covenants in conveyance subject to rents) to transfers of registered estates;

(c) make provision about reference in the register to implied covenants, including provision for the state of the register to be conclusive in relation to whether covenants have been implied.

Land certificates

4. Rules may make provision about—

(a) when a certificate of registration of title to a legal estate may be issued,

(b) the form and content of such a certificate, and

(c) when such a certificate must be produced or surrendered to the registrar.

. . . . . .

Section 134

SCHEDULE 12

TRANSITION

Existing entries in the register

1. Nothing in the repeals made by this Act affects the validity of any entry in the register.

2.—(1) This Act applies to notices entered under the Land Registration Act 1925 (c. 21) as it applies to notices entered in pursuance of an application under section 34(2)(a).

(2) This Act applies to restrictions and inhibitions entered under the Land Registration Act 1925 as it applies to restrictions entered under this Act.

(3) Notwithstanding their repeal by this Act, sections 55 and 56 of the Land Registration Act 1925 shall continue to have effect so far as relating to cautions against dealings lodged under that Act.

(4) Rules may make provision about cautions against dealings entered under the Land Registration Act 1925.

(5) In this paragraph, references to the Land Registration Act 1925 include a reference to any enactment replaced (directly or indirectly) by that Act.

3. An entry in the register which, immediately before the repeal of section 144(1)(xi) of the Land Registration Act 1925, operated by virtue of rule 239 of the Land Registration Rules (S.I. 1925/1093) as a caution under section 54 of that Act shall continue to operate as such a caution.

Existing cautions against first registration

4. Notwithstanding the repeal of section 56(3) of the Land Registration Act 1925, that provision shall continue to have effect in relation to cautions against first registration lodged under that Act, or any enactment replaced (directly or indirectly) by that Act.

Pending applications

5. Notwithstanding the repeal of the Land Registration Act 1925, that Act shall continue to have effect in relation to an application for the entry in the register of a notice, restriction, inhibition or caution against dealings which is pending immediately before the repeal of the provision under which the application is made.

6. Notwithstanding the repeal of section 53 of the Land Registration Act 1925, subsections (1) and (2) of that section shall continue to have effect in relation to an application to lodge a caution against first registration which is pending immediately before the repeal of those provisions.

Former overriding interests

7. For the period of three years beginning with the day on which Schedule 1 comes into force, it has effect with the insertion after paragraph 14 of—

> "15. A right acquired under the Limitation Act 1980 before the coming into force of this Schedule."

8. Schedule 3 has effect with the insertion after paragraph 2 of—

> "2A.—(1) An interest which, immediately before the coming into force of this Schedule, was an overriding interest under section 70(1)(g) of the Land Registration Act 1925 by virtue of a person's receipt of rents and profits, except for an interest of a person of whom inquiry was made before the disposition and who failed to disclose the right when he could reasonably have been expected to do so.
>
> (2) Sub-paragraph (1) does not apply to an interest if at any time since the coming into force of this Schedule it has been an interest which, had the Land Registration Act 1925 (c. 21) continued in force, would not have been an overriding interest under section 70(1)(g) of that Act by virtue of a person's receipt of rents and profits."

9.—(1) This paragraph applies to an easement or profit a prendre which was an overriding interest in relation to a registered estate immediately before the coming into force of Schedule 3, but which would not fall within paragraph 3 of that Schedule if created after the coming into force of that Schedule.

(2) In relation to an interest to which this paragraph applies, Schedule 3 has effect as if the interest were not excluded from paragraph 3.

10. For the period of three years beginning with the day on which Schedule 3 comes into force, paragraph 3 of the Schedule has effect with the omission of the exception.

11. For the period of three years beginning with the day on which Schedule 3 comes into force, it has effect with the insertion after paragraph 14 of—

"15. A right under paragraph 18(1) of Schedule 12."

12. Paragraph 1 of each of Schedules 1 and 3 shall be taken to include an interest which immediately before the coming into force of the Schedule was an overriding interest under section 70(1)(k) of the Land Registration Act 1925.

13. Paragraph 6 of each of Schedules 1 and 3 shall be taken to include an interest which immediately before the coming into force of the Schedule was an overriding interest under section 70(1)(i) of the Land Registration Act 1925 and whose status as such was preserved by section 19(3) of the Local Land Charges Act 1975 (c. 76) (transitional provision in relation to change in definition of "local land charge").

Cautions against first registration

14.—(1) For the period of two years beginning with the day on which section 15 comes into force, it has effect with the following omissions—

(a) in subsection (1), the words "Subject to subsection (3),", and

(b) subsection (3).

(2) Any caution lodged by virtue of sub-paragraph (1) which is in force immediately before the end of the period mentioned in that sub-paragraph shall cease to have effect at the end of that period, except in relation to applications for registration made before the end of that period.

(3) This paragraph does not apply to section 15 as applied by section 81.

15.—(1) As applied by section 81, section 15 has effect for the period of ten years beginning with the day on which it comes into force, or such longer period as rules may provide, with the omission of subsection (3)(a)(i).

(2) Any caution lodged by virtue of sub-paragraph (1) which is in force immediately before the end of the period mentioned in that sub-paragraph shall cease to have effect at the end of that period, except in relation to applications for registration made before the end of that period.

16. This Act shall apply as if the definition of "caution against first registration" in section 132 included cautions lodged under section 53 of the Land Registration Act 1925 (c. 21).

Applications under section 34 or 43 by cautioners

17. Where a caution under section 54 of the Land Registration Act 1925 is lodged in respect of a person's estate, right, interest or claim, he may only make an application under section 34 or 43 above in respect of that estate, right, interest or claim if he also applies to the registrar for the withdrawal of the caution.

Adverse possession

18.—(1) Where a registered estate in land is held in trust for a person by virtue of section 75(1) of the Land Registration Act 1925 immediately before the coming into force of section 97, he is entitled to be registered as the proprietor of the estate.

(2) A person has a defence to any action for the possession of land (in addition to any other defence he may have) if he is entitled under this paragraph to be registered as the proprietor of an estate in the land.

(3) Where in an action for possession of land a court determines that a person is entitled to a defence under this paragraph, the court must order the registrar to register him as the proprietor of the estate in relation to which he is entitled under this paragraph to be registered.

(4) Entitlement under this paragraph shall be disregarded for the purposes of section 131(1).

(5) Rules may make transitional provision for cases where a rentcharge is held in trust under section 75(1) of the Land Registration Act 1925 immediately before the coming into force of section 97.

Indemnities

19.—(1) Schedule 8 applies in relation to claims made before the commencement of that Schedule which have not been settled by agreement or finally determined by that time (as well as to claims for indemnity made after the commencement of that Schedule).

(2) But paragraph 3(1) of that Schedule does not apply in relation to costs and expenses incurred in respect of proceedings, negotiations or other matters begun before 27 April 1997.

Implied indemnity covenants on transfers of pre-1996 leases

20.—(1) On a disposition of a registered leasehold estate by way of transfer, the following covenants are implied in the instrument effecting the disposition, unless the contrary intention is expressed—

(a) in the case of a transfer of the whole of the land comprised in the registered lease, the covenant in sub-paragraph (2), and

(b) in the case of a transfer of part of the land comprised in the lease—

(i) the covenant in sub-paragraph (3), and

(ii) where the transferor continues to hold land under the lease, the covenant in sub-paragraph (4).

(2) The transferee covenants with the transferor that during the residue of the term granted by the registered lease the transferee and the persons deriving title under him will—

(a) pay the rent reserved by the lease,

(b) comply with the covenants and conditions contained in the lease, and

(c) keep the transferor and the persons deriving title under him indemnified against all actions, expenses and claims on account of any failure to comply with paragraphs (a) and (b).

(3) The transferee covenants with the transferor that during the residue of the term granted by the registered lease the transferee and the persons deriving title under him will—

(a) where the rent reserved by the lease is apportioned, pay the rent apportioned to the part transferred,

(b) comply with the covenants and conditions contained in the lease so far as affecting the part transferred, and

(c) keep the transferor and the persons deriving title under him indemnified against all actions, expenses and claims on account of any failure to comply with paragraphs (a) and (b).

(4) The transferor covenants with the transferee that during the residue of the term granted by the registered lease the transferor and the persons deriving title under him will—

(a) where the rent reserved by the lease is apportioned, pay the rent apportioned to the part retained,

(b) comply with the covenants and conditions contained in the lease so far as affecting the part retained, and

(c) keep the transferee and the persons deriving title under him indemnified against all actions, expenses and claims on account of any failure to comply with paragraphs (a) and (b).

(5) This paragraph does not apply to a lease which is a new tenancy for the purposes of section 1 of the Landlord and Tenant (Covenants) Act 1995 (c. 30).

Commonhold and Leasehold Reform Act 2002

(2002 c. 15)

CONTENTS

PART I

COMMONHOLD

Nature of commonhold

. . . . . .

PART 1

COMMONHOLD

Nature of commonhold

Commonhold land

66–001 **1.**—(1) Land is commonhold land if—
(a) the freehold estate in the land is registered as a freehold estate in commonhold land,
(b) the land is specified in the memorandum of association of a commonhold association as the land in relation to which the association is to exercise functions, and
(c) a commonhold community statement makes provision for rights and duties of the commonhold association and unit-holders (whether or not the statement has come into force).

(2) In this Part a reference to a commonhold is a reference to land in relation to which a commonhold association exercises functions.

(3) In this Part—
"commonhold association" has the meaning given by section 34,
"commonhold community statement" has the meaning given by section 31,
"commonhold unit" has the meaning given by section 11,
"common parts" has the meaning given by section 25, and
"unit-holder" has the meaning given by sections 12 and 13.

(4) Sections 7 and 9 make provision for the vesting in the commonhold association of the fee simple in possession in the common parts of a commonhold.

Registration

Application

2.—(1) The Registrar shall register a freehold estate in land as a freehold estate in commonhold land if— **66–002**

(a) the registered freeholder of the land makes an application under this section, and

(b) no part of the land is already commonhold land.

(2) An application under this section must be accompanied by the documents listed in Schedule 1.

(3) A person is the registered freeholder of land for the purposes of this Part if—

(a) he is registered as the proprietor of a freehold estate in the land with absolute title, or

(b) he has applied, and the Registrar is satisfied that he is entitled, to be registered as mentioned in paragraph (a).

Consent

3.—(1) An application under section 2 may not be made in respect of a freehold estate in land without the consent of anyone who— **66–003**

(a) is the registered proprietor of the freehold estate in the whole or part of the land,

(b) is the registered proprietor of a leasehold estate in the whole or part of the land granted for a term of more than than 21 years,

(c) is the registered proprietor of a charge over the whole or part of the land, or

(d) falls within any other class of person which may be prescribed.

(2) Regulations shall make provision about consent for the purposes of this section; in particular, the regulations may make provision—

(a) prescribing the form of consent;

(b) about the effect and duration of consent (including provision for consent to bind successors);

(c) about withdrawal of consent (including provision preventing withdrawal in specified circumstances);

(d) for consent given for the purpose of one application under section 2 to have effect for the purpose of another application;

(e) for consent to be deemed to have been given in specified circumstances;

(f) enabling a court to dispense with a requirement for consent in specified circumstances.

(3) An order under subsection (2)(f) dispensing with a requirement for consent—

(a) may be absolute or conditional, and

(b) may make such other provision as the court thinks appropriate.

Land which may not be commonhold

4. Schedule 2 (which provides that an application under section 2 may not relate wholly or partly to land of certain kinds) shall have effect. **66–004**

Registered details

66–005 **5.**—(1) The Registrar shall ensure that in respect of any commonhold land the following are kept in his custody and referred to in the register—

(a) the prescribed details of the commonhold association;
(b) the prescribed details of the registered freeholder of each commonhold unit;
(c) a copy of the commonhold community statement;
(d) a copy of the memorandum and articles of association of the commonhold association.

(2) The Registrar may arrange for a document or information to be kept in his custody and referred to in the register in respect of commonhold land if the document or information—

(a) is not mentioned in subsection (1), but
(b) is submitted to the Registrar in accordance with a provision made by or by virtue of this Part.

(3) Subsection (1)(b) shall not apply during a transitional period within the meaning of section 8

Registration in error

66–006 **6.**—(1) This section applies where a freehold estate in land is registered as a freehold estate in commonhold land and—

(a) the application for registration was not made in accordance with section 2,
(b) the certificate under paragraph 7 of Schedule 1 was inaccurate, or
(c) the registration contravened a provision made by or by virtue of this Part.

(2) The register may not be altered by the Registrar under Schedule 4 to the Land Registration Act 2002 (c. 9) (alteration of register).

(3) The court may grant a declaration that the freehold estate should not have been registered as a freehold estate in commonhold land.

(4) A declaration under subsection (3) may be granted only on the application of a person who claims to be adversely affected by the registration.

(5) On granting a declaration under subsection (3) the court may make any order which appears to it to be appropriate.

(6) An order under subsection (5) may, in particular—

(a) provide for the registration to be treated as valid for all purposes;
(b) provide for alteration of the register;
(c) provide for land to cease to be commonhold land;
(d) require a director or other specified officer of a commonhold association to take steps to alter or amend a document;
(e) require a director or other specified officer of a commonhold association to take specified steps;
(f) make an award of compensation (whether or not contingent upon the occurrence or non-occurrence of a specified event) to be paid by one specified person to another;
(g) apply, disapply or modify a provision of Schedule 8 to the Land Registration Act 2002 (c. 9) (indemnity).

Effect of registration

Registration without unit-holders

7.—(1) This section applies where— **66–007**

(a) a freehold estate in land is registered as a freehold estate in commonhold land in pursuance of an application under section 2, and

(b) the application is not accompanied by a statement under section 9(1)(b).

(2) On registration—

(a) the applicant shall continue to be registered as the proprietor of the freehold estate in the commonhold land, and

(b) the rights and duties conferred and imposed by the commonhold community statement shall not come into force (subject to section 8(2)(b)).

(3) Where after registration a person other than the applicant becomes entitled to be registered as the proprietor of the freehold estate in one or more, but not all, of the commonhold units—

(a) the commonhold association shall be entitled to be registered as the proprietor of the freehold estate in the common parts,

(b) the Registrar shall register the commonhold association in accordance with paragraph (a) (without an application being made),

(c) the rights and duties conferred and imposed by the commonhold community statement shall come into force, and

(d) any lease of the whole or part of the commonhold land shall be extinguished by virtue of this section.

(4) For the purpose of subsection (3)(d) "lease" means a lease which—

(a) is granted for any term, and

(b) is granted before the commonhold association becomes entitled to be registered as the proprietor of the freehold estate in the common parts.

Transitional period

8.—(1) In this Part "transitional period" means the period between registration of the freehold estate in land as a freehold estate in commonhold land and the event mentioned in section 7(3). **66–008**

(2) Regulations may provide that during a transitional period a relevant provision—

(a) shall not have effect, or

(b) shall have effect with specified modifications.

(3) In subsection (2) "relevant provision" means a provision made—

(a) by or by virtue of this Part,

(b) by a commonhold community statement, or

(c) by the memorandum or articles of the commonhold association.

(4) The Registrar shall arrange for the freehold estate in land to cease to be registered as a freehold estate in commonhold land if the registered proprietor makes an application to the Registrar under this subsection during the transitional period.

(5) The provisions about consent made by or under sections 2 and 3 and Schedule 1 shall apply in relation to an application under subsection (4) as they apply in relation to an application under section 2.

(6) A reference in this Part to a commonhold association exercising functions in relation to commonhold land includes a reference to a case where a

commonhold association would exercise functions in relation to commonhold land but for the fact that the time in question falls in a transitional period.

Registration with unit-holders

66–009 **9.**—(1) This section applies in relation to a freehold estate in commonhold land if—

(a) it is registered as a freehold estate in commonhold land in pursuance of an application under section 2, and

(b) the application is accompanied by a statement by the applicant requesting that this section should apply.

(2) A statement under subsection (1)(b) must include a list of the commonhold units giving in relation to each one the prescribed details of the proposed initial unit-holder or joint unit-holders.

(3) On registration—

(a) the commonhold association shall be entitled to be registered as the proprietor of the freehold estate in the common parts,

(b) a person specified by virtue of subsection (2) as the initial unit-holder of a commonhold unit shall be entitled to be registered as the proprietor of the freehold estate in the unit,

(c) a person specified by virtue of subsection (2) as an initial joint unit-holder of a commonhold unit shall be entitled to be registered as one of the proprietors of the freehold estate in the unit,

(d) the Registrar shall make entries in the register to reflect paragraphs (a) to (c) (without applications being made),

(e) the rights and duties conferred and imposed by the commonhold community statement shall come into force, and

(f) any lease of the whole or part of the commonhold land shall be extinguished by virtue of this section.

(4) For the purpose of subsection (3)(f) "lease" means a lease which—

(a) is granted for any term, and

(b) is granted before the commonhold association becomes entitled to be registered as the proprietor of the freehold estate in the common parts.

Extinguished lease: liability

66–010 **10.**—(1) This section applies where—

(a) a lease is extinguished by virtue of section 7(3)(d) or 9(3)(f), and

(b) the consent of the holder of that lease was not among the consents required by section 3 in respect of the application under section 2 for the land to become commonhold land.

(2) If the holder of a lease superior to the extinguished lease gave consent under section 3, he shall be liable for loss suffered by the holder of the extinguished lease.

(3) If the holders of a number of leases would be liable under subsection (2), liability shall attach only to the person whose lease was most proximate to the extinguished lease.

(4) If no person is liable under subsection (2), the person who gave consent under section 3 as the holder of the freehold estate out of which the extinguished lease was granted shall be liable for loss suffered by the holder of the extinguished lease.

Commonhold unit

Definition

11.—(1) In this Part "commonhold unit" means a commonhold unit specified in a commonhold community statement in accordance with this section. **66–011**

(2) A commonhold community statement must—

(a) specify at least two parcels of land as commonhold units, and

(b) define the extent of each commonhold unit.

(3) In defining the extent of a commonhold unit a commonhold community statement—

(a) must refer to a plan which is included in the statement and which complies with prescribed requirements,

(b) may refer to an area subject to the exclusion of specified structures, fittings, apparatus or appurtenances within the area,

(c) may exclude the structures which delineate an area referred to, and

(d) may refer to two or more areas (whether or not contiguous).

(4) A commonhold unit need not contain all or any part of a building.

Unit-holder

12. A person is the unit-holder of a commonhold unit if he is entitled to be registered as the proprietor of the freehold estate in the unit (whether or not he is registered). **66–012**

Joint unit-holders

13.—(1) Two or more persons are joint unit-holders of a commonhold unit if they are entitled to be registered as proprietors of the freehold estate in the unit (whether or not they are registered). **66–013**

(2) In the application of the following provisions to a unit with joint unit-holders a reference to a unit-holder is a reference to the joint unit-holders together—

(a) section 14(3),

(b) section 15(1) and (3),

(c) section 19(2) and (3),

(d) section 20(1),

(e) section 23(1),

(f) section 35(1)(b),

(g) section 38(1),

(h) section 39(2), and

(i) section 47(2).

(3) In the application of the following provisions to a unit with joint unit-holders a reference to a unit-holder includes a reference to each joint unit-holder and to the joint unit-holders together—

(a) section 1(1)(c),

(b) section 16,

(c) section 31(1)(b), (3)(b), (5)(j) and (7),

(d) section 32(4)(a) and (c),

(e) section 35(1)(a), (2) and (3),

(f) section 37(2),

(g) section 40(1), and

(h) section 58(3)(a).

(4) Regulations under this Part which refer to a unit-holder shall make provision for the construction of the reference in the case of joint unit-holders.

(5) Regulations may amend subsection (2) or (3).

(6) Regulations may make provision for the construction in the case of joint unit-holders of a reference to a unit-holder in—

(a) an enactment,
(b) a commonhold community statement,
(c) the memorandum or articles of association of a commonhold association, or
(d) another document.

Use and maintenance

66–014 **14.**—(1) A commonhold community statement must make provision regulating the use of commonhold units.

(2) A commonhold community statement must make provision imposing duties in respect of the insurance, repair and maintenance of each commonhold unit.

(3) A duty under subsection (2) may be imposed on the commonhold association or the unit-holder.

Transfer

66–015 **15.**—(1) In this Part a reference to the transfer of a commonhold unit is a reference to the transfer of a unit-holder's freehold estate in a unit to another person—

(a) whether or not for consideration,
(b) whether or not subject to any reservation or other terms, and
(c) whether or not by operation of law.

(2) A commonhold community statement may not prevent or restrict the transfer of a commonhold unit.

(3) On the transfer of a commonhold unit the new unit-holder shall notify the commonhold association of the transfer.

(4) Regulations may—

(a) prescribe the form and manner of notice under subsection (3);
(b) prescribe the time within which notice is to be given;
(c) make provision (including provision requiring the payment of money) about the effect of failure to give notice.

Transfer: effect

66–016 **16.**—(1) A right or duty conferred or imposed—

(a) by a commonhold community statement, or
(b) in accordance with section 20,

shall affect a new unit-holder in the same way as it affected the former unit-holder.

(2) A former unit-holder shall not incur a liability or acquire a right—

(a) under or by virtue of the commonhold community statement, or
(b) by virtue of anything done in accordance with section 20.

(3) Subsection (2)—
(a) shall not be capable of being disapplied or varied by agreement, and
(b) is without prejudice to any liability or right incurred or acquired before a transfer takes effect.
(4) In this section—
"former unit-holder" means a person from whom a commonhold unit has been transferred (whether or not he has ceased to be the registered proprietor), and
"new unit-holder" means a person to whom a commonhold unit is transferred (whether or not he has yet become the registered proprietor).

Leasing: residential

17.—(1) It shall not be possible to create a term of years absolute in a residential commonhold unit unless the term satisfies prescribed conditions. **66–017**
(2) The conditions may relate to—
(a) length;
(b) the circumstances in which the term is granted;
(c) any other matter.
(3) Subject to subsection (4), an instrument or agreement shall be of no effect to the extent that it purports to create a term of years in contravention of subsection (1).
(4) Where an instrument or agreement purports to create a term of years in contravention of subsection (1) a party to the instrument or agreement may apply to the court for an order—
(a) providing for the instrument or agreement to have effect as if it provided for the creation of a term of years of a specified kind;
(b) providing for the return or payment of money;
(c) making such other provision as the court thinks appropriate.
(5) A commonhold unit is residential if provision made in the commonhold community statement by virtue of section 14(1) requires it to be used only—
(a) for residential purposes, or
(b) for residential and other incidental purposes.

Leasing: non-residential

18. An instrument or agreement which creates a term of years absolute in a commonhold unit which is not residential (within the meaning of section 17) shall have effect subject to any provision of the commonhold community statement. **66–018**

Leasing: supplementary

19.—(1) Regulations may— **66–019**
(a) impose obligations on a tenant of a commonhold unit;
(b) enable a commonhold community statement to impose obligations on a tenant of a commonhold unit.
(2) Regulations under subsection (1) may, in particular, require a tenant of a commonhold unit to make payments to the commonhold association or a unit-holder in discharge of payments which—
(a) are due in accordance with the commonhold community statement to be made by the unit-holder, or

(b) are due in accordance with the commonhold community statement to be made by another tenant of the unit.

(3) Regulations under subsection (1) may, in particular, provide—

(a) for the amount of payments under subsection (2) to be set against sums owed by the tenant (whether to the person by whom the payments were due to be made or to some other person);

(b) for the amount of payments under subsection (2) to be recovered from the unit-holder or another tenant of the unit.

(4) Regulations may modify a rule of law about leasehold estates (whether deriving from the common law or from an enactment) in its application to a term of years in a commonhold unit.

(5) Regulations under this section—

(a) may make provision generally or in relation to specified circumstances, and

(b) may make different provision for different descriptions of commonhold land or commonhold unit.

Other transactions

66–020 **20.**—(1) A commonhold community statement may not prevent or restrict the creation, grant or transfer by a unit-holder of—

(a) an interest in the whole or part of his unit, or

(b) a charge over his unit.

(2) Subsection (1) is subject to sections 17 to 19 (which impose restrictions about leases).

(3) It shall not be possible to create an interest of a prescribed kind in a commonhold unit unless the commonhold association—

(a) is a party to the creation of the interest, or

(b) consents in writing to the creation of the interest.

(4) A commonhold association may act as described in subsection (3)(a) or (b) only if—

(a) the association passes a resolution to take the action, and

(b) at least 75 per cent. of those who vote on the resolution vote in favour.

(5) An instrument or agreement shall be of no effect to the extent that it purports to create an interest in contravention of subsection (3).

(6) In this section "interest" does not include—

(a) a charge, or

(b) an interest which arises by virtue of a charge.

Part-unit: interests

66–021 **21.**—(1) It shall not be possible to create an interest in part only of a commonhold unit.

(2) But subsection (1) shall not prevent—

(a) the creation of a term of years absolute in part only of a residential commonhold unit where the term satisfies prescribed conditions,

(b) the creation of a term of years absolute in part only of a non-residential commonhold unit, or

(c) the transfer of the freehold estate in part only of a commonhold unit where the commonhold association consents in writing to the transfer.

(3) An instrument or agreement shall be of no effect to the extent that it purports to create an interest in contravention of subsection (1).

(4) Subsection (5) applies where—

(a) land becomes commonhold land or is added to a commonhold unit, and

(b) immediately before that event there is an interest in the land which could not be created after that event by reason of subsection (1).

(5) The interest shall be extinguished by virtue of this subsection to the extent that it could not be created by reason of subsection (1).

(6) Section 17(2) and (4) shall apply (with any necessary modifications) in relation to subsection (2)(a) and (b) above.

(7) Where part only of a unit is held under a lease, regulations may modify the application of a provision which—

(a) is made by or by virtue of this Part, and

(b) applies to a unit-holder or a tenant or both.

(8) Section 20(4) shall apply in relation to subsection (2)(c) above.

(9) Where the freehold interest in part only of a commonhold unit is transferred, the part transferred—

(a) becomes a new commonhold unit by virtue of this subsection, or

(b) in a case where the request for consent under subsection (2)(c) states that this paragraph is to apply, becomes part of a commonhold unit specified in the request.

(10) Regulations may make provision, or may require a commonhold community statement to make provision, about—

(a) registration of units created by virtue of subsection (9);

(b) the adaptation of provision made by or by virtue of this Part or by or by virtue of a commonhold community statement to a case where units are created or modified by virtue of subsection (9).

Part-unit: charging

22.—(1) It shall not be possible to create a charge over part only of an interest in a commonhold unit. **66–022**

(2) An instrument or agreement shall be of no effect to the extent that it purports to create a charge in contravention of subsection (1).

(3) Subsection (4) applies where—

(a) land becomes commonhold land or is added to a commonhold unit, and

(b) immediately before that event there is a charge over the land which could not be created after that event by reason of subsection (1).

(4) The charge shall be extinguished by virtue of this subsection to the extent that it could not be created by reason of subsection (1).

Changing size

23.—(1) An amendment of a commonhold community statement which redefines the extent of a commonhold unit may not be made unless the unit-holder consents— **66–023**

(a) in writing, and

(b) before the amendment is made.

(2) But regulations may enable a court to dispense with the requirement for consent on the application of a commonhold association in prescribed circumstances.

Changing size: charged unit

66–024 **24.**—(1) This section applies to an amendment of a commonhold community statement which redefines the extent of a commonhold unit over which there is a registered charge.

(2) The amendment may not be made unless the registered proprietor of the charge consents—

(a) in writing, and

(b) before the amendment is made.

(3) But regulations may enable a court to dispense with the requirement for consent on the application of a commonhold association in prescribed circumstances.

(4) If the amendment removes land from the commonhold unit, the charge shall by virtue of this subsection be extinguished to the extent that it relates to the land which is removed.

(5) If the amendment adds land to the unit, the charge shall by virtue of this subsection be extended so as to relate to the land which is added.

(6) Regulations may make provision—

(a) requiring notice to be given to the Registrar in circumstances to which this section applies;

(b) requiring the Registrar to alter the register to reflect the application of subsection (4) or (5).

Common parts

Definition

66–025 **25.**—(1) In this Part "common parts" in relation to a commonhold means every part of the commonhold which is not for the time being a commonhold unit in accordance with the commonhold community statement.

(2) A commonhold community statement may make provision in respect of a specified part of the common parts (a "limited use area") restricting—

(a) the classes of person who may use it;

(b) the kind of use to which it may be put.

(3) A commonhold community statement—

(a) may make provision which has effect only in relation to a limited use area, and

(b) may make different provision for different limited use areas.

Use and maintenance

66–026 **26.** A commonhold community statement must make provision—

(a) regulating the use of the common parts;

(b) requiring the commonhold association to insure the common parts;

(c) requiring the commonhold association to repair and maintain the common parts.

Transactions

66–027 **27.**—(1) Nothing in a commonhold community statement shall prevent or restrict—

(a) the transfer by the commonhold association of its freehold estate in any part of the common parts, or
(b) the creation by the commonhold association of an interest in any part of the common parts.

(2) In this section "interest" does not include—
(a) a charge, or
(b) an interest which arises by virtue of a charge.

Charges: general prohibition

28.—(1) It shall not be possible to create a charge over common parts. **66–028**

(2) An instrument or agreement shall be of no effect to the extent that it purports to create a charge over common parts.

(3) Where by virtue of section 7 or 9 a commonhold association is registered as the proprietor of common parts, a charge which relates wholly or partly to the common parts shall be extinguished by virtue of this subsection to the extent that it relates to the common parts.

(4) Where by virtue of section 30 land vests in a commonhold association following an amendment to a commonhold community statement which has the effect of adding land to the common parts, a charge which relates wholly or partly to the land added shall be extinguished by virtue of this subsection to the extent that it relates to that land.

(5) This section is subject to section 29 (which permits certain mortgages).

New legal mortgages

29.—(1) Section 28 shall not apply in relation to a legal mortgage if the creation of the mortgage is approved by a resolution of the commonhold association. **66–029**

(2) A resolution for the purposes of subsection (1) must be passed—
(a) before the mortgage is created, and
(b) unanimously.

(3) In this section "legal mortgage" has the meaning given by section 205(1)(xvi) of the Law of Property Act 1925 (c. 20) (interpretation).

Additions to common parts

30.—(1) This section applies where an amendment of a commonhold community statement— **66–030**
(a) specifies land which forms part of a commonhold unit, and
(b) provides for that land (the "added land") to be added to the common parts.

(2) The amendment may not be made unless the registered proprietor of any charge over the added land consents—
(a) in writing, and
(b) before the amendment is made.

(3)But regulations may enable a court to dispense with the requirement for consent on the application of a commonhold association in specified circumstances.

(4) On the filing of the amended statement under section 33—
(a) the commonhold association shall be entitled to be registered as the proprietor of the freehold estate in the added land, and

(b) the Registrar shall register the commonhold association in accordance with paragraph (a) (without an application being made).

Commonhold community statement

Form and content: general

66–031 **31.**—(1) A commonhold community statement is a document which makes provision in relation to specified land for—

(a) the rights and duties of the commonhold association, and

(b) the rights and duties of the unit-holders.

(2) A commonhold community statement must be in the prescribed form.

(3) A commonhold community statement may—

(a) impose a duty on the commonhold association;

(b) impose a duty on a unit-holder;

(c) make provision about the taking of decisions in connection with the management of the commonhold or any other matter concerning it.

(4) Subsection (3) is subject to—

(a) any provision made by or by virtue of this Part, and

(b) any provision of the memorandum or articles of the commonhold association.

(5) In subsection (3)(a) and (b) "duty" includes, in particular, a duty—

(a) to pay money;

(b) to undertake works;

(c) to grant access;

(d) to give notice;

(e) to refrain from entering into transactions of a specified kind in relation to a commonhold unit;

(f) to refrain from using the whole or part of a commonhold unit for a specified purpose or for anything other than a specified purpose;

(g) to refrain from undertaking works (including alterations) of a specified kind;

(h) to refrain from causing nuisance or annoyance;

(i) to refrain from specified behaviour;

(j) to indemnify the commonhold association or a unit-holder in respect of costs arising from the breach of a statutory requirement.

(6) Provision in a commonhold community statement imposing a duty to pay money (whether in pursuance of subsection (5)(a) or any other provision made by or by virtue of this Part) may include provision for the payment of interest in the case of late payment.

(7) A duty conferred by a commonhold community statement on a commonhold association or a unit-holder shall not require any other formality.

(8) A commonhold community statement may not provide for the transfer or loss of an interest in land on the occurrence or non-occurrence of a specified event.

(9) Provision made by a commonhold community statement shall be of no effect to the extent that—

(a) it is prohibited by virtue of section 32,

(b) it is inconsistent with any provision made by or by virtue of this Part,

(c) it is inconsistent with anything which is treated as included in the statement by virtue of section 32, or

(d) it is inconsistent with the memorandum or articles of association of the commonhold association.

Regulations

32.—(1) Regulations shall make provision about the content of a commonhold community statement. **66–032**

(2) The regulations may permit, require or prohibit the inclusion in a statement of—

(a) specified provision, or

(b) provision of a specified kind, for a specified purpose or about a specified matter.

(3) The regulations may—

(a) provide for a statement to be treated as including provision prescribed by or determined in accordance with the regulations;

(b) permit a statement to make provision in place of provision which would otherwise be treated as included by virtue of paragraph (a).

(4) The regulations may—

(a) make different provision for different descriptions of commonhold association or unit-holder;

(b) make different provision for different circumstances;

(c) make provision about the extent to which a commonhold community statement may make different provision for different descriptions of unit-holder or common parts.

(5) The matters to which regulations under this section may relate include, but are not limited to—

(a) the matters mentioned in sections 11, 14, 15, 20, 21, 25, 26, 27, 38, 39 and 58, and

(b) any matter for which regulations under section 37 may make provision.

Amendment

33.—(1) Regulations under section 32 shall require a commonhold community statement to make provision about how it can be amended. **66–033**

(2) The regulations shall, in particular, make provision under section 32(3)(a) (whether or not subject to provision under section 32(3)(b)).

(3) An amendment of a commonhold community statement shall have no effect unless and until the amended statement is registered in accordance with this section.

(4) If the commonhold association makes an application under this subsection the Registrar shall arrange for an amended commonhold community statement to be kept in his custody, and referred to in the register, in place of the unamended statement.

(5) An application under subsection (4) must be accompanied by a certificate given by the directors of the commonhold association that the amended commonhold community statement satisfies the requirements of this Part.

(6) Where an amendment of a commonhold community statement redefines the extent of a commonhold unit, an application under subsection (4) must be accompanied by any consent required by section 23(1) or 24(2) (or an order of a court dispensing with consent).

(7) Where an amendment of a commonhold community statement has the effect of changing the extent of the common parts, an application under subsection (4) must be accompanied by any consent required by section 30(2) (or an order of a court dispensing with consent).

(8) Where the Registrar amends the register on an application under subsection (4) he shall make any consequential amendments to the register which he thinks appropriate.

Commonhold association

Constitution

66–034 **34.**—(1) A commonhold association is a private company limited by guarantee the memorandum of which—

(a) states that an object of the company is to exercise the functions of a commonhold association in relation to specified commonhold land, and

(b) specifies £1 as the amount required to be specified in pursuance of section 2(4) of the Companies Act 1985 (c. 6) (members' guarantee).

(2) Schedule 3 (which makes provision about the constitution of a commonhold association) shall have effect.

Duty to manage

66–035 **35.**—(1) The directors of a commonhold association shall exercise their powers so as to permit or facilitate so far as possible—

(a) the exercise by each unit-holder of his rights, and

(b) the enjoyment by each unit-holder of the freehold estate in his unit.

(2) The directors of a commonhold association shall, in particular, use any right, power or procedure conferred or created by virtue of section 37 for the purpose of preventing, remedying or curtailing a failure on the part of a unit-holder to comply with a requirement or duty imposed on him by virtue of the commonhold community statement or a provision of this Part.

(3) But in respect of a particular failure on the part of a unit-holder (the "defaulter") the directors of a commonhold association—

(a) need not take action if they reasonably think that inaction is in the best interests of establishing or maintaining harmonious relationships between all the unit-holders, and that it will not cause any unit-holder (other than the defaulter) significant loss or significant disadvantage, and

(b) shall have regard to the desirability of using arbitration, mediation or conciliation procedures (including referral under a scheme approved under section 42) instead of legal proceedings wherever possible.

(4) A reference in this section to a unit-holder includes a reference to a tenant of a unit.

Voting

66–036 **36.**—(1) This section applies in relation to any provision of this Part (a "voting provision") which refers to the passing of a resolution by a commonhold association.

(2) A voting provision is satisfied only if every member is given an opportunity to vote in accordance with any relevant provision of the memorandum or articles of association or the commonhold community statement.

(3) A vote is cast for the purposes of a voting provision whether it is cast in person or in accordance with a provision which—

(a) provides for voting by post, by proxy or in some other manner, and

(b) is contained in the memorandum or articles of association or the commonhold community statement.

(4) A resolution is passed unanimously if every member who casts a vote votes in favour.

Operation of commonhold

Enforcement and compensation

37.—(1) Regulations may make provision (including provision conferring jurisdiction on a court) about the exercise or enforcement of a right or duty imposed or conferred by or by virtue of— **66–037**

(a) a commonhold community statement;
(b) the memorandum or articles of a commonhold association;
(c) a provision made by or by virtue of this Part.

(2) The regulations may, in particular, make provision—

(a) requiring compensation to be paid where a right is exercised in specified cases or circumstances;
(b) requiring compensation to be paid where a duty is not complied with;
(c) enabling recovery of costs where work is carried out for the purpose of enforcing a right or duty;
(d) enabling recovery of costs where work is carried out in consequence of the failure to perform a duty;
(e) permitting a unit-holder to enforce a duty imposed on another unit-holder, on a commonhold association or on a tenant;
(f) permitting a commonhold association to enforce a duty imposed on a unit-holder or a tenant;
(g) permitting a tenant to enforce a duty imposed on another tenant, a unit-holder or a commonhold association;
(h) permitting the enforcement of terms or conditions to which a right is subject;
(i) requiring the use of a specified form of arbitration, mediation or conciliation procedure before legal proceedings may be brought.

(3) Provision about compensation made by virtue of this section shall include—

(a) provision (which may include provision conferring jurisdiction on a court) for determining the amount of compensation;
(b) provision for the payment of interest in the case of late payment.

(4) Regulations under this section shall be subject to any provision included in a commonhold community statement in accordance with regulations made by virtue of section 32(5)(b).

Commonhold assessment

38.—(1) A commonhold community statement must make provision— **66–038**

(a) requiring the directors of the commonhold association to make an annual estimate of the income required to be raised from unit-holders to meet the expenses of the association,
(b) enabling the directors of the commonhold association to make estimates from time to time of income required to be raised from unit-holders in addition to the annual estimate,

(c) specifying the percentage of any estimate made under paragraph (a) or (b) which is to be allocated to each unit,
(d) requiring each unit-holder to make payments in respect of the percentage of any estimate which is allocated to his unit, and
(e) requiring the directors of the commonhold association to serve notices on unit-holders specifying payments required to be made by them and the date on which each payment is due.

(2) For the purpose of subsection (1)(c)—
(a) the percentages allocated by a commonhold community statement to the commonhold units must amount in aggregate to 100;
(b) a commonhold community statement may specify 0 per cent. in relation to a unit.

Reserve fund

66–039 **39.**—(1) Regulations under section 32 may, in particular, require a commonhold community statement to make provision—
(a) requiring the directors of the commonhold association to establish and maintain one or more funds to finance the repair and maintenance of common parts;
(b) requiring the directors of the commonhold association to establish and maintain one or more funds to finance the repair and maintenance of commonhold units.

(2) Where a commonhold community statement provides for the establishment and maintenance of a fund in accordance with subsection (1) it must also make provision—
(a) requiring or enabling the directors of the commonhold association to set a levy from time to time,
(b) specifying the percentage of any levy set under paragraph (a) which is to be allocated to each unit,
(c) requiring each unit-holder to make payments in respect of the percentage of any levy set under paragraph (a) which is allocated to his unit, and
(d) requiring the directors of the commonhold association to serve notices on unit-holders specifying payments required to be made by them and the date on which each payment is due.

(3) For the purpose of subsection (2)(b)—
(a) the percentages allocated by a commonhold community statement to the commonhold units must amount in aggregate to 100;
(b) a commonhold community statement may specify 0 per cent. in relation to a unit.

(4) The assets of a fund established and maintained by virtue of this section shall not be used for the purpose of enforcement of any debt except a judgment debt referable to a reserve fund activity.

(5) For the purpose of subsection (4)—
(a) "reserve fund activity" means an activity which in accordance with the commonhold community statement can or may be financed from a fund established and maintained by virtue of this section,
(b) assets are used for the purpose of enforcement of a debt if, in particular, they are taken in execution or are made the subject of a charging order under section 1 of the Charging Orders Act 1979 (c. 53), and
(c) the reference to a judgment debt includes a reference to any interest payable on a judgment debt.

Rectification of documents

40.—(1) A unit-holder may apply to the court for a declaration that— **66–040**

(a) the memorandum or articles of association of the relevant commonhold association do not comply with regulations under paragraph 2(1) of Schedule 3;

(b) the relevant commonhold community statement does not comply with a requirement imposed by or by virtue of this Part.

(2) On granting a declaration under this section the court may make any order which appears to it to be appropriate.

(3) An order under subsection (2) may, in particular—

(a) require a director or other specified officer of a commonhold association to take steps to alter or amend a document;

(b) require a director or other specified officer of a commonhold association to take specified steps;

(c) make an award of compensation (whether or not contingent upon the occurrence or non-occurrence of a specified event) to be paid by the commonhold association to a specified person;

(d) make provision for land to cease to be commonhold land.

(4) An application under subsection (1) must be made—

(a) within the period of three months beginning with the day on which the applicant became a unit-holder,

(b) within three months of the commencement of the alleged failure to comply, or

(c) with the permission of the court.

Enlargement

41.—(1) This section applies to an application under section 2 if the commonhold association for the purposes of the application already exercises functions in relation to commonhold land. **66–041**

(2) In this section—

(a) the application is referred to as an "application to add land", and

(b) the land to which the application relates is referred to as the "added land".

(3) An application to add land may not be made unless it is approved by a resolution of the commonhold association.

(4) A resolution for the purposes of subsection (3) must be passed—

(a) before the application to add land is made, and

(b) unanimously.

(5) Section 2(2) shall not apply to an application to add land; but the application must be accompanied by—

(a) the documents specified in paragraph 6 of Schedule 1,

(b) an application under section 33 for the registration of an amended commonhold community statement which makes provision for the existing commonhold and the added land, and

(c) a certificate given by the directors of the commonhold association that the application to add land satisfies Schedule 2 and subsection (3).

(6) Where sections 7 and 9 have effect following an application to add land—

(a) the references to "the commonhold land" in sections 7(2)(a) and (3)(d) and 9(3)(f) shall be treated as references to the added land, and

(b) the references in sections 7(2)(b) and (3)(c) and 9(3)(e) to the rights and duties conferred and imposed by the commonhold community statement shall be treated as a reference to rights and duties only in so far as they affect the added land.

(7) In the case of an application to add land where the whole of the added land is to form part of the common parts of a commonhold—

(a) section 7 shall not apply,
(b) on registration the commonhold association shall be entitled to be registered (if it is not already) as the proprietor of the freehold estate in the added land,
(c) the Registrar shall make any registration required by paragraph (b) (without an application being made), and
(d) the rights and duties conferred and imposed by the commonhold community statement shall, in so far as they affect the added land, come into force on registration.

Ombudsman

66–042 **42.**—(1) Regulations may provide that a commonhold association shall be a member of an approved ombudsman scheme.

(2) An "approved ombudsman scheme" is a scheme which is approved by the Lord Chancellor and which—

(a) provides for the appointment of one or more persons as ombudsman,
(b) provides for a person to be appointed as ombudsman only if the Lord Chancellor approves the appointment in advance,
(c) enables a unit-holder to refer to the ombudsman a dispute between the unit-holder and a commonhold association which is a member of the scheme,
(d) enables a commonhold association which is a member of the scheme to refer to the ombudsman a dispute between the association and a unit-holder,
(e) requires the ombudsman to investigate and determine a dispute referred to him,
(f) requires a commonhold association which is a member of the scheme to cooperate with the ombudsman in investigating or determining a dispute, and
(g) requires a commonhold association which is a member of the scheme to comply with any decision of the ombudsman (including any decision requiring the payment of money).

(3) In addition to the matters specified in subsection (2) an approved ombudsman scheme—

(a) may contain other provision, and
(b) shall contain such provision, or provision of such a kind, as may be prescribed.

(4) If a commonhold association fails to comply with regulations under subsection (1) a unit-holder may apply to the High Court for an order requiring the directors of the commonhold association to ensure that the association complies with the regulations.

(5) A reference in this section to a unit-holder includes a reference to a tenant of a unit.

Termination: voluntary winding-up

Winding-up resolution

43.—(1) A winding-up resolution in respect of a commonhold association shall be of no effect unless— **66–043**

(a) the resolution is preceded by a declaration of solvency,

(b) the commonhold association passes a termination-statement resolution before it passes the winding-up resolution, and

(c) each resolution is passed with at least 80 per cent. of the members of the association voting in favour.

(2) In this Part—

"declaration of solvency" means a directors' statutory declaration made in accordance with section 89 of the Insolvency Act 1986 (c. 45),

"termination-statement resolution" means a resolution approving the terms of a termination statement (within the meaning of section 47), and

"winding-up resolution" means a resolution for voluntary winding-up within the meaning of section 84 of that Act.

100 per cent agreement

44.—(1) This section applies where a commonhold association— **66–044**

(a) has passed a winding-up resolution and a termination-statement resolution with 100 per cent of the members of the association voting in favour, and

(b) has appointed a liquidator under section 91 of the Insolvency Act 1986 (c. 45).

(2) The liquidator shall make a termination application within the period of six months beginning with the day on which the winding-up resolution is passed.

(3) If the liquidator fails to make a termination application within the period specified in subsection (2) a termination application may be made by—

(a) a unit-holder, or

(b) a person falling within a class prescribed for the purposes of this subsection.

80 per cent agreement

45.—(1) This section applies where a commonhold association— **66–045**

(a) has passed a winding-up resolution and a termination-statement resolution with at least 80 per cent of the members of the association voting in favour, and

(b) has appointed a liquidator under section 91 of the Insolvency Act 1986.

(2) The liquidator shall within the prescribed period apply to the court for an order determining—

(a) the terms and conditions on which a termination application may be made, and

(b) the terms of the termination statement to accompany a termination application.

(3) The liquidator shall make a termination application within the period of three months starting with the date on which an order under subsection (2) is made.

(4) If the liquidator fails to make an application under subsection (2) or (3)

within the period specified in that subsection an application of the same kind may be made by—

(a) a unit-holder, or
(b) a person falling within a class prescribed for the purposes of this subsection.

Termination application

66–046 **46.**—(1) A "termination application" is an application to the Registrar that all the land in relation to which a particular commonhold association exercises functions should cease to be commonhold land.

(2) A termination application must be accompanied by a termination statement.

(3) On receipt of a termination application the Registrar shall note it in the register.

Termination statement

66–047 **47.**—(1) A termination statement must specify—

(a) the commonhold association's proposals for the transfer of the commonhold land following acquisition of the freehold estate in accordance with section 49(3), and
(b) how the assets of the commonhold association will be distributed.

(2) A commonhold community statement may make provision requiring any termination statement to make arrangements—

(a) of a specified kind, or
(b) determined in a specified manner,

about the rights of unit-holders in the event of all the land to which the statement relates ceasing to be commonhold land.

(3) A termination statement must comply with a provision made by the commonhold community statement in reliance on subsection (2).

(4) Subsection (3) may be disapplied by an order of the court—

(a) generally,
(b) in respect of specified matters, or
(c) for a specified purpose.

(5) An application for an order under subsection (4) may be made by any member of the commonhold association.

The liquidator

66–048 **48.**—(1) This section applies where a termination application has been made in respect of particular commonhold land.

(2) The liquidator shall notify the Registrar of his appointment.

(3) In the case of a termination application made under section 44 the liquidator shall either—

(a) notify the Registrar that the liquidator is content with the termination statement submitted with the termination application, or
(b) apply to the court under section 112 of the Insolvency Act 1986 (c. 45) to determine the terms of the termination statement.

(4) The liquidator shall send to the Registrar a copy of a determination made by virtue of subsection (3)(b).

(5) Subsection (4) is in addition to any requirement under section 112(3) of the Insolvency Act 1986.

(6) A duty imposed on the liquidator by this section is to be performed as soon as possible.

(7) In this section a reference to the liquidator is a reference—

(a) to the person who is appointed as liquidator under section 91 of the Insolvency Act 1986, or

(b) in the case of a members' voluntary winding up which becomes a creditors' voluntary winding up by virtue of sections 95 and 96 of that Act, to the person acting as liquidator in accordance with section 100 of that Act.

Termination

49.—(1) This section applies where a termination application is made under section 44 and— **66–049**

(a) a liquidator notifies the Registrar under section 48(3)(a) that he is content with a termination statement, or

(b) a determination is made under section 112 of the Insolvency Act 1986 (c. 45) by virtue of section 48(3)(b).

(2) This section also applies where a termination application is made under section 45.

(3) The commonhold association shall by virtue of this subsection be entitled to be registered as the proprietor of the freehold estate in each commonhold unit.

(4) The Registrar shall take such action as appears to him to be appropriate for the purpose of giving effect to the termination statement.

Termination: winding-up by court

Introduction

50.—(1) Section 51 applies where a petition is presented under section 124 of the Insolvency Act 1986 for the winding up of a commonhold association by the court. **66–050**

(2) For the purposes of this Part—

(a) an "insolvent commonhold association" is one in relation to which a winding-up petition has been presented under section 124 of the Insolvency Act 1986,

(b) a commonhold association is the "successor commonhold association" to an insolvent commonhold association if the land specified for the purpose of section 34(1)(a) is the same for both associations, and

(c) a "winding-up order" is an order under section 125 of the Insolvency Act 1986 for the winding up of a commonhold association.

Succession order

51.—(1) At the hearing of the winding-up petition an application may be made to the court for an order under this section (a "succession order") in relation to the insolvent commonhold association. **66–051**

(2) An application under subsection (1) may be made only by—

(a) the insolvent commonhold association,

(b) one or more members of the insolvent commonhold association, or

(c) a provisional liquidator for the insolvent commonhold association appointed under section 135 of the Insolvency Act 1986.

(3) An application under subsection (1) must be accompanied by—

(a) prescribed evidence of the formation of a successor commonhold association, and

(b) a certificate given by the directors of the successor commonhold association that its memorandum and articles of association comply with regulations under paragraph 2(1) of Schedule 3.

(4) The court shall grant an application under subsection (1) unless it thinks that the circumstances of the insolvent commonhold association make a succession order inappropriate.

Assets and liabilities

66–052 **52.**—(1) Where a succession order is made in relation to an insolvent commonhold association this section applies on the making of a winding-up order in respect of the association.

(2) The successor commonhold association shall be entitled to be registered as the proprietor of the freehold estate in the common parts.

(3) The insolvent commonhold association shall for all purposes cease to be treated as the proprietor of the freehold estate in the common parts.

(4) The succession order—

(a) shall make provision as to the treatment of any charge over all or any part of the common parts;

(b) may require the Registrar to take action of a specified kind;

(c) may enable the liquidator to require the Registrar to take action of a specified kind;

(d) may make supplemental or incidental provision.

Transfer of responsibility

66–053 **53.**—(1) Where a succession order is made in relation to an insolvent commonhold association this section applies on the making of a winding-up order in respect of the association.

(2) The successor commonhold association shall be treated as the commonhold association for the commonhold in respect of any matter which relates to a time after the making of the winding-up order.

(3) On the making of the winding-up order the court may make an order requiring the liquidator to make available to the successor commonhold association specified—

(a) records;

(b) copies of records;

(c) information.

(4) An order under subsection (3) may include terms as to—

(a) timing;

(b) payment.

Termination of commonhold

66–054 **54.**—(1) This section applies where the court—

(a) makes a winding-up order in respect of a commonhold association, and

(b) has not made a succession order in respect of the commonhold association.

(2) The liquidator of a commonhold association shall as soon as possible notify the Registrar of—

(a) the fact that this section applies,

(b) any directions given under section 168 of the Insolvency Act 1986 (c. 45) (liquidator: supplementary powers),

(c) any notice given to the court and the registrar of companies in accordance with section 172(8) of that Act (liquidator vacating office after final meeting),

(d) any notice given to the Secretary of State under section 174(3) of that Act (completion of winding-up),

(e) any application made to the registrar of companies under section 202(2) of that Act (insufficient assets: early dissolution),

(f) any notice given to the registrar of companies under section 205(1)(b) of that Act (completion of winding-up), and

(g) any other matter which in the liquidator's opinion is relevant to the Registrar.

(3) Notification under subsection (2)(b) to (f) must be accompanied by a copy of the directions, notice or application concerned.

(4) The Registrar shall—

(a) make such arrangements as appear to him to be appropriate for ensuring that the freehold estate in land in respect of which a commonhold association exercises functions ceases to be registered as a freehold estate in commonhold land as soon as is reasonably practicable after he receives notification under subsection (2)(c) to (f), and

(b) take such action as appears to him to be appropriate for the purpose of giving effect to a determination made by the liquidator in the exercise of his functions.

Termination: miscellaneous

Termination by court

55.—(1) This section applies where the court makes an order by virtue of section 6(6)(c) or 40(3)(d) for all the land in relation to which a commonhold association exercises functions to cease to be commonhold land. **66–055**

(2) The court shall have the powers which it would have if it were making a winding-up order in respect of the commonhold association.

(3) A person appointed as liquidator by virtue of subsection (2) shall have the powers and duties of a liquidator following the making of a winding-up order by the court in respect of a commonhold association.

(4) But the order of the court by virtue of section 6(6)(c) or 40(3)(d) may—

(a) require the liquidator to exercise his functions in a particular way;

(b) impose additional rights or duties on the liquidator;

(c) modify or remove a right or duty of the liquidator.

Release of reserve fund

56. Section 39(4) shall cease to have effect in relation to a commonhold association (in respect of debts and liabilities accruing at any time) if— **66–056**

(a) the court makes a winding-up order in respect of the association,
(b) the association passes a voluntary winding-up resolution, or
(c) the court makes an order by virtue of section 6(6)(c) or 40(3)(d) for all the land in relation to which the association exercises functions to cease to be commonhold land.

Miscellaneous

Multiple site commonholds

66–057 **57.**—(1) A commonhold may include two or more parcels of land, whether or not contiguous.

(2) But section 1(1) of this Act is not satisfied in relation to land specified in the memorandum of association of a commonhold association unless a single commonhold community statement makes provision for all the land.

(3) Regulations may make provision about an application under section 2 made jointly by two or more persons, each of whom is the registered freeholder of part of the land to which the application relates.

(4) The regulations may, in particular—
(a) modify the application of a provision made by or by virtue of this Part;
(b) disapply the application of a provision made by or by virtue of this Part;
(c) impose additional requirements.

Development rights

66–058 **58.**—(1) In this Part—

"the developer" means a person who makes an application under section 2, and

"development business" has the meaning given by Schedule 4.

(2) A commonhold community statement may confer rights on the developer which are designed—
(a) to permit him to undertake development business, or
(b) to facilitate his undertaking of development business.

(3) Provision made by a commonhold community statement in reliance on subsection (2) may include provision—
(a) requiring the commonhold association or a unit-holder to co-operate with the developer for a specified purpose connected with development business;
(b) making the exercise of a right conferred by virtue of subsection (2) subject to terms and conditions specified in or to be determined in accordance with the commonhold community statement;
(c) making provision about the effect of breach of a requirement by virtue of paragraph (a) or a term or condition imposed by virtue of paragraph (b);
(d) disapplying section 41(2) and (3).

(4) Subsection (2) is subject—
(a) to regulations under section 32, and
(b) in the case of development business of the kind referred to in paragraph 7 of Schedule 4, to the memorandum and articles of association of the commonhold association.

(5) Regulations may make provision regulating or restricting the exercise of rights conferred by virtue of subsection (2).

(6) Where a right is conferred on a developer by virtue of subsection (2), if he sends to the Registrar a notice surrendering the right—
(a) the Registrar shall arrange for the notice to be kept in his custody and referred to in the register,
(b) the right shall cease to be exercisable from the time when the notice is registered under paragraph (a), and
(c) the Registrar shall inform the commonhold association as soon as is reasonably practicable.

Development rights: succession

59.—(1) If during a transitional period the developer transfers to another person the freehold estate in the whole of the commonhold, the successor in title shall be treated as the developer in relation to any matter arising after the transfer. **66–059**

(2) If during a transitional period the developer transfers to another person the freehold estate in part of the commonhold, the successor in title shall be treated as the developer for the purpose of any matter which—
(a) arises after the transfer, and
(b) affects the estate transferred.

(3) If after a transitional period or in a case where there is no transitional period—
(a) the developer transfers to another person the freehold estate in the whole or part of the commonhold (other than by the transfer of the freehold estate in a single commonhold unit), and
(b) the transfer is expressed to be inclusive of development rights,
the successor in title shall be treated as the developer for the purpose of any matter which arises after the transfer and affects the estate transferred.

(4) Other than during a transitional period, a person shall not be treated as the developer in relation to commonhold land for any purpose unless he—
(a) is, or has been at a particular time, the registered proprietor of the freehold estate in more than one of the commonhold units, and
(b) is the registered proprietor of the freehold estate in at least one of the commonhold units.

Compulsory purchase

60.—(1) Where a freehold estate in commonhold land is transferred to a compulsory purchaser the land shall cease to be commonhold land. **66–060**

(2) But subsection (1) does not apply to a transfer if the Registrar is satisfied that the compulsory purchaser has indicated a desire for the land transferred to continue to be commonhold land.

(3) The requirement of consent under section 21(2)(c) shall not apply to transfer to a compulsory purchaser.

(4) Regulations may make provision about the transfer of a freehold estate in commonhold land to a compulsory purchaser.

(5) The regulations may, in particular—
(a) make provision about the effect of subsections (1) and (2) (including provision about that part of the commonhold which is not transferred);
(b) require the service of notice;
(c) confer power on a court;

(d) make provision about compensation;
(e) make provision enabling a commonhold association to require a compulsory purchaser to acquire the freehold estate in the whole, or a particular part, of the commonhold;
(f) provide for an enactment relating to compulsory purchase not to apply or to apply with modifications.

(6) Provision made by virtue of subsection (5)(a) in respect of land which is not transferred may include provision—

(a) for some or all of the land to cease to be commonhold land;
(b) for a provision of this Part to apply with specified modifications.

(7) In this section "compulsory purchaser" means—

(a) a person acquiring land in respect of which he is authorised to exercise a power of compulsory purchase by virtue of an enactment, and
(b) a person acquiring land which he is obliged to acquire by virtue of a prescribed enactment or in prescribed circumstances.

Matrimonial rights

66–061 **61.** In the following provisions of this Part a reference to a tenant includes a reference to a person who has matrimonial home rights (within the meaning of section 30(2) of the Family Law Act 1996 (c. 27) (matrimonial home)) in respect of a commonhold unit—

(a) section 19,
(b) section 35, and
(c) section 37.

Advice

66–062 **62.**—(1) The Lord Chancellor may give financial assistance to a person in relation to the provision by that person of general advice about an aspect of the law of commonhold land, so far as relating to residential matters.

(2) Financial assistance under this section may be given in such form and on such terms as the Lord Chancellor thinks appropriate.

(3) The terms may, in particular, require repayment in specified circumstances.

The Crown

66–063 **63.** This Part binds the Crown.

General

Orders and regulations

66–064 **64.**—(1) In this Part "prescribed" means prescribed by regulations.

(2) Regulations under this Part shall be made by the Lord Chancellor.

(3) Regulations under this Part—

(a) shall be made by statutory instrument,
(b) may include incidental, supplemental, consequential and transitional provision,
(c) may make provision generally or only in relation to specified cases,
(d) may make different provision for different purposes, and

(e) shall be subject to annulment in pursuance of a resolution of either House of Parliament.

Registration procedure

65.—(1) The Lord Chancellor may make rules about— **66–065**

(a) the procedure to be followed on or in respect of commonhold registration documents, and

(b) the registration of freehold estates in commonhold land.

(2) Rules under this section—

(a) shall be made by statutory instrument in the same manner as land registration rules within the meaning of the Land Registration Act 2002 (c. 9),

(b) may make provision for any matter for which provision is or may be made by land registration rules, and

(c) may provide for land registration rules to have effect in relation to anything done by virtue of or for the purposes of this Part as they have effect in relation to anything done by virtue of or for the purposes of that Act.

(3) Rules under this section may, in particular, make provision—

(a) about the form and content of a commonhold registration document;

(b) enabling the Registrar to cancel an application by virtue of this Part in specified circumstances;

(c) enabling the Registrar, in particular, to cancel an application by virtue of this Part if he thinks that plans submitted with it (whether as part of a commonhold community statement or otherwise) are insufficiently clear or accurate;

(d) about the order in which commonhold registration documents and general registration documents are to be dealt with by the Registrar;

(e) for registration to take effect (whether or not retrospectively) as from a date or time determined in accordance with the rules.

(4) The rules may also make provision about satisfaction of a requirement for an application by virtue of this Part to be accompanied by a document; in particular the rules may—

(a) permit or require a copy of a document to be submitted in place of or in addition to the original;

(b) require a copy to be certified in a specified manner;

(c) permit or require the submission of a document in electronic form.

(5) A commonhold registration document must be accompanied by such fee (if any) as is specified for that purpose by order under section 102 of the Land Registration Act 2002 (c. 9)(fee orders).

(6) In this section—

"commonhold registration document" means an application or other document sent to the Registrar by virtue of this Part, and

"general registration document" means a document sent to the Registrar under a provision of the Land Registration Act 2002.

Jurisdiction

66.—(1) In this Part "the court" means the High Court or a county court. **66–066**

(2) Provision made by or under this Part conferring jurisdiction on a court shall be subject to provision made under section 1 of the Courts and Legal

Services Act 1990 (c. 41) (allocation of business between High Court and county courts).

(3) A power under this Part to confer jurisdiction on a court includes power to confer jurisdiction on a tribunal established under an enactment.

(4) Rules of court or rules of procedure for a tribunal may make provision about proceedings brought—

(a) under or by virtue of any provision of this Part, or
(b) in relation to commonhold land.

The register

66–067 **67.**—(1) In this Part—

"the register" means the register of title to freehold and leasehold land kept under section 1 of the Land Registration Act 2002,
"registered" means registered in the register, and
"the Registrar" means the Chief Land Registrar.

(2) Regulations under any provision of this Part may confer functions on the Registrar (including discretionary functions).

(3) The Registrar shall comply with any direction or requirement given to him or imposed on him under or by virtue of this Part.

(4) Where the Registrar thinks it appropriate in consequence of or for the purpose of anything done or proposed to be done in connection with this Part, he may—

(a) make or cancel an entry on the register;
(b) take any other action.

(5) Subsection (4) is subject to section 6(2).

Amendments

66–068 **68.** Schedule 5 (consequential amendments) shall have effect.

Interpretation

66–069 **69.**—(1) In this Part—

"instrument" includes any document, and
"object" in relation to a commonhold association means an object stated in the association's memorandum of association in accordance with section 2(1)(c) of the Companies Act 1985 (c. 6).

(2) In this Part—

(a) a reference to a duty to insure includes a reference to a duty to use the proceeds of insurance for the purpose of rebuilding or reinstating, and
(b) a reference to maintaining property includes a reference to decorating it and to putting it into sound condition.

(3) A provision of the Law of Property Act 1925 (c. 20), the Companies Act 1985 (c. 6) or the Land Registration Act 2002 (c.9) defining an expression shall apply to the use of the expression in this Part unless the contrary intention appears.

Index of defined expressions

66–070 **70.** In this Part the expressions listed below are defined by the provisions specified.

Expression	*Interpretation provision*
Common parts	Section 25
A commonhold	Section 1
Commonhold association	Section 34
Commonhold community statement	Section 31
Commonhold land	Section 1
Commonhold unit	Section 11
Court	Section 66
Declaration of solvency	Section 43
Developer	Section 58
Development business	Section 58
Exercising functions	Section 8
Insolvent commonhold association	Section 50
Instrument	Section 69
Insure	Section 69
Joint unit-holder	Section 13
Liquidator (sections 44 to 49)	Section 44
Maintenance	Section 69
Object	Section 69
Prescribed	Section 64
The register	Section 67
Registered	Section 67
Registered freeholder	Section 2
The Registrar	Section 67
Regulations	Section 64
Residential commonhold unit	Section 17
Succession order	Section 51
Successor commonhold association	Section 50
Termination application	Section 46
Termination-statement resolution	Section 43
Transfer (of unit)	Section 15
Transitional period	Section 8
Unit-holder	Section 12
Winding-up resolution	Section 43

. . . . . .

SCHEDULES

SCHEDULE 1

APPLICATION FOR REGISTRATION: DOCUMENTS

Introduction

1. This Schedule lists the documents which are required by section 2 to accompany an application for the registration of a freehold estate as a freehold estate in commonhold land.

Commonhold association documents

2. The commonhold association's certificate of incorporation under section 13 of the Companies Act 1985 (c. 6).

3. Any altered certificate of incorporation issued under section 28 of that Act.

4. The memorandum and articles of association of the commonhold association.

Commonhold community statement

5. The commonhold community statement.

Consent

6.—(1) Where consent is required under or by virtue of section 3—

(a) the consent,

(b) an order of a court by virtue of section 3(2)(f) dispensing with the requirement for consent, or

(c) evidence of deemed consent by virtue of section 3(2)(e).

(2) In the case of a conditional order under section 3(2)(f), the order must be accompanied by evidence that the condition has been complied with.

Certificate

7. A certificate given by the directors of the commonhold association that—

(a) the memorandum and articles of association submitted with the application comply with regulations under paragraph 2(1) of Schedule 3,

(b) the commonhold community statement submitted with the application satisfies the requirements of this Part,

(c) the application satisfies Schedule 2,

(d) the commonhold association has not traded, and

(e) the commonhold association has not incurred any liability which has not been discharged.

SCHEDULE 2

LAND WHICH MAY NOT BE COMMONHOLD LAND

"Flying freehold"

1.—(1) Subject to sub-paragraph (2), an application may not be made under section 2 wholly or partly in relation to land above ground level ("raised land") unless all the land between the ground and the raised land is the subject of the same application.

(2) An application for the addition of land to a commonhold in accordance with section 41 may be made wholly or partly in relation to raised land if all the land between the ground and the raised land forms part of the commonhold to which the raised land is to be added.

Agricultural land

2. An application may not be made under section 2 wholly or partly in relation to land if—

(a) it is agricultural land within the meaning of the Agriculture Act 1947 (c. 48),

(b) it is comprised in a tenancy of an agricultural holding within the meaning of the Agricultural Holdings Act 1986 (c. 5), or

(c) it is comprised in a farm business tenancy for the purposes of the Agricultural Tenancies Act 1995 (c. 8).

Contingent title

3.—(1) An application may not be made under section 2 if an estate in the whole or part of the land to which the application relates is a contingent estate.

(2) An estate is contingent for the purposes of this paragraph if (and only if)–

(a) it is liable to revert to or vest in a person other than the present registered proprietor on the occurrence or non-occurrence of a particular event, and

(b) the reverter or vesting would occur by operation of law as a result of an enactment listed in sub-paragraph (3).

(3)The enactments are—

(a) the Schools Sites Act 1841 (c. 38) (conveyance for use as school),

(b) the Lands Clauses Acts (compulsory purchase),

(c) the Literary and Scientific Institutions Act 1854 (c. 112) (sites for institutions), and

(d) the Places of Worship Sites Act 1873 (c. 50) (sites for places of worship).

(4) Regulations may amend sub-paragraph (3) so as to—

(a) add an enactment to the list, or

(b) remove an enactment from the list.

SCHEDULE 3

COMMONHOLD ASSOCIATION

PART 1

MEMORANDUM AND ARTICLES OF ASSOCIATION

Introduction

1. In this Schedule—
(a) "memorandum" means the memorandum of association of a commonhold association, and
(b) "articles" means the articles of association of a commonhold association.

Form and content

2.—(1) Regulations shall make provision about the form and content of the memorandum and articles.

(2) A commonhold association may adopt provisions of the regulations for its memorandum or articles.

(3) The regulations may include provision which is to have effect for a commonhold association whether or not it is adopted under sub-paragraph (2).

(4) A provision of the memorandum or articles shall have no effect to the extent that it is inconsistent with the regulations.

(5) Regulations under this paragraph shall have effect in relation to a memorandum or articles—
(a) irrespective of the date of the memorandum or articles, but
(b) subject to any transitional provision of the regulations.

Alteration

3.—(1) An alteration of the memorandum or articles of association shall have no effect until the altered version is registered in accordance with this paragraph.

(2) If the commonhold association makes an application under this sub-paragraph the Registrar shall arrange for an altered memorandum or altered articles to be kept in his custody, and referred to in the register, in place of the unaltered version.

(3) An application under sub-paragraph (2) must be accompanied by a certificate given by the directors of the commonhold association that the altered memorandum or articles comply with regulations under paragraph 2(1).

(4) Where the Registrar amends the register on an application under sub-paragraph (2) he shall make any consequential amendments to the register which he thinks appropriate.

Disapplication of Companies Act 1985

4.—(1) The following provisions of the Companies Act 1985 (c. 6) shall not apply to a commonhold association—
(a) sections 2(7) and 3 (memorandum), and
(b) section 8 (articles of association).

(2) No application may be made under paragraph 3(2) for the registration of a memorandum altered by special resolution in accordance with section 4(1) of the Companies Act 1985 (objects) unless—
(a) the period during which an application for cancellation of the alteration may be made under section 5(1) of that Act has expired without an application being made,
(b) any application made under that section has been withdrawn, or
(c) the alteration has been confirmed by the court under that section.

PART 2

MEMBERSHIP

Pre-commonhold period

5. During the period beginning with incorporation of a commonhold association and ending when land specified in its memorandum becomes commonhold land, the subscribers (or subscriber) to the memorandum shall be the sole members (or member) of the association.

Transitional period

6.—(1) This paragraph applies to a commonhold association during a transitional period.

(2) The subscribers (or subscriber) to the memorandum shall continue to be members (or the member) of the association.

(3) A person who for the time being is the developer in respect of all or part of the commonhold is entitled to be entered in the register of members of the association.

Unit-holders

7. A person is entitled to be entered in the register of members of a commonhold association if he becomes the unit-holder of a commonhold unit in relation to which the association exercises functions—

(a) on the unit becoming commonhold land by registration with unit-holders under section 9, or
(b) on the transfer of the unit.

Joint unit-holders

8.—(1) This paragraph applies where two or more persons become joint unit-holders of a commonhold unit—

(a) on the unit becoming commonhold land by registration with unit-holders under section 9, or
(b) on the transfer of the unit.

(2) If the joint unit-holders nominate one of themselves for the purpose of this sub-paragraph, he is entitled to be entered in the register of members of the commonhold association which exercises functions in relation to the unit.

(3) A nomination under sub-paragraph (2) must—

(a) be made in writing to the commonhold association, and
(b) be received by the association before the end of the prescribed period.

(4) If no nomination is received by the association before the end of the prescribed period the person whose name appears first in the proprietorship register is on the expiry of that period entitled to be entered in the register of members of the association.

(5) On the application of a joint unit-holder the court may order that a joint unit-holder is entitled to be entered in the register of members of a commonhold association in place of a person who is or would be entitled to be registered by virtue of sub-paragraph (4).

(6) If joint unit-holders nominate one of themselves for the purpose of this sub-paragraph, the nominated person is entitled to be entered in the register of members of the commonhold association in place of the person entered by virtue of—

(a) sub-paragraph (2),
(b) sub-paragraph (5), or
(c) this sub-paragraph.

Self-membership

9. A commonhold association may not be a member of itself.

No other members

10. A person may not become a member of a commonhold association otherwise than by virtue of a provision of this Schedule.

Effect of registration

11. A person who is entitled to be entered in the register of members of a commonhold association becomes a member when the company registers him in pursuance of its duty under section 352 of the Companies Act 1985 (c. 6) (duty to maintain register of members).

Termination of membership

12. Where a member of a commonhold association ceases to be a unit-holder or joint unit-holder of a commonhold unit in relation to which the association exercises functions—

(a) he shall cease to be a member of the commonhold association, but
(b) paragraph (a) does not affect any right or liability already acquired or incurred in respect of a matter relating to a time when he was a unit-holder or joint unit-holder.

13. A member of a commonhold association may resign by notice in writing to the association if (and only if) he is a member by virtue of paragraph 5 or 6 of this Schedule (and not also by virtue of any other paragraph).

Register of members

14.—(1) Regulations may make provision about the performance by a commonhold association of its duty under section 352 of the Companies Act 1985 (c. 6) (duty to maintain register of members) where a person—

(a) becomes entitled to be entered in the register by virtue of paragraphs 5 to 8, or
(b) ceases to be a member by virtue of paragraph 12 or on resignation.

(2) The regulations may in particular require entries in the register to be made within a specified period.

(3) A period specified under sub-paragraph (2) may be expressed to begin from—

(a) the date of a notification under section 15(3),
(b) the date on which the directors of the commonhold association first become aware of a specified matter, or
(c) some other time.

(4) A requirement by virtue of this paragraph shall be treated as a requirement of section 352 for the purposes of section 352(5) (fines).

Companies Act 1985

15.—(1) Section 22(1) of the Companies Act 1985 (initial members) shall apply to a commonhold association subject to this Schedule.

(2) Sections 22(2) and 23 of that Act (members: new members and holding company) shall not apply to a commonhold association.

SCHEDULE 4

DEVELOPMENT RIGHTS

Introductory

1. This Schedule sets out the matters which are development business for the purposes of section 58.

Works

2. The completion or execution of works on—

(a) a commonhold,
(b) land which is or may be added to a commonhold, or
(c) land which has been removed from a commonhold.

Marketing

3.—(1) Transactions in commonhold units.

(2) Advertising and other activities designed to promote transactions in commonhold units.

Variation

4. The addition of land to a commonhold.

5. The removal of land from a commonhold.

6. Amendment of a commonhold community statement (including amendment to redefine the extent of a commonhold unit).

Commonhold association

7. Appointment and removal of directors of a commonhold association.

. . . . . .

INDEX